(♂)+(♀)   dioecious: separate male and female plants

Combinations of these are possible, so that:

(♀̣)+(♀)   is a gynodioecious plant, with distinct female and hermaphrodite individuals.

The order in which the anthers (♂ parts) and stigmas (♀ parts) mature is given by the codes:

pa   protandrous (anthers mature before stigmas)

pg   protogynous (stigmas mature before anthers)

hg   homogamous (anthers and stigmas mature simultaneously)

The habitat (**HAB**) in which the plant is normally found is given.

The soil type (**SOIL**) preferred by the plant is given. Wetness is expressed as:

water   actually in water
wet   waterlogged
damp   wetter than normal, but not waterlogged
moist   typical soil condition
dry   obviously dry, usually crumbly, powdery or rocky

and acidity as:

acid   mainly sandy soils, heaths, moors
calc   (=calcareous): chalk and limestone

Example:

moist-dry; not acid
means that the plant is found on moist or dry soils, but not on acid soils.

The degree of shade (**SHADE**) in which the plant is found is shown on the following scale:

nil   no trees
light   scattered trees, wood edges
mid   typical woodland, e.g. coppice
heavy   complete canopy
deep   as in beechwoods and coniferous plantations

Altitudinal range (**ALT**) is expressed in terms of the usual minimum and maximum heights above sea-level at which the plant grows in Britain, with exceptional records shown in round brackets. Height is given in metres; sl means sea-level.

Example:

sl–600(–900)

means that the plant grows from sea-level to 600m, but has occasionally been found as high as 900m.
[For non-British species the whole information on altitude is enclosed in square brackets, and then refers to the heights at which the plant grows in continental Europe.]

The plant's distribution (**DIST**) in Britain is shown as follows:

E   England
W   Wales
S   Scotland
I   Ireland

with prefixes for north (n), south (s), east (e) and west (w).

(A code in round brackets means that the species is introduced in that region.)

Each of these codes is followed by a figure de̶   ̶ ̶ ̶ ̶order of abundance within each r̶   percentage of 10km²
r̶   ̶ ̶ain where the species
(

l, not persisting, liable to most anywhere.

ie figure refers to the astline occupied.

)

lant can be found in about of northern England, Wales otland, but in only a quarter of thos̶ ̶ ̶ ̶and, where it is introduced rather than native.

RANGE in Europe is described thus:

F   Belgium and France north of the R. Loire
G   Germany, Denmark and Holland
S   The rest of Scandinavia

with prefixes for north (n), south (s), east (e) and west (w).

(A code in brackets means that the species is introduced in that region.)

Each of these codes is followed by a figure denoting the order of abundance within each region, expressed as the percentage of the area of that region where the species occurs.

Example:

Fx, G2, (sS2)

means that the plant can be found in less than a tenth of Belgium and northern France, but in about a quarter of Germany, Denmark and Holland, and about the same in southern Scandinavia, where it is introduced rather than native.

Cross-references direct the reader to further information on the species or group, to be found in the other sections of the book.

Finally, the bold letters **ss**, followed by a number, refer the reader of the appropriate entry in the APPENDIX OF SCARCE SPECIES (pp. 149–159), where closely-related, but not illustrated, species are described briefly.

New Generation Guide
to the

Wild Flowers
of Britain and Northern Europe

Number Nine
The Corrie Herring Hooks Series

New Generation Guide
to the

Wild Flowers
of Britain
and Northern Europe

Alistair Fitter

General Editor
Sir David Attenborough

University of Texas Press
AUSTIN

Dedicated to the new generation: David, Robert and Melanie

ARTISTS
Norman Arlott
Ian Garrard
Sheila Hadley
Alan Harris
Marilyn Leader
David Leigh
Valerie Price
Andrew Robinson
Chris Shields
Fiona Silver
Charles Stitt
Sue Wickison
John Wilkinson

International Standard Book Number 0–292–75535–X
Library of Congress Catalog Card Number 86–51603
Text copyright © 1987 by Alastair Fitter
Illustrations copyright © 1987 by William Collins Sons & Co., Ltd
All rights reserved

First University of Texas Press Edition, 1987

Requests for permission to reproduce material from this work should
be sent to Permissions, University of Texas Press, Box 7819, Austin, Texas 78713–7819.

Filmset by Ace Filmsetting Ltd, Frome

Colour and black-and-white reproduction by
Alpha Reprographics Ltd, Harefield

Made and printed in Great Britain by
William Collins Sons & Co. Ltd, Glasgow

Contents

PART 3: **The Natural History of Wild Flowers**

Seeds

Stems

Leaves

Foreword

Sir David Attenborough

The first requirement of a field guide is that it should enable anyone consulting it to put names to what they find in the field. But anyone whose curiosity is totally satisfied by that achievement, pleasing though it might be, will be missing a great deal. This new-style guide has been prepared for those who want to take their investigations further and to understand why what they find is the way that it is, and how it relates to other organisms around it.

Of course, the process of identification, in itself, has an underlying logic. Even the least experienced naturalist among us quickly recognises that, for example, buttercups are similar to celandines, and that both more closely resemble an anemone than they do a plantain. In coming to such conclusions we are, in fact, speculating about the relationships and therefore the ancestry of flowering plants. Just such considerations have also guided the most expert botanists in classifying plants and listing them in an order that is now broadly accepted everywhere. If their lists and orderings are not to appear arbitrary to those of us who are less expert, we have to have some idea of the way plant families have evolved. That subject, accordingly, occupies the first section of this guide.

The second section is the essential core, the Directory in which all but the rarest flowering plants of Britain and Northern Europe are described in sufficient detail to enable them to be identified.

But having discovered, with the Directory's aid, the name of a flower, the thoughtful naturalist may well go on to ask a great number of questions about it. Most of these are likely to begin with the word 'why?' Why does it not grow taller? Why is it only found in certain areas? Why does this species produce so many seeds when that one produces so few? Why does it live for only one year whereas others live for two years or even more? Until now, the answers to such questions were not to be found in field guides, but only in larger botanical textbooks that are hardly suitable for carrying about the countryside. But that is where such questions may well come to our minds. So this guide contains an Encyclopedia in which the lives of plants are surveyed, starting with their germination from seeds, continuing with their growth and flowering, and ending with their pollination and the production, in turn, of a new generation of seeds. At each stage, the many different solutions evolved by plants to survive the problems with which they are beset are described using, as examples, species in the Directory; and the Directory entries contain page references to the Encyclopedia where their characteristics that are of particular interest are examined in detail.

All of us involved in the preparation of this New Generation Guide hope that these three sections will together enable those who read it not only to identify the wild flowers they find, but also to discover in them a deeper significance and therefore a new delight.

Author's Preface

Dr Alastair Fitter

Natural history is now a major leisure activity. Millions of people choose to spend their spare time in what is left of our countryside, and enhance their enjoyment of it by learning to recognise its inhabitants. There is nothing new in this: many Victorians were keen naturalists, and the first popular identification guides were produced to satisfy that market. The difference today is that both the number of people sharing this interest and their mobility have greatly increased, while the countryside available to them has vastly diminished. Out of this, and out of other impacts of our burgeoning population on its fragile resources, has arisen an environmental awareness, expressed variously in political action, in the growth of conservation societies, and in simple curiosity about the natural world.

If we solve the problem of conserving remnants of our natural environment successfully, it will be because we have learned to understand it better; and much of that understanding will come from the science of ecology. Ecology is about the relations of organisms with each other and with their environment,

and it has grown over the last 100 years from the firm base provided by natural history. It is an inevitable step that the curious naturalist, from knowing what an animal or plant is, should wish to know why it is as it is, and what it does.

This is ecology, and it is one of the few areas of science where the amateur can still make important contributions with little equipment. All that is needed is enthusiasm, and a sufficient understanding of the underlying principles, to allow the right question to be asked. It is surprising how many of the 'obvious' questions as yet have no clear answer. I have tried to point some of these out in this book, and if it arouses in readers some of the necessary curiosity and enthusiasm, it has done its task.

As an ecologist I have long wanted to place in front of the army of enthusiastic amateur naturalists some of the exciting ideas that help to make sense of much of the diversity of the natural world, and explain how it may have evolved. I am very grateful to Crispin Fisher, who conceived the particular format of this series, for making it possible to put that wish into published form.

Part 1: The Evolution of Wild Flowers

THE PLANT KINGDOM

This book is about wild flowers, the most familiar and conspicuous plants. Flowering plants, which include most broad-leaved trees, made their first appearance around 100 million years ago and are at the pinnacle of evolution in the plant kingdom. Plants of more primitive structure had, however, already existed on land for 300 million years, and for over 1000 million (perhaps as many as 2000 million) in the sea. Astonishingly, the tiny primitive plants (phytoplankton) that were floating in those billion-year-old seas were almost indistinguishable from those still there today, while those on land have developed dramatically to survive in an environment that is actually harsher. Although land plants have undergone greater evolutionary change, in terms of evolutionary history it is the marine plants that have the longest record.

There are four great groups of plants:

The **Algae** are structurally simple and live in water or in wet places on land; they are the dominant plants in the sea and on rocky shores.

The **Bryophytes** – mosses and liverworts – are the first true land plants, but both they and the

Pteridophytes – ferns and their allies – are nowadays unable to compete ecologically with the

Spermatophytes – the seed plants – which are most closely and successfully adapted to life on land.

ALGAE

The algae are a heterogenous group and hard to define – they are structurally simple and lack any of the sophistications required for life on land. They include the earliest plants, single-celled plankton and colonies

and filaments of cells. They are primitive, but far from unsuccessful: for a life spent floating in the turbulent surface layers of the oceans, single-celledness cannot be surpassed. Larger plants would simply sink faster. On land (or the shore) size enables neighbours to be overshadowed, but in the sea it gives no such advantage, for there is nothing solid to attach to. This is why these primitive plants have persisted unchanged for so long and why they still dominate two-thirds of the planet's surface.

There are some more complicated algae, particularly the seaweeds, and these too have achieved dominance in a particular habitat, the seashore. By attaching to the surface with a holdfast, they have initiated the game of competing for light, where size *is* an advantage. Living in water, there has been no pressure on algae to become more complex by developing systems for transporting or conserving water, and they can reproduce quite successfully simply by releasing their sex cells into the water in sufficiently huge numbers, leaving their getting together to chance. All other plants, however, either grow on land or have evolved from terrestrial ancestors, and for that step, several developments were necessary.

BRYOPHYTES

These most primitive land-dwelling plants are only partly adapted to life on land. Mostly they are tied to the wetter places for two reasons: first they have few structural devices for obtaining water if it is scarce (they have no roots) or for conserving it; second, they require water to reproduce, for the male gamete to move to the female, just like the algae. Where

A sphagnum bog: only the odd plant of sedge has managed to find a foothold in the dense mat of sphagnum mosses

and for nearly 300 million years they gave the earth its green colour. Unlike the mosses, they were successful even in truly terrestrial habitats and at one time formed huge forests, that we now plunder as coal, which is the fossilised remnant of giant horsetails and other now extinct Pteridophytes. They grew in the very places that now support flowering plants, and those even better-adapted newcomers have ousted the ferns and horsetails. Those Pteridophytes that survive tend to be found in moist and shady places, for although the adult fern can withstand dry conditions, all ferns and their allies still need water for sexual reproduction. That is the most vulnerable point in their life-cycle, and many of the most successful ferns are those that have found a way of circumventing that need: bracken, for example, reproduces mainly vegetatively, by means of long underground rhizomes (still not true roots).

some mosses, and a few algae as well, do grow in places where sometimes there is no water at all, such as the tops of walls and tree-trunks, they survive not by controlling the amount of water they lose, but by drying out totally and becoming dormant, a trick almost impossible for structurally more complex plants, because the desiccation destroys that complexity. As with the algae, however, it is a mistake to think of these primitive features as in some way unsuccessful in evolution, for the Bryophytes have been around for nearly 400 million years, an achievement that *Homo sapiens* may find hard to match. They are in reality superbly fitted to living in very wet places on land, as can be seen by visiting the blanket bog areas of Ireland or north-west Scotland, where mosses of the genus *Sphagnum* are almost the only living thing to be seen for miles.

PTERIDOPHYTES

The Pteridophytes appeared on earth not long after the first land plants.

SPERMATOPHYTES

Seed plants include most of the familiar plants we see. Their domination of the land is largely due to one major development in reproduction (p. 12) and its consequence, the seed. Whereas all other plants require liquid water to reproduce in, because the male sex cells must swim towards the female, the seed plants can reproduce even in deserts. Reproduction is by pollination: the male cells actually grow through the tissue of the plant to reach the female.

The seed plants are divided into two groups, the Gymnosperms and the Angiosperms. In the former the female cells are exposed; in the latter they are protected by being wrapped up and hidden in a special structure called the carpel. These Angiosperms, the true flowering plants, have developed more and more complex methods of ensuring that the male cells reach and fertilise the now hidden female cells; this has resulted in a very great variety of flowers.

LIFE-CYCLES

Sexual reproduction is in essence nothing more than the fusion of two cells to produce a new one with twice as much genetic material. For obvious reasons it must be accompanied by a stage in which cells are produced with half the amount of genetic material, and in this process the material is shuffled as well, so that no two cells are identical. This is true of all sexual organisms, and in the mating of animals the halving is usually followed immediately by the doubling. In plants, however, the cells with half the genes usually start to grow and, in mosses, liverworts and ferns, produce actual plants, which only later form sex cells (without halving the material further). These sex cells then fuse with a cell of the opposite sex and subsequently grow and produce plants of a different character. As a result, plants may have two distinct generations, one with twice the genetic material of the other; indeed in some algae these two generations may be so different that they appear to be distinct species, and have often been named as such in error.

In the bryophytes it is the generation with half the information, known as the haploid, which is what we see as the moss or liverwort plant [1, 2, 3]. It produces the sex cells or gametes [4, 5], without halving the information, and these fuse to make the new cell with twice the information, known as the diploid. This diploid cell starts to grow into a long stalk and capsule [6, 7], attached at the base of the stalk to the haploid parent, and in the capsule the divisions occur which lead to a halving of the information. In this way, haploid spores are produced and these disperse [8] and grow into new moss and liverwort plants [1, 2]. Because the spores are dispersed by wind, whereas the male gametes must swim in water to find the female, the diploid plant (i.e. the stalk and capsule) has become much more resistant than the haploid generation to water loss and is, therefore, more of a land plant. This inability of the haploid plant, which actually produces the gametes, to survive in dry conditions, means that the development of a proper land plant required the diploid plant to become dominant, not the haploid as in the mosses. This is what we see in the ferns. The fern plant that we recognise as male fern

Life-cycle of the moss Mnium.

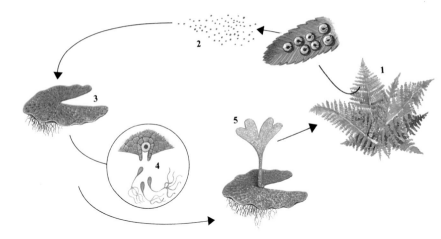

Life-cycle of the fern Dryopteris filix-mas

or bracken is the diploid parent [1]. Just as in the moss capsule, it too produces haploid spores [2] in little pustules under the fronds by a division that halves the amount of genetic material. The spores develop into tiny green plants [3], a few millimetres across, that are haploid and look not unlike a flimsy liverwort. It is these plants that produce the gametes [4], the male still requiring water to swim in, though the female gametes stay put; and when the gametes fuse they restore the diploid generation. Out of the tiny green plant grows the new diploid fern plant [5], but whereas the moss capsule always remains dependent on its haploid parent for nutrition, the fern rapidly becomes independent and soon the dominant generation.

It is these diploid fern plants, though well fitted to growth in dry conditions, that we see typically in moist, shady corners, to which they are restricted solely by the needs of their haploid partner, which can itself be found easily enough by careful searching. Liberation from the need for liquid water for reproduction came only with the seed plants – Spermatophytes. They have reduced the haploid generation even further, and indeed have contained it within the diploid. There are separate male and female plants in the haploid generation, the female reduced to a few cells (the ovule) within its protecting carpel, and the male to a tube, which grows out of the pollen grain. Comparing the life-cycle of a flowering plant with that of a fern, it is clear that the pollen grain is the spore and the tube that grows out of it to fertilise the haploid ovule is the haploid plant, but one that is now quite independent of water.

After fertilisation, the ovule (now diploid) develops into the embryo of a new diploid plant, and the walls of the ovule harden to make a tough coat: together they make the seed. In this form the embryonic plant can survive many vicissitudes and be dispersed. The surrounding carpel develops in one of many possible ways to make a fruit, containing the seeds. It may turn into a nut, a fleshy berry, or a capsule, which can be explosive, dehiscent or simply dry, among other types of fruit. All this is true of the Angiosperms, which could perhaps be better termed the fruiting plants. Those other seed plants, the Gymnosperms, including pines, firs and spruces, have exposed ovules, not enclosed in a carpel, and so cannot form fruits. Where they seem to do so, as in juniper and yew for example, they achieve this by developing a fleshy seed-coat.

13

FLOWERS

All flowering plants have flowers, and the flower is simply a device for ensuring successful fertilisation and the production of seeds, encased in fruits. A typical flower therefore contains the following parts:

> one or more carpels which contain the ovule, awaiting fertilisation;
>
> stamens, which produce the pollen grains from each of which a pollen tube may grow out to fertilise the ovule;
>
> some protective structures, which serve to protect the reproductive structures, and sometimes to attract pollinators which will carry the pollen to another flower.

This is the bare minimum of a hermaphrodite flower, such as wild strawberry, which has both male and female parts. The simplest possible flowers are either male or female and consist of either a carpel or a few stamens, and a few protective scales, as in sedges. The most complex may have both carpels and stamens, the protective structures developed into sepals and petals, which may be modified to attract animals by colour and scent and to reward them with nectar hidden in spurs or tubes, as in orchids. Simplicity and complexity in all this are related to what the flower does: simple flowers tend to be pollinated by either wind or water, while complex structures provide inducements for animal (usually insect) vectors. Confusingly, this difference between flower types bears little relation to other evolutionary trends in flowering plants, for the most primitive of these tend to be insect pollinated, and some of the most highly evolved, such as grasses, are wind-pollinated. Flowers have in fact evolved in two distinct directions – towards simplicity and wind-pollination, and towards complexity

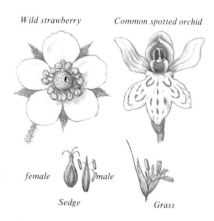

Wild strawberry *Common spotted orchid*

female *male*

Sedge *Grass*

in insect-pollinated flowers (see p. 18).

A 'typical' flower might be somewhere in the middle of this scale. It will have all the structures, but arranged in a simple manner, as in a buttercup. In the centre are the carpels, each containing a single ovule and each surmounted by a tiny stalk, whose top surface is the sensitive area where the pollen grains attach – this is the stigma and its stalk is the style. Around the carpels are the stamens, consisting of a filament topped by a small sac called an anther in which the pollen grains are actually produced. Surrounding this reproductive machinery are two perimeters of scales, one brightly coloured and attractive to insects and the other green and hairy, acting as a protective layer when the flower is in bud. The two layers are together termed the perianth: the outer layer is the calyx, here comprising five sepals, and the inner the corolla, here of five petals. Sepals and petals are not always distinct: where they are, the inner ring is the petals and is usually more brightly-coloured.

Buttercups are pollinated by insects, which are attracted by the brightly-coloured petals and rewarded by nectar secreted from small cups at the

14

Marsh marigold

Creeping buttercup   Annual pearlwort

base of the petals, known as nectaries. This nectar, however, is accessible to small insects without their being forced to brush against either the stigmas or the anthers; many such visits, therefore, do not result in pollination. More complex flowers have the reward placed in such a manner that the insects must pass the anthers first (pp. 279–87). This can be done by having nectar at the end of petals drawn out into spurs (columbine), or fused into a tube (foxglove), or both (toadflax). In an extreme case the corolla tube may be 5cm or more long, as in honeysuckle, restricting access to those insects with long enough tongues, mainly hawkmoths and other long-tongued moths (p. 277).

Whatever the details of the design, all these flowers have the four basic components – stamens, carpels, calyx, corolla. In many flowers these four are effectively reduced to three, either because there are no sepals or, more commonly, no petals, or because the layers of the perianth are indistinguishable. In marsh marigold, the flower looks at first just like a large buttercup, but turns out to have no green sepals; in fact it has no petals, but sepals which look like petals.

Operationally it works just like a buttercup. The common pearlwort has four clear sepals, but usually no petals at all; being self-pollinated it has no need of insects to transport pollen to another flower, and thus no need of colourful petals to attract them.

One of the major divisions in the flowering plants is between those with net-veined leaves and two seed-leaves, or cotyledons (the first leaves which appear on germination and are already present in the embryo) – the dicotyledons, or dicots in botanical slang – and those with parallel-veined leaves and one seed-leaf – the monocots. All the flowers so far have been of dicots. Monocots are similar, but often have indistinguishable petals and sepals; the two are sometimes then called tepals. They may be showy and attractive as in bluebell or unobtrusive as in the wind-pollinated bur-reeds. Wind-pollination is common in the monocots. Grasses and sedges are good examples, and they have much simplified flowers, with carpels, stamens and a few protective scales; the rest would serve no function. There are wind-pollinated dicots too, and they have similarly simplified flowers: the flowers on a hazel catkin, for example, which are all male only, consist of four stamens and a single protective scale, while the female flowerhead, hidden by scales, likewise consists of nothing but carpels and scales. These protective scales, which are not true sepals or petals, are known as bracts.

The separate male and female flowers of hazel

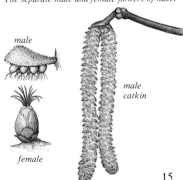

male

male catkin

female

15

TRENDS IN THE EVOLUTION OF FLOWERS

The plants in the Directory section of this book (pp. 29–148) are arranged in systematic order, that is to say in an order which some taxonomists (scientists who classify organisms) believe to represent a scale of evolutionary complexity. Evolution is a complex process, however, involving the continual branching of new lines, which then give rise to further branches, and so on. To convert this into a simple list of families which show an evolutionary progression is impossible – rather like taking all the leaves on a tree and trying to lay them out in order of age.

Systematic order at best then merely reflects evolutionary complexity; it is not an exact picture of it. If the daisy family appears at the end of the dicots and the pink family at the beginning, that means we are fairly sure that the latter has more primitive characteristics, but just because the saxifrages come before the rose family, the same may not apply.

There are some objective criteria for deciding what is primitive and what is advanced: we have fossils of the sorts of plants that existed before the flowering plants evolved, and we have fossils of very early flowering plants. Characters that occur in them are clearly primitive. These very early flowering plants were mainly insect-pollinated but they were not very sophisticated – they had none of the complex mechanisms for ensuring pollen transfer found in some modern flowers (see p. 284). Most botanists believe that the magnolia has about the most primitive flower of any modern flowering plant.

Since those beginnings, there appear to have been two main lines of floral evolution, and they have been in opposite directions. Flowers are basically pollination mechanisms, and plants have adopted two main instruments for transferring pollen – wind and insects. Insect-pollinated flowers have evolved progressively more complex flowers, with more and more sophisticated means of luring, guiding and sometimes trapping or deceiving insects, culminating in the astonishing pollination systems of orchids (see p. 286). Wind-pollinated flowers have developed in quite the opposite direction, progressively losing more and more flower-parts, until in the most advanced of those, the grasses, they consist of little more than stamens, styles and a few scales.

Wind pollination has probably evolved a number of times quite separately; there is no neat series of wind-pollinated groups showing progressive modification. Rather, they often show the characteristics of their insect-pollinated relatives, but much simplified. The most primitive wind-pollinated flowering plants are probably the goosefoot and dock families (though some taxonomists

Ribwort plantain

Hairy wood rush

Magnolia

Fat hen (a goosefoot)

Maiden pink

White dead-nettle

Bog asphodel (a lily)

Branched bur-reed

False oat-grass

Common duckweed

place them much further up the scale). The structure of goosefoot flowers needs to be examined under a lens, which reveals that they in fact have clear similarities to those of the insect-pollinated pink family. Some common ancestor of the two presumably gave rise to both, but by different routes.

Most of the other wind-pollinated dicots are trees, but plantains are another herbaceous group. They have very inconspicuous flowers, but though the sepals and petals are very small and unattractive to insects, it is obvious that they are related to plants such as dead-nettles, foxglove or bellflowers.

The main wind-pollinated herbaceous families, however, are monocots, particularly the rushes, reed-maces, sedges and grasses. Whether or not they actually represent an evolutionary series, they do show quite well the progressive simplification of the flower. Rushes are effectively wind-pollinated lilies and have a flower structure which betrays their relationship, with the same two whorls of tepals.

Bur-reeds and reed-maces have much simpler flowers with no true petals, merely a ring of scales or threads, while sedges may have the same arrangement or nothing at all. Grass flowers represent an extreme development of this evolutionary trend, their flowers consisting of three stamens, a simple ovary with two styles and a few minute scales. Even that is not as far as some wind-pollinated plants have gone: duckweeds rarely flower in Britain, but their minute flowers are unisexual and comprise either one or sometimes two stamens, or a simple ovary.

TRENDS IN INSECT-POLLINATED PLANTS

Wind-pollinated flowers have obviously arisen many times from different insect-pollinated ancestors (p. 16); but insect-pollination is the archetypal mechanism, and shows evolutionary trends rather more clearly. The classification normally adopted reflects these trends: the basic distinction between monocots (p. 15) and dicots rests on quite different sets of characters, but within the dicots pollination has been one of the main evolutionary forces.

The most fundamental division in the dicots is between those plants with free petals, regarded as more primitive, and those with joined petals, often making a tube. Typical free-petal families are the buttercup, pink, cabbage, rose, peaflower and carrot families: all appear in the first half of the Directory.

Dog rose

Tufted vetch

Wild radish (a crucifer)

They are followed by families such as the heather, primrose, labiate, figwort and daisy families, all of which have more or less tubular flowers. The tube enables more precise

pollination mechanisms to evolve in which the insect is guided to nectar well-concealed at the base of the tube, and in so doing must pass and brush against stamens and styles.

Common hemp-nettle (a labiate)

Common figwort

Heather

Primrose

Free-petalled flowers do not have this facility, and in the most primitive forms, where the stamens originate below the ovary (buttercup, pink and cabbage families, for instance), pollination is a relatively hit and miss affair. Originally this must have meant that the chances of successful pollination were less and may explain why the most primitive flower-types, such as buttercups, have so many stamens and styles. A reduction in the number of these is, then, another well-marked evolutionary trend.

If free-petalled flowers cannot form a true tube, they can produce a make-shift one by elongation of the petals, often with a joint so that the petals consist of a narrow upright part (the claw) and a flattened part, held at right angles to the claw (the limb). The limb acts as a display to pollinating insects and the claw forms the tube. This is well seen in pinks and members of the cabbage family.

Although most of the free-petalled flowers are more or less saucer-shaped, and so radially symmetrical, bilateral symmetry has evolved separately a number of times. Some members of the buttercup family (monk's-hood), fumitories, violets and peaflowers are bilaterally symmetrical and their more complex flowers can be seen as aids to attracting insects, particularly in their provision of nectar-bearing spurs.

There is also a tendency for the more advanced families, both those with free and those with joined petals, to have flowers aggregated into heads, which are very conspicuous. In the first group the carrot family is a good example, and in the second the valerian, teasel and daisy families.

Common teasel

Monk's-hood

Common fumitory

Sweet violet

Wild carrot

In flowers with joined petals, some of these trends occur again, but being more advanced none has the really primitive characters, such as masses of stamens and styles. Flowers with anthers and petals developing from beneath the ovary and radially symmetrical petal tubes (primrose and gentian family) are placed earlier in the classification than those with more or less bilaterally symmetrical petals and the petals and stamens atop the ovary (honeysuckle and daisy families).

Common valerian

Spear thistle

Marsh gentian

Daisy

19

There are fewer insect-pollinated families in the monocots and so the trends are less obvious; but the normal arrangement of the main families is water-plaintain, pondweed, lily, iris, orchid. The water-plaintains have simple, radially symmetrical flowers, sometimes (in the water-plantains themselves) with large numbers of carpels, and the petals and sepals arising below them. The pondweed, lily and iris families differ in having few carpels, while the orchids are the most advanced, with

bilaterally symmetrical, often very complex flowers, and the petals and sepals arising below the ovary; their extraordinary pollination mechanisms are explained on p. 286.

The systematic order in which the plants in the Directory section are arranged, then, is not a whim of some ancient botanist, but an attempt to reflect the presumed course of flowering plant evolution. By understanding the pressures that have brought about that evolution, one can more easily learn to identify the plants.

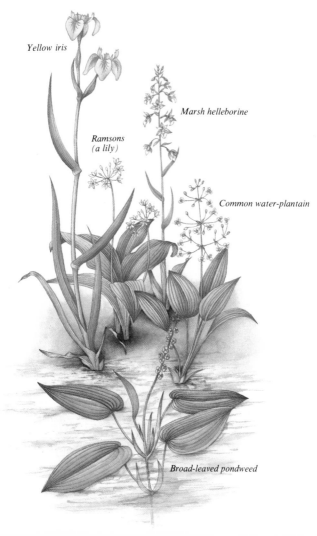

Yellow iris

Marsh helleborine

*Ramsons
(a lily)*

Common water-plantain

Broad-leaved pondweed

Part 2: The Directory of Species

The preceding pages have explained the systems and judgements underlying the classification of wild flowers into groups. The units of this classification are species, into which all living organisms are divided. A species is a group of plants or animals which can interbreed but cannot breed with another species. As a result, the evolutionary pressure of natural selection can act on different species quite independently, because they cannot exchange genetic information, and they may become adapted to quite different ways of life. In practice, many species consist of populations that could potentially interbreed, but are separated geographically and so never do. Such isolated populations may also diverge, and are then known as subspecies – they are species in the process of evolution.

The DIRECTORY of flowers which now follows is ordered to reflect what botanists believe to be an approximation of the order in which the various species evolved. Although this is in many cases and in many ways subjective (and further research and knowledge will doubtless alter and improve our understanding of the progress of plant evolution), the reader will sense some of the background to the conclusions of taxonomists in the information given about each family and species, and in the appearance of the plants themselves.

The seven tables that follow show how the main families of flowering plants differ in those characteristics already picked out in 'Trends' (pp. 16–20). Once the reader has learned to recognise these families, the rest of the classification will fall easily into place.

Over 1,100 wild flower species are illustrated and described, and the reader will find all but the rarest and most inconspicuous flowers growing in Britain and north-west Europe. An APPENDIX OF SCARCE SPECIES, which follows the directory on pp. 149–59, covers every such species for Britain. The directory and appendix together, therefore, represent the complete British flora.

A complete key to the symbols and abbreviations used in the text can be found on the endpapers of this book.

It is important for the user of this guide to be aware that, in order to make the best use of the space available, the paintings of flowering plants in the DIRECTORY are not necessarily to scale with each other. The actual size of part or all of the plant is given in the text for each species.

TABLE 1: MAIN FAMILIES OF DICOTYLEDONS WITH FREE PETALS AND SEPALS, MOSTLY WIND-POLLINATED

FAMILY	Nettle Family p. 29 *Urticaceae*	Dock Family pp. 29–31 *Polygonaceae*	Goosefoot Family pp. 32–34 *Chenopodiaceae*	Pink Family pp. 34–39 *Caryophyllaceae*
TYPICAL GENERA	*Urtica*: nettles *Parietaria*: pellitories	*Rumex*: docks *Polygonum*: bistorts	*Chenopodium*: goosefoots *Atriplex*: oraches	*Silene*: campions *Stellaria*: stitchworts *Dianthus*: pinks
NUMBER OF SEPALS AND PETALS	4–5, undifferentiated	3 2–3	2–5, sometimes joined at base, undifferentiated	4–5 4–5
NUMBER OF STAMENS AND STYLES	4 1	6–8(–9) 1	2–5 1	8–10 2–5
LEVEL OF STAMENS	beneath carpels	beneath carpels	beneath carpels	beneath carpels
SYMMETRY	radial	radial	radial	radial
INFLORESCENCE	spikes	whorls, spikes or in lf-junctions	spikes or in lf-junctions	cymes
FRUITS	dry, not dehiscing, 1-seeded	dry, not dehiscing, 1-seeded	dry, not dehiscing, 1-seeded	capsule
LEAVES	simple, toothed: opposite, alternate	simple, spiral, with stipules	simple, spiral, often mealy or fleshy	simple: opposite
UNUSUAL GENERA	*Soleirolia* is a creeping garden escape.	*Koenigia* is a minute arctic annual.	*Salicornia* has minute lvs and fls and fleshy stems.	*Spergula* has lvs in whorls. *Herniaria* has minute green fls in clusters.
RELATED FAMILIES	HEMP *Cannabaceae* p. 29			PURSLANE *Portulacaceae* p. 32

TABLE 2: SIMPLE DICOTYLEDONS WITH FREE PETALS AND SEPALS: INSECT POLLINATED

FAMILY	Pink Family pp. 34-39 Caryophyllaceae	Buttercup Family pp. 39-44 Ranunculaceae	Crucifers: Cabbage Family pp. 46-51 Cruciferae	Rose Family pp. 55-58 Rosaceae	Peaflower Family pp. 58-65 Papilionaceae
TYPICAL GENERA	Silene: campions Stellaria: stitchworts Dianthus: pinks	Ranunculus: buttercups Anemone: anemones	Brassica: cabbage, rape Cardamine: cuckoo flower Capsella: shepherd's purse	Fragaria: strawberries Potentilla: cinquefoils Rosa: roses	Trifolium: clovers Vicia: vetches Ulex: gorses
NUMBER OF SEPALS AND PETALS	4-5 4-5	usually 3-6 5-∞	4 4	4-5(-8) (0-)4-5(-8)	5 5 (2 lower joined to appear as 1) } joined at base
NUMBER OF STAMENS AND STYLES	2 × no. of sepals 2-5	∞ 1-∞	4 or 6 1	∞ 1-∞	10 fused (or 1+9 fused) 1
LEVEL OF STAMENS	beneath carpels	beneath carpels	beneath carpels	at same level as carpels	at same level as carpels
SYMMETRY	radial	mostly radial, some bilateral	radial	radial	bilateral
INFLORESCENCE	cymes	various: solitary, racemes, cymes	racemes	racemes, cymes, clusters	solitary, racemes, heads
FRUITS	capsule	simple, 1-seeded, mainly dry	capsule: long and thin (siliqua) or short (silicula)	dry, 1-seeded or fleshy	pod
LEAVES	simple, opposite each other on stem	often dissected, spirally round stem	various, spirally round stem	often dissected, alternate, with stipules	usually trefoil or pinnate
UNUSUAL GENERA	Several, but mostly rare.	Many, esp. bilateral fls of Aquilegia and Delphinium. Thalictrum has fls composed mainly of stamens.	Iberis has different sized petals, but fl-type very constant.	Sanguisorba has dense flhds. Alchemilla has green clusters of fls.	Flower type constant and characteristic.
RELATED FAMILIES	MALLOW Malvaceae pp. 70-71 CRANESBILL Geraniaceae pp. 65-67	WATER-LILY Nymphaceae p. 44	POPPY Papaveraceae p. 45-46	SAXIFRAGE Saxifragaceae pp. 53-55 STONECROP Crassulaceae pp. 52-53 SUNDEW Droseraceae p. 52	none

TABLE 3: DICOTYLEDONS WITH FREE PETALS AND SEPALS: INSECT-POLLINATED

FAMILY	Cranesbill Family pp. 65-67 *Geraniaceae*	Spurge Family pp. 67-68 *Euphorbiaceae*	Willowherb Family pp. 74-75 *Onagraceae*	Carrot Family pp. 77-81 *Umbelliferae*
TYPICAL GENERA	*Geranium*: cranesbills *Erodium*: storksbills	*Euphorbia*: spurges	*Epilobium*: willowherbs	*Anthriscus*: cow parsley *Conopodium*: pignut *Angelica*: angelica
NUMBER OF SEPALS AND PETALS	5 5	0(-3) 0	(2)4 or 5 (2)4 or 5	0-5 5
NUMBER OF STAMENS AND STYLES	10 1 (3-5 stigmas)	1 (*Euphorbia*) or 8-10 3 or 2	1 or 8 5 or 1	5 2
LEVEL OF STAMENS	beneath carpel	beneath carpel	above carpel	above carpel
SYMMETRY	radial	radial	radial or slightly bilateral	radial
INFLORESCENCE	cymes	clusters, cymes, umbels	racemes	umbels
FRUITS	capsule	capsule	capsule	dry, not dehiscing
LEAVES	dissected, often lobed; alternate	simple; alternate	simple; spiral or opposite	dissected, usually pinnate, often feathery
UNUSUAL GENERA		*Mercurialis* has 3-sepalled fls in whorled spikes.	*Circaea* has 2 petals and sepals.	*Sanicula* has lobed lvs and fls in clusters. *Eryngium* is spiny and has fls in heads.
RELATED FAMILIES	WOOD-SORREL *Oxalidaceae* p. 67 FLAX *Linaceae* p. 67 ST JOHN'S-WORT *Guttiferae* pp. 71-72		LOOSESTRIFE *Lythraceae* p. 76	DOGWOOD *Cornaceae* p. 76

TABLE 4: DICOTYLEDONS WITH JOINED PETALS AND SEPALS

FAMILY	Heath Family pp. 82–84 *Ericaceae*	Primrose Family pp. 84–86 *Primulaceae*	Borage Family pp. 91–93 *Boraginaceae*	Bedstraw Family pp. 89–90 *Rubiaceae*
TYPICAL GENERA	*Calluna*: heather *Erica*: heaths *Vaccinium*: bilberry	*Primula*: primrose *Lysimachia*: loosestrifes	*Myosotis*: forget-me-nots *Echium*: viper's bugloss	*Galium*: bedstraws *Sherardia*: field madder
NUMBER OF SEPALS AND PETALS	4–5 / 4–5	5 / 5 or 0	5 / 5	0, 4–6 / (3–)4(–5)
NUMBER OF STAMENS AND STYLES	(5), 8 or 10 / 1	5 / 1	5 / 1	4 / 2
LEVEL OF STAMENS	above or beneath carpel	beneath carpel	beneath carpel	above carpel
SYMMETRY	radial	radial	radial	radial
INFLORESCENCE	racemes or solitary	various	cymes	cymes, often contracted into clusters or whorls
FRUITS	capsule or berry	capsule	4 nutlets	2-lobed nutlet
LEAVES	simple; alternate: evergreen	simple	simple, often rough-hairy; alternate	simple, narrow; whorled
UNUSUAL GENERA		*Hottonia* has feathery lvs.	*Mertensia* is bluish, hairless and creeping.	*Rubia* has a berry.
RELATED FAMILIES	WINTERGREEN *Pyrolaceae* pp. 81–82	SEA-LAVENDER AND THRIFT *Plumbaginaceae* p. 86 GENTIAN *Gentianaceae* pp. 87–88		

TABLE 5: DICOTYLEDONS WITH TUBULAR FLOWERS

FAMILY	Labiate Family pp. 93–97 *Labiatae*	Figwort Family pp. 98–103 *Scrophulariaceae*	Bellflower Family pp. 107–109 *Campanulaceae*	Daisy Family pp. 109–120 *Compositae*
TYPICAL GENERA	*Thymus*: thymes *Lamium*: dead-nettles *Ajuga*: bugle	*Digitalis*: foxglove *Linaria*: toadflaxes *Rhinanthus*: yellow rattle	*Campanula*: bellflowers	*Bellis*: daisy *Taraxacum*: dandelions *Cirsium*: thistles
NUMBER OF SEPALS AND PETALS	5 4–5 (2-lobed)	4 or 5 5 (often 2-lobed)	5 5	hairs + 5-toothed tube (disc floret) or long flap (ray floret)
NUMBER OF STAMENS AND STYLES	2 or 4 1 (2 stigmas)	4 1 (1 or 2 stigmas)	5 1 (2–5 stigmas)	5 1 (2 stigmas)
LEVEL OF STAMENS	beneath carpel	beneath carpel	above carpel	above carpel
SYMMETRY	bilateral	bilateral	radial	bilateral
INFLORESCENCE	whorls or heads	racemes	racemes	heads (solitary or in branching spikes)
FRUITS	4 nutlets	capsule	capsule	dry, not dehiscent, 1-seeded; often with parachute
LEAVES	simple: opposite	various: opposite	simple: spiral	various
UNUSUAL GENERA	*Mentha* and *Lycopus* have radially symmetrical fls with 4 equal lobes.	*Verbascum* has 5 stamens. *Veronica* has 2 stamens and flat 4-lobed fls.	*Jasione* and *Phyteuma* have fls in heads.	*Tussilago* and *Petasites* have fls that appear before lvs.
RELATED FAMILIES	VERVAIN *Verbenaceae* p. 93	BROOMRAPE *Orobanchaceae* p. 104	PLANTAIN *Plantaginaceae* pp. 105–106	VALERIAN *Valerianaceae* p. 106 TEASEL *Dipsacaceae* p. 107

TABLE 6: INSECT-POLLINATED MONOCOTYLEDONS

FAMILY	Water-plantain Family p. 121 *Alismataceae*	Lily Family pp. 123–126 *Liliaceae*	Iris Family pp. 129–130 *Iridaceae*	Orchid Family pp. 130–135 *Orchidaceae*
TYPICAL GENERA	*Alisma*: water-plantains *Sagittaria*: arrowhead	*Convallaria*: lily-of-the-valley *Hyacinthoides*: bluebells	*Iris*: flags *Gladiolus*: gladiolus	*Orchis*: manikin orchids *Dactylorhiza*: spotted orchids *Ophrys*: insect orchids
NUMBER OF SEPALS AND PETALS	3 similar 3	3 similar 3	3 similar 3	3 3 often similar
NUMBER OF STAMENS AND STYLES	6–∞ 6–∞	6 1	3 1 (3 stigmas)	1 2
LEVEL OF STAMENS	beneath carpel	beneath carpel	above carpel	above carpel
SYMMETRY	radial	radial	radial	bilateral
INFLORESCENCE	whorls or racemes	racemes	solitary or racemes	racemes
FRUITS	dry, not dehiscing, 1-seeded	capsule or berry	capsule	capsule
LEAVES	simple, often floating	simple, narrow: often all from root	narrow: from roots	narrow
UNUSUAL GENERA		*Allium* has fls in heads.		*Cypripedium* has 2 stamens and 3 stigmas. *Neottia, Corallorhiza* and *Epipogium* have no lvs nor green colour.
RELATED FAMILIES	FLOWERING RUSH: *Butomaceae* p. 121	DAFFODILS: *Amaryllidaceae* pp. 128–129		

TABLE 7: WIND-POLLINATED MONOCOTYLEDONS

FAMILY	Pondweed Family pp. 122–123 Potamogetonaceae	Rush Family pp. 127–128 Juncaceae	Sedge Family pp. 135–139 Cyperaceae	Grass Family pp. 140–148 Gramineae
TYPICAL GENERA	Potamogeton: pondweeds	Juncus: rushes Luzula: wood-rushes	Carex: sedges	Poa: meadow-grass Agrostis: bent-grass Alopecurus: foxtail
NUMBER OF SEPALS AND PETALS	4, undifferentiated	3 similar 3	absent or scales	absent; replaced by 2 bracts
NUMBER OF STAMENS AND STYLES	4 4	3 or 6 3	2–3 2–3	3 2
LEVEL OF STAMENS	beneath carpel	beneath carpel	beneath carpel	beneath carpel
SYMMETRY	radial	radial	radial	bilateral
INFLORESCENCE	racemes	cymes or heads	spikelets in racemes or heads	spikelets in racemes or clusters
FRUITS	dry, not dehiscing nor fleshy; 1-seeded	capsule	nut-like	dry, not dehiscing, 1-seeded
LEAVES	floating or submerged, alternate; stipules	grass-like or cylindrical	grass-like	narrow with sheath round stem
UNUSUAL GENERA	Groenlandia has opposite or whorled lvs.		Eleocharis has no lvs. Eriophorum has woolly fruits.	All grasses are distinctively related. Phragmites may be over 2 m tall.
RELATED FAMILIES	EEL-GRASS: Zosteraceae p. 122		BUR-REEDS: Sparganiaceae p. 135 REED-MACES: Typhaceae p. 135	

DICOTYLEDONS

The dicotyledons are the largest main group of flowering plants, characterized by their two cotyledons (seed-leaves), net-veined leaves, and often 4- or 5-petalled flowers.

MISTLETOE FAMILY
Loranthaceae
Woody hemiparasites, growing on trees, with green leaves and small simple flowers, male and female often separate.

SANDALWOOD FAMILY
Santalaceae
Often hemiparasitic, with simple leaves and small hermaphrodite flowers; sepals or petals only. (Bastard toadflax)

HEMP FAMILY
Cannabiaceae
Herbs with lobed leaves and separate male and female flowers. (Hop)

○ **Mistletoe**
Viscum album
Short–tall; on trees. Woody evergreen hemiparasite, forking regularly; lvs yellowish, oblong, leathery; fls small, green, 4-petalled; fr a white sticky berry. LH perenn. GERM spr. FL 2–4; fr 11–1. POLL ins (d). SEX (♂) + (♀); occ. (♂ + ♀). HAB on deciduous trees, mainly apple and poplar; in G on conifers too. ALT sl–100(–1300 in G). DIST sE2, nE1, W2. RANGE F3, G3, S1.
See p. 222.

○ **Bastard toadflax**
Thesium humifusum
Low–short. Hemiparasite; lvs v. narrow, 1-veined; fls 3mm, dull greenish-white, petal tube 5-lobed. LH perenn; rootstock. GERM spr; disp. by ants. FL 6–8. POLL ins(h); self. SEX (♀). HAB dry calcareous grassland, mainly on chalk. SOIL dry; calc. SHADE nil. ALT sl–150. DIST E2. RANGE F2.
See p. 224, 266.

● **Hop**
Humulus lupulus
Tall. Clockwise climber, with square stems, deeply 3–5 lobed lvs. and ♂ fls in branching clusters, or ♀ in 'cones' on separate plants. LH perenn; rootstock. GERM spr. FL 7–9. POLL wind. SEX (♂) + (♀). HAB hedges, scrub, fens, wet woods. SOIL moist–wet; not acid. SHADE nil–heavy. ALT sl–200. DIST sE4, nE3, W3, S2, I3. RANGE F4, G4, S3.
See p. 191, 270.

NETTLE FAMILY
Urticaceae
Mostly herbs, often with stinging hairs and unlobed leaves. Male and female flowers separate, on the same or separate plants, with 4 or 5 inconspicuous lobed petals. Exotic species have extremely potent poisons in stinging hairs. Often associated with man-affected habitats.
See p. 182, 239, 250, 251, 257, 273.

● **Nettle**
Urtica dioica
Mid–v.tall. Stems creeping, rooting, bearing upright stems with stinging hairs; lvs short-stalked, toothed in opposite pairs; fls in catkin-like spikes. LH perenn; rootstock. GERM aut–spr. FL 6–9. POLL wind. SEX (♂) + (♀). HAB fens, wet woods; near buildings, in fields, hedges. SOIL wet–moist, not acid; favours high phosphate levels. SHADE nil–mid. ALT sl–800. DIST E5, W5, S5, I5. RANGE F5, G5, S5.
ssI.

● **Annual nettle**
Urtica urens
Short–mid. Like nettle, but lvs long-stalked, ♂ and ♀ fls on same plant; stinging hairs less powerful. LH ann. GERM spr–sum. FL 5–9. POLL wind. SEX (♂ + ♀). HAB arable weed. SOIL moist–dry; acid–calc. SHADE nil. ALT sl–200(–400). DIST E4, W2, S3, I2. RANGE F4, G5, S4.
See p. 183, 264, 271.

● **Pellitory-of-the-wall**
Parietaria judaica
Short–mid. Branching, red-stemmed, hairy, with alternate lvs; fls in small clusters. LH perenn; rootstock. GERM spr. FL 5–10. POLL wind. SEX (♀) + (♂) + (♀) pg. HAB rocks, walls, stony banks. SOIL moist–dry; not acid. SHADE nil–light. HAB rocks, walls, stony banks. ALT sl–200. DIST sE4, nE1, W1, S2. RANGE F3, G1.
See p. 262.

Large pellitory
Parietaria officinalis
Mid. Like Pellitory-of-the-wall, but little-branched, with longer lvs, much longer than stalks. LH perenn. GERM ? FL 6–9. POLL wind. SEX (♀) + (♂) + (♀) pg. HAB bare ground, walls, woods. SOIL moist–dry; acid–calc. SHADE nil–mid. ALT [sl–500(–1000)]. RANGE F2, G2.

DOCK FAMILY
Polygonaceae
Docks, knotgrasses and bistorts. Mainly herbs with a sheath (ochrea) round the stem where each entire leaf joins. 'Petals' persisting in flower and becoming hard in docks and known as valves. Many are found in waste places, a few in natural grassland, wet places, etc.
See p. 16, 257, 272, 289, 293.

29

● **Bistort**
Polygonum bistorta
Short–mid. Forms
large clumps; stems
unbranched; lvs oval
or triangular; fls pink,
in dense cylindrical
spikes, up to 8cm long.
LH perenn; short
rhizome. GERM spr. FL
6–9. POLL ins. SEX (♀)
pa. HAB old meadows.
SOIL damp–moist;
acid–calc. SHADE nil–
light. ALT sl–350. DIST
sE2, nE4, W2, S2, I1.
RANGE F3, G3, S2.
See p. 271.

● **Knotgrass**
Polygonum aviculare
V. low–low; but
spreading. Sprawling,
much-branched, with
small narrow lvs and
tiny fls in lf-junctions.
LH ann. GERM spr. FL
6–10. POLL self. SEX
(♀). HAB bare ground,
cultivated and un-
cultivated. SOIL moist–
dry; acid–calc. SHADE
nil. ALT sl–500. DIST
E5, W5, S5, I5. RANGE
F5, G5, S5.
See p. 243, 261, 273.
ss2. ss3. ss4.

● **Amphibious bistort**
Polygonum amphibium
Low–short; but
spreading. Floating in
water, with oblong lvs,
or on land with nar-
rower lvs, rounded at
base; fls in dense
spikes up to 5cm long.
LH perenn; rooted
nodes. GERM spr. FL
6–9. POLL ?ins. SEX
(♂)+(♀); (♀); (♀+♀).
HAB slow or still water
and waterside mud and
grassland. SOIL water-
moist; not acid. SHADE
nil. ALT sl–200. DIST
E4, W3, S3, I3. RANGE
F4, G4, S3.

● **Water-pepper**
Polygonum hydropiper
Short–mid. Branching
weak-stemmed,
ochreae straight-edged;
lvs narrow; fls greenish
in broken, lfy spike;
burning taste. LH ann.
GERM spr. FL 7–9. POLL
self. SEX (♀). HAB bare,
damp mud and in
shallow water. SOIL
damp–wet; acid–calc.
SHADE nil. ALT sl–200
(–400). DIST E4, W4,
S3, I4. RANGE F5, G5,
S3.

○ **Small water-pepper**
Polygonum minus
Short. Like Water-
pepper but smaller, lvs
less than 5cm long,
ochreae fringed, fls
pinkish. LH ann. GERM
spr. FL 8–9. POLL self.
SEX (♀). HAB damp,
sparsely grassy places.
SOIL wet–damp; not
calc. SHADE nil. ALT
sl–300. DIST E1, W1,
S1, I1. RANGE F2, G3,
S1.
ss5.

● **Redshank**
Polygonum persicaria
Short–mid. Weak-
stemmed, branching,
with narrow, normally
dark-spotted lvs;
ochreae fringed; fls
pink or white, in loose
spikes. LH ann. GERM
spr. FL 6–10. POLL self.
SEX (♀). HAB bare
ground, often by
water. SOIL wet–moist;
acid–calc. SHADE nil.
ALT sl–400. DIST E5,
W5, S3, I5. RANGE F5,
G5, sS4, nS1.

● **Pale persicaria**
*Polygonum
lapathifolium*
Short–tall. Like Red-
shank, but larger, lvs
not dark-blotched;
ochreae straight-edged;
fl-spike larger, denser;
fls rarely pink. LH ann.
GERM spr. FL 6–10.
POLL self. SEX (♀). HAB
bare ground and by
ponds. SOIL wet–moist;
acid–calc. SHADE nil.
ALT sl–400. DIST E4,
W3, S2, I2. RANGE F5,
G5, sS4, nS2.

○ **Alpine bistort**
Polygonum viviparum
Low–short. Lvs v.
narrow on stem; fl-
spike narrow with
white fls at top and
reddish-purple bulbils
at base. LH perenn;
short rhizome, bulbils.
GERM ? FL 6–8. POLL
ins, but rarely sets
seed. SEX (♀); (♂);
(♀); (♂+♀). HAB damp
grassland and rocks,
mainly in mountains.
SOIL damp; acid–calc.
SHADE nil (sl–)
100–1250. DIST E1,
W1, S3, I1. RANGE F1,
G1, S5.
See p. 293.

○ **Buckwheat**
Fagopyrum esculentum
Short–mid. Lvs large,
pointed heart-shaped,
all on stems; fls in
branching spikes. LH
ann. GERM ? FL 7–9.
POLL ins(h). SEX (♂+♀)
heterostylous; (♂).
HAB disturbed ground.
SOIL moist, not acid.
SHADE nil. ALT sl–100.
DIST once cultivated,
now casual mainly in
sE. RANGE cultivated
and casual F, G, S.

● **Black bindweed**
Bilderdykia convolvulus
Mid–v.tall. Clockwise
climber, with broad
arrow-shaped lvs, and
loose lfy spikes of
pinkish-green fls. LH
ann. GERM spr. FL
7–10. POLL self. SEX
(♀). HAB disturbed
ground. SOIL damp–
moist; acid–calc.
SHADE nil–light. ALT
sl–400. DIST E5, W3,
S3, I3. RANGE F5, G5,
S4.
See p. 193. **ss6.**

● **Japanese knotweed**
Reynoutria japonica
V.tall. Large and fast-growing, with large rounded-triangular lvs and zigzag stems; fl-spike branching. LH perenn; creeping rhizome. GERM ? FL 8–10. POLL ? SEX (♀'). HAB disturbed ground, roadsides; increasingly spreading into more natural habitats. SOIL moist–dry; acid–calc. SHADE nil–light. ALT sl–200. DIST (E,W,S,I) spreading. RANGE (F, G,S) spreading.

● **Curled dock**
Rumex crispus
Tall. Lvs very long (to 30cm), rather narrow, with very wavy edges; fls in close whorls; all 3 fr valves with tubercles, toothed. LH perenn; rootstock. GERM spr. FL 6–10. POLL wind. SEX (♀').. HAB disturbed ground, sometimes in woods; a distinct subspecies on shingle beaches. SOIL damp–dry; acid–calc. SHADE nil–mid. ALT sl–500. DIST E5, W5, S5, I5. RANGE F5, G5, S3.
See p. 215. **ss7**.

● **Broad-leaved dock**
Rumex obtusifolius
Tall. Lvs large and broad, lower heart-shaped at base, sometimes wavy-edged; fls in well-spaced whorls; only 1 fr valve tubercled, untoothed. LH perenn; rootstock. GERM aut–spr. FL 6–10. POLL wind. SEX (♀'). HAB disturbed ground. SOIL damp–dry; acid–calc. SHADE nil–light. ALT sl–500. DIST E5, W5, S5, I5. RANGE F5, G5, sS3.
See p. 273. **ss8**.

● **Water dock**
Rumex hydrolapathum
V.tall. The largest dock, much branched, with lvs up to 1m or more long; fls in close whorls; all 3 fr valves tubercled, untoothed. LH perenn; rootstock. GERM spr. FL 7–9. POLL wind. SEX (♀'). HAB in or by still or slow water. SOIL water–wet; not acid. SHADE nil–light. ALT sl–100. DIST sE4, nE2, W2, S2, I2. RANGE F4, G4, sS2. **ss9**.

○ **Marsh dock**
Rumex palustris
Mid-tall. Lvs long and narrow; fls in lfy whorls; whole plant turning yellow in fr; fr valves toothed, swollen. LH ann or short-lived perenn. GERM aut. FL 6–9. POLL wind. SEX (♀'). HAB muddy watersides. SOIL damp–moist; acid–calc. SHADE nil. ALT sl–100. DIST E2, W1. RANGE F2, G3, sS1. **ss10**.

● **Wood dock**
Rumex sanguineus
Mid-tall. Like Clustered dock, but stem straight, branches more upright, lvs narrow oval, and fl-spikes less lfy; only 1 fr valve tubercled. LH perenn; rootstock. GERM spr. FL 6–8. POLL wind. SEX (♀'). HAB mainly woods, but also in disturbed and grassy places. SOIL wet–moist; not acid. SHADE nil–heavy. ALT sl–300. DIST E4, W4, sS4, nS1. RANGE F4, G4, sS1.

● **Clustered dock**
Rumex conglomeratus
Mid-tall. Stem zigzag, branches spreading; lvs often narrowed in middle; fls in well-spaced, lfy whorls; all 3 fr-valves tubercled. LH perenn; rootstock. GERM spr. FL 6–8. POLL wind. SEX (♀'). HAB grassy places and wood edges. SOIL damp–moist; acid–calc. SHADE nil–mid. ALT sl–300. DIST E4, W3, S2, I4. RANGE F4, G4, sS1. **ss11**.

● **Common sorrel**
Rumex acetosa
Mid-tall. Lvs arrow-shaped, upper clasping stem, ochreae fringed; fls in whorls in loose, branching spikes, turning orange. LH perenn; rootstock. GERM spr. FL 5–7. POLL wind. SEX (♂) + (♀). HAB typical of old grassland, but also in more disturbed grassy places, open woods, mountains, etc. SOIL damp–moist; acid–calc. SHADE nil–light. ALT sl–1300. DIST E5, W5, S5, I5. RANGE F5, G5, S5.
See p. 170, 270.

● **Sheep's sorrel**
Rumex acetosella
Low–short. Delicate with narrow, arrow-shaped lvs, the lobes bent forwards, all stalked; fls in very sparse, branching spikes. LH perenn; root buds. GERM aut–spr. FL 5–9. POLL wind. SEX (♂) + (♀). HAB heathy and grassy places on poor, often sandy soils with sparse vegetation. SOIL moist–dry; not calc. SHADE nil. ALT sl–1000. DIST E5, W5, S5, I5. RANGE F5, G5, S5.
See p. 270, 272.

○ **Mountain sorrel**
Oxyria digyna
Low–short. Lvs fleshy, kidney-shaped, mostly from roots; fr with two valves, no tubercles. LH perenn; rootstock. GERM ? FL 7–8. POLL wind. SEX (♀'). HAB stony places in mountains. SOIL damp; not acid. SHADE nil. ALT (sl–) 200–1250. DIST nE1, W1, S3, I1. RANGE G1, S4.

PURSLANE FAMILY
Portulacaceae
Herbs, with simple, often fleshy leaves and hermaphrodite flowers with 2 sepals and, usually, 5 petals, joined at the base to make a short tube.

● **Blinks**
Montia fontana
V.low–low; spreading. Weak and often red-stemmed, with pairs of small lvs, widest near top; fls 2–3mm, in loose clusters, each with 3 stamens. LH persistent ann. GERM spr. FL 4–10. POLL self (fls open only in sun). SEX (♀) hg. HAB wet grassland, spring, slow muddy streams, wet rocks. SOIL water–damp; acid–calc. SHADE nil. ALT sl–1000. DIST nE4, sE2, W4, S4, I2. RANGE F3, G4, S5.
See p. 261. **ss12.**

● **Spring beauty**
Montia perfoliata
Short. Lower lvs long-stalked, one opposite pair encircling stem, all fleshy; fls 4–5mm, each with 5 stamens. LH ann. GERM win–spr. FL 4–7. POLL ins(d); self. SEX (♀). HAB disturbed ground, roadsides, sand-dunes. SOIL moist-dry; not calc. SHADE nil–mid. ALT sl–100. DIST (E3, W2, S2, I2); spreading.

○ **Pink purslane**
Montia sibirica
Short-mid. Like Spring beauty but lvs not encircling stem; fls 15–20mm, pink, petals notched. LH persistent ann. GERM ? FL 4–7. POLL ins(d, h). SEX (♀) pa. HAB damp woods, often by streams. SOIL damp–moist; not calc. SHADE light–heavy. ALT sl–100. DIST (E3, W3, S3, I1); spreading. RANGE (F1).

GOOSEFOOT FAMILY
Chenopodiaceae
Mainly herbs, with simple, often fleshy or mealy leaves. All have obscure, greenish, 3–5 petalled flowers either hermaphrodite or with separate ♂ or ♀ flowers on each plant (oraches, sea purslane). A very high proportion can tolerate salty soils, and the family is important in saltmarsh communities.
See p. 16, 17, 229, 257.

● **Good King Henry**
Chenopodium bonus-henricus
Mid. Lvs large (to 10cm), little-toothed, triangular; almost lfless fl-spikes; the only perennial goosefoot. LH perenn; rootstock. GERM sl–spr. FL 5–8. POLL wind. SEX (♀) pg. HAB lightly disturbed ground, often near farms. SOIL damp–moist; acid–calc. SHADE nil. ALT sl–250. DIST E3, W2, S2, I2. RANGE F3, G4, sS2.

● **Fat hen**
Chenopodium album
Short-tall. Very variable; stem reddish and lvs deep green, but hidden by thick white meal; lvs rather narrow, widest in middle, toothed. LH ann. GERM spr. FL 6–10. POLL wind. SEX (♀) pg. HAB disturbed ground. SOIL damp–dry; acid–calc. SHADE nil. ALT sl–300. DIST E5, W4, S4, I4. RANGE F5, G5, S4.
See p. 17, 170, 215, 243. **ss13.**

○ **Fig-leaved goosefoot**
Chenopodium ficifolium
Mid–tall. Lvs large (to 8cm), 3-lobed, the middle lobe much the largest. LH ann. GERM spr. FL 7–9. POLL wind. SEX (♀) pg. HAB disturbed, fertile ground. SOIL moist; not acid. SHADE nil. ALT sl–100. DIST seE3, nwE1. RANGE F2, G2, and casual.

○ **Maple-leaved goosefoot**
Chenopodium hybridum
Tall. Lvs triangular, with large teeth; fls in lfless branching clusters. LH ann. GERM spr. FL 7–10. POLL wind. SEX (♀) pg. HAB disturbed ground. SOIL moist; not acid. SHADE nil. ALT sl–100. DIST sE2. RANGE F3, G3, sS3.
ss14.

○ **Nettle-leaved goosefoot**
Chenopodium murale
Mid. Lvs triangular or diamond-shaped, with pointed, curved teeth; fls in dense, branching clusters. LH winter ann. GERM aut. FL 6–9. POLL wind. SEX (♀) pg. HAB disturbed ground, sand dunes. SOIL moist–dry; acid-calc. SHADE nil. ALT sl–100. DIST E2, W2, S1, I1. RANGE F3, G3, sS1.

● **Many-seeded goosefoot**
Chenopodium polyspermum
Mid–tall. Sprawling, reddish, square-stemmed, with untoothed, oval lvs and loose, lfy fl-spikes. LH ann. GERM spr. FL 7–10. POLL wind. SEX (♀) pg. HAB cultivated ground. SOIL moist–dry; not acid. SHADE nil. ALT sl–200. DIST sE3, nE2, W2, I1. RANGE F4, G4, sS2. **ss15**.

● **Red goosefoot**
Chenopodium rubrum
Mid. Very variable, reddish, hairless; lvs diamond-shaped or triangular, much toothed; fls in dense, often lfy spikes. LH ann. GERM spr. FL 7–10. POLL wind. SEX (♀) pg. HAB disturbed, fertile ground, especially near sea. SOIL damp–moist; acid–calc. SHADE nil. ALT sl–200. DIST sE4, nE1, S1, I1. RANGE F4, G4, sS2. **ss16**.

● **Babington's orache**
Atriplex glabriuscula
Low–short; procumbent. Bracts of ♀ fls thick, fused; lvs triangular, stems mealy; often red in autumn. LH ann. GERM spr. FL 7–9. POLL small ins, mainly self. SEX (♂+♀). HAB maritime sand and shingle. SOIL dry; mainly calc. SHADE nil. ALT sl. DIST coastal: E2, W2, S2, I1. RANGE coastal: F2, G2, S2, s. to Brittany. **ss17**.

● **Spear-leaved orache**
Atriplex prostrata
Mid–tall. Very like Babington's orache, but taller, erect, and not turning red; bracts of ♀ fls thin. LH ann. GERM spr. FL 7–10. POLL small ins, mainly self. SEX (♂+♀). HAB sea-shores, disturbed ground. SOIL moist–dry; not acid. SHADE nil. ALT sl–100(–400). DIST sE4, nE2, W2, S2, I2. RANGE coastal: F4, G4, S2.

● **Grass-leaved orache**
Atriplex littoralis
Mid–tall. Lvs very narrow; bracts of ♀ fls joined at base with a pointed at tip. LH ann. GERM spr–sum. FL 7–8. POLL small ins, mainly self. SEX (♂+♀). HAB salt-marshes, muddy banks by sea. SOIL damp to wet; saline. SHADE nil. ALT sl. DIST coastal: eE4, sE2, wE2, W2, S2, I1. RANGE coastal, F3, G3, S3; inland, F1, G1, S1.

● **Common orache**
Atriplex patula
Tall. Similar to Spear-leaved orache, but lvs less triangular and more mealy. LH ann. GERM mainly spr. FL 7–9. POLL small ins, mainly self. SEX (♂+♀). HAB less coastal than other oraches; disturbed ground. SOIL moist; not acid. SHADE nil. ALT sl–200(–400). DIST E5, W4, S3, I4. RANGE F5, G5, S3. *See p. 243.*

● **Sea beet**
Beta vulgaris ssp. *maritima*
Mid–tall; sprawling. Lvs leathery, often red-tinged, untoothed; fls in small clusters of 2–3; 'petals' persistent, swollen at base in fr. LH ann or monocarpic perenn; rootstock. GERM win onwards. FL 6–9. POLL wind; not self. SEX (♀) pa. HAB drift line of sand and shingle beaches; dry banks near the sea. SOIL moist to dry; saline. SHADE nil. ALT sl. DIST coastal: sE4, nE3, W4, S1, I3. RANGE coastal: F5, G3, sS1.

● **Sea purslane**
Halimione portulacoides
Mid–tall. Like oraches (♂ and ♀ fls separate) but grey lvs entire, opposite at woody base of stem; bracts of ♀ fls fused to top. LH woody perenn; rhizome. GERM win onwards. FL 7–10. POLL wind. SEX (♂+♀). HAB upper salt-marsh and along drainage channels. SOIL wet; saline. SHADE nil–light (under reeds). ALT sl. DIST coastal: E4, W4, I2. RANGE coastal: F4, G4.

● **Glasswort**
Salicornia europaea agg.
Low–short. Stems swollen, fleshy; lvs reduced to scales and fused with the stem; fls minute, at the joints of the stem; 1–2 stamens. LH ann. GERM spr. FL 8–9. POLL ? SEX (♀). HAB open muddy sand and shingle, often near low tide. SOIL wet; saline. SHADE nil. ALT sl. DIST coastal: E4, W4, S2, I4. RANGE coastal: F4, G4, S2. *See p. 205.*

○ **Perennial glasswort**
Arthrocnemum perenne
Short. Like Glasswort but stems creeping and woody at base, forming large tussocks; turns orange or red. LH woody perenn; rooting stems. GERM ? FL 4–9. POLL ? SEX (♀). HAB gravelly salt-marshes. SOIL wet; saline. SHADE nil. ALT sl. DIST coastal: seE2, nwE1, W1, S1, I1. RANGE coastal: F2.

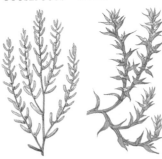

● **Annual seablite**
Suaeda maritima
Low–short; erect or
prostrate. Lvs fleshy,
½-cylindrical, pointed
at the top; often red;
fls tiny, in small groups
among upper lvs. LH
ann. GERM spr–early
sum. FL 7–10. POLL
wind; self. SEX (♂) and
(♀). HAB bare mud,
muddy sand, salt-
marshes. SOIL wet,
saline. SHADE nil. ALT
sl. DIST coastal: E3,
W3, S2, I3. RANGE
coastal: F4, G4, S2
(not arctic).

● **Prickly saltwort**
Salsola kali
Short–mid; prostrate.
Lvs narrow, fleshy,
tapering into a spiny
tip; fls solitary, sur-
rounded by bracts,
persisting in fr. LH ann.
GERM late spr. FL 7–9.
POLL wind. SEX (♂).
HAB along seaward
edge of foredunes;
rarely inland in bare
sandy places or waste
ground. SOIL dry; not
acid. SHADE nil. ALT sl.
DIST coastal: E3, W3,
S3, I3. RANGE coastal,
F3, G3, sS2; inland,
F1, G1.
See p. 205.

PINK FAMILY
Caryophyllaceae
A large family with
about 22 genera and
75 species native to the
British Isles, all of
which are herbs (i.e.
non woody). Most
have leaves in opposite
pairs, a few in whorls.
Leaves always un-
toothed and simple,
either narrow or oval.
Flowers have 5 (rarely
4) petals and sepals,
the petals often not-
ched and not joined.
Flowers commonly in
terminal flowerheads,
loosely branching and
of indefinite growth
(cymes), often giving
long flowering periods.
Fruit a dry capsule,
often forming a censer-
type dispersal mech-
anism. Ecologically a
very heterogeneous
family.
*See p. 16, 17, 18, 19,
173, 191, 210, 214, 249,
257, 263, 277, 282, 298,
299.*

● **Thyme-leaved
sandwort**
Arenaria serpyllifolia
Low–short. Oval lvs;
inconspicuous fls,
5–8mm, petals shorter
than sepals. LH ann or
short-lived perenn.
GERM sum–aut. FL 5
onwards. POLL self;
ins. SEX (♂) hg. HAB
bare ground in grassy
and heathy places;
walls. SOIL dry; not
acid. SHADE nil. ALT
sl–400 (–600). DIST E4,
W3, S2, I2. RANGE F4,
G4, S3.
See p. 209. **ss 18**.

● **Three-nerved
sandwort**
Moehringia trinervia
Low–short. Lvs oval
with 3–5 conspicuous
veins; fls 5–6mm,
petals shorter than
sepals. LH ann or
short-lived perenn.
GERM ? FL 5–6. POLL
self; ins. SEX (♂). HAB
mainly deciduous
woodland, in sparse
vegetation. SOIL moist;
fertile; not acid. SHADE
mid–heavy. ALT sl–300
(–400). DIST E4, W4,
S3, I2. RANGE F4, G4,
S3.
See p. 209, 246.

○ **Fine-leaved
sandwort**
Minuartia hybrida
Low. Branching, but
erect; lvs narrow; fls
5–6mm, petals half as
long as white-edged
sepals; styles 3. LH
ann. GERM aut. FL 5–8.
POLL ins. SEX (♂).
HAB dry bare places:
walls, rocks, sandy and
gravelly ground. SOIL
dry; not acid. SHADE
nil. ALT sl–200(–300).
DIST sE2, nE1, W1, I1.
RANGE F3, G2.
ss19.

○ **Cyphel**
Minuartia sedoides
V.low–low. Forms neat
cushions, with closely
overlapping narrow
lvs; fls 4–5mm diam,
5 yellowish sepals, 0
petals, 3 short styles.
LH perenn; winter-
green. GERM ? FL 6–8.
POLL ins(d); self ? SEX
(♀+♂); (♂) rare. HAB
open stony ground at
high altitude. SOIL
moist; base-poor to
base-rich. SHADE nil.
ALT 500–1300. DIST S1.
RANGE G1, alpine.

○ **Spring sandwort**
Minuartia verna
V.low–low. Forms
loose cushions, often
straggling; lvs narrow,
3-veined; fls 8–10mm,
petals longer than
sepals; styles 3. LH
perenn; wintergreen.
GERM ? FL 5–9. POLL
ins. SEX (♂) pa; (♀+♂)
and (♀) also occur.
HAB dry rocks and
short grassland on
limestone; particularly
on debris contamina-
ted by lead-mining.
SOIL dry; not acid.
SHADE nil. ALT sl–900.
DIST E1, W1, S1, I1.
RANGE F1, G2, S1.
See p. 219, 262, 282
ss20. ss21.

● **Sea sandwort**
Honkenya peploides
V.low–low. Creeping
with fleshy, yellow-
green, oval lvs; fls
7–10mm, petals pale
green, as long as ♂ fls,
or shorter than ♀ fls'
sepals; fr conspicuous.
LH perenn; stolons.
GERM ? FL 5–8. POLL
ins, wind, wind-blown
sand or self. SEX (♂);
(♂); (♀). HAB fore-
shore; forms tiny
foredunes in sand and
shingle. SOIL dry; not
acid. SHADE nil. ALT sl.
DIST coastal: E5, W5,
S5, I5. RANGE coastal:
F5, G5, S3.
See p. 205.

● **Lesser stitchwort**
Stellaria graminea
Short–tall. Stems
square; lvs narrow; fls
6–12mm, petals not-
ched to over half-way,
as long as sepals;
styles 3. LH perenn;
creeping rootstock,
stems may root. GERM
? FL 5–8. POLL ins(d,
h, c). SEX (♂) pa;
(♂+♀), (♀). HAB open
woods, heathland,
scrub, tall grassland.
SOIL well-drained,
moist to dry; not calc.
SHADE nil to mid. ALT
sl–400 (–600). DIST
E5, W5, S4, I4. RANGE
F5, G5, S5.

Small-flowered chickweed
Stellaria longifolia
Short. Very like Lesser stitchwort but has rough stems and very small fls (2–4mm). LH perenn. GERM ? FL 6–8. POLL ins. SEX (♀). HAB woods. SOIL damp–moist; acid–calc. SHADE mid–heavy. ALT [sl–1500]. RANGE G1, S4.

● **Greater stitchwort**
Stellaria holostea
Short–mid. Stems square, rough; lvs narrow, greyish, rough-edged and unstalked; fls 20–30mm, petals notched to half-way, longer than sepals; styles 3. LH perenn; creeping rootstock. GERM ? FL 4–6. POLL ins(d, c); self. SEX (♀) pa; (♀) and (♀ + ♀) rare. HAB woods, hedges. SOIL damp to moist; not calc. SHADE nil to heavy. ALT sl–500(–800). DIST E5, W5, S3, I3. RANGE F5, G5, S1.

○ **Wood stitchwort**
Stellaria nemorum
Short–mid. Stems round, evenly hairy; lvs stalked, oval; fls to 18mm, petals notched over half-way, longer than sepals; styles 3. LH perenn; stolons. GERM ? FL 5–7. POLL ins(d, c). SEX (♀) pa. HAB damp woods, shady streamsides. SOIL damp to moist; not acid. SHADE light to heavy. ALT sl–400 (–900). DIST nE2, W1, sS2. RANGE F1, G2, S4. **ss22.**

● **Bog stitchwort**
Stellaria alsine
Low–short; but spreading. Stems square; lvs unstalked; fls 4–6mm, petals notched, shorter than sepals. LH perenn; rooted nodes. GERM ? FL 5–7. POLL ins(d); self. SEX (♀) pa. HAB springs, muddy streams, wet woods. SOIL wet–damp; not calc. SHADE nil–mid. ALT sl–1000. DIST E4, W5, S5, I4. RANGE F5, G5, sS4.

● **Common chickweed**
Stellaria media
Low–short; spreading. Variable; stems round with a line of hairs; lower lvs long-stalked, upper lvs unstalked; fls to 10mm, petals deeply notched, equalling sepals; styles 3. LH persistent ann. GERM any. FL 1–12. POLL ins(h, d); self. SEX (♀) slightly pa. HAB disturbed ground, damp woods. SOIL damp–moist; acid–calc. SHADE nil–light. ALT sl–750. DIST E5, W5, S5, I5. RANGE F5, G5, S5.
See p. 174, 215, 243, 263, 296. **ss23.**

○ **Marsh stitchwort**
Stellaria palustris
Low–mid; spreading. Stems square, some with no fls; lvs greyish, narrow; fls 12–18mm, petals split to base; styles 3. LH perenn; creeping rootstock. GERM ? FL 5–7. POLL ins(d). SEX (♀) pa. HAB grassy marshes, fens. SOIL damp–moist; not acid. SHADE nil. ALT sl–100. DIST E2, W1, S1, I1. RANGE F2, G3, sS3.

● **Water chickweed**
Myosoton aquaticum
Short–tall; straggling. Weak-stemmed with large oval lvs, the upper unstalked; fls 12–15mm, petals notched half-way, longer than sepals; styles 5. LH persistent ann or short-lived perenn; buds on stem base. GERM ? FL 6–11. POLL ins(d, h, c). SEX (♀) pa; (♀). HAB marshes, woods, near water. SOIL wet-damp; not acid. SHADE nil–mid. ALT sl–100. DIST sE4, nE1, W1. RANGE F3, G4, sS2.
See p. 192, 263.

● **Field mouse-ear**
Cerastium arvense
Low–short; spreading. Hairy, lvs narrow, straight-sided; prostrate shoots without fls; upright shoots with fls 12–20mm, petals notched half-way; styles 5. LH perenn; creeping rootstock. GERM ? FL 4–9. POLL ins(d, h). SEX (♀) pa; (♀). HAB grassland, roadsides, open banks. SOIL dry; not acid. SHADE nil. ALT sl–200. DIST eE3, nE2, W2, S2, I1. RANGE F3, G4, S3.
See p. 191, 280.

○ **Alpine mouse-ear**
Cerastium alpinum
V.low–low; spreading. Like Field mouse-ear but densely long-hairy, lvs narrowed at base; fls 15–20(–25)mm. LH perenn, creeping woody stems. GERM ? FL 6–8. POLL ins. SEX (♀) pa. HAB mountain rocks. SOIL damp-moist; not calc. SHADE nil. ALT 500–1250. DIST nE1, W1, S2. RANGE G1, S3. **ss24.**

○ **Starwort mouse-ear**
Cerastium cerastoides
V.low–low. Like Field mouse-ear but hairless (except for line of hairs on stem); lvs curved; fls 9–12mm; styles 3. LH perenn; creeping woody stems. GERM ? FL 7–8. POLL ins(d); self. SEX (♀) hg. HAB mountain rocks. SOIL damp–moist; not acid. SHADE nil. ALT 750–1250. DIST S1. RANGE G1, S3.

○ **Sea mouse-ear**
Cerastium diffusum
Low–short. Stickily
hairy, branching, with
oval lvs, lfy bracts and
4-petalled and 4-styled
fls, 3–4mm; petals
slightly notched,
shorter than sepals.
LH winter ann. GERM
aut. FL 4–7. POLL ins
(d); rarely self. SEX (♀)
hg. HAB sand-dunes;
inland rare on dis-
turbed ground. SOIL
dry; calc. SHADE nil.
ALT sl. DIST coastal,
E5, W5, S5, I5; inland,
E1, W1, S1, I3. RANGE
coastal: F5, G5, S3.
See p. 214. **ss25.**

● **Common mouse-ear**
Cerastium fontanum
Short–mid. Hairy, dull
grey-green; prostrate
shoots with no fls,
erect shoots with fls,
5–8mm; petals longer
than sepals, notched
½-way; styles 5. LH
short-lived perenn;
creeping rootstock.
GERM spr. FL 4–10.
POLL ins(d); self. SEX
(♀) pa. HAB grass and
bare places. SOIL
damp–dry; acid–calc.
SHADE nil–light. ALT
sl–1250. DIST E1, W1,
S1, I5. RANGE F5, G5,
S5.
See p. 214. **ss26.**

● **Sticky mouse-ear**
Cerastium glomeratum
Low–short. Stickily
hairy (at top of stem),
yellowish-green, all
shoots flg; fls in small,
dense clusters rarely
opening; sepals hairy,
petals notched, equal-
ling sepals; styles 5.
LH persistent ann.
GERM ? BL 4–10. POLL
self. SEX (♀) hg. HAB
bare and sparsely
grassy ground, walls.
SOIL moist–dry; acid–
calc. SHADE nil. ALT
sl–600. DIST E4, W3,
S3, I2. RANGE F5, G5,
S2.

● **Little mouse-ear**
*Cerastium
semidecandrum*
V.low–low. Hairy and
branched with long-
stalked lvs; fls 5mm,
petals shorter than
sepals, slightly not-
ched; bracts white-
edged; styles 5. LH
persistent ann. GERM
aut. FL 3–5. POLL self.
SEX (♀) hg. HAB bare,
sandy ground. SOIL
dry; not acid. SHADE
nil. ALT sl–400. DIST
E3, W2, S2, I2. RANGE
F4, G5, sS4.
See p. 188. **ss27.**

● **Corn spurrey**
Spergula arvensis
Low–short. Stems
weak, bent, with
whorls of very narrow
lvs, channelled under-
neath, stickily hairy;
fls 5–8mm in widely
branching clusters;
styles 5. LH ann. GERM
aut–spr. FL 5–9. POLL
ins(d); self; fls open
morning only. SEX (♀)
hg. HAB arable weed.
SOIL moist–dry; not
calc. SHADE nil. ALT
sl–400. DIST E1, W1,
S1, I4. RANGE F4, G5,
S4.
*See p. 210, 243, 261,
263, 282.*

● **Lesser sea spurrey**
Spergularia marina
Low. Slightly hairy, all
shoots flg, more or less
prostrate, bearing
whorls of very narrow,
fleshy lvs; fls 5–8mm,
pink, petals shorter
than sepals; styles 3.
LH ann. GERM aut–spr.
FL 5–9. POLL self; fls
often closed, occasion-
ally cleistogamous. SEX
(♀). HAB dry parts of
saltmarshes. SOIL wet–
moist; saline. SHADE
nil. ALT sl. DIST
coastal, E4, W4, S4,
I4; inland, E1, W1, S1.
RANGE coastal, F4, G4,
S4; inland F1, G1, S1.
See p. 191.

● **Greater sea spurrey**
Spergularia media
Low–short. Hairless,
some shoots with no
fls; lvs narrow, fleshy
whorled; fls 8–12mm,
dull pink, petals longer
than sepals; styles 3.
LH perenn; rootstock.
GERM ? FL 6–9. POLL
ins;d). SEX (♀) pa; (♀).
HAB muddy salt-
marshes. SOIL wet–
damp; saline. SHADE
nil. ALT sl. DIST
coastal: seE5, E1, W1,
S1, I3. RANGE coastal:
F5, G5, S2.
See p. 191.

● **Rock sea spurrey**
Spergularia rupicola
Low. Stickily hairy,
some stems not flg;
lvs narrow, short,
fleshy worled; fls
8–10mm, deep pink,
petals equalling sepals;
styles 3. LH perenn;
rootstock. GERM ? FL
6–9. POLL ins(d). SEX
(♀) pa. HAB maritime
rocks. SOIL moist–dry;
acid–calc. SHADE nil.
ALT sl. DIST coastal:
swE, W4, swS2, I3.
RANGE coastal: F2.
See p. 191.

● **Sand spurrey**
Spergularia rubra
Low–short. Slightly
sticky, lvs narrow,
greyish, whorled; fls
3–5mm, pale pink,
shorter than sepals;
styles 3. LH persistent
ann. GERM aut–spr. FL
5–9. POLL ins(d) in fine
weather; self. SEX (♀)
hg; (♀+♀); (♀). HAB
open sandy ground.
SOIL dry; not calc.
SHADE nil. ALT sl–300.
DIST sE4, nE2, W2, S2,
I1. RANGE F4, G4, sS4.
See p. 245.

○ **Corn cockle**
Agrostemma githago
Mid–tall. Hairy, with
narrow, greyish lvs;
fls 30–50mm; sepals
hairy with narrow
tubes longer than
petals. LH ann. GERM
aut–spr. FL 5–8. POLL
ins(h, l). SEX (♀) hg–pa.
HAB arable fields. SOIL
moist–dry; acid–calc.
SHADE nil. ALT sl–50.
DIST eE1. RANGE F2,
G3, S2; declining.

● **Annual pearlwort**
Sagina apetala
V.low–low. Creeping, all stems flg, lvs needle-like; fls 3–4mm, 4 green sepals, no petals. LH ann. GERM aut–spr. FL 4–8. POLL ins, self. SEX (♀) pa. HAB bare ground, paths. SOIL damp–moist; not acid. SHADE nil. ALT sl–300. DIST seE5, nwE1, W1, S1, I2. RANGE F4, G3, sS1.
See p. 161, 294.

● **Procumbent pearlwort**
Sagina procumbens
V.low–low. Creeping from central non-flg rosette; fls 4mm, 4–5 green sepals, petals whitish, often missing. LH perenn; rosette. GERM ? FL 5–9. POLL self. SEX (♀) hg. HAB bare places, paths, lawns, damp rocks in mountains. SOIL moist; acid–calc. SHADE nil. DIST E5, W5, S5, I5. RANGE F5, G5, S5.

○ **Sea pearlwort**
Sagina maritima
Low. Like Annual pearlwort but lvs pointed, fleshy; sepals upright not spreading in fr. LH ann. GERM ? FL 5–9. POLL self. SEX (♀) hg. HAB maritime rocks, dune-slacks, rarely on mountains. SOIL wet–moist; not calc. SHADE nil. ALT sl. DIST coastal: E1, W1, S1, I2. RANGE F2, G2, S2.

○ **Knotted pearlwort**
Sagina nodosa
Low. Flg stems erect from basal rosette; lvs in pairs, with clusters (knots) on stem; fls 5–10mm, petals longer than sepals; styles 5. LH perenn; rosettes. GERM ? FL 7–9. POLL ins(d); self. SEX (♀) pa; (♀). HAB on sparsely vegetated sand and peat. SOIL damp; acid–calc. SHADE nil. ALT sl–600. DIST E1, W1, S1, I3. RANGE F2, G3, S3.

○ **Alpine pearlwort**
Sagina saginoides
V.low. Like Procumbent pearlwort, but with fls in central rosette; fls 4mm, with 5 sepals and 5 shorter, white petals; styles 5. LH perenn; rootstock. GERM ? FL 7–9. POLL ins(d), rarely open; self. SEX (♀) hg. HAB mountain rocks. SOIL damp; calc. SHADE nil. ALT 600–1250. DIST S2. RANGE F1, G1, S4.
ss28.

○ **Heath pearlwort**
Sagina subulata
Low. Central rosette non-flg; flg shoots slightly sticky-hairy; lvs long-pointed; fls 4mm, with 5 white petals, shorter than sepals; styles 5. LH perenn; rootstock. GERM spr. FL 6–8. POLL self. SEX (♀) hg. HAB sand or rocks. SOIL moist-dry; not calc. SHADE nil. ALT sl–800. DIST E1, W1, S1, I2. RANGE F2, G2, S2.

○ **Berry catchfly**
Cucubalus baccifer
Tall. Downy; stems easily broken; fls 15–20mm, nodding, petals deeply notched; fr a black berry. LH perenn; rhizome. GERM spr. FL 7–9. POLL ins. SEX (♀)pa. HAB disturbed and shady places. SOIL moist–dry; acid–calc. SHADE nil-mid. ALT sl–50. DIST E1. RANGE F2, G2.

○ **Annual knawel**
Scleranthus annuus
Low. Branching, weak-stemmed, yellowish-green, with narrow lvs in pairs clasping stem; fls clustered, no petals, 5 sepals white-edged; fr a nut. LH persistent ann. GERM aut–spr. FL 4–10. POLL ins(d, h); self. SEX (♀) hg. HAB bare sandy ground. SOIL dry; not calc. SHADE nil. ALT sl–350. DIST E3, W1, S1, I2. RANGE F4, G4, S3.
See p. 270. **ss29**.

○ **Perennial knawel**
Scleranthus perennis
Low–short. Woody-stemmed at base; lvs bluish, curved, often in small tufts up stem; fls with no petals and white-edged sepals. LH perenn; woody stems. POLL self; ins? SEX (♀) hg. HAB sandy fields. SOIL dry; acid–calc. SHADE nil. ALT sl–200. DIST E1, W1. RANGE F2, G3, sS3.

○ **Fringed rupturewort**
Herniaria ciliolata
V.low, creeping ever-green mat-former. Slightly hairy, lvs small, oval; fls 2mm, green, in tight clusters among lvs; stems. GERM ? FL 7–8. POLL ins(ants); self. SEX (♀) hg. HAB maritime sand and rocks. SOIL dry; calc. SHADE nil. ALT sl–50. DIST E1. RANGE F1.
ss30. **ss31**.

○ **Moss campion**
Silene acaulis
V.low–low, cushion forming. Lvs narrow, pointed; fls 10–12mm, petals notched, almost flush with cushion. LH perenn; stems. GERM spr. FL 6–8. POLL ins(l, d, h). SEX (♀) pa; (♂); (♀). HAB mountain rocks. SOIL damp–dry; not acid. SHADE nil. ALT (sl–)300–1250. DIST E1, W1, S3, I1. RANGE G1, S3.
See p. 258, 271, 299.

● **White campion**
Silene pratensis
Mid–tall. Lvs narrow oval, very hairy; fls 20–30mm, white, evening-scented; capsule with prominent teeth. LH short-lived perenn; rootstock. GERM aut–spr. FL 5–10. POLL ins(l). SEX (♂)+(♀). HAB disturbed ground, roadsides. SOIL moist–dry; acid–calc. SHADE nil. ALT sl–400. DIST E5, W4, S3, I2. RANGE F5, G4, S3.
See p. 174, 180, 259, 278, 288, 289, 292, 299.

● **Red campion**
Silene dioica
Mid–tall. Lf-stalks with a flange; fls 18–25mm, pink to deep red, occasionally paler (hybridizes with white campion); capsule with teeth down-turned. LH perenn; creeping rootstock. GERM aut–spr. FL 3–11. POLL ins(h, l). SEX (♂)+(♀). HAB deciduous woods, hedges, cliffs. SOIL damp–moist; not acid; fertile. SHADE nil–heavy. ALT sl–1000. DIST E5, W5, S5, I3. RANGE F5, G5, S5.
See p. 2, 180, 288, 289.

○ **Night-flowering catchfly**
Silene noctiflora
Short–mid. Lvs sticky; fls 15–18mm, rolling shut in the daytime to show yellowish petal undersides. LH ann. GERM aut–spr. FL 6–9. POLL ins(l, h). SEX (♀) pa. HAB arable fields. SOIL dry; calc. SHADE nil. ALT sl–100. DIST E3, W1, sS1. RANGE F2, G3, S2.
See p. 259, 278.

● **Sea campion**
Silene maritima
Low–short, patch-forming. Some shoots not flowering; fls 20–25mm, in small groups; sepal-tube inflated; capsule cylindrical. LH perenn; rootstock. GERM aut. POLL ins(l, h). SEX (♀) pa; (♂)+(♀); (♂+♀). HAB coastal shingle, cliffs; also on gravelly soils in mountains. SOIL moist–dry; not acid. SHADE nil. ALT sl–100, 250–1000. DIST coastal: E4, W3, S3, I3. RANGE F4, G2, S1.
See p. 249, 295, 299.

● **Bladder campion**
Silene vulgaris
Mid–tall. All shoots flg, fls in large numbers in each group; fls 15–20mm, petals notched, sepal-tube inflated; capsule oval. LH perenn; rootstock. GERM aut–spr. FL 5–9. POLL ins(l, h). SEX (♀) pa; (♂)+(♀); (♂+♀); (♀+♂). HAB grassy places, often slightly disturbed. SOIL dry; not acid. SHADE nil–light. ALT sl–300. DIST E5, W4, S3, I3. RANGE F5, G5, S4.
See p. 295.

○ **Small-flowered catchfly**
Silene gallica
Short–mid. Sticky-hairy; fls 10–12mm, in short spikes and all facing to one side. LH ann. GERM spr. FL 6–10. POLL ins(d); self. SEX (♀) pa. HAB bare, often sandy places. SOIL dry; acid–calc. SHADE nil. ALT sl–100. DIST E2, W1, I1. RANGE F3, G2.

○ **Sand catchfly**
Silene conica
Short. Stickily hairy; fls 4–5mm, pink, sepal-tube swollen in fruit, sticky. LH ann. GERM aut. FL 5–7. POLL ins(d); self. SEX (♀) pa. HAB bare sandy ground. SOIL dry; not calc. SHADE nil. ALT sl–100. DIST E2. RANGE F3, G1, (S1).
See p. 263.

○ **Nottingham catchfly**
Silene nutans
Mid–tall. Lvs widest above middle; fls 15–20mm, nodding in one-sided spikes; petals deeply split, rolling back in daytime. LH perenn; rootstock. GERM aut–spr. FL 5–8. POLL ins(l, h). SEX (♀) pa; rarely (♂)+(♀). HAB rocky and gravelly, bare but undisturbed ground. SOIL dry; calc. SHADE nil. ALT sl–250. DIST E1, W1, S1. RANGE F3, G3, S2.
See p. 1, 259, 271, 278, 299. **ss32.**

○ **Spanish catchfly**
Silene otites
Mid–tall. Lvs broadest near tip; fls 3–4mm, yellowish, in whorls in branching spikes. LH perenn; rootstock. GERM ? FL 6–9. POLL ins(l, h); wind. SEX (♀) pa; (♀)+(♂). HAB sandy grassland and heaths. SOIL dry; not acid. SHADE nil. ALT 50–100. DIST E1. RANGE F2, G2.
See p. 271, 299.

○ **Alpine catchfly**
Lychnis alpina
Low. Tufted; lvs narrow; fls 8–12mm, in tight clusters, petals deeply notched. LH perenn; rootstock. GERM spr. FL 6–7. POLL ins(l); self. SEX (♀) pa. HAB stony ground in mountains. SOIL dry; not acid. SHADE nil. ALT E600, S900. DIST E1, S1. RANGE F1, G1, S3.

● **Ragged robin**
Lychnis flos-cuculi
Mid-tall. Some shoots not flg, with lvs broadest near tip; fls with 4-lobed ragged petals. LH perenn; rootstock. GERM aut–spr. FL 5–8. POLL ins(l, h). SEX (♀) pa. HAB fens, meadows and woods. SOIL wet–damp; not acid. SHADE nil–mid. ALT sl–600. DIST E5, W5, S5, I5. RANGE F5, G5, S3.
See p. 164, 276, 299.

○ **Sticky catchfly**
Lychnis viscaria
Mid. Stems lfy, sticky beneath nodes; fls 18–20mm in branching, whorled spikes; petals slightly notched. LH perenn; rootstock. GERM ? FL 6–8. POLL ins(h,l). SEX (♀). HAB rocks, cliffs. SOIL dry; calc. SHADE nil. ALT sl–450. DIST W1, S1. RANGE F1, G4, S3.
See p. 271, 280.

● **Soapwort**
Saponaria officinalis
Mid–tall. Lvs to 10cm; fls 25mm, pale pink, in stalked clusters; petal tube longer than sepals; styles 2. LH perenn; rhizomes and stolons. GERM spr. FL 6–9. POLL ins(l). SEX (♀) pa. HAB hedges, roadsides, woods. SOIL damp–moist; not acid. SHADE nil–light. ALT sl–300. DIST E3, W1, S1, I2. RANGE F2, G3, S1.
See p. 213.

Annual gypsophila
Gypsophila muralis
Low. Much-branched; lvs very narrow, bluish; fls 4mm, petals notched, in loose clusters. LH ann. GERM ? FL 6–9. POLL ins(d, h). SEX (♀) pa. HAB sandy grassland and heaths. SOIL damp–moist; not calc. SHADE nil–light. ALT [sl–200]. RANGE F2, G3, S1.

○ **Maiden pink**
Dianthus deltoides
Short–mid. Roughly hairy, some shoots not flg; fls 15–20mm, petals spotted, fringed. LH perenn; creeping rootstock. GERM aut. FL 6–9. POLL ins(l). SEX (♀) pa. HAB grassy, often sandy places. SOIL dry; not acid. SHADE nil–light. ALT sl–200. DIST E2, W2, S2. RANGE F2, G3, S3.
See p. 17. **ss33**.

○ **Cheddar pink**
Dianthus gratianopolitanus
Low. Tufted, with creeping non-flg shoots; fls 20–30mm, borne singly, petals fringed. LH perenn; rootstock. GERM ? spr. FL 5–7. POLL ins(l). SEX (♀) pa. HAB rocky grassland. SOIL dry; calc. SHADE nil. ALT 50–200. DIST E1. RANGE F1, G2.

Carthusian pink
Dianthus carthusianorum
Short. With non-flg shoots and narrow; fls 20mm, deep bright red, in tight clusters enfolded by brown bracts. LH perenn; rootstock. GERM ? FL 6–8. POLL ins(l). SEX (♀) pa, (♀). HAB sandy, grassy places and open woods. SOIL dry; acid–calc. SHADE nil–mid. ALT [sl–2400]. RANGE F2, G3. **ss34**.

○ **Wild pink**
Dianthus plumarius
Short. With non-flg shoots and rough-edged lvs; fls 25–35mm, very fragrant, petals deeply lobed. LH perenn; rootstock. GERM aut. FL 6–8. POLL ins(l). SEX (♀) pa. HAB rocks and stony places. SOIL dry; calc. SHADE nil. ALT ? DIST (E1, W1, S1). RANGE (F1, G1).

BUTTERCUP FAMILY
Ranunculaceae
A heterogeneous collection of primitive plants, some 'buttercup-like', with simple saucer-shaped flowers and many stamens and styles, others with complex, bilaterally symmetrical flowers. Fruits usually dry, sometimes dehiscent, 1-seeded. Many have very poisonous leaves and fruits. Characteristic of undisturbed habitats and mostly perennial including many marsh, water and woodland plants.
See p. 14, 18, 19, 183, 202, 248, 257, 269, 273, 274, 280, 281, 282, 289, 296.

○ **Stinking hellebore**
Helleborus foetidus
Mid–tall. Evergreen; lvs deeply lobed into 5 or more segments, all on stem; fls 15–30mm, nodding, bell-shaped, petal-less; sepals purple-tipped. LH perenn; rootstock. GERM spr; ant-dispersed. FL 1–4. POLL ins(d, h). SEX (♀) pg. HAB open woods, scrub. SOIL moist–dry; calc. SHADE nil–mid. ALT sl–200. DIST E2, W2, but widely naturalised. RANGE F3, G2.
See p. 190, 282.

○ **Green hellebore**
Helleborus viridis
Short. Two summer-green, deeply-lobed root lvs; fls more open than Stinking hellebore, 30–50mm, green, petal-less. LH perenn; rootstock. GERM spr. FL 2–4. POLL ins(d, h). SEX (♀) pg. HAB deciduous woods. SOIL moist; calc. SHADE light-deep. ALT sl–200. DIST E2, W2, but widely naturalised. RANGE F2, G2.

○ **Nigella**
Nigella arvensis
Low–short. Lvs feathery, with thread-like segments; fls with 5 blue, petal-like sepals, veined green, and many stamens. LH ann. GERM aut–spr. FL 6–9. POLL ins. SEX (♀). HAB arable fields, disturbed ground. SOIL moist–dry; not acid. SHADE nil. ALT sl–100. DIST casual E. RANGE F2, G3; and casual.

○ **Winter aconite**
Eranthis hyemalis
Low. Lvs deeply 5-lobed, after fls (4–5); fls 20–30mm petal-less, with 6 yellow sepals, sitting on a ring of 3 small lvs on an otherwise bare stem. LH perenn; rhizome. GERM spr. FL 1–3. POLL ins(d, h); self. SEX (♀) hg. HAB woods. SOIL moist; not acid. SHADE light–heavy. ALT sl–100. DIST widely naturalised. RANGE naturalised F, G.
See p. 183.

○ **Globeflower**
Trollius europaeus
Short–mid. Lvs 3–5 lobed and toothed; fls 20–30mm, petal-less, sepals yellow, incurved, making a globe-like shape. LH perenn; rootstock. GERM spr. FL 5–7(–8). POLL ins(d, h, c); self. SEX (♀) hg. HAB grassland, rock-ledges and open woods. SOIL wet–moist; not acid. SHADE nil–mid. ALT sl–1000. DIST nE3, W2, S4, I1. RANGE F1, G3, S4.
See p. 258, 294.

● **Marsh marigold**
Caltha palustris
Short–mid. Lvs rounded or heart-shaped, glossy dark green, few on stems; fls 10–45mm, petal-less with 5 yellow sepals. LH perenn; rhizomes. GERM spr–sum. FL 3–8. POLL ins(d, h, c). SEX (♀) hg. HAB meadows, fens, springs, streamsides, woods. SOIL wet–damp; not acid. SHADE nil–mid. ALT sl–1100. DIST E5, W4, S5, I4. RANGE F5, G5, S5.
See p. 15, 190, 294.

● **Meadow buttercup**
Ranunculus acris
Short–tall. Hairy; lvs irregularly 3-lobed, the lobes unstalked; fls 15–25mm, on smooth, hairy stalks, with sepals pressed against sepals. LH perenn; rootstock. GERM spr–sum. FL 4–7(–9). POLL ins(h, d, l, c). SEX (♀) pg, rarely (♂) + (♀). HAB meadows; rock-ledges and springs in mountains. SOIL damp–moist; not acid. SHADE nil–light. ALT sl–1250. DIST E5, W5, S5, I5. RANGE F5, G5, S5.
See p. 162, 190, 282.
ss35.

Woolly buttercup
Ranunculus lanuginosus
Mid. Very hairy; lvs shallowly 3-lobed, toothed; fls 25–40mm, sepals pointing slightly downwards. LH perenn; rootstock. GERM ? FL 5–7. POLL ins(d, h, c). SEX (♀) pg. HAB woods. SOIL damp–moist; acid–calc. SHADE light–heavy. ALT [sl–2000]. RANGE F1, G3.

● **Bulbous buttercup**
Ranunculus bulbosus
Short. Hairy, with swollen base to stem; lvs 3-lobed, all lobes stalked; fls 15–30mm, on ridged stalks, sepals down-turned. LH perenn; stem-tuber. GERM spr. FL 4–6. POLL ins(h, d, l, c). SEX (♀), (♀ + ♀). HAB grassland. SOIL dry; not acid. SHADE nil. ALT sl–600. DIST E5, W4, S4, I4. RANGE F5, G5, sS3.
See p. 213, 252.

○ **Hairy buttercup**
Ranunculus sardous
Short–mid. Hairy; lvs shiny, 3-lobed, lobes stalked; fls 10–25mm, on hairy, ridged stalks; sepals down-turned. LH ann. GERM aut–spr. FL 5–10. POLL ins(d, h). SEX (♀). HAB disturbed ground, arable fields. SOIL damp–moist; not acid. SHADE nil. ALT sl–100. DIST E2, W2, S2. RANGE F4, G3, sS1.
ss36.

● **Creeping buttercup**
Ranunculus repens
Short(–mid). Slightly hairy, with long runners; lvs lobed, the middle long-stalked; fls 20–30mm, on smooth stalks, sepals pressed against petals. LH perenn; stolons. FL 5–9. GERM spr–sum–aut. POLL ins(d, h, c). SEX (♀) pa. HAB grassland, woods, bare ground. SOIL wet–moist; not acid. SHADE nil–mid. ALT sl–800. DIST E4, W5, S5, I5. RANGE F5, G5, S5.
See p. 15, 177, 217, 251.

○ **Greater spearwort**
Ranunculus lingua
Tall–v.tall. Almost hairless; lvs long (to 250mm), narrow, toothed; fls 25–30mm, on smooth stalks. LH perenn; stolons. GERM ins(d, c). SEX (♀) pg. HAB marshes, fens, woods. SOIL water–wet; not acid. SHADE nil–mid. ALT sl–200. DIST E2, W2, S2, I2. RANGE F2, G3, sS2.
See p. 281.

● **Lesser spearwort**
Ranunculus flammula
Low–mid. Hairless, creeping stems, rooting at intervals; lvs very variable, oval to narrow; fls 10–20mm, on ridged stalks. LH perenn; rooting stems. FL 6–9. POLL ins(d, h, c); self. SEX (♀) pa. HAB grassy and bare places. SOIL water–moist; acid–calc. SHADE nil–light. ALT sl–1000. DIST E4, W5, S5, I5. RANGE F4, G5, S3.
ss37.

● **Lesser celandine**
Ranunculus ficaria
Low–short. Hairless, with a rosette of glossy dark-green, pale-veined lvs; fls 20–30mm, with 8–12 narrow, pointed petals. LH perenn; root tubers; bulbils at lf-bases in shade. FL 3–5. POLL ins(d, h, c). SEX (♀) hg/pa. HAB woods, hedges, grassland. SOIL damp–moist; not acid. SHADE nil–heavy. ALT sl–750. DIST E5, W5, S4, I3. RANGE F5, G5, sS3.
See p. 174, 253, 276, 293, 297.

● **Goldilocks buttercup**
Ranunculus auricomus
Short–mid. Lower lvs shallowly lobed, upper finger-like; fls 5–10mm with 0–5 petals, often malformed. LH perenn; rootstock. GERM spr. FL 4–5. POLL apo. SEX (♀) pa. HAB woods. SOIL moist; not acid. SHADE light–mid. ALT sl–400. DIST E4, W1, S1, I2. RANGE F1, G1, S4.

● **Celery-leaved buttercup**
Ranunculus sceleratus
Short–tall. Lvs lobed, stems furrowed; fls 5–10mm, petals only as long as sepals; frs very numerous. LH persistent ann. GERM spr; requires light. BL 5–9. POLL ins(d) or self. SEX (♀) pg. HAB muddy edge of fresh water. SOIL water–wet; not acid. SHADE nil. ALT sl–100. DIST sE4, E3, W3, S2, I3. RANGE Fe, G4, S2.
See p. 190. **ss38**.

Large white buttercup
Ranunculus platanifolius
Mid–tall. Lvs large, 5-lobed; fls 15–20mm, white, long-stalked. LH perenn; rootstock. GERM ? FL 5–7. POLL ins(h, d). SEX (♀). HAB woods, meadows. SOIL damp–moist; not acid. SHADE nil–mid. ALT [sl–2500]. RANGE F2, G2, S2.

Glacier buttercup
Ranunculus glacialis
Low. Lvs lobed, slightly fleshy; fls to 30mm, white or pinkish. LH perenn; rootstock. GERM ? FL 7–8. POLL ins(d, l. h). SEX (♀ + ♂) pa. HAB stony ground in high mountains. SOIL moist; not calc. SHADE nil. ALT [2000–4000]. RANGE F1, G1, S2.

● **Common water crowfoot**
Ranunculus aquatilis
Floating. Submerged lvs feathery, floating lvs toothed; fls 10–20mm; short-stalked. LH short-lived perenn. GERM sum–aut. FL 4–9. POLL ins(c, d, h); self. SEX (♀) pg. HAB still and slow fresh water. SOIL water; not acid. SHADE nil. ALT sl–600. DIST E4, W3, S3, I3. RANGE F3, G2, S1.
See p. 167, 202, 203.

● **Pond water crowfoot**
Ranunculus peltatus
Floating; submerged lvs feathery, floating lvs rounded, little toothed; fls 15–20mm, petals 5 or more, long-stalked. LH short-lived perenn. GERM ? FL 5–8. POLL ins(c, d, h). SEX (♀) pg. HAB still and slow fresh water; not acid. SHADE nil. ALT sl–400. DIST sE5, nE2, W3, S2, I4. RANGE F4, G3, S3.
ss39.

41

● **Thread-leaved water crowfoot**
Ranunculus trichophyllus
Submerged; no floating lvs; fls 8–10mm; short-stalked. LH perenn. GERM ? FL 5–7. POLL ins(d, c, h). SEX (♀) pg. HAB still fresh water. SOIL water; acid–calc. SHADE nil–light. ALT sl–500. DIST E3, W2, S2, I3. RANGE F3, G3, S3.
See p. 202.

● **River water crowfoot**
Ranunculus fluitans
Submerged, stems to 5m; lvs all long and narrow, to 30cm; fls 20–30mm, short-stalked. LH perenn; rhizome. GERM sum. FL 5–8. POLL ins(d, h, c). SEX (♀). HAB fast fresh water. SOIL water; not acid. SHADE nil. ALT sl–150. DIST E3, W3, sS1, I1. RANGE F3, G4, S1.
See p. 190, 202, 216.
ss40.

● **Fan-leaved water crowfoot**
Ranunculus circinatus
Submerged; no floating lvs; submerged lvs circular in outline; fls 10–20mm, long-stalked. LH perenn. GERM aut. FL 6–8. POLL ins(d, c, h). SEX (♀). HAB still and slow fresh water. SOIL water; not acid. SHADE nil. ALT sl–150. DIST sE3, nE1, sS1, I1. RANGE F3, G3, S1.

● **Ivy-leaved water crowfoot**
Ranunculus hederaceus
Creeping, rooting on stem; lvs ivy-shaped; fls 2–5mm, petals equalling sepals. LH short-lived perenn. GERM aut. FL 4–9. POLL self. SEX (♀). HAB mud or shallow water. SOIL water–wet; acid–calc. SHADE nil. ALT sl–700. DIST E3, W3, S3, I3. RANGE F3, nG2, sS1.
See p. 202. **ss41. ss42**.

○ **Alpine meadow-rue**
Thalictrum alpinum
Low. Lvs all from roots, 2-trefoil; fls with minute petals and 10–20 long, violet stamens with yellow anthers. LH perenn; rootstock. GERM sum. FL 5–7. POLL wind. SEX (♀) pg. HAB stony alpine grassland. SOIL damp–moist; not acid. SHADE nil. ALT sl (in n)–1250. DIST nE1, W1, S3, I1. RANGE G1, S4.

● **Common meadow-rue**
Thalictrum flavum
Tall. Lvs 2-pinnate with narrow lflts; fls in dense clusters, with minute petals and conspicuous, upright, yellow stamens. LH perenn; rhizome. GERM spr. FL 6–8. POLL ins(h, d); wind. SEX (♀) pg. HAB meadows and fens. SOIL wet–damp; not acid. SHADE nil–light. ALT sl–150. DIST sE3, ne2, W2, S1, I2. RANGE F4, G3, S3.
See p. 281.

○ **Lesser meadow-rue**
Thalictrum minus
Short–tall. Lvs 3–4-pinnate, lflts broader; fls in loose clusters, as Common meadow-rue, but stamens drooping. LH perenn; rhizome, often stolons too. GERM aut. FL 6–8. POLL ins(d); wind; occasionally apo. SEX (♀) pg. HAB grassy and rocky places. SOIL damp–dry; acid–calc. SHADE nil–mid. ALT sl–750. DIST E2, W2, S2, I2. RANGE F3, G3, S1.

○ **Baneberry**
Actaea spicata
Mid. Lvs pinnate; forms dense clumps with a canopy of lvs and fls in emergent spikes; fr a black berry. LH perenn; rhizome. GERM spr. FL 5–7. POLL ins(c, d). SEX (♀) pg. HAB woods, often ash, and limestone pavements. SOIL moist; calc. SHADE light–heavy. ALT 100–400. DIST nE1. RANGE F2, G3, S5.

● **Traveller's joy**
Clematis vitalba
V.tall; climbing. Lvs pinnate, stalks twining; fls 4-petalled, in branching clusters; fr long-plumed. LH woody perenn. GERM ? FL 7–9. POLL ins(h, d). SEX (♀) pg. HAB woods, scrub. SOIL dry; calc. SHADE nil–mid. ALT sl–400. DIST sE4, W3; introduced elsewhere. RANGE F4, G4.
See p. 162, 190, 194.

Alpine clematis
Clematis alpina
Tall, scrambling. Lvs 2-pinnate, twining; fls 30–40mm, violet; fr long-plumed. LH woody perenn. GERM ? FL 5–7. POLL ins(h). SEX (♀) hg. HAB rocky woods. SOIL moist; calc. SHADE nil–mid. ALT [1000–2500]. RANGE G1, S1.

○ **Monk's-hood**
Aconitum napellus
Tall. Lvs deeply lobed, hairless; fls with tall hood 20mm high in unbranched spikes. LH perenn; rootstock. GERM ? FL 5–7. POLL ins(h). SEX (♂) pa. HAB woods, stream-banks, roadsides. SOIL damp–moist; not acid. ALT sl–150. DIST swE2, sW2. RANGE sF2, sG2. *See p. 19, 241, 257.*

Wolfsbane
Aconitum vulparia
Tall. Like Monk's-hood but fls yellow with a longer, narrow-er hood; spikes branching. LH perenn; rootstock. GERM ? FL 6–7. POLL ins(h). SEX (♂) pa. HAB woods. SOIL damp–moist; not acid. SHADE mid-deep. ALT [sl–2000]. RANGE eF1, sG3.

Northern wolfsbane
Aconitum septentrionale
Mid–tall. Like Wolf's-bane, but with hairy fls, often violet, the hood more pyramidal, broader at base. LH perenn; rootstock. GERM spr? FL 7–8. POLL ins(h). SEX (♂). HAB woods. SOIL damp–moist; acid–calc. SHADE light–heavy. ALT [sl–2000]. RANGE S4.

○ **Forking larkspur**
Consolida regalis
Short. Stems softly hairy; lvs feathery; fls 15–18mm with very long spur to 15mm. LH ann. GERM spr. FL 6–8. POLL ins(h, l). SEX (♂) pa. HAB arable fields. SOIL dry; calc. SHADE nil. ALT sl–100. DIST (E, W, S). RANGE eF2, G3, sS2; introduced elsewhere.

○ **Columbine**
Aquilegia vulgaris
Mid–tall. Lvs mostly from root, 2-trefoil; fls with petal-like sepals and long-spurred petals. LH perenn; rootstock. GERM spr. FL 5–7. POLL ins(h). SEX (♂) pa. HAB open woods, roadsides. SOIL moist-dry; calc. SHADE nil–mid. ALT sl–400. DIST E3, W3, S1, I1. RANGE F3, G3, S2. *See p. 15, 259.*

Yellow pheasant's-eye
Adonis vernalis
Short. Lvs feathery; fls 40–80mm, yellow, with 12–20 petals. LH perenn; rootstock. GERM ?, seeds distrib. by ants. FL 4–5. POLL ins(h, c, d). SEX (♂). HAB grassland. SOIL dry; calc. SHADE nil. ALT [sl–1500]. RANGE eF2, sG2, sS1.

○ **Pheasant's-eye**
Adonis annua
Low–short. Lvs feath-ery; fls 15–25mm with 5–8 scarlet petals, dark-spotted at base. LH ann. GERM spr. FL 6–7. POLL ins(h). SEX (♂) hg. HAB arable fields. SOIL dry; calc. SHADE nil. ALT sl–100. DIST (sE1). RANGE F2, G1.

● **Wood anemone**
Anemone nemorosa
Low–short. 3 deeply-lobed lvs forming whorl beneath solitary fl 20–40mm; fl has no petals but 6–12 petal-like sepals. LH perenn; rhizome. GERM spr; seeds distrib. by ants. FL 3–5. POLL ins(d, h); self. FL 3–5. POLL ins(d, h); self. HAB woods, upland meadows. SOIL moist; not acid. SHADE nil–heavy. ALT sl–1250. DIST E5, W5, S4, I3. RANGE F5, G5, S3. *See p. 171, 174, 190, 198, 253, 279, 281, 297.*

○ **Yellow anemone**
Anemone ranunculoides
Low–short. Like Wood anemone but hairy, stem lvs unstalked, fls yellow, with 5–8 sepals. LH perenn; rhizome. GERM spr. FL 3–5. POLL ins(d, h). SEX (♂) pg. HAB woods. SOIL moist; not acid. SHADE light–heavy. ALT [sl–1500]. DIST (sE2). RANGE eF2, G3, S2.

○ **Pasque flower**
Pulsatilla vulgaris
Short. Very hairy, with feathery lvs; fls bell-shaped, 50–80mm, eventually nodding. LH perenn; rootstock. GERM sum. FL 4–5. POLL ins(h). SEX (♂) pg. HAB grassland. SOIL dry; calc. SHADE nil. ALT sl–250. DIST sE1. RANGE F2, G3, sS2.

WATER-LILY FAMILY
Nymphaeaceae
A small family of water plants, all rooting in mud with floating, hairless leaves on long stalks. The flowers are large, solitary, and have few to many petals. The seeds have a spongy attachment which enables them to float. All grow in still or slow-flowing fresh water.
See p. 173, 274.

Pale pasque flower
Pulsatilla vernalis
Low. Lvs less feathery than Pasque flower, more buttercup-like; fls creamy-white inside, violet outside. LH perenn; rootstock. GERM sum? FL 4–7. POLL ins(d, l, c); self. SEX (♂) pg. HAB heaths, open woods, mountain meadows. SOIL damp; not calc. SHADE nil–mid. ALT [sl–3000]. RANGE eF1, G2, S2.

Small pasque flower
Pulsatilla pratensis
Low–short. Very like Pasque flower, but fls drooping, 40mm, pale to dark purple; fr-stem elongating. LH perenn; rootstock. GERM spr–sum. FL 5–6. POLL ins(h). SEX (♂). HAB grassland, open woods. SOIL dry; acid–calc. SHADE nil–light. ALT [sl–400]. RANGE eG1, sS1.
See p. 282.

Hepatica
Hepatica nobilis
Low. Lvs 3-lobed, un-toothed, long-lived, purplish; fls 15–25mm, with 3 sepal-like bracts and 6–7(–10) petal-like sepals. LH perenn; rootstock. GERM seeds dispersed by ants. FL 3–5. POLL ins(c, d, h, l). SEX (♂) hg. HAB woods. SOIL dry–moist; acid–calc. SHADE nil–heavy. ALT [sl–3600]. RANGE F1, G4, sS4.
See p. 259.

● **Yellow water-lily**
Nuphar lutea
Floating; lvs up to 40cm across, oval; fls with 5–6 yellow sepals, 40–60mm, held clear of water. LH perenn; rhizome. GERM early sum. FL 6–9. POLL ins(d). SEX (♂) pg. HAB still and slow fresh water. SOIL water; acid–calc. SHADE nil. ALT sl–500. DIST sE5, nE2, W2, S2, I2. RANGE F5, G5, S3.
See p. 222. **ss43**.

FUMITORY FAMILY
Fumariaceae
Scrambling or climbing, mainly annual weeds, with several-times pinnate leaves, and spikes of characteristic flowers. Each has 2 sepals, 4 petals, 1 or 2 of which have a spur or sac, and 2 stamens. The bottom petal is important in identification. Fumitories *Fumaria* are annual weeds, with twisting leaf-stalks, but some *Corydalis* spp. are perennial.
See p. 19, 283.

● **White water-lily**
Nymphaea alba
Floating; lvs less than 30cm, circular; fls with 20–25 petals, up to 200mm across, held flush with water surface. LH perenn; rhizome. GERM early sum. FL 7–8. POLL ins(d); self. SEX (♂) hg. HAB still fresh water. SOIL nil. SHADE nil. ALT sl–400. DIST E4, W3, S3, I3. RANGE F3, G3, sS3.
See p. 166, 197, 198.

● **Climbing corydalis**
Corydalis claviculata
Climbing, with branching stems and lvs ending in a twining tendril; fls 5–6mm long, in long-stalked spikes. LH ann. GERM spr. FL 6–9. POLL ins(h); self. SEX (♂). HAB woods, rocky places. SOIL damp–moist; not acid. SHADE light-mid. ALT sl–500. DIST E3, W3, S3, I1. RANGE nwF2, nG2, sS1.
See p. 194, 246, 283.

○ **Yellow corydalis**
Corydalis lutea
Short. Lvs without tendrils; fls yellow, 12–18mm long. LH perenn; rootstock. GERM spr. FL 5–9. POLL ins(h); self. SEX (♂). HAB walls. SOIL dry; not acid. SHADE nil. ALT sl–200. DIST introduced. RANGE introduced.

○ **Bulbous corydalis**
Corydalis solida
Short. Stem unbranched, with few, many-times divided lvs; fls 15–25mm, spur straight. LH perenn; tuber. GERM spr. FL 4–5. POLL ins(h). SEX (♂) hg. HAB woods, shady places. SOIL moist; not calc. SHADE light–heavy. ALT sl–50. DIST (seE1). RANGE F3, G3, sS2.

POPPY FAMILY
Papaveraceae
Mainly annuals, with large, showy flowers whose petals are often crumpled like tissue paper. The stems exude a milky juice when broken, which probably acts as a defence against insects. Annuals tend to be arable weeds (especially in genus *Papaver*) but several others are perennial.
See p. 242, 279, 281.

● **Ramping fumitory**
Fumaria capreolata
Mid–tall. Scrambling; fls 10–12mm long, dark-tipped, in dense, 20-fld spikes; fr-stalk bent. LH ann. GERM aut–spr. FL 5–9. POLL self. SEX (♀). HAB disturbed ground, roadsides, hedges. SOIL moist–dry; not acid. SHADE nil–light. ALT sl–100. DIST E2, W2, S1, I2. RANGE F3, G1. **ss44. ss45.**

● **Wall fumitory**
Fumaria muralis
Mid–tall. Scrambling; fls 9–12mm, all pink, in 10–12-fld spikes. LH ann. GERM aut–spr. FL 5–10. POLL self. SEX (♀). HAB disturbed ground. SOIL moist–dry; acid–calc. SHADE nil. ALT sl–100. DIST E2, W2, S2, I2. RANGE nwF2; introduced G. **ss46. ss47.**

● **Common fumitory**
Fumaria officinalis
Tall. Scrambling; fls 6–8mm long, pink, dark-tipped, up to 40 in each spike. LH ann. GERM spr. FL 5–10. POLL ins(d, h); self. SEX (♀) hg. HAB disturbed ground. SOIL dry; acid–calc. SHADE nil. ALT sl–300. DIST E5, W4, S4, I3. RANGE F5, G4, S4.
See p. 19, 183, 283.

○ **Small fumitory**
Fumaria parviflora
Mid–tall. Scrambling; fls 5–6mm long, pale, pink-tipped, in 20-fld spikes. LH ann. GERM spr. FL 6–9. POLL self. SEX (♀). HAB disturbed ground. SOIL dry; calc. SHADE nil. ALT sl–100. DIST sE2, nE1, S1. RANGE F3, wG1. **ss48. ss49.**

● **Prickly poppy**
Papaver argemone
Short–mid. Stiffly hairy; fls 20–60mm, pale scarlet; fr capsule ribbed and bristly. LH ann. GERM spr. FL 5–7. POLL ins(h, d); self. SEX (♀) hg. HAB disturbed ground. SOIL dry; not acid. SHADE nil. ALT sl–200. DIST E3, W2, S2, I2. RANGE F3, G3, sS2.

● **Long-headed poppy**
Papaver dubium
Short–mid. Stiffly hairy; fls mid-scarlet, 30–70mm, on hairy stalks, the hairs flattened; capsule long. LH ann. GERM aut. FL 6–8. POLL ins(d, h, c); self. SEX (♀) hg. HAB disturbed ground. SOIL moist–dry; acid–calc. SHADE nil. ALT sl–400. DIST E5, W3, S3, I3. RANGE F4, G5, S2. **ss50.**

● **Common poppy**
Papaver rhoeas
Short–mid. Rough, hairy; fls deep scarlet, 70–100mm, with spreading hairs; capsule rounded. LH ann. GERM win–spr. FL 6–10. POLL ins(c, h, d). SEX (♀) hg. HAB disturbed ground. SOIL dry; not acid. SHADE nil. ALT sl–300. DIST E5, W4, S3, I4. RANGE F5, G5, S2.
See p. 163, 188, 243, 281. **ss51.**

Arctic poppy
Papaver radicatum
Low–short. Stiffly hairy, with deeply-lobed lvs; fls yellow; capsule oval, brown-hairy. LH perenn. GERM sum? FL 7. POLL ins(d, c). SEX (♀). HAB stony ground. SOIL damp–dry; acid–calc. SHADE nil. ALT [(sl in arctic–) 500–2000]. RANGE S2.

● **Yellow horned poppy**
Glaucium flavum
Mid–tall. Lvs wavy-edged, bluish, hairless; fls 60–90mm; pods up to 300mm long. LH perenn; tap-root. GERM spr. FL 6–9. POLL ins(d, h). SEX (♀) pg. HAB sea shingle, rarely inland. SOIL dry; not acid. SHADE nil. ALT sl. DIST coastal: E3, W3, S1, I2. RANGE coastal: F3, G1, S1, casual inland.

45

○ **Welsh poppy**
Meconopsis cambrica
Mid. Coarsely-lobed lvs from roots and on stem; fls 50–70mm, with hairy sepals. LH perenn; rootstock. GERM spr. FL 6–8. POLL ins(d, c). SEX (♀). HAB rocks and open woods. SOIL damp–moist; acid–calc. SHADE nil–mid. ALT sl–600. DIST swE2, W2, I2, introduced elsewhere. RANGE F1, introduced elsewhere.

● **Greater celandine**
Chelidonium majus
Mid–tall. Stems brittle, with orange juice, lvs coarsely pinnate; fls 20–25mm, in small clusters. LH perenn; rootstock. GERM sprsum. FL 4–9. POLL ins(c, h, d); self. SEX (♀) hg. HAB hedges, disturbed ground. SOIL moist; acid–calc. SHADE nil–light. ALT sl–200. DIST E4, W4, S2, I2. RANGE F5, G5, sS3.
See p. 253, 263.

CABBAGE FAMILY
Cruciferae
A highly distinctive family, with four petals arranged in a cross, and capsule-like fruits that are either long and thin (siliqua) or shorter (silicula), and open from the base. Flowers secrete copious nectar in many cases. A high proportion are weeds or annuals of naturally open places; several are important crop species, particularly in the genus *Brassica*.
See p. 18, 19, 188, 219, 239, 240, 257, 262, 282.

● **Rape**
Brassica napus
Tall. Greyish, coarsely lobed lvs, some half-clasping the stem; fls 20–35mm, in a rounded spike, the buds on top. LH ann or bienn. GERM imm. FL 4–8. POLL ins(h); self. SEX (♀) pg. HAB relict of cultivation and by streams. SOIL damp–moist; acid–calc. SHADE nil. ALT sl–200. DIST casual. RANGE casual.

● **Black mustard**
Brassica nigra
Tall. Lvs bright green, all stalked, bristly; fls 12–15mm; capsules small pressed to stem. LH ann. GERM spr. FL 6–8. POLL ins(d). SEX (♀). HAB sea-cliffs and by streams, also associated with cultivation. SOIL moist; not acid. SHADE nil–light. ALT sl–400. DIST E3, W3, S1, I1. RANGE F3, G3, sS2.
ss52.

○ **Wild cabbage**
Brassica oleracea
Tall. Hairless; lvs greyish, some clasping the almost woody stem and leaving scars; fls 30–40mm, in long spikes, the fls at the base. LH short-lived perenn; tap-root. GERM spr. FL 5–9. POLL ins(h); self. SEX (♂) hg. HAB sea-cliffs, cultivated forms (cabbage, etc.) often occur as casuals. SOIL dry; calc. SHADE nil. ALT sl–200. DIST coastal: sE2, W2. RANGE F1.
See p. 240, 262, 269.

● **Turnip**
Brassica rapa
Tall. Lvs green, the lower bristly and coarsely-lobed, the upper clasping the stem; fls 20mm, in a flattened spike, the fls above the buds. LH ann or bienn. GERM imm. FL 4–8. POLL ins(h); self. SEX (♀) pg. HAB disturbed ground, especially by streams. SOIL moist; acid–calc. SHADE nil. ALT sl–200. DIST E4, W4, S2, I4. RANGE F4, G4, S3.

○ **Wallflower cabbage**
Rhynchosinapis cheiranthos
Mid–tall. Stem leafy; lvs pinnately lobed; fls 15–25mm; siliqua beaded. LH bienn. GERM imm. FL 6–8. POLL ins(d, h, l); self. SEX (♀) hg. HAB casual or bare ground. SOIL dry; not calc. SHADE nil. DIST E2, W2, S2. RANGE F3, G1.

● **White mustard**
Sinapis alba
Mid–tall. Lvs roughly hairy, deeply lobed, the end lobe largest; fls 20–25mm; siliqua with a long curved beak. LH winter ann. GERM aut. FL 6–8. POLL ins(h, d). SEX (♀) hg. HAB waste places, disturbed ground. SOIL moist–dry; acid–calc. SHADE nil. ALT sl–300. DIST E4, W4, S3, I3. RANGE F4, G3, S2.

● **Charlock**
Sinapis arvensis
Mid–tall. Lvs coarsely lobed; fls 15–20mm; siliqua with a short straight beak. LH ann. GERM imm or spr. FL 4–10. POLL ins(h, d). SEX (♀) pg. HAB disturbed ground. SOIL damp–dry; not acid. SHADE nil. ALT sl–400. DIST E5, W5, S4, I5. RANGE F5, G5, S4.
See p. 243.

● **Annual wall rocket**
Diplotaxis muralis
Short–mid. Lvs lobed, mostly in a rosette; fls 10–12mm, pale yellow; siliqua held at an angle, short-stalked. LH winter ann, sometimes persistent. GERM aut. FL 6–9. POLL ins(h, d); self. SEX (♀) hg. HAB rocks, walls, disturbed ground. SOIL dry; not acid. SHADE nil. ALT sl–200. DIST E3, W2, S1, I2. RANGE F4, G3, Sq. **ss53.**

● **Sea radish**
Raphanus maritimus
Mid–tall. Lvs coarsely lobed; fls 25–40mm, yellow or rarely white; siliqua beaded, not easily breaking, long-beaked. LH short-lived perenn. GERM spr. FL 6–8. POLL ins(h, d). SEX (♀). HAB sandy shores, cliffs. SOIL dry; not calc. SHADE nil. ALT sl–200. DIST E4, W3, S3, I3. RANGE F5, G5, S3.

● **Wild radish**
Raphanus raphanistrum
Mid. Lvs coarsely and bluntly lobed; fls 25–30mm, yellow or white, veined purple; pods breaking easily between seeds. LH ann. GERM spr. FL 5–9. POLL ins (h, d). SEX (♀); hg. HAB disturbed ground. SOIL moist–dry; not calc. SHADE nil. ALT sl–200. DIST E4, W2, S3, I3. RANGE F5, G5, S3.
See p. 18, 243.

● **Sea rocket**
Cakile maritima
Short–mid. Lvs pinnately lobed, fleshy; fls 10–20mm, lilac; fr oval, thick-stalked. LH ann. GERM spr. FL 6–9. POLL ins(c, d, l, h); self. SEX (♀) hg. HAB sandy shores. SOIL dry; not acid. SHADE nil. ALT sl. DIST coastal: E5, W5, S4, I4. RANGE F5, G5, S4.

● **Sea kale**
Crambe maritima
Mid. Massive, fleshy, greyish; lvs large, wavy-edged; fls 10–15mm, in large flattened clusters; frs bell-shaped. LH perenn; rootstock. GERM spr. FL 6–8. POLL ins(h, d); self. SEX (♀). HAB sandy and shingly coasts. SOIL dry; not acid. SHADE nil. ALT sl. DIST coastal: E3, W1, S1, I1. RANGE coastal: F2, G2, sS2.

● **Field pepperwort**
Lepidium campestre
Short–mid. Greyish, densely hairy; lvs narrow, clothing the stem; fls 2–3mm, the petals larger than the sepals; frs round and flat, notched. LH persistent ann. GERM aut–spr. FL 5–8. POLL self, rarely ins(d). SEX (♀) pg. HAB grassy and disturbed ground. SOIL dry; acid–calc. SHADE ALT sl–200. DIST E3, W2, S2, I2. RANGE F4, G4, sS2.
See p. 182.

● **Smith's pepperwort**
Lepidium heterophyllum
Short–mid. Like Field pepperwort but shorter, fls 3–4mm, anthers violet; frs with the style persisting in the notch. LH perenn; rootstock. GERM ? FL 5–8. POLL self. SEX (♀). HAB disturbed and grassy places. SOIL dry; acid–calc. SHADE nil. ALT sl–350. DIST wE5, eE2, W5, S3, I2. RANGE F3, G1, (S1).

● **Narrow-leaved pepperwort**
Lepidium ruderale
Short. Usually hairless, smelling of cress; lower lvs pinnate; fls 2mm, green and petalless; frs notched. LH persistent ann. GERM aut–spr. POLL self. SEX (♀). HAB disturbed ground. SOIL moist–dry; not acid. SHADE nil. ALT sl–100. DIST E3 (mainly near coasts), W1, S1. RANGE F3, G3, S2.

● **Swinecress**
Coronopus squamatus
Low–short, prostrate. Lvs pinnately-lobed; fls 2–3mm, in spikes opposite the lvs; fr 2-lobed but not notched. LH persistent ann. GERM spr. FL 6–9. POLL self, ins(d). SEX (♀) pg. HAB disturbed, often trodden ground. SOIL moist–dry; acid–calc. SHADE nil. ALT sl–200. DIST sE5, nE2, W2, S2. RANGE F3, G3, S2.

● **Lesser swinecress**
Coronopus didymus
Low–short, prostrate. Resembles Swinecress but lvs feathery, strong-smelling; fls less than 2mm, sometimes with petals; fr notched. LH persistent ann. GERM spr. FL 7–9. POLL self. SEX (♀). HAB disturbed ground. SOIL moist–dry; acid–calc. SHADE nil. ALT sl–100. DIST sE3, nE1, W2, S1. RANGE wF4, nG2, S1.

● Hoary cress
Cardaria draba
Mid–tall. Hairless but greyish; lvs clasping stem; fls 5–6mm, in flat clusters; fr not splitting. LH perenn; rootstock and stolons. GERM spr. FL 5–6. POLL ins(d, h); self. SEX (♀) pg. HAB disturbed and grassy places. SOIL dry; not acid. SHADE nil. ALT sl–200. DIST eE4, wE2, W2, S1, I1; spreading. RANGE F4, G4, sS2.
See p. 262.

○ Wild candytuft
Iberis amara
Low–short. Lvs toothed, scattered up stem; fls 6–8mm, white or lilac, two petals larger than the others; fr ball-shaped. LH persistent ann. GERM spr. FL 6–9. POLL ins(h, d); self. SEX (♀) hg. HAB bare and sparsely grassy places. SOIL dry; calc. SHADE nil. ALT sl–300. DIST sE2. RANGE F3, wG1.
See p. 169.

Buckler mustard
Biscutella laevigata
Short–mid. Lvs lobed, hairy; upper simple; fls 5–10mm, fr 2-lobed, the style persisting between them. LH perenn; rootstock. GERM ? FL 5–7. POLL ins(h, d); in poor weather fls do not open, then self. SEX (♀) pg. HAB rocky, sometimes disturbed ground. SOIL dry; calc. SHADE nil. ALT [200–2000]. RANGE F1, G2.

○ Alpine pennycress
Thlaspi alpestre
Short. Lvs in a rosette, untoothed, some clasping stem; fls 4–8mm, anthers violet; fr heart-shaped. LH monocarpic or short-lived (2–4 yrs) perenn. GERM spr. FL 5–7. POLL ins(h, d); self. SEX (♀) hg. HAB rocky and stony places. SOIL dry; calc; often on old mining wastes. SHADE nil (–light on acid soil). ALT 100–800. DIST E1, W1, S1. RANGE F1, G2, S3.
See p. 219.

● Field pennycress
Thlaspi arvense
Short–mid. Strong-smelling; lvs toothed, scattered on stem, not in rosette; fls 4–6mm, anthers yellow; fr with broad wings, notched; dead stems prominent in winter. LH monocarpic; ann or longer-lived perenn. GERM imm–spr. FL 5–8. POLL ins(d, h); self. SEX (♀) hg. HAB disturbed ground, arable fields. SOIL damp–dry; acid–calc. SHADE nil. ALT sl–300. DIST seE5, nwE3, W3, S2, I2. RANGE F4, G5, S4.
See p. 243, 282. **ss54**.

● Shepherd's cress
Teesdalia nudicaulis
Low–mid. Pinnately lobed lvs almost all in rosette; fls 2mm, 2 petals longer than others; fr flattened, winged, notched. LH ann. GERM sum–spr. FL 5–9. POLL ins; self. SEX (♀) hg. HAB disturbed and bare ground. SOIL dry; not calc. SHADE nil. ALT sl–400. DIST E2, W2, S2, I1. RANGE F2, G3, sS1.
See p. 244. **ss55**.

● Shepherd's purse
Capsella bursa-pastoris
Low–mid. Rosette of pinnately lobed lvs and simple lvs on stems; fls 2–4mm; fr triangular, notched. LH persistent ann. GERM imm–any. FL 1–12. POLL ins(h, c); self; (♀). HAB disturbed ground. SOIL moist–dry; acid–calc. SHADE nil. ALT sl–500. DIST E5, W5, S5, I5. RANGE F5, G5, S5.
See p. 189, 243, 248, 249.

● English scurvy-grass
Cochlearia anglica
Low–short. Fleshy; rosette lvs tapering to stalk, upper clasping stem; fls 10–15mm; fr flattened. LH bienn or short-lived perenn. GERM spr–sum. FL 4–7. POLL ins(d, c); self. SEX (♀). HAB coastal mud. SOIL wet; saline. SHADE nil. ALT sl. DIST coastal: E3, W3, S2, I3. RANGE coastal: F2, G2.

● Early scurvy-grass
Cochlearia danica
V. low to low. Fleshy; lvs ivy-shaped at base of stem, single and stalked higher up; fls 4–5mm; fr swollen. LH winter ann. GERM aut. FL 1–7. POLL ins; self. SEX (♀) hg. HAB sandy and rocky places, mainly coastal. SOIL dry; not acid. SHADE nil. ALT sl. DIST coastal: E4, W4, S3, I3; inland E casual. RANGE F4, G4, sS3.

● Common scurvy-grass
Cochlearia officinalis
Low to mid. Fleshy, very variable; lvs rounded, heart or kidney-shaped; fls 8–10mm, ball-shaped. LH persistent ann, bienn, or short-lived perenn; tap-root. GERM spr. FL 3–8. POLL ins(d, c); self. SEX (♀) hg. HAB salt-marshes, cliffs, banks; mountain rocks. SOIL wet–moist; acid–calc. SHADE nil. ALT sl–800. DIST sE3 coastal, nE4, W3 coastal, S3, I4. RANGE coastal: F3, G4, S4; inland F1, G2.
See p. 205, 262.

○ **Honesty**
Lunaria annua
Mid–tall. Lvs toothed, pointed, rough-hairy, upper unstalked; fls 25–35mm, red-purple; fr large, flat, almost circular and transparent. LH persistent ann (to 3 yrs). GERM spr. FL 4–6. POLL ins (h, l, d), self. SEX (♂️) hg. HAB garden escape. SOIL moist; not acid. SHADE nil–mid. ALT ? DIST casual. RANGE casual.

○ **Perennial honesty**
Lunaria rediviva
Tall. Hairy; lvs pointed, toothed, all stalked; fls 20–25mm; fr a flat, elliptical, translucent pod. LH perenn. GERM spr. FL 5–7. POLL ins(h, d, c, l); self. SEX (♂️) hg. HAB woods. SOIL damp–moist; not acid. SHADE mid–heavy. ALT [sl–1200]. DIST casual. RANGE eF2, G3, sS1.

○ **Twisted whitlow-grass**
Draba incana
Low–mid. Hairy, oblong lvs in a rosette and clothing stems; fls 3–5mm, with notched petals; fr more than 6mm long, twisted when ripe. LH short-lived perenn; rootstock. GERM ? FL 5–7. POLL self. SEX (♂️) hg. HAB rocky and sandy places. SOIL dry; not acid. SHADE nil. ALT sl–1100. DIST nE1, W1, S2, I1. RANGE S3. **ss56**.

○ **Wall whitlow-grass**
Draba muralis
Low–short. Hairy; lvs in rosette and scattered on stems, broad oval; fls 2–3mm, petals entire; fr to 6mm long, straight. LH winter ann, sometimes persisting. GERM aut. FL 4–6. POLL ins; self. SEX (♂️). HAB rocks and walls. SOIL dry; calc. SHADE nil. ALT sl–400. DIST E1, widely casual. RANGE F2, G1, sS1. *See p. 244*. **ss57**.

● **Common whitlow-grass**
Erophila verna
V.low–low. Very variable; lvs in rosette, entire or toothed; fls 3–6mm, petals deeply notched (4 appear as 8); fr flattened. LH winter ann or ephemeral. GERM spr–aut. FL 2–6. POLL self. SEX (♂️) hg. HAB bare ground, rocks, walls, sand-dunes. SOIL dry; acid–calc. SHADE nil. ALT sl–750. DIST E5, W3, S4, I3. RANGE F5, G5, sS4. *See p. 174, 188, 244, 261*.

● **Horseradish**
Armoracia rusticana
Tall. Very large, long-stalked, crinkled root lvs and short-stalked, narrow stem lvs; fls 8–10mm, in dense spikes; fr ball-shaped. LH perenn; taproot. GERM spr? FL 5–7. POLL ins(d, c, h); self. SEX (♂️) hg. HAB cultivated; naturalised in grassy places. SOIL damp–moist; not acid. SHADE nil. ALT sl–200. DIST sE5, nE3, W3, S2, I2. RANGE F4, G4, sS3. **ss58**.

● **Large bittercress**
Cardamine amara
Short–mid. No rosette; lvs pinnate, lower and upper similar; fls 10–15mm, anthers violet. LH perenn; creeping rootstock, stolons. GERM imm. FL 4–6. POLL ins(d, h, c). SEX (♂️), (♂️+♀) hg. HAB wet woods, stream-sides, fens. SOIL wet–damp; not v. acid. SHADE nil–heavy. ALT sl–400. DIST E3, W3, S2, I1. RANGE F3, G4, S3.

● **Wavy bittercress**
Cardamine flexuosa
Short–mid. Lvs in a sparse rosette, and on stem, all pinnate, with at least 11 lflts; fls 5–8mm with 6 stamens. LH short-lived perenn; rootstock. GERM imm. FL 4–9. POLL ? SEX (♂️). HAB woods and stream-sides. SOIL damp; not acid. SHADE nil–heavy. ALT sl–1250. DIST E4, W5, S4, I3. RANGE F3, G3, S3.

● **Hairy bittercress**
Cardamine hirsuta
Low–short. Smaller than Wavy bittercress, with most lvs in rosette, each with fewer lflts; fls less than 5mm, with 4 stamens. LH ann, sometimes persisting. GERM imm. FL 3–10. POLL self. SEX (♂️) hg. HAB bare ground. SOIL damp–moist; acid–calc. SHADE nil. ALT sl–1200. DIST E5, W5, S5, I4. RANGE F5, G4, sS2. *See p. 243*. **ss59**.

○ **Narrow-leaved bittercress**
Cardamine impatiens
Mid. Lvs with many, lobed lflts, clasping stem; fls 5–6mm, with no or narrow petals. LH ann or bienn. GERM spr. FL 5–8. POLL ins(d, c); self. SEX (♂️). HAB woods and rocks. SOIL damp–moist; not acid. SHADE nil–mid. ALT sl–400. DIST E2, W2, S1. RANGE F2, G3, S2. *See p. 168*.

● **Cuckoo flower
(Lady's smock)**
Cardamine pratensis
Short–mid. Lvs pin-
nate, in rosette with
large lflts; narrow lflts
on stem; fls 12–20mm,
lilac or white, anthers
yellow. LH perenn;
rootstock, stolons,
leaf-sprouts. GERM spr.
FL 4–6. POLL ins(h, d,
l). SEX (♀), (♂+♀), (♀)
pg. HAB meadows, fens,
woods. SOIL water–
moist; not acid. SHADE
nil–mid. ALT sl–1000.
DIST E5, W5, S5, I5.
RANGE F5, G5, S5.
*See p. 170, 217, 253,
262, 276, 293.* **ss60**.

● **Common wintercress**
Barbarea vulgaris
Mid–tall. Deep glossy
green; lvs pinnately-
lobed in rosette be-
coming simple up
stem; fls 7–10mm; fr
square-edged, 15–
25mm long, held up-
right. LH persistent
ann. GERM aut. FL 5–8.
POLL ins(d, h, c); self.
SEX (♂) hg. HAB grassy
and disturbed places.
SOIL damp–moist; not
acid. SHADE nil–light.
ALT sl–200. DIST E5,
W3, S4, I3. RANGE
F4, G3, S4.
ss61.

● **Hairy rockcress**
Arabis hirsuta
Short–mid. Hairy; lvs
simple, in rosette and
pressed to stem; fls
3–5mm; fr to 50mm,
pressed to stem. LH
bienn or short-lived
perenn; taproot. GERM
spr. FL 6–8. POLL
ins(d, h). SEX (♀) pg.
HAB grassy places,
walls, rocks. SOIL dry;
calc. SHADE nil. ALT
sl–800. DIST E3, W3,
S3, I3. RANGE F4, G4,
S4.
ss62. ss63.

○ **Alpine rockcress**
Arabis alpina
Low–mid. Mat-form-
ing; lvs toothed, hairy,
greyish, clasping stem;
fls 6–10mm, white. LH
perenn; stolons. GERM
? spr. FL 6–8. POLL
ins; self. SEX (♀) hg.
HAB mountain rocks.
SOIL wet–moist; calc.
SHADE nil. ALT (sl–)850.
DIST S1. RANGE G2, S3.

● **Watercress**
Nasturtium officinale
Short–mid, creeping.
Lvs pinnate, strong-
tasting; fls 4–6mm; fr
12–18mm long, held
horizontally. LH
perenn, often short-
lived; tap-root, rooting
stems. GERM spr ? FL
5–9. POLL ins(h, d);
self. SEX (♀) hg. HAB
flowing water. SOIL
water; not acid. SHADE
nil. ALT sl–350. DIST
E5, W5, S3, I5. RANGE
F5, G5, sS1.
See p. 253.

● **Great yellowcress**
Rorippa amphibia
Mid–tall. Variable; lvs
long, narrow, toothed,
ribbed, yellow–green;
fls 6–7mm; fr long-
stalked. LH perenn;
stolons. GERM spr. FL
6–8. POLL ins(h, d),
self. SEX (♀) hg. HAB
in and by water. SOIL
water–damp; acid–
calc. SHADE nil–light.
ALT sl–100. DIST E3,
W1, I2. RANGE F3,
G4, sS1.

● **Marsh yellowcress**
Rorippa palustris
Low–mid. Lvs pin-
nately-lobed; fls 3mm,
pale yellow, petals
shorter than sepals.
LH persistent ann.
GERM spr. FL 6–9. POLL
ins(d); self. SEX (♀) hg.
HAB damp, bare
ground. SOIL wet–
moist; acid–calc. SHADE
nil–light. ALT sl–300.
DIST sE5, nE3, W3, S2,
I2. RANGE F5, G5, S4.
See p. 253. **ss64**.

● **Creeping yellowcress**
Rorippa sylvestris
Mid. Weak-stemmed;
lvs pinnately cut, upper
unstalked; fls 5mm,
petals longer than
sepals. LH perenn;
rootstock, stolons.
GERM spr. FL 6–8. POLL
ins(h, d); ? self. SEX
(♀) hg. HAB streams
and ponds. SOIL water–
damp; acid–calc.
SHADE nil. ALT sl–150.
DIST E4, W2, S2, I2.
RANGE F4, G5, S2.

○ **Hoary stock**
Matthiola incana
Mid–tall. Hairy; stem
woody at base; lvs
narrow, entire, greyish;
fls 30–50mm, fragrant;
fr softly hairy. LH
perenn; tap-root.
GERM ? FL 5–7. POLL
ins(l, h); self. SEX (♀)
hg. HAP sea-cliffs. SOIL
dry; not acid. SHADE
nil. ALT sl–50. DIST
sE1, W1.

○ **Sea stock**
Matthiola sinuata
Mid. Hairy; stem lfy
throughout; lvs lobed,
whitish; fls 20–30mm,
fragrant; fr stickily-
hairy. LH bienn. GERM
? FL 6–8. POLL ins(l).
SEX (♀) hg. HAB sea-
cliffs, sand-dunes.
SOIL dry; calc. SHADE
nil. ALT sl. DIST sE1,
W1. RANGE F1.

○ **Dame's violet**
Hesperis matronalis
Mid–tall. Hairy; stems branching; lvs narrow, toothed, short-stalked; fls 15–20mm, very fragrant, with deeply lobed stigma. LH short-lived perenn; tap-root, woody stem-base. GERM imm. FL 5–7. POLL ins(l, h, d). SEX (♀); hg. HAB garden escape, roadsides, etc. SOIL moist; not acid. SHADE nil–mid. ALT sl–400. DIST and RANGE widespread casual.

○ **Treacle mustard**
Erysimum cheiranthoides
Short–tall. Sparsely hairy; lvs narrow, rosette lvs soon dying; fls 5–6mm; fr 4-angled, hairy. LH persistent ann. GERM spr. FL 6–8. POLL ins(h, d, l); self. SEX (♀). HAB disturbed ground. SOIL moist–dry; not acid. SHADE nil. ALT sl–400. DIST sE3, nE1, W1, S1, I1. RANGE F3, G4, S4.

● **Garlic mustard**
Alliaria petiolata
Short–tall. Garlic-smelling when damaged; lvs toothed, heart-shaped, long-stalked; fls 6mm; fr 4-angled. LH bienn; root-buds. GERM spr. FL 4–7. POLL ins(c, d, h); self. SEX (♀) hg. HAB hedges, wood-edges. SOIL moist–dry; not acid. SHADE nil–mid. ALT sl–250. DIST E5, W5, S3, I3. RANGE F5, G5, S2.
See p. 262.

● **Tall rocket**
Sisymbrium altissimum
Mid–tall. Root lvs pinnate, short-lived; stem lvs feathery; fls 10–12mm; fr to 100mm long, held at an angle. LH winter ann, sometimes persisting. GERM aut. FL 6–8. POLL ins; self ? SEX (♀) hg. HAB disturbed ground. SOIL dry; acid–calc. SHADE nil. ALT sl–200. DIST and RANGE casual throughout.

● **Hedge mustard**
Sisymbrium officinale
Mid–tall. Roughly hairy; lvs pinnately lobed; fls 3mm, in dense spikes on spreading branches; fr closely pressed to stem. LH ann, sometimes persisting. GERM spr. FL 5–9. POLL self. SEX (♀) hg. HAB disturbed ground. SOIL moist–dry; acid–calc. SHADE nil. ALT sl–250. DIST E5, W5, S4, I5. RANGE F5, G5, S3.

○ **Eastern rocket**
Sisymbrium orientale
Mid–tall. Hairy; rosette lvs lobed, soon dying; stem lvs simple; fls 7–8mm, pale yellow; fr to 100mm, held at an angle. LH persistent ann. GERM aut–spr. FL 6–8. POLL ins?; self. SEX (♀). HAB disturbed ground. SOIL dry; not acid. SHADE nil. ALT sl–200. DIST and RANGE casual throughout.

● **Thale cress**
Arabidopsis thaliana
Low–mid. Rosette lvs toothed, hairy; stem lvs entire, hairless, unstalked; fls 3mm; fr ribbed. LH persistent ann. GERM spr. FL 3–10. POLL self. SEX (♀) hg; (♀ + ♂). HAB bare and disturbed ground, walls. SOIL dry; not calc. SHADE nil–light. ALT sl–700. DIST E4, W2, S3, I2. RANGE F4, G3, S3.
See p. 261, 262.

MIGNONETTE FAMILY
Resedaceae
A small family with only one native British genus. Plants often have pinnate or pinnately-lobed leaves and long spikes of flowers, with variable numbers (4–7) of slender petals. Weld was formerly extensively used as a dye-plant.
See p. 245.

● **Wild mignonette**
Reseda lutea
Mid. Stem ridged, rather stout, solid, clothed with small lvs; fls 6mm, greenish-yellow, 6-petalled. LH bienn or short-lived perenn; tap-root. GERM aut–spr. FL 6–8. POLL ins(h, d, c); self. SEX (♀ + ♂) pa. HAB disturbed ground. SOIL dry; calc. SHADE nil. ALT sl–200. DIST sE4, nE2, W2, S1, I1. RANGE F4, G3, S1.

● **Weld**
Reseda luteola
Tall to v.tall. Stem ridged, hollow; lvs narrow, unlobed, in a rosette which withers in second year; fls 4–5mm, pale yellow-green, 4-petalled. LH bienn; tap-root. GERM aut. FL 6–9. POLL ins(d, h); self. SEX (♀) hg. HAB disturbed ground. SOIL dry; calc. SHADE nil. ALT sl–250. DIST sE4, nE3, W3, S2, I3. RANGE F4, G3, sS2.
See p. 215, 245.

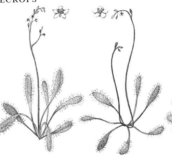

SUNDEW FAMILY
Droseraceae
A small family of insectivorous plants, with a rosette of heavily modified leaves, each with a covered with long hairs, each with a sticky tip, which trap insects and then curve inwards to hold them. The insects are then digested by enzymes secreted from the leaves and contribute to the plant's nutrition (see p. 238). Flowers are inconspicuous and often fail to open at all (cleistogamous).
See p. 233.

○ **Great sundew**
Drosera anglica
Short. Lvs all in rosette, up to 30mm long, narrow; flg stem arising from centre of rosette, much longer than lvs; fls 5–6mm. LH perenn; rootstock. GERM spr. FL 7–8. POLL self. SEX (♀). HAB peat bogs and fens. SOIL wet; acid–calc. SHADE nil. ALT sl–500(–900). DIST E1, W1, S3, I2. RANGE F2, G3, S4.

○ **Oblong-leaved sundew**
Drosera intermedia
V.low–low. Lvs in a rosette, oblong on long stalks; flg stalk arising from side of rosette and curving upwards; fls 5–6mm. LH perenn; rootstock. GERM spr. FL 7–8. POLL self. SEX (♀). HAB wet heaths and moors, on peat. SOIL wet–damp; acid. SHADE nil. ALT sl–300. DIST E2, W2, S2, I2. RANGE F2, G3, sS3.

● **Common sundew**
Drosera rotundifolia
Low–short. Lvs in a rosette, circular, long-stalked; flg stem arising from centre of rosette, longer than lvs; fls 5–6mm. LH perenn; rootstock. GERM spr. FL 6–8. POLL self. SEX (♀). HAB bogs, heaths, moors. SOIL wet–damp; acid. SHADE nil. ALT sl–750. DIST E3, W4, S4, I4. RANGE F3, G4, S4.

STONECROP FAMILY
Crassulaceae
Fleshy ('succulent') herbs, mostly with small, unstalked, hairless leaves. Flowers often conspicuous, brightly-coloured, usually with 5 petals and sepals. Carpels not joined, equal in number to the petals. Typically grow in dry places where water supply is intermittent; the fleshy leaves enable them to store water and so survive as perennials in habitats otherwise normally dominated by annuals.
See p. 204, 249.

● **Navelwort**
Umbilicus rupestris
Short. Lvs mostly from roots, circular, fleshy, the stem joining in the centre beneath a depression in the upper surface; fls bell-shaped, 8–10mm long, in long spikes. LH perenn; rootstock. GERM spr. FL 6–8. POLL ins(?); self. SEX (♀) pa. HAB rocks, walls, banks. SOIL dry; not calc. SHADE nil–light. ALT sl–500. DIST wE4, eE1, W5, wS2, I4. RANGE wF4.
See p. 204.

○ **Roseroot**
Rhodiola rosea
Short. Greyish, often purplish; lvs fleshy, large, densely clothing stem; fls 5–6mm, 4-petalled yellowish, in dense heads. LH perenn; rootstock. GERM ? FL 5–7. POLL ins(d, h). SEX (♂) + (♀), (♂ + ♀). HAB rocks in mountains and by sea in n. SOIL moist; acid–calc. SHADE nil. ALT sl–1250. DIST nE1, W1, S3, I1. RANGE F1, G1, S3.

● **Orpine**
Sedum telephium
Short–mid. Greyish; stems reddish, with toothed, oval unfleshy lvs; fls 9–12mm, pale purplish-red, in dense clusters. LH perenn; rootstock. GERM spr? FL 7–9. POLL ins(d, h); self. SEX (♀) pa. HAB open woods, hedges, grassy banks. SOIL moist–dry; acid–calc. ALT sl–400. DIST E3, W3, S3. RANGE F4, G5, sS3.

● **Biting stonecrop**
Sedum acre
V.low–low, creeping and mat-forming. Hot-tasting stems hidden by small, blunt fleshy lvs; fls 10–12mm, scattered along stems. LH perenn; evergreen. GERM imm–spr. FL 5–7. POLL ins(d, h); self. SEX (♀) pa. HAB bare ground, walls. SOIL dry; not acid. SHADE nil. ALT sl–400. DIST E5, W5, S4, I3. RANGE F5, G5, S3.
See p. 204.

● **White stonecrop**
Sedum album
Low, creeping and mat-forming. Lvs almost cylindrical, well-spaced, up to 12mm long; fls 6–9mm, in branching, flattened heads. LH perenn; evergreen. GERM imm–spr. FL 6–8. POLL ins(d, h); self. SEX (♀) pa. HAB rocks and wall-tops. SOIL dry; acid–calc. SHADE nil. ALT sl–300. DIST E3, W3, S2, I3; mostly introduced. RANGE F3, G3, S2.

● **English stonecrop**
Sedum anglicum
V.low, creeping and
mat-forming. Greyish,
often reddening; lvs to
5mm, cylindrical,
clothing stem; fls
10–12mm, scattered on
stems. LH perenn;
evergreen. GERM imm–
spr. FL 6–9. POLL
ins(d, h); self. SEX (♀)
pa. HAB rocks, sparsely
grassy banks. SOIL d.v;
not calc. SHADE nil.
ALT sl–1100. DIST
wE3, eE1, W3, S3, I4.
RANGE wF3, wS2.
ss65. ss66.

○ **Rock stonecrop**
Sedum forsteranum
Short. Often greyish;
non-flg stems creeping,
ending in rosettes; flg
stems erect, with scat-
tered, narrow lvs; fls
12mm, 5–8-petalled, in
dense, flattened clus-
ters. LH perenn; ever-
green. GERM spr. FL
6–7. POLL ins(d, h);
self. SEX (♀) pa. HAB
rocks. SOIL dry; acid–
calc. SHADE nil–mid.
ALT sl–300. DIST swE1,
W2; and naturalised.
RANGE F3, wG1.

○ **Reflexed stonecrop**
Sedum reflexum
Short. Non-flg shoots
lfy all over, with no
rosette; lvs cylindrical;
fls 15mm, 7-petalled.
LH perenn; evergreen.
GERM spr. FL 6–8. POLL
ins(h, d, l). SEX (♀).
HAB rocks, walls. SOIL
dry; not acid. SHADE
nil. ALT sl–200. DIST
(E3, W3, S2, I1).
RANGE F4, G3, S2.

○ **Hairy stonecrop**
Sedum villosum
Low. Hairy; stems
erect, sparsely lfy; lvs
narrow, flattened; fls
6mm, pink, long-
stalked. LH short-lived
perenn. GERM ? FL 6–8.
POLL ins(d, h); self.
SEX (♀) pa. HAB
streamsides, rocks, in
mountains. SOIL wet–
moist; acid–calc.
SHADE nil. ALT 50–
1000. DIST nE2, S1.
RANGE F1, G3, S1.

**Hen-and-chickens
houseleek**
Jovibarba sobolifera
Low–short. Lvs fleshy,
forming a ball-like
rosette; fls bell-shaped,
6-petalled, on a lfy
stem. LH perenn;
stolons. GERM ? FL 7–8.
POLL ins. SEX (♀). HAB
sandy and rocky
grassland. SOIL dry;
not calc. SHADE nil.
ALT [sl–200]. RANGE
G2.
See p. 204.

**SAXIFRAGE
FAMILY**
Saxifragaceae
Small plants with
simple, toothed or
lobed leaves, often in
a rosette, and showy,
5-petalled flowers with
10 stamens and 5
styles. Fruit a forked
capsule. Characteristic
of upland habitats,
with a few lowland
species.
See p. 16, 269, 293.

**GRASS OF
PARNASSUS
FAMILY**
Parnassiaceae
Closely related to the
saxifrages but with
only 5 fertile stamens
in the solitary flower.
(Grass of Parnassus)

● **Opposite-leaved
golden saxifrage**
*Chrysosplenium
oppositifolium*
Low, creeping, patch-
forming. Lvs rounded,
blunt-toothed, in
opposite pairs; fls
3–4mm, with no petals.
LH perenn; evergreen.
GERM spr–sum. FL 3–7.
POLL ins(d, c); self.
SEX (♀) pg. HAB
stream-banks, springs.
SOIL wet–damp; acid–
calc. SHADE nil–heavy.
ALT sl–1100. DIST swn
E5, eE1, W5, S5, I4.
RANGE F4, G3, wS1.
See p. 282.

○ **Alternate-leaved
golden saxifrage**
*Chrysosplenium
alternifolium*
Like Opposite-leaved
golden saxifrage but
lvs heart-shaped,
toothed, alternate; fls
5–6mm. LH perenn;
evergreen, stolons.
GERM spr. FL 4–7. POLL
ins(d, c); self. SEX (♀)
hg. HAB stream banks.
SOIL wet–damp; acid–
calc. SHADE nil–mid.
ALT sl–900. DIST E2,
W2, S3. RANGE eF3,
G4, S3.
See p. 282.

● **Starry saxifrage**
Saxifraga stellaris
Low–short. Lvs
toothed, all in rosette;
fls 10–15mm, long-
stalked; anthers red.
LH perenn. GERM ? FL
6–8. POLL ins(d); self.
SEX (♀) pa–pg. HAB
rocks, stream sides, in
mountains. SOIL wet–
damp; acid–calc.
SHADE nil. ALT 200–
1400. DIST nE1, W1,
S3, I1. RANGE F1, G1,
S3.

○ **St Patrick's
cabbage**
Saxifraga spathularis
Low–mid. Lvs toothed,
long-stalked, in
rosette; margin trans-
lucent; fls 8–10mm,
red-spotted, in branch-
ing clusters. LH perenn;
evergreen. GERM spr.
FL 6–7. POLL ins(d, h);
self. SEX (♀). HAB
rocks. SOIL damp–
moist; acid. SHADE
nil–mid. ALT 200–1000.
DIST I2.
ss67.

53

○ **Arctic saxifrage**
Saxifraga nivalis
V.low–low. Lvs
toothed, purplish un-
derneath, all in rosette;
fls 5–6mm, in a dense
head. LH perenn;
evergreen. GERM ? FL
7–8. POLL ins(d); self.
SEX (♀) hg–pg. HAB
mountain rocks. SOIL
damp; not calc. SHADE
nil. ALT 400–1300.
DIST nE1, W1, S2, I1.
RANGE S3.

● **Rue-leaved saxifrage**
Saxifraga tridactylites
V.low–low. Sticky-
hairy, red-tinged; lvs
ivy-shaped, sometimes
entire; fls 4–5mm, flhd
branching. LH winter
ann. GERM aut. FL 4–6.
POLL self. SEX (♀)
hg–pg. HAB walls,
rocks, bare sandy
ground. SOIL dry; acid–
calc. SHADE nil. ALT
sl–700. DIST sE4, nE2,
W1, S1, I2. RANGE F5,
G4, S2.
See p. 174, 175.

● **Yellow saxifrage**
Saxifraga aizoides
Low. Non-flg stems
creeping; flg stems
erect, with narrow,
unstalked lvs, and up
to 10 fls, 8–12mm,
well-spaced. LH
perenn; evergreen.
GERM spr. FL 6–9. POLL
ins(d, h, l); ?self. SEX
(♀) pa. HAB stream
sides, rocks, in moun-
tains. SOIL wet–moist;
not acid. SHADE nil.
ALT sl (in n)–1200.
DIST nE1, S3, I1.
RANGE F1, G2, S3.
ss68.

● **Meadow saxifrage**
Saxifraga granulata
Short–mid. Lvs lobed,
mostly in rosette, with
bulbils at base of stalk;
fls 20–30mm, in loose
clusters. LH perenn;
bulbils. GERM aut. FL
4–6. POLL ins(d, h).
SEX (♀) pa. HAB grassy
places. SOIL moist; not
acid. SHADE nil–light.
ALT sl–500. DIST E3,
W2, S2, I1. RANGE F3,
G4, S3.

○ **Highland saxifrage**
Saxifraga rivularis
V.low. Lvs bluntly ivy-
shaped, long-stalked,
most from roots; fls
6–10mm, few. LH
perenn; stolons, bul-
bils. GERM ? FL 7–8.
POLL ins(d); self. SEX
(♀) pg. HAB mountain
rocks. SOIL wet–damp;
not calc. SHADE nil.
ALT 900–1200. DIST S1.
RANGE S3.

○ **Drooping saxifrage**
Saxifraga cernua
V.low–low. Lvs poin-
ted ivy-shaped, with
bulbils at base of stalk;
fls 15–25mm, partly or
entirely replaced by
red bulbils. LH perenn;
bulbils. GERM not
fruiting. FL 7. POLL
rare. SEX (♀) pa–fl.
HAB mountain rocks.
SOIL damp–moist;
calc. SHADE nil. ALT
900–1200. DIST S1.
RANGE G1, S2.
See p. 293.

● **Mossy saxifrage**
Saxifraga hypnoides
Low, creeping, mat-
forming. Most shoots
non-flg, sometimes
with bulbils; lvs nar-
row, 3-lobed, hairy;
fls 10–15mm. LH
perenn; evergreen.
GERM spr. FL 5–7.
POLL ins. SEX (♀) pa.
HAB rocks, grassy
places. SOIL damp;
acid–calc. SHADE nil–
light. ALT sl–1300.
DIST nE2, W2, S3, I1.
RANGE F1.
See p. 276.

○ **Tufted saxifrage**
Saxifraga cespitosa
Low, tufted, forming
tiny cushions. Lvs 3-
lobed, sticky-hairy; fls
8–10mm, greenish. LH
perenn; evergreen.
GERM ? FL 5–7. POLL
ins(d); ? self. SEX (♀)
pg. HAB mountain
rocks. SOIL damp–
moist; not acid. SHADE
nil. ALT 600–1100. DIST
W1, S1. RANGE S3.
ss69.

○ **Purple saxifrage**
Saxifraga oppositifolia
V.low–low, creeping,
mat-forming. Lvs tiny,
in 4 dense rows, often
lime-encrusted; fls
10–20mm, purple. LH
perenn; evergreen.
GERM spr. FL 3–5, 7–8.
POLL ins(d, l); self.
SEX (♀) pa then hg.
HAB mountain rocks.
SOIL moist; calc. SHADE
nil. ALT (sl–)400–1200.
DIST nE1, W1, S3, nI1.
RANGE F1, G2, S3.

Mountain saxifrage
Saxifraga cotyledon
Short. Lvs pointed,
fleshy, in a cupped
rosette, yellowing in
winter; fls white in a
long-stalked, loose
cluster. LH perenn;
evergreen. GERM ? FL
7–8. POLL ins. SEX
(♀). HAB rocks. SOIL
moist; not acid nor
calc. SHADE nil. ALT
[sl–2000]. RANGE S3.

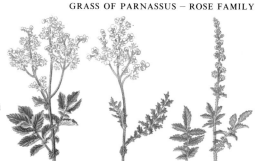

● **Grass of Parnassus**
Parnassia palustris
Short. Lvs heart-
shaped, long-stalked,
most from roots; fls
solitary, 15–30mm, on
a long stalk with a
single lf, petals veined.
LH perenn; rootstock.
GERM spr–sum. FL
6–10. POLL ins(d, c, h);
self. SEX (♀) pa. HAB
moors, marshes. SOIL
wet–damp; acid–calc.
SHADE nil. ALT sl–800.
DIST sE1, nE3, W1, S4,
I3. RANGE F3, G4, S5.
*See p. 249, 257, 262,
276, 278.*

ROSE FAMILY
Rosaceae
A very distinctive
family, typified by the
roses, with 5 petals and
sepals and often a ring
of 5 more sepals out-
side them, called the
epicalyx. All have
large numbers of
stamens. Leaves have
stipules at the base of
the stalk. Otherwise a
very disparate family,
including many trees
(not covered here),
shrubs and herbs.
Found in a wide
variety of habitats, but
most are perennials.
*See p. 16, 18, 239, 248,
249, 257, 262, 269, 291,
298.*

● **Meadowsweet**
Filipendula ulmaria
Tall. Lvs pinnate, with
red stalk, and small
lflts between up to 5
pairs of larger ones;
fragrant fls, 5–10mm,
in dense clusters. LH
perenn; rhizome. GERM
spr. FL 6–9. POLL ins(h,
d, c); self. SEX (♀) pa;
(♀+♂)+(♂). HAB
meadows, marshes,
fens. SOIL wet–damp;
not acid. SHADE nil–
mid. ALT sl–900. DIST
E5, W5, S5, I5. RANGE
F5, G5, S5.

● **Dropwort**
Filipendula vulgaris
Short–mid. Lvs pin-
nate, with up to 8 pairs
of lflts, few on stem;
fls 10–15mm, in looser
clusters than Meadow-
sweet. LH perenn;
rhizome, root tubers.
GERM spr. FL 5–8. POLL
ins(h, d, c); self. SEX
(♀) hg. HAB short
grassland. SOIL dry;
calc. SHADE nil. ALT
sl–350. DIST sE3, nE2,
W2, S1. RANGE F3, G3,
sS3.

● **Agrimony**
Agrimonia eupatoria
Mid. Lvs pinnate; fls
5–8mm, in a long
spike; fr grooved and
spiny. LH perenn; root-
stock. GERM spr. FL
6–8. POLL ins(d, h);
self. SEX (♀). HAB
grassy places. SOIL
moist–dry; not acid.
SHADE nil–light. ALT
sl–500. DIST E5, W5,
S3, I4. RANGE F5, G5,
sS3.
See p. 172, 263. **ss70.**

● **Salad burnet**
Sanguisorba minor
Short. Lvs pinnate
with reddish midrib
and many lflts; fls
small, with no petals
and conspicuous yellow
stamens and red styles,
in round heads. LH
perenn; rootstock.
GERM spr. FL 5–9. POLL
ins(h). SEX (♀+♂+♀).
HAB short grassland.
SOIL dry; calc. SHADE
nil. ALT sl–500. DIST
E4, W3, sS1, I2. RANGE
F4, G3, sS1.
See p. 219, 271, 273.

● **Great burnet**
Sanguisorba officinalis
Mid–tall. Lvs pinnate
with few lflts; fls small,
with no petals; sta-
mens short. LH perenn;
rootstock. GERM imm.
FL 6–8. POLL ins(d, h,
l); self. SEX (♀) hg.
HAB tall grassland. SOIL
wet–moist; not acid.
SHADE nil–light. ALT
sl–400. DIST E3, W2,
sS1, I1. RANGE F3,
G4, sS1.
See p. 237.

○ **Alpine lady's-
mantle**
Alchemilla alpina
Low–short. Lvs deeply
5-lobed, sticky under-
neath; fls 3mm, yel-
lowish-green, with no
petals, in clusters.
LH perenn; rootstock.
GERM ? FL 6–8. POLL
apo. SEX (♀). HAB
mountain grassland.
SOIL moist; acid–calc.
SHADE nil. ALT (100–)
400–1300. DIST nE1,
S3, I1. RANGE F1, G2,
S3.

● **Lady's-mantle**
Alchemilla vulgaris
Low–mid. Lvs 5–7-
lobed, usually to about
half way; fls 3–5mm,
yellow–green, with no
petals, in clusters. LH
perenn; rootstock.
GERM spr. FL 6–9. POLL
apo. SEX (♀). HAB
grassland. SOIL damp–
dry; acid–calc. SHADE
nil–light. ALT sl–1200.
DIST sE2, nE4, W3,
S5, I3. RANGE F3, G5,
S5.
See p. 263, 291.

● **Parsley piert**
Aphanes arvensis
V. low–low; prostrate.
Lvs lobed, the stipules
enclosing the fls, each
with a single stamen.
LH ann. GERM aut–spr.
FL 4–10. POLL self. SEX
(♀). HAB bare ground.
SOIL dry; acid–calc.
SHADE nil. ALT sl–500.
DIST sE4, nE2, W2, S1,
I3. RANGE F4, G4, sS1.

● **Field rose**
Rosa arvensis
Tall, forming bushes.
Thorns curved; fls 30–
50mm, white, the
styles joined to make a
column; hips red. LH
perenn; stems. GERM
spr. FL 6–8. POLL ins(h,
d, l); self. SEX (♀) hg.
HAB hedges, scrub. SOIL
moist–dry; not acid.
SHADE nil–mid. ALT
sl–400. DIST E4, W3,
I3. RANGE F4, swG4. -

○ **Burnet rose**
Rosa pimpinellifolia
Short–mid. Suckering;
stems with dense,
straight prickles; lvs
with 3–5 pairs of lflts;
fls 25–40mm, creamy-
white, fr dark purple.
LH perenn; stems,
suckers. GERM spr. FL
5–7. POLL ins(d, h, l).
SEX (♀). HAB open
places, dunes, grass-
land. SOIL dry; calc.
SHADE nil. ALT sl–500.
DIST E2, W2, S2, I2.
RANGE F3, G2, sG1.

● **Dog rose**
Rosa canina
V.tall, scrambling.
Stems and prickles
curved; lvs usually
hairless; fls 40–50mm,
pink or white, the
styles not fused. LH
perenn; stems. GERM
spr. FL 6–7. POLL ins(h,
d, c, l), self; apo. SEX
(♀). HAB fens, woods,
scrub, hedges. SOIL
damp–dry; acid–calc.
SHADE nil–mid. ALT
sl–500. DIST E5, W5,
S4, I4. RANGE F5, G5,
sS2.
*See p. 18, 192, 207,
236, 298.*

● **Sweet briar**
Rosa rubiginosa
Tall–v.tall. Straight-
stemmed, prickles
curved; lvs with dense,
sticky hairs; fls 30mm,
pink. LH perenn; stems.
GERM spr. FL 6–7. POLL
ins(d, h, l). SEX (♀).
HAB scrub, open
woods. SOIL dry; calc.
SHADE nil–mid. ALT
sl–200. DIST seE4,
nwE2, W2, S2, I2.
RANGE F2, G4, sS2.

● **Downy rose**
Rosa tomentosa
Tall–v.tall. Stems
curved; prickles heavy,
curved or straight; fls
35–40mm, sepals not
falling. LH perenn;
stems. GERM spr. FL
6–7. POLL ins(d, h, l).
SEX (♀). HAB woods,
scrub. SOIL moist–dry;
not calc. SHADE nil–
light. ALT sl–400. DIST
E3, W3, S2, I1. RANGE
F3, G4, sS2.

● **Soft rose**
Rosa mollis
Tall. Straight-stem-
med; prickles straight;
lvs hairy; fls 30–50mm,
sepal persisting on
fruit. LH perenn; stems,
suckers. GERM spr. FL
6–8. POLL ins(d, h, l).
SEX (♀). HAB open
woods, scrubs, rocky
places. SOIL moist;
acid–calc. SHADE nil–
light. ALT sl–600. DIST
sE1, nE3, W2, S4, I2.
RANGE F1, G2, S4.

● **Dewberry**
Rubus caesius
Short–mid. Thin,
round stems, rooting;
prickles few, flimsy;
lvs with 3 lflts; fls 15–
25mm, white; fr
bluish, with few, large
fruitlets. LH perenn;
bienn stems, rooting
nodes. GERM aut–spr.
FL 6–9. POLL ins(d, h,
c). SEX (♀). HAB tall
grassland, scrub, fens.
SOIL wet–dry; not acid.
SHADE nil–mid. ALT
sl–300. DIST eE5, wE3,
W3, sS2, I3. RANGE
F5, G5, sS2.

● **Bramble**
Rubus fruticosus
Short–v.tall. Very
variable; stems arch-
ing, ridged, stiff, with
strong prickles; lvs
with 3–5 lflts; fls 20–
30mm, white or pink,
fr red, turning black.
LH perenn; bienn
stems rooting at tips.
GERM aut–spr. FL 5–10.
POLL apo. SEX (♀). HAB
woods, scrub, dis-
turbed ground. SOIL
wet–dry; acid–calc.
SHADE nil–heavy. ALT
sl–350. DIST E5, W5,
S4, I5. RANGE F5, G5,
sS3.
*See p. 192, 251, 277,
280, 282.*

○ **Cloudberry**
Rubus chamaemorus
Short, creeping. No
prickles; lvs rounded,
lobed; fls rare, white,
15–25mm; fr orange.
LH perenn; rhizome.
GERM spr. FL 6–8. POLL
ins(h, d). SEX (♂) + (♀).
SHADE nil. ALT 200–
1200. DIST nE1, W1,
S3, nI1. RANGE G1, S5.

○ **Arctic bramble**
Rubus arcticus
Low–short; creeping.
Spineless; all lvs
trefoil, wrinkled; fls
15–25mm, with long
sepals; fr ripening red.
GERM spr? FL 6–7. POLL
ins. SEX (♀). HAB
moors. SOIL moist;
acid–calc. SHADE nil.
ALT [sl–1500]. DIST
?S1. RANGE S4.

● **Raspberry**
Rubus idaeus
Tall–v.tall. Prickles hair-like; lvs with 3–5 lflts; fls small, with thin upright petals; fr red. LH perenn; suckering, bienn; stems. GERM spr. FL 5–8. POLL ins(d, h); self. SEX (♀). HAB open woods, heaths. SOIL damp–dry; acid–calc. SHADE nil–mid. ALT sl–800. DIST E4, W5, S5, I4. RANGE wF2, eF5, G5, S5.
See p. 277, 282.

○ **Stone bramble**
Rubus saxatilis
Low–mid, creeping. No prickles; lvs with 3 lflts; fls 10mm, petals small, sometimes upright. LH perenn; stolons. GERM spr. FL 6–8. POLL ins(d, h); self. SEX (♀) pg. HAB rocks, woods. SOIL moist; calc. SHADE nil–mid. ALT sl–1000. DIST nE2, W2, S3, I2. RANGE eF1, G3, S5.

● **Wild strawberry**
Fragaria vesca
Low–short, creeping. Rooting; lvs with 3 silky-hairy lflts; fls 12–18mm; fr a tiny strawberry. LH perenn; stolons. GERM spr–sum. FL 4–7. POLL ins(d, h, l). SEX (♀) pg. HAB woods, scrub, open grassland. SOIL dry; not acid. SHADE nil–heavy. ALT sl–750. DIST E5, W5, S4, I5. RANGE F5, G5, S4.
See p. 14, 162, 217, 251. **ss71.**

○ **Shrubby cinquefoil**
Potentilla fruticosa
Tall shrub. Lvs pinnate, with hairy, untoothed lflts; fls 15–20mm, in sparse clusters. LH perenn; stems. GERM ? FL 5–7. POLL ins(d, h). SEX (♂)+(♀). HAB rocky ground. SOIL damp–moist; not acid. SHADE nil. ALT 200–750. DIST E1, I1. RANGE S1.
See p. 270.

● **Marsh cinquefoil**
Potentilla palustris
Short–mid. Lvs pinnate, end lflt largest; fls 20–30mm, with thin petals shorter than conspicuous red-purple sepals. LH perenn; rhizome. GERM spr–sum. FL 5–7. POLL ins(d, h). SEX (♀) pa. HAB marshes, fens, ponds. SOIL water–wet; acid. SHADE nil–light. ALT sl–900. DIST sE2, nE4, W4, S4, I5. RANGE F2, G4, S5.

Barren strawberry
Potentilla sterilis
Low. Hairy; lvs with 3 lflts, bluish above, silvery beneath; fls 10–15mm, petals shallowly notched; fr a dry capsule. LH perenn; rootstock, stolons. GERM spr. FL 2–5. POLL ins(d, h); self. SEX (♀) hg. HAB open grassy places, woods. SOIL dry; acid–calc. SHADE nil–mid. ALT sl–600. DIST E5, W5, S3, I4. RANGE F5, G3, sS1. **ss72.**

White cinquefoil
Potentilla alba
Low–short. Hairy; lvs with 5 very narrow lobes, silvery-white underneath; fls 15–20mm. LH perenn. GERM ? FL 4–5. POLL ins. SEX (♀). HAB grassy and rocky places. SOIL dry; not calc. SHADE nil–mid. ALT [sl–1000]. RANGE eF1, G3.

● **Tormentil**
Potentilla erecta
Low–short, patch-forming. Root lvs with 3 rounded lflts, soon dying; stem lvs with 3 narrow, toothed lflts and 2 lf-like stipules; fls 6–12mm, 4-petalled. LH perenn; rootstock. GERM spr–sum. FL 5–9. POLL ins(d, h, l, c). SEX (♀) pa–hg. HAB grassland, heaths, moors. SOIL damp–dry; not calc. SHADE nil–light. ALT sl–1000. DIST E5, W5, S5, I5. RANGE F5, G5, S5.
See p. 213, 219, 276, 278.

● **Trailing tormentil**
Potentilla anglica
Low–short; long, procumbent rooting. Root lvs persisting, stem lvs with 5 lflts and 2 untoothed stipules; fls 14–18mm, mostly 4-petalled, some with 5. LH perenn; rootstock, rooting stems. GERM spr–sum. FL 6–9. POLL ins. SEX (♀). HAB wood-edges, heaths. SOIL moist–dry; not acid. SHADE nil–mid. ALT sl–400. DIST E3, W3, S2, I3. RANGE F2, G3, sS1.

● **Creeping cinquefoil**
Potentilla reptans
Low–short; long, procumbent, rooting. Root lvs long-stalked, with 5 lflts; stem lvs similar; fls 17–25mm, 5-petalled. LH perenn; rootstock, rooting stems. FL 6–9. POLL ins(h, d). SEX (♀) hg; (♂+♀)+ (♀). HAB bare and sparsely grassy places. SOIL dry; not acid. SHADE nil–light. ALT sl–400. DIST E5, W4, S3, I5. RANGE F5, G5, sS3.
See p. 251, 278.

○ **Spring cinquefoil**
Potentilla tabernaemontani
Low; mat-forming, creeping and rooting. Root lvs with 5, stem lvs 3 lflts, stipules narrow; fls 10–20mm. LH perenn; rootstock, rooting stems. GERM spr. FL 4–6. POLL apo. SEX (♀). HAB grassy, rocky ground. SOIL dry; calc. SHADE nil. ALT sl–300. DIST E2, W1, S1. RANGE F3, G3, sS2.
See p. 291.

○ **Alpine cinquefoil**
Potentilla crantzii
Low–short; prostrate, not rooting and mat-forming. Lvs as in Spring cinquefoil; fls 15–25mm, often orange-centred. LH perenn; rootstock. GERM spr–sum. FL 6–7. POLL apo. SEX (♀). HAB mountain rocks. SOIL moist; calc. SHADE nil. ALT 100–1000. DIST nE1, W1, S2. RANGE F1, G1, S4.
See p. 291.

○ **Hoary cinquefoil**
Potentilla argentea
Short. Stems hairy; lvs with 5 pinnately-lobed lflts, white-hairy underneath; fls 10–15mm. LH perenn; rootstock. GERM spr–sum. FL 6–9. POLL ins(h), apo. SEX (♀). HAB sandy grassland. SOIL dry; not calc. SHADE nil. ALT sl–100. DIST seE3, nwE1, W1, S1. RANGE F3, G4, S4.

○ **Norwegian cinquefoil**
Potentilla norvegica
Short–mid. Hairy, upright; lvs with 3 toothed lflts; fls 10–15mm, sepals hairy, as long as petals, enlarging in fr. LH ann or short-lived perenn; tap-root. GERM spr. FL 6–9. POLL ins. SEX (♀) hg. HAB disturbed ground. SOIL dry; not calc. SHADE nil. ALT sl–100. DIST (E2, W2, S2, I2). RANGE G2, S4, (F2).

● **Silverweed**
Potentilla anserina
Low; creeping and rooting. Lvs pinnate, silvery; fls 15–20mm, solitary, sparse. LH perenn; stolons. GERM sum. FL 5–8. POLL ins(d, hc, c); self in poor weather. SEX (♀) pa–pg; (♀+♀)+(♀) rare. HAB disturbed and grassy places. SOIL damp; acid–calc. SHADE nil. ALT sl–400. DIST E5, W5, S4, I5. RANGE F5, G4, S4.
See p. 217, 251.

● **Water avens**
Geum rivale
Mid. Root lvs pinnate, stem lvs trefoil; fls nodding, bell-shaped, petals 8–15mm long, apricot-coloured; sepals pinkish purple; fr with hairy, hooked style. LH perenn; rhizome. GERM imm. FL 4–9. POLL ins(h); self. SEX (♀) pg; (♀+♂)+(♂). HAB marshes, rocks. SOIL wet–damp; acid–calc. SHADE nil–heavy. ALT sl–1000. DIST sE3, nE5, W4, S5, I4. RANGE eF2, G4, S5.
See p. 258, 259.

● **Herb bennet**
Geum urbanum
Mid. Root lvs pinnate, stem lvs trefoil with large stipules; fls 8–15mm; style persisting as hook on hairy fr. Hybridises with Water avens. LH perenn; rhizome. GERM spr. FL 5–9. POLL ins(h); self. SEX (♀) pg; (♀+♂). HAB woods, scrub, hedges. SOIL moist; acid–calc. SHADE light–heavy. ALT sl–500. DIST E5, W5, S4, I4. RANGE F5, G5, sS4.
See p. 2, 162, 172, 237.

○ **Mountain avens**
Dryas octopetala
Low; creeping under-shrub. Lvs oblong, with rounded teeth, silvery underneath; fls 25–40mm, 8- or more-petalled; fr with long feathery styles. LH perenn; stems. GERM ? FL 5–7. POLL ins(h, d, l, c); self. SEX (♀) pg; (♀+♀); (♀+♂); (♂)+(♀). HAB mountain rocks. SOIL moist–dry; calc. SHADE nil. ALT sl (in n)–1000. DIST nE1, W1, S2, I1. RANGE F1, G2, S3.
See p. 270.

PEAFLOWER FAMILY
Leguminosae
A highly characteristic family, with pinnate or trefoil (in clovers) leaves and distinctive flowers. Each flower has 5 petals, 2 joined making a case surrounding the stamens and style; two at each side (wings) and one at the top (standard) often bent back. Most fix nitrogen from the air with the aid of bacteria in root nodules, and so are commonest on infertile, nitrogen-poor soils.
See p. 18, 19, 195, 221, 226, 229, 258, 268, 269, 277, 283, 284.

○ **Alpine milk-vetch**
Astragalus alpinus
Low–short. Lvs pinnate ending in a lflt; fls 10mm long, pale blue-violet, in loose heads; pod hairy, brown. LH perenn; rootstock. GERM sum. FL 7. POLL ins(h, l). SEX (♀). HAB mountain rocks. SOIL moist; calc. SHADE nil. ALT 600–800. DIST S1. RANGE G1, S3.

○ **Purple milk-vetch**
Astragalus danicus
Low–short. Lvs pinnate, ending in a lflt; fls 15mm long, deep violet, in long-stalked dense heads; pod white, hairy. LH perenn; rootstock. GERM ? FL 5–7. POLL ins(h). SEX (♀). HAB short turf. SOIL dry; calc. SHADE nil. ALT sl–200. DIST E2, S1, I1. RANGE F1, G2, S1.
See p. 284.

○ **Wild liquorice**
Astragalus glycyphyllos
Tall. Thick-stemmed; lvs pinnate, ending in a lflt; lflts few; fls 10–15mm long in loose clusters; pods to 35mm long. LH perenn; rootstock. GERM spr. FL 6–8. POLL ins(h). SEX (♀). HAB grassland, scrub. SOIL dry; not acid. SHADE nil–mid. ALT sl–150. DIST E2, W1, S1. RANGE F3, G4, sS3.

○ **Yellow milk-vetch**
Oxytropis campestris
Low short. Lvs hairy, pinnate, ending in a lflt; lflts 10–20mm; fls 15–20mm long, cream, streaked purple, in dense heads. LH perenn; rootstock. GERM ? FL 6–7. POLL ins(h). SEX (♀). HAB mountain rocks. SOIL moist; calc. SHADE nil. ALT 600–700. DIST S1. RANGE G1, S1.

○ **Mountain milk-vetch**
Oxytropis halleri
Low–short. Like Yellow milk-vetch, but lflts 5–8mm, fls 20mm, purple; heads longer-stalked. LH perenn; rootstock. GERM ? FL 6–7. POLL ins(h). SEX (♀). HAB mountain rocks. SOIL moist; calc. SHADE nil. ALT sl–600. DIST S1. RANGE G1.

Scorpion senna
Coronilla emerus
Tall–v.tall. Not spiny; lvs greyish-green; fls in loose clusters; pods up to 100mm long. LH perenn; shrub. GERM ? FL 4–6. POLL ins(h). SEX (♀). HAB scrub, open woods. SOIL dry; calc. SHADE nil–mid. ALT [sl–1800]. RANGE F2, G1, S1.

○ **Crown vetch**
Coronilla varia
Mid. Straggling; lflts oblong; fls 12mm long, pinkish-purple in long-stalked heads. Pod angled, bearded. LH perenn; rootstock. GERM aut. FL 6–8. POLL ins(h). SEX (♀). HAB bare and grassy places. SOIL moist–dry; calc. SHADE nil–light. ALT sl–100[–1500]. DIST (E3). RANGE F3, G3.

● **Gorse**
Ulex europaeus
Tall–v.tall. Sharply spiny; lvs spiny, not trefoil except in seedlings, ridged; fls 15mm long, wings longer than keel; golden-yellow. LH perenn; shrub. GERM spr. FL (1–)3–5(–12). POLL ins(h, d, c). SEX (♀). HAB grassland, heaths, open woods. SOIL dry; not calc. SHADE nil–light. ALT sl–600. DIST E5, W5, S5, I5. RANGE F4, G4, sS1.
See p. 236, 278, 284, 298.

● **Western gorse**
Ulex gallii
Short–v.tall. Spiny; lvs as unridged spines; fls 10–12mm long, bright yellow; wings longer than keel. LH perenn; shrub. GERM spr–aut. FL 7–10. POLL ins(h). SEX (♀). HAB heaths, grassland. SOIL dry; acid. SHADE nil. ALT sl–700. DIST wE3, eE1, W4, S1, sI3. RANGE wF3.

○ **Dwarf gorse**
Ulex minor
Short–tall. Spiny, forming neat clumps; lvs as unridged spines; fls 8–10mm long, pale yellow, wings as long as keel. LH perenn; shrub. GERM spr–aut. FL 7–10. POLL ins(h). SEX (♀). HAB heaths. SOIL dry; acid. SHADE nil. ALT sl–250. DIST sE3, nE1. RANGE wF2.

● **Broom**
Cytisus scoparius
Tall–v.tall; can be prostrate by sea. Stems green, angled; lvs trefoil, deciduous; fls 20mm long, on long stalks. Pods to 40mm, black. LH perenn; shrub. GERM spr–sum. FL 4–6. POLL ins(h), not self. SEX (♀). HAB heaths, open woods, waste ground. SOIL dry; not calc. SHADE nil–mid. ALT sl–300 (–600). DIST E4, W4, S4, I4. RANGE F4, G4, sS2.
See p. 168, 196, 278, 284.

Clustered broom
Chamaecytisus supinus
Short–mid; prostrate.
Stems hairy, slightly
spiny; lvs trefoil; fls
20–25mm long, in
cluster at end of stem.
LH perenn; shrub.
GERM ?; seeds dis-
persed by ants. FL 5–7.
POLL ins(h). SEX (♂️).
HAB open woods,
scrub, heaths. SOIL
dry; acid. SHADE nil–
mid. ALT [sl–600].
RANGE F2, G1.

● **Petty whin**
Genista anglica
Short–mid. Spiny,
slender-stemmed; lvs
simple, pointed, oval;
fls 8–19mm long,
standard shorter than
keel; pods swollen. LH
perenn; shrub. GERM
sum. FL 4–6. POLL
ins(h). SEX (♂️). HAB
heaths. SOIL wet–dry;
acid. SHADE nil. ALT
sl–600(–800). DIST
E3, W2, S3. RANGE F3,
nG3, sS1.
See p. 284.

○ **Hairy greenweed**
Genista pilosa
Short. Stems spineless,
ridged; lvs oval, blunt,
long-lived; fls 10mm
long; pods hairy. LH
perenn; shrub. GERM
aut. FL 5–6. POLL
ins(h); not self. SEX
(♂️). HAB heaths, grass-
land, cliffs. SOIL dry;
acid. SHADE nil. ALT
sl(–500). DIST seE1,
W1. RANGE F3, G3,
sS1.

● **Dyer's greenweed**
Genista tinctoria
Mid; can be prostrate
by sea. Stems slender,
not spiny; lvs simple,
narrow, to 30mm; fls
15mm long, standard
as long as keel; pods
not swollen nor hairy.
LH perenn; shrub.
GERM aut. FL 6–8. POLL
ins(h), self. SEX (♂️).
HAB grassland, heaths.
SOIL moist–dry; not
calc. SHADE nil-light.
ALT sl–200. DIST sE4,
nE2, W2, sS1. RANGE
F4, G4.
See p. 284.

Black broom
Lembotropis nigricans
Tall–v.tall. Lvs trefoil;
fls 7–10mm long, in
dense spikes, wings
shorter than keel; pods
hairy. LH perenn;
shrub. GERM ? FL 6–7.
POLL ins(h). SEX (♂️).
HAB rocks and scrub.
SOIL dry; not acid.
SHADE nil–mid. ALT
[sl–1500]. RANGE G2.

Winged broom
*Chamaespartium
sagittale*
Low–short; prostrate.
Stems winged, green,
almost lfless, rooting;
fls 12–15mm long, in
dense clusters; pods
hairy. LH perenn;
shrub. GERM ? FL 5–9.
POLL ins(h); not self.
SEX (♂️). HAB grassy
places, open woods.
SOIL dry; not calc.
SHADE nil–mid. ALT
[sl–1200]. RANGE F3,
G2.

○ **Bladder senna**
Colutea arborescens
V.tall. Lvs pinnate,
lflts rounded; fls 20mm
long, in few-flowered
hanging spikes; pods
enormously inflated.
LH perenn; shrub.
GERM spr. FL 6–8. POLL
ins(h). SEX (♂️). HAB
rocky and disturbed
ground, open woods.
SOIL dry; not acid.
SHADE nil–mid. ALT
[sl–1000]. DIST widely
naturalised. RANGE F3,
G2 and naturalised.

○ **Tree lupin**
Lupinus arboreus
V.tall. Lvs palmate
with 7–11 pointed lflts;
fls yellowish, 15mm
long, in whorls in a
long spike; pod hairy.
LH perenn; shrub.
GERM spr–sum. FL 5–8.
POLL ins(h). SEX (♂️).
HAB waste ground,
sandy soils. SOIL dry;
not calc. SHADE nil.
ALT sl–100. DIST
naturalised in south.
ss73.

● **Tufted vetch**
Vicia cracca
Tall–v.tall. Scrambl-
ing; lvs pinnate, with
6–12 pairs of lflts;
tendrils branched; fls
10–12mm long, in
dense spikes; pods
brown. LH perenn;
rootstock, stolons.
GERM imm. FL 6–8.
POLL ins(h, d). SEX (♂️).
HAB hedges, scrub, tall
grassland, fens. SOIL
damp–moist; not acid.
SHADE nil–mid. ALT sl–
400. DIST E5, W5, S4,
I5. RANGE F5, G5, S4.
See p. 18.

○ **Fodder vetch**
Vicia villosa
Mid. Lvs pinnate with
6–8 pairs of lflts; fls
12–15mm long, with
swollen sepal tube;
very variable. LH
persistent ann. GERM
spr. FL 6–10. POLL
ins(h). SEX (♂️). HAB
disturbed ground. SOIL
moist–dry; not acid.
SHADE nil. ALT sl–200.
DIST widespread casual.
RANGE F3, G4, S3.
ss74.

○ **Wood vetch**
Vicia sylvatica
Tall. Sprawling; lvs
with 6–10 pairs of
lflts; tendrils branched
fls 15–20mm long,
purple-veined; pods
black. LH perenn;
rootstock. GERM ? FL
6–8. POLL ins(h). SEX
(♀). HAB woods, scrub
cliffs. SOIL moist–dry;
not acid. SHADE nil–
mid. ALT sl–400(–700).
DIST E2, W2, S3, I2.
RANGE eF1, G3, S4.
ss75.

● **Bush vetch**
Vicia sepium
Mid–tall. Climbing;
lvs with 3–9 pairs of
lflts, tendrils branched;
fls 12–15mm long,
streaked pinkish-
purple; pods black. LH
perenn; rootstock.
GERM aut–spr. FL 4–10.
POLL ins(h). SEX (♀).
HAB tall grassland,
scrub. SOIL damp–
moist; not acid. SHADE
nil–mid. ALT sl–400
(–800). DIST E5, W5,
S5, I5. RANGE F5, G5,
S4.

● **Common vetch**
Vicia sativa
Short–tall. Scrambling;
lvs with 4–8 pairs of
lflts, tendrils usually
branched; fls 10–30mm
long, in pairs, bright
purplish-pink; pods
brown or black. LH
ann, sometimes over-
wintering. GERM spr.
FL 4–9. POLL ins(h, l),
self. SEX (♀). HAB bare
ground, hedges. SOIL
damp–moist; not acid.
SHADE nil. ALT sl–300.
DIST E5, W5, S5, I5.
RANGE F5, G5, S5.

○ **Spring vetch**
Vicia lathyroides
Low; prostrate. Lvs
with 2–3 pairs of lflts
and unbranched ten-
drils; fls 5–8mm long,
borne singly; pods
black. LH winter ann.
GERM aut. FL 4–5. POLL
self, sometimes
cleistogamous. SEX
(♀). HAB bare and
open grassy places.
SOIL dry; not acid.
SHADE nil. ALT sl. DIST
E2, W1, S2, I1. RANGE
F3, G3, sS2.
See p. 244.

● **Hairy tare**
Vicia hirsuta
Short. Lvs with 4–8
pairs of alternating
lflts; tendrils branched;
fls 4–5mm long, dirty
violet; pods small,
hairy. LH ann. GERM
imm. FL 5–8. POLL
ins(h, l), self. SEX (♀).
HAB open grassy
places. SOIL moist–dry;
not acid. SHADE nil.
ALT sl–300. DIST E4,
W3, S2, I2. RANGE F5,
G5, S3.

● **Smooth tare**
Vicia tetrasperma
Mid. Like Hairy tare
but 3–6 pairs of lflts;
tendrils unbranched;
fls 4–8mm, bluer; pod
hairless. LH ann. GERM
aut–spr. FL 5–8. POLL
ins(h), self. SEX (♀).
HAB open grassy
places. SOIL moist–dry;
not acid. SHADE nil.
ALT sl–100. DIST sE4,
nE2, W2, sS1. RANGE
F5, G5, sS3.
ss76.

○ **Yellow vetch**
Vicia lutea
Short–mid, often pros-
trate. Tufted; lflts 3–9
pairs; tendrils often
branched; fls 20–
30mm long, usually
single; pods hairy. LH
ann, sometimes over-
wintering. FL 6–9. POLL
ins(h). SEX (♀). HAB sea cliffs
and shingle. SOIL dry;
not acid. SHADE nil.
ALT sl. DIST coastal;
E2, W1, S1. RANGE
coastal: F2. Casual
inland (F, G).

○ **Broad-leaved
everlasting pea**
Lathyrus latifolius
V.tall. Climbing; lvs
with 1 pair of broad
lflts and tendrils; stems
winged; fls 20–30mm
long, sepal teeth longer
than tube. LH perenn;
rootstock. GERM aut.
FL 7–9. POLL ins(h).
SEX (♀). HAB waste
places, scrub. SOIL
moist; not acid. SHADE
nil–light. ALT sl–200.
DIST widespread garden
escape. RANGE G2,
sS3; and garden
escape.

○ **Narrow-leaved
everlasting pea**
Lathyrus sylvestris
V.tall. Climbing, stems
winged; 1 pair of
narrow lflts, tendrils
branched; fls 15–20mm
long, dull pink, sepal
teeth shorter than
tube. LH perenn;
rootstock. GERM spr.
FL 7–9. POLL ins(h).
SEX (♀). HAB scrub,
open woods; waste
ground. SOIL moist;
not acid. SHADE nil–
mid. ALT sl–100. DIST
sE3, nE1, W1, S1;
also garden escape.
RANGE F4, G4, sS3.

● **Meadow vetchling**
Lathyrus pratensis
Mid–tall. Scrambling;
stems angled; lvs with
large stipules, 1 pair of
lflts and usually
branched tendrils; fls
15–20mm long. LH
perenn; rootstock.
GERM aut–spr. FL 5–8.
POLL ins(h), self. SEX
(♀). HAB meadows,
fens. SOIL wet–moist;
not acid. SHADE nil–
light. ALT sl–400. DIST
E5, W5, S4, I5. RANGE
F5, G5, S5.

Spring pea
Lathyrus vernus
Low–short. Lvs with
2–4 prs of oval,
pointed, bright green
lflts and no tendrils;
fls red-purple, turning
blue then greenish. LH
perenn; rhizome. GERM
spr? FL 4–5. POLL ins
(h). SEX (♀). HAB
woods, scrub,
meadows. SOIL dry;
calc. SHADE nil–heavy.
ALT [sl–1500]. RANGE
eF2, G4, S3.

● **Bitter vetchling**
Lathyrus montanus
Short. Stems winged;
lvs with 2–4 pairs of
lflts and no tendrils;
fls 10–15mm long,
crimson fading blue.
LH perenn; rootstock.
GERM spr. FL 4–7. POLL
ins(h). SEX (♀). HAB
open woods, grassland,
heaths. SOIL moist–
dry; acid. SHADE nil–
mid. ALT sl–500(–800).
DIST E4, W5, S5, I4.
RANGE F3, G4, sS4.
See p. 195.

○ **Sea pea**
Lathyrus japonicus
Short–mid; prostrate.
Stems angled; lvs
slightly fleshy, with 3–4
pairs of lflts; tendrils
sometimes branched;
sometimes absent; fls
15–20mm long, purple,
fading blue. LH
perenn; rootstock.
GERM ? FL 6–8. POLL
ins(h, l). SEX (♀). HAB
sand and shingle by
sea. SOIL dry; calc.
SHADE nil. ALT sl. DIST
coastal: E1, S1.
RANGE coastal: G1, S2.
See p. 195.

○ **Marsh pea**
Lathyrus palustris
Tall. Climbing; stems
winged; lvs with 2–4
pairs of narrow lflts;
tendrils branched; fls
15–20mm long. LH
perenn; rootstock.
GERM aut–spr. FL 6–7.
POLL ins(h). SEX (♀).
HAB fens, marshes.
SOIL wet–damp; calc.
SHADE nil–light. ALT
sl–100. DIST E1, W1,
I1. RANGE F2, G2, S2.

○ **Tuberous pea**
Lathyrus tuberosus
Tall. Scrambling;
stems angled; one pair
of oval lflts; tendrils
long, branched; fls
15–18mm long. LH
perenn; root tubers.
GERM aut. FL 6–7. POLL
ins(h). SEX (♀). HAB
bare and grassy places.
SOIL moist; not acid.
DIST introduced: E3,
W1, S1. RANGE F2,
G4; introduced S2.

○ **Grass vetchling**
Lathyrus nissolia
Mid–tall. Lf midrib
expanded, with no
lflts nor tendrils, to
look like a grass lf;
fls 15mm long. LH
ann. GERM aut. FL
POLL ins(h, l); self.
SEX (♀). HAB meadows.
SOIL moist; not acid.
SHADE nil. ALT sl–100.
DIST sE3, W1. RANGE
F2, G1.

○ **Yellow vetchling**
Lathyrus aphaca
Mid–tall. Scrambling;
lvs reduced to long,
unbranched tendrils;
stipules large and lf-
like; fls 10–12mm long.
LH ann. GERM aut. FL
5–8. POLL ins(h); self.
SEX (♀). HAB grassland.
SOIL dry; acid–calc.
SHADE nil. ALT sl–100.
DIST sE2. RANGE F3,
G2.

○ **Sainfoin**
Onobrychis viciifolia
Mid. Lvs with 6–12
pairs of lflts and 1
terminal; fls 10–12mm
long, with short wings.
LH perenn; rootstock.
GERM spr. FL 6–9. POLL
ins(h); not self. SEX (♀).
HAB grassland, and
often cultivated. SOIL
dry; calc. SHADE nil.
ALT sl–200. DIST sE2,
nE1. RANGE F4, G3.
See p. 268.

● **Rest-harrow**
Ononis repens
Short–mid. Hairy,
woody at stem base;
lvs trefoil; fls 10–15mm
long, wings as long as
keel. LH perenn;
rhizome. GERM aut–
spr. FL 7–9. POLL
ins(h). SEX (♀). HAB
grassland. SOIL dry;
not acid. SHADE nil.
ALT sl–200(–350). DIST
E4, W3, S3, I2.
RANGE F5, G5, S2.
See p. 284. **ss77.**

● **Spiny rest-harrow**
Ononis spinosa
Mid. Stems woody,
spiny, with 2 lines of
hairs; lvs trefoil; fls
10–15mm long, wings
shorter than keel. LH
perenn; rootstock.
GERM aut–spr. FL 6–9.
POLL ins(h). SEX (♀).
HAB grassland. SOIL
dry; acid–calc. SHADE
nil. ALT sl–200. DIST
seE4, nwE2, W2, S1.
RANGE F4, G4, sS1.

● **Kidney vetch**
Anthyllis vulneraria
Low–mid, sometimes prostrate. Lvs pinnate, with silky hairs; fls 12–15mm long, yellow, orange or red, in dense heads. LH short-lived perenn. GERM aut–spr. FL 4–9. POLL ins(h, l). SEX (♀). HAB short grassland. SOIL dry; calc. SHADE nil. ALT sl–400(–800). DIST E4, W3, S2, I3. RANGE F4, G4, S3.
See p. 241.

○ **White melilot**
Melilotus alba
Tall. Lvs trefoil; fls 4–5mm in loose, long-stalked spikes, white; pods brown, hairless. LH bienn. GERM spr. FL 7–10. POLL ins(h). SEX (♀). HAB disturbed ground. SOIL dry; not acid. SHADE nil. ALT sl–200. DIST E3, W1, S1, I1. RANGE F4, G4, S3.

○ **Tall melilot**
Melilotus altissima
Tall. Lvs trefoil; fls 5–6mm, yellow, in long, dense stalked spikes; wings as long as keel; pods black, hairy. LH bienn. GERM sum, aut, spr. FL 6–9. POLL ins(h). SEX (♀). HAB disturbed ground. SOIL moist–dry; not acid. SHADE nil. ALT sl–200. DIST E3, W2, S2, I1. RANGE F3, G3, S2.
See p. 245.

● **Common melilot**
Melilotus officinalis
Mid–tall. Lvs trefoil; fls as Tall melilot but standard longer than keel; pods brown, hairless. LH ann–bienn. GERM sum–spr. FL 6–9. POLL ins(h). SEX (♀). HAB disturbed ground. SOIL moist–dry; not acid. SHADE nil. ALT sl–200. DIST E4, W2, S2, I1. RANGE F5, G5, S3.
See p. 245, 284.

● **Lucerne**
Medicago sativa
Mid–tall. Lvs large, trefoil; fls 8–10mm, purple or yellow in short, dense spikes; pods spirally coiled. LH perenn; rootstock. GERM any. FL 6–9. POLL ins(h, l); self. SEX (♀). HAB grassland, bare ground. SOIL moist–dry; not acid. SHADE nil–light. ALT sl–200. DIST ssp *falcata* E1; ssp *sativa* widespread escape from cultivation. RANGE F4, G4, S3.
See p. 226, 227.

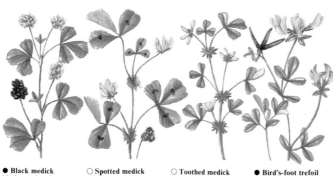

● **Black medick**
Medicago lupulina
Low–mid; prostrate. Lvs trefoil, lflts with a minute point; fls 2–4mm in round heads; pods black, spirally coiled. GERM any. FL 4–10. POLL ins(h); self. SEX (♀). HAB grassy and disturbed ground. SOIL moist–dry; acid–calc. SHADE nil. ALT sl–200 (–400). DIST E5, W4, S3, I4. RANGE F5, G5, S3.
See p. 243, 244.

○ **Spotted medick**
Medicago arabica
Short–mid; prostrate. Lvs trefoil, dark-spotted; fls 4–6mm, in loose heads on stalks shorter than lvs; pods spiny, spirally coiled. LH ann. GERM spr. FL 4–9. POLL ins(h); self. SEX (♀). HAB grassy and disturbed ground. SOIL dry; not acid or calc. SHADE nil. ALT sl–100. DIST sE3, nE1, W1. RANGE F3, G2.

○ **Toothed medick**
Medicago polymorpha
Short–mid; prostrate. Like Spotted medick but fls 3–4mm; lvs un-spotted, and flhd-stalks as long as lvs. FL 5–8. POLL self. SEX (♀). HAB bare ground. SOIL dry; not acid nor calc. SHADE nil. ALT sl. DIST sE2; casual elsewhere. RANGE F3, G2.
ss78.

● **Bird's-foot trefoil**
Lotus corniculatus
Short; prostrate. Lvs with 5 lflts, but appearing trefoil; fls 12–15 mm, in a whorl-like head; pods spreading. LH perenn; rootstock. GERM aut–spr. FL 5–9. POLL ins(h); self. SEX (♀). HAB grassy and bare ground. SOIL dry; calc. SHADE nil. ALT sl–400 (–800). DIST E5, W5, S5, I5. RANGE F5, G5, S4.
See p. 240, 258, 268, 283, 284. **ss79**. **ss80**.

○ **Narrow-leaved bird's-foot trefoil**
Lotus tenuis
Mid–tall. Delicate, as Bird's-foot trefoil but fls 2–4 together, 10mm; lflts narrower. LH perenn; rootstock. GERM spr? FL 6–8. POLL ins(h). SEX (♀). HAB grassland. SOIL dry; calc. SHADE nil. ALT sl–100. DIST sE3, nE1, W1. RANGE F3, G3, sS1.

● **Greater bird's-foot trefoil**
Lotus uliginosus
Short–tall. Straggling, hollow-stemmed; lvs trefoil, lflts large; fls 10–12mm, up to 12 in a head; sepal teeth spreading. LH Perenn; stolons. GERM spr. FL 6–8. POLL ins(h). SEX (♀♂). HAB tall grassland, ditches, marshes. SOIL wet–damp; not acid. SHADE nil–light. ALT sl–300(–500). DIST E4, W4, S3, I3. RANGE F4, G4, sS2.

○ **Horseshoe vetch**
Hippocrepis comosa
Short; prostrate. Lvs pinnate, ending in a lflt; fls 8–10mm in a whorl-like head on a long stalk; pods twisted like a string of horseshoes. LH perenn; rootstock. GERM spr–sum. FL 5–8. POLL ins(h). SEX (♀♂). HAB short grassland. SOIL dry; calc. SHADE nil. ALT sl–300(–500). DIST E2, W1. RANGE F4, G3.
See p. 284.

● **Bird's-foot**
Ornithopus perpusillus
V.low–short; prostrate. Variable; lvs pinnate, unstalked; fls 3–5mm, streaked red, in sparse heads; pods beaded, claw-like. LH ann, sometimes overwintering. GERM spr, aut. FL 5–8. POLL ins(h, d); self. SEX (♀♂) hg. HAB bare and lightly grassy places. SOIL dry; not calc. SHADE nil. ALT sl–300. DIST E3, W3, S2, I1. RANGE F3, G3, sS1. **ss81**.

● **Hop trefoil**
Trifolium campestre
Low–short. Hairy; lvs trefoil, lflts with no point (cf Black medick, p. 63); fls 4–6 mm, brown when dead and covering pods. LH ann, sometimes persisting. GERM spr. FL 5–9. POLL ins(h, d, l). SEX (♀♂). HAB grassland. SOIL moist–dry; not acid. SHADE nil. ALT sl–200(–350). DIST E4, W4, S3, I3. RANGE F5, G5, sS3.

● **Lesser trefoil**
Trifolium dubium
Low–short; prostrate. Lvs trefoil; fls 3mm, standard brown when dead, folded over pod; heads with 3–15 fls. LH ann. GERM aut, spr. FL 5–9. POLL ins(h); self. SEX (♀♂). HAB bare and grassy places. SOIL moist, not acid. SHADE nil. ALT sl–300 (–500). DIST E5, W5, S5, I5. RANGE F5, G5, sS3.

○ **Slender trefoil**
Trifolium micranthum
V.low–low; prostrate. Lvs trefoil; fls 2–3mm, 2–6 in a head; standard notched, fl-stalks long, slender. LH ann. GERM aut, spr. FL 6–8. POLL ins(h); self. SEX (♀♂). HAB bare and sparsely grassy places. SOIL dry, not calc. SHADE nil. ALT sl–200. DIST E3, W2, I1. RANGE F3, G1.
See p. 269.

● **Red clover**
Trifolium pratense
Short–mid. Lvs trefoil, usually white-marked; stipules hair-pointed; fls 15–18mm in dense, rounded heads. LH perenn; rootstock. GERM aut, spr. FL 5–9. POLL ins(h, l). SEX (♀♂). HAB grassland. SOIL moist–dry; not acid. SHADE nil. ALT sl–400 (–800). DIST E5, W5, S5, I5. RANGE F5, G5, S5
See p. 170, 174, 213 225, 227, 268. **ss82**.

● **Zigzag clover**
Trifolium medium
Short–mid. Lvs trefoil, lflts narrow, faintly white-marked; fls 15–18mm, purplish-red, in rounded heads. LH perenn; rhizomes. GERM aut. FL 6–9. POLL ins(h, l). SEX (♀♂). HAB grassland. SOIL moist–dry; not acid. SHADE nil. ALT sl–400. DIST E4, W4, S3, I2. RANGE F4, G5, sS4, nS1.

● **White clover**
Trifolium repens
Low–short; creeping. Stems rooting at nodes; lvs trefoil; fls 10mm, in loose heads, brown when dead; sepal teeth short. LH perenn; rooting nodes, evergreen. GERM spr–sum. FL 5–9. POLL ins(h). SEX (♀♂). HAB grassland. SOIL moist–dry; acid–calc. SHADE nil. ALT sl–600(–900). DIST E5, W5, S5, I5. RANGE F5, G5, S5.
See p. 200, 217, 240, 249, 251, 268, 278. **ss83**.

● **Alsike clover**
Trifolium hybridum
Short–mid. Lvs trefoil, lflts unmarked; stipules pointed; fls 6–8mm long in rounded heads; sepal teeth long. LH short-lived perenn; rootstock. GERM aut, spr. FL 6–9. POLL ins(h). SEX (♀♂). HAB grassland, roadsides. SOIL moist; not acid. SHADE nil. ALT sl–300. DIST E4, W3, S3, I3. RANGE eF2, G5, S4.

○ **Strawberry clover**
Trifolium fragiferum
Low–short; creeping, rooting at nodes. Lvs trefoil, stipules pointed; fls 5–6mm, in rounded heads; fruiting heads with dead fls resemble strawberries. LH short-lived perenn; rooting nodes. GERM aut, spr. FL 6–9. POLL ins(h). SEX (♀̇). HAB grassland. SOIL damp–moist; not acid, often saline. SHADE nil. ALT sl–100. DIST seE4, nwE1, W1, S1, I1. RANGE F4, G3, sS2.

○ **Knotted clover**
Trifolium striatum
Low–short, often prostrate. Lvs trefoil, downy; fls 5–8mm in egg-shaped heads, half-hidden by lvs when young. LH ann, sometimes persistent. GERM aut. FL 5–7. POLL ins(h). SEX (♀̇). HAB sparsely grassy places. SOIL dry; not acid nor calc. SHADE nil. ALT sl–100. DIST E3, W2, sS1, I1. RANGE F3, G3, sS1.
See p. 269. **ss84. ss85.**

○ **Rough clover**
Trifolium scabrum
Low; often prostrate. Lvs trefoil, downy, veins thick and curved; fls in small, unstalked, egg-shaped heads. LH ann. GERM aut. FL 5–7. POLL ins(h). SEX (♀̇). HAB bare and sparsely grassy places; not acid. SHADE nil. ALT sl. DIST E2, W2, S1, I1. RANGE F2, G1.

● **Sea clover**
Trifolium squamosum
Short. Lvs trefoil, downy, stipules narrow; fls 6–8mm, in short-stalked heads, above 2 lvs; sepal teeth spreading, star-like. LH ann. GERM ? FL 6–7. POLL ins(h). SEX (♀̇). HAB short turf. SOIL damp–moist; saline. SHADE nil. ALT sl. DIST coastal: E2, W2. RANGE coastal: F2.

● **Hare's-foot clover**
Trifolium arvense
Low–short. Lvs trefoil; lflts narrow, hairy; fls 3–4mm in long, almost cylindrical heads, with prominent sepal teeth. LH winter ann, sometimes persisting. GERM aut, rarely spr. FL 6–9. POLL ins(h, d, l); self. SEX (♀̇). HAB open grassland. SOIL dry; not calc. SHADE nil. ALT sl–200. DIST E4, W3, S2, I2. RANGE F4, G5, sS4, nS1. **ss86.**

○ **Crimson clover**
Trifolium incarnatum
Short–mid. Lvs trefoil; lflts broad; fls 10–15mm in long, almost cylindrical, heads, usually crimson; sepal teeth long. LH ann, often persisting. GERM spr. FL 6–7. POLL ins(h); self. SEX (♀̇). HAB grassland, mainly cultivated. SOIL moist–dry; calc. SHADE nil. ALT sl–200. DIST E3, W2, S1, I1; and casual. RANGE F3; casual G, S.

○ **Burrowing clover**
Trifolium subterraneum
Low; prostrate. Lvs trefoil, hairy; fls 8–12mm, some sterile with no petals; fruiting heads grow into ground, 'planting' seeds. LH winter ann. GERM aut. FL 5–6. POLL ins(h); self, sometimes cleistogamous. SEX (♀̇). HAB open grassland. SOIL dry; not acid. SHADE nil. ALT sl. DIST mainly coastal: sE2, W1, I1. RANGE F3, G1. **ss87. ss88.**

CRANESBILL FAMILY
Geraniaceae
A very recognisable family, with deeply lobed, often hairy leaves and showy, flat, 5-petalled flowers. The style with 5 stigmas and the 10 stamens are often conspicuous, and the fruit, ending in a long beak (hence 'cranesbill' and 'storksbill') is characteristic. Ecologically varied, including woodland and grassland perennials and annuals. Rarely on wet ground. *See p. 199, 211, 269, 282.*

● **Common storksbill**
Erodium cicutarium
Low–mid. Stems sticky, hairy; lvs twice pinnate; fls 12–14mm, petals soon falling; 5 stamens sterile; fr beak to 40mm, twisted. LH ann, often persisting. GERM sum–aut. FL 4–9. POLL ins(h, l, c); self. SEX (♀̇) hg–pa; (♀̇ + ♀). (♀̇ + ♂). HAB bare and sparsely grassy places. SOIL dry; acid–calc. SHADE nil. ALT sl–200 (–350). DIST E4, W2, S2, I2. RANGE F5, G4, sS4, nS1.
See p. 182. **ss89.**

○ **Sea storksbill**
Erodium maritimum
V.low–low; prostrate. Stiffly hairy; lvs deeply lobed, long-stalked; fls 6–8mm, petals shorter than sepals; fr beak 10mm. LH ann or bienn. GERM spr–sum. FL 5–8. POLL ins(h, c); self. SEX (♀̇). HAB bare and sparsely grassy, sandy places. SOIL dry; calc. SHADE nil. ALT sl. DIST coastal: swE3, neE1, W3, eI2. RANGE F3, G2.

○ **Bloody cranesbill**
Geranium sanguineum
Short–mid. Clump-
forming; lvs deeply
lobed, less so in shade;
fls 25–35mm, bright
purple, solitary. LH perenn;
rhizome. GERM aut.
FL 7–8. POLL ins(h, d,
c, l); self. SEX (♀) pa.
HAB short grassland,
scrub, rocks, open
woods. SOIL dry; calc.
SHADE nil–mid. ALT
sl–300. DIST seE1,
nwE3, W2, S2, I1.
RANGE F2, G3, sS3.
See p. 199, 282.

● **Meadow cranesbill**
Geranium pratense
Mid–tall. Stems
stickily-hairy; lvs
deeply lobed; fls 25–
35mm, blue, in pairs;
fr beak to 25mm. LH
perenn; rhizome.
GERM spr. FL 6–9. POLL
ins(h, d, c). SEX (♀) pa;
(♂ + ♀). HAB tall
grassland. SOIL damp–
moist; not acid. SHADE
nil–light. ALT sl–300
(–500). DIST E4, W3,
S3, I1. RANGE eF2,
G4, sS2.
See p. 262, 264.

● **Wood cranesbill**
Geranium sylvaticum
Mid–tall. Stems
stickily-hairy; lvs less
deeply lobed than
Meadow cranesbill;
fls 20–30mm, purplish-
blue; fr beak to 25mm.
LH perenn; rhizome.
GERM aut. FL 6–8. POLL
ins(h, l, d); not self.
SEX (♂) pa. HAB
meadows, woods,
rock-ledges. SOIL
damp–moist; acid–
calc. SHADE nil–heavy.
ALT sl–600(–1000). DIST
nE3, W1, S3, I1.
See p. 168, 262, 263.

Marsh cranesbill
Geranium palustre
Mid–tall. Lvs deeply
lobed, lobes little
toothed; fls purplish,
30mm; fr-stalks bent
downwards. LH
perenn; rhizome.
GERM ? FL 7–8. POLL
ins(h, d); not self. SEX
(♂ + ♀) pa. HAB
meadows, woods. SOIL
damp–dry; not acid.
SHADE nil–mid. ALT
[sl–900]. RANGE eFx,
G4, sS1.

● **Hedgerow
cranesbill**
Geranium pyrenaicum
Mid. Lvs lobed to
half-way; fls 12–18mm,
petals purple, notched;
fr beak 10mm. LH
short-lived perenn;
rootstock. GERM aut.
FL 5–9. POLL ins(d, c);
self. SEX (♂) pa. HAB
hedges, roadsides. SOIL
moist, not acid. SHADE
nil–light. ALT sl–300.
DIST sE4, nE2, W3,
S2, I2. RANGE F4, G4,
sS3.

● **Herb robert**
Geranium robertianum
Short–med. Foetid;
stems red; lvs deeply
5-lobed, reddening;
fls 15–20mm, petals
slightly notched; fr
beak 10–20mm. LH
persistent ann. GERM
spr. FL 4–11. POLL
(♂) pa. HAB woods,
rocks, shingle. SOIL
moist–dry; acid–calc.
SHADE nil–deep. ALT
sl–500 (–700). DIST E5,
W5, S5, I5. RANGE F5,
G5, S4.
See p. 256, 259, 262.
ss90.

● **Shining cranesbill**
Geranium lucidum
Short. Hairless; lvs
shallowly lobed,
glossy; fls 15mm in
pairs; fr beak 10mm.
LH ann, sometimes
persisting. GERM spr.
FL 5–8. POLL ins(h, d,
c); self. SEX (♀). HAB
rocks, banks. SOIL
damp–moist; not calc.
SHADE light–deep. ALT
sl–400 (–600). DIST
E3, W4, S3, I2.
RANGE F3, G1, sS2.
See p. 199, 262.

● **Dove's-foot
cranesbill**
Geranium molle
Short; half-prostrate.
Hairy; lvs rounded,
lobed to about half-
way; fls 5–10mm,
petals notched; fr
beak 5–8mm. LH
persistent ann. GERM
imm. FL 4–9. POLL
ins(h); self. SEX (♂ + ♀)
pa–hg. HAB grassland.
SOIL moist–dry; acid–
calc. SHADE nil. ALT
sl–300(–500). DIST E5,
W4, S3, I4. RANGE F5,
G5, sS2.
See p. 261.

○ **Round-leaved
cranesbill**
Geranium rotundifolium
Short. Hairy; lvs
rounded, scarcely
lobed; fls 10–12mm,
petals not notched; fr
beak 10–15mm. LH
ann. GERM spr? FL 6–7.
POLL ins(h); self. SEX
(♂) hg. HAB bare and
stony places. SOIL dry;
not acid. SHADE nil.
ALT sl–200. DIST sE3.
RANGE F3, G2.

● **Small-flowered
cranesbill**
Geranium pusillum
Short. Downy; lvs
deeply lobed, lobes
narrow; fls 3–6mm;
5 stamens sterile; fr
beak 5–6mm. LH
persistent ann. GERM
aut. FL 6–9. POLL
ins(d, h); self. SEX (♂)
pg. HAB bare and
sparsely grassy places.
SOIL dry; not acid.
SHADE nil. ALT sl–200.
DIST E4, W3, S2, I1.
RANGE F5, G5, sS3.
See p. 261.

WOOD SORREL FAMILY
Oxalidaceae
Leaves are clover-like (trefoil) and show sleep movements, folding down at night. Flowers cup-shaped. Several species are grown in gardens and found as escapes.

FLAX FAMILY
Linaceae
Slender-stemmed with simple leaves and 5-petalled flowers with papery petals, often falling early.

● **Cut-leaved cranesbill**
Geranium dissectum
Short–mid. Straggling; lvs very deeply lobed, lobes toothed; fls 6–10mm on stalks 5–15mm; sepals hairy; fr beak 7–12mm. LH ann. GERM imm. FL 5–9. POLL ins(h, d); self. SEX (♀) pg–hg. HAB disturbed ground, open grassland. SOIL moist–dry; acid–calc. SHADE nil. ALT sl–300 (–400). DIST E5, W4, S3, I5. RANGE F5, G5, sS2.
See p. 199.

● **Long-stalked cranesbill**
Geranium columbinum
Short–mid. Lvs very deeply lobed; fls 12–15mm on stalks up to 60mm; flhd even longer-stalked; fr beak 15–20mm. LH ann–bienn. GERM imm. FL 6–8. POLL ins(d, h); self. SEX (♀) hg; (♂ +♀); (♀). HAB sparsely grassy places. SOIL dry; calc. SHADE nil. ALT sl–250. DIST E3, W2, S2, I2. RANGE F5, G4, sS2.
See p. 262, 263.

● **Wood sorrel**
Oxalis acetosella
Low. Creeping; lvs trefoil, long-stalked, from rhizome; fls singly on long stalks, nodding, veined. LH perenn; rhizome. GERM spr–sum. FL 4–5. POLL ins(d, c); self, cleistogamous. SEX (♀). HAB woods, mountain ledges. SOIL moist; acid–calc. SHADE nil–deep. ALT sl–1200. DIST E4, W5, S5, I5. RANGE F5, G5, S4.
See p. 169, 200, 202, 246, 252.

○ **Yellow oxalis**
Oxalis corniculata
Low. Stems prostrate, rooting, hairy; lvs numerous, long-stalked, trefoil; lflts small, bell-shaped. LH ann or short-lived perenn. GERM spr–sum. FL 5–10. POLL ins; self. SEX (♀). HAB bare ground. SOIL damp; acid–calc. SHADE nil–light. ALT sl–300. DIST (E3, W3, S2, I2). RANGE (F3, G3, S2).

SPURGE FAMILY
Euphorbiaceae
A distinctive family with untoothed leaves and obscure flowers, often in conspicuous clusters. Spurge flowers have neither petals nor sepals, but are compound: a central ♀ flower with 3 styles is surrounded by several ♂ flowers, each with 1 anther. This head is enclosed in a bract with several glands. Mercuries have 3 tiny sepals. Many have milky juice.

○ **Pale flax**
Linum bienne
Mid. Lvs narrow, alternate, unstalked; fls 15–20mm, pale blue; sepals pointed. LH persistent ann or short-lived perenn. GERM spr. FL 5–9. POLL ins(h, d). SEX (♀). HAB grassland. SOIL dry; calc. SHADE nil. ALT sl–100. DIST sE2, W2, I2. RANGE wF2.

○ **Perennial flax**
Linum perenne
Mid. Greyish; lvs narrow, alternate, unstalked; fls 25–35mm, clear blue; inner sepals blunt. LH perenn; rootstock. GERM spr. FL 5–8. POLL ins(h, d). SEX (♀). HAB grassland. SOIL dry; calc. SHADE nil. ALT sl–300. DIST eE1, sS1. RANGE eF1, G2.
See p. 266.

● **Purging flax**
Linum catharticum
Low–short. Lvs oblong, opposite, unstalked; fls 8–12mm, white, in branching cluster. LH ann, sometimes persisting. GERM spr. FL 5–9. POLL ins(d); self. SEX (♀) hg. HAB short grassland, heaths. SOIL moist–dry; acid–calc. SHADE nil. ALT sl–500(–800). DIST E5, W5, S5, I5. RANGE F5, G5, S3.
See p. 181. **ss91.**

● **Wood spurge**
Euphorbia amygdaloides
Mid–tall. Downy, often orange-tinged; lvs narrow; fl bracts joined, with crescent-shaped glands. LH perenn; rootstock, evergreen. GERM spr. FL 4–5. POLL ins(d). SEX (♂ +♀). HAB woods, scrub. SOIL moist; not acid. SHADE light–heavy. ALT sl–400. DIST sE4, W3; introduced elsewhere. RANGE F5, wG3.
See p. 276.

● **Sea spurge**
Euphorbia paralias
Short–mid. Un-
branched; lvs greyish,
fleshy, densely clothing
stem, midrib obscure;
glands crescent-
shaped. LH perenn.
rootstock. GERM spr.
FL 4–8. POLL ins(d).
SEX (♂+♀). HAB
coastal sand. SOIL dry;
calc. SHADE nil. ALT sl.
DIST coastal: E3, W4,
I3. RANGE coastal: F4,
G1.
See p. 205.

● **Portland spurge**
Euphorbia portlandica
Low–short. Branched
stem; lvs as in Sea
spurge, but midrib
prominent; glands
crescent-shaped. LH
short-lived perenn.
GERM spr. FL 5–9.
POLL ins(d). SEX
(♂+♀). HAB coastal
sand. SOIL dry; calc.
SHADE nil. ALT sl. DIST
coastal: wE3, W4, sS1,
I3. RANGE coastal:
wF3.

● **Sun spurge**
Euphorbia helioscopia
Short–mid. Lvs oval,
toothed; fls in a
spreading, flat-topped
cluster; bracts con-
spicuous, sometimes
yellow-green. LH ann.
GERM spr. FL 4–10(–4).
POLL ins(d). SEX
(♂+♀). HAB disturbed
ground. SOIL moist;
acid–calc. SHADE nil.
ALT sl–400. DIST E5,
W5, S3, I4. RANGE F5,
G5, sS4.

● **Petty spurge**
Euphorbia peplus
Short. Branching stems
with blunt oval lvs;
glands crescent-
shaped; fr capsule
winged. LH ann. GERM
spr. FL 4–10(–4). POLL
ins(d). SEX (♂+♀). HAB
disturbed ground. SOIL
moist; acid–calc.
SHADE nil. ALT sl–400.
DIST E5, W4, S2, I3.
RANGE F5, G5, sS3.

● **Dwarf spurge**
Euphorbia exigua
Low–short. Slender,
greyish; lvs small,
narrow, clothing stem;
glands crescent-shaped.
LH ann. GERM spr.
FL 5–10. POLL ins(d).
SEX (♂+♀). HAB
disturbed ground. SOIL
moist; not acid. SHADE
nil. ALT sl–200. DIST
sE4, nE2, W2, S1, I2.
RANGE F4, G3, sS1.
ss92.

○ **Broad-leaved spurge**
Euphorbia platyphyllos
Short–tall. Lvs long,
toothed at the tip,
clasping stem; fls
yellow, glands roun-
ded; fr warty. LH ann.
GERM spr. FL 6–9. POLL
ins(d). SEX (♂+♀). HAB
disturbed ground. SOIL
moist, not calc. SHADE
nil. ALT sl–100. DIST
sE2. RANGE F3, G3.
ss93.

○ **Caper spurge**
Euphorbia lathyrus
Mid–tall. Lvs in 4
ranks along stem,
greyish; glands cres-
cent-shaped; fr swol-
len. LH bienn. GERM
spr. FL 6–7. POLL
ins(d). SEX (♂+♀). HAB
woods, disturbed
ground. SOIL moist;
not acid. SHADE nil–
mid. ALT sl–100. DIST
casual. RANGE casual:
F, G.
ss94.

● **Annual mercury**
Mercurialis annua
Short–mid. Branching,
hairless; lvs oval,
stalked; ♂ fls on long
spikes, ♀ fls unstalked
at lf-junctions. LH ann.
GERM spr. FL 5–10(–12).
POLL wind; ins(h, d).
SEX (♂)+(♀); rarely
(♂+♀). HAB disturbed
ground. SOIL moist–
dry; not acid. SHADE
nil. ALT sl–200. DIST
sE4, nE1, W2, sS1, I2.
RANGE F5, G4.
See p. 270.

● **Dog's mercury**
Mercurialis perennis
Short. Unbranched,
hairy; lvs oval, stalked.
♂ and ♀ fls on long
stalks. LH perenn;
rhizome. GERM aut. FL
(12–)2–4. POLL wind;
ins(d). SEX (♂)+(♀);
rarely (♂+♀). HAB
woods; mountain
rocks. SOIL moist; not
acid. SHADE nil–heavy.
ALT sl–1000. DIST E5,
W5, S4, I1. RANGE F5,
G5, sS2.
*See p. 169, 208, 213,
246.*

BALSAM FAMILY
Balsaminaceae
A small family of
mostly tropical species;
only one species is
native. Flowers are
remarkable and wholly
characteristic – sus-
pended, with 5 petals
making lip, hood and
spur. Stems fleshy,
leaves sometimes with
non-floral nectaries,
which may encourage
ants and provide
defence from cater-
pillars. Fruits ex-
plosive.
See p. 168.

○ **Touch-me-not balsam**
Impatiens noli-tangere
Mid. Lvs many-toothed; fls 30–35mm, yellow, hanging from horizontal spikes beneath lvs; spur long, curved. LH ann. GERM spr. FL 7–9. POLL ins(h); self (cleisto-gamous). SEX (♀). HAB woods. SOIL damp; not calc. SHADE light-heavy. ALT sl–250. DIST E2, W1. RANGE eF4, G5, S3.
See p. 168, 246, 261.

○ **Orange balsam**
Impatiens capensis
Mid. Like Touch-me-not balsam, but lvs with few teeth; fls 20–30mm long, orange, spur more sharply curved. LH ann. GERM spr. FL 6–8. POLL ins(h); self. SEX (♀). HAB river banks. SOIL nil–light. ALT sl–100. DIST (sE2, W1). RANGE (F1).

● **Small balsam**
Impatiens parviflora
Mid–tall. Lvs finely toothed; fls 5–15mm, pale yellow; spur almost straight. LH ann. GERM spr. FL 6–9. POLL ins(h); self. SEX (♀). HAB woods, disturbed ground. SOIL moist; not acid. SHADE light–heavy. ALT sl–150. DIST (E3, W1, S1). RANGE (F3, G3, sS2).

● **Himalayan balsam**
Impatiens glandulifera
Tall–v.tall. Stems purplish; lvs long, in 2's or 3's; fls large, to 40mm, purplish. LH ann. GERM spr. FL 7–11. POLL ins(h); self. SEX (♀). HAB river banks, woods. SOIL wet–moist; not acid. SHADE nil–heavy. ALT sl–300. DIST (E5, W5, S3, I5). RANGE (F3, G3, sS3).
See p. 176, 188, 210, 296.

MILKWORT FAMILY
Polygalaceae
A small family with only 1 genus in our flora. All have simple, unstalked, hairless leaves. Flowers have 3 petals and 5 sepals (2 large, coloured and petal-like), and 8 stamens, fused into a petal-like tube. Fruits 2-lobed, often hanging. Plants of grassy and heathy places. Flowers are very variable in colour.

○ **Dwarf milkwort**
Polygala amarella
V.low–low; prostrate. Lower lvs in rosette; stem lvs widest at tip; fls 2–5mm long, pink to blue. LH perenn; woody stem and rosette. GERM ? FL 6–8. POLL ins. SEX (♀). HAB short grassland. SOIL damp–dry; calc. SHADE nil. ALT 200–450. DIST nE1. RANGE eF2, G3, S2.

● **Heath milkwort**
Polygala serpyllifolia
Low–short. Lvs all on stem, in opposite pairs, those at the top largest; fls 5 6mm, normally blue. LH perenn; woody stem. GERM spr–sum. FL 5–8. POLL ins. SEX (♀). HAB poor grassland, heaths. SOIL moist–dry; not calc. SHADE nil–light. ALT sl–600(–1000). DIST wE4, eE2, W4, S5, I4. RANGE F3, G3, wS2.

● **Common milkwort**
Polygala vulgaris
Low–short. Differs from Heath milkwort in alternate lvs; fls 6–8mm, often pink or white. LH perenn; woody stem. GERM aut. FL 5–9. POLL ins. SEX (♀). HAB short grassland. SOIL moist–dry; not acid. SHADE nil. ALT sl–400(–600). DIST E4, W4, S4, I4. RANGE F4, G5, sS4.
ss95.

DAPHNE FAMILY
Thymelaeaceae
Mainly shrubs, with simple, alternate unstalked lvs, often glossy. *Daphne* spp have no petals, but 4 petal-like sepals. Fls are in clusters at the lf bases. Both British species are found in calcareous woodland.

○ **Mezereon**
Daphne mezereum
V.tall. Fls appear on bare stems; fls 8–12mm, pinkish-purple, scented; lvs not glossy; fr a red berry. LH perenn; shrub. GERM spr. FL 2–4. POLL ins(h, d, l); self. SEX (♀) hg. HAB woods. SOIL moist–dry; calc. SHADE light–heavy. ALT sl–200. DIST E2 and widely naturalised. RANGE eF2, G4, S3.

○ **Spurge laurel**
Daphne laureola
Mid–tall. Lvs dark
green, leathery; fls
10mm, yellow–green,
in small clusters; fr a
black berry. LH
perenn; shrub. GERM ?
FL 1–4. POLL ins(l, h).
SEX (♀). HAB woods,
scrub. SOIL dry; calc.
SHADE light–heavy.
ALT sl–250. DIST sE4,
nE2, W3, (S2). RANGE
F3, wG1.

CURRANT FAMILY
Grossulariavene
A family of one genus,
Ribes. Most species are
familiar garden soft
fruit plants. All are
shrubs, mostly with
palmately lobed leaves
and spikes of small
4–5-petalled flowers.
Fruits are berries,
varying greatly in
colour.

● **Red currant**
Ribes rubrum
Tall–v.tall. Lvs aroma-
tic; fls purple-tipped,
up to 20 in a spike; fr
bright red, to 10mm.
LH perenn; shrub.
GERM spr. FL 4–5. POLL
ins(h). SEX (♀) hg.
HAB woods, hedges,
fens. SOIL damp–moist;
not acid. SHADE nil–
mid. ALT sl–400. DIST
E4, W3, S3, I2. RANGE
F3, nG3, sS2.
ss96.

● **Black currant**
Ribes nigrum
Tall–v.tall. Lvs aro-
matic; fls in few-
flowered spikes; fr
black, to 15mm. LH
perenn; shrub. GERM
aut. FL 4–5. POLL
ins(h); self. SEX (♀) hg.
HAB woods, hedges.
SOIL damp–moist;
acid–calc. SHADE nil–
mid. ALT sl–300. DIST
E4, W3, S3, I2. RANGE
F3, G3, S3.

● **Gooseberry**
Ribes uva-crispa
Tall. Stems very spiny;
fls singly or in pairs,
petals reflexed; fr
green, hairy, to 20mm.
LH perenn; shrub.
GERM spr. FL 3–5. POLL
ins(h). SEX (♀) pa.
HAB hedges, scrub,
rarely woods. SOIL
moist; acid–calc.
SHADE nil–mid. ALT
sl–300. DIST E5, W5,
S4, I2. RANGE F5, G5,
S4.
See p. 162.

MALLOW FAMILY
Malvaceae
A family with showy
fls and usually pal-
mately-lobed leaves.
Petals 5, often notched,
usually purplish-pink;
fls often have an outer
ring of sepals
(epicalyx) below the
true sepals.
See p. 257.

● **Musk mallow**
Malva moschata
Mid–tall. Lvs palmate
at base, deeply dis-
sected at top of stem;
fls 40–60mm, with 3
unjoined outer sepals.
LH perenn; rootstock.
GERM aut. FL 7–8. POLL
ins(h); self. SEX (♀) pa.
HAB grassland, scrub.
SOIL dry; not acid.
SHADE nil–light. ALT
sl–300. DIST sE4, nE2,
W4, S2, I2. RANGE
F5, G4, sS3.
See p. 203.

● **Dwarf mallow**
Malva neglecta
Short–mid; usually
prostrate. Lvs with
shallow, pointed lobes;
fls 15–20mm, outer
sepals very narrow,
petals much longer
than sepals. LH persis-
tent ann. GERM aut.
FL 6–9. POLL ins(h, d);
self. SEX (♀). HAB
disturbed ground. SOIL
dry; acid–calc. SHADE
nil. ALT sl–200. DIST
seE5, nwE2, W2, S2,
I2. RANGE F5, G5,
sS2.

● **Common mallow**
Malva sylvestris
Mid–tall. Stem lvs
well-lobed, dark-
spotted; fls 25–40mm,
in small clusters;
petals more than twice
as long as sepals. LH
perenn; rootstock.
POLL ins(h); self.
SEX (♀). HAB bare
places, roadsides. SOIL
dry; not acid. SHADE
nil. ALT sl–200(–300).
DIST E5, W4, S2, I2.
RANGE F5, G5, sS2.

○ **Tree mallow**
Lavatera arborea
Tall–v.tall. Stem thick,
woody; lvs softly
hairy; fls 30–40mm,
veined; outer sepals
joined, 3-lobed. LH
bienn. GERM spr? FL
4–9. POLL ins(h, d).
SEX (♀) pa. HAB bare
and rocky places by
sea. SOIL dry; not acid.
SHADE nil. ALT sl–100.
DIST coastal: swE2,
W2. RANGE coastal:
wF2.
ss97.

○ **Marsh mallow**
Althaea officinalis
Tall. Softly hairy; lvs greyish; fls 25–30mm, outer sepals forming a 6–9-lobed cup. LH perenn; rootstock (used to make marshmallows). GERM aut–spr. FL 8–9. POLL ins(h); self. SEX (♀) pa. HAB meadows, saltmarshes; near coast in Britain. SOIL wet–damp; saline. SHADE nil. ALT sl. DIST coastal: sE2, W2, I2. RANGE F3, G2, sS1.

ST JOHN'S-WORT FAMILY
Hypericaceae
A small and distinctive family with only 1 native genus. Leaves are single, in opposite pairs and usually dotted with translucent glands. Flowers are flat, with 5 sepals and petals, and very numerous stamens. Mainly grassland plants.
See p. 210.

● **Tutsan**
Hypericum androsaemum
Mid–tall. Shrubby with broad lvs and fls 20mm, sepals almost as long as petals; fr a dark purple berry. LH perenn; shrub. GERM spr. FL 6–8. POLL ins(h, d, l); self. SEX (♀) hg. HAB woods, cliffs. SOIL damp–moist; not calc. SHADE nil–heavy. ALT sl–400(–600). DIST wE4, eE2, W4, wS3, I5. RANGE wF4, eF2.

● **Perforate St John's-wort**
Hypericum perforatum
Mid–tall. Stems with 2 ridges; lvs narrow with many translucent dots; fls 20mm, edged with black dots. LH perenn; rhizome, root-buds. GERM spr. FL 7–9. POLL ins(h, d); self. SEX (♀) hg. HAB grassland, open woods. SOIL moist–dry; not acid. SHADE nil–light. ALT sl–300(–400). DIST E5, W5, S3, I3. RANGE F5, G5, sS4.

● **Imperforate St John's-wort**
Hypericum maculatum
Mid. Stems square, unwinged; lvs almost undotted; fls 20mm, black-dotted on petals not margins. LH perenn; rhizome. GERM spr. FL 6–8. POLL ins(h, d); self. SEX (♀) hg. HAB woods, hedges. SOIL moist; not calc. SHADE light–mid. ALT sl–300. DIST E3, W4, S3, I4. RANGE F3, G5, S4.

● **Hairy St John's-wort**
Hypericum hirsutum
Mid–tall. Softly hairy, with round stems; lvs with translucent dots, unstalked; fls 10–15mm long, pale yellow. LH perenn; rootstock. GERM spr. FL 7–9. POLL ins(h, d); self. SEX (♀) hg. HAB shady and grassy places. SOIL damp–moist; calc. SHADE nil–mid. ALT sl–400. DIST sE4, nE2, W3, S2, I1. RANGE F5, G4, S2.

○ **Pale St John's-wort**
Hypericum montanum
Mid–tall. Softly hairy; lvs not dotted, but dark edged; fls 10–15mm, very pale, scented. LH perenn; rootstock. GERM imm. FL 6–8. POLL ins(h, d); self. SEX (♀) hg. HAB shady and grassy places. SOIL moist–dry; calc. SHADE nil–mid. ALT sl–300. DIST E2, W2. RANGE F3, G3, sS3.

● **Square-stemmed St John's-wort**
Hypericum tetrapterum
Mid. Stems square, winged; lvs unstalked, with translucent dots; fls 10mm, pale yellow. LH perenn; stolons. GERM spr–sum. FL 7–9. POLL ins(h, d). SEX (♀) hg. HAB grassy places, often near water. SOIL damp–moist; not calc. SHADE nil. ALT sl–350. DIST E5, W5, S3, I5. RANGE F4, G4, sS1. **ss98**.

● **Slender St John's-wort**
Hypericum pulchrum
Mid. Stems round, slender, red-tinged; lvs unstalked, oval, with translucent dots; fls 15mm, petals with red and black dots. LH perenn; rootstock. GERM spr. FL 7–9. POLL ins(h, d); self. SEX (♀) hg. HAB grassland, heaths, open woods. SOIL moist–dry; not calc. SHADE nil–light. ALT sl–500(–800). DIST E4, W5, S5, I5. RANGE F4, G4, wS2. *See p. 219.* **ss99**.

● **Trailing St John's-wort**
Hypericum humifusum
Low; creeping. Stems very fine; lvs unstalked with translucent dots; fls 10mm, scattered; sepals different sizes. LH short-lived perenn; stems. GERM spr–sum. FL 7–10. POLL ins(d); self; cleistogamous. SEX (♀) hg. HAB heaths, moors, bare ground. SOIL dry; acid. SHADE nil–light. ALT sl–300(–500). DIST E4, W4, S3, I3. RANGE F5, G4, sS1. **ss100**.

71

○ **Marsh St John's-wort**
Hypericum elodes
Short; creeping. Stems rooting at nodes; lvs grey-hairy, rounded; fls 10–15mm, half-opening. LH perenn; rooting nodes. GERM spr; seeds v. long-lived. FL 6–9. POLL ins(h, d); self. SEX (♀) hg. HAB marshes, shallow water. SOIL water–wet; acid. SHADE nil. ALT sl–400. DIST swE3, neE1, W2, wS2, wI3. RANGE F4, nwG2.

VIOLET FAMILY
Violaceae
A very distinctive family with toothed leaves usually on long stalks, with stipules at base. Flowers flat, with 5 petals, 4 spreading, 1 forming a lip and spur. Flowers normally borne singly on a long stalk. Most have seeds dispersed by ants. Most produce cleisto-gamous flowers in summer, after normal flowering time.
See p. 250, 257, 266, 283.

● **Sweet violet**
Viola odorata
Low. Lvs rounded, much larger in sum-mer; fls 15mm, fra-grant; white forms common; sepals blunt. LH perenn; stolons and rhizome. GERM spr. FL 3–5. POLL ins(h); cleistogamous fls self. SEX (♀). HAB woods, scrub, hedges. SOIL moist–dry; acid–calc. SHADE nil–mid. ALT sl–200. DIST E5, W3, S2, I2. RANGE F5, G4, sS3.
See p. 19, 199, 209, 250, 261, 278.

● **Hairy violet**
Viola hirta
Low. Like Sweet violet, but hairier, without stolons, lvs narrower and fls paler, unscented. LH perenn; rhizome. GERM spr-sum. FL 4–5. POLL ins(h); cleistogamous fls self. SEX (♀). HAB grassland. SOIL dry; calc. SHADE nil–light. ALT sl–600. DIST sE4, nE2, W2, S2, I1. RANGE F4, G4, sS3.
See p. 219, 250.

● **Common dog violet**
Viola riviniana
Low. Lvs heart-shaped, in a rosette; stipules feathery; fls 12–20mm, spur paler. Sepals pointed. LH perenn; rootstock, root-buds. GERM spr–sum. FL 3–5. POLL ins(h); cleisto-gamous fls self. SEX (♀). HAB woods, grass-land, heaths, rocks. SOIL moist–dry; acid–calc. SHADE nil–heavy. ALT sl–1000. DIST E5, W5, S5, I5. RANGE F5, G5, S4.
See p. 169, 250, 252, 261. **ss101.**

● **Early dog violet**
Viola reichenbachiana
Low. Very like Com-mon dog violet, but lvs narrower, fls paler, spur same colour as petals. LH perenn; rootstock. GERM spr-sum. FL 3–5 (before Common dog violet). POLL ins(h). SEX (♀). HAB woods. SOIL moist–dry; calc. SHADE light–heavy. ALT sl–250(–600). DIST sE4, nE2, W2, sS1, I2. RANGE F4, G4, sS2.
See p. 209.

Eastern dog violet
Viola mirabilis
Low. Like Common dog violet but stem with a line of hairs, stipules untoothed and spur even paler. LH perenn; rootstock. GERM ? FL 4–5. POLL ins(d, h, l); cleisto-gamous fls self. SEX (♀). HAB woods. SOIL damp–moist; acid–calc. SHADE nil–mid. ALT [sl–2500]. RANGE eF1, G3, S3.

○ **Heath dog violet**
Viola canina
V.low–short. Lvs oval; no rosette; fls 10–15mm, pale blue-violet, spur yellowish or whitish; sepals painted. LH perenn; rhizome. GERM spr-sum. FL 4–6. POLL ins(h); cleistogamous fls self. SEX (♀). HAB grassland, heaths, fens. SOIL damp–dry; not calc. SHADE nil–light. ALT sl–200(–400). DIST E3, W2, S2, I2. RANGE F4, G5, S5.
See p. 209, 250.

○ **Pale dog violet**
Viola lactea
Low. Lvs narrow, oval, no rosette; fls 15–20mm, dull bluish-white, spur greenish; sepals pointed. LH perenn; rhizome. GERM ? FL 5–6. POLL ins(h). SEX (♀). HAB heaths. SOIL moist–dry; acid. SHADE nil. ALT sl–100. DIST sE2, W1, I1. RANGE F2.

○ **Fen violet**
Viola persicifolia
Short. Lvs heart-shaped, no rosette; fls 10–15mm, pale bluish-white, often veined, spur greenish. LH perenn; rhizome, root-buds. GERM spr. FL 5–6. POLL ins(h). SEX (♀). HAB grassland, fens. SOIL damp; calc. SHADE nil. ALT sl–100. DIST E1. RANGE eF1, G2, sS2.
See p. 249.

72

● **Marsh violet**
Viola palustris
Low. No above-ground stems; lvs arising in tufts from rhizomes; fls 10–15mm, lilac, veined darker; sepals blunt. LH perenn; rhizome. GERM spr–sum. FL 4–7. POLL ins(h); cleisto-gamous fls self. SEX (♀). HAB marshes, fens, woods. SOIL wet–damp; acid–calc. SHADE nil–mid. ALT sl–1250. DIST sE2, nE4, W4, S5, I4. RANGE F2, G4, S5.
See p. 250, 282.

Northern marsh violet
Viola epipsila
Low–short. Lvs in opposite pairs, slightly hairy; fls 15–20mm, longer-spurred. LH perenn; rhizome. GERM ? FL 5–8. POLL ins(h); cleistogamous fls self. SEX (♀). HAB marshes, fens, woods. SOIL wet–damp; not calc. SHADE nil–heavy. ALT [sl–2000]. RANGE neG2, S5.

● **Yellow wood violet**
Viola biflora
Low; creeping. Slightly hairy; lvs tufted, heart-shaped; fls 15–18mm, yellow, often in pairs. LH perenn; rhizome. GERM ? FL 6–8. POLL ins(d, h, l); cleisto-gamous fls self. SEX (♀). HAB mountain woods. SOIL damp–moist; acid–calc. SHADE nil–mid. ALT [500–2500]. RANGE F1, G1, S3.

● **Mountain pansy**
Viola lutea
Low. Lfs in tufts, hairy; stipules deeply lobed; fls 20–35mm, flat, on stalks more than 50mm long. LH perenn; rhizome. GERM spr. FL 5–8. POLL ins(h, d, l). SEX (♀). HAB upland grassland. SOIL moist–dry; calc. SHADE nil. ALT 200–600(–1000). DIST E1, nE2, W2, S3, I1. RANGE F1, G1.
See p. 219.

● **Wild pansy**
Viola tricolor
V.low–short. Variable, branching; lvs oval, toothed; stipules leafy, lobed; fls 10–25mm, flat, often blue and yellow; fl-stalks usually less than 60mm. LH persistent ann or short-lived perenn. GERM spr. FL 4–10. POLL ins(h); self. SEX (♀). HAB disturbed and grassy places; sand-dunes (dwarf forms). SOIL moist–dry; acid–calc. SHADE nil. ALT sl–300 (–600). DIST E4, W4, S4, I2. RANGE F3, G5, S5.
See p. 243, 279.

● **Field pansy**
Viola arvensis
Low–short. Very vari-able; like Wild pansy but fls less than 15mm, creamy-yellow, petals little larger than sepals. LH ann, sometimes persisting. GERM spr. FL 4–10. POLL ins(h); self. SEX (♀). HAB disturbed ground. SOIL moist–dry; acid–calc. SHADE nil–light. DIST E4, W2, S3, I3. RANGE F5, G5, S4.
See p. 209, 243. **ss102.**

ROCK-ROSE FAMILY
Cistaceae
A small family of herbs and shrubs, mainly Mediterranean, but with a few nor-thern species. All have untoothed leaves, single 5-petalled flowers with many stamens. The petals are short-lived and often fall on the day the flowers open. Characteristic of dry places.
See p. 219.

● **Hoary rock-rose**
Helianthemum canum
Low. Greyish, hairy dwarf shrub; lvs nar-row; fls 10–15mm, the style S-shaped. LH perenn; shrub. GERM ? FL 5–6(–7). POLL ins(h). SEX (♀) pg. HAB rocky grassland. SOIL dry; calc. SHADE nil. ALT sl–500. DIST nE1, W1, I1. RANGE F3, G1.

● **Common rock-rose**
Helianthemum nummularium
Low–short. Branches woody; lvs green on top, oval, with narrow stipules; fls 20–25mm, style straight. LH perenn; shrub. GERM spr. FL 5–9. POLL ins(h, d, l); self. SEX (♀) pg. HAB grassland, rocks. SOIL dry; calc. SHADE nil–light. ALT sl–400(–600). DIST E3, W2, S3, I1. RANGE F4, G4, sS3.
ss103.

○ **Spotted rock-rose**
Tuberaria guttata
Low–short. Lvs in rosette, soon dying; fls 10–20mm, dark-centred; petals fall in morning of opening. LH ann. GERM spr. FL 5–8. POLL ins; self, may be cleistogamous. SEX (♀). HAB bare coastal grassland and heaths. SOIL dry; not acid. SHADE nil. ALT sl–100. DIST W1, I1. RANGE F2, G1.

SEA HEATH FAMILY
Frankeniaceae
A small family with one British species (Sea heath). Rather heather-like leaves, but simple 5-petalled, flat flowers with 6 stamens. Most of the family grow in salty places.

GOURD FAMILY
Cucurbitaceae
A large tropical family with one British species (White bryony) which has 5-petalled flowers joined at the base. The family includes gourds, melons and cucumbers.

○ **Sea heath**
Frankenia laevis
V.low; prostrate. Mat-forming, heathy; lvs narrow, opposite, dense; fls 5–8mm, un-stalked. LH perenn; evergreen. GERM ?imm. FL 7–8. POLL ins. SEX (♀). HAB damp coastal sand, drier salt-marshes. SOIL damp–moist; saline. SHADE nil. ALT sl. DIST coastal: sE2. RANGE coastal: wF2.

● **White bryony**
Bryonia cretica
V.tall, climbing. Stem to 4m, climbing by tendrils at lf-base; lvs lobed; fls greenish; fr a red berry. LH perenn; rootstock. GERM spr–sum. FL 5–9. POLL ins(h). SEX (♂) + (♀). HAB scrub, hedges. SOIL moist–dry; not acid. SHADE nil–mid. ALT sl–200. DIST sE5, nE2, W3. RANGE F4, G2.
See p. 195, 213, 278.

WILLOWHÉRB FAMILY
Onagraceae
Very distinctive 4-petalled flowers (2 in Enchanter's night-shade), and rather narrow toothed leaves. Up to 10 stamens; petals not joined. Common in wet places and woods; most are opportunist species, with very large seed production.
See p. 165, 257, 269.

○ **Alpine enchanter's nightshade**
Circaea alpina
Short. Lvs oval, heart-shaped at base, toothed; fls 2-petalled, 2–3mm; fl-stalk length-ening after flg. LH perenn; root tuber. GERM sum. FL 7–8. POLL ins(d); self. SEX (♀). HAB woods. SOIL moist; acid. SHADE light–heavy. ALT 100–450. DIST nE1, W1, S1. RANGE eF1, G3, S4.

● **Enchanter's nightshade**
Circaea lutetiana
Short–mid. Lvs oval, little-toothed; fls 4–8mm, petals deeply notched; fl-stalk lengthening during flg. LH perenn; rootstock. GERM spr. FL 6–9. POLL ins(d); self. SEX (♀) hg. HAB woods, shady gardens. SOIL moist; acid–calc. SHADE light–heavy. DIST E5, W5, S3, I5. RANGE F5, G5, sS2.
See p. 172, 263, 276.

● **Common evening primrose**
Oenothera biennis
Tall. Lvs long, narrow, reddening; fls 40–50mm, sepals green. LH bienn. GERM spr. FL 6–9. POLL ins(l, h); self. SEX (♀). HAB disturbed ground, sand-dunes. SOIL dry; acid–calc. SHADE nil. ALT sl–100. DIST casual: E4, W2, S2, I1. RANGE casual: F5, G5, sS3.
See p. 279.

● **Large-flowered evening primrose**
Oenothera erythrosepala
Tall. Stems red-hairy; lvs less narrow, crink-led; fls 60–80mm, sepals red-striped. LH bienn. GERM spr. FL 6–9. POLL ins(l, h); self. SEX (♀). HAB disturbed ground, sand-dunes. SOIL dry; acid–calc. SHADE nil. ALT sl–100. DIST E3, W2, S1, I1. RANGE casual: F4, G3, sS2.

● **Rosebay willowherb**
Epilobium angustifolium
Mid–tall. Forms large patches; lvs long, narrow, spirally up stem; fls 20–30mm, lower petals largest, splayed. LH perenn; root-buds. GERM spr. FL 7–9. POLL ins(h). SEX (♀) pa. HAB dis-turbed ground, road-sides, open woods. SOIL moist–dry; acid–calc. SHADE nil–mid. ALT sl–600(–1000). DIST E5, W5, S5, I3. RANGE F5, G5, S5.
See p. 206, 246, 247, 250, 256, 262, 263.

● **Great willowherb**
Epilobium hirsutum
Tall–v.tall. Very hairy; lvs opposite, clasping stem; fls 15–25mm, stigma 4-lobed; seed pod to 80cm. LH perenn; stolons. GERM spr. FL 7–8. POLL ins(h); self. SEX (♀) pa. HAB marshes, stream-sides, ditches. SOIL wet-damp; acid–calc. SHADE nil–light. ALT sl–350. DIST E5, W5, S3, I5. RANGE F5, G5, sS2.
See p. 177, 233, 239.

● **Hoary willowherb**
Epilobium parviflorum
Mid. Very hairy; lvs alternate, not clasping stem; fls 6–10mm, stigma prominently 4-lobed; stolons, lf-rosettes. GERM aut. FL 7–8. POLL ins(h); self. SEX (♀) hg. HAB marshes. SOIL wet–damp; not acid. SHADE nil. ALT sl–300. DIST E5, W4, S3, I4. RANGE F5, G5, sS3. *See p. 280.*

● **Broad-leaved willowherb**
Epilobium montanum
Mid. Lvs pointed, oval, opposite, short-stalked; fls 6–8mm, stigma 4-lobed, petals notched. LH perenn; stolons, lf-rosettes. GERM imm, spr. FL 6–8. POLL ins(h, d); self. SEX (♀) hg. HAB disturbed ground, woods, walls. SOIL moist–dry; acid–calc. SHADE nil–mid. ALT sl–400(–800). DIST E5, W5, S5, I5. RANGE F5, G5, S4. *See p. 207.* **ss104.**

● **Square-stemmed willowherb**
Epilobium tetragonum
Mid. Stem 4-angled; lvs narrow, unstalked, shiny; fls 6–8mm, stigma not lobed; petals slightly notched. LH perenn; stolons, lf-rosettes. GERM spr. FL 6–8. POLL self. SEX (♀) hg. HAB woods, fens, disturbed ground. SOIL wet–moist; acid–calc. SHADE nil–mid. ALT sl–200. DIST sE4, nE1, W2, I1. RANGE F5, G4, sS3.

● **Short-fruited willowherb**
Epilobium obscurum
Mid. Like Square-stemmed willowherb, but lvs dull green, and sepal tube sticky-hairy; no rosettes in winter. LH perenn; stolons. GERM imm. FL 6–8. POLL self. SEX (♀) hg. HAB marshes, fens, woods. SOIL damp; acid–calc. SHADE nil–heavy. ALT sl–300 (–600). DIST E4, W4, S4, I4. RANGE F4, G4, S3.

○ **American willowherb**
Epilobium adenocaulon
Mid. Stem 4-angled; lvs opposite, short-stalked; fls 4–6mm, stigma not 4-lobed. LH perenn; lf-rosettes. GERM imm. FL 6–8. POLL self. SEX (♀) hg. HAB woods, disturbed ground. SOIL damp; not calc. SHADE nil–mid. ALT sl–200. DIST (sE4, nE1, W3, S2). RANGE (F4, G2, S3).

● **Pale willowherb**
Epilobium roseum
Mid. Stem 2-angled, sticky-hairy; lvs clearly stalked; fls 4–6mm, very pale; stigma not lobed. LH perenn; stolons, lf-rosettes. GERM aut–spr. FL 6–8. POLL self. SEX (♀) hg. HAB shady places. SOIL damp–moist; not calc. SHADE nil–mid. ALT sl–200. DIST E3, W4, S2, I2. RANGE F4, G4, sS3.

● **Marsh willowherb**
Epilobium palustre
Short–mid. Stems slender, hairy; lvs narrow, unstalked; fls 4–6mm, stalk curved; stigma unlobed. LH perenn; stolons. GERM aut. FL 6–8. POLL ins(d); self. SEX (♀). HAB marshes, springs. SOIL wet–damp; not calc. SHADE nil–light. ALT sl–800. DIST sE4, nE5, W5, S5, I5. RANGE F4, G5, S5. *See p. 164.*

○ **Alpine willowherb**
Epilobium anagallidifolium
Low; creeping. Stems upright, stolons creeping; stolons lfy; fls 4–5mm, sepals reddish; fl-spike nodding. LH perenn; stolons. GERM spr. FL 7–8. POLL self. SEX (♀). HAB mountain-springs, flushes. SOIL water–wet; not calc. SHADE nil. ALT 250–1250. DIST nE1, S3. RANGE F1, G1, S3.

○ **Chickweed willowherb**
Epilobium alsinifolium
Low; creeping. Like Alpine willowherb, but stolons below-ground; fls 8–10mm, purplish; lvs pointed, toothed. LH perenn; stolons. GERM ? FL 7–8. POLL self. SEX (♀). HAB mountain-springs, flushes. SOIL water–wet; not acid. SHADE nil. ALT 150–1000. DIST nE2, S3. RANGE F1, G1, S3.

● **New Zealand willowherb**
Epilobium brunnescens
V.low; creeping. Stems rooting; lvs often red-tinged; fls 3–4mm, long-stalked, borne singly. LH perenn; rooting nodes. GERM ? FL 6–7. POLL self. SEX (♀). HAB streamsides, rocks. SOIL wet; acid–calc. SHADE nil. ALT 100–1000. DIST sE1, nE3, W3, S4, I3. RANGE ? *See p. 217.*

**WATER MILFOIL
FAMILY**
Haloragaceae
See p. 257, 271.

**MARE'S-TAIL
FAMILY**
Hippuridaceae

**WATER
STARWORT
FAMILY**
Callitrichaceae
3 families of water
plants with very in-
conspicuous flowers
which either have no
petals, inconspicuous
petals, or petals that
soon fall. Flowers are
often monosexual.

● **Alternate water
milfoil**
*Myriophyllum
alterniflorum*
Short–tall. Lvs pin-
nate, with up to 18
segments, feathery, 4 in
a whorl; ♂ fls 4–5mm,
yellowish, above
petal-less ♀ fls in
whorled spikes. LH
perenn; rhizome. GERM
spr–sum. FL 6–8. POLL
wind on water surface.
SEX (♂ + ♂ + ♀) pa. HAB
still or slow fresh
water; not
calc. SHADE nil. ALT
sl–400(–700). DIST E2,
W2, S4, I3. RANGE F2,
nG3, S4.

● **Spiked water milfoil**
Myriophyllum spicatum
Tall–v.tall. Lvs pin-
nate, with 25–35
segments, feathery, 4 in
a whorl; fls in whorls
of 4, lowest ♀, upper ♂,
reddish, 3–4mm. LH
perenn; rhizome. GERM
spr–sum. FL 6–7. POLL
wind on water surface.
HAB still or slow fresh
water; still or not
acid. SHADE nil. ALT
sl–500. DIST seE4,
nwE2, W2, S2, I4.
RANGE F3, G5, S2.
See p. 203. **ss105.**

● **Mare's-tail**
Hippuris vulgaris
Mid–tall in water; low
on land. Lvs narrow,
whorled, sharp-tipped;
fls small at lf-bases,
petals reduced to a
tiny ring. LH perenn;
rhizome. GERM ? FL
6–7. POLL wind. SEX
(♂ + ♀) pg. HAB still
and slow fresh water.
SOIL water; not acid.
SHADE nil. ALT sl–300
(–500). DIST E4, W3,
S3, I3. RANGE F3, G4,
S5.
See p. 203, 257. **ss106.
ss107.**

● **Water starwort**
*Callitriche
stagnalis* agg.
Short–tall; smaller on
mud. A difficult group
of species, with
various-shaped, entire
lvs, often in rosettes;
fls tiny, petalless; fr 4
nutlets. LH ann–
perenn; lf-rosettes.
GERM spr. FL 4–9. POLL
wind, water. SEX
(♂ + ♀). HAB still and
flowing fresh water;
mud. SOIL water–
damp; acid–calc.
SHADE nil–light. ALT
sl–1000. DIST E5, W4,
S4, I4. RANGE F4, G5,
See p. 274, 275.

**DOGWOOD
FAMILY**
Cornaceae
Mainly shrubs with
simple leaves and
heads of 4-petalled
flowers. Dwarf cornel
is herbaceous.
See p. 257.

**LOOSESTRIFE
FAMILY**
Lythraceae
Square-stemmed plants
with usually 6-petalled,
sometimes minute
flowers.

IVY FAMILY
Araliaceae
Ivy is the only British
species in this mainly
tropical family.
Flowers 5-petalled.

○ **Dwarf cornel**
Cornus suecica
Low; creeping. Stems
upright; lvs opposite,
strongly-veined; fls
3–4mm in heads sur-
rounded by 4 large
white bracts. LH
perenn; rhizome. GERM
spr–sum. FL 6–8. POLL
ins(d, h). SEX (♀) pa.
HAB heaths, moors.
SOIL damp–moist; not
calc. SHADE nil. ALT
200–800. DIST nE1, S3.
RANGE nG2, S4.
See p. 295.

● **Purple loosestrife**
Lythrum salicaria
Tall. Lvs narrow, un-
stalked in pairs or 3's;
fls 10–15mm in
whorled spikes. LH
perenn; rhizome. GERM
ins(h, d). SEX (♀) hg;
heterostylous with 3
flower types. HAB
Fens, marshes, and by
water. SOIL wet–damp;
not acid. SHADE nil–
light. ALT sl–400. DIST
E5, W4, S2, I5. RANGE
F5, G5, sS4.
See p. 167, 267, 279.

● **Water purslane**
Lythrum portula
Low–short; creeping.
Stems rooting; lvs
small; fls 1–2mm,
petals soon falling,
leaving bell-shaped
sepal tube. LH ann;
sometimes persisting.
GERM sum–aut. FL
6–10. POLL self. SEX
(♀). HAB bare mud.
SOIL damp; not calc.
SHADE nil. ALT sl–400.
DIST sE4, nE2, W3, S3,
I3. RANGE F3, G3,
sS3.
ss108. ss109. ss110.

●**Ivy**
Hedera helix
Creeping or climbing.
Stems woody; lvs
glossy, evergreen, only
lobed on non-flg
shoots; fls 3–6mm,
yellow-green, only in
sun; fr a black berry.
LH perenn; rooting
nodes, evergreen.
GERM spr–sum. FL
9–11. POLL ins(h, d, l).
SEX (♀); pg–hg–pa.
HAB woods, hedges,
walls, rocks. SOIL
moist–dry; acid–calc.
SHADE nil–heavy. ALT
sl–500. DIST E5, W5,
S5, I5. RANGE F5, G5,
sS2.
*See p. 2, 197, 221, 282,
297.*

CARROT FAMILY
Umbelliferae
Herbs with distinctive pinnate leaves (often feathery) and flowers in umbels – flat-topped heads in which several stalks arise from a single point; often the umbels are compound. Flowers have 5, usually white or yellow, petals, some of which may be larger than others. Fruit is dry, often flattened or ridged.
See p. 18, 19, 183, 187, 245, 248, 265, 276, 285.

● **Marsh pennywort**
Hydrocotyle vulgaris
V.low–short; creeping; lvs circular, the long stalk entering in the centre; fls small, pinkish, beneath lvs. LH perenn; rooting nodes. GERM sum–aut. FL 6–8. POLL ins(h, d); self. SEX (♀) hg. HAB marshes, fens, wet grassland. SOIL water–damp; acid–calc. SHADE nil–light. ALT sl–500. DIST E4, W4, S3, I4. RANGE F4, G4, sS3.

● **Sanicle**
Sanicula europaea
Mid. Lvs 5-lobed, shiny dark green, long-stalked; fls pale pink in dense clusters. LH perenn; rootstock. GERM spr–sum. FL 5–7. POLL ins(h, d). SEX (♀ + ♂) pg. HAB woods. SOIL moist–dry; not acid. SHADE light–heavy. ALT sl–400. DIST E4, W5, S3, I3. RANGE F5, G5, sS3.
See p. 271.

○ **Astrantia**
Astrantia major
Mid–tall. Lvs 5–7-lobed, long-stalked; fls white, in heads surrounded by pinkish-green bracts. LH perenn; rootstock. GERM ? FL 6–9. POLL ins(c, d, l); wind. SEX (♀ + ♂) pa. HAB woods, meadows. SOIL damp–moist; acid–calc. SHADE nil–mid. ALT sl–200; mountains in F, G. DIST (E2). RANGE F1, G3.

● **Sea holly**
Eryngium maritimum
Mid. Lvs rounded, strongly spiny-toothed, blue-grey; fls 8–10mm in dense heads, blue, surrounded by spiny bracts. LH perenn; rootstock. GERM spr–sum. FL 7–8. POLL ins(h, d, c). SEX (♀ + ♂) pa. HAB coastal sand and shingle. SOIL dry; not acid. SHADE nil. ALT sl. DIST coastal: E3, W2, S1, I2. RANGE coastal: F3, G3, sS2.
See p. 236, 237, 295, 298.

○ **Field eryngo**
Eryngium campestre
Mid. Branching, yellow-green; root lvs pinnate, spiny; fls 2–3mm in heads with spiny bracts. LH perenn; rootstock. GERM spr. FL 7–8. POLL ins(h, d, c). SEX (♀). HAB grassland. SOIL dry; acid–calc. SHADE nil. ALT sl–100. DIST E1. RANGE F4, G3.

○ **Bur chervil**
Anthriscus caucalis
Mid–tall. Lvs 3-pinnate, slightly hairy; fls 2mm; no bracts beneath umbel; fl-stalks thickening in fr. LH ann. GERM spr. FL 5–6. POLL ins(h, d); self. SEX (♀ + ♂). HAB bare ground. SOIL dry; not calc. SHADE nil. ALT sl. DIST seE3, nwE2, W1, S1, I1. RANGE F3, G3, sS1.

● **Cow parsley**
Anthriscus sylvestris
Tall. Lvs 2–3 pinnate; fls 3–4mm; no bracts beneath umbel; fr black, short-beaked. LH perenn; rootstock. GERM spr. FL 4–6. POLL ins(h). SEX (♀ + ♂) pa. HAB roadsides, hedges, woods. SOIL moist; not acid. SHADE nil–mid. ALT sl–400(–800). DIST E5, W5, S5, I5. RANGE F5, G5, S5.
See p. 176, 212, 213, 264, 271.

● **Sweet cicely**
Myrrhis odorata
Tall. Lvs large, 2–3 pinnate, strongly aniseed-scented when crushed; fls 2–4mm; fr large, ridged. LH perenn; rootstock. GERM spr. FL 5–7. POLL ins(h, d, c). SEX (♀ + ♂) pa. HAB roadsides, hedges. SOIL moist; acid–calc. SHADE nil–mid. ALT sl–500. DIST sE1, nE4, W3, S4, I2. RANGE eF2, G4, sS3.
See p. 265.

● **Rough chervil**
Chaerophyllum temulentum
Mid–tall. Stem hairy, purple-dotted; lvs 2–3 pinnate, downy; fls 2mm; no bracts beneath umbel. LH bienn. GERM spr. FL 5–7. POLL ins(h, d, c). SEX (♀ + ♂) pa. HAB hedges, woods. SOIL moist; acid–calc. SHADE nil–mid. ALT sl–400. DIST E5, W5, S3, I2. RANGE F5, G5, sS2.
See p. 271.

● **Upright hedge parsley**
Torilis japonica
Short–tall. Lvs usually 2-pinnate; fls 2–3mm, white, outer petals larger; 4–6 bracts beneath umbel; fr with hooked spines. LH ann, sometimes persisting. GERM spr. FL 7–9. POLL ins, self. SEX (♀ + ♂) pa. HAB hedges, grassy places. SOIL dry; acid–calc. SHADE nil–mid. ALT sl–400. DIST E5, W5, S3, I5. RANGE F5, G5, sS3.
ss111. ss112.

○ **Caraway**
Carum carvi
Mid. Branching; lvs hairless, 2–3-pinnate with narrow lflts; fls 2–3mm, usually without bracts. LH bienn. GERM aut. FL 6–7. POLL ins(h). SEX (♀) pa + (♀). HAB grassland, disturbed ground. SOIL moist; not acid. SHADE nil. ALT sl–100[–1000]. DIST (E2, W1, S1, I1). RANGE eF2, G5, S5.

● **Wild carrot**
Daucus carota
Mid–tall. Lvs 3-pinnate, feathery; fls 2–4mm, white, sometimes red-edged; pinnate bracts beneath umbel; umbel concave in fr. LH bienn, sometimes persisting. GERM spr–sum. FL 6–9. POLL ins(d, c). SEX (♀). HAB grassy places, often by sea. SOIL dry; not acid. SHADE nil. ALT sl–200 (–400). DIST sE5, nE3, W3, S2, I4. RANGE F5, G5, sS3.
See p. 19, 213, 245.

● **Pignut**
Conopodium majus
Mid. Lvs 2–3-pinnate, lower short-lived; lf-lobes grass-like; fls 1–3mm; 0–2 bracts beneath umbel; fr egg-shaped, styles upright. LH perenn; root tuber. GERM spr. FL 5–6. POLL ins. SEX (♀). HAB grassy and shady places. SOIL moist–dry; acid–calc. SHADE nil–mid. ALT sl–500(–700). DIST E5, W5, S5, I3. RANGE wF3, G1, wS2.
See p. 183, 253. **ss113.**

● **Greater burnet saxifrage**
Pimpinella major
Tall. Stems ridged; lvs 1-pinnate; fls 2–3mm, often pinkish, with styles longer than petals. LH perenn; rootstock. GERM spr. FL 6–7. POLL ins(h). SEX (♀ + ♂) pa. HAB grassy places, hedges, woods. SOIL moist; acid–calc. SHADE nil–mid. ALT sl–300. DIST E3, S1, I2. RANGE F4, G5, sS2.

● **Burnet saxifrage**
Pimpinella saxifraga
Mid–tall. Stems slightly ridged; lower lvs 1-pinnate, stem lvs 2-pinnate; fls 2mm, styles shorter than petals; no bracts beneath umbels. LH perenn; rootstock. GERM spr. FL 5–9. POLL ins(h). SEX (♀ + ♂) pa. HAB grassland. SOIL dry; not acid. SHADE nil–light. ALT sl–400 (–800). DIST E5, W5, S3, I3. RANGE F5, G5, S4.

○ **Shepherd's needle**
Scandix pecten-veneris
Short–mid. Lvs 2–3-pinnate, lflts narrow; fls 1mm, in small umbels; fr very long (to 70mm). LH ann. GERM spr. FL 5–8. POLL ins. SEX (♀ + ♂) pa. HAB arable fields. SOIL moist; not acid. SHADE nil. ALT sl–200(–300). DIST seE4, nwE2, W1, S1, I1. RANGE F4, G2, sS1.

● **Ground elder**
Aegopodium podagraria
Mid–tall. Carpeting, forming a canopy of 2-trefoil lvs; fls white, 1mm, with no bracts. LH perenn; rhizome. GERM spr. FL 6–8. POLL ins(d, h). SEX (♀). HAB gardens, waste ground; woods in F, G, S. SOIL moist; not acid. SHADE nil–heavy. ALT sl–400. DIST E5, W5, S5, I5. RANGE F5, G5, sS4.
See p. 250, 251.

○ **Moon carrot**
Seseli libanotis
Mid. Stems ridged, with dead lf-stalks at base; lvs 2–3-pinnate; fl-stalks downy; bracts present. LH short-lived perenn; rootstock. GERM spr–sum. FL 7–9. POLL ins(h, c). SEX (♀ + ♂) pa. HAB grassland. SOIL dry; calc. SHADE nil. ALT sl–150. DIST sE1. RANGE F2, G2, sS2.

● **Fool's parsley**
Aethusa cynapium
Low–tall. Stems ridged; lvs 2–3-pinnate; no bracts beneath umbel, but conspicuous bracts inside it. LH ann-bienn. GERM spr. FL 6–9. POLL ins(d, h). SEX (♀) pg–pa. HAB disturbed ground. SOIL moist; acid–calc. SHADE nil. ALT sl–250. DIST E5, W4, S2, I3. RANGE F5, G4, sS4.
See p. 263.

○ **Honewort**
Trinia glauca
Low–short. Stems greyish, with dead lf-stalks at base; lvs 3-pinnate, grey; ♂ and ♀ fls on separate plants. LH perenn; rootstock. GERM ? FL 5–6. POLL ins. SEX (♂)+(♀). HAB grass-land. SOIL dry; calc. SHADE nil. ALT sl–200. DIST sE1. RANGE F2, G1.

● **Giant hogweed**
Heracleum mantegazzianum
V.tall. Enormous (to 5m), with thick red-blotched stems; umbels up to 50cm across; causes painful skin lesions. LH bienn. GERM spr. FL 6–8. POLL ins. SEX (♀). HAB waste places, gravelly riversides. SOIL moist; not acid. SHADE nil–light. ALT sl–200. DIST naturalised and wide-spread E, W, S, I. RANGE naturalised and spreading F, G, S.
See p. 188.

● **Hogweed**
Heracleum sphondylium
Tall–v.tall. Never above 2m; stems hollow; lvs 1-pinnate, hairy, lflts broad; outer fls larger than inner. LH bienn, often persisting. GERM spr. FL 4–10. POLL ins(h, d). SEX (♂+♂)+(♀) pa. HAB grassy places. SOIL moist; not acid. SHADE nil–light. ALT sl–1000. DIST E5, W5, S5, I5. RANGE F5, G5, S3.
See p. 186, 245.

● **Wild angelica**
Angelica sylvestris
Tall–v.tall. Stems hollow, purplish; lvs 2–3-pinnate, stalks inflated around stem; umbels large, with no or few bracts. LH perenn. GERM spr–sum. FL 7–9. POLL ins(h, d, c). SEX (♀) pa. HAB fens, meadows, woods. SOIL wet–damp; not acid. SHADE nil–heavy. ALT sl–800. DIST E5, W5, S5, I5. RANGE F5, G5, S5.

○ **Garden angelica**
Angelica archangelica
Tall–v.tall. Like Angelica but stems green and fls greenish-white; fr with corky wings. LH perenn. GERM spr–sum. FL 7–9. POLL ins. SEX (♀). HAB disturbed ground, riversides, marshes. SOIL damp–moist; not acid. SHADE nil–light. ALT sl–100. DIST naturalised E2. RANGE eF1, G2, S4.

● **Hemlock**
Conium maculatum
Tall–v.tall. Stem purple-dotted; lvs 3–4-pinnate, strong-smelling, poisonous; fr rounded, ridged. LH bienn or winter ann. GERM aut. FL 6–8. POLL ins. SEX (♀). HAB disturbed ground, near water. SOIL damp–moist; not acid. SHADE nil–light. ALT sl–250. DIST E5, W4, S3, I3. RANGE F5, G5, sS3.
See p. 240, 276.

● **Fine-leaved water dropwort**
Oenanthe aquatica
Mid–v.tall. Spreading, bushy, hollow-stemmed; lvs feathery, 3–4-pinnate; umbels opposite lvs. LH short-lived perenn; stolons. GERM spr. FL 6–9. POLL ins(h, d, c). SEX (♂+♂) pa. HAB still water, often dry in summer. SOIL water–damp; not acid. SHADE nil–mid. ALT sl–200. DIST E3, W2, S1, I2. RANGE F4, G4, sS3.
See p. 167. **ss114**

● **Hemlock water dropwort**
Oenanthe crocata
Tall–v.tall. Poisonous; stems ridged; lvs 3–4-pinnate, stalks enfolding stem; upper and lower bracts obvious. LH perenn. GERM spr–sum. FL 6–8. POLL ins. SEX (♂+♂) pa. HAB ditches, wet grass-land. SOIL water–damp; not calc. SHADE nil–light. ALT sl–300. DIST wE4, eE2, W4, S2, I3. RANGE wF3.
See p. 276.

● **Tubular water dropwort**
Oenanthe fistulosa
Mid. Greyish; lvs 1-pinnate, with gutter-like stalks, segments narrow; umbels becoming spherical in fr. LH perenn; root tubers. GERM aut–spr. FL 6–9. POLL ins(c, d, h). SEX (♂+♂) pa. HAB shallow water, marshes, wet grassland. SOIL water–damp; acid–calc. SHADE nil. ALT sl–150. DIST seE4, nwE2, W2, S1, I2. RANGE F3, G3, sS1.

○ **Parsley water dropwort**
Oenanthe lachenalii
Mid–tall. Lvs 2-pinnate, with narrow segments; umbels with slender branches; fr small, 2mm, egg-shaped. LH perenn; rootstock. GERM sum. FL 6–9. POLL ins. SEX (♂+♂) pa. HAB marshes, fens. SOIL wet–damp; not acid. SHADE nil. ALT sl–100. DIST E3, W2, S1, I2. RANGE F2, G2, sS1.
ss115. ss116

○ **Greater water parsnip**
Sium latifolium
V.tall. Stems hollow, ridged; lvs 1-pinnate, lflts large; submerged lvs feathery; umbels with leaf-like bracts beneath. LH perenn; rootstock. GERM spr–sum. FL 6–8. POLL ins(c, d, h). SEX (♀). HAB ponds, ditches, fens, marshes. SOIL water–wet; not acid. SHADE nil. ALT sl–150. DIST sE2, W1, I1. RANGE F3, G3, sS3.
See p. 216, 265.

○ **Cowbane**
Cicuta virosa
Tall–v.tall. Poisonous; stems ridged, hollow; lvs 2–3-pinnate; umbels large, spreading; fr small, rounded. LH perenn; rootstock. GERM sum. FL 7–8. POLL ins(d, h). SEX (♀ + ♂). HAB ditches, marshes, water-margins. SOIL wet; acid–calc. SHADE nil–light. ALT sl–150. DIST E1, W1, S1, I1. RANGE F1, G3, S3.

○ **Cambridge milk parsley**
Selinum carvifolia
Mid–tall. Stems hollow, strongly ridged; lvs 2–3-pinnate, finely pointed; fl-stalks rough; fr rounded. LH perenn; rootstock. GERM spr. FL 7–10. POLL ins. SEX (♀). HAB fens, grassland. SOIL wet–damp; calc. SHADE nil. ALT sl–100. DIST E1. RANGE F3, G3, sS3.

● **Lesser water parsnip**
Berula erecta
Mid–tall. Weak-stemmed; lvs 1-pinnate, lflts large, 7 or more pairs; umbels opposite lvs; fr spherical. LH perenn; stolons. GERM spr. FL 7–9. POLL ins(h, d, c). SEX (♀). HAB ditches, ponds, marshes. SOIL water–wet; acid–calc. SHADE nil. ALT sl–200. DIST E4, W2, S2, I3. RANGE F5, G5, sS1.
See p. 216, 265.

● **Wild celery**
Apium graveolens
Mid. Stem ridged; lvs yellowish, celery-scented, 1-pinnate, lflts toothed; umbels often unstalked, with no bracts. LH bienn. GERM aut–spr. FL 6–8. POLL ins;d). self. SEX (♀) pa. HAB mainly coastal meadows. SOIL damp; saline. SHADE nil. ALT sl. DIST coastal E4, W2, S1, I3; inland E1. RANGE coastal F5, G4, sS1; inland F1, G2.

● **Fool's watercress**
Apium nodiflorum
Low–mid, prostrate. Trailing; lvs 1-pinnate, watercress-like; lflts toothed; umbels un-stalked, opposite lvs; fr rounded; rooting nodes. GERM spr–sum. FL 6–9. POLL ins(h, d, c). SEX (♀). HAB streams, ditches, muddy ponds. SOIL water; not acid. SHADE nil. ALT sl–250. DIST E4, W4, S2, I5. RANGE F5, wG2.
ss117. ss118.

○ **Stone parsley**
Sison amomum
Tall. Foul-smelling, purple-tinged, slender-stemmed; lvs 1-pinnate, lflts toothed; bracts beneath and within umbels. LH bienn or short-lived perenn. GERM ? FL 7–9. POLL ins. SEX (♀). HAB grassy places. SOIL moist–dry; not acid. SHADE nil. ALT sl–200. DIST sE4, W1. RANGE F4.
ss119.

○ **Milk parsley**
Peucedanum palustre
Tall–v.tall. Stems short, hollow; lvs 2–4-pinnate; bracts beneath umbels narrow, down-turned. Fr rounded. LH bienn or short-lived perenn. GERM spr–sum. FL 7–9. POLL ins(h, d, c, l). SEX (♀ + ♂) pa. HAB marshes, fens. SOIL damp; calc. SHADE nil–mid. ALT sl–100. DIST E1. RANGE F2, G3, S4.
ss120.

○ **Masterwort**
Peucedanum ostruthium
Mid–v.tall. Lvs trefoil, with swollen sheaths round hollow stem; lflts broad; flhds 50–100mm across. LH perenn; rootstock. GERM spr? FL 6–7. POLL ins. SEX (♀). HAB grassland. SOIL moist–damp; acid–calc. SHADE nil. ALT 100–400. DIST E2, S2. RANGE eF1, G2, sS2.

Sermountain
Laserpitum latifolium
Tall–v.tall. Lvs 1–2-pinnate, sometimes trefoil; lflts inflated round stem; bracts beneath umbels down-turned. LH perenn; rootstock. GERM ? FL 6–8. POLL ins(h, d, c). SEX (♀). HAB rocks, shady places. SOIL moist–dry; not acid. SHADE nil–mid. ALT [sl–2000]. RANGE F2, G4, sS3.

● **Scots lovage**
Ligusticum scoticum
Short–tall. Stems reddish, lvs deep glossy green, 2-trefoil; lflts broad, toothed; stalks inflated round stem. LH perenn; rootstock. GERM ? FL 6–8. POLL ins. SEX (♀). HAB coastal rocks. SOIL dry; acid–calc. SHADE nil. ALT sl. DIST coastal: S4, nI2. RANGE coastal: S3.

● **Wild parsnip**
Pastinaca sativa
Mid–tall. Stems hollow, ridged; lvs rough, 1-pinnate; lflts broad, toothed; fls yellow; fr winged. LH bienn. GERM spr. FL 7–8. POLL ins(d, h). SEX (♀+♂) pa. HAB disturbed and grassy ground. SOIL dry; calc. SHADE nil. ALT sl–250. DIST seE4, nwE2, W2, S2, I3. RANGE F4, G4, S3.
See p. 245.

● **Alexanders**
Smyrnium olusatrum
Tall–v.tall. Lvs 3-trefoil, deep dark glossy green; stalks inflated around stem; fls yellow, in dense umbels. LH bienn. GERM spr. FL 4–6. POLL ins. SEX (♀). HAB hedges, woods, waste ground, mainly by sea. SOIL moist; acid–calc. SHADE nil–mid. ALT sl. DIST naturalised: E3, W3, S1, I3. RANGE naturalised: F2, G1.
See p. 278.

● **Rock samphire**
Crithmum maritimum
Short. Fleshy; lvs 1–2-pinnate with finger-like lobes; fls yellow; bracts beneath umbel. LH perenn; woody stem-base. GERM spr. FL 6–9. POLL ins. SEX (♀). HAB sea-cliffs. SOIL dry; acid–calc. SHADE nil. ALT sl–200. DIST coastal: swE5, neE1, W4, S1, I4. RANGE coastal: F4.

● **Fennel**
Foeniculum vulgare
Tall. Strong-smelling. Lvs greyish, 3–4-pinnate, feathery; fls yellow; no bracts beneath umbels. LH bienn or short-lived perenn. GERM aut–spr. FL 7–9. POLL ins. SEX (♀). HAB disturbed ground, mainly near sea. SOIL moist–dry; not acid. SHADE nil. ALT sl–150. DIST sE3, nE1, W3, S1, I2. RANGE F3, G2.

● **Pepper saxifrage**
Silaum silaus
Mid–tall. Lvs 2–3-pinnate, segments narrow, finely toothed; fls dull yellow; no bracts beneath umbel. LH perenn; rootstock. GERM spr. FL 6–9. POLL ins(h). SEX (♀). HAB grassland. SOIL damp–moist; acid–calc. SHADE nil. ALT sl–300. DIST E4, W1, S1. RANGE F4, G3.

WINTERGREEN FAMILY
Pyrolaceae
Evergreen herbs, with usually rounded, often slightly leathery leaves and 5-petalled flowers with a conspicuous central style. Dependent on an associated mycorrhizal fungus, and often in deep shade.
See p. 259, 298.

BIRD'S-NEST FAMILY
Monotropaceae
Like wintergreens but with no green chlorophyll, and so wholly dependent on mycorrhiza. Can grow in shade too deep for green plants.
(Yellow bird's-nest).

DIAPENSIA FAMILY
Diapensiaceae
A small family represented here by a single species.
(Diapensia).

○ **One-flowered wintergreen**
Moneses uniflora
Low. Lvs rounded, in a loose rosette; fls 12–15mm, solitary, nodding; style straight. LH perenn; evergreen, rhizome. GERM ? FL 5–7. POLL ins(h, d, c); self. SEX (♀) hg. HAB coniferous woods. SOIL damp–moist; not calc. SHADE light–heavy. ALT sl–100. DIST S1. RANGE eF1, G3, S4.

○ **Toothed wintergreen**
Orthilia secunda
Low. Lvs oval, yellowish, in rosettes; fls greenish, 5mm, along one side of spike; style protruding. LH perenn; evergreen, rhizome. GERM ? FL 6–8. POLL ins. SEX (♀) pg. HAB woods, mountain rocks. SOIL damp–moist; acid–calc. SHADE nil–heavy. ALT 50–700. DIST nE1, W1, S2, I1. RANGE eF1, G4, S5.
See p. 265.

○ **Intermediate wintergreen**
Pyrola media
Short. Lvs rounded, deep green, in rosette; fls 10mm, cup-shaped, in a loose spike, petals pinkish; style longer than fl. LH perenn; evergreen, rhizome. GERM ? FL 6–8. POLL ins(h, d); self. SEX (♀) hg. HAB woods, wet moors. SOIL damp–moist, not calc. SHADE nil–mid. ALT sl–500. DIST nE1, W1, S3, nI1. RANGE eF1, G2, S3.

81

● **Common wintergreen**
Pyrola minor
Short. Lvs oval, pale green, in rosette; fls 5–8mm, cup-shaped, pinkish, in a dense spike; style shorter than fl. LH perenn; evergreen, rhizome. GERM spr. FL 6–8. POLL ins(h, d); self. SEX (♀) pa–hg. HAB woods, moors, rocks. SOIL damp–dry; acid–calc. SHADE nil–heavy. ALT sl–x200. DIST E2, W1, S3, I2. RANGE F2, G4, S5.
See p. 266.

○ **Round-leaved wintergreen**
Pyrola rotundifolia
Short. Lvs rounded, glossy green, long-stalked; fls x2–15mm, flat, white, in a loose spike; style curved. LH perenn; evergreen, rhizome. GERM ? FL 6–9. POLL ins(h, d); self. SEX (♀) pa. HAB woods, dune-slacks, fens, bogs. SOIL wet–moist; not acid. SHADE nil–mid. ALT sl–750. DIST E2, Wx, S2, I1. RANGE eF2, G3, S3.

Yellow wintergreen
Pyrola chlorantha
Low–short. Lvs all in rosette, elliptical, long-stalked, evenly toothed; fls with prominent curved style. LH perenn; rootstock. GERM ? spr. FL 6–7. POLL ins. SEX (♀) HAB woods. SOIL damp–moist; acid. SHADE mid–heavy. ALT [sl–800]. RANGE eF1, G3, S4.

○ **Diapensia**
Diapensia lapponica
V.low–low. Cushion-forming dwarf shrub with small, crowded, leathery lvs, and fls 10–20mm. LH perenn; shrub. GERM ? FL 5–6. POLL ins(d). SEX (♀) pg. HAB mountain rocks, moors. SOIL moist–dry; acid. SHADE nil. ALT 800. DIST S1. RANGE S3.

○ **Yellow bird's-nest**
Monotropa hypopitys
Low–short. Whole plant pale brownish-yellow; lvs reduced to scales; fls 10–15mm in nodding spikes, becoming upright in fr. LH perenn; rootstock. GERM ? FL 6–8. POLL ins(h, c). SEX (♀) hg. HAB beech and pine woods; dune-slacks. SOIL moist–dry; acid–calc. SHADE nil–deep. ALT sl–200(–400). DIST E2, W1, S1, I1. RANGE F3, G4, sS3.
See p. 222, 230.

HEATHER FAMILY
Ericaceae
Shrubs with evergreen, often leathery or needle-like leaves and typically bell-shaped flowers. Characteristic of infertile soils, both dry (heaths) and wet (bogs). Associated with a unique sort of mycorrhizal fungus.
See p. 18.

CROWBERRY FAMILY
Empetraceae
Very like, and sometimes included in, the Heath family, but flowers flat, and petals and sepals similar. (Crowberry).

● **Heather**
Calluna vulgaris
Short–mid. Woody, evergreen; lvs very narrow, in dense rows, margins rolled down; sepals longer than, but same colour as, petals. LH perenn; woody. GERM aut–spr. FL 7–9. POLL ins(h, d, l); wind. SEX (♀) pa. HAB heaths, moors, bogs, pine-woods. SOIL wet–dry; acid. SHADE nil–light. ALT sl–1000. DIST E4, W5, S5, I5. RANGE F4, G5, S5.
See p. 18, 176, 177, 207, 248, 257, 258.

○ **Dorset heath**
Erica ciliaris
Short–mid. Woody evergreen; lvs oval, in whorls of 3; fls 8–10mm, flask-shaped, deep pink. LH perenn; woody. GERM spr. FL 6–9. POLL ins(h, d, l). SEX (♀). HAB heaths. SOIL dry; acid. SHADE nil. ALT sl–100. DIST sE1, I1. RANGE wF2.

● **Bell heather**
Erica cinerea
Short–mid. Woody evergreen, with lfy short shoots; lvs narrow, in whorls of 3; fls 5–6mm, purple-red, almost spherical. LH perenn; woody. GERM spr. FL 7–9. POLL ins (h, d, l); self. SEX (♀) pg. HAB heaths, moors. SOIL moist–dry; acid. SHADE nil–1250. DIST E3, W4, S5, I4. RANGE F4, wW1.
See p. 273, 285.

● **Cross-leaved heath**
Erica tetralix
Low–mid. Woody evergreen; lvs greyish, edges rolled right under, in whorls of 4; fls 6–7mm, open flask-shaped, pale pink. LH perenn; woody. GERM ins(h); self. SEX (♀) pa. HAB bogs, wet heaths and moors. SOIL wet–moist; acid. SHADE nil. ALT sl–700. DIST E3, W4, S5, I4. RANGE F3, nG3, swS3.
ss121. ss122.

○ **Cornish heath**
Erica vagans
Mid–tall. Woody evergreen; lvs narrow, in whorls of 4–5; fls long-stalked, 3–4mm, bell-shaped, on lfy stalks. LH perenn; woody. GERM ? FL 7–8. POLL ins(h, d, l). SEX (♀). HAB heaths. SOIL dry; acid. SHADE nil. ALT sl–100. DIST swE1. RANGE wF2. **ss123**.

○ **Mountain heath**
Phyllodoce caerulea
Low. Lvs very narrow, like spruce tree; fls bell-shaped, nodding on long stalks, in clusters of 2–6. LH perenn; shrub. GERM ? FL 6–7. POLL ins. SEX (♀). HAB moors, rocks. SOIL dry; acid. SHADE nil. ALT 750. DIST S1. RANGE S4.

○ **Bog rosemary**
Andromeda polifolia
Low–short, creeping. Hairless dwarf shrub; lvs narrow, shiny grey on top; fls 5–7mm, bell-shaped on long erect stalks. LH perenn; woody. GERM aut (following shedding). FL 5–7. POLL ins(h, l). SEX (♀) hg. HAB bogs. SOIL wet; acid. SHADE nil. ALT sl–500. DIST nE2, W1, sS1, I2. RANGE F1, G3, S5.

Arctic rhododendron
Rhododendron lapponicum
Low–mid. Lvs oval, leathery, rusty-hairy underneath; fls bell-shaped, reddish-violet. LH perenn; woody, evergreen. GERM ? FL 6–7. POLL ins. SEX (♀). HAB heaths, rocks. SOIL moist–dry; not acid. SHADE nil. ALT [600–2000]. RANGE S2.

● **Bilberry**
Vaccinium myrtillus
Short–mid. Deciduous dwarf shrub; stems green, ridged; lvs oval, grass-green; fls 6–8mm, pink, flask-shaped, hanging; fr a black berry. LH perenn; woody. GERM aut–spr. FL 4–7. POLL ins(h, d, l); self. SEX (♀) pa. HAB heaths, moors, woods. SOIL moist–dry; acid. SHADE nil–mid. ALT sl–1250. DIST seE2, nwE4, W5, S5, I4. RANGE F3, G5, S5. *See p. 258.*

○ **Northern bilberry**
Vaccinium uliginosum
Short–mid. Deciduous dwarf shrub; stems round, brown; lvs bluish-green; fls 4–5mm, flask-shaped; fr a black berry. LH perenn; woody. GERM spr–sum. FL 5–6. POLL ins(h, l); self. SEX (♀) pa. HAB moors. SOIL moist–dry; acid. SHADE nil. ALT (100–)400–1000. DIST nE1, S3. RANGE eF1, G3, S5.

○ **Cranberry**
Vaccinium oxycoccus
Low; creeping. Rooting dwarf shrub; lvs small, dark green, well-spaced; fl 8–10mm, petal lobes bent back, stamens pointing forwards; fr a red berry. LH perenn; woody. GERM spr. FL 6–8. POLL ins(h); self. SEX (♀) pa. HAB bogs. SOIL wet–damp; acid. SHADE nil. ALT sl–750. DIST sE1, nE3, W2, S3, I2. RANGE F1, G3, S4. *See p. 258.* **ss124**.

● **Cowberry**
Vaccinium vitis-idaea
Low–short. Evergreen dwarf shrub; lvs glossy, dark green; fls 5–6mm, pale pink, bell-shaped; fr a red berry. LH perenn; woody. GERM sum. FL 6–8. POLL ins(h); self. SEX (♀) hg. HAB moors, pine-woods. SOIL moist–dry; acid. SHADE nil–mid. ALT (50–)300–1100. DIST sE1, nE3, W2, S4, I2. RANGE eF2, G4, S5. *See p. 258.*

○ **Bearberry**
Arctostaphylus uva-ursi
Low; creeping. Rooting evergreen dwarf shrub; lvs dark green, leathery; fls pink, 4–6mm, bell-shaped; fr a red berry. LH perenn; woody. GERM spr. FL 4–7. POLL ins(h); self. SEX (♀) pa. HAB moors, pine-woods. SOIL dry; acid. SHADE nil–light. ALT (sl–)200–900. DIST nE1, S3, nI1. RANGE eF1, G2, S4.

○ **Black bearberry**
Arctous alpina
Low; creeping. Deciduous dwarf shrub, much branched; lvs bright green; fls white, 4mm; fr a black berry. LH perenn; woody. GERM spr–sum. FL 5–8. POLL ins(h); self. SEX (♀) pg. HAB rocky moors. SOIL moist; acid. SHADE nil. ALT (100–)300–800. DIST nS2. RANGE eF1, sG2, S4.

83

○ **Wild azalea**
*Loiseleuria
procumbens*
V.low–low; creeping.
Mat-forming, ever-
green dwarf shrub; lvs
small, leathery, in
pairs; fls 4–5mm, flat,
in dense clusters. LH
perenn; woody. GERM
spr–sum. FL 5–7. POLL
ins(d, h, l). SEX (♀) pg,
later hg. HAB stony
mountain heaths. SOIL
dry; not calc. SHADE
nil. ALT 500–1100. DIST
S3. RANGE S3.

Cassiope
Cassiope hypnoides
V.low–low; creeping.
Mossy, mat-forming,
evergreen dwarf
shrub; lvs cypress-like
on stems; fls bell-
shaped, long-stalked,
white with pink sepals.
LH perenn; woody.
GERM spr–sum. FL 6–8.
POLL ins(h, l). SEX (♀).
HAB mountain heaths.
SOIL moist–dry; acid–
calc. SHADE nil. ALT
[1000–3000]. RANGE
S3.

Arctic cassiope
Cassiope tetragona
Low–short. More
upright than Cassiope,
with 4 ranks of tiny
oval lvs up stems; fl-
stalks downy. LH
perenn; evergreen.
GERM ? FL 7. POLL ins.
SEX (♀). HAB heaths,
stony ground. SOIL
dry; calc. SHADE nil.
ALT [sl–1000]. RANGE
nS2.

○ **Labrador tea**
Ledum palustre
Short–tall. Evergreen
shrub, resembling
dwarf rhododendron;
stem and leathery lvs
with rusty down; fls
with 5 separate petals.
LH perenn; woody.
GERM spr. FL 5–7. POLL
ins(h, l). SEX (♀). HAB
bogs, woods. SOIL
wet–damp; acid–calc.
SHADE nil–mid. ALT
100[–500]. DIST E1, S1.
RANGE G1, S3.

● **Crowberry**
Empetrum nigrum
Low–short; creeping.
Evergreen dwarf shrub,
mat-forming and
rooting; lvs narrow,
edges rolled under,
clothing stem; fls
1–2mm, flat, 1–3
together at lf-junc-
tions; fr a black berry.
LH perenn; woody.
GERM sum. FL 4–6.
POLL ins(h, d, l); wind.
SEX (♂) + (♀). HAB
moors, dry bogs and
stony mountain heaths.
SOIL moist–dry; acid.
SHADE nil. ALT sl–800.
DIST sE1, nE3, W2,
S4, I2. RANGE eF1, G2,
S3.
See p. 243, ss125.

**PRIMROSE
FAMILY**
Primulaceae
Mostly perennial
herbs, with mainly un-
divided oval or oblong
leaves. Flowers 5-
petalled, flat, some-
times with a tube in
the centre. Fruit a dry
capsule. Mainly plants
of undisturbed
habitats. Some have
heterostylous flowers
(see p. 269) in which
various individuals
have stamens and
styles of different but
complementary
lengths.
*See p. 18, 19, 211, 257,
266, 269.*

○ **Bird's-eye primrose**
Primula farinosa
V.low–low. Lvs in
rosette, broadest near
tip, white beneath; fls
8–12mm, magenta, in
a cluster on a common
stalk; petals deeply
notched. LH perenn;
lf-rosette. GERM spr.
FL 5–7. POLL ins(h, l).
SEX (♀) heterostylous.
HAB grassland. SOIL
damp; calc. SHADE nil.
ALT sl–500. DIST nE2,
See p. 258, 266.

○ **Scottish primrose**
Primula scotica
V.low–low. Lvs in
rosette, broadest in
middle, white beneath;
fls 6–9mm, purple;
petals slightly notched;
sepal teeth blunt. LH
short-lived perenn;
rosette. GERM ? FL 5–9
in two spells. POLL
ins(h). SEX (♀). HAB
grassland. SOIL damp;
not acid. SHADE nil.
ALT sl–50. DIST nS1.
See p. 266.

○ **Oxlip**
Primula elatior
Short. Lvs hairy,
sharply distinguished
from stalk, in rosette;
fls 15–18mm, long-
stalked in a cluster
atop a common stalk;
pale yellow. LH perenn;
rhizome. GERM spr. FL
4–5. POLL ins(h, l);
self. SEX (♀) hetero-
stylous. HAB woods.
SOIL damp; calc.
SHADE light–heavy. ALT
50–150. DIST eE1.
RANGE eF3, G4, sS1.
See p. 266.

● **Cowslip**
Primula veris
Low–short. Lvs
downy, like Oxlip, in
rosette; fls 10–15mm,
orange-yellow, short-
stalked, in a cluster
atop a common stalk;
hybridises with
Primrose. LH perenn;
rhizome. GERM spr. FL
4–5. POLL ins(h, l). SEX
(♀) heterostylous. HAB
grassland, scrub. SOIL
dry; not acid. SHADE
nil–light. ALT sl–400
(–750). DIST E4, W3,
S2, I2. RANGE F4, G4,
S3.
See p. 266, 278.

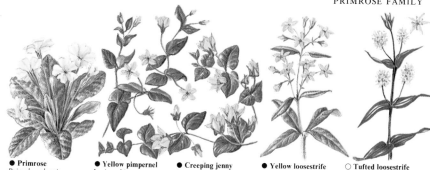

● **Primrose**
Primula vulgaris
Low. Lvs almost hair-
less, narrowing to
stalk, in rosette; fls
25–30mm, long-
stalked; common stalk
not seen; hybrid with
cowslips resembles
oxlip. LH perenn;
rhizome. GERM spr;
seeds dispersed by ants.
FL (12–)3–5(–6). POLL
ins(h, l); self. SEX (♀)
heterostylous. HAB
woods, scrub, banks,
cliffs. SOIL moist; acid–
calc. SHADE nil–heavy.
ALT sl–400(–800). DIST
E4, W5, S4, I4. RANGE
F4, G2, wS1.
See p. 2, 18, 198, 253.

● **Yellow pimpernel**
Lysimachia nemorum
V.low–low; creeping.
Lvs oval, pointed, in
opposite pairs; fls 10–
15mm, flat, on long,
thin stalks, singly at
lf-junctions; sepal-
teeth narrow. LH
perenn; rooting nodes.
GERM spr–sum. FL 5–9.
POLL ins(h, d); self.
SEX (♀) hg. HAB woods,
shady places. SOIL
damp–moist; acid–
calc. SHADE light–
heavy. ALT sl–600
(–800). DIST E4, W5,
S4, I4. RANGE F3, G3,
sS1.

● **Creeping jenny**
Lysimachia nummularia
Low; creeping. Lvs
rounded, often heart-
shaped, pointed, in
opposite pairs; fls
15–25mm, bell-
shaped; stalks thick,
shorter than lvs; sepal-
teeth oval. LH perenn;
rooting nodes. GERM
spr. FL 6–8. POLL
ins(h, d); self. SEX (♀)
hg. HAB meadows,
woods. SOIL damp–
moist; not acid. SHADE
nil–mid. ALT sl–200.
DIST E4, W3, sS2, I2.
RANGE F4, G5, sS3.

● **Yellow loosestrife**
Lysimachia vulgaris
Tall–v.tall. Lvs spear-
shaped in whorls of 3,
sometimes 2 or 4; fls
15–20mm in long-
stalked, lfy, branching
spikes. LH perenn;
rhizome. GERM spr–
sum. FL 7–8. POLL
ins(h, d); self. SEX (♀)
hg. HAB fens, tall
grassland, damp
woods. SOIL damp–
moist; not acid. SHADE
nil–mid. ALT sl–300.
DIST E3, W2, S2, I3.
RANGE F4, G5, sS4.
See p. 210, 259.

○ **Tufted loosestrife**
Lysimachia thyrsiflora
Mid. Lvs narrow, in
opposite pairs, un-
stalked; fls in dense
balls on long stalks,
but rarely produced.
LH perenn; rhizome.
GERM spr–sum. FL 6–7.
POLL ins(h) sum. SEX (♀)
HAB marshes, lake
margins. SOIL wet–
water; not calc. SHADE
nil–mid. ALT sl–150.
DIST nE1. RANGE eF1,
G3, S3.

● **Water violet**
Hottonia palustris
Aquatic; short–mid.
Lvs submerged,
whorled, pinnate,
feathery; fls 20–25mm
in whorled spikes. LH
short-lived perenn;
rooting stems. GERM
imm. FL 5–6. POLL
ins(h). SEX (♀) hetero-
stylous. HAB ponds,
ditches. SOIL water; not
acid. SHADE nil–light.
ALT sl–100. DIST E2,
W1. RANGE F3, G4,
sS3.
*See p. 166, 203, 214,
261, 266, 274.*

● **Chickweed
wintergreen**
Trientalis europaea
Low–short. Lvs in
whorl of 5–6; stem lvs
small, few; fls long-
stalked, 5–9-petalled,
15–20mm, arising from
whorl. LH perenn;
rhizome. GERM spr.
FL 5–8. POLL ins, self.
SEX (♀) pg. HAB
conifer woods, moors.
SOIL moist; acid.
SHADE nil–mid. ALT
(sl–)200–800. DIST
nE2, S3. RANGE eF1,
G3, S5.

● **Brookweed**
Samolus valerandi
Low–mid. Lvs blunt,
alternate up stem; fls
long-stalked, 2–4mm,
in a branching spike.
LH perenn; rhizome.
GERM spr–sum. FL 6–8.
POLL self. SEX (♀) hg.
HAB bare ground near
sea. SOIL damp; not
acid. SHADE nil. ALT
sl(–150). DIST E3, W2,
S2, I4. RANGE F2, G2,
sS2.

● **Scarlet pimpernel**
Anagallis arvensis
Low–short. Sprawling,
square-stemmed; lvs
pointed; fls 12–15mm,
scarlet or blue; sepal
teeth projecting
between petal lobes.
LH ann; sometimes
persisting. GERM spr–
sum. FL 5–10. POLL
ins, self. SEX (♀). HAB
disturbed ground,
dunes. SOIL moist–dry;
not acid. SHADE nil.
ALT sl–300. DIST E4,
W4, S2, I4. RANGE F5,
G4, sS3.

○ **Chaffweed**
Anagallis minima
V.low. Tiny; lvs oval,
alternating up stem,
almost hiding minute
pinkish fls, 1mm or
less. LH ann. GERM
aut–spr. FL 6–8. POLL
self ? SEX (♀). HAB
bare, sandy heaths.
SOIL damp–moist; acid.
SHADE nil. ALT sl–50.
DIST coastal: E3, W2,
S2, I2. RANGE F4, G3,
sS3.
See p. 188, 261.

85

SEA-LAVENDER FAMILY
Plumbaginaceae
A mainly coastal family of perennials with simple undivided leaves and 5-petalled flowers, surrounded by dry, papery bracts.

● **Bog pimpernel**
Anagallis tenella
V.low–low; creeping. Stems rooting; lvs rounded or heart-shaped; fls 10–15mm on long, slender stalks. LH perenn; rooting nodes. GERM spr–sum. FL 5–9. POLL ins, self. SEX (♀). HAB dune-slacks, bogs, fens, heaths. SOIL damp; acid–calc. SHADE nil. ALT sl–300(–500). DIST E3, W4, S3, I4. RANGE F4, wG1.

● **Sea milkwort**
Glaux maritima
Low; creeping. Lvs narrow, fleshy, opposite; fls 5mm with no petals; sepals pink; unstalked at lf-bases. LH perenn; rooting nodes. GERM sum. FL 5–9. POLL ins, self. SEX (♀) pg. HAB salt-marshes, coastal rocks. SOIL damp–moist; saline. SHADE nil. ALT sl(–100). DIST coastal: E5, W5, S4, I5. RANGE coastal, F5, G5, S4; inland, G1.
See p. 205, 248.

● **Thrift**
Armeria maritima
Low–short. Lvs v. narrow, in a dense basal cluster; fls in dense, spherical cluster, each 8–10mm. LH perenn; rootstock. GERM imm. FL 4–7(–9). POLL ins(d, l, h, c). SEX (♀) pa. HAB sea-cliffs, salt-marshes, mountain rocks. SOIL wet–dry; saline or not acid. SHADE nil. ALT sl; 300–1250. DIST coastal, E4, W5, S5, I5; inland, E1, S1. RANGE coastal, F5, G5, S3; inland, G3, S2.
See p. 249.

○ **Rock sea-lavender**
Limonium binervosum
Low–short. Lvs 3-veined, in rosette; stems branching from base, bearing 1-sided spikes of lavender-coloured fls, 8–10mm. LH perenn; rootstock. GERM ? FL 7–9. POLL ins(d, h), wind, self. SEX (♀) + (♀). HAB sea-cliffs. SOIL dry; saline. SHADE nil. ALT sl–50. DIST coastal: E2, W3, S1, I2. RANGE coastal: F2.

BOGBEAN FAMILY
Menyanthaceae
A small aquatic family, closely related to the Gentians, but with leaves alternate not in opposite pairs, and petals often falling early. Both species here have obviously fringed petals.

○ **Lax-flowered sea-lavender**
Limonium humile
Low–short. Lvs narrow, long-stalked, with pinnate veins; stems branching from below middle, with fls. 8–10mm, scattered along branches. LH perenn; rootstock. GERM spr–sum. FL 7–9. POLL ins(d, h), wind, self. SEX (♀) + (♀). HAB salt-marshes. SOIL wet; saline. SHADE nil. ALT sl. DIST coastal: E2, W2, I3. RANGE coastal: wF1, sS2.

● **Common sea-lavender**
Limonium vulgare
Low–short. Lvs narrowly eliptical, pinnate-veined; stems branching from above middle, with fls, 8–10mm, in dense flat-topped clusters. LH perenn; rootstock. GERM spr–sum. FL 7–9. POLL ins(d, h), wind, self. SEX (♀) + (♀). HAB salt-marshes. SOIL wet; saline. SHADE nil. ALT sl. DIST coastal: E4, W2, S1. RANGE coastal: F3, G3, sS2.
See p. 167, 249. **ss 126**

● **Bogbean**
Menyanthes trifoliata
Short (above water). Lvs with three broad lobes above water; fls 15–20mm, pink and white, fringed, in long spikes. LH perenn; rhizome. GERM spr–sum. FL 4–6. POLL ins(h, l). SEX (♀) pg, heterostylous. HAB shallow lakes, marsh and bog pools. SOIL water; acid. SHADE nil. ALT sl–700(–900). DIST E3, W4, S4, I4. RANGE F3, G4, S5.

○ **Fringed water-lily**
Nymphoides peltata
Floating. Lvs rounded, glossy dark green above, purple beneath; fls 30mm, fringed; lvs smaller than true water-lilies (p. 47). LH perenn; rhizome. GERM aut, on exposed mud. FL 6–9. POLL ins(h, l). SEX (♀) pg, hetero-stylous. HAB lakes, ponds. SOIL water; not acid. SHADE nil. ALT sl–100. DIST E1, but widely naturalised. RANGE F2, G2; naturalised S.

GENTIAN FAMILY
Gentianaceae
A well-defined family of herbaceous plants with opposite leaves and usually 4 or 5-petalled flowers joined into a tube and persisting around the fruit. Flowers are in branching clusters, often contracted into heads or whorls.
See p. 19, 210, 245, 278.

● **Common centaury**
Centaurium erythraea
V.low–mid. Lvs 3–7-veined, in rosette; a few on stem; fls 10–12mm, unstalked, in dense clusters on long, branching stalks. LH ann–bienn. GERM aut. FL 6–9. POLL ins(d, h, c); self. SEX (♀). HAB sparsely grassy places, dunes. SOIL dry; not acid. SHADE nil–light. ALT sl–250. DIST E4, W3, S2, I4. RANGE F5, G4, sS2. *See p. 259.* **ss127.**

○ **Seaside centaury**
Centaurium littorale
V.low–short. Lvs narrow, 3-veined, in rosette; fls 12–14mm, unstalked, in dense clusters. LH ann. GERM any. FL 7–8. POLL ins(d, h, c); self. SEX (♀) hg. HAB dunes, coastal sand. SOIL dry; calc. SHADE nil. ALT sl. DIST coastal: E2, W2, S2, I1. RANGE coastal: F1, G4, sS4.

○ **Lesser centaury**
Centaurium pulchellum
V.low–low. Variable: small, unbranched or larger, well-branched; lvs all on stems; fls stalked, 5–8mm in loose, branching clusters. LH ann. GERM spr–sum. FL 6–9. POLL ins(d, h, c); self. SEX (♀) hg. HAB grassland, salt-marshes. SOIL damp; not acid. SHADE nil. ALT sl. DIST sE3, nE1. W1. RANGE F5, G3, sS2. **ss128.**

● **Yellow-wort**
Blackstonia perfoliata
Short–mid. Lvs greyish, in rosette and in opposite pairs on stems; fls 10–15mm, 6–8-petalled in loose branching clusters. LH ann. GERM spr–sum. FL 6–10. POLL self. SEX (♀) hg. HAB open grassland, dunes, disturbed ground. SOIL dry; calc. SHADE nil–light. ALT sl–250. DIST sE4, nE2, W2, I2. RANGE F4, G1.

○ **Yellow centaury**
Cicendia filiformis
V.low–low. Variably branched; lvs narrow; fls 3–6mm, 4-petalled, singly on long stalks. LH ann. GERM spr–sum. FL 6–10. POLL self; fls open morning only. SEX (♀) hg. HAB open sandy and peaty ground. SOIL damp–moist; acid–calc. SHADE nil. ALT sl. DIST sE2, W1, sI2. RANGE F3, nG2.

○ **Alpine gentian**
Gentiana nivalis
Low. Slender, sometimes branched, with weak rosette; fls 15–18mm, solitary, 5-lobed. LH ann. GERM spr. FL 6–9. POLL self; ? ins. SEX (♀). HAB mountain rocks, moors. SOIL moist; calc. SHADE nil. ALT 700–1000. DIST S1. RANGE G1 (Alps), S4. *See p. 258.*

○ **Marsh gentian**
Gentiana pneumonanthe
Short. Lvs narrow, on stems, lower v. small; fls long-tubed (to 40mm) lobes scarcely spreading, green-striped outside. LH perenn; rootstock. GERM sum. FL 7–9. POLL ins(h); self; cleistogamous. SEX (♀) pa. HAB wet heaths. SOIL wet; acid. SHADE nil. ALT sl–200. DIST E2, W1. RANGE F3, G4, sS3.

○ **Spring gentian**
Gentiana verna
V.low–low. Rosette lvs making tufts; stem lvs clothing stem; fls 30–40mm, solitary, long-tubed. LH perenn; rootstock. GERM spr? FL 4–6. POLL ins(l). SEX (♀). HAB short grassland. SOIL moist–dry; calc. SHADE nil. ALT sl in I; 300–750. DIST nEl, I1. RANGE eF1, G2.

Great yellow gentian
Gentiana lutea
Tall. Large-leaved, bluish-green; fls 5–9-petalled in dense whorls above lvs clasping stem. LH perenn; rootstock. GERM spr. FL 7–9. POLL ins(d, h, l, c). SEX (♀). HAB alpine meadows. SOIL moist; acid–calc. SHADE nil. ALT [250–2500]. RANGE sF2, sG2. *See p. 213.*

Cross gentian
Gentiana cruciata
Mid. Lvs thick, narrow, oval, upper unstalked or clasping stem; fls 4-lobed in dense clusters, green outside. LH perenn. GERM ? FL 6–9. POLL ins. SEX (♀). HAB grassland, woods. SOIL moist–dry; calc. SHADE nil–mid. ALT [sl–2000]. RANGE eF2, G3.

Purple gentian
Gentiana purpurea
Short–mid. Stout-stemmed, with lf-pairs cupping clusters of purple fls, yellowish inside; petal-tube 5-8-lobed. LH perenn; rootstock. GERM ? FL 7–8. POLL ins(h). SEX (♀) pg. HAB meadows, open conifer woods. SOIL damp–moist; acid. SHADE nil–light. ALT [500–2500]. RANGE sG1, sS1.

● **Autumn gentian**
Gentianella amarella
Low–short. Lvs in rosette in first yr; flg stem produced later; fls in clusters, tube 15–20mm long, fringed at the throat, purplish. LH bienn, rarely ann. GERM spr–sum. FL 8–9. POLL ins(h); self. SEX (♀). HAB short grassland, dunes. SOIL dry; calc. SHADE nil. ALT sl–600. DIST E4, W2, S2, I3. RANGE G2, S3.

○ **Early gentian**
Gentianella anglica
Low. Very like Autumn gentian and best told by widely spaced upper lvs, upright (not spreading) sepal teeth, and earlier flg. LH bienn. GERM spr. FL 5–6. POLL ins(h); self. SEX (♀). HAB short grassland. SOIL dry; calc. SHADE nil. ALT sl–100. DIST sE2.

○ **Chiltern gentian**
Gentianella germanica
Low–mid. Like Autumn gentian but lvs broader and petal-tube longer (25–35mm), opening wider at mouth. LH ann or bienn. GERM spr. FL 9–10. POLL ins(h); self. SEX (♀). HAB short grassland, bare chalk. SOIL dry; calc. SHADE nil. ALT sl–250. DIST sE2. RANGE F3, G3.
See p. 266.

○ **Dune gentian**
Gentianella uliginosa
V.low–low. Unbranched with few lvs or with many stems, ending in long-stalked fls 10–20mm long, with unequal-sized sepal-teeth. LH ann or bienn. GERM spr. FL 8–11. POLL ins(h); self. SEX (♀). HAB dune slacks. SOIL damp; calc. SHADE nil. ALT sl. DIST sW2. RANGE F2, G2.

● **Field gentian**
Gentianella campestris
Low–short. Lvs mostly on stem; fls 15–25mm long, violet-blue, with 4-petal lobes, 2 more conspicuous than others. LH ann or bienn. GERM spr–sum. FL 7–10. POLL ins(h, l); self. SEX (♀). HAB grassland. SOIL moist–dry; not calc. SHADE nil. ALT sl–800. DIST E2, W2, S4, I2. RANGE F2, G3, S4.
See p. 244, 245.

BINDWEED FAMILY
Convolvulaceae
Climbing or creeping plants with often large, trumpet-shaped flowers. Dodders are wholly parasitic, with no green colouring, and twist round hosts; their flowers, though small, are clearly related to bindweeds.
See p. 220, 257, 296.

PHLOX FAMILY
Polemoniaceae
A small family with a single European genus, in many ways most like Gentians. (Jacob's ladder)

● **Hedge bindweed**
Calystegia sepium
Tall–v.tall. Climbing anti-clockwise, with large arrow-shaped lvs and fls 30–35mm; sepals enclosed by bracts. LH perenn; rhizome, stolons. GERM aut–sum. POLL ins(l, h); not self. SEX (♀). HAB disturbed ground, hedges, woods, fens. SOIL wet-moist; acid–calc. SHADE nil–mid. ALT sl–350. DIST E4, W4, S3, I5. RANGE F5, G5, sS3.
See p. 193, 256.

● **Great bindweed**
Calystegia sylvatica
Tall–v.tall. Very like Hedge bindweed but fls 60–75mm, sometimes pink-striped, with overlapping bracts. LH perenn; rhizome, stolons. GERM spr–sum. FL 6–9. POLL ins(l, h). SEX (♀). HAB hedges, disturbed ground. SOIL moist; not acid. SHADE nil–light. ALT sl–200. DIST and RANGE widely naturalised.

BEDSTRAW FAMILY
Rubiaceae
Distinctive family with square, often rough stems and whorls of narrow, pointed leaves. Flowers in clusters, long-tubed, with 4 spreading petal lobes. Fruit usually 2-lobed.
See p. 187, 210, 257.

● **Sea bindweed**
Calystegia soldanella
Low; creeping. Lvs thick, kidney-shaped, long-stalked; fls 25–40mm, pink, striped white; sepals longer than bracts. LH perenn; rhizomes. GERM spr? FL 6–8. POLL ins(h). SEX (♀). HAB sand-dunes. SOIL dry; calc. SHADE nil. ALT sl. DIST coastal: E3, W4, S2, I2. RANGE coastal: F4, G3.
See p. 205.

● **Field bindweed**
Convolvulus arvensis
Mid–tall or creeping. Twines anti-clockwise (*cf* Black Bindweed, p. 33); lvs arrow-shaped; fls 20–30mm, with small bracts beneath sepals. LH perenn; rhizome. GERM aut. FL 6–9. POLL ins(d, h); self. SEX (♀) hg. HAB disturbed ground. SOIL moist–dry; acid–calc. SHADE nil. ALT sl–250. DIST E5, W5, S3, I4. RANGE F5, G5, sS4.

● **Common dodder**
Cuscuta epithymum
Tall; climbing. Red stems twine anti-clockwise round host, bearing clusters of pink, bell-shaped fls, 5–10mm, with pointed lobes. LH ann, sometimes persisting. GERM spr. FL 6–10. POLL ins(h); self. SEX (♀). HAB heaths; on gorse, heather and other plants. SOIL dry; acid. SHADE nil. ALT sl–200. DIST E3, W2, S1, I2. RANGE F3, G3, sS3.
See p. 220. **ss129**.

○Jacob's ladder
Polemonium caeruleum
Mid–tall. Lvs pinnate, with pointed lflts; fls 20–30mm, with prominent stamens and styles. LH perenn; rhizome. GERM spr. FL 6–8. POLL ins(h). SEX (♀)+(♀) pa. HAB grassy and rocky places. SOIL moist; calc. SHADE nil–mid. ALT 150–600. DIST nE2; and widely naturalised. RANGE eF1, G2, S3; and naturalised.

● **Field madder**
Sherardia arvensis
Low–short. More or less prostrate; lvs prickly in whorls of 4–6; fls 3–4mm, almost hidden by long bracts; sepals 4–6, enlarging in fr. LH ann. GERM imm. FL 5–9. POLL ins(d, h); self. SEX (♀)+(♀) pa. HAB disturbed ground, grassland. SOIL moist; not acid. SHADE nil. ALT sl–350. DIST E4, W4, S2, I3. RANGE F5, G5, sS3.

● **Squinancywort**
Asperula cynanchica
Low–short. Weak-stemmed; branching; lvs v.narrow, in 4s, some short; fls 3–4mm, pink out, white inside. LH perenn; rootstock. GERM spr. FL 6–9. POLL ins(d); self. SEX (♀)+(♀) pa–hg. HAB short grassland. SOIL dry; calc. SHADE nil. ALT sl–300. DIST sE3, nE1, W2, I2. RANGE F4, G3.

○ **Blue woodruff**
Asperula arvensis
Low–short. Lvs v. narrow in well-separated whorls of 6–9; fls 4mm, bright blue, in tight heads, surrounded by long bracts. LH ann. GERM ? SEX (♀). HAB disturbed ground. SOIL moist–dry; not acid. SHADE nil. ALT [sl–600]. DIST casual. RANGE F3, G3.

● **Woodruff**
Galium odoratum
Short–mid. Patch-forming; stems unbranched, with lvs in 6–9's, prickly; fls 5–6mm in terminal clusters; fr bristly. LH perenn; rhizome. GERM win–spr. FL 4–6. POLL ins(d, h); self. SEX (♀) pa–hg. HAB woods. SOIL moist; calc. SHADE mid–heavy. ALT sl–300(–650). DIST E4, W5, S4, I3. RANGE F4, G5, S3.

● **Hedge bedstraw**
Galium mollugo
Mid–tall. Much branched, often scrambling; lvs in 6–8's, prickly; fls 3–4mm in loose clusters; fr black. GERM aut–spr. FL 6–9. POLL ins(d, c); self. SEX (♀) pa. HAB hedges, rough grassland. SOIL moist; not acid. SHADE nil–light. ALT sl–250(–400). DIST sE5, nE3, W3, S3, I2. RANGE F5, G5, S3.
See p. 263.

● **Northern bedstraw**
Galium boreale
Short–mid. Lvs in 4's,
3-veined; fls 3mm in a
terminal cluster; fr
with many hooked
bristles. LH perenn;
rhizome. GERM spr?
FL 6–8. POLL ins(d);
self. SEX (♀) pa. HAB
rocky and stony grass-
land. SOIL moist; not
acid. SHADE nil–light.
ALT sl–1000. DIST nE2,
W2, S4, I2. RANGE F2,
G4, S4.

● **Heath bedstraw**
Galium saxatile
Short; creeping. Lvs in
4–8's with forward
pointing prickles,
blackening when dry;
fls 3mm in small
clusters; fr sharply
warty. LH perenn;
rooting stems. GERM
aut. FL 6–8. POLL
ins(d, c). SEX (♀) pa.
HAB heaths, poor grass-
land. SOIL dry; acid.
SHADE nil–light. ALT
sl–1200. DIST E4, W5,
S5, I5. RANGE F4, G4,
swS3.
See p. 219.

○ **Slender bedstraw**
Galium pumilum
Short; creeping. Like
Heath bedstraw but
prickles pointing
backwards; plants
drying green; fls 4mm
in long-stalked, flat-
topped heads; fr with
blunt warts. LH
perenn; rooting stems.
GERM spr. FL 6–7. POLL
ins(d, c). SEX (♀) pa.
HAB short grassland.
SOIL dry; calc. SHADE
nil. ALT sl–250. DIST
E2. RANGE F3, G3.

○ **Limestone bedstraw**
Galium sterneri
Short; creeping. Like
Slender bedstraw, but
lvs pricklier, fls
3–4mm; fr with
pointed warts. LH
perenn; rooting stems.
GERM spr. FL 6–7. POLL
ins(d, c). SEX (♀) pa.
HAB rocky grassland.
SOIL dry; calc. SHADE
nil. ALT 150–750. DIST
nE2, W1, S2, I2.
RANGE sS2.

● **Marsh bedstraw**
Galium palustre
Mid–tall; scrambling.
Stems rough, turning
black when dry; lvs in
4–6's, blunt-tipped;
fls 3–4.5mm in loose,
spreading clusters. LH
perenn; rhizome. GERM
aut–sum. FL 6–8. POLL
ins(d, c); self. SEX
(♀) pa. HAB marshes,
fens. SOIL wet–damp;
acid calc. SHADE nil–
mid. ALT sl–600. DIST
E5, W5, S5, I5.
RANGE F5, G5, S4.
ss130.

● **Fen bedstraw**
Galium uliginosum
Short–mid. Stems
rough with down-
turned prickles, not
blackening; lvs in
6–8's, pointed-tipped;
fls 2.5–3mm in tight
clusters. LH perenn;
rhizome. GERM spr.
FL 7–8. POLL ins(d, c);
self. SEX (♀) pa. HAB
fens. SOIL wet; calc.
SHADE nil–mid. ALT
sl–500. DIST E4, W2,
S3, I2. RANGE F3, G5,
S4.

● **Lady's bedstraw**
Galium verum
Low–short; sprawling.
Blackens when dry;
lvs v. narrow, edges
rolled under, glossy
dark green, in 8–12's;
fls 2–4mm, yellow;
abundant. LH perenn;
stolons. GERM aut. FL
6–9. POLL ins(d, c);
self. SEX (♀) pa. HAB
short grassland. SOIL
dry; not acid. SHADE
nil–light. ALT sl–600.
DIST E4, W4, S4, I4.
RANGE F5, G4, S3.
See p. 210, 219.

● **Common cleavers
(Goose-grass)**
Galium aparine
Short–tall; scrambling.
Stems and lvs climbing
by many backward-
pointing prickles; lvs
in 6–8's; fls 2mm, in
stalked clusters; fr
bristly. LH ann. GERM
aut–win. FL 5–8. POLL
ins(d, c); self. SEX (♀)
pa. HAB hedges, dis-
turbed and rocky
ground. SOIL damp–dry;
acid–calc. SHADE nil–
heavy. ALT sl–450.
DIST E5, W5, S5, I5.
RANGE F5, G5, S3.
See p. 172, 192, 237.
ss131. ss132.

○ **Wild madder**
Rubia peregrina
Short–v.tall; scramb-
ling. Stem woody at
base, prickly above;
lvs oval, leathery, in
4–6's; fls 5mm, in
loose clusters; fr a
black berry. LH
perenn; rhizome. GERM
spr? FL 6–8. POLL
ins(d, c). SEX (♀) HAB
scrub, stony ground.
SOIL dry; acid–calc.
SHADE nil–mid. ALT
sl–250. DIST swE2, W2,
I2. RANGE wF2.

● **Crosswort**
Cruciata laevipes
Short–mid. Lvs
yellowish, hairy,
3-veined, in 4's; fls
2–3mm, pale greenish-
yellow; fr stalks bent
down. LH perenn;
rhizome. GERM spr. FL
4–6. POLL ins(d, c).
SEX (♀+♂) pa. HAB
grassland, scrub. SOIL
moist; acid–calc.
SHADE nil–light. ALT
sl–350(–500). DIST E4,
W4, S3. RANGE F3, G4.
See p. 271.

BORAGE FAMILY
Boraginaceae
Nearly all are roughly hairy, with undivided leaves. Flowers have either a long tube with a more or less bell-shaped upper part, or a short tube and 5 spreading petal-lobes, as in forget-me-nots. Buds often pink, flowers often blue. Flower spikes usually 1-sided, coiled initially. *See p. 256, 266, 279.*

● **Common comfrey**
Symphytum officinale
Mid–tall. Massive, clumped; lvs broad, running into winged stems; fls 15mm long, cream or purple, with long sepal-teeth. LH perenn; rootstock. GERM any. FL 5–6. POLL ins(h). SEX (♀) hg. HAB streamsides, fens. SOIL damp; not acid. SHADE nil–light. ALT sl–100 (–300). DIST E4, W4, S3, I2. RANGE F5, G5, sS3.
See p. 241, 266.

● **Russian comfrey**
Symphytum × uplandicum
Mid–tall. A hybrid involving Common comfrey, and differing in its less winged stems and always purple-blue fls. LH perenn; rootstock. GERM ? FL 6–8. POLL ins? SEX (♀). HAB roadsides, disturbed ground. SOIL moist; acid–calc. SHADE nil. ALT sl–250. DIST and RANGE widespread.

● **Houndstongue**
Cynoglossum officinale
Mid–tall. Lvs grey with silky hairs, narrow; fls 10mm, maroon, in clusters lengthening in fr; fr with hooked spines. LH bienn. GERM spr. FL 5–8. POLL ins. SEX (♀) pg. HAB sand-dunes, grassland. SOIL dry; calc. SHADE nil–light. ALT sl–250(–400). DIST E3, W2, S2, I1. RANGE F4, G4, sS3.
See p. 283. **ss133.**

● **Amsinckia**
Amsinckia intermedia
Mid. Lvs spear-shaped, with short bristles; fls 4–6mm, orange, on outside of coiled spikes. LH ann. GERM aut. FL 5–9. POLL ins. SEX (♀). HAB disturbed ground. SOIL dry; not acid. SHADE nil. ALT sl–200. DIST introduced and spreading. RANGE introduced weed: F2, G3.

● **Corn gromwell**
Buglossoides arvense
Short–mid. Stems branching only near top; lvs oval below, upper narrower; fls 3–4mm, yellowish-white. LH ann, often overwintering. GERM aut–spr. FL 4–9. POLL ins(h, d, l); self. SEX (♀) pg. HAB arable fields. SOIL moist; not acid. SHADE nil. ALT sl–200. DIST sE4, nE2, W1. RANGE F4, G4, S3.

○ **Purple gromwell**
Buglossoides purpuro-caeruleum
Mid. Stem creeping with upright flg stems; lvs narrow; fls 12–15mm, purple at first, then blue. LH perenn; woody stem. GERM spr. FL 4–6. POLL ins(h). SEX (♀) pg. HAB woods. SOIL moist–dry; calc. SHADE light–heavy. ALT sl–200. DIST swE1, W1. RANGE F3, G2.

● **Common gromwell**
Lithospermum officinale
Mid–tall. Much-branched, with spear-shaped lvs, prominently veined; fls 3–4mm dull white, in lfy clusters. LH perenn; rootstock. GERM spr–sum. FL 5–7. POLL ins(h, d). SEX (♀). HAB open woods, scrub. SOIL dry; not acid. SHADE nil–mid. ALT sl–200. DIST sE3, nE1, W1. RANGE F3, G3, sS2.

○ **Lungwort**
Pulmonaria officinalis
Short. Lvs mostly from roots, oval, softly hairy, pale-blotched; fls 10–12mm, bluish-purple. LH perenn; rhizome. GERM spr. FL 3–5. POLL ins(h, d). SEX (♀) pa. HAB woods, hedges. SOIL damp-moist; not acid. SHADE nil–mid. ALT sl–200. DIST mostly natural-ised: E3, W3, S3. RANGE eF2, G4, sS3.
See p. 266. **ss134.**

● **Wood forget-me-not**
Myosotis sylvatica
Short–mid. Lvs ob-long, hairy; fls 5–10mm, blue, long-stalked, with hairy sepal-tube. LH perenn; rhizome. GERM spr. FL 4–7. POLL ins(h, d, l); self. SEX (♀) hg. HAB woods. SOIL damp–moist; not acid. SHADE light–heavy. ALT sl–400. DIST E3, W2, S2. RANGE eF2, G4, sS2.
ss135.

● **Field forget-me-not**
Myosotis arvensis
Short. Lvs in rosette
and on flg stem,
hairy; fls 3–5mm, dull
blue, petal-lobes
cupped; sepal tube
hairy. LH ann, some-
times persisting. GERM
spr, aut. FL 4–10. POLL
ins(d, h, l); self. SEX
(♀') hg. HAB disturbed
ground, woods. SOIL
moist–dry; acid–calc.
SHADE nil–mid. ALT
sl–200(–500). DIST E5,
W5, S5, I5. RANGE F5,
G5, S4.

● **Early forget-me-not**
Myosotis ramosissima
V.low–short. Often
tiny; lvs hairy; fls
2mm, blue, petal-tube
shorter than spreading
sepal-tube. LH ann.
GERM aut–win. FL 4–5.
POLL ins?; self. SEX
(♀'). HAB bare ground.
SOIL dry; acid–calc.
SHADE nil. ALT sl–200
(–400). DIST E4, W2,
S2, I2. RANGE F4, G4,
sS4.
See p. 244, 261.

● **Changing forget-
me-not**
Myosotis discolor
Low–short. Lvs hairy;
fls 2mm, yellow at
first, turning blue, in
coiled spikes; short-
stalked; sepal-teeth
upright. LH ann. GERM
aut. FL 5–6. POLL
ins(h, d); self. SEX (♀')
hg. HAB bare ground.
SOIL dry; not calc.
SHADE nil. ALT sl–500.
DIST E4, W3, S4, I3.
RANGE F4, G3, sS3.

● **Water forget-me-not**
Myosotis scorpioides
Short–mid. Stems
creeping then erect;
hairs on stems and
sepals few and flat-
tened; fls 5–10mm; fr
black, short-stalked.
LH perenn; rhizome,
stolons. GERM imm.
FL 6–9. POLL ins(h, d,
l). SEX (♀') hg. HAB
wet places. SOIL water–
damp; acid–calc.
SHADE nil–mid. ALT
sl–450. DIST E5, W4,
S4, I4. RANGE F5, G5,
sS4.
See p. 216, 217, 251.
ss136.

● **Creeping forget-me-
not**
Myosotis secunda
Short–mid. Resembles
Water forget-me-not,
but fls 4–6mm, sepal
teeth larger, and dark
brown fr on longer
stalks. LH perenn;
stolons. GERM imm.
FL 5–8. POLL ins(h, d).
SEX (♀') hg. HAB
marshes, peaty soils.
SOIL water–wet; not
calc. SHADE nil. ALT
sl–800. DIST E3, W4,
S4, I3. RANGE F2.

● **Tufted forget-me-not**
Myosotis laxa
Short–mid. Stems
erect, lvs almost hair-
less; fls 2–4mm, petals
rounded; sepal teeth
very long; fr dark
brown, long-stalked.
LH ann or bienn. GERM
imm. FL 5–8. POLL
ins(h, d). SEX (♀') hg.
HAB marshes, stream
sides. SOIL water–wet;
acid–calc. SHADE nil–
light. ALT sl–500. DIST
E4, W4, S4, I4. RANGE
F4, nG4, S3.

● **Viper's bugloss**
Echium vulgare
Mid–tall. Very rough-
hairy; fls 15–18mm
long, opening pink,
then blue; stamens
and style much longer
than petal-tube. LH
bienn or short-lived
perenn. GERM spr–
sum. FL 5–9. POLL
ins(h, d, l). SEX (♀'). pa.
HAB disturbed ground,
dunes. SOIL dry; not
acid. SHADE nil–mid.
ALT sl–100(–350). DIST
sE4, nE2, W2, S1, I1.
RANGE F5, G4, sS3.
See p. 299. **ss137.**

● **Green alkanet**
*Pentaglottis
sempervirens*
Mid–tall. Lvs oval,
rough with hairs; fls
10–12mm, blue, white-
centred, flat, like a
forget-me-not, in lfy
clusters. LH perenn;
rootstock. GERM aut?
FL 4–7. POLL ins. SEX
(♀'). HAB open woods;
hedges. SOIL moist; not
acid. SHADE nil–mid.
ALT sl–200. DIST sE4,
nE2, W2, S2, I2.
RANGE F2, eG1.

● **Bugloss**
Lycopsis arvensis
Short–mid. Lvs nar-
row, crinkle-edged,
with rough hairs; fls
5–6mm in dense
clusters, elongating in
fr. LH winter or spring
ann. GERM aut, spr. FL
4–9. POLL ins(h, d, l).
SEX (♀'). HAB disturbed,
sandy ground. SOIL
dry; not calc. SHADE
nil. ALT sl–200(–400).
DIST E4, W2, S3, I2.
RANGE F4, nG4, sS4.
See p. 256.

○ **Alkanet**
Anchusa officinalis
Short–mid. Lvs softly
hairy, spear-shaped;
fls 10mm in coiled
branching clusters. LH
ann, bienn or short-
lived perenn. GERM
aut–spr. FL 6–8. POLL
ins. SEX (♀'). HAB
disturbed and grassy
places. SOIL dry; not
calc. SHADE nil. ALT
[sl–300]. DIST casual.
RANGE eG2; and
casual.

○ **Oyster plant**
Mertensia maritima
V.low–low, prostrate.
Forms large blue-grey
mats; lvs hairless,
fleshy; fls 5–8mm, pink
at first, turning blue;
fr fleshy, yellowish. LH
perenn. GERM ? FL 6–8.
POLL ins?; self. SEX (♀).
HAB shingle. SOIL dry;
saline. SHADE nil. ALT
sl. DIST coastal: nE1,
S3, nI2. RANGE
coastal: nG1, wS4.
See p. 205, 266.

VERVAIN FAMILY
Verbenaceae

LABIATE FAMILY
Labiatae
Labiates are a large
family with square
stems, opposite and
often hairy and aro-
matic leaves, and 2-
lipped flowers (the
upper lip can be very
small in bugles and
germanders). The
vervain family has only
one British representa-
tive (*Verbena*) and
differs mainly in the
5-lobed petal tube.
*See p. 17, 18, 187, 210,
257, 266, 271, 283, 285.*

● **Vervain**
Verbena officinalis
Mid. Stem woody at
base, square; lvs
pinnately lobed; fls
4–5mm, in dense
spikes that elongate in
fr. LH short-lived
perenn; rootstock.
GERM aut–spr. FL 6–10.
POLL ins(h, d, l); self.
SEX (♀) hg. HAB bare
ground, roadsides.
SOIL dry; not acid.
SHADE nil. ALT sl–150.
DIST sE4, nE1, W2, I2.
RANGE F5, G4, sS2.

● **Bugle**
Ajuga reptans
Short. Stolons lfy and
rooting, forming
rosettes; flg stems lfy,
lvs shallowly toothed;
fls 1-lipped. LH perenn;
rhizome, stolons. GERM
sum–aut. FL 4–6. POLL
ins(h, l); self. SEX (♀)
hg. HAB woods, grass-
land. SOIL damp; not
acid. SHADE nil–heavy.
ALT sl–750. DIST E5,
W5, S4, I4. RANGE F5,
G5, sS2.
See p. 277, 285.

○ **Pyramidal bugle**
Ajuga pyramidalis
Short. No runners;
stem hairy all round;
lvs hairy; fls purplish-
blue, smaller than
Bugle. LH perenn;
rhizome. GERM sum.
FL 5–7. POLL ins(h);
self. SEX (♀) pa–hg.
HAB grassy and rocky
places. SOIL moist–dry;
acid–calc. SHADE nil.
ALT sl–500. DIST nE1,
nS2, wI1. RANGE F2,
G2, S4.
ss138.

● **Skullcap**
Scutellaria galericulata
Short–mid. Lvs spear-
shaped, shallowly
toothed; fls 10–20mm
long, in pairs up stem.
LH perenn; rhizome.
GERM spr–sum. FL 6–9.
POLL ins(h, d). SEX
(♂ +♀) hg. HAB
marshes, fens, river-
sides. SOIL wet–damp;
acid–calc. SHADE nil–
mid. ALT sl–400. DIST
E4, W2, S3, I2. RANGE
F5, G5, S3.
See p. 169. **ss139.**

○ **Lesser skullcap**
Scutellaria minor
Low. Delicate, with
thick stems and small,
untoothed lvs; fls
6–10mm long, spotted,
in pairs up stem. LH
perenn; rhizome.
GERM spr–sum. FL
7–10. POLL ins(h, d).
SEX (♀). HAB wet
heaths. SOIL wet–damp;
acid. SHADE nil–light.
ALT sl–450. DIST sE4,
nE2, W3, wS2, I2.
RANGE F4, G3.

○ **Cut-leaved
germander**
Teucrium botrys
Short. Lvs pinnately
cut, softly hairy; fls
12–15mm, 1-lipped, in
1-sided lfy whorls. LH
perenn; rhizome,
stolons. GERM spr.
FL 6–10. POLL ins(h);
self. SEX (♀). HAB bare
ground. SOIL dry;
calc. SHADE nil. ALT
sl–100. DIST sE1.
RANGE F3, G3.

○ **Wall germander**
Teucrium chamaedrys
Short. Lvs glossy,
with deep, rounded
teeth, slightly hairy;
fls 12–15mm in short,
tight, lfy spikes; 1-
lipped. LH perenn;
rhizome. GERM spr–
sum. FL 5–9. POLL
ins(h); self. SEX (♀);
pa. HAB walls, bare
ground. SOIL dry; calc
SHADE nil–light. ALT
[sl–1250]. DIST oc-
casionally naturalised.
RANGE F3, sG3.
ss140.

Mountain germander
Teucrium montanum
Low–short. Creeping,
woody; lvs narrow
oval, white with hairs
beneath, edges rolled
under; fls 10–12mm;
1-lipped. LH perenn;
woody stem. GERM
spr? FL 5–8. POLL
ins(h). SEX (♀). HAB
rocks and stony
ground. SOIL dry; calc.
SHADE nil–light. ALT
[sl–1500]. RANGE F4,
sG3.

93

● **Wood sage**
Teucrium scorodonia
Short. Branching,
softly hairy; lvs
pointed oval, wrinkled;
fls 12–15mm, 1-lipped,
with long stamens. LH
perenn; rhizome. GERM
spr. FL 6–9. POLL
ins(h). SEX (♀) pa. HAB
woods, heaths, rocks.
SOIL moist–dry; not
calc. SHADE nil–mid.
ALT sl–500. DIST E4,
W5, S4, I3. RANGE F4,
G3, sS2.
See p. 285.

● **Self-heal**
Prunella vulgaris
Low–short. Downy;
lvs oval with shallow
teeth; fls 10–15mm
long, 2-lipped, upper
lip hooded, in dense
heads; sepal-tube 2-
lipped. LH perenn;
rhizome. GERM aut–spr.
FL 6–10. POLL ins(h).
SEX (♂+♀) pa–hg. HAB
grassland, open woods.
SOIL moist; acid–calc.
SHADE nil–light. ALT
sl–750. DIST E5, W5,
S5, I5. RANGE F5, G5,
S4.
See p. 271, 277. **ss141.**

Large self-heal
Prunella grandiflora
Short–mid. Very like
Self-heal, but larger
with stalked flhds and
fls 20–25mm long. LH
perenn; rhizome. GERM
spr? FL 7–9. POLL
ins(h). SEX (♂), (♀+♀),
(♀)+(♀); pa–hg. HAB
grassland. SOIL moist;
not acid. SHADE nil–
light. ALT[sl–1800].
RANGE eF3, sG3, S1.

● **Ground ivy**
Glechoma hederacea
Short. Stems creeping,
rooting; lvs hairy,
aromatic, rounded;
fls 15–20mm, long-
tubed, in whorls. LH
perenn; rooting stems.
GERM spr–sum. FL 3–6.
POLL ins(h). SEX
(♀+♀) pa. HAB woods,
hedges. SOIL damp–
moist; acid–calc.
SHADE light-heavy. ALT
sl–400. DIST E5, W5,
S4, I4. RANGE F5, G5,
S3.
See p. 209, 270, 271.

○ **Catmint**
Nepeta cataria
Mid–tall. Grey-
downy, smelling of
mint; lvs sharply
toothed; fls 12mm
long, red-dotted, in
whorls, upper con-
densed into a head. LH
perenn; rootstock.
GERM imm. FL 6–9.
POLL ins(h). SEX (♀) pa.
HAB bare, grassy and
rocky ground. SOIL
dry; not acid. SHADE
nil–light. ALT sl–100.
DIST E3, W1; natura-
lised in I. RANGE eF3,
G3, naturalised in S.

○ **Bastard balm**
Melittis melissophyllum
Mid. Hairy, aromatic,
resembling dead-
nettles, but sepal tube
2-lipped and fls 25–
40mm long, pink-
spotted. LH perenn;
rhizome. GERM spr?
FL 5–7. POLL ins(h, l).
SEX (♀); pa. HAB open
woods, hedges. SOIL
moist; not acid. SHADE
light–mid. ALT sl–150.
DIST sE2. RANGE F4,
G2.

● **Black horehound**
Ballota nigra
Mid–tall. Hairy,
foetid; lvs rounded,
long-stalked; fls 12–
18mm, in whorls; sepal
teeth hair-pointed. LH
perenn; rhizome. GERM
aut. FL 6–9. POLL
ins(h). SEX (♀) pa.
HAB disturbed ground,
roadsides. SOIL dry;
not acid. SHADE nil.
ALT sl–200. DIST E4,
W3, sS2; naturalised
in I. RANGE F5, G4,
sS3.

● **White dead-nettle**
Lamium album
Short–mid. Lvs
roughly hairy, nettle-
shaped, long-stalked;
fls 18–20mm long,
upper lip hooded. LH
perenn; rhizome. GERM
spr. FL 3–11. POLL
ins(h). SEX (♀) hg.
HAB hedges, disturbed
ground. SOIL moist;
acid–calc. SHADE nil–
light. ALT sl–300. DIST
E5, W4, S3, I2. RANGE
F5, G5, S3.
See p. 17, 266.

○ **Spotted dead-nettle**
Lamium maculatum
Short–mid. Resembles
White dead-nettle, but
has a strong, rather
unpleasant smell,
spotted lvs and
pinkish fls, 20–25mm.
LH perenn; rhizome.
GERM ? FL 5–8. POLL
ins(h). SEX (♀). HAB
woods, disturbed
ground. SOIL moist;
not calc. SHADE nil–
mid. ALT [sl–2000].
DIST garden escape.
RANGE F3, G3.

● **Henbit dead-nettle**
Lamium amplexicaule
Low–short. Lvs
rounded, toothed,
upper unstalked; fls
10–15mm long with a
long tube; sepal-tube
hairy. LH ann, or
winter ann. GERM any.
FL 3–10. POLL ins(h);
self. SEX (♀). HAB
disturbed ground. SOIL
moist–dry; not calc.
SHADE nil. ALT sl–450.
DIST E4, W2, S2, I1.
RANGE F4, G5, S3.

○ **Cut-leaved dead-nettle**
Lamium hybridum
Low–mid. Lvs deeply and irregularly toothed, running into stalks; fls 8–12mm long, tube hidden by sepals. LH ann. GERM any. FL 3–10. POLL ins(h); self. SEX (♀). HAB disturbed ground. SOIL moist; acid–calc. SHADE nil. ALT sl–300. DIST E3, W2, S2, I2. RANGE F2, G2, S3.

● **Red dead-nettle**
Lamium purpureum
Low–mid. Lvs rounded, with even shallow teeth; often purplish; fls 10–15mm long, tube longer than sepals. LH ann. GERM any. FL (1–)3–10(–12). POLL ins(h); self. SEX (♀) hg. HAB disturbed ground. SOIL moist; acid–calc. SHADE nil. ALT sl–300(–600). DIST E5, W4, S4, I3. RANGE F5, G5, S3.
See p. 243, 296.

○ **Red hemp-nettle**
Galeopsis angustifolia
Short–tall. Lvs downy, narrow, with few, shallow teeth; fls 15–25mm long, tube longer than sepals. LH ann. GERM spr. FL 7–9. POLL ins(h); self. SEX (♀). HAB arable fields. SOIL moist; not acid. SHADE nil. ALT sl–350. DIST sE4, nE2, W2, I1. RANGE F3, G3, sS1.

Downy hemp-nettle
Galeopsis segetum
Short–mid. Lvs oval, well-toothed, with silky hairs; fls 20–30mm long, all pale yellow. LH ann. GERM spr. FL 7–9. POLL ins(h); self. SEX (♀). HAB arable fields, walls, rocks. SOIL moist–dry; acid–calc. SHADE nil–light. ALT [sl–1200]. DIST rare casual. RANGE eF3, nwG3.

● **Large-flowered hemp-nettle**
Galeopsis speciosa
Mid–tall. Much-branched, with stiff hairs; fls 20–40mm long, pale yellow, lower lip purple; orange-centred. LH ann. GERM spr. FL 7–9. POLL ins(h); self. SEX (♀). HAB arable fields, disturbed ground. SOIL moist; not calc (often peaty). SHADE nil–light. ALT sl–400. DIST sE1, nE4, W3, S4, I2. RANGE F2, G3, S4.

● **Common hemp-nettle**
Galeopsis tetrahit
Mid–tall. Branching, stem rough-hairy and swollen at lf-junctions; lvs deeply toothed; fls 15–20mm long, sometimes white. LH ann. GERM spr. FL 7–9. POLL ins; self. SEX (♀). HAB woods, fens, disturbed ground. SOIL damp–moist; acid–calc. SHADE nil–mid. ALT sl–400. DIST E5, W5, S5, I4. RANGE F5, G5, S5.
See p. 18.

● **Yellow archangel**
Lamiastrum galeobdolon
Short–mid. Stems creeping, with upright flg stems; lvs nettle-like; fls 18–20mm long, lower lip red-streaked. LH perenn; stolons. GERM spr–sum. FL 5–6. POLL ins(h). SEX (♀) hg. HAB woods. SOIL damp–moist; not acid. SHADE light–heavy. ALT sl–300. DIST E4, W3, S1, I1. RANGE F5, G4, sS2.
See p. 2, 191, 254, 284.

Jupiter's distaff
Salvia glutinosa
Mid–tall. Clumped, with large lvs, heart-shaped at base and fls 30–45mm long. LH perenn; rootstock. GERM spr. FL 7–9. POLL ins(h). SEX (♀) pa, (♂+♀), (♂)+(♀). HAB woods. SOIL moist; acid–calc. SHADE mid–heavy. ALT [200–1200]. RANGE eF1, sG2.
See p. 285.

○ **Wild sage**
Salvia nemorosa
Mid–tall. Lvs narrow oblong, heart-shaped at base; fls 10–14mm long in whorled spikes, with purple bracts. LH perenn; rootstock. GERM ? FL 6–8. POLL ins(h). SEX (♀) pa, (♂+♀). HAB bare ground. SOIL dry; not acid. SHADE nil. ALT [sl–800]. DIST casual. RANGE F2, G3.

○ **Wild clary**
Salvia verbenaca
Mid–tall. Stems purplish, lvs often deeply toothed; fls 12–15mm long (5–8mm when cleistogamous) in whorled spikes; sepal-tube hairy. LH perenn; rootstock. GERM ? FL 6–9. POLL ins(h); self (cleistogamous). SEX (♀). HAB grassland. SOIL dry; not acid. SHADE nil. ALT sl–150. DIST seE3, nwE1, W1, S1, I2. RANGE F3, G4, S2.

○ **Meadow clary**
Salvia pratensis
Mid–tall. Lvs oblong, little toothed; fls 15–25mm long (♀ fls 10mm), the upper lip bent up into a hood. LH perenn; rootstock. GERM aut. FL 6–7. POLL ins(h). SEX (♂ + ♀) pa–hg. HAB grassland. SOIL dry; calc. SHADE nil. ALT sl–100. DIST sE2; occ. casual. RANGE F4, G4; casual in S.
See p. 285.

○ **Limestone wound-wort**
Stachys alpina
Mid–tall. Softly hairy; lvs heart-shaped, long-stalked; fls 15–20mm long, sepal-teeth shorter than sepal-tube. LH perenn; rootstock. GERM ? FL 6–8. POLL ins. SEX (♂). HAB open woods. SOIL moist–dry; calc. SHADE light–mid. ALT 150–250. DIST E1, W1. RANGE F2, G3.
ss142.

● **Field woundwort**
Stachys arvensis
Low–short. Weak-stemmed, hairy; lvs heart-shaped; fls 6–8mm long, tube concealed by sepals. LH ann. GERM aut, spr. FL 4–10. POLL self. SEX (♂). HAB arable fields. SOIL moist–dry; acid. SHADE nil. ALT sl–400. DIST E4, W4, S2, I3. RANGE F5, G4, sS2.

● **Marsh woundwort**
Stachys palustris
Mid–tall. Lvs spear-shaped, short-stalked (upper unstalked); fls 12–15mm long, pale purple; sepal teeth long. LH perenn; rhizome, root tubers. GERM imm. FL 7–9. POLL ins(h). SEX (♂) pa. HAB marshes, fens, watersides. SOIL wet–damp; acid–calc. SHADE nil–light. ALT sl–350. DIST E4, W5, S4, I5. RANGE F5, G5, S3.
See p. 167.

● **Hedge woundwort**
Stachys sylvatica
Mid–tall. Rough-hairy, foul-smelling; lvs heart-shaped, long-stalked; fls 12–15mm long, red-purple; sepal teeth long. LH perenn; rhizome. GERM spr–sum. FL 6–9. POLL ins(h). SEX (♂) pa. HAB woods, hedges. SOIL moist; acid–calc. SHADE nil–heavy. ALT sl–400. DIST E5, W5, S5, I5. RANGE F5, G5, S3.
See p. 239, 283.

● **Betony**
Stachys officinalis
Short–mid. Lvs oblong, regularly toothed, mostly in rosette; fls 15–18mm long, in dense spikes. LH perenn. GERM spr–sum. FL 6–10. POLL ins(h). SEX (♂) hg–pa. HAB grassland, heaths. SOIL dry; not calc. SHADE nil–light. ALT sl–450. DIST E4, W5, S2, I2. RANGE F4, G5, sS1.

● **Water mint**
Mentha aquatica
Short–tall. Purple-stemmed, mint-scented; lvs oval; stamens protruding from fls, which are mostly in a head. LH perenn; rhizome. GERM aut–spr. FL 7–9. POLL ins(h). SEX (♂) pa + (♀). HAB marshes, fens, water-margins. SOIL water–damp; acid–calc. SHADE nil–mid. ALT sl–400. DIST E5, W5, S5, I5. RANGE F5, G5, sS2.
See p. 184, 250, 271.

● **Corn mint**
Mentha arvensis
Short–mid. Aromatic, but not minty; lvs variable, hairy; fls with protruding stamens, in dense whorls. LH perenn; rhizome. GERM spr–sum. FL 7–9. POLL ins(h). SEX (♂) pa + (♀). HAB arable fields, open woods, grassy places. SOIL damp–dry; acid–calc. SHADE nil–mid. ALT sl–350. DIST E4, W4, S3, I3. RANGE F5, G5, S3.
See p. 283.

○ **Round-leaved mint**
Mentha suaveolens
Tall. Apple-scented; stem densely white-hairy; lvs oval or rounded, wrinkled, grey beneath; fls in dense spikes. LH perenn; rhizome. GERM spr. FL 8–9. POLL ins(h). SEX (♂) pa. HAB disturbed ground, ditches. SOIL wet–damp; acid–calc. SHADE nil. ALT sl–250. DIST E2, W2, S1, I2. RANGE F3, G3, sS1.

● **Spearmint**
Mentha spicata
Tall. Slightly pepper-mint-scented; lvs spear-shaped, grey beneath; fls in long spikes. LH perenn; rhizome. GERM spr. FL 7–10. POLL ins(h). SEX (♂) pa. HAB disturbed ground. SOIL damp–moist; acid–calc. SHADE nil. ALT sl–200. DIST widely casual. RANGE F2, G4, S2; and casual.

○ **Pennyroyal**
Mentha pulegium
Low–short; prostrate. Lvs small, oval, strongly scented; fls in whorls, not at top of stem; sepal teeth unequal. LH perenn; rhizome. GERM ? FL 7–10. POLL ins(h). SEX (♀); pa. HAB sandy ground. SOIL damp; acid. SHADE nil. ALT sl–200. DIST E2, W2, I1. RANGE F2, G2.

● **Gipsywort**
Lycopus europaeus
Mid–tall. Lvs spear-shaped, unstalked, regularly and sharply toothed; fls 3mm long in tight whorls. LH perenn; rhizome. GERM spr–sum. FL 7–9. POLL ins(h, d). SEX (♂+♀) pa. HAB fens, marshes, water-sides. SOIL water–damp; acid–calc. SHADE nil–heavy. ALT sl–200. DIST E4, W3, S2, I3. RANGE F5, G5, sS4.

○ **Lesser calamint**
Calamintha nepeta
Mid. Much-branched; lvs grey-hairy, with few teeth; fls 10–15mm long, hairs at tip of sepal-tube. LH perenn; rhizome. GERM ? FL 7–9. POLL ins(h, d, l). SEX (♀). HAB grassy places. SOIL dry; calc. SHADE nil. ALT sl–150. DIST sE2, W1. RANGE F3, G1.

● **Common calamint**
Calamintha sylvatica
Mid. Little branched; lvs with many teeth; fls 10–20mm long (larger in shady places). LH perenn; rhizome. GERM aut. FL 7–9. POLL ins(h, d, l). SEX (♀). HAB grassy places, woods. SOIL moist–dry; calc. SHADE nil–heavy. ALT sl–200. DIST sE4, nE2, W2, I2. RANGE F4, G3.

● **Wild basil**
Clinopodium vulgare
Mid–tall. Hairy, slightly aromatic; lvs scarcely toothed; fls 15–10mm long in whorls; bracts bristly; sepals hairy. LH perenn; rhizome. GERM spr. FL 7–9. POLL ins(h, l). SEX (♂+♀) pa. HAB grassland, scrub. SOIL dry; calc. SHADE nil–light. ALT sl–400. DIST E4, W4, S3, I2. RANGE F5, G5, S3.

● **Marjoram**
Origanum vulgare
Mid–tall. Aromatic; stems purplish; lvs oval, untoothed; fls 6–8mm long in heads with purple bracts. LH perenn; rootstock. GERM aut–spr. FL 7–9. POLL ins(h, d, l). SEX (♂+♀) pa. HAB grassy places, scrub. SOIL dry; calc. SHADE nil–light. ALT sl–400. DIST sE4, nE3, W4, S3, I3. RANGE F5, G4, S3. *See p. 271.*

● **Basil thyme**
Acinos arvensis
Low–short. Hairy, but not aromatic; lvs small, oval, scarcely toothed; fls 7–10mm long, in few-fld whorls. LH winter ann. GERM aut. FL 6–9. POLL ins(h). SEX (♀). HAB arable fields, disturbed ground. SOIL dry; calc. SHADE nil. ALT sl–300. DIST E4, W2, S1, I1. RANGE F4, G4, S3.

○ **Large thyme**
Thymus pulegioides
Low–short; prostrate. Aromatic; woody-stemmed; stems 4-angled, hairy on angles; fls in long whorled spikes. LH perenn; woody stems. GERM aut. FL 7–8. POLL ins(h, d, l). SEX (♀) pa+(♀). HAB grass-land. SOIL dry; calc. SHADE nil. ALT sl–250. DIST sE3, W1, S1. RANGE F4, G5, S3.

● **Wild thyme**
Thymus serpyllum agg.
V.low–low; prostrate. Mat-forming, slightly aromatic; stems 4-angled, hairy on 2 sides; lvs small; fls in rounded heads. LH perenn; rooting stems. GERM aut. FL 6–9. POLL ins(h, d, l). SEX (♀) pa+(♀). HAB grassy, heathy sandy and rocky places. SOIL dry; acid–calc. SHADE nil. ALT sl–1200. DIST E4, W5, S5, I4. RANGE F4, G2, sS4. *See p. 277.*

NIGHTSHADE FAMILY
Solanaceae
An economically important family, including potato, tomato and many poisonous plants. Leaves are often large, alternate. Flowers usually with 5 joined petals, sometimes bell-shaped. Fruit is normally a berry, red, yellow or black, often poisonous.
See p. 262.

● **Bittersweet**
Solanum dulcamara
Mid–v.tall; scrambling. Stems woody, sometimes twining; lvs lobed at base; fls 10–12mm, petals bent back; anthers in a column; fr red. LH perenn; woody stems. GERM spr–sum. FL 5–9. POLL ins. SEX (♀). HAB woods, hedges, fens, shingle beaches. SOIL wet–dry; not acid. SHADE nil–mid. ALT sl–300. DIST E5, W4, S3, I3. RANGE F5, G5, S3.
See p. 163, 193.

● **Black nightshade**
Solanum nigrum
Mid. Lvs usually untoothed; fls 5–8mm, petals turned back; anthers in a loose column; fr black. LH ann. GERM spr. FL 7–9. POLL ins. SEX (♀). HAB disturbed ground. SOIL moist–dry; acid–calc. SHADE nil. ALT sl–250. DIST E4, W2; casual in S and I. RANGE F4, G4, S3.

● **Deadly nightshade**
Atropa belladonna
Tall–v.tall. Bushy, with large oval lvs, sometimes paired; fls 25–30mm, bell-shaped, deep dull purple; fr black, deadly. LH perenn; rootstock. GERM spr–sum. FL 6–9. POLL ins. SEX (♀). HAB scrub, stony ground. SOIL dry; calc. SHADE nil–mid. ALT sl–250. DIST sE4, nE2, W2, S1, I1. RANGE F3, G4. *See p. 240, 241.*

● **Henbane**
Hyoscyamus niger
Mid–tall. Lvs sharp-toothed, sticky-hairy, poisonous; fls 20–30mm, cream veined purple; fr a capsule. LH ann–bienn. GERM aut–spr. FL 5–9. POLL ins. SEX (♀). HAB disturbed ground, often sandy. SOIL dry; acid–calc. SHADE nil. ALT sl–200. DIST E3, W2, S1, I1. RANGE F3, G4, S3.

FIGWORT FAMILY
Scrophulariaceae
A rather variable family with several flower-types. They may be flat, 4–5-petalled flowers, the petals joined in a very short tube, as in mulleins and speedwells; open tubes, as in foxgloves; or 2-lipped, with the lips closed (toadflaxes) or open (yellow rattle, lousewort). Leaves are very variable. Several species are hemi-parasites.
See p. 15, 17, 18, 224, 238, 239, 245, 266, 269, 277, 279, 283.

○ **White mullein**
Verbascum lychnitis
Tall–v.tall. Stems angled; lvs white-powdery below; fls white, 15–20mm, in a branching spike; anthers with white hairs. LH bienn. GERM aut–spr. FL 6–9. POLL ins(d, l); self. SEX (♀) hg. HAB disturbed ground. SOIL dry; calc. SHADE nil. ALT sl–200. DIST E2, W2, S1. RANGE F4, G3.
ss143.

● **Dark mullein**
Verbascum nigrum
Tall. Stems angled; lvs pale-hairy below; fls 10–25mm; anthers with purple hairs. LH bienn. GERM aut–spr. FL 6–9. POLL ins(d, l); self. SEX (♀) hg. HAB disturbed and grassy places. SOIL dry; not acid. SHADE nil. ALT sl–200. DIST E3, W2, S1. RANGE F4, G4, S3.
ss144. ss145.

● **Great mullein**
Verbascum thapsus
Tall–v.tall. Lvs and stems densely white-hairy all over; fls 15–30mm; 3 anthers with white hairs, 2 hairless. LH bienn. GERM aut–spr. FL 6–8. POLL ins(d, l); self. SEX (♀) hg. HAB disturbed ground. SOIL dry; acid–calc. SHADE nil. ALT sl–300. DIST E4, W4, S3, I2. RANGE F5, G5, S3.
See p. 245.

● **Water figwort**
Scrophularia auriculata
Tall. Stem with 4 prominent wings; fls 10mm, upper lip brown; sepal-tube pale-edged. LH perenn; rhizome. GERM aut–spr. FL 6–9. POLL ins(h). SEX (♀) pg. HAB watersides. SOIL wet–damp; acid–calc. SHADE nil–heavy. ALT sl–250. DIST E4, W3, S1, I3. RANGE F5, wG1.
See p. 167, 258.

● **Common figwort**
Scrophularia nodosa
Mid–tall. Stem 4-angled, not winged; lvs pointed, toothed; fls 10mm, upper lip brown; sepal-tube with narrow brown edge. LH perenn; rhizome. GERM imm. FL 6–9. POLL ins(h). SEX (♀) pg. HAB woods, hedges. SOIL damp; acid–calc. SHADE nil–mid. ALT sl–450. DIST E5, W5, S4, I4. RANGE F5, G5, S3.
See p. 18, 266. **ss146.**

○ **Green figwort**
Scrophularia umbrosa
Mid–tall. Stem broadly winged; lvs toothed; fls 10–12mm, upper lip green-brown; sepal teeth with pale edge. LH perenn; rhizome. GERM aut–spr. FL 7–9. POLL ins(h). SEX (♀) pg. HAB woods. SOIL damp; not calc. SHADE light–mid. ALT sl–250. DIST E2, W1, S2, I1. RANGE eF2, G4, sS1.

● **Snapdragon**
Antirrhinum majus
Mid–tall. Stems woody, branching; lvs narrow; fls 30–40mm long, in long spikes, lips closed. LH perenn; woody stem-base. GERM spr–sum. FL 5–10. POLL ins(h); self. SEX (♀) hg. HAB walls, rocks. SOIL dry; not acid. SHADE nil. ALT sl–200. DIST widely naturalised. RANGE widely naturalised F, G.
See p. 248.

○ **Lesser snapdragon**
Misopates orontium
Mid. Lvs very narrow; fls 10–15mm long, lips closed, in lfy spikes, with narrow green sepals. LH ann. GERM imm. FL 7–10. POLL ins(h); self. SEX (♀) hg. HAB bare and disturbed, often sandy ground. SOIL dry; not calc. SHADE nil. ALT sl–750. DIST E2, W2, I1. RANGE F4, G4, sS2.

● **Pale toadflax**
Linaria repens
Mid–tall. Lvs very narrow; fls 7–15mm long, pale lilac, veined darker with orange throat and short spur. LH perenn; rhizome. GERM spr. FL 6–9. POLL ins(h). SEX (♀). HAB bare and grassy places. SOIL dry; not acid. SHADE nil. ALT sl–200. DIST E3, W3, S2, I1. RANGE F4, G2, sS3. **ss14".**

○ **Purple toadflax**
Linaria purpurea
Mid–tall. Lvs crowded, very narrow; fls 7–10mm, with a long, curved spur, in dense spikes. LH perenn; rootstock. GERM spr. FL 6–8. POLL ins(h). SEX (♀). HAB walls, disturbed ground. SOIL moist–dry; not acid. SHADE nil. ALT sl–150. DIST widely naturalised. RANGE widely naturalised.

○ **Prostrate toadflax**
Linaria supina
Low–short. Sprawling; lvs narrow; fls 10–15mm, in short, tight spikes. LH ann. GERM aut. FL 6–9. POLL ins(h). SEX (♀). HAB sandy ground. SOIL dry; calc. SHADE nil. ALT sl. DIST sE1. RANGE F3.

● **Common toadflax**
Linaria vulgaris
Mid–tall. Lvs very narrow; fls 15–25mm long, yellow, lip darker, long-spurred. LH perenn; rhizome. GERM spr. FL 6–10. POLL ins(h). SEX (♀). HAB grassland, hedges. SOIL moist; not acid. SHADE nil–light. ALT sl–300. DIST E5, W5, S3, I2. RANGE F5, G5, S4.
See p. 180, 262, 283, 299.

● **Ivy-leaved toadflax**
Cymbalaria muralis
Low; trailing. Stems long; lvs ivy-shaped, glossy, thick, often purplish; fls 8–10mm long, in long slender stalks. LH perenn; rooting stems. GERM spr–sum. FL 5–11. POLL ins(h); self. SEX (♀). HAB walls. SOIL dry; not acid. SHADE nil. ALT sl–300. DIST very widely naturalised. RANGE widely naturalised F, G.
See p. 166.

● **Sharp-leaved fluellen**
Kickxia elatine
Short–mid; prostrate. Lvs arrow-shaped; fls 7–9mm long, on long, slender, hairless stalks; spur straight. LH ann. GERM spr. FL 7–10. POLL ins. SEX (♀). HAB arable fields. SOIL moist–dry; acid–calc. SHADE nil. ALT sl–200. DIST sE4, nE1, W2. RANGE F4, G3, S2.
See p. 283.

● **Round-leaved fluellen**
Kickxia spuria
Short–mid; prostrate. Lvs rounded; fls 8–11mm long, on long, slender, hairy stalks; spur curved. LH ann. GERM spr. FL 7–10. POLL ins; self (cleistogamous). SEX (♀). HAB arable fields. SOIL moist–dry; acid–calc. SHADE nil. ALT sl–150. DIST sE4, W1. RANGE F4, G2.
See p. 283.

99

● **Monkey flower**
Mimulus guttatus
Short–mid. Fleshy-stemmed, with opposite lvs; fls 25–45mm, 2-lipped, lips open; yellow with few red spots. LH perenn; rhizome. GERM spr. FL 6–9. POLL ins(h). SEX (♂) hg. HAB river gravels, rocks. SOIL wet–damp; acid–calc. SHADE nil. ALT sl–600. DIST sE2, nE4, W3, S4, I2. RANGE eF1, G3, S2. *See p. 285.*

○ **Mudwort**
Limosella aquatica
Low; creeping. Lvs long-stalked in rosettes; fls 2–5mm, petals shorter than sepals. LH ann. GERM spr. FL 6–10. POLL ins; self. SEX (♂). HAB mud. SOIL wet–damp; acid–calc. SHADE nil. ALT sl–450. DIST E2, W1, S1, I1. RANGE F3, G3, S3. *See p. 259.* **ss148**.

● **Foxglove**
Digitalis purpurea
Tall–v.tall. Lvs large, spear-shaped; grey-downy; fls 30–40mm long, tubular, spotted inside, in long, many-fld spikes. LH bienn or short-lived perenn. GERM aut–spr. FL 6–9. POLL ins(h). SEX (♂) pa. HAB woods, heaths, rocks. SOIL moist–dry; acid. SHADE nil–mid. ALT sl–700. DIST E4, W5, S5, I5. RANGE F4, G2, wS2.
See p. 15, 17, 163, 207, 240, 241, 245, 259, 262, 277, 282.

Small yellow foxglove
Digitalis lutea
Mid–tall. Lvs hairless, strongly ribbed; fls 15–20mm long, hairless, lips almost closed. LH short-lived perenn. GERM ? FL 6–8. POLL ins(h). SEX (♂) pa. HAB woods, rocks. SOIL dry; calc. SHADE nil–mid. ALT [sl–1200]. RANGE F4, G2.

Large yellow foxglove
Digitalis grandiflora
Tall. Lvs hairy below; fls 30–40mm long, brown-veined, hairy outside. LH perenn. GERM ? FL 6–9. POLL ins(h). SEX (♂) pa. HAB woods, rocks. SOIL moist–dry; acid–calc. SHADE nil–mid. ALT [sl–1500]. RANGE eF1, G3.

● **Fairy foxglove**
Erinus alpinus
Low. Tufted; lvs spoon-shaped, in rosette; fls with 5-toothed petal-lobes, in short, dense spikes. LH perenn. GERM spr. FL 5–10. POLL ins(h). self. SEX (♂). HAB walls. SOIL dry; acid–calc. SHADE nil. ALT sl–250. DIST naturalised: E3, W1, S2, I2. RANGE F1.

● **Red bartsia**
Odontites verna
Short–mid. Purple-tinged hemiparasite; lvs narrow, toothed; fls 8–10mm, 2-lipped, in lfy spikes. LH ann. GERM spr–sum. FL 6–9. POLL ins(h). SEX (♂). HAB grassy and disturbed places. SOIL damp–moist; acid–calc. SHADE nil. ALT sl–400. DIST E5, W5, S4, I2. RANGE F5, G5, S3.
See p. 225.

Yellow odontites
Odontites lutea
Short–mid. Branching, often purple-tinged hemiparasite; lvs toothed; fls 6mm, 2-lipped, in 1-sided spikes. LH ann. GERM spr. BL 7–9. POLL ins. SEX (♂). HAB grassland. SOIL moist–dry; not acid. SHADE nil. ALT [100–800]. RANGE F2, G2.

○ **Alpine bartsia**
Bartsia alpina
Low–short. Parasitic on other roots; lvs un-stalked; fls 20mm long, 2-lipped, among purplish bracts. LH perenn; rhizome. GERM spr? FL 7–8. POLL ins(h). SEX (♂). HAB rocks, grassy places, marshes. SOIL damp–moist; not acid. SHADE nil. ALT 250–800. DIST nE1, S1. RANGE seF1, sG1, S4.
See p. 224.

○ **Yellow bartsia**
Parentucellia viscosa
Low–mid. Parasitic on roots; lvs narrow, toothed; fls 20mm long, 2-lipped, the upper lip hooded. LH ann. GERM spr. FL 6–9. POLL ins(h, d). SEX (♂). HAB grassland. SOIL damp–moist; acid–calc. SHADE nil. ALT sl–200. DIST sE2, nE1, W2, S1, I2. RANGE wF2, nG1.

○ **Spiked speedwell**
Veronica spicata
Low–mid. Downy, un-branched; lvs oval in rosette, narrow on stem; fls 5mm, in dense pyramidal spikes. LH perenn; rhizome. GERM aut. FL 7–10. POLL ins(d, h). SEX (♀). HAB grassy and rocky places. SOIL dry; acid–calc. SHADE nil. ALT sl–400. DIST E1, W1. RANGE F1, G2, S2.

Large speedwell
Veronica austriaca
Short–mid. Hairy, branching; lvs toothed, unstalked; fls 8–10mm, in long, loose spikes; 5-sepals. LH perenn; rhizome. GERM ? FL 6–8. POLL ins(d). SEX (♀). HAB grassland. SOIL dry; acid–calc. SHADE nil. ALT 100–1250. RANGE F2, G3.

● **Germander speedwell**
Veronica chamaedrys
Low–short; prostrate. Patch-forming, sprawl-ing stem with 2 lines of hairs; fls 10mm, in spikes of 10–20. LH perenn; rooting stems. GERM aut–spr. FL 4–6. POLL ins(d, h). SEX (♀) hg. HAB grassland, hedges, open woods. SOIL moist-dry; acid–calc. SHADE nil–light. ALT sl–800. DIST E5, W5, S5, I5. RANGE F5, G5, S4.
See p. 261, 276, 279.

● **Wood speedwell**
Veronica montana
Low–short; creeping. Stem hairy all round; lvs stalked; fls 6–8mm, violet-blue, in few-fld spikes. LH perenn; rooting stems. GERM spr–sum. FL 4–7. POLL ins(d, h). SEX (♀). HAB woods. SOIL damp–moist; acid–calc. SHADE light–heavy. ALT sl–300. DIST E4, W4, S3, I3. RANGE F4, G4, sS1.
See p. 209.

○ **Rock speedwell**
Veronica fruticans
Low. Stems woody at base; lvs unstalked and untoothed; fls 10mm, deep bright blue with a red centre. LH perenn; woody stem. GERM spr. FL 7–8. POLL ins(d); self. SEX (♀) hg. HAB rocks. SOIL damp–moist; not acid. SHADE nil. ALT 500–1000. DIST S1. RANGE eF1, sG1, S3.

● **Common field speedwell**
Veronica persica
Low–short; sprawling. Lvs short-stalked; fls 8–12mm, lower petal very pale; fl-stalks longer than lvs; fr lobes spreading. LH ann. GERM any. FL 1–12. POLL ins(d); self. SEX (♀) hg. HAB dis-turbed ground. SOIL moist; acid–calc. SHADE nil. ALT sl–300. DIST E5, W5, S4, I4. RANGE F5, G4, S2.
See p. 174, 215, 243, 296.

● **Green field speedwell**
Veronica agrestis
Low. Lvs light green, toothed; fls 4–8mm, usually all pale blue, on short stalks; sepal teeth blunt. LH ann. GERM any. FL 3–11. POLL ins(d, h); self. SEX (♀) hg. HAB dis-turbed ground. SOIL moist–dry; acid–calc. SHADE nil–light. ALT sl–450. DIST E4, W4, S3, I3. RANGE F4, G4, S3.

● **Grey field speedwell**
Veronica polita
Low. Lvs dull, grey green, downy; fls 4–8mm, bright blue, on short stalks; sepal teeth blunt. LH ann. GERM any. FL 3–11. POLL ins(d); self. SEX (♀) hg. HAB disturbed ground. SOIL moist–dry; not calc. SHADE nil. ALT sl–300. DIST E4, W2, S2, I2. RANGE F4, G4, sS2.

● **Ivy-leaved speedwell**
Veronica hederifolia
Low–short; prostrate. Lvs ivy-like, hairy; fls 3–5mm, dull lilac or blue, solitary and long-stalked; sepals longer than petals. LH ann. GERM win–spr. FL 3–8. POLL self. SEX (♀). HAB disturbed ground. SOIL moist–dry; acid–calc. SHADE nil. ALT sl–400. DIST E4, W4, S3, I3. RANGE F5, G4, S2.
ss149.

● **Thyme-leaved speedwell**
Veronica serpyllifolia
Low–short. Stems creeping, flg shoots erect; lvs oval, hairless; fls 5–6mm, dark-streaked; bracts longer than stalks. LH perenn; rooting stems. GERM spr–sum. FL 4–10. POLL ins(d); self. SEX (♀). HAB grassy places. SOIL moist; acid–calc. SHADE nil–light. ALT sl–1250. DIST E5, W5, S5, I5. RANGE F5, G5, S4.

○ **Alpine speedwell**
Veronica alpina
Low. Scarcely creeping; lvs broad oval; fls 5–6mm, deep blue, in few-fld spikes; bracts longer than stalks. LH perenn; rootstock. GERM spr. FL 7–8. POLL ins(d); self. SEX (♀). HAB rocks. SOIL damp–moist; acid–calc. SHADE nil. ALT 350–1250. DIST S2. RANGE sG1, S3.

● **Heath speedwell**
Veronica officinalis
Low–short. Creeping, mat-forming, hairy; fls 5–6mm, lilac-blue, in long-stalked spikes. LH perenn; rooting stems. GERM spr–sum. FL 5–8. POLL ins(d, h). SEX (♀) pg–pa. HAB grassland, heaths. SOIL dry; not calc. SHADE nil–light. ALT sl–800. DIST E5, W5, S5, I5. RANGE F5, G5, S4.

● **Wall speedwell**
Veronica arvensis
Low–short. Hairy; lvs toothed; fls 2–3mm, bright blue, hidden by narrow bracts. LH ann. GERM win–spr. FL 3–10. POLL ins(h, d); self. SEX (♀). HAB bare ground, walls. SOIL dry; acid–calc. SHADE nil. ALT sl–800. DIST E5, W5, S5, I5. RANGE F5, G5, S3.
ss150. ss151.

● **Brooklime**
Veronica beccabunga
Short–mid. Rather fleshy, with glossy, short-stalked oval lvs; fls 7–8mm in paired spikes. LH perenn; rooting stems. GERM spr–sum. FL 5–9. POLL ins(d, h); self. SEX (♀) pg. HAB still and slow water, meadows. SOIL water–wet; acid–calc. SHADE nil–light. ALT sl–800. DIST E5, W5, S4, I5. RANGE F5, G5, S3.
See p. 263.

● **Water speedwell**
Veronica anagallis-aquatica
Short. Rather fleshy, with spear-shaped un-stalked lvs; fls 5–6mm, pale blue, in many-fld, paired spikes. LH perenn; rooting stems. GERM spr–sum. FL 6–8. POLL ins(d); self. SEX (♀). HAB water and mud. SOIL water–wet; not acid. SHADE nil–light. ALT sl–400. DIST E4, W3, S2, I3. RANGE F5, G5, S2.
See p. 216.

● **Pink water speedwell**
Veronica catenata
Short. Very like Water speedwell, but with larger fls, pink fls, and spreading fruits. LH perenn; rooting stems. GERM aut. FL 6–8. POLL ins(d); self. SEX (♀). HAB water and mud. SOIL water–wet; not acid. SHADE nil. ALT sl–250. DIST E4, W2, S1, I3. RANGE F3, G4, sS2.

● **Marsh speedwell**
Veronica scutellata
Short–mid. Lvs very narrow; fls 6–7mm, purple-streaked, in loose, few-fld spikes. LH perenn; rooting stems. GERM spr. FL 6–8. POLL ins(d); self. SEX (♀). HAB water, meadows. SOIL water–wet; not calc. SHADE nil. ALT sl–500. DIST E4, W4, S4, I4. RANGE F4, G4, S4.
See p. 192.

● **Slender speedwell**
Veronica filiformis
V.low–low. Downy, mat-forming; lvs rounded; fls 8–12mm, abundant, on very long stalks. LH perenn; rooting stems. GERM no fruit produced. FL 4–6. POLL ? SEX (♀). HAB grassy places. SOIL moist; not acid. SHADE nil–light. ALT sl–300. DIST E4, W4, S3, I3. RANGE F3, G3, S2.

● **Eyebright**
Euphrasia officinalis agg.
Low–short. Variable (a collection of many v. similar spp.); hemi-parasite; lvs toothed; fls 4–12mm, purple-veined, with large, toothed bracts. LH ann. GERM spr–sum. FL 6–10. POLL ins(h, d); self. SEX (♀) pg, hg. HAB grassland. SOIL moist–dry; acid–calc. SHADE nil–light. ALT sl–1250. DIST E4, W4, S5, I3. RANGE F4, G4, G5, S5.
See p. 225, 263, 279.

● **Yellow rattle**
Rhinanthus minor
Short–mid. Hemi-parasite; lvs parallel-sided, regularly toothed; fls 15–20mm long; sepal tube greatly inflated. LH ann. GERM spr. FL 5–9. POLL ins(h); self. SEX (♀). HAB grassland. SOIL moist–dry; acid–calc. SHADE nil. ALT sl–600(–1000). DIST E4, W5, S5, I5. RANGE F5, G5, S5.
See p. 176, 225, 263, 295.

Lapland lousewort
Pedicularis lapponica
Short. Hemiparasite;
lvs v.narrow; fls 20–
25mm, 2-lipped; sepal
tube slightly inflated.
LH perenn; rootstock.
GERM ? FL 6–8. POLL
ins. self. SEX (♀). HAB grassland, moors. SOIL
moist; not calc. SHADE
nil. ALT [sl–2000].
RANGE S3.

● **Marsh lousewort**
Pedicularis palustris
Low–mid. Hemipara-
site; purple-tinged,
with a single branching
stem; lvs pinnately
cut; fls 20–25mm,
sepals hairy. LH ann–
bienn. GERM spr–sum.
FL 5–9. POLL ins(h).
SEX (♀). HAB heaths,
moors. SOIL wet–damp;
acid. SHADE nil. ALT
sl–500. DIST E3, W4,
S5, I5. RANGE F3, G4,
S5.
See p. 295.

● **Lousewort**
Pedicularis sylvatica
Low–short. Hemi-
parasite; many un-
branched stems; lvs
pinnately cut; fls 20–
25mm; sepal-tube
hairless. LH perenn;
rootstock. GERM spr.
FL 4–7. POLL ins(h).
SEX (♀). HAB heaths,
bogs. SOIL wet–damp;
not calc. SHADE nil–
mid. ALT sl–500(–800).
DIST E4, W5, S5, I5.
RANGE F4, G3, sS4.
*See p. 213, 224, 225,
295.*

Moor king
*Pedicularis sceptrum-
carolinae*
Mid–tall. Thick-
stemmed, unbranched
hemiparasite; lvs
pinnately lobed; fls
30–35mm, in dense
spikes. LH perenn;
rootstock. GERM spr.
FL 6–8. POLL ins(h). SEX
(♀). HAB grassland,
moors. SOIL damp; not
acid. SHADE nil–mid.
ALT [sl–1000]. RANGE
G1, S3.

Variegated lousewort
Pedicularis oederi
Low. Stem hairy at lf-
junctions; lvs pinnately
lobed, lobes rounded;
fls yellow on lower lips,
red-brown on upper,
with 2 red spots. LH
perenn. GERM ? FL 6–8.
POLL ins(h); self. SEX
(♀). HAB grassland.
SOIL damp–moist; not
acid. SHADE nil. ALT
[500–1500]. RANGE sG1,
S2.

● **Common cow-wheat**
Melampyrum pratense
Low–mid. Slender,
spreading hemipara-
site; lvs spear-shaped;
fls 10–16mm, with 2
closed lips, the lower
straight. LH ann. GERM
spr. FL 5–9. POLL
ins(h); self. SEX (♀).
HAB grassland, heaths,
open woods. SOIL
moist; acid–calc.
SHADE nil–mid. ALT sl–
900. DIST E4, W5, S5,
I4. RANGE F5, G5, S5.

○ **Small cow-wheat**
*Melampyrum
sylvaticum*
Low–short. Resembles
Common cow-wheat,
but fls 8–10mm, deep
yellow, lips open, lower
lip bent. LH ann. GERM
spr. FL 6–8. POLL
ins(h); self. SEX (♀).
HAB rocky woods. SOIL
moist; acid. SHADE
light–mid. ALT 200–
400. DIST nE1, S2.
RANGE G2, S5.

Wood cow-wheat
*Melampyrum
nemorosum*
Short. Hemiparasitic;
lvs triangular, short-
stalked, toothed; fls
15–20mm, orange, with
bright purple bracts.
LH ann. GERM ? FL 6–9.
POLL ins(h). SEX (♀). HAB
woods. SOIL moist; not
calc. SHADE light–
heavy. ALT sl–1000.
RANGE eG2, sS2.

○ **Crested cow-wheat**
Melampyrum cristatum
Short–mid. Hemipara-
site; lvs narrow; fls
12–18mm, upper lip
purple, lower yellow,
in dense spikes with
purple bracts. LH ann.
GERM spr. FL 6–9. POLL
ins(h); self. SEX (♀).
HAB grassland, scrub,
wood-edges. SOIL dry;
not acid. SHADE nil–
mid. ALT sl–100. DIST
eE1. RANGE F3, G3,
sS3.

○ **Field cow-wheat**
Melampyrum arvense
Short–mid. Resembles
Crested cow-wheat but
fls 20–25mm, both lips
pink, throat yellow, in
a looser spike. LH ann.
GERM spr. FL 6–9. POLL
ins(h); self. SEX (♀).
HAB grassy and arable
fields. SOIL dry; not
acid. SHADE nil. ALT
sl–100. DIST E1. RANGE
F3, G3, sS2.

BROOMRAPES

**BROOMRAPE
FAMILY**
Orpbanchaceae
A family of parasites,
none of which has
chlorophyll, and so
wholly dependent for
nutrition on their hosts.
Leaves scale-like and
flowers 2-lipped,
brownish or purplish.
It is important for
identification to notice
surrounding species to
determine hosts.
See p. 221, 296.

● **Toothwort**
Lathraea squamaria
Low–short. Lvs and
stems pinkish-cream;
fls in a 1-sided spike,
with the style longer
than the petals. LH
perenn; rhizome. GERM
spr? FL 4–6. POLL
ins(h); self, cleistoga-
mous. SEX (♀) pg. HAB
woods, on elm and
hazel. SOIL moist; calc.
SHADE light–heavy. ALT
sl–300. DIST E3, W3,
S2, I1. RANGE F3, G4,
sS3.
See p. 2, 222, 223, 265.

○ **Greater broomrape**
*Orobanche rapum-
genistae*
Short–tall. Stem
yellow-brown, scaly at
base; fls 20–25mm
long, upper lip un-
lobed; stigmas yellow.
LH perenn; tuber.
GERM spr. FL 5–7. POLL
ins(h). SEX (♀) hg. HAB
on gorse and broom.
SOIL dry; acid. SHADE
nil. ALT sl–100. DIST
E2, W2, S1, I1. RANGE
F2, G2.

○ **Knapweed
broomrape**
Orobanche elatior
Short–mid. Often red-
tinged; sepal-teeth
split, shorter than 18–
25mm petal-tube;
stigmas yellow. LH
perenn; tuber. GERM
spr? FL 6–7. POLL ins.
SEX (♀). HAB parasitic
on Greater knapweed.
SOIL dry; calc. SHADE
nil. ALT sl–150. DIST
E2, W1. RANGE eF1,
G2, sS1.
See p. 221.

● **Common broomrape**
Orobanche minor
Short–mid. Stem
yellow- or red-brown;
fls 10–18mm long,
upper lip toothed;
stigmas purple. LH ann.
GERM spr. FL 6–9. POLL
ins(h). SEX (♀) hg. HAB
many plants, esp. pea-
flower and daisy
families. SOIL moist–
dry; acid–calc. SHADE
nil. ALT sl–100. DIST
sE4, nE1, W1, I2.
RANGE F4, G3, sS1.
See p. 221. **ss152.**

○ **Thyme broomrape**
Orobanche alba
Low–short. Stems deep
red-purple; fls 15–20
mm long, red-purple;
stamens purple. LH
ann. GERM spr. FL 6–8.
POLL ins(h). SEX (♀)
hg. HAB on thyme in
rocky grassland. SOIL
dry; not acid. SHADE
nil. ALT sl–100. DIST
E1, S1, I1. RANGE F3,
G2.
ss153.

○ **Thistle broomrape**
Orobanche reticulata
Short–mid. Stem
purplish-yellow; fls
15–25mm, dark-
spotted; stigmas
purple. LH perenn;
tuber. GERM spr? FL
6–7. POLL ins. SEX (♀).
HAB parasitic on
thistles. SOIL dry; calc.
SHADE nil. ALT 100–
150. DIST nE1. RANGE
F2, G3.

○ **Ivy broomrape**
Orobanche hederae
Low–mid. Stem purp-
lish-brown; fls 12–20
mm long, cream,
purple-veined; stigmas
yellow. LH ann. GERM
spr. FL 6–7. POLL
ins(h). SEX (♀) hg. HAB
on ivy. SOIL dry; calc.
SHADE nil. ALT sl–100.
DIST sE2, W1, sS1, I2.
RANGE F3, G1.
See p. 221.

○ **Purple broomrape**
Orobanche purpurea
Short–mid. Stem
bluish-purple; fls 20–
30mm, more strongly
blue, upper lip sharply
2-lobed. LH perenn;
tuber. GERM spr? FL
6–7. POLL ins; self. SEX
(♀). HAB parasitic on
Yarrow and other
composites. SOIL dry;
not acid. SHADE nil.
ALT sl–150. DIST E1,
W1. RANGE F3, G2.
See p. 221.

○ **Clove-scented
broomrape**
*Orobanche
caryophyllacea*
Short–mid. Stem
yellow, scaly below;
fls 20–30mm long,
yellowish; stigmas
purple. LH ann. GERM
spr. FL 6–7. POLL
ins(h). SEX (♀) hg. HAB
on bedstraws. SOIL
dry; calc. SHADE nil.
ALT sl–50. DIST seE1.
RANGE F3, G3.

104

**GLOBULARIA
FAMILY**
Golbulariaceae
A small family, with 2-
lipped flowers in heads.
(Globularia)

**BUTTERWORT
FAMILY**
Lentibulariaceae
Carnivorous plants
which catch animals
either on sticky leaves
(butterworts) or in
aquatic traps (bladder-
worts). Flowers 2-
lipped and spurred.
See p. 233, 257, 274.

Globularia
Globularia elongata
Low–short. Lower lvs
oval, notched at tip,
upper narrow; fls in a
round head. LH
perenn; rhizome. GERM
? FL 4–6. POLL ins. SEX
(♀). HAB grassland,
rocks. SOIL dry; acid–
calc. SHADE nil. ALT
[200–1500]. RANGE F3,
sG2.

○ **Pale butterwort**
Pinguicula lusitanica
V.low–low. Lvs yellow-
ish, rolled at the edges,
less than 20mm, all in
rosette; fls 6–7mm,
lilac, spur 2–4mm. LH
perenn; rosette. GERM ?
FL 6–10. POLL ins(h);
self. SEX (♀). HAB
moors, bogs, wet
heaths. SOIL wet–damp;
acid. SHADE nil. ALT sl–
500. DIST wE2, W1,
wS3, I2. RANGE wF2.

● **Common butterwort**
Pinguicula vulgaris
Low. Lvs yellow-green,
rolled in at edges, over
20mm long, all in
rosette; fls violet, 10–
15mm long. LH perenn;
rootless bud. GERM
sum–aut. FL 5–8. POLL
ins(h). SEX (♀). HAB
bogs, wet heaths, rocks.
SOIL wet; acid–
calc. SHADE nil. ALT sl–
1000. DIST sE2, nE4,
W4, S5, I3. RANGE F2,
G3, S5.
ss154.

○ **Greater bladderwort**
Utricularia vulgaris
Short–mid; aquatic.
All stems with feathery
lvs and tiny animal-
catching bladders; fls
12–18mm long. LH
perenn; detached buds.
GERM ? FL 7–8. POLL
ins(h). SEX (♀). HAB
deep water. SOIL water;
acid–calc. SHADE nil.
ALT sl–400(–650). DIST
E2, W2, S2, I3. RANGE
F3, G4, S4.

○ **Lesser bladderwort**
Utricularia minor
Low–short; aquatic.
Some stems with
feathery lvs, others
colourless with
bladders; fls 6–8mm
long, pale yellow. LH
perenn; detached buds.
GERM ? FL 6–9. POLL
ins(h). SEX (♀). HAB
shallow, often peaty
water. SOIL water; not
calc. SHADE nil. ALT sl–
700. DIST E2, W2, S2,
I3. RANGE F2, G3, S3.
ss155.

PLANTAIN FAMILY
Plantaginaceae
Often mistaken for
monocots because of
their rosette of strongly
ribbed, often narrow
leaves. Flowers 4-
petalled and small, in
dense, long-stalked
spikes. Long stamens
and colourful anthers
are most conspicuous
features.
*See p. 17, 181, 248,
257.*

● **Buck's-horn
plantain**
Plantago coronopus
V.low–low. Downy;
lvs greyish, pinnately
lobed, 1-veined; fl-
spike 5–40mm long, its
stalk slightly longer
than lvs. LH ann, bienn
or short-lived perenn.
GERM spr. FL 5–9. POLL
wind. SEX (♀) pg. HAB
bare or grassy sandy
ground, mainly by sea.
SOIL dry; acid–calc.
SHADE nil. ALT sl–100
(–350). DIST coastal:
E5 (2 inland), W5, S4,
I5. RANGE coastal: F5
(2 inland), G4, sS2.
See p. 199, 205, 215.
ss156a.

● **Ribwort plantain**
Plantago lanceolata
Low–mid. Lvs long,
narrow, strongly
ribbed; fls 4mm,
brown, with cream
anthers; spikes to
60mm, green, on long
ridged stalks. LH
perenn, rootstock.
GERM aut–spr. FL 4–10.
POLL wind; ins(d, c).
SEX (♀) pg. HAB grass-
land. SOIL moist–dry;
acid–calc. SHADE nil–
light. ALT sl–800. DIST
E5, W5, S5, I5. RANGE
F5, G5, S3.
See p. 16, 273.

● **Greater plantain**
Plantago major
Low–short. Lvs oval,
ribbed; fls 3mm,
anthers purple at first;
spikes to 150mm, as
long as stalks. LH
perenn; rootstock.
GERM spr. FL 5–9. POLL
wind. SEX (♀) pg. HAB
trampled grassy and
disturbed ground. SOIL
moist; acid–calc.
SHADE nil. ALT sl–300
(–600). DIST E5, W5,
S5, I5. RANGE F5, G5,
S4.
See p. 180, 217.

● **Sea plantain**
Plantago maritima
Low–short. Lvs very narrow, fleshy, 3–5-veined; fls 3mm, anthers yellow; spikes to 60mm, rarely more, shorter than stalks. LH perenn; rootstock. GERM spr–sum. FL 6–9. POLL wind. SEX (♀) pg. HAB saltmarshes, mountains. SOIL wet; saline. SHADE nil. ALT sl(–800). DIST coastal: E5, W5, S5, I5; inland S2. RANGE coastal: F4, G4 (inland 1), S4. *See p. 205.*

● **Hoary plantain**
Plantago media
Short. Downy, lvs oval, short-stalked; fls 2mm, stamens purplish; spikes to 60mm on long, unridged stalks. LH perenn; rootstock. GERM spr. FL 5–8. POLL ins(h, d, c); wind. SEX (♀) pg. HAB grassland. SOIL dry; calc. SHADE nil. ALT sl–300(–500). DIST E4, W2, S1, I1. RANGE F4, G3, S4.

● **Shoreweed**
Littorella uniflora
V.low–low; prostrate. Turf-forming, with creeping stolons and rosettes of cylindrical, narrow lvs; fls 4–6mm, only out of water. LH perenn; stolons. GERM ? FL 6–8. POLL wind. SEX (♂+♀). HAB sandy and gravelly lake-shores. SOIL water; acid. SHADE nil. ALT sl–750. DIST sE2, nE4, W3, S5, I4. RANGE F2, G3, S3. **ss156b.**

MOSCHATEL FAMILY
Adoxaceae
A family containing one species only (Moschatel), with no obvious relationships. It has a clock-face-like head of 5 4-petalled flowers.

VALERIAN FAMILY
Valerianaceae
A small family of opposite-leaved herbs with heads of small 5-petalled flowers. *See p. 277, 283.*

● **Moschatel**
Adoxa moschatellina
Low. Patch-forming, with twice-trefoil lvs and small green fls with yellow anthers. LH perenn; rhizome. GERM spr. FL 3–5. POLL ins(d); self. SEX (♀) pa–pg. HAB woods, mountain rocks. SOIL moist; not acid. SHADE nil–heavy. ALT sl–750. DIST E4, W4, S3, I1. RANGE F4, G4, S2.

● **Marsh valerian**
Valeriana dioica
Short. Creeping runners; root lvs un-toothed; stem lvs pinnately lobed; fls 5mm (♂). 2mm (♀), on separate plants. LH perenn; stolons. GERM spr–sum. FL 5–6. POLL ins(d, h, c). SEX (♂)+(♀). HAB marshes, meadows. SOIL wet–damp; not acid. SHADE nil–mid. ALT sl–600. DIST E4, W3, S2. RANGE F3, G4, sS2. *See p. 164, 182, 270, 271.*

● **Common valerian**
Valeriana officinalis
Short–v.tall. No runners; lvs all pin-nate; fls 5mm, in dense clusters. LH perenn; rhizome. GERM spr–sum. FL 6–8. POLL ins (d, h, c). SEX (♀) pa. HAB grassland, marshes, woods. SOIL wet–dry; not acid. SHADE nil–mid. ALT sl–800. DIST E5, W5, S5, I5. RANGE F5, G5, sS3. *See p. 19, 241, 262.*

● **Red valerian**
Centranthus ruber
Mid–tall. Lvs greyish; upper toothed, un-stalked, unlike lower; fls 5mm, red-pink or white, with long tube and spur. LH perenn; rootstock. GERM sum–aut. FL 5–9. POLL ins (l, h). SEX (♀) pa. HAB walls, rocks. SOIL dry; not acid. SHADE nil. ALT sl–200. DIST sE4, nE2, W4, S2, I2. RANGE F4, G1.

● **Cornsalad**
Valerianella locusta
Low–mid. Delicate, branching; lvs un-stalked, little toothed; fls 1–2mm, in heads surrounded by bracts. LH ann. GERM win–spr. FL 4–8. POLL self. SEX (♀) hg. HAB arable fields, dunes, walls. SOIL moist–dry; acid–calc. SHADE nil. ALT sl–350. DIST E3, W3, S2, I3. RANGE F4, G4, sS2. *See p. 257.*

HONEYSUCKLE FAMILY
Caprifoliaceae
Mostly large shrubs (e.g. Elder, Fly honey-suckle, but including woody climbers, dwarf shrubs and herbs. Leaves in opposite pairs; flowers open, bell-shaped or tubular, with 5 joined petals. *See p. 19, 277.*

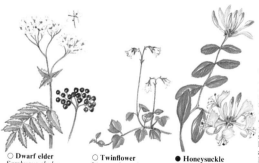

○ **Dwarf elder**
Sambucus ebulus
Tall. Strong-smelling, clumped; lvs pinnate; fls small, in flat-topped clusters to 100mm; fr black. LH perenn; rhizome. GERM spr. FL 7–8. POLL ins(d, h, c); self. SEX (♀). HAB disturbed ground, roadsides. SOIL moist; not acid. SHADE nil–light. ALT sl–250. DIST E3, W2, S1, I2. RANGE F3, G3.

○ **Twinflower**
Linnaea borealis
V.low to low; creeping. Mat-forming; lvs rounded, long-stalked; fls 8–10mm, bell-shaped in pairs on long upright stalks. LH perenn; rooting stems. GERM spr? FL 6–8. POLL ins(d); self. SEX (♀) hg. HAB conifer woods. SOIL moist; acid. SHADE light–heavy. ALT 100–750. DIST nE1, S2. RANGE nG1, S5.
See p. 172, 173.

● **Honeysuckle**
Lonicera periclymenum
Tall–v.tall; climbing. Stems twining or sprawling, woody and flaky; lvs oval; fls long-tubed (to 50mm), in heads, all fls in one plane. LH perenn; woody stems. GERM spr. FL 6–9. POLL ins (l, h); self. SEX (♀). HAB woods, hedges, scrub. SOIL moist–dry; not calc. SHADE nil–mid. ALT sl–500. DIST E5, W5, S5, I5. RANGE F5, G3, wS2.
See p. 193, 259, 278.

TEASEL FAMILY
Dipsacaceae
An attractive family, similar to the Daisy family in having heads of flowers, either flat or round, usually with prominent stamens and styles. The flowers have 4 or 5 petal-lobes and a short tube. Leaves in opposite pairs.
See p. 277, 283, 298.

● **Field scabious**
Knautia arvensis
Mid–tall. Rather coarse, hairy, with pinnately-lobed lvs; fls in flat heads, to 40mm, outer fls with large outer petal lobes. LH perenn; rootstock. POLL ins(h, l). SEX (♀) + (♀) pa. HAB grassy places. SOIL dry; acid–calc. SHADE nil. ALT sl–350. DIST E5, W4, S2, I4. RANGE F5, G5, S3.
See p. 271.

● **Small scabious**
Scabiosa columbaria
Short–mid. Lvs pinnate, slightly hairy; fls in flat heads, 15–25mm, outer fls with large outer petal lobes. LH perenn; rootstock. GERM spr–sum. FL 6–10. POLL ins(h, l). SEX (♀ + ♀) pa. HAB grassland. SOIL dry; calc. SHADE nil. ALT sl–400 (–600). DIST E4, W1, S1. RANGE F4, G3, sS2.
See p. 283.

● **Devil's-bit scabious**
Succisa pratensis
Short–tall. Hairy; lvs narrow oval, narrower on stem, untoothed; fls in rounded heads, 15–25mm. LH perenn; rootstock. GERM spr. FL 6–10. POLL ins(h, l). SEX (♀) + (♀) pa. HAB grassland. SOIL damp–moist; acid–calc. SHADE nil–light. ALT sl–800. DIST E5, W5, S5, I5. RANGE F5, G5, S3.
See p. 276.

● **Teasel**
Dipsacus fullonum
Tall–v.tall. Prickly; stems ridged; lvs spear-shaped, pustulate; fls in large (to 80mm;, egg-shaped, spiny heads. LH bienn. GERM aut–spr. FL 7–8. POLL ins(h); self. SEX (♀). HAB disturbed ground, roadsides, stream sides. SOIL damp–moist; not acid. SHADE nil–light. ALT sl–200. DIST sE5, nE3, W3, S1, I2. RANGE F5, G4.
See p. 19, 237.

○ **Small teasel**
Dipsacus pilosus
Mid–tall. Prickly; stem angled; lvs stalked, with a pair of lflts, at base; fls in rounded, spiny heads to 25mm. LH bienn. GERM spr. FL 7–9. POLL ins(h, d). SEX (♀) pa. HAB woods, watersides. SOIL damp; not acid. SHADE light–mid. ALT sl–250. DIST E3, W1. RANGE F2, G3, S1.
See p. 237.

BELLFLOWER FAMILY
Campanulaceae
Stems often have milky juice, and simple, alternate leaves. Flowers bell-shaped in bellflowers, 1 or 2-lipped in lobelias, or short-tubed in heads and resembling daisy family in rampions. Most are perennials of undisturbed habitats.
See p. 17, 249, 257, 263, 269, 298.

○ **Spiked rampion**
Phyteuma spicatum
Mid–tall. Lvs oval, heart-shaped at base, long-stalked; fls in dense oblong heads; style prominent. LH perenn; rootstock. GERM spr–sum. FL 5–8. POLL ins(h, d, l, c); self. SEX (♀) pa. HAB scrub, grassland. SOIL dry; not acid. SHADE nil–mid. ALT sl–50. DIST sE1. RANGE F3, G4, sS1.

Round-headed rampion
Phyteuma tenerum
Low–short. Root lvs narrow to broad, toothed; stem-lvs narrow; fls 8–10mm, blue, in round heads. LH perenn; tuber. GERM spr? FL 7–8. POLL ins. SEX (♀). HAB short grassland. SOIL dry; calc. SHADE nil. ALT sl–100. DIST sE2. RANGE F2, wG1.

● **Sheep's-bit scabious**
Jasione montana
Low–mid. Lvs narrow, wavy-edged, hairy; fls in dense, rounded heads, up to 35mm. LH short-lived perenn; rootstock. GERM imm. FL 5–9. POLL ins(h, d, l, c); self. SEX (♀) pa. HAB grassy, heathy and rocky places. SOIL dry; acid. SHADE nil–light. ALT sl–400(–900). DIST wE4, eE2, W5, S2, I3. RANGE F3, G3, sS3.

● **Clustered bellflower**
Campanula glomerata
V.low–short. Root lvs long-stalked in a loose rosette; fls 15–20mm, deeply lobed; sepal teeth pointed. LH perenn; rootstock. GERM spr. FL 6–10. POLL ins(h, d, l, c); self. SEX (♀) pa. HAB grassland. SOIL dry; calc. SHADE nil. ALT sl–300. DIST E3, W1, S1. RANGE F3, G4, S2.
See p. 259, 263, 266.

● **Giant bellflower**
Campanula latifolia
Tall–v.tall. Stem bluntly angled; lvs pointed oval, finely toothed; fls 40–55mm, often white. LH perenn; rootstock. GERM spr. FL 7–8. POLL ins(h, d, l, c); self. SEX (♀) pa. HAB woods. SOIL moist; not acid. SHADE light–heavy. ALT sl–400. DIST sE2, nE4, W2, S3. RANGE eF1, G2, S2.

● **Nettle-leaved bellflower**
Campanula trachelium
Tall. Stems sharply angled; lvs unevenly toothed; sepal teeth pointed, erect. LH perenn; rootstock. GERM spr–sum. FL 7–9. POLL ins(h, d, l, c); self. SEX (♀) pa. HAB woods, scrub. SOIL moist; not acid. SHADE light–heavy. ALT sl–300. DIST sE4, nE1, W2. RANGE F4, G4, sS2.

○ **Creeping bellflower**
Campanula rapunculoides
Mid. Stems rounded, slender; lvs finely toothed; fls 20–30mm, sepal teeth hairy, spreading. LH perenn; rootstock. GERM spr–sum. FL 7–9. POLL ins (h, d, l, c); self. SEX (♀) pa. HAB disturbed ground, woods. SOIL moist; not acid. SHADE nil–mid. ALT sl–250. DIST (E3, W2, S2, I2). RANGE F3, G4, S3.

○ **Spreading bellflower**
Campanula patula
Mid. Stems rough, angled; fls 15–20mm, with spreading lobes, in a loose, much-branched cluster. LH short-lived perenn; rootstock. GERM aut. FL 7–9. POLL ins(h, d, l, c); self. SEX (♀) pa. HAB woods, hedges, walls. SOIL moist–dry; not acid. SHADE nil–mid. ALT sl–200. DIST sE1, W1. RANGE eF1, G3, S3.

● **Peach-leaved bellflower**
Campanula persicifolia
Mid. Lvs narrow, finely-toothed, hairless; fls 25–35mm, in erect spikes. LH perenn; rootstock. GERM aut. FL 5–8. POLL ins(h, d, l, c); self. SEX (♀) pa. HAB woods, scrub, disturbed ground. SOIL moist; acid–calc. SHADE nil–mid. ALT sl–250. DIST (E3, W2, S3). RANGE F4, G4, S3.

● **Harebell**
Campanula rotundifolia
Short–mid. Delicate; lower lvs rounded, upper very narrow; fls 15–18mm, long-stalked. LH perenn; stolons. GERM aut–spr. FL 7–10. POLL ins(h, d, l, c); self. SEX (♀) pa. HAB grassland, heaths. SOIL dry; acid–calc. SHADE nil–light. ALT sl–1250. DIST E4, W5, S5, I2. RANGE F4, G5, S5.
See p. 257.

Bearded bellflower
Campanula barbata
Low–short. Lvs oblong, hairy, mostly in rosette; fls 15–25mm, with long white hairs inside. LH perenn; rootstock. GERM spr? FL 6–8. POLL ins(h, d, l, c); self. SEX (♀) pa. HAB shady and rocky places. SOIL moist; not acid. SHADE nil–mid. ALT [800–2300]. RANGE sG1, S1.

○ **Ivy-leaved bellflower**
Wahlenbergia hederacea
V.low–low; creeping. Stems slender; lvs ivy-shaped on long stalks; fls 6–10mm, bell-shaped, fine stalked. LH perenn; GERM spr–sum. FL 7–8. POLL ins (♀) pa. HAB heaths, woods, moors. SOIL peaty, damp; acid. SHADE nil–mid. ALT sl–300(–500). DIST swE2, W3, wS1, I2. RANGE F2, wG1.

● **Venus's looking-glass**
Legousia hybrida
Low–short. Lvs oblong, wavy-edged; fls with a tube 15–30mm long, and spreading petal lobes, 8–15mm, shorter than sepals. LH ann. GERM spr. FL 5–8. POLL ins(h, d); self. SEX (♀) pa. HAB arable fields. SOIL moist–dry; calc. SHADE nil. ALT sl–150. DIST sE3, nE1. RANGE F3, G2.

● **Water lobelia**
Lobelia dortmanna
Short–mid. Lvs very narrow, in a dense, submerged rosette; stems lfless, with a few, nodding 2-lipped fls 15–20mm. LH perenn; stolons. GERM spr. FL 7–8. POLL ins(h, d). SEX (♀). HAB gravelly lakes. SOIL water; acid. SHADE nil. ALT sl–150. DIST nE1, W2, S4, I2. RANGE wF1, nG2, S3.

● **Heath lobelia**
Lobelia urens
Short–mid. Lvs oblong, toothed, mainly on stem; fls 10–15mm, 2-lipped, erect. LH perenn; rootstock. GERM ? FL 8–9. POLL ins(h, d, l). SEX (♀). HAB heaths, woods. SOIL damp–moist; acid. SHADE nil–mid. ALT sl–100. DIST sE1. RANGE F2.

DAISY FAMILY
Compositae
The largest and one of the most characteristic families, with compound heads, containing usually many small florets. These are of two kinds: disc florets which have a short tube, and ray florets which have a long flap on the end of the tube. The heads may have just disc florets (rayless, as in thistles), just ray florets (as in dandelions), or both (rayed, as in daisy). The fruit has fine hairs, a pappus, often forming a parachute.
See p. 16, 18, 19, 162, 169, 212, 221, 237, 248, 259, 263, 265, 269, 277, 283, 289, 290, 291, 295, 296, 298.

● **Hemp agrimony**
Eupatorium cannabinum
Mid–tall. Stems purplish, downy; lvs deeply 5-lobed; flhds rayless, small, in dense clusters. LH perenn; rootstock. GERM spr–sum. FL 7–9. POLL ins(d, h, c, l); self. SEX (♀) pa. HAB woods, marshes, disturbed ground. SOIL damp–moist; not acid. SHADE nil–mid. ALT sl–250. DIST sE4, nE2, W4, S2, I3. RANGE F5, G5, sS3.
See p. 277.

● **Canadian goldenrod**
Solidago canadensis
Tall–v.tall. Lvs spear-shaped, downy, strongly veined; flhds 5mm, shortly-rayed; in 1-sided spikes. LH perenn; rhizome. GERM spr. FL 7–9. POLL ins(d, h); self. SEX (♀) pa. HAB disturbed ground. SOIL moist; not acid. SHADE nil–light. ALT sl–250. DIST AND RANGE widely naturalised.

● **Goldenrod**
Solidago virgaurea
Low–tall. Lvs oval or spear-shaped, often hairless; flhds 6–10mm, rayed, in branching clusters. LH perenn; rootstock. GERM aut–spr. FL 7–9. POLL ins (d, h); self. SEX (♀) pa. HAB open woods, heaths, rocks. SOIL moist–dry; not calc. SHADE nil–mid. ALT sl–1100. DIST E4, W5, S4, I3. RANGE F4, G5, S5.
See p. 249, 271, 277.

● **Michaelmas daisy**
Aster novae-belgii
Mid–tall. Lvs narrow, stem lfy; flhds 25–40 mm, rays purple, discs yellow; in lfy branching spikes. LH perenn; rhizome. GERM spr–sum. FL 8–11. POLL ins(d, h, c, l); self. SEX (♀) pa. HAB disturbed ground. SOIL moist–dry; acid–calc. SHADE nil–light. ALT sl–250. DIST AND RANGE widely naturalised.

109

● **Sea aster**
Aster tripolium
Short–tall. Lvs fleshy, hairless, becoming narrow up stem; flhds 10–20mm, rays purplish (or absent), discs yellow. LH perenn; rhizome. GERM spr–sum. FL 7–10. POLL ins (d, h, c); self. SEX (♀) pa. HAB salt-marshes, sea-cliffs. SOIL wet–dry; saline. SHADE nil. ALT sl. DIST coastal: E4, W2, S3, I4; rarely inland. RANGE coastal: F4, G5, S4; rarely inland.
See p. 271.

○ **Goldilocks**
Aster linosyris
Low–mid. Lvs very narrow, overlapping on stem; flhds 12–18 mm, rayless, in a flat-topped cluster. LH perenn; rootstock. GERM spr? FL 8–10. POLL ins(d, h, l, c); self. SEX (♀) pa. HAB rocks, grassland. SOIL dry; calc. SHADE nil–light. ALT sl–100. DIST wE1, W1. RANGE F2, G2, sS1.

● **Canadian fleabane**
Conyza canadensis
Low–tall. Branching, with few narrow lvs on stem; flhds 3–5mm, discs yellow, rays pale rays pale mauve. LH ann. GERM spr–sum. FL 8–10. POLL ins(d, h). SEX (♀) pa. HAB disturbed ground, dunes. SOIL dry; not acid. SHADE nil. ALT sl–250. DIST sE4, nE1, W2. RANGE F4, G4, sS2.

● **Ploughman's spikenard**
Inula conyza
Short–tall. Lower lvs oval, stalked, downy; stems reddish; flhds 10mm, rays small or absent. LH short-lived perenn; rootstock. GERM spr–sum. FL 7–9. POLL ins(d, h); self. SEX (♀) pa. HAB scrub, rocks, grassy places. SOIL dry; not acid. SHADE nil–mid. ALT sl–250. DIST sE4, nE2, W2. RANGE F4, G3, sS1.
See p. 247.

● **Golden samphire**
Inula crithmoides
Short–tall. Fleshy, with narrow lvs clothing stem; flhds 20–25mm, ray-florets long. LH perenn; rootstock. GERM spr? FL 7–10. POLL ins(d, h, c); self. SEX (♀) pa. HAB sea cliffs, salt-marshes. SOIL wet–dry; saline. SHADE nil. ALT sl–100. DIST coastal; sE3, W2, sI2. RANGE coastal: F2.

○ **Elecampane**
Inula helenium
Tall–v.tall. Massive with large densely downy lvs; flhds 60–80mm, rays long, narrow. LH perenn; rootstock. GERM ? FL 7–8. POLL ins(h, l); self. SEX (♀) pa. HAB disturbed ground, roadsides. SOIL moist; acid–calc. SHADE nil. ALT sl–200. DIST AND RANGE widely naturalised.

○ **Irish fleabane**
Inula salicina
Mid. Lvs stiff, not or slightly toothed; flhds 25–30mm, borne singly or in small clusters. LH perenn; stolons. GERM spr? FL 7–8. POLL ins (h, d, l); self. SEX (♀) pa. HAB marshes, rocks, lake shores. SOIL wet–damp; not acid. SHADE nil–light. ALT sl–50. DIST I1. RANGE F2, G3, sS2.

● **Daisy**
Bellis perennis
V.low–low. Lvs spoon-shaped, in a rosette; flhds 15–25mm, rays white, often red outside, on hairy stalks. LH perenn; evergreen rosette. GERM sum–aut. FL 1–12. POLL ins(h, d, c); self. SEX (♂+♀) pa. HAB short grassland. SOIL moist; acid–calc. SHADE nil. ALT sl–800. DIST E5, W5, S5, I5. RANGE F5, G5, S2.
See p. 19, 201, 259, 265, 296.

● **Scentless mayweed**
Matricaria perforata
Short–mid. Sprawling; lvs feathery, 2–3-pinnate; flhds 15–40mm, rays white, less than 20. LH ann, sometimes persisting. GERM aut–spr. FL 4–10. POLL ins(h, d); self. SEX (♀) pa. HAB disturbed ground. SOIL moist–dry; acid–calc. SHADE nil. ALT sl–300 (–500). DIST E5, W5, S4, I4. RANGE F5, G5, S4.

● **Sea mayweed**
Matricaria maritima
Short–mid; prostrate. Stems short, much branched; lvs feathery, fleshy; flhds 30–50mm, rays more than 20. LH perenn; rootstock. GERM aut–spr. FL 5–9. POLL ins(h, d); self. SEX (♀) pa. HAB coastal sand, shingle and rocks. SOIL moist–dry; saline. SHADE nil. ALT sl–100. DIST coastal: E3, W2, S4, I4. RANGE coastal: F2, G3, S4.
See p. 249.

● **Scented mayweed**
Chamomilla recutita
Short–mid. Stems
branched; lvs feathery,
2–3-pinnate, scented;
flhds 10–25mm, rays
15, down-turned. LH
ann. GERM aut. FL 5–8.
POLL ins(d, h); self.
SEX (♀) pa. HAB dis-
turbed ground. SOIL
moist–dry; not calc.
SHADE nil. ALT sl–200.
DIST E4, W2, S1.
RANGE F5, G5, S3.

● **Pineapple mayweed**
Chamomilla suaveolens
Low–short. Smells of
pineapple when
crushed; lvs feathery,
2–3-pinnate; flhds 5–
10mm, with no rays.
LH ann. GERM aut. FL
5–10. POLL ins(d); self.
SEX (♀). HAB disturbed
and trampled ground.
SOIL moist–dry; acid–
calc. SHADE nil. ALT sl–
300(–500). DIST E5,
W5, S5, I5. RANGE F5,
G5, S4.

○ **Lawn chamomile**
Chamaemelum nobile
Low–short. Scented;
lvs feathery, 2–3-pin-
nate; flhds 15–25mm;
rays female, showing
styles. LH perenn;
rhizome. GERM spr. FL
6–7. POLL ins(d, h, c);
self. SEX (♀) pa. HAB
sandy grassland. SOIL
dry; acid–calc. SHADE
nil. ALT sl–200(–400).
DIST sE3, W2, I2.
RANGE wF3.

● **Corn chamomile**
Anthemis arvensis
Short–mid. Branching,
aromatic; lvs feathery,
hairy; flhds 20–30mm,
rays female, showing
styles LH ann. GERM
aut. FL 6–8. POLL ins
(h, d); self. SEX (♀) pa.
HAB arable fields, dis-
turbed ground. SOIL
dry; calc. SHADE nil.
ALT sl–200. DIST E3,
W2, S1. RANGE F4, G5,
S3.

● **Stinking chamomile**
Anthemis cotula
Short–mid. Branching,
unpleasantly scented;
lvs feathery, hairless;
flhds 10–25mm; rays
down-turned with
neither stamens nor
styles. LH ann. GERM
aut. FL 7–9. POLL ins
(d, c); self. SEX (♀) pa.
HAB arable fields. SOIL
moist; acid–calc.
SHADE nil. ALT sl–200.
DIST E4, W2, S2, I2.
RANGE F3, G3, S2.

○ **Yellow chamomile**
Anthemis tinctoria
Short–mid. Lvs 2-
pinnate, white with
down; flhds 25–40mm,
on long, grooved
stalks; rays with styles
only. LH short-lived
perenn. GERM spr. FL
7–8. POLL ins(h, d, l,
c); self. SEX (♀) pa.
HAB disturbed ground.
SOIL dry; not acid.
SHADE nil. ALT sl–200.
DIST E casual. RANGE
eF1, G3, S4.

● **Blue fleabane**
Erigeron acer
Low–mid. Stems red-
dish, rough–hairy; lvs
narrow, untoothed,
hairy; flhds 10–20mm;
rays erect, short. LH
ann–bienn. GERM imm.
FL 6–9. POLL ins; self.
SEX (♀) pa. HAB grassy
and bare ground. SOIL
dry; calc. SHADE nil.
ALT sl–200(–400). DIST
sE4, nE2, W2, S1, I2.
RANGE F4, G4, S5.
See p. 271.

○ **Alpine fleabane**
Erigeron borealis
Low–short. Lvs hairy,
mostly in rosette; flhds
15–20mm, hairy out-
side; rays long, spread-
ing. LH perenn;
rhizome. GERM spr.
FL 7–8. POLL ins; self.
SEX (♀) pa. HAB rocks.
SOIL moist; calc. SHADE
nil. ALT 800–1100. DIST
S1. RANGE S3.

● **Gallant soldier**
Galinsoga parviflora
Short–mid. Lvs
toothed, yellowish,
white–hairy; flhds 3–
5mm, with 5 3-lobed
rays. LH ann. GERM
spr–sum. FL 5–10. POLL
ins; self. SEX (♀). HAB
disturbed ground. SOIL
moist; acid–calc.
SHADE nil. ALT sl–250.
DIST E3, W2, S1.
RANGE F3, G3, S2.
ss157.

● **Mountain
everlasting**
Antennaria dioica
Low–short. Lvs white-
woolly beneath; in
rosettes; flhds 5–15mm,
on lfy stalks; rayless,
but with spreading
bracts. LH perenn;
stolons. GERM sum–
aut. FL 6–7. POLL apo.
SEX (♂) + (♀) + (♀).
HAB heaths, rocks,
rocks, moors. SOIL dry;
not acid. SHADE nil.
ALT 200–800. DIST sE1,
nE3, W2, S4, I3.
RANGE eF2, G4, S5.

111

● **Common cudweed**
Filago vulgaris
Low–short. Stem
much-branched at base
and top; stem and
narrow lvs white–
woolly. Flhds 5mm in
dense clusters. LH ann.
GERM spr. FL 7–8. POLL
ins; self. SEX (♀). HAB
heaths, fields, tracks
on sandy soils. SOIL
dry; acid. SHADE nil.
ALT sl–300. DIST E4,
W3, S2, I2. RANGE F3,
G3.

○ **Red-tipped cudweed**
Filago lutescens
Low–short. Lvs finely
pointed, with yellow
hairs; flhds in clusters
of 10–20, with red-
tipped bracts. LH ann.
GERM spr. FL 7–8. POLL
self. SEX (♀). HAB
sandy ground. SOIL
dry; acid. SHADE nil.
ALT sl–50. DIST eE1.
RANGE F2, G2, sS2.

○ **Broad-leaved
cudweed**
Filago pyramidata
Low–short. Stem
branching from base;
and spoon-shaped lvs
hairy; flhds 5mm,
shorter than lvs. LH
ann. GERM spr. FL 7–8.
POLL ins; self. SEX (♀).
HAB sandy fields, dis-
turbed ground. SOIL
dry; acid. SHADE nil.
ALT sl–200. DIST sE2.
RANGE F3, G1.

● **Small cudweed**
Logfia minima
Low. Stem branching
from middle; and
narrow lvs grey–
woolly; flhds 3–4mm
in clusters; bracts
hairless at tip. LH ann.
GERM imm. FL 6–9.
POLL ins; self. SEX (♀).
HAB sandy fields,
heaths. SOIL dry; acid.
SHADE nil. ALT sl–200
(–350). DIST E3, W3,
S2, I2. RANGE F3, G4,
sS3.

○ **Field cudweed**
Logfia arvensis
Low–mid. Stem
branching near top,
white; lvs narrow,
white; flhds 4–5mm,
with narrow, white
hair-tipped bracts. LH
ann. GERM spr. FL 7–9.
POLL ins; self. SEX (♀).
HAB disturbed, sandy
ground. SOIL dry; acid.
SHADE nil. ALT [sl–400].
DIST casual in E.
RANGE F2, G3, S3.

● **Marsh cudweed**
Filaginella uliginosa
Low–short. Woolly,
much-branched; lvs
oblong; flhds 3–4mm,
in small clusters, sur-
rounded by longer lvs.
LH ann. GERM spr–sum.
FL 7–10. POLL ins; self.
SEX (♀). HAB bare,
sandy ground. SOIL
damp–moist; acid.
SHADE nil. ALT sl–350.
DIST E4, W5, S4, I3.
RANGE F5, G5, S4.
ss158.

○ **Highland cudweed**
Omalotheca norvegica
Low–short. Lvs spear-
shaped, 3-veined; flhds
5–7mm, with brown
bracts, along top
quarter of stem. LH
perenn; rootstock.
GERM spr? FL 8–9. POLL
ins; self. SEX (♀). HAB
mountain rocks. SOIL
moist; not calc. SHADE
nil. ALT 800–1200. DIST
S1. RANGE G1, S4.

○ **Dwarf cudweed**
Omalotheca supina
V.low–low. Tufted; lvs
very narrow and short,
woolly; flhds 6–8mm,
in short dense clusters,
longer than lvs. LH
perenn; rhizome. GERM
spr? FL 7–8. POLL ins;
self. SEX (♀). HAB
mountain rocks. SOIL
moist; not calc. SHADE
nil. ALT 500–1400. DIST
S3. RANGE G1, S3.

● **Heath cudweed**
Omalotheca sylvatica
Low–mid. White–
woolly; lvs very
narrow, 1-veined;
flhds 2mm (6mm long),
in a long lfy spike,
occupying more than ½
the stem. LH perenn;
rootstock. GERM spr.
FL 7–9. POLL ins; self.
SEX (♀). HAB woods,
heaths, grassland. SOIL
moist–dry; acid. SHADE
nil–mid (–800). DIST E3, W2,
S4, I2. RANGE F3, G4,
S4.

● **Common fleabane**
Pulicaria dysenterica
Short–mid. Stems
woolly; lvs arrow–
shaped, clasping stem,
woolly beneath; flhds
15–30mm, rays low.
LH perenn; stolons.
GERM any. FL 7–10.
POLL ins(d); self. SEX
(♀) pa. HAB grassland,
marshes. SOIL damp;
not calc. SHADE nil–
light. ALT sl–300. DIST
E4, W4, S1, I3. RANGE
F5, G2.
See p. 210, 211.

112

○ **Small fleabane**
Pulicaria vulgaris
Low–mid. Branched;
lvs oval, narrowed to
base, unstalked; flhds
10mm, rays very short.
LH ann. GERM aut–win.
FL 8–9. POLL ins; self.
SEX (♀) pa. HAB bare
sandy places, ponds
wet in winter. SOIL
damp; not calc. SHADE
nil. ALT sl–150. DIST
sE1. RANGE F2, G3,
sS1.

Arnica
Arnica montana
Short–mid. Lvs spear-
shaped, downy, mainly
in rosette; flhds 40–
80mm, rays very long,
narrow, single. LH
perenn; rootstock.
GERM ? FL 6–8. POLL
ins(h, d, l); self. SEX
(♀) pa. HAB grassland,
open woods. SOIL
moist; not acid. SHADE
nil–light. ALT [200–
2000]. RANGE eF1, G4,
sS4.

● **Leopard's-bane**
*Doronicum
pardalianches*
Mid–tall. Patch-form-
ing, rosette-lvs hairy,
heart-shaped; flhds
40–60mm, rays long,
numerous. LH perenn;
stolons. GERM aut. FL
5–7. POLL ins(h, d, l,
c); self. SEX (♀) pa.
HAB woods. SOIL
moist; acid–calc.
SHADE light–mid. ALT
sl–400. DIST (E3, W3,
S3). RANGE F2, G2.
See p. 271.

● **Winter heliotrope**
Petasites fragrans
Short. Patch-forming;
lvs rounded, to 20cm,
always present; flhds
scented, in loose few-
fld spike. LH perenn;
rhizome. GERM spr? FL
12–3. POLL ins(h, d);
self. SEX (♂)+(♀). HAB
stream sides, disturbed
ground. SOIL damp–
moist; acid–calc.
SHADE nil–light. ALT
sl–200. DIST E3, W2,
S1, I4. RANGE F2.

● **Butterbur**
Petasites hybridus
Short. Patch-forming;
lvs heart-shaped,
downy beneath, up to
1m, dying in winter;
flhds in dense spikes,
before spring lvs. LH
perenn; rhizome. GERM
spr–sum. FL 3–5. POLL
ins(h). SEX (♂)+(♀).
HAB grassland, woods,
streams, by roads. SOIL
wet–moist; acid–calc.
SHADE nil–mid. ALT sl–
400. DIST E4, W4, S3,
I3. RANGE F5, G4, sS3.
See p. 191, 198, 250.

● **Coltsfoot**
Tussilago farfara
Low. Patch-forming;
lvs heart-shaped, to
20cm, dying in winter;
flhds 15–35mm, on
white stalks with
purple scales; before
leaves. LH perenn;
stolons. GERM sum.
FL 2–4. POLL ins(h, d);
self. SEX (♀) pa. HAB
disturbed ground. SOIL
wet–dry; acid–calc.
SHADE nil. ALT sl–400
[–1000]. DIST E5, W5,
S5, I5. RANGE F5, G5,
S5.
See p. 191. **ss159**.

● **Yarrow**
Achillea millefolium
Short–mid. Lvs grey-
ish, 2–3-pinnate, aro-
matic; flhds 4–6mm, in
dense, flat clusters;
rays short, notched. LH
perenn; stolons. GERM
win–spr. FL 6–11. POLL
SEX (♀+♀) pa. HAB
grassy places. SOIL
moist–dry; acid–calc.
SHADE nil–light. ALT
sl–1250. DIST E5, W5,
S5, I5. RANGE F5, G5,
S5.
See p. 221, 296.

● **Sneezewort**
Achillea ptarmica
Short–mid. Lvs
narrow, pointed, un-
stalked, finely toothed;
flhds 12–18mm, in
loose clusters; rays
longer than Yarrow.
LH perenn; rhizome.
GERM spr. FL 7–9. POLL
ins(h, d); self. SEX (♀)
pa. HAB grassland,
marshes. SOIL damp;
not calc. SHADE nil–
mid. ALT sl–750. DIST
E4, W5, S5, I3. RANGE
F3, G5, S4.

● **Sea wormwood**
Artemisia maritima
Short–mid. Grey,
strongly aromatic; lvs
2-pinnate, woolly;
flhds 1–2mm, rayless,
drooping in lfy, branch-
ing spikes. LH perenn;
rootstock. GERM spr.
FL 8–10. POLL wind.
SEX (♀). HAB salt-
marshes. SOIL damp;
saline. SHADE nil. ALT
sl. DIST coastal: E4,
W2, S1, I1. RANGE
coastal: F4, G4, sS2.

● **Mugwort**
Artemisia vulgaris
Tall. Stems reddish,
ridged; lvs pinnately
lobed, dull green
above, grey beneath;
flhds 2–3mm, oval, in
dense, lfy spikes. LH
perenn; rootstock.
GERM spr. FL 7–9. POLL
wind. SEX (♀). HAB
disturbed ground. SOIL
moist–dry; acid–calc.
SHADE nil. ALT sl–400.
DIST E5, W4, S3, I3.
RANGE F5, G5, S4.
See p. 273.

113

● **Wormwood**
Artemisia absinthium
Mid–tall. Stems grooved; lvs 1–3-pinnate, white-downy on both sides; flhds 2–4 mm, bell-shaped, drooping. LH perenn; rootstock. GERM spr. FL 7–8. POLL wind. SEX (♀). SOIL moist– dry; acid–calc. SHADE nil. ALT sl–350. DIST E3, W2, S1, I1. RANGE F3, G3, S3.

○ **Field wormwood**
Artemisia campestris
Short–mid. Almost hairless and unscented; lower lvs 2–3-pinnate, upper narrow, un-divided; flhds 3–4mm, in a long, branching spike. LH perenn; rhizome. GERM spr–sum. FL 8–9. POLL wind. SEX (♀). HAB heaths, grassland. SOIL dry; acid–calc. SHADE nil. ALT sl–100. DIST eE1. RANGE F2, G3, sS2.

● **Nodding bur-marigold**
Bidens cernua
Low–mid. Lvs narrow, unstalked in pairs; flhds 15–25mm, drooping, with no rays; surrounded by lf-like bracts. LH ann. GERM spr–sum. FL 7–9. POLL ins(h, d); self. SEX (♀). HAB mud, wet in winter. SOIL damp– moist; acid–calc. SHADE nil. ALT sl–200. DIST E4, W2, S2, I3. RANGE F4, G4, S2.

● **Trifid bur-marigold**
Bidens tripartita
Short–mid. Lvs 3-lobed, stalked, in pairs; flhds 15–25mm, up-right, with no rays; bracts lf-like. LH ann. GERM spr–sum. FL 7–10. POLL ins(h, d); self. SEX (♀). HAB water-sides. SOIL damp– moist; acid–calc. SHADE nil. ALT sl–200. DIST E4, W3, S1, I2. RANGE F5, G5, sS4.

● **Ox-eye daisy**
Leucanthemum vulgare
Short–mid. Lvs deep dark green, toothed, clasping stem; flhds 25–50mm, solitary, rays long. LH perenn; rootstock. GERM sum– aut. FL 5–9. POLL ins (h, d, l. c); self. SEX (♀). HAB grassland. SOIL moist–dry; not acid. SHADE nil. ALT sl–400(–800). DIST E5, W5, S4, I5. RANGE F5, G5, S4.
See p. 249.

● **Feverfew**
Tanacetum parthenium
Short–mid. Strongly aromatic; lvs yellow green, pinnately-lobed; flhds 10–25mm, rays short, broad, notched. LH perenn; rootstock. GERM spr? FL 6–9. POLL ins(d, h); self. SEX (♀). HAB disturbed ground, walls. SOIL dry; not acid. SHADE nil. ALT sl–250. DIST naturalised: E4, W2, S3, I1. RANGE naturalised widely

● **Tansy**
Tanacetum vulgare
Mid–tall. Strongly aromatic; lvs 1–2-pinnate, dark green; flhds 6–12mm, rayless, in flattened clusters. GERM spr. FL 7–10. POLL ins(d, h, c); self. SEX (♀). HAB disturbed ground. SOIL moist– dry; acid–calc. SHADE nil. ALT sl–250. DIST E4, W4, S3, I3. RANGE F5, G5, S4.

● **Corn marigold**
Chrysanthemum segetum
Short–mid. Lvs grey-ish, deeply toothed, upper clasping stem; flhds 35–60mm, rays long, broad. LH ann. GERM spr. FL 6–10. POLL ins(d, h, c, l); self. SEX (♀) pa. HAB cornfields. SOIL moist; acid. SHADE nil. ALT sl–300. DIST E4, W3, S3, I4. RANGE F3, G3, S3.
See p. 242.

● **Ragwort**
Senecio jacobaea
Mid–tall(v.tall). Lvs deeply pinnately lobed, end-lobe blunt; flhds 15–25mm, in dense, flat-topped clusters. LH perenn; rootstock. GERM imm–spr. FL 6–10. POLL ins(d, h, c, l); self. SEX (♀ + ♀) pa. HAB grassland. SOIL moist–dry; acid–calc. SHADE nil–light. ALT sl– 400 (–700). DIST E5, W5, S5, I5. RANGE F5, G5, S2.
See p. 240, 263, 277, 296. **ss160.**

● **Hoary ragwort**
Senecio erucifolius
Mid–tall. Like Rag-wort, but lvs greyish, finely toothed, end lobe pointed; flhds 15–20mm, in loose clus-ters. LH perenn; root-stock. GERM spr. FL 7–8. POLL ins(d, h); self. SEX (♀) pa. HAB grassland. SOIL damp– dry; not acid. SHADE nil. ALT sl–200. DIST E4, W2, I1. RANGE F4, G4, sS1.

● **Marsh ragwort**
Senecio aquaticus
Mid(–tall). Branches spreading; all lvs pinnately-lobed and toothed; flhds 25–30 mm, in loose clusters. LH short-lived perenn. GERM aut–spr. FL 7–8. POLL ins(h, d, l); self. SEX (♀') pa. HAB marshes, grassland. SOIL damp; acid calc. SHADE nil–light. ALT sl–400. DIST E4, W5, S4, I5. RANGE F4, G4, sS1.
See p. 164.

○ **Fen ragwort**
Senecio paludosus
Tall–v.tall. Hairy; lvs narrow, saw-edged; flhds 30–40mm in a flat-topped cluster. LH perenn; rhizome. GERM aut–spr. FL 6–7. POLL ins(d, h, l); self. SEX (♀') pa. HAB marshes, ditches. SOIL wet; calc. SHADE nil. ALT sl–50. DIST eE1. RANGE F1, G3, sS1.

● **Oxford ragwort**
Senecio squalidus
Short. Branching; lvs pinnately lobed, clasping stem; flhds 15–20mm, bracts black-tipped. LH persistent annual. GERM spr. FL 4–11. POLL ins (d, h, c); self. SEX (♀' + ♀) pa. HAB walls, waste ground. SOIL dry; not acid. SHADE nil. ALT sl–250. DIST (E5, W3, S2, I2). RANGE (F3, G?).
See p. 288, 289.

○ **Alpine ragwort**
Senecio fuchsii
Mid–tall. Lvs narrow, oval, finely toothed, hairless; flhds 15–25 mm, rays few, in branching clusters. LH perenn; rhizome. GERM spr. FL 7–9. POLL ins; self. SEX (♀') pa. HAB woods. SOIL moist; acid–calc. SHADE light–heavy. ALT [100–2000]. DIST (nE1). RANGE eF2, G4.

● **Groundsel**
Senecio vulgaris
Low–mid. Lvs coarsely lobed, hairy or hairless; flhds 4–5mm, with or without rays; outer bracts black-tipped, short. LH ann. GERM any. FL 1–12. POLL ins; self. SEX (♀') pa. HAB disturbed ground. SOIL moist–dry; acid–calc. SHADE nil. ALT sl–500. DIST E5, W5, S5, I5. RANGE F5, G5, S4.
See p. 174, 188, 215, 243, 248, 288, 289.

● **Sticky groundsel**
Senecio viscosus
Short–mid. Lvs dark, greyish-green, stickily hairy, pinnately lobed; flhds 8mm, rayed, outer bracts longer than in Groundsel. LH ann. GERM spr. FL 6–9. POLL ins(h, d); self. SEX (♀') pa. HAB disturbed ground, bare sandy places. SOIL dry; acid. SHADE nil–light. ALT sl–250. DIST E4, W3, S3, I1. RANGE F4, G4, S3.

● **Heath groundsel**
Senecio sylvaticus
Mid. Lvs yellowish, slightly sticky, deeply lobed; flhds 5mm, outer bracts very short. LH ann. GERM imm. FL 7–9. POLL ins(d, h); self. SEX (♀'). HAB open, sandy ground. SOIL dry; acid. SHADE nil–light. ALT sl–350. DIST E4, W4, S3, I2. RANGE F3, G4, S3.

● **Carline thistle**
Carlina vulgaris
Low–mid. Lvs spiny, pinnately lobed, in rosette, dying after 1 yr; flhd 20–40mm, clustered, spiny; bracts resemble rays. LH bienn. GERM spr. FL 7–9. POLL ins(h); self. SEX (♀'). HAB short grassland. SOIL dry; calc. SHADE nil. ALT sl–400. DIST sE4, nE2, W2, S2, I3. RANGE F4, G4, sS4.
See p. 219, 246, 294, 295.

Stemless carline thistle
Carlina acaulis
Low. Lvs spiny, pinnately lobed, in rosette, persisting; flhd 30–50mm, unstalked, solitary; bracts resembling rays. LH short-lived perenn. GERM spr? FL 5–9. POLL ins(h, l); self. SEX (♀'). HAB grassy and rocky places. SOIL moist–dry; calc. SHADE nil. ALT [250–1500]. RANGE eF2, sG3.

○ **Alpine sawwort**
Saussurea alpina
Low–mid. Hairy; lvs toothed, spear-shaped, white beneath; flhds 15–20mm, rayless, the disc florets long. LH perenn; stolons. GERM spr? FL 8–9. POLL ins (h, d); self. SEX (♀') pa. HAB grassy and rocky places. SOIL moist; acid–calc. SHADE nil. ALT (50–)500–1200. DIST nE1, nW1, S3, I1. RANGE G1, S4.

● **Greater burdock**
Arctium lappa
Tall. Bushy; lvs large, heart-shaped, solid-stalked, grey beneath; flhds 30–40mm, on long stalks. LH bienn. GERM any. FL 7–9. POLL ins(h, l); self. SEX (♀). HAB disturbed ground. SOIL moist; not acid. SHADE nil–light. ALT sl–150. DIST sE4, W2, I1. RANGE F5, G5, sS2. *See p. 282.*

● **Lesser burdock**
Arctium minus
Tall. Bushy; lvs narrow oval, green beneath, hollow-stalked; flhds 15–40mm, short or unstalked. LH bienn. GERM any. FL 7–9. POLL ins(h, l); self. SEX (♀). HAB woods, disturbed ground. SOIL moist; acid–calc. SHADE nil–mid. ALT sl–300. DIST E5, W5, S5, I5. RANGE F5, G5, S3. *See p. 237.*

○ **Cabbage thistle**
Cirsium oleraceum
Tall. Stems not winged; lvs narrow, pinnately lobed, softly spiny; flhds 25–40mm, rayless, straw-coloured. LH perenn; rootstock. GERM imm. FL 7–9. POLL ins(h, l); self. SEX (♀) hg. HAB fens, marshes. SOIL wet–damp; not acid. SHADE nil–light. ALT sl–200. DIST (E1, S1). RANGE F4, G5, sS1.

● **Creeping thistle**
Cirsium arvense
Mid–tall. Stems not winged; lvs spiny-lobed; flhds 15–25mm, with rough, not spiny, purplish bracts. LH perenn; root buds. GERM spr–sum. FL 6–9. POLL ins(h, d, l, c); self. SEX (♂)+(♀). HAB disturbed ground, fields. SOIL moist; acid–calc. SHADE nil–light. ALT sl–700. DIST E5, W5, S5, I5. RANGE F5, G5, S4. *See p. 251.*

● **Spear thistle**
Cirsium vulgare
Mid–v.tall. Stem winged, spiny; lvs deeply lobed, very spiny; flhds 20–40mm, solitary. LH bienn. GERM aut–spr. FL 7–9. POLL ins(h, l); self. SEX (♀) hg. HAB disturbed ground, fields. SOIL moist–dry; not acid. SHADE nil. ALT sl–600. DIST E5, W5, S5, I5. RANGE F5, G5, S3. *See p. 19, 236, 237, 295.*

● **Woolly thistle**
Cirsium eriophorum
Mid–v.tall. Stems not winged; lvs very spiny, white–woolly, the narrow lobes in two planes; flhds 40–70mm, with cottony bracts. LH bienn. GERM aut. FL 7–9. POLL ins(h, l). self. SEX (♀) hg. HAB grassy and disturbed places. SOIL dry; calc. SHADE nil. ALT sl–250. DIST E3, W1. RANGE F4, G2. *See p. 237.*

● **Meadow thistle**
Cirsium dissectum
Short–tall. Stem unwinged, almost lfless; lvs spear-shaped, prickle-edged, cottony; flhds 20–25mm, solitary. LH perenn; stolons. GERM sum–aut. FL 6–9. POLL ins (h, d, l); self. SEX (♀) hg. HAB fens, meadows. SOIL damp; not acid. SHADE nil. ALT sl–300 (–500). DIST sE4, W2, nE1, I4. RANGE F3, G1. **ss161.**

● **Melancholy thistle**
Cirsium helenioides
Mid–tall. Very like Meadow thistle, but taller, lvs more cottony and flhds 30–50mm. LH perenn; stolons. GERM aut? FL 7–8. POLL ins(h); self. SEX (♀) hg. HAB meadows, scrub, stream banks. SOIL damp–moist; acid–calc. SHADE nil–light. ALT sl–800. DIST nE4, W1, S4, I1. RANGE F1, G2, S5.

● **Dwarf thistle**
Cirsium acaule
Low–short. Lvs very spiny, in rosette; flhds 25–50mm, not or shortly stalked, solitary. LH perenn; rhizome. GERM aut. FL 6–9. POLL ins(h, l); self. SEX (♀)+(♀). HAB short grassland. SOIL dry; calc. SHADE nil. ALT sl–250. DIST sE4, nE1, W2. RANGE F4, G3, sS2.

● **Marsh thistle**
Cirsium palustre
Mid–v.tall. Stem winged, spiny; lvs hairy and weakly spiny; flhds 10–15mm, often white. LH bienn. GERM spr. FL 7–9. POLL ins(h, d, l); self. SEX (♀)+(♀). HAB marshes, woods. SOIL damp–moist; acid–calc. SHADE nil–mid. ALT sl–750. DIST E5, W5, S5, I5. RANGE F5, G5, S4. *See p. 167, 276.*

● **Welted thistle**
Carduus acanthoides
Mid–tall. Stem winged, spiny, except at top; lvs softly spiny; flhds 10–20mm, bracts weakly spiny. LH bienn. GERM imm. FL 6–9. POLL ins(h, l); self. SEX (♀). HAB grassy and disturbed ground. SOIL moist; acid–calc. SHADE nil. ALT sl–350. DIST E4, W3, S2, I2. RANGE F5, G5, S4. **ss162.**

● **Musk thistle**
Carduus nutans
Mid–tall. Stem winged, spiny, except at top, white cottony; lvs deeply spiny-lobed; flhds 30–50mm, solitary, nodding. LH bienn. GERM imm. FL 6–9. POLL ins(h, l); self. SEX (♀) hg. HAB disturbed and grassy places. SOIL moist–dry; calc. SHADE nil. ALT sl–500. DIST E4, W3, S1. RANGE F4, G4, S2.

○ **Brown knapweed**
Centaurea jacea
Short–mid. Lvs spear-shaped, hairy; flhds 10–20mm, rayless, the outer disc-florets ray-like; bracts brown, toothed. LH perenn; rootstock. GERM sum–aut. FL 8–9. POLL ins(h, d, l); self. SEX (♀). HAB grassy and disturbed places. SOIL dry; not acid. SHADE nil. ALT sl–200. DIST sE2. RANGE F2, G5, S3.

● **Black knapweed**
Centaurea nigra
Short–mid. Lvs spear-shaped, hairy or cottony; flhds 20–40 mm, rayless, the outer disc-florets sometimes ray-like; bracts dark-brown with hair-like teeth. LH perenn; rootstock. GERM spr? FL 6–9. POLL ins(h, d, l, c); self. SEX (♀). HAB grassy places. SOIL moist–dry; acid–calc. SHADE nil–light. ALT sl–600. DIST E5, W5, S5, I5. RANGE F4, G1, S2.

● **Greater knapweed**
Centaurea scabiosa
Mid–tall. Lvs pinnately-lobed, slightly hairy; flhds 30–50mm, rayless, the outer disc-florets greatly enlarged; bracts green, with dark brown toothed edges. LH perenn; rootstock. GERM imm. FL 6–9. POLL ins(h, l, d); self. SEX (♀). HAB grassland. SOIL dry; not acid. SHADE nil. ALT sl–300. DIST E4, W2, S2, I2. RANGE F4, G4, S3.

○ **Red star-thistle**
Centaurea calcitrapa
Short–mid. Branching; lvs pinnately lobed; flhds 8–10mm, rayless; bracts with long, sharp spines. LH bienn. GERM spr. FL 7–9. POLL ins(h, d); self. SEX (♀). HAB disturbed ground. SOIL dry; acid–calc. SHADE nil. ALT sl–50. DIST sE1, casual elsewhere. RANGE F3, G2, and casual.

○ **Cornflower**
Centaurea cyanus
Mid–tall. Lvs pinnately lobed, upper unlobed, grey–downy; flhds 15–30mm, rayless, outer disc-florets much enlarged. LH ann. GERM aut–spr. FL 6–8. POLL ins(h, d, l); self. SEX (♀). HAB cornfields, disturbed ground. SOIL moist–dry; acid–calc. SHADE nil. ALT sl–200. DIST E2, W1, S1, I1. RANGE F4, G4, S3.

Perennial cornflower
Centaurea montana
Mid. Creeping, with erect flg stems; lvs narrow, greyish; flhds 60–80mm, outer florets ray-like. LH perenn; rhizome. GERM spr? FL 5–8. POLL ins. SEX (♀). HAB grassland. SOIL moist; not acid. SHADE nil–mid. ALT [200–1500]. RANGE F2, G3.

○ **Cotton thistle**
Onopordum acanthium
Mid–v.tall. Stem winged, spiny, white–cottony; lvs spiny-lobed; flhds 30–50mm, rayless; bracts cottony at base, spiny. LH bienn. GERM spr. FL 7–9. POLL ins(h); self. SEX (♀). HAB disturbed and bare, sandy ground. SOIL dry; not calc. SHADE nil. ALT sl–200. DIST seE3, nwE1, W1, S1, I1. RANGE F4, G3, sS2.

● **Sawwort**
Serratula tinctoria
Mid–tall. Knapweed-like; lvs pinnately lobed, lobes finely toothed; flhds rayless, 15mm; bracts dark. LH perenn; rootstock. GERM spr? FL 7–9. POLL ins(h, d); self. SEX (♀), (♂ + ♀), (♀); (♂) rare. HAB grassland, open woods. SOIL damp–moist; calc. SHADE nil–mid. ALT sl–450. DIST E3, W4, S1, I1. RANGE F4, G4, sS2.

● Goatsbeard
Tragopogon pratensis
Mid. Lvs very long
and narrow, densely
up stem; flhds 15–20
mm, bracts longer than
florets; fr forming a
clock. LH ann, or
short-lived perenn.
GERM imm. FL 5–8.
POLL ins(h, d); self.
SEX (♀⁺). HAB grassland,
roadsides. SOIL moist–
dry; acid–calc. SHADE
nil. ALT sl–350. DIST
E5, W3, S2, I2. RANGE
F5, G5, S3.
See p. 162, 259. **ss163**.

● Chicory
Cichorium intybus
Mid–tall. Lvs pin-
nately-lobed, upper
clasping stems; flhds
25–40mm, in small un-
stalked clusters. LH
perenn; rootstock.
GERM spr? FL 6–9. POLL
ins(h); self. SEX (♀⁺).
HAB grassland, road-
sides. SOIL dry; calc.
SHADE nil. ALT sl–250.
DIST sE4, nE2, W2,
S2, I1. RANGE F4, G4,
sS3.
See p. 259.

○ Alpine sow-thistle
Cicerbita alpina
Tall–v.tall. Un-
branched stems with
russet hairs; lower lvs
pinnately lobed with
winged stalks, upper
clasping stem; flhds
20–30mm, dull purp-
lish-blue, short-lived.
LH herb perenn; root-
stock. GERM ? FL 7–8.
POLL ins(h, c, l). SEX
(♀⁺). HAB rock ledges.
SOIL moist; mildly
acid. SHADE nil–light.
ALT 500–1100. DIST S1.
RANGE F1, G2, S4.

○ Prickly lettuce
Lactuca serriola
Mid–v.tall. Stems and
lvs prickly; lvs loosely
clasping stem, turned
vertically away from
sun (n–s); flhds 11–
13mm in branching
spikes; fr greyish. LH
winter ann or bienn.
GERM aut. FL 7–9. POLL
self. SEX (♀⁺). HAB bare
ground, roadsides,
dunes. SOIL dry; not
acid. SHADE nil. ALT sl–
100. DIST seE3, E1, W1.
RANGE F4, G3, S1.
See p. 201.

○ Great lettuce
Lactuca virosa
Tall–v.tall. Like Prickly
lettuce but lvs horizon-
tal, tightly clasping
stem; fr blackish. LH
winter ann or bienn.
GERM aut. FL 7–9. POLL
ins. SEX (♀⁺). HAB bare
and sparsely grassy
places. SOIL dry; not
acid. SHADE nil–light.
ALT sl–200. DIST seE3,
nE1, W1, S1. RANGE
F3, G2.
ss164.

Purple lettuce
Prenanthes purpurea
Mid–v.tall. Lvs clasp-
ing stem; flhds 12–15
mm, few-flowered,
purple, hanging face-
down on long stalks.
LH herb perenn; root-
stock. GERM ? FL 7–9.
POLL ins(c, h, d). SEX
(♀⁺). HAB upland
woods. SOIL damp–
moist. SHADE light–
heavy [ALT 100–1800].
RANGE F1, G3.

● Wall lettuce
Mycelis muralis
Mid–tall. Lvs delicate,
often tinged red,
deeply lobed with end-
lobe large, lower long-
stalked, upper clasping
stem; flhds 12–15mm
with 4–5 pale yellow
fls, upright; bracts in 2
rows. LH herb perenn;
rootstock. GERM aut–
spr. FL 6–9. POLL ins
(h, d) or self. SEX (♀⁺).
HAB bare ground in
shade; walls, rocks,
bare chalk; often under
beech. SOIL dry; often
calc. SHADE light–
heavy. ALT sl–400.
DIST E4, W4, S2, I2.
RANGE F4, G4, S3.
See p. 248, 259.

**● Perennial sow-
thistle**
Sonchus arvensis
Tall–v.tall. Stem with
milky juice; lvs lobed,
softly spiny, clasping
stem, bases rounded;
flhds 40–50mm; bracts
with sticky dull yellow
hairs. LH herb perenn;
rhizome. GERM aut–
spr. FL 7–10. POLL ins
(h, l, c, d); self. SEX
(♀⁺). HAB by streams,
fens, marshes, grassy
banks, coasts; an
arable weed. SOIL
damp–dry; not acid.
SHADE nil–light. ALT
sl–400. DIST E5, W4,
S2, I3. RANGE F5, G5,
S3.
ss165.

● Prickly sow-thistle
Sonchus asper
Short–tall. Stem with
milky juice; lvs prickly,
toothed, shiny, tightly
clasping stem; flhds
20mm, deep yellow. LH
persistent ann. GERM
aut–spr. FL 6–9. POLL
ins(h, l, d). SEX (♀⁺).
HAB disturbed ground.
SOIL moist–dry; not
acid. SHADE nil. ALT sl–
400. DIST E5, W5, S5,
I5. RANGE F5, G5, S3.

● Smooth sow-thistle
Sonchus oleraceus
Short–v.tall. Stem with
milky juice; lvs lobed,
dull green, loosely
clasping stem; flhds
20–25mm, pale yellow.
LH persistent ann.
GERM aut–spr. FL 6–10.
POLL ins(h, d). SEX (♀⁺).
HAB disturbed ground.
SOIL moist–dry; not
acid. SHADE nil. ALT sl–
400. DIST E5, W5, S3,
I4. RANGE F5, G5, S3.

● **Bristly ox-tongue**
Picris echioides
Mid–tall. Stems bristly,
branching, leafy; lvs
deeply toothed, clasp-
ing stem; flhds 20–25
mm, surrounded by
large bracts; fr with
white hairs. LH per-
sistent ann. GERM spr.
FL 6–11. POLL ins(h);
or self. SEX (♀). HAB
disturbed ground. SOIL
moist–dry, not acid.
SHADE nil. ALT sl–200.
DIST seE4, E2, W2, I1.
RANGE F4, G1.
See p. 237.

● **Hawkweed ox-
tongue**
Picris hieracioides
Short–tall. Like Bristly
ox-tongue but lvs un-
toothed; flhds 25–35
mm; bracts small; fr
hairs cream. LH bienn
or short-lived perenn.
GERM spr. FL 7–9. POLL
ins(h, d) or self. SEX
(♀). HAB open grass-
land. SOIL dry; calc.
SHADE nil. ALT sl–200.
DIST seE3, E2, W2, I1.
RANGE F4, G3, S1.
See p. 245.

● **Nipplewort**
Lapsana communis
Short–tall. Lvs stalked,
toothed or lobed, on
stems; flhds numerous,
10–20mm, open in
morning and in sun
only; frs prominent
within persistent
bracts. LH ann, some-
times overwintering.
GERM aut–spr. FL 6–10.
POLL ins(h, d, l); self.
SEX (♀). HAB disturbed
ground, hedges,
wood-edges, walls.
SOIL moist–dry; not
acid. SHADE nil–mid.
ALT sl–400. DIST E5,
W5, S3, I4. RANGE F5,
G5, S3.
See p. 259.

● **Dandelion**
*Taraxacum hamatum
(Vulgaria)*
Low–short. Lvs all in
rosette, deeply lobed;
flhds 35–55mm, soli-
tary on hollow stalks
with milky juice;
bracts often down-
turned. LH perenn;
rootstock and rosette.
GERM sum–aut. FL 1–
12, peaking 4–6. POLL
apo. SEX (♀). HAB
grassy places. SOIL
damp–moist; not acid.
SHADE nil–light. ALT sl–
1200. DIST E5, W5, S5,
I5. RANGE F5, G5, S5.
*See p. 170, 212, 213,
215.* **ss166**

● **Lesser dandelion**
*Taraxacum
brachyglossum
(Erythrosperma)*
V.low–low. Smaller
than other dandelions;
lvs all in a rosette,
deeply toothed; flhd
20–30mm, solitary on
hollow stalks with
milky juice. LH perenn;
rootstock and rosette.
GERM sum–aut. FL 4–5
(–7). POLL apo. SEX (♀).
HAB chalk grassland,
sand-dunes, heaths,
walls. SOIL dry; often
calc. SHADE nil. ALT sl–
500. DIST sE4, nE2,
W2, S2, I2. RANGE F4,
G4, S3.
ss167.

● **Red-veined
dandelion**
*Taraxacum faeroense
(Spectabilia)*
Low–short. Like Dan-
delion but lvs often
spotted, purple-stalked,
shallow-lobed; flhds
30–40(–50)mm; bracts
up-turned. LH perenn;
rootstock and rosette.
GERM spr–sum. FL 5–7.
POLL apo. SEX (♀). HAB
wet mountain grass-
land, flushes; damp
heaths. SOIL wet–moist;
not acid. SHADE nil.
ALT sl–1000. DIST sE2,
nE4, W2, S4, I2.
RANGE F2, G2, S5.
ss168. ss169.

○ **Smooth cat's-ear**
Hypochaeris glabra
Short. Lvs hairless,
widely lobed or
toothed, all in rosette;
flhds 15–25mm on
branching, almost
lfless stalks, opening in
sun. LH winter ann.
GERM aut. FL 6–10.
POLL ins(d, l, c); self.
SEX (♀). HAB open
grassy and sandy
places. SOIL dry; rather
acid. SHADE nil. ALT sl–
200. DIST E2, W1, S1,
I1, declining. RANGE
F2, G3, S1.
ss170.

○ **Spotted cat's-ear**
Hypochaeris maculata
Short–mid. Lvs large,
hairy, purple-spotted,
shallowly toothed, all
in rosette; flhds 30–45
mm, solitary or on
branching almost lfless
stalks. LH perenn;
rootstock and rosette.
GERM spr. FL 6–8. POLL
ins(h, d). SEX (♀). HAB
limestone grassland
and sea cliffs. SOIL dry;
calc. SHADE nil(–mid in
G). ALT sl–100. DIST
E1, W1. RANGE F1,
G3, S3.

● **Common cat's-ear**
Hypochaeris radicata
Short–mid. Lvs hairy,
deeply toothed, all in
rosette; flhds 25–40
mm on branching
stems bearing several
scale-like lvs. LH
perenn; rootstock and
rosette. GERM aut. FL
6–9. POLL ins(h, d, l).
SEX (♀). HAB most
types of grassland.
SOIL moist–dry; not
acid. SHADE nil. ALT
sl–500. DIST E5, W5,
S5, I5. RANGE F5, G5,
S2.

● **Autumn hawkbit**
Leontodon autumnalis
Low–mid. Lvs hairless,
more or less deeply
toothed, all in rosette;
flhds 15–35mm on
branching stalks with
several scale lvs near
top; outer florets
streaked red under-
neath. LH perenn;
rootstock and rosette.
GERM sum–aut. FL 7–
11. POLL ins(d, h);
self. SEX (♀). HAB
grassland. SOIL moist–
dry; not acid. SHADE
nil–light. ALT sl–800.
DIST E5, W5, S5, I5.
RANGE F5, G5, S5.
See p. 265, 276, 296.

● **Rough hawkbit**
Leontodon hispidus
Short–mid. Lvs hairy, shallowly lobed, in rosette; flhds 25–40 mm on unbranched leafless stalks, drooping in bud. LH perenn; rootstock and rosette. GERM ? FL 6–10. POLL ins(h, d, c, l); self. SEX (♀). HAB grassland. SOIL moist–dry; often clayey; mainly calc. SHADE nil. ALT sl–500. DIST E5, W5, S2, I2. RANGE F5, G5, S2.

● **Lesser hawkbit**
Leontodon taraxacoides
Low–short. Lvs lobed, hairy, in rosette; flhds 12–20mm on unbranched stalks without scale lvs; outer florets greyish underneath. LH perenn, often short-lived; rootstock and rosette. GERM spr–sum. FL 6–10. POLL ins(h). SEX (♀). HAB grassland. SOIL dry; mainly calc. SHADE nil. ALT sl–500. DIST E3, W3, S1, I3. *See p. 247.*

○ **Rough hawksbeard**
Crepis biennis
Mid–tall. Lvs coarsely lobed, upper clasping stem, not arrow-shaped; flhds 20–35 mm; outer bracts spreading. LH bienn. GERM sum. FL 6–7. POLL ins(h); apo. SEX (♀). HAB roadsides, disturbed ground. SOIL moist–dry; not acid. SHADE nil. ALT sl–200. DIST E3, W1, S1, I2. RANGE F5, G5, sS2.

● **Smooth hawksbeard**
Crepis capillaris
Short–tall. Lvs pinnately arrow-lobed, clasping stem; flhds 10–20mm, outer florets reddish beneath. LH ann, sometimes persisting. GERM sum. FL 6–10. POLL ins(h, d); self. SEX (♀). HAB grassland, disturbed ground. SOIL dry; acid–calc. SHADE nil. ALT sl–450. DIST E5, W5, S4, I5. RANGE F5, G5, sS2.

● **Marsh hawksbeard**
Crepis paludosa
Mid–tall. Stem reddish; lvs dull green, waisted, pointed, toothed, clasping stem; flhds 15–25mm; bracts with black, sticky hairs. LH perenn; rootstock. GERM imm. FL 7–9. POLL ins(h, d); self. SEX (♀). HAB marshes, springs, woods. SOIL wet–damp; acid–calc. SHADE nil–mid. ALT sl–500(–800). DIST nE4, W2, S4, I2. RANGE eF2, G5, S4. **ss171.**

● **Beaked hawksbeard**
Crepis vesicaria
Short–mid. Stems hairy, branching; lvs pinnately lobed, arrow-shaped round stem; flhds 15–25mm, outer florets orange beneath. LH bienn. GERM imm. FL 5–7. POLL ins(h, d); self. SEX (♀). HAB disturbed ground. SOIL dry; not acid. SHADE nil. ALT sl–250. DIST sE4, nE1, W2, S1, I3. RANGE F5. G2.
See p. 265. **ss172.**

● **Leafy hawkweed**
Hieracium umbellatum agg.
Mid–tall. Stems hairy; lvs narrow, clothing stem; flhds 20–30mm, in flat-topped clusters. LH perenn; rootstock. GERM spr. FL 6–10. POLL apo. SEX (♀). HAB grassland, heaths, rocks. SOIL moist–dry; acid–calc. SHADE nil–mid. ALT sl–400. DIST E3, W4, S3, I2. RANGE F5, G5, S4. **ss173.**

● **Common hawkweed**
Hieracium vulgatum agg.
Short–tall. Lvs narrow, elliptical, in some rosette and on stem; flhds 15–25mm; bracts sticky. LH perenn; rootstock. GERM aut–spr. FL 7–8. POLL apo. SEX (♀). HAB woods, rocks. SOIL moist–dry; acid–calc. SHADE nil–mid. ALT sl–600. DIST E5, W5, S5, I2. RANGE F5, G5, S5.

○ **Alpine hawkweed**
Hieracium alpinum agg.
Low. Whole plant long silky-hairy; lvs oval, in rosette; flhds 25–35mm, usually solitary. LH perenn; rootstock. GERM spr? FL 7–8. POLL apo. SEX (♀). HAB mountain rocks. SOIL moist; acid–calc. SHADE nil. ALT 500–1250. DIST nE?, W1, S3. RANGE G1, S3.

● **Mouse-ear hawkweed**
Pilosella officinarum
Low–short. Lvs in rosette, with long, sparse hairs; greyish; runners lfy; flhds 20–30mm, solitary. LH perenn; stolons. GERM spr. FL 5–9. POLL apo. SEX (♀). HAB bare ground, grassland, rocks. SOIL dry; acid–calc. SHADE nil. ALT sl–500(–800). DIST E5, W5, S5, I5. RANGE F5, G5, sS5.

MONOCOTYLEDONS

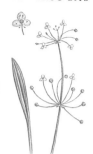

**MONO-
COTYLEDONS**
Narrow-leaved plants, with flower parts in threes or sixes (see p. 15).

WATER-PLANTAIN FAMILY
Alismataceae
Aquatic plants with long-stalked leaves and flowers with 2 whorls of flower parts, 3 petal-like and 3 sepal-like.
See p. 20, 197.

● **Common water-plantain**
Alisma plantago-aquatica
Short–tall. Lvs large, oval; sometimes small and floating; fls 8–10 mm, petals rounded; fr long-beaked. LH perenn. GERM aut–spr. FL 6–9. POLL ins(d). SEX (♀). HAB ponds, ditches, slow water. SOIL water; acid–calc. SHADE nil. ALT sl–400. DIST E5, W4, S2, I4. RANGE F5, G5, S3.
See p. 20, 166.

○ **Narrow-leaved water-plantain**
Alisma lanceolatum
Short–tall. Differs from Common water-plantain in its narrow, tapering lvs, pink fls and short-beaked fr. LH perenn. GERM aut–spr. FL 6–9. POLL ins (d). SEX (♀). HAB still water. SOIL water; not acid. SHADE nil. ALT sl–50. DIST sE3, nE1, W1, S1, I1. RANGE F2, G4, sS1.
ss174.

○ **Lesser water-plantain**
Baldellia ranunculoides
Low–short. Sometimes creeping; lvs very narrow; fls 10–15mm, in a flat-topped cluster or 2 whorls. LH perenn; stolons. GERM ? FL 6–9. POLL ins. SEX (♀). HAB shallow, often peaty water. SOIL water–wet; not calc. SHADE nil. ALT sl–150. DIST E2, W2, S1, I3. RANGE wF3, nG3, sS1.

FLOWERING RUSH FAMILY
Butomaceae
A small aquatic family, resembling water-plantains. Flowers with parts in two whorls of 3, the inner petal-like.

FROG-BIT FAMILY
Hydrocharitaceae
An aquatic family, often almost wholly submerged. Flowers as in Flowering rush.

● **Arrowhead**
Sagittaria sagittifolia
Mid–tall. Lvs strap-like in water, oval floating, and arrow-shaped above surface; fls 20mm, purple-centred. LH perenn; buds on stolons. GERM spr. FL 7–8. POLL ins. SEX (♂ +♀). HAB slow and still water. SOIL water; acid–calc. SHADE nil. ALT sl–200. DIST sE4, nE2, W2, I2. RANGE F4, G4, S3.
See p. 198, 203, 271.

● **Flowering rush**
Butomus umbellatus
Tall. Lvs very long and narrow, 3-sided and sedge-like; fls with different-length stalks. LH perenn; rhizome. GERM spr. FL 7–8. POLL ins(h, d, l). SEX (♀). HAB shallow, slow and still water. SOIL water; not acid. SHADE nil–light. ALT sl–150. DIST sE4, nE2, W2, I2. RANGE F3, G4. S2.
See p. 167.

○ **Frog-bit**
Hydrocharis morsus-ranae
Floating. Lvs rounded, floating, long-stalked, glossy; fls 20mm, yellow-centred. LH perenn; buds on stolons. GERM never fruiting. FL 7–8. POLL ? SEX (♀). HAB still water. SOIL water; calc. SHADE nil. ALT sl–50. DIST E3, W2, I2. RANGE F2, G3, S2.
ss175.

○ **Water soldier**
Stratiotes aloides
Floating. Submerged except when flowering; lvs spine-toothed, in rosettes; fls 30–40mm. LH perenn. GERM never fruiting. FL 6–8. POLL ? SEX (♂) + (♀). HAB still water; calc. SHADE nil. ALT sl–50. DIST E2, S1. RANGE F2, G3, S2.

RANNOCH RUSH FAMILY
Scheuchzeriaceae
A family with only 1 member.

ARROW-GRASS FAMILY
Juncaginaceae
A small family of plantain-like plants, with small green flowers in long spikes. (*Triglochin*)

EEL-GRASS FAMILY
Zosteraceae
The only wholly marine family; leaves narrow, strap-like. Flowers small green.

PONDWEED FAMILY
Potamogetonaceae
An aquatic family, in fresh water. Unusually for monocots, they have 4 petals.
See p. 20, 257, 274.

● **Canadian pondweed**
Elodea canadensis
Submerged. Lvs in whorls of 3, oblong, finely toothed; most plants ♀; fls 5mm, floating. LH perenn; buds. SEX (♂) + (♀). GERM never fruiting. FL 5–9. POLL water. HAB slow water. SOIL water; acid–calc. SHADE nil. ALT sl–150. DIST E4, W2, S2, I2. RANGE F4, G4, S2. *See p. 203, 274.* **ss176.**

○ **Rannoch rush**
Scheuchzeria palustris
Low–short. Lvs very narrow; fls 4mm, with 6 narrow sepals and no petals, in a loose, few-fld spike. LH perenn; rhizome. GERM spr–sum. FL 6–7. POLL wind. SEX (♀). HAB wet bogs. SOIL wet; acid. SHADE nil. ALT 350. DIST S1. RANGE F1, G2, S4.

● **Sea arrow-grass**
Triglochin maritimum
Short–mid. Lvs v. narrow, upright, all from roots; fls small, in a spike that elongates in fr; fr less than 4mm. LH perenn; rhizome. GERM spr. FL 6–9. POLL wind. SEX (♀). pg. HAB grassy salt-marshes. SOIL wet; saline. SHADE nil. ALT sl. DIST coastal: E3, W3, S4, I4. RANGE coastal: F3, G4 (and 1 inland), S5.

● **Marsh arrow-grass**
Triglochin palustris
Short–mid. Like Sea arrow-grass, but has furrowed lvs and fr-spike not elongating; fr 8–10mm. LH perenn; rhizome. GERM spr. FL 5–8. POLL wind. SEX (♀) pg. HAB marshes, grassland. SOIL wet–damp; acid–calc. SHADE nil. ALT sl–600 (–800). DIST E4, W3, S4, I4. RANGE F3, G4, S5. *See p. 172, 262, 273.*

● **Eel-grass**
Zostera marina
Submerged. Lvs very long and narrow, strap-shaped; fls in long branching spikes, male and female alternating in 2 rows. LH perenn; rhizome. GERM ? FL 6–9. POLL water. SEX (♂ + ♀). HAB marine mud at and below low tide mark. SOIL water; saline. SHADE nil. ALT sl. DIST coastal: E2, W2, S2, I2. RANGE coastal: F2, G3, S3. *See p. 202, 274, 275.* **ss177. ss178.**

● **Broad-leaved pondweed**
Potamogeton natans
Submerged. Floating lvs oval, jointed to stalk; submerged lvs narrow; fls in spikes above water surface. LH perenn; rhizome. GERM spr–sum. FL 5–9. POLL wind. SEX (♀). HAB shallow water. SOIL water; acid–calc. SHADE nil. ALT sl–600. DIST E5, W3, S3, I3. RANGE F4, G5, S4. *See p. 20, 274.* **ss179.**

● **Bog pondweed**
Potamogeton polygonifolius
Submerged. Floating lvs oval, unjointed, often reddish; submerged lvs spear-shaped; fls in short, aerial spikes. LH perenn; rhizome. GERM spr–sum. FL 5–10. POLL wind. SEX (♀). HAB still, shallow, often peaty water. SOIL water; not calc. SHADE nil. ALT sl–700. DIST E3, W4, S5, I4. RANGE F3, nG3, sS3.

○ **Various-leaved pondweed**
Potamogeton gramineus
Submerged. Variable; resembling Bog pondweed, but floating lvs sometimes absent; submerged lvs narrower; acid. LH perenn; rhizome, buds on stolons. GERM spr–sum. FL 6–9. POLL wind. SEX (♀). HAB still and slow water. SOIL water; acid. SHADE nil. ALT sl–700. DIST E2, W1, S3, I2. RANGE F2, G3, S4.

○ **Reddish pondweed**
Potamogeton alpinus
Submerged. Floating, lvs narrow oval, un-jointed, leathery; submerged lvs reddish, narrowed at each end; fr spike dense. LH perenn; rhizome. GERM spr–sum. FL 6–9. POLL wind. SEX (♀). HAB still and slow water. SOIL water; acid. SHADE nil. ALT sl–1000. DIST E3, W1, S3, I2. RANGE F1, G4, S4.

122

○ **Shining pondweed**
Potamogeton lucens
Submerged. All lvs
submerged, narrow to
oblong; fl stalk
thickened beneath
spike. LH perenn;
rhizome, buds. GERM
spr–sum. FL 6–9. POLL
wind. SEX (♀). HAB
still and slow water.
SOIL water; calc. SHADE
nil. ALT sl–400. DIST
E3, W1, S1, I2. RANGE
F3, G3, S2.
ss180.

● **Perfoliate pondweed**
*Potamogeton
perfoliatus*
Submerged. All lvs
submerged, clasping
stem, narrow to
rounded; fl stalk not
thickened. LH perenn;
rhizome, buds on
stolons. GERM spr–
sum. FL 6–9. POLL
wind. SEX (♀). HAB
still and slow water.
SOIL water; acid–calc.
SHADE nil. ALT sl–700.
DIST E4, W2, S2, I2.
RANGE F4, G5, S4.

● **Curled pondweed**
Potamogeton crispus
Submerged. All lvs
submerged, very
narrow, toothed and
wavy-edged; stems 4-
angled; fr spike short.
LH perenn; rhizome,
buds. GERM spr–sum.
FL 5–10. POLL wind.
SEX (♀). HAB still and
slow water. SOIL water;
acid–calc. SHADE nil.
ALT sl–400. DIST E5,
W2, S2, I3. RANGE F4,
G4, sS2.
ss181. ss182.

● **Small pondweed**
*Potamogeton
berchtoldii*
Submerged. All lvs
submerged, very
narrow, less than 2mm
wide, short, 3-veined;
fr spike short, short-
stalked. LH perenn;
buds. GERM spr–sum.
FL 6–9. POLL wind. SEX
(♀). HAB still and slow
water. SOIL water;
acid–calc. SHADE nil.
ALT sl–150. DIST E3,
W3, S2, I2. RANGE F3,
G4. S3.
See p. 203, 274. **ss183**.
ss184.

● **Lesser pondweed**
Potamogeton pusillus
Submerged. Extremely
like Small pondweed,
and best distinguished
by rolled (not flat)
stipules at lf-bases. LH
perenn; buds. GERM
spr–sum. FL 6–9. POLL
wind. SEX (♀). HAB
still and slow water.
SOIL water; calc or
brackish. SHADE nil.
ALT sl–300(–500). DIST
E4, W2, S2, I1. RANGE
F4, G4, S1.
See p. 274. **ss185**.

○ **Blunt-leaved
pondweed**
*Potamogeton
obtusifolius*
Submerged. All lvs
submerged, narrow,
but more than 2mm
wide, the tip rounded
with a tiny point; fr
spike longer than Small
pondweed. LH perenn;
buds. GERM spr–sum.
FL 6–9. POLL wind. SEX
(♀). HAB still and slow
water. SOIL water;
acid–calc. SHADE nil.
ALT sl–200. DIST E2,
W2, S2, I2. RANGE F2,
G3, S2.
ss186. ss187.

● **Fennel pondweed**
Potamogeton pectinatus
Submerged. All lvs
submerged, dark green,
very narrow, with
white-edged stipules;
fls in pairs along stem,
submerged. LH perenn;
rhizome. GERM spr–
sum. FL 5–9. POLL
water. SEX (♀). HAB
still and flowing water.
SOIL water; not acid.
SHADE nil. ALT sl–250.
DIST E4, W2, S2, I2.
RANGE F4, G5, S2.
*See p. 203, 216, 217,
274.* **ss188. ss189**.
ss190. ss191.

LILY FAMILY
Liliaceae
A large and attractive,
much cultivated family,
with recognisable
flowers, which have 3
petals and 3 sepals,
often indistinguishable.
Leaves and growth
habit vary greatly, but
most have bulbs or
other storage organs,
and grow in undis-
turbed habitats.
See p. 17, 20, 293.

False helleborine
Veratrum album
Mid–tall. Stems thick;
lvs broad, folded along
the veins, in 3's; fls 6-
petalled, in long dense
spikes. LH perenn.
GERM spr? FL 7–8. POLL
ins(d, h, l). SEX (♀) pa.
HAB grassland. SOIL
moist–dry; acid–calc.
SHADE nil–light. ALT
[700–2000]. RANGE sF1,
sG2.

● **Lily-of-the-valley**
Convallaria majalis
Low–short. Patch-
forming; lvs oval, in a
pair on stem, almost
opposite; fls bell-
shaped, nodding,
stalked, in a spike. LH
perenn; rhizome. GERM
spr. FL 5–6. POLL ins
(h, d); self. SEX (♀) pa.
HAB woods, usually
deciduous. SOIL dry;
not acid. SHADE light–
heavy. ALT sl–250. DIST
E3, W2, S1. RANGE F4,
G5, S4.
See p. 253.

○ **May lily**
Maianthemum bifolium
Low–short. Lvs long heart-shaped, in a pair on stem, but not opposite; fls 4-petalled, 4mm, in a dense spike. LH perenn; rhizome. GERM spr–sum. FL 5–7. POLL ins(h, d); self. SEX (♀) pg. HAB woods, often coniferous. SOIL moist; not calc. SHADE mid-heavy. ALT 150–200. DIST E1. RANGE F3, G5, S4.

○ **Snowdon lily**
Lloydia serotina
Low. Lvs very narrow, long from roots, short on stem; fls 6-petalled, 20mm, purple-veined, usually solitary. LH perenn; bulb. GERM spr? FL 5–6. POLL ins(d). SEX (♀); pa. HAB mountain rocks. SOIL moist; not acid. SHADE nil. ALT 500–800. DIST W1. RANGE sG1. **ss192**.

St Bernard's lily
Anthericum liliago
Mid. Lvs all from roots, very long and narrow; fls 30–50mm, star-like, 6-petalled. LH perenn. GERM ? FL 5–6. POLL ins(h, d). SEX (♀). HAB grassland, rocks, open woods. SOIL dry; not acid. SHADE nil–mid. ALT [100–1500]. RANGE F3, G3, sS1.
See p. 266.

○ **Scottish asphodel**
Tofieldia pusilla
Low. Lvs in a flattened fan, sword-shaped, all from roots; fls 6-petalled, 5mm, off-white, in a short spike. LH perenn; rhizome. GERM spr? FL 6–8. POLL ins; self. SEX (♀) hg. HAB moors, stream sides. SOIL wet; acid. SHADE nil–mid. ALT (50–)400–900. DIST nE1, S3. RANGE sG1, S4. **ss193**.

German asphodel
Tofieldia calyculata
Low–short. Lvs yellowish, like Scottish asphodel, but larger on stem; fls yellow-green, 5–6mm, in a long spike. LH perenn; rhizome. GERM ? FL 7–8. POLL ins(h, d, l, c); self. SEX (♀) pg. HAB moors, bogs. SOIL wet–damp; calc. SHADE nil. ALT [200–2000]. RANGE G2, sS1.

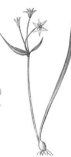

● **Bog asphodel**
Narthecium ossifragum
Low–mid. Lvs sword-shaped, in a flattened fan; fls 15mm, anthers orange; whole spike orange in fr. LH perenn; rhizome. GERM spr? FL 7–8. POLL ins. SEX (♀). HAB bogs, moors, wet heaths. SOIL wet–damp; not calc. SHADE nil. ALT sl–1000. DIST wW4, eE1, W4, S5, I4. RANGE wF4, eF1, nG3, wS3.
See p. 17.

○ **Fritillary**
Fritillaria meleagris
Short–mid. Lvs very narrow, dull green on stem; fls bell-shaped, 30–50mm, solitary, nodding, chequered. LH perenn; bulb. GERM spr. FL 4–5. POLL ins (h); self. SEX (♀). HAB grassland. SOIL damp-moist; not acid. SHADE nil. ALT sl–100. DIST sE2. RANGE F2, G2, sS2.

○ **Butcher's broom**
Ruscus aculeatus
Mid–tall. Small almost lfless shrub with stems flattened to resemble spiny, leathery lvs, bearing fls on mid-surface. LH perenn; rhizome. GERM sum. FL 1–4. POLL ins. SEX (♂)+(♀). HAB woods, scrub. SOIL dry; acid–calc. SHADE nil–mid. ALT sl–200. DIST sE2, and widely naturalised. RANGE F3.
See p. 185.

○ **Martagon lily**
Lilium martagon
Tall. Lvs in dense whorls along stem; fls 40mm, petals rolled back, nodding. LH perenn; bulb. GERM spr. FL 6–7. POLL ins(l); self. SEX (♀) hg. HAB woods, scrub, grassy places. SOIL moist; not acid. SHADE nil–mid. ALT sl–100. DIST swE1, and widely naturalised. RANGE F2, G4.
See p. 252.

○ **Yellow star of Bethlehem**
Gagea lutea
Low–short. Lvs solitary, bluebell-like, 3–5-ridged on back; fls 6-petalled, 20mm, green-striped outside. LH perenn; bulb. GERM spr. FL 4–5. POLL ins (d, c); self. SEX (♀) pg. HAB woods, grassy places. SOIL damp-moist; not acid. SHADE nil–heavy. ALT sl–350. DIST E2, S1. RANGE eF2, G4, S3.
See p. 253.

Meadow gagea
Gagea pratensis
Low. Lvs solitary, very narrow, grey-green, keeled beneath; fls paler than Yellow star of Bethlehem. LH perenn; bulb. GERM spr. FL 3–4. POLL ins (d, c); self. SEX (♀) pg. HAB grassland. SOIL moist–dry; calc. SHADE nil–light. ALT [sl–500]. RANGE eF1, G3, sS2. **ss194.**

Belgian gagea
Gagea spathacea
Low–short. Lvs very narrow, in pairs; fls very like Yellow star of Bethlehem, but petals narrower. LH perenn; bulb. GERM spr. FL 4–5. POLL ins(d, c); self. SEX (♀) pg. HAB grassland, woods. SOIL damp; not calc. SHADE light–heavy. ALT [sl–300]. RANGE neF1, nG3, sS2.

○ **Wild tulip**
Tulipa sylvestris
Mid. Lvs narrow, from roots, but ridged; fls loosely bell-shaped, solitary, 30–50mm long. LH perenn; bulb. GERM spr. FL 4–5. POLL ins; self. SEX (♀) hg. HAB grassy places. SOIL moist–dry; acid–calc. SHADE nil–light. ALT sl–100. DIST occasionally naturalised. RANGE F2, sG2, and naturalised.

● **Ramsons**
Allium ursinum
Short–mid. Carpeting, strongly garlic-smelling; lvs stalked, elliptical; stem lfless, ending in a ball-like cluster of star-like fls. LH perenn; bulb. GERM spr. FL 4–6. POLL ins(h, d, l, c); self. SEX (♀) pa. HAB woods. SOIL damp–moist; acid–calc. SHADE light–heavy. ALT sl–300(–450). DIST E4, W5, S3, I3. RANGE F4, G3, S2.
See p. 20, 179, 252, 294.

● **Crow garlic**
Allium vineale
Mid–tall. Lvs almost cylindrical, hollow, sheathing stem; flhd a dense ball of bulbils, usually with a few long-stalked fls; stamens long. LH perenn; bulb. GERM spr ? FL 6–7. POLL ins; self. SEX (♀) pa. HAB grassy and disturbed places. SOIL dry; not acid. SHADE nil. ALT sl–300(–450). DIST sE4, nE2, W2, S1, I2. RANGE F5, G4, sS2.
See p. 293.

○ **Field garlic**
Allium oleraceum
Mid–tall. Lvs cylindrical or flat, sheathing stem; flhds as in Crow garlic, but usually with some fls; stamens short. LH perenn; bulb. GERM spr ? FL 6–8. POLL ins; self. SEX (♀) pa. HAB grassland. SOIL moist–dry; not acid. SHADE nil. ALT sl–350. DIST sE1, nE3, W1, S1. RANGE F4, G3, S3.

○ **Chives**
Allium schoenoprasum
Short–mid. Tufted; lvs cylindrical, all from roots; fls 10–16mm long, each a spreading bell, in a dense head. LH perenn; bulb. GERM imm. FL 6–8. POLL ins (h, d, l, c); self. SEX (♀) pa. HAB rocky ground. SOIL dry; not acid. SHADE nil. ALT sl–200. DIST E1, W1, S1. RANGE F1, G1, S2.
See p. 213.

○ **Sand leek**
Allium scorodoprasum
Mid–tall. Lvs strap-shaped, flat, sheathing the stem; flhd with purple bulbils and few long-stalked fls. LH perenn; bulb. GERM imm. FL 6–8. POLL ins (h, d, l, c); self. SEX (♀) pa. HAB grassy and disturbed, sandy ground. SOIL dry; not acid. SHADE nil–light. ALT sl–200. DIST nE2, S2, (I2). RANGE G2, sS2. **ss195.**

German garlic
Allium senescens
Short–mid. Stem angled; lvs narrow, all from roots; fls long-stalked in a dense, rounded head. LH perenn; bulb. GERM spr ? FL 6–7. POLL ins (h, d, l, c); self. SEX (♀) pa. HAB sandy grassland. SOIL dry; not acid. SHADE nil. ALT [200–2000]. RANGE sF2, sG3, sS1.

○ **Round-headed leek**
Allium sphaerocephalon
Mid–tall. Lvs almost cylindrical, hollow, sheathing stem; fls long-stalked, in a large, dense head. LH perenn; bulb. GERM spr ? FL 6–8. POLL ins; self. SEX (♀) pa. HAB rocks, dunes, grassland. SOIL dry; calc. SHADE nil. ALT sl–50. DIST sE1. RANGE F3, G1.

● **Bluebell**
Hyacinthoides non-scriptus
Short–mid. Forms dense stands; lvs strap-shaped, all from roots; fls 15–20mm long, bell-shaped, drooping in a 1-sided spike. LH perenn; bulb. GERM win–spr. FL 4–6. POLL ins(d, c). SEX (♀) hg. HAB woods, hedges, cliffs. SOIL moist; acid–calc. SHADE (nil–)light–heavy. ALT sl–400 (–700). DIST E5, W5, S4, I4. RANGE wF5, eF2.
See p. 15, 206, 246, 252.

○ **Autumn squill**
Scilla autumnalis
Low–short. Lvs very narrow, appearing after fls; fls 10mm, star-like, with no bracts, in a short spike. LH perenn; bulb. GERM spr? FL 8–10. POLL ins. SEX (♀) hg. HAB coastal grass-land, usually sandy. SOIL dry; calc. SHADE nil. ALT sl–50. DIST sE1. RANGE F3.

○ **Spring squill**
Scilla verna
Low. Lvs narrow, appearing with fls; fls 12–15mm, star-like, with a bract at the base of each stalk. LH perenn; bulb. GERM aut. FL 4–6. POLL ins. SEX (♀). HAB coastal grassland, mainly on cliffs. SOIL dry; not acid. SHADE nil. ALT sl–400. DIST coastal: wE2, W2, S2, I2. RANGE coastal: wF2. wS1.
ss196.

○ **Grape hyacinth**
Muscari atlanticum
Low–short. Lvs very narrow, channelled; fls flask-shaped, blue fringed white, 5mm long. LH perenn; bulb. GERM spr? FL 4–5. POLL ins; self. SEX (♀) pg. HAB grassland. SOIL dry; not acid. SHADE nil. ALT sl–150. DIST sE1. RANGE F3, G2.
See p. 252.

○ **Meadow saffron**
Colchicum autumnale
Low–short. Lvs ob-long, dead before flg; fls crocus-like, with a long tube appearing direct from ground. LH perenn; corm. GERM spr. FL 8–10. POLL ins (h, d); self. SEX (♀) pg. HAB grassland, woods. SOIL damp–moist; calc. SHADE nil–mid. ALT sl–150. DIST E2, W1, I1. RANGE F3, G4.
See p. 252, 257.

● **Common Solomon's seal**
Polygonatum multiflorum
Mid–tall. Stem arch-ing, lvs elliptical, held like wings above the stem; fls hanging in small groups, 10–15 mm long, in pairs; rhizome. GERM spr. FL 5–6. POLL ins(h); self. SEX (♀) hg. HAB woods. SOIL moist; acid–calc. SHADE light–heavy. ALT sl–250. DIST E2, W1, and rarely naturalised. RANGE F4, G5, sS3.
See p. 253.

○ **Angular Solomon's seal**
Polygonatum odoratum
Short. Like Common Solomon's seal but fls 20mm, solitary or in pairs; petal tube straight-sided. LH perenn; rhizome. GERM spr. FL 6–7. POLL ins (h); self. SEX (♀) hg. HAB woods. SOIL moist; calc. SHADE mid–heavy. ALT sl–500. DIST E1, W1. RANGE F2, G4, S3.

○ **Whorled Solomon's seal**
Polygonatum verticillatum
Mid–tall. Lvs narrow, in whorls of 4–6; fls in small groups, hanging on a common stalk. LH perenn; rhizome. GERM ? FL 6–7. POLL ins(h); self. SEX (♀) hg. HAB woods. SOIL moist; acid. SHADE mid–heavy. ALT 200. DIST S1. RANGE F1, G2, S4.

● **Common star of Bethlehem**
Ornithogalum umbellatum
Low–short. Lvs long, with a central white strip; fls 30mm, spreading, bell-shaped, petals green-striped on back. LH perenn; bulb. GERM aut–win. FL 5–6. POLL ins; self. SEX (♀). HAB grassland. SOIL moist–dry; acid–calc. SHADE nil. ALT sl–200. DIST E3, W1, S2. RANGE F3, G4, sS3.
See p. 263.

● **Herb paris**
Paris quadrifolia
Short–mid. Lvs oval in an unstalked whorl of 4 near top of stem; fls with 4–6 sepals and 4–6 fine petals. LH perenn; rhizome. GERM spr. FL 5–7. POLL ins (d); self. SEX (♀) pg. HAB woods. SOIL damp–moist; calc. SHADE mid–heavy. ALT sl–300. DIST E3, W3, S2. RANGE F4, G4, S5.

RUSH FAMILY
Juncaceae
Rushes usually have
narrow, often cylindri-
cal leaves and incin-
spicuous flowers, which
on close inspection
resemble small, dull
lily flowers, with 2
whorls of 3 brown or
green 'tepals'. Typic-
ally on rather infertile
soils.

● **Heath rush**
Juncus squarrosus
Short–mid. Tufted,
with very fine, wiry
lvs; fls dark brown,
silvery-edged; fr
brown. LH perenn;
rootstock. GERM spr–
sum. FL 5–7. POLL
wind. SEX (♀) pg. HAB
moors, heaths. SOIL
damp–dry; acid. SHADE
nil. ALT sl–1000. DIST
sE2, nE5, W5, S5, I4.
RANGE F3, G3, S3.
See p. 297. **ss197.**
ss198. ss199.

● **Slender rush**
Juncus tenuis
Mid–tall. Lvs narrow,
with white ears at base;
bracts longer than
flhd; fruit greyish. LH
perenn. GERM ? FL 6–7.
POLL wind. SEX (♀).
HAB bare ground,
tracks. SOIL damp;
acid. SHADE nil. ALT
sl–350. DIST E4, W4,
S4, I2. RANGE F5, G4,
sS3.

● **Saltmarsh rush**
Juncus gerardi
Short–mid. Patch-
forming, with lfy
stems; lvs narrow; fls
dark brown, in spread-
ing, branching clusters;
fr pale brown. LH
perenn; rhizome. GERM
spr–sum. FL 6–7. POLL
wind. SEX (♀) pg. HAB
salt-marshes. SOIL wet;
saline. SHADE nil. ALT
sl. DIST coastal; E4,
W5, S5, I5. RANGE
coastal: F5, G5, S4;
inland: F1, G2.
ss200.

● **Toad rush**
Juncus bufonius
Low–short. Lvs
narrow; fls in clusters
branching from half-
way along stem;
greenish, in small
groups. LH ann. GERM
any. FL 5–9. POLL
wind; self (cleistoga-
mous). SEX (♀). HAB
bare and disturbed
ground. SOIL wet–
damp; acid–calc.
SHADE nil. ALT sl–600.
DIST E5, W5, S5, I5.
RANGE F5, G5, S5.
ss201.

● **Hard rush**
Juncus inflexus
Mid–tall. Tufted;
stems greyish, lfless,
prominently ridged; fls
in a loose cluster,
beneath a long bract.
LH perenn; rhizome.
GERM spr–sum. FL 5–7.
POLL wind. SEX (♀) pg.
HAB grassland, moors.
SOIL damp–moist; not
acid. SHADE nil–light.
ALT sl–400. DIST E5,
W4, S3, I4. RANGE F5,
G4, sS1.
ss202. ss203.

● **Soft rush**
Juncus effusus
Mid–v.tall. Tufted;
stems green, faintly
ridged; fls either in a
loose or dense cluster.
GERM spr. FL 6–8. POLL
wind. SEX (♀) pg. HAB
grassland, woods,
moors. SOIL wet–moist;
acid–calc. SHADE nil–
mid. ALT sl–800. DIST
E5, W5, S5, I5. RANGE
F5, G5, S3.
*See p. 161, 177, 234,
235.*

● **Compact rush**
Juncus conglomeratus
Mid–tall. Very like
Soft rush, but stems
more ridged just
beneath fls, which are
always in a tight
cluster. LH perenn;
rhizome. GERM spr. FL
5–7. POLL wind. SEX
(♀) pg. HAB grassland,
woods, moors. SOIL
wet–moist; not calc.
SHADE nil–mid. ALT sl–
750. DIST E5, W5, S5,
I3. RANGE F5, G5, S3.

● **Sea rush**
Juncus maritimus
Tall. Tufted, with lvs
at base of stem; fls
pale straw, in a loose
cluster, beneath a
sharp bract; fr brown.
LH perenn; rhizome.
GERM spr–sum. FL 7–8.
POLL wind. SEX (♀) pg.
HAB salt marshes. SOIL
damp; saline. SHADE
nil. ALT sl. DIST
coastal: E4, W3, S3,
I4. RANGE coastal: F4,
G4, sS2.
ss204.

● **Jointed rush**
Juncus articulatus
Short–mid. Lvs
flattened; fls in clusters
of 5–15, inner tepals
blunt; fr abruptly
narrowed to break. LH
perenn; rhizome. GERM
spr. FL 6–9. POLL wind.
SEX (♀) pg. HAB grassy
places, marshes, moors.
SOIL wet–damp; not
calc. SHADE nil–light.
ALT sl–600(–800). DIST
E5, W5, S5, I5. RANGE
F5, G5, S3.

● **Sharp-flowered rush**
Juncus acutiflorus
Mid–tall. More up-right than Jointed rush; lvs cylindrical; fls in clusters of 5–10, tepals fine-pointed; fr gradually tapering. LH perenn; rhizome. GERM spr. FL 7–9. POLL wind. SEX (♀) pg. HAB marshes, grassland. SOIL wet–damp; not calc. SHADE nil–mid. ALT sl–600. DIST E3, W4, S4, I4. RANGE F4, G3, sS1.
ss205.

● **Blunt-flowered rush**
Juncus subnodulosus
Mid–tall. Lvs cylindrical; fls in clusters of 5–10, straw-coloured, the tepals blunt; fr abruptly narrowed to beak. LH perenn; rhizome. GERM spr. FL 7–9. POLL wind. SEX (♀) pg. HAB fens, marshes. SOIL wet–damp; calc. SHADE nil–light. ALT sl–200. DIST E3, W2, S1, I3. RANGE F4, G3, sS1.

● **Bulbous rush**
Juncus bulbosus
Low; sprawling. Stems swollen at base, sometimes very long; lvs thread-like; fls in branched clusters, often replaced by green plantlets. LH perenn; rooting nodes. GERM spr? FL 6–9. POLL wind. SEX (♀) pg. HAB bogs, heaths, temporary pools. SOIL wet; acid. SHADE nil–light. ALT sl–1000. DIST E4, W5, S5, I5. RANGE F4, G3, S4.
See p. 293. **ss206. ss207.**

● **Hairy wood-rush**
Luzula pilosa
Short. Lvs grass-like, with few long, white hairs; mostly from roots; fls dark brown, long-stalked, turned down in fr. LH perenn; stolons. GERM sum. FL 4–6. POLL wind. SEX (♀). HAB woods. SOIL moist; acid–calc. SHADE light–deep. ALT sl–500(–700). DIST E5, W5, S4, I3. RANGE F5, H5, S5.
See p. 16. **ss208.**

● **Great wood-rush**
Luzula sylvatica
Mid–tall. Large, tufted, lvs 5–20mm wide, shiny; fls in a broadly spreading cluster, dark brown. LH perenn; stolons. GERM spr–sum. FL 4–6. POLL wind. SEX (♀). HAB woods, rocks, moors. SOIL damp; acid. SHADE nil–mid. ALT sl–1000. DIST sE3, nE5, W5, S5, I4. RANGE F4, G3, wS2.

● **Field wood-rush**
Luzula campestris
Low–short. Loosely tufted; lvs conspicuously long-hairy; fls in dense clusters, with bright yellow anthers on short stamen filaments. LH perenn; stolons. GERM sum–aut. FL 3–5. POLL wind. SEX (♀) pg. HAB grassland. SOIL dry; not acid. SHADE nil. ALT sl–600(–1000). DIST E5, W5, S5, I4. RANGE F5, G5, S3.

● **Heath wood-rush**
Luzula multiflora
Short. Tufted; lvs to 6mm wide; fls in long-stalked clusters or a single dense head; filaments as long as anthers. LH perenn. GERM sum–aut. FL 4–6. POLL wind. SEX (♀). HAB heaths, moors, grassy woods. SOIL moist–dry; acid. SHADE nil–light. ALT sl–1000. DIST E5, W5, S5, I5. RANGE F5, G5, S5.
ss209. ss210.

○ **Spiked wood-rush**
Luzula spicata
Low–short. Lvs grooved, often hairless; fls in a dense, drooping spike; fr as long as tepals. LH perenn. GERM spr? FL 6–7. POLL wind. SEX (♀). HAB stony and grassy places. SOIL moist; acid. SHADE nil. ALT sl–1000[–3000]. DIST nE1, S3. RANGE sG1, S4.

DAFFODIL FAMILY
Amaryllidaceae
All have parallel-sided, often fleshy leaves from roots, and conspicuous flowers, arising either directly from bulb or corm or on a leafless stalk. Flowers sheathed in bud, with 2 rings of 3 petals each, often with an inner trumpet.

● **Wild daffodil**
Narcissus pseudo-narcissus
Short. Lvs greyish, as long as fl-stalk; fls with inner trumpet and petals spreading or not; nodding. LH perenn, bulb. GERM win–spr. FL 3–4. POLL ins(h). SEX (♀) hg. HAB woods, grassland, and as a garden escape. SOIL moist; acid–calc. SHADE nil–mid. ALT sl–300. DIST E3, W3; and widely naturalised. RANGE F3; naturalised in F and G.
See p. 213, 294.

○ **Summer snowflake**
Leucojum aestivum
Mid. Lvs to 15mm
wide; fls bell-shaped,
15–20mm long, in
clusters of 3–6; stalks
unequal. LH perenn;
bulb. GERM spr. FL 4–5.
POLL ins(h). SEX (♀)
hg. HAB grassland,
scrub. SOIL wet–damp;
not acid. SHADE nil–
mid. ALT sl–100. DIST
sE1, I1. RANGE F2, G1.

○ **Spring snowflake**
Leucojum vernum
Short. Lvs to 10mm
wide; fls bell-shaped,
20–25mm long, soli-
tary; sheath green. LH
perenn; bulb. GERM
spr. FL 2–3. POLL ins
(h). SEX (♀). HAB
scrub, grassland. SOIL
damp; calc. SHADE
nil–mid. ALT sl–100.
DIST sE1. RANGE F2,
G3.

● **Snowdrop**
Galanthus nivalis
Short. Lvs greyish, to
4mm wide; fls bell-
shaped, 15–20mm long,
green outside, solitary;
sheath split. LH
perenn; bulb. GERM
spr. FL 1–3. POLL ins
(h). SEX (♀) hg. HAB
woods, stream sides.
SOIL damp; acid–calc.
SHADE nil–mid. ALT sl–
200. DIST widely
naturalised. RANGE F3,
G2, and widely
naturalised.
*See p. 252, 258, 279,
296.*

YAM FAMILY
Dioscoreaceae
A tropical family with
a single northern
European representa-
tive (Black bryony).

ARUM FAMILY
Araceae
Another tropical
family, with a few
European representa-
tives, of very different
vegetative appearance,
but with flowers em-
bedded in a central
spike (spadix), some-
times surrounded by a
sheath (spathe).

● **Black bryony**
Tamus communis
V.tall; climbing.
Clockwise twiner with
no tendrils and heart-
shaped lvs; fls 4–5mm,
6-petalled, in spikes.
LH perenn; tuber.
GERM win–spr. FL 5–8.
POLL ins(h, d). SEX (♂)
+(♀). HAB woods,
scrub. SOIL moist–dry;
not acid. SHADE nil–
mid. ALT sl–250. DIST
E4, W4, I1. RANGE F5,
wG1.
See p. 195.

● **Lords-and-ladies**
Arum maculatum
Mid. Lvs large, arrow-
shaped, often black-
spotted, glossy, all
from roots; fls with
cylindrical purple
spadix and large
spathe; fr an orange
berry. LH perenn;
tuber. GERM win–spr
(after 2 yrs). FL 4–5.
POLL ins(d). SEX (♂ +
♀) pg. HAB woods,
hedges. SOIL moist;
calc. SHADE light–deep.
ALT sl–200(–350). DIST
E5, W5, S3, I4. RANGE
F5, G4, sS1.
*See p. 163, 252, 253,
285.*

○ **Sweet flag**
Acorus calamus
Tall. Iris-like, with
flattened, unstable,
crinkled lvs; fls yellow-
ish, spadix wedge from
stalk. LH perenn;
rhizome. GERM no
fruits. FL 5–7. POLL
ins? SEX (♀) pg. HAB
shallow water edges.
SOIL water; not acid.
SHADE nil. ALT sl–100.
DIST naturalised: E2,
W1, S1, I1. RANGE
naturalised: F3, G4,
sS3.

○ **Bog arum**
Calla palustris
Short. Lvs heart-
shaped, unspotted; flg
spadix green; spathe
white, not enclosing
spadix. LH perenn;
rhizome. GERM spr–
Sum. FL 6–7. POLL ins
(d). SEX (♀) pg. HAB
bogs, swamps. SOIL
water–wet; acid–calc.
SHADE nil–mid. ALT sl–
100. DIST rarely
naturalised. RANGE G3,
S3.

IRIS FAMILY
Iridaceae
A distinctive family
with sword-shaped or
linear leaves. Flowers
of true Irises have 3
spreading outer petals,
3 upright inner petals,
and 3 petal-like styles.
Irises are extensively
cultivated, and may
escape.
See p. 20.

○ **Stinking iris**
Iris foetidissima
Mid–tall. Lvs foul-
smelling when bruised;
fls purplish-grey, to
80mm; fr splitting to
reveal orange seeds.
LH perenn; rhizome.
GERM spr–sum. FL 5–7.
POLL ins(h). SEX (♀).
HAB hedges, woods,
sea-cliff scrub. SOIL
moist–dry; calc. SHADE
light–heavy. ALT sl–
200. DIST sE3, W2; and
naturalised. RANGE F3.
See p. 171.

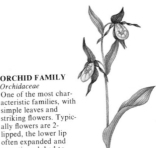

● **Yellow iris**
Iris pseudacorus
Mid–v.tall. Lvs long,
ridged; stem flattened,
branched; fls to 100
mm, in pairs or 3's. LH
perenn; rhizome.
GERM spr–sum. FL 6–8.
POLL ins(h). SEX (♂).
HAB marshes, water
edges. SOIL water–wet;
not acid. SHADE nil–
mid. ALT sl–300. DIST
E5, W5, S5, I5. RANGE
F5, G5, sS4.
See p. 20, 250, 257.

○ **Gladiolus**
Gladiolus illyricus
Mid–tall. Lvs greyish,
iris-like; fls 6-petalled,
petals 25–30mm; 3–8
in a spike. LH perenn;
corm. GERM spr? FL
6–7. POLL ins. SEX (♂).
HAB grassland, heaths,
open woods. SOIL
moist–dry; acid. SHADE
nil–light. ALT sl–50.
DIST sE1. RANGE wF1.
See p. 252.

○ **Spring crocus**
Crocus albiflorus
Low. Lvs very narrow,
appearing with fls; fls
purple or white, on a
long, pale tube. LH
perenn; corm. GERM
spr? FL 3–4. POLL ins.
SEX (♂). HAB grassland.
SOIL moist; not acid.
SHADE nil. ALT sl–100.
DIST (E, W, S). RANGE
sF1, sG1, and natural-
ised.
ss211.

ORCHID FAMILY
Orchidaceae
One of the most char-
acteristic families, with
simple leaves and
striking flowers. Typic-
ally flowers are 2-
lipped, the lower lip
often expanded and
sometimes lobed to
resemble an insect.
Many have long spurs.
Orchids have complex
life-cycles and many
are threatened by
collecting and habitat
destruction.
*See p. 16, 20, 229, 230,
257, 269, 277, 285, 286,
296.*

○ **Lady's slipper**
Cypripedium calceolus
Short–mid. Lvs oval,
ribbed; fls with 4 long
maroon petals, each
60–90mm, and a huge,
inflated yellow lower
lip. LH perenn;
rhizome. GERM spr. FL
6. POLL ins(h, d, c).
SEX (♂). HAB grassland,
scrub. SOIL dry; calc.
SHADE nil–light. ALT
ALT 200. DIST nE1.
RANGE F1, G2, S2.
See p. 286.

Calypso
Calypso bulbosa
Low–short. Has a
single, elliptical, ribbed
lf, and a single fl with
a large, hollow lower
lip on a purple stem.
LH perenn; rhizome.
GERM spr. FL 5–6. POLL
ins. SEX (♂). HAB coni-
fer woods, marshes.
SOIL damp–moist; not
calc. SHADE light–
heavy. ALT [sl–400].
RANGE S2.

Black vanilla orchid
Nigritella nigra
Low–short. Lvs
narrowly oblong, up
stem; fls dark purple,
spurred, vanilla-
scented, in a dense
spike. LH perenn;
rhizome. GERM ? FL
6–8. POLL ins(l). SEX
(♂). HAB mountain
grassland. SOIL moist;
not acid. SHADE nil.
ALT [200–1000]. RANGE
sG1, S2.

● **Bee orchid**
Ophrys apifera
Short–mid. Lvs oblong
in rosette, and smaller
up stem; fls with long
pink sepals, small
green petals and large
lower lip bee-like. LH
perenn; tubers. GERM
spr. FL 6–7. POLL self.
SEX (♂). HAB grassland.
SOIL dry; calc. SHADE
nil. ALT sl–250. DIST
E3, W2, I2. RANGE F4,
G3.
See p. 286, 287.

○ **Late spider orchid**
Ophrys fuciflora
Low–short. Like Bee
orchid, but petals and
sepals pink, and lower
lip much broader. LH
perenn; tubers. GERM
spr. FL 6–7. POLL ins
(h). SEX (♂). HAB grass-
land. SOIL dry; calc.
SHADE nil. ALT sl–100.
ALT sl–100. DIST sE1.
RANGE F2, G2.
See p. 286, 287.

○ **Early spider orchid**
Ophrys sphegodes
Low–short. Like Bee
orchid, but petals and
sepals green and lower
lip much longer, blue-
marked. LH perenn;
tubers. GERM spr. FL
4–6. POLL ins(h). SEX
(♂). HAB grassland.
SOIL dry; calc. SHADE
nil. ALT sl–150. DIST
sE1. RANGE F3, G2.
See p. 286, 287.

● **Fly orchid**
Ophrys insectifera
Short–mid. Lvs few, narrowly elliptical; fls with green sepals, hair-like brown petals, and lower lip lobed, fly-like. LH perenn; tubers. GERM spr. FL 5–6. POLL ins(h, d). SEX (♀). HAB woods, scrub, grassland. SOIL damp–dry; calc. SHADE nil–heavy. ALT sl–300. DIST E3, W1, I2. RANGE F3, G3, S2.
See p. 286, 287.

● **Early purple orchid**
Orchis mascula
Short–mid. Lvs in rosette, and smaller up stem, dark-spotted; fls purple, pink or white, hooded; spur long, pointed upwards. LH perenn; tubers. GERM spr. FL 4–6. POLL ins(h, l). SEX (♀). HAB woods, scrub, grassland. SOIL moist; not acid. SHADE nil–heavy. ALT sl–500 (–850). DIST E4, W4, S3, I2. RANGE F5, G4, S2.
See p. 253, 287.

○ **Military orchid**
Orchis militaris
Short–mid. Lvs in rosette, narrower up stem; fls hooded; lower lip 3-lobed, the central lobe forking into 2 long and 1 short tooth. LH perenn; tubers. GERM spr. FL 5–6. POLL ins(h, l). SEX (♀). HAB woods, scrub, grassland. SOIL moist–dry; calc. SHADE nil–mid. ALT sl–150. DIST sE1. RANGE F2, G3, sS1.
See p. 286.

● **Green-winged orchid**
Orchis morio
Low–mid. Lvs in rosette and on stem; fls with green-veined hood and shortly 3-lobed lower lip; spike loose. LH perenn; tubers. GERM spr. FL 5–6. POLL ins(h, l). SEX (♀). HAB grassland. SOIL moist; not acid. SHADE nil–light. ALT sl–300. DIST sE3, nE1, W2, S1, I2. RANGE F3, G4, sS1.
See p. 246.

Meadow orchid
Orchis palustris
Short–mid. Lvs narrow, in rosette and up stem; unspotted; fls in a loose spike, with an open hood and 3-lobed lip. LH perenn; tubers. GERM spr. FL 5–6. POLL ins(h, l). SEX (♀). HAB meadows. SOIL damp; acid–calc. SHADE nil. ALT sl–300]. RANGE F3, G3, sS1.

○ **Lady orchid**
Orchis purpurea
Mid–tall. Lvs mainly in rosette, oval, shiny; sepals and petals forming hood; lower-lip 3-lobed, the central lobe forked. LH perenn; tubers. GERM spr. FL 5–6. POLL ins(h, l). SEX (♀). HAB woods, scrub. SOIL moist; calc. SHADE light–heavy. ALT sl–100. DIST sE1. RANGE F2, G2.
See p. 286.

○ **Monkey orchid**
Orchis simia
Short. Lvs oblong; fls hooded, the lower lip with long thin lobes resembling arms and legs of monkey, with tooth between legs. LH perenn; tubers. GERM spr. FL 5–6. POLL ins(h, l). SEX (♀). HAB grassland. SOIL dry; calc. SHADE nil–light. ALT sl–150. DIST E1. RANGE F3, wG1.
See p. 286.

○ **Burnt orchid**
Orchis ustulata
Low–short. Lvs narrow oblong; fls with maroon hood and pale, spotted, 4-lobed lip; fl-spike dark at top with unopened buds. LH perenn; tubers. GERM spr. FL 5–6. POLL ins(h, l). SEX (♀). HAB short grassland. SOIL dry; calc. SHADE nil. ALT sl–250. DIST E2. RANGE F2, G3, sS1.

● **Pyramidal orchid**
Anacamptis pyramidalis
Short–mid. Lvs narrow, on stems; fls with 3-lobed lower lip and long spur, in a very dense, pyramidal spike. LH perenn; tubers. GERM spr. FL 6–8. POLL ins(l). SEX (♀). HAB grassland, dunes. SOIL moist–dry; calc. SHADE nil. ALT sl–300. DIST E3, W1, S1, I2. RANGE F3, G2, sS1.
See p. 287.

● **Common spotted orchid**
Dactylorhiza fuchsii
Short–mid. Rosette lvs oval–oblong, narrower up stem, all dark-spotted; fls in a long spike, lower lip equally 3-lobed. LH perenn; tubers. GERM spr. FL 6–8. POLL ins(h, d, c). SEX (♀). HAB grassland, scrub. SOIL moist–dry; not acid. SHADE nil–light. ALT sl–500. DIST E4, W4, S3, I4. RANGE F4, G4, S2.
See p. 14, 253, 286, 287, 288.

● **Heath spotted orchid**
Dactylorhiza maculata
Short–mid. Like Common spotted orchid, but lvs narrower, and central lobe of lip much smaller. LH perenn; tubers. GERM spr. FL 6–8. POLL ins(h, d, c). SEX (♀). HAB marshes, heaths, bogs. SOIL wet–moist; acid. SHADE nil–light. ALT sl–1000. DIST wE4, eE2, W4, S4, I4. RANGE F3, G4, S5.

● **Early marsh orchid**
Dactylorhiza incarnata
Short–mid. Lvs yellow-green, unspotted, hooded at tip; fls variable in colour; lower lip with side lobes folded back. LH perenn; tubers. GERM spr. FL 5–7. POLL ins(d, h). SEX (♀). HAB marshes, meadows, fens. SOIL wet–damp; not acid. SHADE nil. ALT sl–600. DIST E3, W2, S3, I4. RANGE F3, G3, S3. *ss212.*

● **Southern marsh orchid**
Dactylorhiza praetermissa
Short–mid. Lvs long, spear-shaped, un-spotted; fls in dense spike with long bracts, lower lip slightly toothed, flat; spur short. LH perenn; tubers. GERM spr. FL 6–7. POLL ins(h, d, l, c). SEX (♀). HAB marshes, fens. SOIL wet–damp; calc. SHADE nil. ALT sl–300. DIST sE4, nE1, W2. RANGE nF2, wG1. *See p. 288.*

● **Northern marsh orchid**
Dactylorhiza purpurella
Short mid. Like Southern marsh orchid, but lvs often spotted; fls deep purple, lip untoothed; spur longer. LH perenn; tuber. GERM spr. FL 6–7. POLL ins(h, d, l, c). SEX (♀). HAB marshes, fens, grass-land. SOIL wet–moist; not acid. SHADE nil. ALT sl–400. DIST sE1, nE2, W2, S4, I2. RANGE nG1, sS1. *ss213.*

Elder-flowered orchid
Dactylorhiza sambucina
Short. Lvs glossy, un-spotted, pale; fls either lemon yellow with green bracts, or pink-purple with red bracts. LH perenn; tubers. GERM spr. FL 4–6. POLL ins(h, d). SEX (♀). HAB grassland. SOIL moist; not calc. SHADE nil. ALT [sl–1500]. RANGE F2, G2, sS2.

● **Fragrant orchid**
Gymnadenia conopsea
Short–mid. Lvs narrow, unspotted; fls very fragrant, hooded; sepals spreading and spur very long (to 15 mm); tubers. GERM spr. FL 6–8. POLL ins(l). SEX (♀). HAB grassland, fens. SOIL damp–dry; calc. SHADE nil–light. ALT sl–400(–600). DIST E4, W2, S3, I2. RANGE F4, G4, S3. *See p. 277, 283, 287, 288.*

○ **Man orchid**
Aceras anthropophorum
Short–mid. Lvs ob-long, glossy, upper clasping stem; fls yellow-green, with a tight hood and a mani-kin-shaped lip. LH perenn; tubers. GERM spr. FL 5–6. POLL ins(d, h). SEX (♀). HAB grass-land, scrub. SOIL dry; calc. SHADE nil–light. ALT sl–150. DIST sE2. RANGE F3, G1. *ss214.*

○ **Musk orchid**
Herminium monorchis
Low. Lvs yellowish in a pair near stem base; fls green, sweet-scented, lip 3-lobed, central lobe longest. LH perenn; tubers. GERM spr. FL 6–7. POLL ins(d, h, c). SEX (♀). HAB grassland. SOIL damp–dry; calc. SHADE nil. ALT sl–200. DIST sE2. RANGE F2, G3, S2.

● **Frog orchid**
Coeloglossum viride
Low–short. Stem lfy; lvs rounded to narrow; fls yellowish, hooded, the lower lip strap-like, toothed, brownish. LH perenn; tubers. GERM spr. FL 6–7. POLL ins (d, h, c). SEX (♀). HAB grassland, rocks. SOIL damp–dry; acid–calc. SHADE nil. ALT sl–900. DIST E3, W2, S3, I3. RANGE F4, G4, S5. *See p. 288.* **ss215.**

○ **Lesser twayblade**
Listera cordata
Low–short. Lvs oval to heart-shaped, in a pair on stem; fls green, red-tinged; lower lip lobed. LH perenn; rhizome. GERM spr. FL 6–8. POLL ins(d, h). SEX (♀). HAB conifer woods, moors, bogs. SOIL wet–damp; acid. SHADE nil–mid. ALT [sl–]150–800. DIST sE1, nE2, W1, S4, I2. RANGE eF1, G2, S5.

● **Common twayblade**
Listera ovata
Short–mid. Lvs oval in a single pair on stem; fls yellow-green, lip strap-shaped, forked, to 15mm. LH perenn; rhizome. GERM spr. FL 6–7. POLL ins(h, d, c). SEX (♀). HAB woods, grassland. SOIL moist; acid–calc. SHADE nil–heavy. ALT sl–600. DIST E5, W4, S3, I4. RANGE F5, G5, S3.
See p. 287.

● **Greater butterfly orchid**
Platanthera chlorantha
Short–mid. One pair of broad lvs at stem-base; few smaller lvs on stem; fls with spreading petals and sepals, entire lip and long spur. LH perenn; tubers. GERM spr. FL 6–7. POLL ins(l). SEX (♀). HAB woods, grassland. SOIL moist–dry; not acid. SHADE nil–mid. ALT sl–500. DIST sE4, nE2, W2, S3, I3. RANGE F5, G4, S3.
See p. 287.

● **Lesser butterfly orchid**
Platanthera bifolia
Short(–mid). Very like Greater butterfly orchid, but lvs narrower, and pollensacs parallel, not converging upwards. LH perenn; tubers. GERM spr. FL 6–7. POLL ins(l). SEX (♀). HAB woods, moors, grassland. SOIL damp–dry; acid–calc. SHADE nil–mid. ALT sl–400. DIST E2, W2, S3, I3. RANGE F4, G4, S4.
See p. 287.

○ **White helleborine**
Cephalanthera damasonium
Short–mid. Lvs narrow oval, bluish; fls rarely opening and so appearing almost tubular; in lfy spikes. LH perenn; rhizome. GERM spr. FL 5–6. POLL self. SEX (♀). HAB woods. SOIL moist–dry; calc. SHADE heavy–deep. ALT sl–250. DIST sE2. RANGE F3, G3, sS1.

○ **Narrow-leaved helleborine**
Cephalanthera longifolia
Short–mid. Like White helleborine, but lvs narrow, dull green; fls smaller, slightly open, spike less lfy. LH perenn; rhizome. GERM spr. FL 5–6. POLL ins(h). SEX (♀). HAB woods. SOIL moist–dry; calc. SHADE mid–deep. ALT sl–250. DIST E2, W1, S1, I1. RANGE eF2, G3, sS1.

○ **Red helleborine**
Cephalanthera rubra
Short–mid. Slightly sticky-hairy; lvs narrow; fls pink–purple, half-open, revealing a whitish, tongue-like lip. LH perenn; rhizome. GERM spr. FL 6–7. POLL ins(h). SEX (♀). HAB woods, scrub. SOIL dry; calc. SHADE mid–deep. ALT sl–150. DIST sE1. RANGE F2, G3, sS2.

○ **White frog orchid**
Leucorchis albida
Low–short. Lvs keeled, narrowing up stem; fls 2–3mm, twisted on stalks, greenish-white, fragrant. LH perenn; tubers. GERM ? FL 5–6. POLL ins(l). SEX (♀). HAB grassland. SOIL damp–moist; not calc. SHADE nil. ALT sl–600 [–2500]. DIST E1, W1, S3, I2. RANGE F1, G2, S3.

○ **Autumn lady's-tresses**
Spiranthes spiralis
Low–short. Lvs in a rosette beside flg stalk and producing, in next year, a spike with a spiral row of small fragrant fls. LH perenn; tubers. GERM spr. FL 8–9. POLL ins(h). SEX (♀). HAB grassland. SOIL moist–dry; calc. SHADE nil. ALT sl–200. DIST sE3, nE1, W2, I2. RANGE F3, G3.
ss216.

○ **Creeping lady's-tresses**
Goodyera repens
Low–short. Rosette lvs oval; stem lvs smaller; fls unspurred, lip tongue-like, in a spirally twisted spike. LH perenn; rhizome and stolons. GERM spr. FL 7–8. POLL ins(h). SEX (♀). HAB conifer woods. SOIL moist; acid. SHADE light–heavy. ALT sl–300. DIST E1, S2. RANGE F1, G2, S4.
See p. 161, 296.

○ **Dark red helleborine**
Epipactis atrorubens
Short–mid. Stem purple-tinged, hairy; lvs in 2 opposite rows; fls red-purple, bluish outside; open. LH perenn; rhizome. GERM spr. FL 6–7. POLL ins (h). SEX (♀). HAB woods, rocks, grassland. SOIL moist–dry; calc. SHADE nil–light. ALT sl–500. DIST nE1, W1, S1, I1. RANGE F2, G2, S2.

● **Broad-leaved helleborine**
Epipactis helleborine
Mid–tall. Stem hairy, sometimes purple-tinged; lvs oval, spirally up stem; fls reddish to green, open; lip curved under. LH perenn; rhizome. GERM spr. FL 7–9. POLL ins(h). SEX (♂). HAB woods. SOIL moist; not acid. SHADE light–deep. ALT sl–300. DIST E4, W3, S2, I2. RANGE F5, G5, sS3. *See p. 230, 286.*

○ **Narrow-lipped helleborine**
Epipactis leptochila
Short–mid. Yellowish-green, like Broad-leaved helleborine, but lvs in 2 rows up stem, and fls green, nodding, lip pointed. LH perenn; rootstock. GERM spr. FL 7–8. POLL self. SEX (♂). HAB woods. SOIL moist–dry; calc. SHADE mid–deep. ALT sl–200. DIST sE2, W1. RANGE F1, G2. **ss217.**

○ **Marsh helleborine**
Epipactis palustris
Short–mid. Lvs narrow oval, folded upwards; fl parts dull purple-brown and hairy out-side, inner white, held horizontally. LH perenn; rhizome. GERM spr. FL 7–8. POLL ins(h, l, d). SEX (♂). HAB marshes, fens, dune-slacks. SOIL wet–damp; calc. SHADE nil–light. ALT sl–150. DIST E2, W2, S1, I2. RANGE F3, G3, sS2. *See p. 20, 286.*

○ **Green-flowered helleborine**
Epipactis phyllanthes
Short–mid. Lvs in 2 ranks, becoming narrow up stem; fls numerous, hanging straight down, scarcely open. LH perenn; rhizome. GERM spr. FL 7–9. POLL self; apo? SEX (♂). HAB woods, dunes. SOIL dry; calc. SHADE nil–deep. ALT sl–200. DIST sE2, W1, I1. RANGE nG1.

○ **Violet helleborine**
Epipactis purpurata
Short–mid. Whole plant purple-tinged; lvs spirally up stem; fls pale greenish inside, violet outside. LH perenn; rootstock. GERM spr. FL 8–9. POLL ins(h). SEX (♂). HAB woods. SOIL moist; calc. SHADE mid–deep. ALT 50–250. DIST sE3. RANGE eF1, G2. *See p. 252.*

● **Bird's-nest orchid**
Neottia nidus-avis
Short–mid. Whole plant yellow-brown without chlorophyll; lvs reduced to scales on stem; fls hooded, lip 2-lobed. LH perenn; rhizome. GERM spr. FL 5–7. POLL ins(h, d, c); self. SEX (♂). HAB woods. SOIL moist; calc. SHADE heavy-deep. ALT sl–250. DIST E3, W2, S2, I2. RANGE F4, G4, S2. *See p. 222, 230.*

○ **Coralroot orchid**
Corallorhiza trifida
Low–short. Stem yellowish or greenish-brown and no true lvs; fls with 3-lobed lip, red-spotted. LH perenn; rhizome. GERM spr. FL 5–7. POLL ins(h, d). SEX (♂). HAB woods, dune-slacks. SOIL damp; acid–calc. SHADE nil–heavy. ALT sl–400. DIST nE1, S2. RANGE eF1, G3, S5. *See p. 230.*

○ **Ghost orchid**
Epipogium aphyllum
Low. Lacks chloro-phyll and lvs; stem yellowish or pinkish; fls yellowish, tinged with pinkish-mauve lip on top. LH perenn; rhizome. GERM spr. FL 6–9. POLL ins(h). SEX (♂). HAB woods, dune-slacks. SOIL damp–dry; calc. SHADE deep. ALT 50–150. DIST sE1. RANGE eF1, G3, S3. *See p. 230.*

○ **Bog orchid**
Malaxis paludosa
V.low–low. Lvs less than 10mm, rounded, near stem-base, often fringed with bulbils; fls tiny, twisted so that lip is on top. LH perenn; bulb. GERM spr. FL 7–9. POLL ins(h, d, c). SEX (♂). HAB *Sphagnum* bogs. SOIL wet; acid. SHADE nil. ALT sl–500. DIST E1, W1, S2, I1. RANGE F1, G2, S3. *See p. 253.*

○ **Fen orchid**
Liparis loeselii
Low–short. Like Bog orchid, but lvs larger (more than 25mm long), 1 pair; lip of fl in any position relative to fl. LH perenn; bulb. GERM spr. FL 6–7. POLL ins. SEX (♂). HAB fens, dune slacks. SOIL wet–damp; calc. SHADE nil–light. ALT sl–50. DIST sE1, W1. RANGE F1, G3, S1.

Violet bird's-nest orchid
Limodorum abortivum
Mid. Violet-coloured,
lfless; fls 40mm,
yellow-tinged, spurred.
LH perenn; tuber.
GERM ? FL 5–7. POLL
ins? SEX (♀). HAB
mainly coniferous
woods. SOIL moist–
dry; calc. SHADE heavy.
ALT [200–800]. RANGE
eF2, wG1.

**DUCKWEED
FAMILY**
Lemnaceae
Floating plants, not
differentiated into
stem and leaves, but
with roots arising
directly from a small,
green, sometimes leafy
plate; some species
have no roots at all.
Flowers minute and
rarely seen.
See p. 17, 214.

● **Fat duckweed**
Lemna gibba
Floating. Disc swollen,
particularly under-
neath, 3–5mm across,
each with 1 root. LH
perenn by budding.
GERM ? FL 7. POLL
water. SEX (♂ + ♀). HAB
still water. SOIL water;
acid–calc. SHADE nil.
ALT sl–200. DIST E3,
W1, I1. RANGE F3, G4,
S2.
ss218.

● **Common duckweed**
Lemna minor
Floating. Disc flat,
1.5–4mm across, bud-
ding, each with 1 root;
fls in sunny places. LH
perenn by budding.
GERM win–spr. FL 6–7.
POLL water. SEX (♂ + ♀).
HAB still water. SOIL
water; acid–calc.
SHADE nil–light. ALT
sl–500. DIST E5, W4,
S3, I4. RANGE F5, G5,
S3.
See p. 17. **ss219.**

● **Ivy-leaved duckweed**
Lemna trisulca
Just submerged. Discs
floating just below sur-
face, oval, with a stalk,
and usually daughter
discs attached to it. LH
perenn by budding.
GERM ? FL 5–7. POLL
water. SEX (♂ + ♀). HAB
still water. SOIL water;
acid–calc. SHADE nil–
light. ALT sl–300. DIST
E4, W2, S2, I3. RANGE
F4, G4, S2.

BUR-REED FAMILY
Sparganiaceae
Aquatic plants with
iris-like or floating
leaves and dense,
round, rather spiky,
football-like flower-
heads. Actual flowers
are very inconspicuous.
See p. 15, 17, 264, 269.

**REED-MACE
FAMILY**
Typhavene
Leaves again iris-like,
very long; flowers in a
long, dense spadix.
See p. 17.

● **Branched bur-reed**
Sparganium erectum
Tall–v.tall. Lvs are 3-
sided at base; fls in a
branching spike, ♂
flhds small, above ♀.
LH perenn; rhizome.
GERM spr–sum. FL 6–8.
POLL wind. SEX (♂ + ♀).
HAB still and slow
water. SOIL
water–wet; acid–calc.
SHADE nil–light. ALT
sl–400. DIST E5, W4,
S3, I4. RANGE F5, G4,
S2.
See p. 17.

● **Unbranched bur-
reed**
Sparganium simplex
Short–mid. Lvs long
and narrow, either 3-
sided and upright or
flat and floating; small
♂ heads above ♀ heads.
LH perenn; rhizome.
GERM spr–sum. FL 6–8.
POLL wind. SEX (♂ + ♀).
HAB still and slow,
shallow water. SOIL
water; not acid. SHADE
nil. ALT sl–200. DIST
E4, W2, S2, I3. RANGE
F3, G4, S4.
ss220. ss221.

● **Bulrush (Reed-
mace)**
Typha latifolia
Tall–v.tall. Lvs 10–
20mm wide; ♀ spike,
fat, chocolate-brown,
cylindrical, joining ♂
spike. LH perenn;
rhizome. GERM spr–
sum. FL 6–7. POLL
wind. SEX (♂ + ♀). HAB
reed-swamps, still and
slow water. SOIL water;
acid–calc. SHADE nil–
light. ALT sl–500. DIST
E5, W3, S2, I4. RANGE
F5, G5, S3.
*See p. 179, 257, 264,
271.*

● **Lesser bulrush**
Typha angustifolia
Tall–v.tall. Lvs 5mm
wide; ♀ fls in narrow,
chocolate-brown, cyl-
indrical spike, separ-
ated from smaller ♂
spike. LH perenn;
rhizome. GERM spr–
sum. FL 6–7. POLL
wind. SEX (♂ + ♀). HAB
still and slow water.
SOIL water; not acid.
SHADE nil. ALT sl–250.
DIST sE4, nE1, W1, S1,
I1. RANGE F4, G4, sS3.

135

SEDGE FAMILY
Cyperaceae
Sedges have no obvious petals or sepals, but the stamens and styles, which are in separate flowers in most species, are enclosed by a small scale called a glume, which is important for identification. The flowers are grouped in spikelets containing male and female flowers except in *Carex* and *Kobresia* which have them in separate spikes. Stems are usually 3-angled. See p. 11, 14, 15, 17, 172, 257, 264, 271.

○ **Wood club-rush**
Scirpus sylvaticus
Mid–tall. Lvs flat, 5–20mm wide; fls in loose, branching clusters, above lf-like bracts; spikelets 3–4 mm. LH perenn; rhizome. GERM spr-sum. FL 5–7. POLL wind. SEX (♂+♀). HAB marshes, woods, watersides. SOIL wet–damp; not acid. SHADE nil–mid. ALT sl–200. DIST E3, W2, S2, I2. RANGE F5, G5, S3. ss222.

● **Sea club-rush**
Scirpus maritimus
Mid–tall. Stems with broad, keeled lvs; flhd a dense cluster of un-stalked spikelets, 10–20mm; bracts long, lf-like. LH perenn. GERM spr. FL 6–8. POLL wind. SEX (♂+♀). HAB shallow brackish and salt water. SOIL water; saline. SHADE nil. ALT sl. DIST E3, W3, S3, I3. RANGE F3, G4, S3. ss223.

● **Common club-rush**
Scirpus lacustris
Tall–v.tall. Stems round, lfless above water; spikelets 5–8 mm, in tight groups on long stalks; 3 styles. Grey club-rush (ssp. *tabernaemontani*) is greyish and has 2 styles. LH perenn; rhizome. GERM spr-sum. FL 6–8. POLL wind. SEX (♂+♀). HAB slow, often deep water. SOIL water; acid–calc. SHADE nil. ALT sl–300. DIST E4, W3, S3, I4. RANGE F3, G5, S4. ss224.

● **Bristle club-rush**
Scirpus setaceus
V.low–low(–short). Stems round, lvs thread-like; spikelets in a single egg-shaped head, with a bract continuing the stem; fr black. LH ann, often persisting. GERM spr-sum. FL 5–7. POLL wind. SEX (♂+♀). HAB usually bare, sandy ground, or in short turf. SOIL damp; not calc. SHADE nil. ALT sl–600. DIST E3, W4, S4, I3. RANGE F3, G4, sS2. ss225.

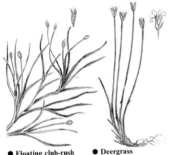

● **Floating club-rush**
Scirpus fluitans
Floating. Stems long, floating or submerged; lvs narrow; fls in a single spikelet just above water. LH perenn. GERM imm. FL 5–7. POLL wind. SEX (♂+♀). HAB still and slow water. SOIL water; acid. SHADE nil. ALT sl–400. DIST E3, W3, S2, I3. RANGE F3, G2, sS2.

● **Deergrass**
Scirpus cespitosus
Low–short. Tufted with almost lfless stems (a tiny lf near base), and a single spikelet with two large glumes. LH perenn. GERM spr-sum. FL 5–6. POLL wind. SEX (♂+♀). HAB moors, heaths, bogs. SOIL damp–moist; acid. SHADE nil. ALT sl–1100. DIST E2, W4, S5, I4. RANGE F3, G3, S5.

● **Flat sedge**
Blysmus compressus
Low–mid. Stems rounded, lfy; lvs flat; spikelets 5–7mm in a flattened head, 20mm long; fr with long, brown bristles. LH perenn; rhizome. GERM spr? FL 6–7. POLL wind. SEX (♂+♀). HAB marshes, open grassy places. SOIL wet–damp; acid–calc. SHADE nil. ALT sl–450. DIST E3, W2, S1. RANGE F3, G3, sS3. ss226.

● **Common cotton-grass**
Eriophorum angustifolium
Short–mid. Stem rounded, lfy; lvs long, channelled, 3-sided at tip; spikelets in a loose, nodding cluster, cottony in fr. LH perenn; rhizome. GERM spr. FL 4–5. POLL wind. SEX (♂+♀) pg. HAB bogs, moors. SOIL wet; acid. SHADE nil–light. ALT sl–1100. DIST E4, W5, S5, I5. RANGE F4, G4, S5. ss227. ss228.

● **Hare's-tail cotton-grass**
Eriophorum vaginatum
Mid. Tussock-forming; lvs narrow, top lf with an inflated sheath round stem; fls in a single, upright spike-let; cottony in fr. LH perenn; rhizome. GERM spr-sum. FL 4–5. POLL wind. SEX (♂+♀) pg. HAB bogs, moors. SOIL wet–damp; acid. SHADE nil. ALT sl–800. DIST sE2, nE4, W4, S5, I4. RANGE F2, G3, S5. See p. 264.

● **Common spike-rush**
Eleocharis palustris
Low–mid. Variable;
forms groups of small
tufts; top sheath on
stem lfless; fls in a
single spikelet, with a
short glume at base.
LH perenn; rhizome.
GERM spr–sum. FL 5–8.
POLL wind. SEX (♂+♀).
HAB marshes, by
water. SOIL wet–damp;
acid–calc. SHADE nil.
ALT sl–400. DIST E5,
W4, S4, I3. RANGE F5,
G5, S3.
ss229. ss230. ss231.

● **Needle spike-rush**
Eleocharis acicularis
Low–mid. Stems 4-
angled, slender; top
sheath lfless; fls in a
single spikelet, 4mm,
with a glume 2mm
long at its base. LH
perenn; rhizome.
GERM spr–sum. FL 7–
10. POLL wind. SEX
(♂+♀). HAB on mud
by water, dry in
summer. SOIL damp;
acid–calc. SHADE nil.
ALT sl–250. DIST E2,
W2, S2, I2. RANGE F3,
G4, S4.
ss232. ss233.

○ **Great fen sedge**
Cladium mariscus
Tall–v.tall. Forms ex-
tensive stands; stems
round; lvs very long,
saw-edged, bent in an
arch; fls in clusters;
spikelets 3–4mm. LH
perenn; rhizome.
GERM sum. FL 7–8.
POLL wind. SEX (♂+
♀). HAB reed-swamps;
fens. SOIL wet–damp;
not acid. SHADE nil–
mid. ALT sl–250. DIST
E3, W2, S2, I2. RANGE
F3, G2, S2.
See p. 237.

○ **White beak-sedge**
Rhynchospira alba
Short–mid. Tufted;
stems rounded with lfy
stems; spikelets 4–5
mm, whitish-brown,
each with 1–2 fls, and
several glumes. LH
perenn. GERM spr. FL
6–9. POLL wind. SEX
(♂+♀). HAB bogs,
moors, heaths. SOIL
wet–damp; acid.
SHADE nil. ALT sl–450.
DIST E2, W2, S3, I3.
RANGE F2, G2, S4.
ss234.

● **Black bog-rush**
Schoenus nigricans
Short–tall. Tufted;
stems rounded, lfy at
base; lvs v. narrow;
spikelets 5–8mm, v.
dark, 1–4 fld; bract
much longer than flhd.
LH perenn. GERM spr.
FL 5–7. POLL wind. SEX
(♂+♀). HAB fens,
wet–damp; acid–calc.
SHADE nil. ALT sl–300
(–500). DIST E2, W2,
S4, I4. RANGE F3, G2,
sS1.
ss235.

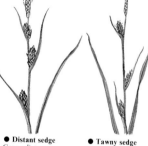

Northern false sedge
Kobresia myosuroides
Low–short. Lvs
narrow; fl-spike with
up to 20 spikelets, each
with 2 fls, one ♂ above
one ♀. LH perenn;
rhizome. GERM ? FL 6–
9. POLL wind. SEX (♂+
♀). HAB stony places.
SOIL moist–dry; acid–
calc. SHADE nil. ALT
[sl–3000]. RANGE sG1,
S3.
ss236.

● **Distant sedge**
Carex distans
Short–tall. Tufted; lvs
greyish; flhd with 1♂
spike above 2–3 ♀
spikes, 10–30mm,
with bracts shorter
than flhd. LH perenn;
rhizome. GERM spr–
sum. FL 5–6. POLL
wind. SEX (♂+♀) pa.
HAB rocks, marshes;
especially by sea. SOIL
wet–damp; calc or
saline. SHADE nil. ALT
sl–250. DIST E3, W3,
S2, I3. RANGE F4, G3,
S2.
ss237.

● **Tawny sedge**
Carex hostiana
Short–mid. Loosely
tufted; lvs yellowish;
flhds with 1♂ spike
and 1–3 ♀ spikes, less
than 15mm, spaced
out; bracts shorter
than flhd. LH perenn;
rhizome. GERM spr–
sum. FL 5–6. POLL
wind. SEX (♂+♀) pa.
HAB fens, marshes. SOIL
wet–damp; calc. SHADE
nil–light. ALT sl–500
(–750). DIST E3, W3,
S4, I3. RANHE F3, G3,
S2.
ss238.

● **Green-ribbed sedge**
Carex binervis
Mid–tall. Often tufted;
lvs dark green; flhds
with 1♂ spike above
2–3 ♀, spaced out;
glumes purplish;
bracts short. LH
perenn; rhizome. GERM
spr. FL 5–6. POLL wind.
SEX (♂+♀) pa. HAB
moors, heaths, grass-
land. SOIL moist–dry;
acid. SHADE nil. ALT sl–
800. DIST E3, W5, S5,
I4. RANGE F3, wG1,
wS2.
ss239.

● **Common yellow
sedge**
Carex viridula
Low–mid. Tufted; lvs
often longer than
stems; ♂ spike sur-
rounded by 1–3 egg-
shaped ♀ spikes, often
with 1 lower down
stem. LH perenn;
rhizome. GERM spr–
sum. FL 5–6. POLL
wind. SEX (♂+♀) pa.
HAB fens, marshes,
grassy and stony
ground. SOIL wet–
damp; acid–calc.
SHADE nil. ALT sl–1000.
DIST E4, W5, S5, I5.
RANGE F4, G4, S3.
ss240.

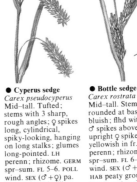

● **Long-bracted sedge**
Carex extensa
Short–mid. Tufted;
stem sometimes
rounded; lvs greyish,
grooved; ♂ spike
above cluster of 2–4 ♀
spikes; bracts v. long.
LH perenn; rhizome.
GERM spr. FL 6–7. POLL
wind. SEX (♂+♀) pa.
HAB salt-marshes,
coastal rocks. SOIL wet–
damp; saline. SHADE
nil. ALT sl–50. DIST
coastal: E3, W3, S3,
I3. RANGE coastal: F3,
G3, sS3.

● **Wood sedge**
Carex sylvatica
Short–mid. Tufted;
lvs up to 6mm wide,
yellowish; ♀ spikes
long, narrow, droop-
ing on long stalks. LH
perenn; rhizome. GERM
spr. FL 5–7. POLL
wind. SEX (♂+♀) pa.
HAB woods. SOIL damp–
moist; not acid. SHADE
light–heavy. ALT sl–
600. DIST E5, W4, S3,
I3. RANGE F5, G5, sS3.
ss241. ss242.

● **Cyperus sedge**
Carex pseudocyperus
Mid–tall. Tufted;
stems with 3 sharp,
rough angles; ♀ spikes
long, cylindrical,
spiky-looking, hanging
on long stalks; glumes
long-pointed. LH
perenn; rhizome. GERM
spr–sum. FL 5–6. POLL
wind. SEX (♂+♀) pa.
HAB slow and still
water. SOIL water–wet;
not acid. SHADE nil.
ALT sl–100. DIST E3,
W1, S1, I2. RANGE F3,
G3, sS3.
See p. 172.

● **Bottle sedge**
Carex rostrata
Mid–tall. Stems
rounded at base and
bluish; flhd with 2–4
♂ spikes above 2–5
upright ♀ spikes;
yellowish in fr. LH
perenn; rhizome. GERM
spr–sum. FL 6–7. POLL
wind. SEX (♂+♀) pa.
HAB peaty ground. SOIL
water–wet; acid.
SHADE nil. ALT sl–900.
DIST sE2, nE4, W2, S5,
I5. RANGE F4, G4, S5.

● **Bladder sedge**
Carex vesicaria
Mid–tall. Very like
Bottle sedge but dark
green, with sharply 3-
angled ♀ spikes
usually drooping. LH
perenn; rhizome. GERM
sum–aut (2nd year). FL
6–7. POLL wind. SEX
(♂+♀) pa. HAB fens,
peaty ground, lakes.
SOIL water–wet; acid–
calc. SHADE nil. ALT sl–
450. DIST E3, W2, S3,
I2. RANGE F3, G4, S5.

● **Greater pond-sedge**
Carex riparia
Tall–v.tall. Patch-
forming; stems sharply
3-angled; lvs to 15mm
wide; ♂ spikes dark
brown, 3–6 above 1–5
♀ spikes, lower nod-
ding. LH perenn;
rhizome. GERM spr. FL
5–6. POLL wind. SEX
(♂+♀) pa. HAB still
and slow water,
marshes. SOIL water–
wet; not acid. SHADE
nil–light. ALT sl–150.
DIST sE4, nE2, W2, S1,
I2. RANGE F4, G4, sS2.
See p. 271.

● **Lesser pond-sedge**
Carex acutiformis
Tall–v.tall. Like
Greater pond sedge:
lvs to 10mm,♂ spikes
purplish, 2–3; fr 4mm
long (not 8), flattened
(not swollen). LH
perenn; rhizome. GERM
spr–sum. FL 6–7. POLL
wind. SEX (♂+♀) pa.
HAB still and slow
water, woods. SOIL
water–wet; acid–calc.
SHADE nil–mid. ALT sl–
350. DIST sE4, nE2,
W3, S2, I2. RANGE F4,
G5, sS2.

○ **Pendulous sedge**
Carex pendula
Tall–v.tall. Tussock-
forming, spreading;
lvs to 20mm wide; ♀
spikes long (to 150
mm), drooping. LH
perenn; rhizome. GERM
aut–spr. FL 5–6. POLL
wind. SEX (♂+♀) pa.
HAB woods, by streams.
SOIL damp–moist; not
acid. SHADE light–
heavy. ALT sl–150.
DIST sE4, nE2, W3, S2,
I2. RANGE F4, G2.

● **Carnation sedge**
Carex panicea
Low–mid. Lvs bluish
on both sides; flhd
with 1 ♂ spike above
1–3 ♀; lowest bract
shorter than flhd. LH
perenn; rhizome. GERM
sum. FL 5–6. POLL
wind. SEX (♂+♀) pa.
HAB grassland, moors,
fens. SOIL damp; not
acid nor calc. SHADE
nil. ALT sl–1100. DIST
E5, W5, S5, I5. RANGE
F5, G5, S5.
ss243. ss244.

● **Glaucous sedge**
Carex flacca
Low–mid. Lvs bluish
only underneath; flhd
with 2–3 ♂ spikes
above 2–4 ♀; lowest
bract as long as flhd.
LH perenn; rhizome.
GERM spr–sum. FL 5–6.
POLL wind. SEX (♂+
♀) pa. HAB grassland,
fens, marshes. SOIL
wet–dry; not acid.
SHADE nil–light. ALT
sl–800. DIST E5, W5,
S5, I5. RANGE F5, G5,
S2.

● **Hairy sedge**
Carex hirta
Mid. Lvs and stems hairy; ♂ and ♀ spikes spaced out, the ♀ yellowish; bracts long. LH perenn; rhizome. GERM sum. FL 5–6. POLL wind. SEX (♂ + ♀) pa. HAB grassland, woods. SOIL damp–moist; not acid. SHADE nil–mid. ALT sl–350. DIST E5, W4, S3, I3. RANGE F5, G5, S3. **ss245. ss246.**

● **Pill sedge**
Carex pilulifera
Low–short. Tufted; stems curved, lvs short; ♂ spike solitary, unstalked; ♀ spikes few-flowered, rounded. LH perenn; rhizome. GERM spr–sum. FL 5–6. POLL wind. SEX (♂ + ♀) pa. HAB grassland, heaths, moors. SOIL dry; acid. SHADE nil. ALT sl–1100. DIST E4, W4, S5, I3. RANGE F4, G5, S4. **ss247. ss248.**

● **Spring sedge**
Carex caryophyllea
Low(–short). Loosely tufted; lvs dark green; ♂ spike solitary, yellow anthers conspicuous; ♀ spike clustered, lower bract sheathing. LH perenn; rhizome. GERM spr? FL 4–5. POLL wind. SEX (♂ + ♀) pa. HAB grassland. SOIL dry; calc. SHADE nil. ALT sl–400 (–650). DIST E4, W3, S2, I2. RANGE F5, G5, S3. *See p. 271.* **ss249. ss250. ss251. ss252.**

● **Tufted sedge**
Carex elata
Mid–tall. Forms large tussocks; lvs slightly bluish; ♂ spikes narrow, very dark; ♀ fls with black glumes and 2 (not 3) styles. LH perenn; rhizome. GERM spr–sum. FL 5–6. POLL wind. SEX (♂ + ♀) pa. HAB fens, ditches, woods. SOIL water–damp; not acid. SHADE nil–mid. ALT sl–100. DIST E3, W2, I3. RANGE F4, G3, sS3.

● **Slender tufted sedge**
Carex acuta
Tall. Tufted; lvs long. ♂ spikes dark; ♀ spikes long and narrow (4–5mm wide), with dark, pointed glumes and 2 styles. LH perenn; rhizome. GERM spr. FL 5–6. POLL wind. SEX (♂ + ♀) pa. HAB marshes, watersides. SOIL wet–damp; acid–calc. SHADE nil–light. ALT sl–200. DIST E3, W3, S2, I2. RANGE F4, G4, S4. **ss253. ss254. ss255.**

● **Common sedge**
Carex nigra
Low–mid. Variable, sometimes tufted; flhd with 1 long ♂ spike above 1–2 smaller ones; ♀ spikes short-stalked, glumes black and 2 styles. LH perenn; rhizome. GERM spr–sum. FL 5–7. POLL wind. SEX (♂ + ♀) pa. HAB marshes, grassland. SOIL wet–moist; acid–calc. SHADE nil–light. ALT sl–1000. DIST E5, W5, S5, I5. RANGE F5, G5, S5. *See p. 14.* **ss256. ss257. ss258. ss259. ss260. ss261. ss262.**

● **Greater tussock sedge**
Carex paniculata
Tall–v.tall. Makes enormous tussocks; lvs up to 7mm wide, dark green, v. long; spikes all similar, in a long head. LH perenn; rhizome. GERM spr–sum. FL 5–6. POLL wind. SEX (♂ + ♀) pa. HAB marshes, fens, woods. SOIL wet; not acid. SHADE nil–mid. ALT sl–200(–450). DIST sE5, nE3, W3, S2, I3. RANGE F4, G4, S2. *See p. 271.* **ss264.**

● **False fox-sedge**
Carex otrubae
Tall. Tufted; stems sharply 3-angled; lvs up to 10 mm wide; spikes all similar, yellowish-green, turning brown, in a dense head. LH perenn; rhizome. GERM spr–sum. FL 5–7. POLL wind. SEX (♂ + ♀) pa. HAB grassland. SOIL damp; not acid. SHADE nil–light. ALT sl–200. DIST E4, W3, S2, I2. RANGE F5, G4, S2. **ss265. ss266.**

● **Brown sedge**
Carex disticha
Mid–tall. Stems stiff, stout, longer than lvs; spikes more than 15 in flhd, all similar, with styles at top and bottom of flhd. LH perenn; rhizome. GERM sum. FL 6–7. POLL wind. SEX (♀ + ♀) pa. HAB marshes, fens, grassland. SOIL wet–moist; acid–calc. SHADE nil. ALT sl–350. DIST E4, W2, S2, I3. RANGE F4, G5, S3. **ss267.**

● **Sand sedge**
Carex arenaria
Low–mid. Stems often curved, in long spaced lines, as long as lvs; spikes less than 15 in flhd, top spikes ♂. LH perenn; rhizome. GERM spr–sum. FL 6–7. POLL wind. SEX (♂ + ♀) pa. HAB sand-dunes, sandy fields. SOIL dry; not acid. SHADE nil. ALT sl(–200). DIST coastal: E4, W5, S5, I4; and inland. RANGE coastal: F5, G5, S2; and inland. *See p. 214, 250.*

● **Grey sedge**
Carex divulsa
Mid(–tall). Tufted; lvs channelled, shorter than stems; spikes all similar, spaced along stem, but crowded near top. LH perenn; rhizome. GERM spr. FL 6–7. POLL wind. SEX (♀+♂) pa. HAB grassland. SOIL moist–dry; calc. SHADE nil. ALT sl–200. DIST sE4, nE1, W2, I2. RANGE F3, G4, sS2.

● **Spiked sedge**
Carex spicata
Mid(–tall). Like Grey sedge, but often red-tinged; spikes crowded into a head 20–30mm long. LH perenn; rhizome. GERM sum. FL 6–7. POLL wind. SEX (♀+♀). HAB banks, grassland, marshes. SOIL wet–dry; not acid. SHADE nil–light. ALT sl–200. DIST sE4, nE2, W2, S1, I2. RANGE F5, G5, sS4.
ss268.

● **Star sedge**
Carex echinata
Low–mid. Tufted, with short, narrow lvs and wiry stems; spikes all similar, star-like, upper ♀ on top and ♂ below; rest all ♀. LH perenn; rhizome. GERM spr–sum. FL 5–7. POLL wind. SEX (♂+♀) pa. HAB marshes, grassy places, woods, bogs. SOIL wet; not calc. SHADE nil–light. ALT sl–1000. DIST E4, W5, S5, I5. RANGE F4, G4, S5.

● **Remote sedge**
Carex remota
Mid. Tufted; lvs grass-green, narrow; spikes all similar, narrow, with v. long lf-like bracts. LH perenn; rhizome. GERM spr–sum. FL 6–7. POLL wind. SEX (♂+♀) pa. HAB woods. SOIL wet–damp; acid–calc. SHADE light–heavy. ALT sl–300. DIST E5, W5, S4, I4. RANGE F5, G5, sS3.

● **Oval sedge**
Carex ovalis
Mid–tall. Tufted; stems lfy at base only; spikes all similar, oval, close together, each ♀ at top, ♂ at base. LH perenn; rhizome. GERM late spr. FL 6–7. POLL wind. SEX (♂+♀) pa. HAB grassland, heaths, moors. SOIL dry; acid. SHADE nil–light. ALT sl–600. DIST E4, W5, S5, I4. RANGE F4, G5, sS5, nS2.
ss269. ss270.

● **White sedge**
Carex curta
Mid. Tufted. Lvs pale green, as long as stems; spikes all similar, ♀ on top and ♂ at base; ♀ glumes v. pale. LH perenn; rhizome. GERM spr. FL 6–8. POLL wind. SEX (♂+♀) pa. HAB heaths, bogs. SOIL wet; acid. SHADE nil. ALT sl–1100. DIST E3, W5, S4, I3. RANGE F1, G4, S5.
ss271.

● **Flea sedge**
Carex pulicaris
Low–short. Tufted; lvs v. fine, stiff; fls in a single spike, ♂ at top; ♀ fls spaced, turned down when fruiting. LH perenn; rhizome. GERM spr–sum. FL 5–6. POLL wind. SEX (♂+♀) pa. HAB grassland, fens, marshes. SOIL wet–damp; calc. SHADE nil. ALT sl–1000. DIST eE2, wE4, W4, S5, I5. RANGE F3, G2, S3.
ss272. ss273.

● **Dioecious sedge**
Carex dioica
Low–short. Lvs thread-like; ♂ and ♀ plants separate, each with a single spike; fruits spreading. LH perenn; rhizome. GERM spr–sum. FL 5–6. POLL wind. SEX (♂)+(♀). HAB fens, marshes. SOIL wet; not acid. SHADE nil. ALT sl–800. DIST E2, W2, S4, I2. RANGE F1, G3, S5.
See p. 270.

GRASS FAMILY
Gramineae
Grass flowerheads consist of spikelets containing one or more flowers. Each flower consists of two scales and the stamens and styles, and each spikelet has two scales (the glumes) enclosing the flowers. Any of the scales may have a long hair called an awn. The spikelets may be in a spike or a branching cluster. Grass leaves have a small flap called a ligule between leaf and stem – its shape and size are important. Grasses are economically important, including cereals and major forage plants. *See p. 15, 16, 17, 173, 177, 257, 269, 273.*

● **Giant fescue**
Festuca gigantea
Tall–v.tall. Lvs shiny, up to 18mm wide, their base wrapped claw-like round the stem; stem purplish at nodes; spikelets with long awns. LH perenn. GERM imm. FL 7–8. POLL wind. SEX (♀) pa. HAB woods. SOIL damp–moist; not acid. SHADE light–heavy. ALT sl–350. DIST E5, W4, S3, I3. RANGE F5, G5, sS3.

● **Meadow fescue**
Festuca pratensis
Mid–tall. Lvs 2–4mm
wide; spikelets 10–
12mm, unawned, in
branching clusters,
one branch of each
pair with only one
spikelet. LH perenn.
GERM imm. FL 6–7.
POLL wind. SEX (♀) pa.
HAB grassland. SOIL
moist; not acid. SHADE
nil. ALT sl–200(–500).
DIST E5, W4, S3, I4.
RANGE F5, G5, S4.
See p. 273.

● **Tall fescue**
Festuca arundinacea
Tall–v.tall. Tussock-
forming; lvs to 10mm
wide, their bases
wrapped claw-like
round stem; all
branches of clusters
have several spikelets,
10–18mm. LH perenn.
GERM imm. FL 5–7.
POLL wind. SEX (♀) pa.
HAB grassland. SOIL
damp–moist; acid–
calc. SHADE nil–light.
ALT sl–300. DIST E4,
W3, S3, I3. RANGE F4,
G3, S2.
ss274.

● **Red fescue**
Festuca rubra
Low–mid(–tall). Non-
flg shoots with thread-
like lvs; flg shoots
with flat lvs to 3mm
wide, their sheaths
joined round stem;
spikelets 7–10mm,
awned. LH perenn;
stolons. GERM imm. FL
5–6. POLL wind. SEX
(♀) pa. HAB grassland,
from saltmarshes to
mountains. SOIL wet–
dry; acid–calc. SHADE
nil–light. ALT sl–1000.
DIST E5, W5, S5, I5.
RANGE F5, G5, S5.
See p. 247, 254. **ss275.**
ss276. ss277.

● **Sheep's fescue**
Festuca ovina
Low–mid. Tufted; lvs
all thread-like, their
sheaths open at back
of stem; spikelets
5–6mm, awned, often
bluish. LH perenn.
GERM imm. FL 6–7.
POLL wind. SEX (♀) pa.
HAB grassland, heaths,
moors. SOIL dry; acid–
calc. SHADE nil. ALT
sl–1300. DIST E5, W5,
S5, I5. RANGE F5, G5,
S5.
See p. 293. **ss278.**
ss279.

● **Viviparous fescue**
Festuca vivipara
Low–short. Like
Sheep's fescue, but fls
replaced by tiny green
plantlets that form
new plants. LH perenn.
GERM none. FL none.
POLL none. SEX none.
HAB mountain grass-
land, rocks, moors.
SOIL moist–dry; acid–
calc. SHADE nil. ALT
sl–1000. DIST nE2, W2,
S4, I3. RANGE S3.
See p. 292, 293.

● **Perennial ryegrass**
Lolium perenne
Short–tall. Tufted; lvs
flat, folded when
emerging; spikelets
5–15mm, unawned and
unstalked, alternating
up stalk. LH perenn.
GERM imm. FL 5–10.
POLL wind. SEX (♀) pa.
HAB grassy and dis-
turbed ground; very
widely sown. SOIL
moist; not acid. SHADE
nil. ALT sl–500. DIST
E5, W5, S5, I5. RANGE
F5, G5, S3.

● **Italian ryegrass**
Lolium multiflorum
Short–tall. Like
Perennial ryegrass, but
lvs rolled when emerg-
ing and spikelets
awned; hybrids inter-
mediate between them
occur. LH ann–bienn.
GERM imm. FL 6–7.
POLL wind. SEX (♀) pa.
HAB cultivated and
disturbed ground. SOIL
moist–dry; not acid.
SHADE nil. ALT sl–300.
DIST E5, W3, S3, I3.
RANGE F5, G5, S2.

● **Dune fescue**
Vulpia fasciculata
Low–mid. Lvs short,
rolled; sheaths in-
flated; spikelets 10–
15mm, awned, in
1-sided spikes. LH ann.
GERM aut. FL 5–6.
POLL cleistogamous:
self. SEX (♀). HAB
sand-dunes. SOIL dry;
calc. SHADE nil. ALT sl.
DIST coastal: E3, W3,
S1, I1. RANGE coastal:
F3.
ss280.

● **Squirreltail fescue**
Vulpia bromoides
Low–mid. Stem
ridged; sheaths not in-
flated; flhd a shortly
branching cluster;
upper glume of each
spikelet long, awned,
3-nerved. LH ann. GERM
imm. FL 5–7. POLL
cleistogamous: self.
SEX (♀). HAB heaths,
sandy and disturbed
ground. SOIL dry; acid–
calc. SHADE nil. ALT
sl–400. DIST sE5, nE3,
W4, S3, I4. RANGE F5,
G3, sS2.

○ **Rat's-tail fescue**
Vulpia myuros
Low–mid. Stem
smooth; flhd branch-
ing, nodding; upper
glume of each spikelet
v. fine, not nerved. LH
ann. GERM imm. FL
5–7. POLL cleisto-
gamous: self. SEX (♀).
HAB sandy ground,
walls. SOIL dry; not
calc. SHADE nil. ALT
sl–200. DIST sE3, W3,
I2. RANGE F3, G2.
ss281.

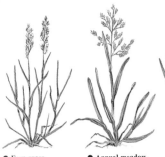

● **Fern grass**
Desmazeria rigida
Low. Stem and flhd
stiff; spikelets short-
stalked, 2–4mm in 1-
sided branches. LH
ann. GERM imm. FL
5–7. POLL wind. SEX
(♀) pa. HAB bare
ground, walls, rocks.
SOIL dry; calc. SHADE
nil. ALT sl–350. DIST
sE5, nE2, W2, S1, I3.
RANGE F3.
ss282.

● **Annual meadow-
grass**
Poa annua
Low–short. Lvs flat,
wrinkled near base;
spikelets 3–5mm, in
long, spreading
branches. LH ann or
short-lived perenn.
GERM imm. FL 1–12.
POLL wind, self or
cleistogamous. SEX (♀)
pa. HAB disturbed
ground, grassland. SOIL
moist; acid–calc.
SHADE nil–light. ALT sl–
1200. DIST E5, W5, S5,
I5. RANGE F5, G5, S5.
ss283.

○ **Bulbous meadow-
grass**
Poa bulbosa
Short. Tufted; stems
swollen at base;
spikelets purplish in a
dense cluster, often
replaced by plantlets
(viviparous). LH
perenn. GERM imm. FL
4–5. POLL wind. SEX
(♀) pa. HAB bare and
sparsely grassy places.
SOIL dry; not acid.
SHADE nil. ALT sl–50.
DIST sE2. RANGE F3,
G3, sS2.
ss284.

● **Rough meadow-
grass**
Poa trivialis
Short–tall. Tufted,
rough-stemmed; lvs
with long, pointed
ligule; spikelets 2–4mm
in a narrow, much-
branched cluster. LH
perenn. GERM imm. FL
5–7. POLL wind. SEX
(♀). HAB grassland,
woods. SOIL damp–
moist; acid–calc.
SHADE nil–mid. ALT
sl–500(–750). DIST E5,
W5, S5, I5. RANGE F5,
G5, S5.
ss285.

● **Smooth meadow-
grass**
Poa pratensis
Low–mid. Tufted,
smooth-stemmed; lvs
with v. short, blunt
ligule; spikelets 4–
6mm in a branching
cluster. LH perenn;
stolons. GERM imm.
FL 4–6. POLL wind. SEX
(♀) pa. HAB grassland.
SOIL moist–dry; acid–
calc. SHADE nil. ALT
sl–600(–900). DIST
E5, W5, S5, I5. RANGE
F5, G5, S5.
See p. 251, 273. **ss286**.
ss287.

● **Wood meadow-
grass**
Poa nemoralis
Mid–tall. Slender,
with lvs held horizon-
tally and v. short (or
no) ligule; flhd with
many spikelets on long
stalks. LH perenn.
GERM imm. FL 6–7.
POLL wind. SEX (♀) pa.
HAB woods, rocks.
SOIL moist; acid–calc.
SHADE nil–heavy. ALT
sl–500. DIST E4, W4,
S4, I3. RANGE F5, G5,
S5.

○ **Alpine meadow-
grass**
Poa alpina
Low–short. Tufted;
lvs 3–5mm wide, short
and stiff; ligule long,
rounded, often ragged;
spikelets often re-
placed by plantlets.
LH perenn; rootstock.
GERM ? FL 6–8. POLL
wind. SEX (♀). HAB
grassland, mountain
rocks. SOIL moist;
acid–calc. SHADE nil.
ALT (300–)600–1000.
DIST nE1, W1, S3, I1.
RANGE F1, G1, S4.
See p. 292. **ss288**.
ss289.

● **Reflexed saltmarsh
grass**
Puccinellia distans
Short–mid. Tufted;
ligule short, rounded;
spikelets 4–6mm on
long branches, pointed
downwards when
fruiting. LH perenn.
GERM spr. FL 6–7. POLL
wind. SEX (♀) pa. HAB
saltmarshes, coastal
rocks, roadsides. SOIL
damp; saline. SHADE
nil. ALT sl(–50). DIST
coastal: E4, W2, S2,
I2; and by major
roads. RANGE S3, F2,
G3.

● **Common saltmarsh
grass**
Puccinellia maritima
Low–short. Tufted but
sward-forming; spike-
lets 6–12mm on
upright branches,
making a narrow flhd.
LH perenn; stolons.
GERM spr? FL 6–7.
POLL wind. SEX (♀) pa.
HAB saltmarshes. SOIL
wet–damp; saline.
SHADE nil. ALT sl. DIST
coastal: E5, W5, S4,
I5; rare inland. RANGE
coastal: F5, G5, S3.
ss290. **ss291**.

● **Cock's-foot**
Dactylis glomerata
Mid–tall. Tussock-
forming, stems flatten-
ed at base; spikelets
crowded into dense
clusters on long stalks.
LH perenn. GERM imm.
FL 4–10. POLL wind.
SEX (♀) pa. HAB grass-
land, woods. SOIL
moist; acid–calc.
SHADE nil–mid. ALT sl–
400(–700). DIST E5,
W5, S5, I5. RANGE F5,
G5, S4.
See p. 273, 292.

● **Crested dog's-tail**
Cynosurus cristatus
Short–mid. Tufted, stems tough, lvs narrow; spikelets with short awns, in two rows but all facing same direction. LH perenn. GERM imm. FL 6–8. POLL wind. SEX (♀) pa. HAB grassland. SOIL moist–dry; acid–calc. SHADE nil. ALT sl–600. DIST E5, W5, S5, I5. RANGE F5, G5, S2.
See p. 292.

● **Whorl grass**
Catabrosa aquatica
Low–mid. Creeping and rooting or floating; lvs up to 10mm wide, with long, blunt ligules; spikelets 3–5mm, in alternating branching clusters. LH perenn; rooting nodes. GERM imm. FL 5–8. POLL wind. SEX (♀) pa. HAB ditches, mud, sandy beaches where streams outfall. SOIL water–wet; not acid. SHADE nil. ALT sl–300. DIST E3, W2, S2. RANGE F3, G3, S2.

○ **Loose silky-bent**
Apera spica-venti
Short–mid. Lvs to 10mm wide, rough; spikelets 2–3mm, each with 1 fl and an awn up to 12mm long. LH ann. GERM aut. FL 6–7. POLL wind. SEX (♀) pa. HAB sandy fields. SOIL dry; not calc. SHADE nil. ALT sl–50. DIST E2, W1, S1. RANGE F3, G5, S3.

● **Quaking grass**
Briza media
Short–mid. Lvs narrow, with short, blunt ligules; spikelets 5mm, shaped like a Chinese lantern, quaking. LH perenn; rhizome. GERM imm. FL 5–8. POLL wind. SEX (♀) pa. HAB grassland. SOIL damp–dry; not acid. SHADE nil. ALT sl–500(–650). DIST E5, W4, S4, I3. RANGE F5, G5, sS4, nS1.
See p. 273. **ss292.**

○ **Blue moor-grass**
Sesleria albicans
Short–mid. Tufted; lvs short, greyish, all near stem-base; spikelets 5–8mm, purplish, in a dense spike. LH perenn; rhizome. GERM aut–spr. FL 4–6. POLL wind. SEX (♀) pa. HAB grassland, stony ground. SOIL damp–dry; calc. SHADE nil. ALT sl–900. DIST nE2, S2, I2. RANGE F2, G2.
See p. 201.

○ **Mountain melick**
Melica nutans
Short–mid. Lvs smooth; spikelets 6–7mm, oval, with two dark glumes; in a 1-sided spike, nodding. LH perenn. GERM spr. FL 5–7. POLL wind. SEX (♀). HAB woods, rocks. SOIL moist; calc. SHADE nil–mid. ALT 100–500. DIST nE2, W2, S3. RANGE eF2, G4, S5.

● **Wood melick**
Melica uniflora
Mid. Lvs rough beneath; stem hairy; spikelets 4–5mm, with dark glumes; upright in a sparse, spreading cluster. LH perenn. GERM spr. FL 5–7. POLL wind. SEX (♀). HAB woods. SOIL moist–dry; not acid. SHADE light–heavy. ALT sl–500. DIST E5, W5, sS4, nS1, I2. RANGE F4, G5, sS2.

● **Reed sweet-grass**
Glyceria maxima
Tall–v.tall. Forms large clumps; stems short, lvs up to 20mm wide; ligules rounded, with a point; spikelets 5–8mm in spreading clusters. LH perenn; rhizome. GERM spr–sum. FL 6–8. POLL wind. SEX (♀) pa. HAB still and slow water, marshes. SOIL water–wet; not acid. SHADE nil–mid. ALT sl–200. DIST sE5, nE3, W3, S2, I2. RANGE F4, G4, S3.

● **Floating sweet-grass**
Glyceria fluitans
Mid–tall. Creeping and rooting, often floating; smooth-stemmed; spikelets 15–30mm in a narrow, branching cluster. LH perenn; rooting nodes. GERM spr. FL 5–8. POLL wind. SEX (♀) pa. HAB still or slow water, marshes. SOIL water–wet; acid–calc. SHADE nil–light. ALT sl–600. DIST E5, W5, S5, I5. RANGE F5, G5, sS5, nS1.
ss293.

● **Plicate sweet-grass**
Glyceria plicata
Mid–tall. Very like Floating sweet-grass but stems rough, fl-cluster spreading, ligule blunt (not pointed). LH perenn; rooting nodes. GERM spr. FL 6–8. POLL wind. SEX (♀) pa. HAB in and by water. SOIL water–wet; not acid. SHADE nil. ALT sl–400. DIST E4, W3, S2, I3. RANGE F4, G4, sS2.

● **Barren brome**
Bromus sterilis
Mid–tall. Stem hair-less, lf-sheaths downy; spikelets 20–30mm, singly on long, droop-ing branches; awns 20–35mm long. LH ann. GERM imm. FL 5–7. POLL wind. SEX (♀) pa. HAB bare and disturbed ground. SOIL dry; acid–calc. SHADE nil. ALT sl–350. DIST E5, W4, S3, I3. RANGE F5, G5, S2.

○ **Drooping brome**
Bromus tectorum
Short–tall. Like Barren brome, but lvs hairy, spikelets 10–15mm, 4 or more on each branch; awns 10–20mm. LH ann. GERM imm. FL 5–7. POLL wind. SEX (♀) pa. HAB disturbed ground. SOIL dry; acid–calc. SHADE nil. ALT sl–100. DIST E1, casual. RANGE F4, G4, S3.

● **Hairy brome**
Bromus ramosus
Tall–v.tall. Lvs to 15mm wide, hairy; spikelets 20–30mm, long-stalked, on hanging branches; whole flhd arched. LH perenn. GERM aut–spr. FL 7–8. POLL wind. SEX (♀) pa. HAB woods. SOIL moist; not acid. SHADE light–heavy. ALT sl–350. DIST E5, W4, S3, I3. RANGE F4, G4, S2.
ss294.

● **Upright brome**
Bromus erectus
Tall. Tufted; upper lvs flat, lower rolled at edges; spikelets 20–35mm, awned, on up-right branches. LH perenn. GERM imm? FL 5–7. POLL wind. SEX (♀) pa. HAB grass-land. SOIL dry; calc. SHADE nil. ALT sl–250. DIST sE4, nE2, W2, S1, I2. RANGE F1, G3, S2.

● **Soft brome**
Bromus hordeaceus
Low–tall. Variable; lvs flat, with short ligule and hairy sheaths; spikelets 10–25mm, hairy, awned. LH ann–bienn. GERM imm. FL 5–7. POLL wind; self. SEX (♀) pa. HAB grassland, bare ground, dunes. SOIL dry; acid–calc. SHADE nil. ALT sl–500. DIST E5, W4, S4, I4. RANGE F5, G5, S4.
ss295. ss296. ss297.

● **Tor grass**
Brachypodium pinnatum
Mid–tall. Lvs stiff, flat, 3mm wide, rolled at edges, yellowish; spikelets 20–35mm, v. narrow, unstalked; awn v. short. LH perenn; rhizome. GERM spr. FL 6–8. POLL wind. SEX (♀) pa. HAB grassland. SOIL dry; calc. SHADE nil. ALT sl–250. DIST sE4, nE2, W2, S1, I2. RANGE F5, G4, S2.

● **False brome**
Brachypodium sylvaticum
Mid–tall. Lvs soft, to 12mm wide, often yellowish; spikelets 10–25mm, narrow, unstalked; awns con-spicuous. LH perenn. GERM spr. FL 7–8. POLL wind. SEX (♀) pa. HAB woods, scrub, grass-land. SOIL dry; not acid. SHADE nil–mid. ALT sl–350. DIST E5, W5, S4, I4. RANGE F5, G5, S2.

● **Bearded couch**
Elymus caninus
Mid–tall. Tufted; stems downy at lf-junctions; spikelets 10–18mm, with a long awn; glumes stay on spike after fr falls. LH perenn. GERM spr? FL 7–8. POLL wind. SEX (♀) pa. HAB woods, rocks. SOIL moist; not acid. SHADE nil–mid. ALT sl–400(–600). DIST E5, W5, S4, I3. RANGE F4, G5, S5.

● **Common couch**
Elymus repens
Mid–tall. Stems hair-less; lvs green, flat; spikelets 10–15mm, with pointed but usually unawned glumes, falling with fr. LH perenn; rhizome. GERM imm. FL 6–8. POLL wind. SEX (♀) pa. HAB disturbed ground, fields. SOIL moist–dry; acid–calc. SHADE nil–light. ALT sl–300(–450). DIST E5, W4, S4, I5. RANGE F5, G5, S5.

● **Sand couch**
Elymus farctus
Mid. Non-flg shoots, creeping, flg stems upright; lvs bluish, ribbed, hairy; spike breaking between spikelets. LH perenn; rhizome. GERM spr–sum. FL 6–8. POLL wind. SEX (♀) pa. HAB coastal sand. SOIL dry; calc. SHADE nil. ALT sl. DIST coastal: E4, W3, S4, I4. RANGE coastal: F4, G4, S2.
See p. 216. **ss298**.

○ **Lyme grass**
Leymus arenarius
Tall–v.tall. Stems thick, lvs broad (to 15mm), bluish-grey; spikelets 20mm, paired, alternating up stem. LH perenn; rhizome. GERM spr. FL 6–8. POLL wind. SEX (♀) pa. HAB dunes. SOIL dry; calc. SHADE nil. ALT sl. DIST coastal: E3, W2, S4, I2. RANGE coastal: F1, G4, S5; inland: G2, S2.

○ **Wood barley**
Hordelymus europaeus
Mid–tall. Tufted; lf-sheaths hairy; spike-lets 10–15mm, in 3's up stem, each one flowered in a narrow spike. LH perenn. GERM ? FL 6–7. POLL wind. SEX (♀) pa. HAB woods. SOIL moist; calc. SHADE mid–heavy. ALT sl–250. DIST E3, W2, I1. RANGE F2, G3, S1.

● **Wall barley**
Hordeum murinum
Short–mid. Lvs wrapped claw-like round stems; spike-lets 8–12mm in groups of 3, the outer two sterile or ♂ only; glumes hairy. LH ann. GERM imm. FL 5–10. POLL wind. SEX (♀ + ♂) pa. HAB roadsides, disturbed ground. SOIL dry; not acid. SHADE nil. ALT sl–300. DIST E5, W3, S2, I2. RANGE F5, G4, S2.

● **Sea barley**
Hordeum marinum
Short. V. like Wall barley, but lvs nar-rower, bluish, without claws round stem; glumes narrow, hair-less. LH ann. GERM imm? FL 6–7. POLL wind. SEX (♀ + ♂) pa. HAB disturbed and grassy places by sea. SOIL moist–dry; saline. SHADE nil. ALT sl. DIST coastal: E3, W1, S1. RANGE coastal: F3, G2.

● **Meadow barley**
Hordeum secalinum
Mid. Lvs shortly claw-like at base; spikelets 8–10mm, as in Wall barley; glumes bristle-like; spikes 20–50mm long. LH perenn. GERM imm. FL 6–7. POLL wind. SEX (♀ + ♂) pa. HAB grass-land. SOIL damp–moist; not acid. SHADE nil. ALT sl–150. DIST sE4, nE2, W2, I1. RANGE F4, G2, sS1.

● **Wild oat**
Avena fatua
Mid–tall. Spikelets 20–25mm, long-stalked, hanging each with 2–3 fls and long glumes: awns v. long, twisted. LH ann. GERM aut–spr. FL 6–9. POLL wind. SEX (♀) pa. HAB arable fields, disturbed ground. SOIL moist; acid–calc. SHADE nil. ALT sl–250. DIST E4, W1, S2, I2. RANGE F4, G4, S3.

● **Downy oat-grass**
Avenula pubescens
Mid–tall. Lvs and sheaths green and hairy; spikelets 10–15mm, upright; glumes large; in a spreading cluster. LH perenn. GERM sum–aut. FL 5–7. POLL wind. SEX (♀) pa. HAB grassland. SOIL dry; not acid. SHADE nil. ALT sl–500. DIST E4, W3, S2, I2. RANGE F5, G5, S3.

● **Meadow oat-grass**
Avenula pratensis
Mid–tall. Lvs fur-rowed, bluish, hairless; spikelets 15–20mm, upright, in a narrow, spike-like cluster. LH perenn. GERM aut. FL 6. POLL wind. SEX (♀) pa. HAB grassland. SOIL moist–dry; not acid. SHADE nil. ALT sl–500 (–800). DIST sE4, nE2, W2, S3. RANGE F3, G4, S3.

● **False oat-grass**
Arrhenatherum elatius
Tall–v.tall. Stems sometimes swollen at base; roots yellow; spikelets 7–10mm, 2-flowered, one ♂, the other ♀ or both. LH perenn. GERM imm. FL 6–9. POLL wind; self. SEX (♀ + ♂ + ♀) pa. HAB grassy and disturbed ground. SOIL moist–dry; acid–calc. SHADE nil–light. ALT sl–500. DIST E5, W5, S5, I5. RANGE F5, G5, S3. *See p. 17, 271, 272, 273.*

● **Crested hair-grass**
Koeleria macrantha
Short–mid. Stems with dead lf-bases persist-ing; lvs rolled or flat; spikelets 2–5mm, purplish; glumes silvery-edged, unequal. LH perenn. GERM aut. SEX (♀) pa. HAB grass-land, rocks. SOIL dry; not acid. SHADE nil. ALT sl–500. DIST E4, W3, S3, I2. RANGE F4, G3, sS1. **ss299. ss300.**

145

● **Yellow oat-grass**
Trisetum flavescens
Short–mid(–tall). Lvs and sheaths downy; ligule v. short; spikelets 3–6mm, 2–4-flowered, yellowish, with a bent awn; in a branching, narrow cluster. LH perenn; stolons. GERM summ–aut. FL 5–6. POLL wind. SEX (♀) pa. HAB grassland. SOIL moist–dry; not acid. SHADE nil. ALT sl–500. DIST E5, W4, S3, I3. RANGE F5, G5, S2.

● **Tufted hair-grass**
Deschampsia cespitosa
Tall–v.tall. Forms large tussocks; lvs ridged, rough, dark green; ligules 4–8mm; spikelets 3–4mm, silvery, awned. LH perenn. GERM imm. FL 6–8. POLL wind. SEX (♀) pa. HAB grassland. SOIL wet–moist; acid–calc. SHADE nil–mid. ALT sl–1100. DIST E5, W5, S5, I5. RANGE F5, G5, S5.
See p. 212, 213, 273, 292. **ss301.**

● **Wavy hair-grass**
Deschampsia flexuosa
Mid–tall. Tufted; lvs v. fine, with short ligules; spikelets 4–5mm, silvery, with a bent awn. LH perenn. GERM any. FL 5–7. POLL wind. SEX (♀) pa. HAB heaths, moors, woods, bare ground. SOIL moist–dry; acid. SHADE nil–heavy. ALT sl–1100. DIST E4, W5, S5, I5. RANGE F4, G5, S5.

● **Early hair-grass**
Aira praecox
Low. Lf-sheaths smooth; spikelets 2mm, in dense spikes, enclosed in silvery sheaths at first. LH ann. GERM aut. FL 4–6. POLL wind. SEX (♀) pa. HAB bare, sandy and rocky ground, heaths. SOIL dry; acid. SHADE nil. ALT sl–400(–600). DIST E4, W5, S5, I5. RANGE F4, G3, S2.
See p. 244.

● **Silver hair-grass**
Aira caryophyllea
Low–short. Lf-sheaths rough; spikelets 2–3mm, long-stalked; in a spreading cluster. LH ann. GERM aut–spr. FL 5–6. POLL wind. SEX (♀) pa. HAB bare, sandy and stony places. SOIL dry; not calc. SHADE nil. ALT sl–400 (–600). DIST E4, W4, S4, I4. RANGE F4, G4, sS2.

○ **Holy grass**
Hierochloe odorata
Mid. Lvs flat, aromatic, bright green; spikelets 4–5mm, rounded, each with 3 florets, 2 ♂ and 1 ♀. LH perenn; rhizome. GERM imm. FL 3–5. POLL wind. SEX (♀ + ♂). HAB marshes, woods. SOIL water–wet; not calc. SHADE nil–mid. ALT 100–300 [–1500]. DIST S1, nI1. RANGE G2, S4.

● **Sweet vernal grass**
Anthoxanthum odoratum
Short–mid. Lvs flat, with a few long hairs; spikelets 7–10mm, with a bent awn, in a spike-like cluster; smells of fresh hay when dry. LH perenn. GERM aut–spr. FL 4–6. POLL wind. SEX (♀) pg. HAB grassland. SOIL wet–dry; acid–calc. SHADE nil–light. ALT sl–1000. DIST E5, W5, S5, I5. RANGE F5, G5, S5.
See p. 273.

○ **Grey hair-grass**
Corynephorus canescens
Short(–mid). Tufted; lvs greyish, thread-like, with swollen, purplish, sheaths; spikelets 3–4mm, purplish, in a narrow cluster. LH perenn. GERM imm. FL 6–7. POLL wind. SEX (♀) pa. HAB sandy grassland. SOIL dry; acid–calc. SHADE nil. ALT sl. DIST E1, S1. RANGE F2, nG4, sG1, sS1.

● **Yorkshire fog**
Holcus lanatus
Mid–tall. Tufted, grey-downy all over; purple striped at base; spikelets 3–4mm, often purple, with a single small hooked awn, shorter than glumes. LH perenn. GERM imm. FL 5–8. POLL wind. SEX (♀ + ♂) pa. HAB grassland, disturbed ground. SOIL damp–moist; acid–calc. SHADE nil–light. ALT sl–400 (–600). DIST E5, W5, S5, I5. RANGE F5, G5, S3.

● **Creeping soft-grass**
Holcus mollis
Mid. Like Yorkshire fog but not tufted; green, downy only at stem-joints; spikelets whitish-green; awn longer than glumes. LH perenn. GERM imm. FL 6–8. POLL wind. SEX (♀ + ♂) pa. HAB woods, sandy grassland, heaths. SOIL moist–dry; acid. SHADE nil–mid. ALT sl–500. DIST E5, W5, S5, I4. RANGE F4, G5, S3.
See p. 271.

● **Velvet bent**
Agrostis canina
Short–mid; prostrate.
Runners with tufts of
lvs; flg stems with flat
lvs and pointed
ligules, 2–3mm long;
spikelets 2–4mm,
1-fld, purplish,
awned. LH perenn;
stolons. GERM imm.
FL 6–8. POLL wind. SEX
(♀) pa. HAB grassland,
ditches. SOIL water–
damp; acid–calc.
SHADE nil–light. ALT
sl–1000. DIST E4, W5,
S4, I4. RANGE F4, G4,
S4.
ss302.

● **Common bent**
Agrostis capillaris
Low–mid. Sometimes
tufted; lvs flat, ligules
v. short, rounded;
spikelets 2–4mm, 1-fld,
often purplish, un-
awned; in spreading
flhds. LH perenn;
rhizome. GERM imm.
FL 6–8. POLL wind. SEX
(♀) pa. HAB grassland.
SOIL moist; not calc.
SHADE nil–light. ALT
sl–1200. DIST E5, W5,
S5, I5. RANGE F5, G5, S5.
See p. 254. **ss303**.

● **Creeping bent**
Agrostis stolonifera
Short–tall. Runners
creeping up to 2m;
ligules long (to 5mm),
pointed or ragged;
spikelets 2–3mm, 1-fld,
unawned; in spreading
flhds, contracted in fr.
LH perenn; stolons.
GERM imm. FL 6–8.
POLL wind. SEX (♀) pa.
HAB grassland, dis-
turbed ground. SOIL
wet–dry; acid–calc.
SHADE nil–light. ALT
sl–750. DIST E5, W5,
S4, I5. RANGE F5, G5,
S4.
See p. 217, 272.

● **Marram**
Ammophila arenaria
Tall. Lvs rolled,
ridged, bluish inside,
stiff, sharp-pointed;
spikelets 12–15mm,
1-fld, in a dense spike.
LH perenn; rhizome.
GERM spr. FL 6–8. POLL
wind. SEX (♀) pa. HAB
sand dunes. SOIL dry;
calc. SHADE nil. ALT sl.
DIST coastal: E5, W5,
S5, I5. RANGE coastal:
F4, G5, S3.
See p. 201, 214, 216.

● **Wood small-reed**
*Calamagrostis
epigeios*
Tall–v.tall. Tufted;
stem stout, with 2–4
joints; lvs hairless,
ligule to 12mm; spike-
lets 5–7mm, 1-fld, in a
branching flhd. LH
perenn. GERM imm.
FL 6–8. POLL wind. SEX
(♀) pa. HAB woods,
fens, ditches. SOIL
damp; not acid. SHADE
nil–mid. ALT sl–200.
DIST E4, W3, S2, I2.
RANGE F4, G5, S4.
See p. 251.

○ **Purple small-reed**
*Calamagrostis
canescens*
Tall. Like Wood small-
reed but stem with 4–6
joints, lvs hairy on
top, ligule 1–2mm,
spikelets 4–5mm. LH
perenn. GERM imm?
FL 6–7. POLL wind. SEX
(♀) pa. HAB fens,
woods. SOIL wet–damp;
not acid. SHADE nil–
heavy. ALT sl–100
(–300). DIST E2, W1,
S1. RANGE F3, G4, S3.
ss304. ss305.

● **Timothy**
Phleum pratense
Tall–v.tall. Lvs rough,
ligule short; spikelets
1-fld; glumes awned,
packed into a dense
cylindrical head, up to
300mm long. LH
perenn. GERM imm. FL
6–8. POLL wind. SEX
(♀) pa. HAB grassland.
SOIL moist; not acid.
SHADE nil. ALT sl–400.
DIST E5, W5, S5, I5.
RANGE F5, G5, S4.
See p. 273. **ss306**.

● **Sand cat's-tail**
Phleum arenarium
V.low–low. Lvs short,
with swollen sheaths
and ligules to 7mm;
spikelets 3mm, 1-fld,
in short, oval heads.
LH ann. GERM aut. FL
5–6. POLL wind. SEX
(♀) pa. HAB coastal
sand, rare inland. SOIL
dry; not acid. SHADE
nil. ALT sl. DIST coastal:
E3, W3, S2, I2. RANGE
coastal: F5, G4,
sS2: inland: F1, G1.
See p. 214, 244. **ss307**.

● **Meadow foxtail**
Alopecurus pratensis
Mid–tall. Tufted; lvs
broad (4–8mm) with
short ligules; spikelets
4–5mm, 1-fld, with
awn inside the floret,
not on the glume. LH
perenn. GERM aut–spr.
FL 4–6. POLL wind. SEX
(♀) pg. HAB grassland.
SOIL damp–moist; not
acid. SHADE nil. ALT
sl–400. DIST E5, W5,
S4, I4. RANGE F5, G5,
S4.
ss308.

● **Marsh foxtail**
Alopecurus geniculatus
Short–mid. Stems bent
at the joints; spike-
lets 2–3mm, 1-fld, in
short, cylindrical flhds,
with conspicuous
orange or purple
anthers. LH perenn;
rooting stems. GERM
imm. FL 6–8. POLL
wind. SEX (♀) pg. HAB
grassland, marshes;
shallow, still water.
SOIL water–damp;
acid–calc. SHADE nil.
ALT sl–600. DIST E4,
W4, S4, I3. RANGE F4,
G4, S5.
ss309. ss310.

● **Black grass**
Alopecurus myosuroides
Short–mid. Lvs rough,
ligule up to 5mm long;
spikelets 4–7mm,
1-fld, with a long awn,
in a narrow, pointed,
cylindrical head. LH
ann. GERM spr. FL 5–8.
POLL wind. SEX (♀) pg.
HAB arable fields, dis-
turbed ground. SOIL
moist; not acid. SHADE
nil. ALT sl–200. DIST
sE4, nE2, W2, S2.
RANGE F5, G4, S2.

● **Reed canary-grass**
Phalaris arundinacea
Tall–v.tall. Lvs rough,
broad (10–18mm),
with a long, ragged
ligule; spikelets 2–3-fld,
only 1 floret fully
developed, in branch-
ing, lobed clusters. LH
perenn; rhizome.
GERM aut–spr. FL 6–8.
POLL wind. SEX (♀ + ♂)
pa. HAB marshes, fens,
woods. SOIL wet–damp;
not acid. SHADE nil–
mid. ALT sl–400. DIST
E5, W5, S4, I4. RANGE
F5, G5, S4.

● **Common reed**
Phragmites australis
V.tall. Covers huge
areas; dead stems
surviving winter; lvs
v. broad, 10–20mm or
more, with a hairy
ligule; spikelets with
long, silky hairs. LH
perenn; rhizome. GERM
spr–sum. FL 8–10. POLL
wind. SEX (♀) pa. HAB
marshes, fens, water-
edges, woods. SOIL
water-moist; acid–calc.
SHADE nil–mid. ALT
sl–400. DIST E5, W4,
S4, I5. RANGE F5, G5,
S4.
See p. 188, 251.

● **Wood millet**
Milium effusum
Tall–v.tall. Loosely
tufted; lvs 5–10mm
wide, ligule 5mm,
pointed; fls in whorls,
on long, drooping
stalks; some short-
stalked. LH perenn.
GERM spr. FL 5–7. POLL
wind. SEX (♀) pa. HAB
woods. SOIL moist; not
acid. SHADE light–
heavy. ALT sl–300.
DIST E4, W3, S3, I3.
RANGE F5, G5, S5.

● **Heath grass**
Danthonia decumbens
Short–mid. Tufted; lvs
flat with a ring of hairs
for ligule; spikelets
7–10mm, rounded,
with large glumes. LH
perenn. GERM aut–spr.
FL 6–8. POLL SEX self
(cleistogamous); rarely
wind. SEX (♀). HAB
heaths, sandy and peaty
grassland. SOIL dry;
acid. SHADE nil–light.
ALT sl–600. DIST E4,
W5, S5, I5. RANGE F4,
G4, S3.

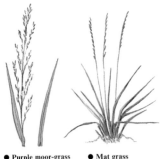

● **Purple moor-grass**
Molinia caerulea
Mid–v.tall. Tussock-
forming; lvs dying in
winter but persisting;
ligule a ring of hairs;
spikelets 6–10mm,
usually purplish. LH
perenn. GERM aut–spr.
FL 7–9. POLL wind. SEX
(♀) pa. HAB marshes.
moors, heaths, woods.
SOIL wet–damp; acid
(–calc). SHADE nil–mid.
ALT sl–800. DIST E4,
W5, S5, I5. RANGE F4,
G4, S5.

● **Mat grass**
Nardus stricta
Low–short. Lvs v. fine,
tough; white but per-
sistent when dead;
spikelets 1-fld, in 2
rows on a 1-sided
spike. LH perenn. GERM
spr. FL 6–8. POLL wind.
SEX (♀) pg. HAB moors,
heaths, upland grass-
land. SOIL damp–dry;
acid. SHADE nil. ALT
sl–1000. DIST sE3,
nE5, W5, S5, I4.
RANGE F2, G4, S5.
See p. 234.

● **Common cord-grass**
Spartina anglica
Tall. Coarse, loosely
tufted; lvs yellowish,
to 15mm wide; ligule a
ring of hairs; spikelets
in narrow spikes; 4–5
spikes on each stem.
LH perenn; rhizome.
GERM spr? FL 8–11.
POLL wind. SEX (♀) pg.
HAB tidal mud. SOIL
tidal water. SHADE nil.
ALT sl. DIST coastal:
E4, W4, S2, I2. RANGE
coastal: F4, G4.
See p. 289, 297. **ss311**.

APPENDIX OF SCARCE SPECIES IN BRITAIN

The species in this appendix have not appeared in the form of a colour illustration in the preceding pages. Here they are described in terms of their similarity to and their differences from more familiar species that are the subject of a full and detailed entry in the directory.

The DIRECTORY and this APPENDIX together represent the complete British flora except for trees and shrubs.

1. Hemp *Cannabis sativa* (Cannabaceae)
Like Nettle (p. 29) but has finger-lobed leaves and no stinging hairs; disturbed ground. Casual.

2. Sea knotgrass *Polygonum maritimum*
Like Knotgrass (p. 30) but perennial, with rolled leaves; sea-shores. E1.

3. Ray's knotgrass *Polygonum oxyspermum*
Like Sea Knotgrass (above) but has longer fruit. E3, W2, S1, I3.

4. Slender hare's-ear *Bupleurum tenuissimum* (Umbelliferae)
Like Knotgrass (p. 30) but has grey leaves and yellow flowers; grassland. E1.

5. Tasteless water-pepper *Polygonum mite*
Like Small water-pepper (p. 30) but has broader leaves and a nodding flower-spike. E3, W1, I2.

6. Copse bindweed *Bilderdykia dumetorum*
Like Black bindweed (p. 30) but has white flowers and long-stalked, shiny fruit; hedges. E1.

7. Northern dock *Rumex longifolius*
Like Curled dock (p. 31) but has dense flower-spikes and unswollen fruit-valves. nE1, S3.

8. Fiddle dock *Rumex pulcher*
Like Broad-leaved dock (p. 31) but has leaves narrowest in middle; all fruit-valves swollen. sE2.

9. Scottish dock *Rumex aquaticus*
Like Water dock (p. 31) but has shorter leaves and unswollen fruit-valves. S1.

10. Golden dock *Rumex maritimus*
Like Marsh dock (p. 31) but bright yellow in fruit. E1, W1, I1.

11. Shore dock *Rumex rupestris*
Like Clustered dock (p. 31) but thick-stemmed and greyish; sea-shores. E1.

12. Iceland purslane *Koenigia islandica* (Polygonaceae)
Like Blinks (p. 32) but has broader leaves

and 3-petalled flowers; mountain gravels. S1.

13. Oak-leaved goosefoot *Chenopodium glaucum*
Like Fat hen (p. 32) but has green stems and leaves grey beneath only. E2, W1, S1.

14. Upright goosefoot *Chenopodium urbicum*
Like Maple-leaved goosefoot (p. 32) but has oval leaves. E2, W1.

15. Stinking goosefoot *Chenopodium vulvaria*
Like Many-seeded goosefoot (p. 33) but has mealy flowers and smells of old fish; saltmarshes. E2, W1, S1.

16. Small red goosefoot *Chenopodium botryodes*
Like Red goosefoot (p. 33) but has leaves scarcely toothed, and dead flower-parts hiding fruit; saltmarshes. seE2.

17. Frosted orache *Atriplex laciniata*
Like Babington's orache (p. 33) but silvery-grey. E3, W2, S2, I2.

18. Lesser thyme-leaved sandwort *Arenaria leptocladus*
Like Thyme-leaved sandwort (p. 34) but has smaller flowers (3–5mm) and narrower sepals. E3, W2, S2, I3.

19. Teesdale sandwort *Minuartia stricta*
Like Fine-leaved sandwort (p. 34) but a small tufted perennial; petals as long as sepals. nE1.

20. Arctic sandwort *Arenaria norvegica*
Like Spring sandwort (p. 34) but has small oval leaves; flowers 8–12mm. nE1, S1.

21. Mountain sandwort *Minuartia rubella*
Like Arctic sandwort (above) but much smaller; flowering stems nearly leafless. S1.

22. Greater chickweed *Stellaria neglecta*
Like Wood stitchwort (p. 35) but has petals only as long as sepals, or sometimes absent. E3, W3, S1, I1.

23. Lesser chickweed *Stellaria pallida*
Like Common chickweed (p. 35) but has smaller flowers (4–8mm) and all leaves stalked. sE2, nE1, W1, S1, I1.

24. Arctic mouse-ear *Cerastium arcticum*
Like Alpine mouse-ear (p. 35) but has
shorter hairs. W1, S2.

25. Grey mouse-ear *Cerastium brachypetalum*
Like Sea mouse-ear (p. 36) but has petals
much shorter than sepals and 10 (not 5)
stamens. E1.

26. Upright chickweed *Moenchia erecta*
Like Common mouse-ear (p. 36) but grey.
with entire petals and 4 styles. sE2, W1.

27. Dwarf mouse-ear *Cerastium pumilum*
Like Little mouse-ear (p. 36) but more
upright; petals as long as sepals. Limestone
grassland. sE2.

28. Snow pearlwort *Sagina intermedia*
Like Alpine pearlwort (p. 37) but smaller
with no rosette and larger leaves. S2.

29. Strapwort *Corrigiola litoralis*
Like Annual knawel (p. 37) but greyish with
red stems and oval leaves alternating up
stem; gravel. sE1.

30. Smooth rupturewort *Herniaria glabra*
Like Fringed rupturewort (p. 37) but has no
white stipules, and flowers in spikes; sandy
ground. eE1.

31. Coral necklace *Illecebrum verticillatum*
Like Smooth rupturewort (above) but has
white flowers. E1.

32. Italian catchfly *Silene italica*
Like Nottingham catchfly (p. 38) but has
upright flowers. sE1.

33. Deptford pink *Dianthus armeria*
Like Maiden pink (p. 39) but smaller flowers
in leafy clusters. sE2.

34. Childling pink *Petrorhagia nanteuilli*
Like Carthusian pink (p. 39) but has much
smaller, pink flowers. sE1.

35. Corn buttercup *Ranunculus arvensis*
Like Meadow buttercup (p. 40) but hairless,
and has small flowers and spiny fruit; bare
ground. E3, W2, S1.

36. Small-flowered buttercup *Ranunculus
parviflorus*
Like Hairy buttercup (p. 40) but has smaller
flowers and rounded leaves; dry ground.
sE2, W2, I1.

37. Creeping spearwort *Ranunculus reptans*
Like Lesser spearwort (p. 41) but creeps and
roots at each node; wet gravel. nE1, S1.

38. Adder's-tongue spearwort *Ranunculus
ophioglossifolius*
Like Celery-leaved buttercup (p. 41) but has
undivided leaves. sE1.

39. Brackish water crowfoot *Ranunculus baudotii*
Like Pond water crowfoot (p. 41) but has
flowers 10–20mm; brackish water. E2, W2,
S1, I1.

40. Chalk-stream crowfoot *Ranunculus
penicillatus*
Like River water crowfoot (p. 42) but has
shorter, paler leaves; chalk streams. E2.

41. Round-leaved crowfoot *Ranunculus
omiophyllus*
Like Ivy-leaved water crowfoot (p. 42) but
has flowers 8–12mm. E2, W3, S2, I2.

42. Three-lobed crowfoot *Ranunculus tripartitus*
Like Ivy-leaved water crowfoot (p. 42) but
has finely divided submerged leaves too.
sE2, W1.

43. Least water-lily *Nuphar pumila*
Like Yellow water-lily (p. 44) but has flowers
to 30mm. E1, S2.

44. Purple fumitory *Fumaria purpurea*
Like Ramping fumitory (p. 45) but has
purple flowers. E2, W1, S1, I1.

45. Western fumitory *Fumaria occidentalis*
Like Ramping fumitory (p. 45) but has wide
flat edges to lower petal of each flower.
swE1.

46. False fumitory *Fumaria bastardii*
Like Wall fumitory (p. 45) but has flat edges
to lower petal of each flower; flowers
9–11mm. E2, W2, S1, I3.

47. Martin's fumitory *Fumaria martinii*
Like False fumitory (above) but has flowers
11–13mm. sE1.

48. French fumitory *Fumaria densiflora*
Like Small fumitory (p. 45) but has pink
flowers 6–7mm. E2, S2.

49. Chalk fumitory *Fumaria vaillantii*
Like Small fumitory (p. 45) but has flat
leaflets and pink flowers; on chalk. sE2.

50. Babington's poppy *Papaver lecoqii*
Like Long-headed poppy (p. 45) but has
yellow stem-juice and brown (not violet)
anthers. E3, W2, S1, I2.

51. Rough poppy *Papaver hybridum*
Like Common poppy (p. 45) but smaller and
bristly-hairy, with smaller crimson flowers.
E2, W1, I1.

52. Isle of Man cabbage *Rhynchosinapis
monensis*
Like Black mustard (p. 46) but has pinnately
lobed leaves in rosette; flowers to 25mm;
coastal sand. E1, W1, S1.

53. Perennial wall rocket *Diplotaxis tenuifolia*
Like Annual wall rocket (p. 47) but perennial,
greyish; flowers 15–30mm; pods upright.
E3, W2, S1.

54. Perfoliate pennycress *Thlaspi perfoliatum*
Like Field pennycress (p. 48) but has greyish
leaves in rosette and clasping stem;
perennial; stony places, on limestone. E1.

55. Hutchinsia *Hornungia petraea*
Like Shepherd's cress (p. 48) but has pinnate leaves in rosette and on stem; on limestone. E1, W1.

56. Rock whitlow-grass *Draba norvegica*
Like Twisted whitlow-grass (p. 49) but has less toothed leaves and untwisted pods; stem leafless. S1.

57. Yellow whitlow-grass *Draba aizoides*
Like Wall whitlow-grass (p. 49) but tufted, with yellow flowers. W1.

58. Dittander *Lepidium latifolium*
Like Horseradish (p. 49) but has narrower, straight-edged leaves and smaller flowers. E2, W2.

59. Northern rock-cress *Cardaminopsis petraea*
Like Hairy bittercress (p. 49) but has lobed leaves, and flowers 5–8mm; mountain rocks. W1, S2, I1.

60. Coralroot bittercress *Cardamine bulbifera*
Like Cuckoo flower (p. 50) but has all leaves on stem, upper simple, with purple bulbils at base; woods. E1.

61. Small-flowered wintercress *Barbarea stricta*
Like Common wintercress (p. 50) but has end lobe of leaf longest, and flowers 5–6mm. E2, W1, S1.

62. Bristol rock-cress *Arabis stricta*
Like Hairy rock-cress (p. 50) but has fewer, larger flowers, 5–6mm. E1.

63. Tower mustard *Arabis glabra*
Like Hairy rock-cress (p. 50) but has pinnately-lobed hairless leaves, and flowers 5–6mm. E2.

64. Iceland yellowcress *Rorippa islandica*
Like Marsh yellowcress (p. 50) but creeping and has long-stalked pods. E1, S3, I1.

65. Mossy stonecrop *Crassula tillaea*
Like English stonecrop (p. 53) but much smaller, with flowers 1–2mm; damp ground. sE2.

66. Water tillaea *Crassula aquatica*
Like Mossy stonecrop (above) but has 4 (not 3) petals. S1.

67. Kidney saxifrage *Saxifraga hirsuta*
Like St Patrick's cabbage (p. 53) but has long-stalked, hairy leaves. sI1.

68. Marsh saxifrage *Saxifraga hirculus*
Like Yellow saxifrage (p. 54) but has stem leafy only at base, and solitary flowers; bogs. nE1, S1, nI1.

69. Irish saxifrage *Saxifraga rosacea*
Like Tufted saxifrage (p. 54) but has pointed leaf-lobes. I1.

70. Fragrant agrimony *Agrimonia procera*
Like Agrimony (p. 55) but larger, aromatic, and has ungrooved fruit. E3, W3, S2, I3.

71. Sibbaldia *Sibbaldia procumbens*
Like Wild strawberry (p. 57) but smaller, tufted, and has no runners; flowers 5mm, yellowish; mountains. S2.

72. Rock cinquefoil *Potentilla rupestris*
Like Barren strawberry (p. 57) but has no runners, pinnate root leaves, and flowers 15–25mm; rocks. W1, S1.

73. Garden lupin *Lupinus polyphyllus*
Like Tree lupin (p. 60) but flowers blue, purple, pink, white or yellow; the commonest herbaceous lupin. Garden escape.

74. Bithynian vetch *Vicia bithynica*
Like Fodder vetch (p. 60) but has flowers 1–3 together, 15–20mm long; keel very pale. E2, W1, S1.

75. Upright vetch *Vicia orobus*
Like Wood vetch (p. 61) but has pink flowers and no tendrils; scrub. E1, W2, S1, I1.

76. Slender tare *Vicia tenuissima*
Like Smooth tare (p. 61) but has flowers in 2–5s, each 6–9mm. sE2.

77. Small rest-harrow *Ononis reclinata*
Like Rest-harrow (p. 62) but a small, sticky annual, with flowers 5–10mm and hanging pods; cliff-tops. sE1, W1.

78. Bur medick *Medicago minima*
Like Toothed medick (p. 63) but has spiny pods. sE1.

79. Hairy bird's-foot trefoil *Lotus subbiflorus*
Like Bird's-foot trefoil (p. 63) but is a hairy annual with long-stalked flowers, and pods 6–12mm. swE1, W1.

80. Slender bird's-foot trefoil *Lotus angustissimus*
Like Hairy bird's-foot trefoil (above) but has short-stalked flowers, and pods 20–30mm. sE1.

81. Orange bird's-foot *Ornithopus pinnatus*
Like Bird's-foot (p. 64) but hairless and has orange flowers. swE1.

82. Sulphur clover *Trifolium ochroleucon*
Like Red clover (p. 64) but has yellowish flowers. eE1.

83. Western clover *Trifolium occidentale*
Like White clover (p. 64) but has unmarked, rounded leaflets and smaller flowers. wE2, W1.

84. Clustered clover *Trifolium glomeratum*
Like Knotted clover (p. 65) but hairless and has rounded flowerheads. sE2.

85. Twin-flowered clover *Trifolium bocconei*
Like Knotted clover (p. 65) but has paler flowers and leaflets hairless on top. swE1.

86. Upright clover *Trifolium strictum*
Like Hare's-foot clover (p. 65) but has very narrow leaflets and long-stalked heads of bright pink flowers. E1, W1.

87. Fenugreek *Trifolium ornithopodioides*
Like Burrowing clover (p. 65) but hairless;
flowers pink, not persisting. sE2, W1, I1.

88. Suffocated clover *Trifolium suffocatum*
Like Burrowing clover (p. 65) but has dense
green and white flowers in unstalked heads
beneath leaves. sE2.

89. Musk storksbill *Erodium moschatum*
Like Common storksbill (p. 65) but has
pinnately lobed leaves, sticky hairs and
larger flowers. E2, W1, I2.

90. Little robin *Geranium purpureum*
Like Herb robert (p. 66) but has smaller
flowers and yellow (not orange) pollen in
anthers. sE1, W1.

91. Allseed *Radiola linoides*
Like Purging flax (p. 67) but minute, with
tiny 4-petalled flowers; damp and acid
soils. E2, W2, S1, I2.

92. Purple spurge *Euphorbia peplis*
Like Dwarf spurge (p. 68) but fleshy,
prostrate and red-stemmed; coastal sand.
E1.

93. Upright spurge *Euphorbia serrulata*
Like Broad-leaved spurge (p. 68) but delicate;
limestone woods. E1, W1.

94. Irish spurge *Euphorbia hyberna*
Like Caper spurge (p. 68) but not greyish,
and has alternate leaves; woods. E1, I2.

95. Chalk milkwort *Polygala calcarea*
Like Common milkwort (p. 69) but has
bright blue or white flowers and blunt
leaves, some in rosette; on chalk. sE2.

96. Mountain currant *Ribes alpinum*
Like Red currant (p. 70) but has flower
spikes upright, male and female on
separate plants. E1, W1 and naturalised.

97. Small tree-mallow *Lavatera cretica*
Like Tree-mallow (p. 70) but smaller, has
paler flowers and shallowly-lobed leaves.
sE1.

98. Wavy St John's-wort *Hypericum undulatum*
Like Square-stemmed St John's-wort (p. 71)
but has flowers 20mm, petals red-tinged
beneath. swE1, W1.

99. Irish St John's-wort *Hypericum canadense*
Like Slender St John's-wort (p. 71) but
delicate, with a square stem, and flowers
6mm; damp ground. I1.

100. Flax-leaved St John's-wort *Hypericum
linarifolium*
Like Trailing St John's-wort (p. 71) but
upright, with narrow leaves and reddish
petals; dry, acid rocks. swE1, W1.

101. Teesdale violet *Viola rupestris*
Like Common dog-violet (p. 72) but smaller,
softly hairy and has flowers 10–15mm;
upland grassland. nE1.

102. Dwarf pansy *Viola kitaibeliana*
Like Field pansy (p. 73) but tiny; flowers
4–8mm; dunes. swE1.

103. White rock-rose *Helianthemum appeninum*
Like Common rock-rose (p. 73) but has
greyish, inrolled, narrow leaves and white
flowers. swE1.

104. Spear-leaved willowherb *Epilobium
lanceolatum*
Like Broad-leaved willowherb (p. 75) but has
narrower, longer-stalked leaves and pale
flowers. E3, W2.

105. Whorled water milfoil *Myriophyllum
verticillatum*
Like Spiked water milfoil (p. 76) but has
pinnate bracts beneath flowers. E2, W1, I2.

106. Rigid hornwort *Ceratophyllum demersum*
(Ceratophyllaceae)
Like Mare's-tail (p. 76) but floats submerged
and uprooted. It has stiff, narrow,
branching dark green leaves and a
3-spined fruit. E3, W2, S2, I1.

107. Soft hornwort *Ceratophyllum submersum*
Like Rigid hornwort (above) but softer, pale
green, and has 1-spined fruit. E2, W1.

108. Grass poly *Lythrum hyssopifolia*
Like Water purslane (p. 76) but more upright
with narrow leaves. sE1.

109. Hampshire purslane *Ludwigia palustris*
Like Water purslane (p. 76) but has pointed
leaves and flowers in pairs. sE1.

110. Waterwort *Elatine hexandra*
Like Water purslane (p. 76) but has narrow,
whorled leaves; often in water. E1, W1,
S1, I1.

111. Spreading bur parsley *Torilis arvensis*
Like Upright hedge parsley (p. 78) but has
no bracts or sometimes 1, and fewer stalks
in the flowerhead; arable fields. E2, W1.

112. Knotted bur parsley *Torilis nodosa*
Like Upright hedge parsley (p. 78) but
prostrate, with flowerheads opposite
leaves; bare ground. E3, W2, S1, I1.

113. Great pignut *Bunium bulbocastanum*
Like Pignut (p. 78) but larger and with many
bracts beneath flowerhead. E1.

114. River water dropwort *Oenanthe fluviatilis*
Like Fine-leaved water dropwort (p. 79) but
floats on water; leaves 2-pinnate. E2, I2.

115. Corky-fruited water dropwort *Oenanthe
pimpinelloides*
Like Parsley water dropwort (p. 79) but has
long-beaked fruit. sE2, W1.

116. Narrow-leaved water dropwort *Oenanthe
silaifolia*
Like Parsley water dropwort (p. 79) but has
hollow stems and narrow leaflets. E2.

117. Creeping marshwort *Apium repens*
Like Fool's watercress (p. 80) but roots at every node. E1.

118. Lesser marshwort *Apium inundatum*
Like Fool's watercress (p. 80) but grows under water; leaflets very narrow. E2, W2, S1, I2.

119. Corn parsley *Petroselinum segetum*
Like Stone parsley (p. 80) but smells of parsley. sE3, W1.

120. Hog's fennel *Peucedanum officinale*
Like Milk parsley (p. 80) but has long, narrow leaflets and yellow flowers; grassland. sE1.

121. Mackay's heath *Erica mackaiana*
Like Cross-leaved heath (p. 82) but has leaves dark green above, white below; flowers brighter, deeper pink. I1.

122. St Dabeoc's heath *Daboecia cantabrica*
Like Cross-leaved heath (p. 82) but has larger leaves and flowers, the flowers flask-shaped. I1.

123. Irish heath *Erica erigena*
Like Cornish heath (p. 83) but up to 2m tall, with red not brown anthers; bogs. I1.

124. Small cranberry *Vaccinium microcarpum*
Like Cranberry (p. 83) but has almost triangular leaves. S2.

125. Mountain crowberry *Empetrum hermaphroditum*
Like Crowberry (p. 84) but has hermaphrodite flowers; mountains. nE1, W1, S3.

126. Matted sea-lavender *Limonium bellidifolium*
Like Common sea-lavender (p. 86) but has much-branched stems, only the upper with flowers. eE1.

127. Perennial centaury *Centaurium scilloides*
Like Common centaury (p. 87) but perennial, with non-flowering stems, and larger flowers; cliffs. swE1, W1.

128. Slender centaury *Centaurium tenuiflorum*
Like Lesser centaury (p. 87) but has branches of flowerhead parallel. sE1.

129. Greater dodder *Cuscuta europaea*
Like Common dodder (p. 89) but has blunt petals, longer than styles; often on nettles. E2, W1.

130. Slender marsh bedstraw *Galium debile*
Like Marsh bedstraw (p. 90) but smaller with pointed leaves and often pinkish flowers. E1.

131. Corn cleavers *Galium tricornutum*
Like Common cleavers (p. 90) but has short-stalked flowers and no prickles on fruit; arable fields. E2.

132. Wall bedstraw *Galium parisiense*
Like Common cleavers (p. 90) but has downward-pointing leaves and green flowers; fruit smooth; walls. E2.

133. Green houndstongue *Cynoglossum germanicum*
Like Houndstongue (p. 91) but no smell and smaller flowers; woods. E2.

134. Narrow-leaved lungwort *Pulmonaria longifolia*
Like Lungwort (p. 91) but has narrower leaves and smaller flowers. sE1.

135. Alpine forget-me-not *Myosotis alpestris*
Like Wood forget-me-not (p. 91) but smaller, with deep blue flowers and short-stalked fruit; mountains. nE1, S1.

136. Pale forget-me-not *Myosotis stolonifera*
Like Water forget-me-not (p. 92) but has rounded leaves and pale flowers. nE1, S1.

137. Purple viper's bugloss *Echium lycopsis*
Like Viper's bugloss (p. 92) but has less rough leaves, red flowers turning purple, and 2 prominent stamens. sE1.

138. Ground-pine *Ajuga chamaepitys*
Like Pyramidal bugle (p. 93) but annual with pinnate leaves and yellow flowers; dry bare ground. sE1.

139. Spear-leaved skullcap *Scutellaria hastifolia*
Like Skullcap (p. 93) but has arrow-shaped leaves and longer flowers. sE1.

140. Water germander *Teucrium scordium*
Like Wall germander (p. 93) but has downy, greyish, oblong leaves, and flowers all up stem; damp ground. sE1.

141. Cut-leaved self-heal *Prunella laciniata*
Like Self-heal (p. 94) but has pinnate leaves and cream flowers. sE2, W1.

142. Downy woundwort *Stachys germanica*
Like Limestone woundwort (p. 96) but white, hairy. sE1.

143. Hoary mullein *Verbascum pulverulentum*
Like White mullein (p. 98) but has thick white down round stems, and broader leaves. sE1 and casual.

144. Moth mullein *Verbascum blattaria*
Like Dark mullein (p. 98) but has narrower, shiny leaves and long-stalked flowers. E2, W1.

145. Twiggy mullein *Verbascum virgatum*
Like Dark mullein (p. 98) but has hairless leaves, and flowers in groups of up to 5. swE1 and casual.

146. Balm-leaved figwort *Scrophularia scorodonia*
Like Common figwort (p. 98) but downy, with wrinkled, heart-shaped leaves. sE1, sW1.

147. Small toadflax *Chaenorrhinum minus*
Like Pale toadflax (p. 99) but much smaller,
with lip of flower ajar. E4, W3, S2, I3.

148. Welsh mudwort *Limosella subulata*
Like Mudwort (p. 100) but has very narrow
leaves. W1.

149. Cornish moneywort *Sibthorpia europea*
Like Ivy-leaved speedwell (p. 101) but
perennial, with rounded leaves and pinkish,
5-petalled flowers; shady places. sE2, W1.

150. Spring speedwell *Veronica verna*
Like Wall speedwell (p. 102) but has
pinnately lobed leaves. eE1.

151. Fingered speedwell *Veronica triphyllos*
Like Wall speedwell (p. 102) but has long-
stalked flowers and lobed leaves. eE1.

152. Ox-tongue broomrape *Orobanche loricata*
Like Common broomrape (p. 104) but has
flowers 15–20mm; on ox-tongues and
hawksbeards. E1.

153. Carrot broomrape *Orobanche amethystea*
Like Thyme broomrape (p. 104) but has
yellow flowers, veined purple; on wild
carrot. seE1.

154. Large-flowered butterwort *Pinguicula
grandiflora*
Like Common butterwort (p. 105) but has
flowers 25–30mm. sI2.

155. Intermediate bladderwort *Utricularia
intermedia*
Like Lesser bladderwort (p. 105) but has
bladders on non-green stems only;
flowers 8–12mm. E1, S3, I2.

156a. Mousetail *Myosurus minimus*
(Ranunculaceae)
Like Buck's-horn plantain (p. 105) but has
narrow, simple leaves and 5–7-petalled
flowers; bare, damp ground. E2.

156b. Awlwort *Subularia aquatica*
Like Shoreweed (p. 106) but annual, with
no stolons, and tiny 4-petalled flowers in
a long spike. nE1, nW1, S2, I1.

157. Shaggy soldier *Galinsoga ciliata*
Like Gallant soldier (p. 111) but with longer
ray-florets. E3, W2, S1.

158. Jersey cudweed *Gnaphalium luteoalbum*
Like Marsh cudweed (p. 112) but has
oblong leaves, not overtopping flowerheads. eE1.

159. Purple coltsfoot *Homogyne alpina*
Like Coltsfoot (p. 113) but has smaller
leaves, purple underneath, and purple
flowers; mountains. S1.

160. Field fleawort *Senecio integrifolius*
Like Ragwort (p. 114) but has a rosette of
grey, oval leaves and fewer flowerheads.
E2, W1.

161. Tuberous thistle *Cirsium tuberosum*
Like Meadow thistle (p. 116) but has all
leaves pinnately lobed; flowerheads 25–
30mm; dry grassland. E1, W1.

162. Slender thistle *Carduus tenuiflorus*
Like Welted thistle (p. 117) but has flowerheads 8–10mm; leaves white underneath;
near coast. E2, W2, S1, I2.

163. Viper's grass *Scorzonera humilis*
Like Goat's-beard (p. 118) but has shorter
leaves and florets larger than bracts. E1.

164. Least lettuce *Lactuca saligna*
Like Great lettuce (p. 118) but smaller, not
prickly and has greyish, pinnately lobed
leaves. E1.

165. Marsh sow-thistle *Sonchus palustris*
Like Perennial sow-thistle (p. 118) but has
pointed leaf-lobes clasping stem, and
flowerheads 30–40mm; marshes, fens. E1.

166. Dandelion *Taraxacum*
Section *Vulgaria* (p. 119) includes many very
similar species.

167. Lesser dandelion *Taraxacum*
Section *Erythrosperma* (p. 119) includes
many similar species.

168. Red-veined dandelion *Taraxacum*
Section *Spectabilia* (p. 119) includes many
similar species.

169. Marsh dandelion *Taraxacum*
Section *Palustria* has unspotted leaves, and
bracts closely pressed to flowerheads.

170. Lamb's succory *Arnoseris minima*
Like Smooth cat's-ear (p. 119) but has
flowerheads 6–10mm on a swollen stalk.
E1.

171. Northern hawksbeard *Crepis mollis*
Like Marsh hawksbeard (p. 120) but has
scarcely toothed leaves, and fruits with
pure white hairs. nE2, S1.

172. Stinking hawksbeard *Crepis foetida*
Like Beaked hawksbeard (p. 120) but has an
unpleasant smell, and flowerheads nodding
in bud. sE1.

173. Hawkweeds *Hieracium* (p. 120)
There are literally hundreds of hawkweeds,
only identifiable by specialists. A few
common or distinctive types only are
shown.

174. Ribbon-leaved water-plantain *Alisma
gramineum*
Like Narrow-leaved water-plantain (p. 121)
but has very narrow leaves, and flowers
5–6mm usually closed. E1, W1.

175. Floating water-plantain *Luronium natans*
(Alismataceae)
Like Frog-bit (p. 121) but has elliptical
leaves, and flowers, 12–15mm. E1, W1.

176. Esthwaite waterweed *Elodea nuttallii*
Like Canadian pondweed (p. 122) but has narrower, pointed, pale green leaves in whorls of 4. E1, I1.

177. Narrow-leaved eel-grass *Zostera angustifolia*
Like Eel-grass (p. 122) but has narrower leaves (2–3mm wide). E3, W2, S3, I2.

178. Dwarf eel-grass *Zostera nana*
Like Eel-grass (p. 122) but has shorter, narrower (1mm wide), 1-veined leaves. E2, W1, S2, I2.

179. Fen pondweed *Potamogeton coloratus*
Like Broad-leaved pondweed (p. 122) but has translucent, net-veined leaves. E2, W1, S1, I2.

180. Long-stalked pondweed *Potamogeton praelongus*
Like Shining pondweed (p. 123) but has blunt leaves and unthickened flowerstalks. E2, W1, S2, I2.

181. Holly-leaved naiad *Najas marina*
Like Curled pondweed (p. 123) but has prickly leaves in opposite pairs, and separate male and female plants. eE1.

182. Opposite-leaved pondweed *Groenlandia densa*
Like Curled pondweed (p. 123) but has leaves in opposite pairs. E3, W1, S1, I2.

183. Hair-like pondweed *Potamogeton trichoides*
Like Small pondweed (p. 123) but has hair-like leaves. E2, S1.

184. Shetland pondweed *Potamogeton rutilus*
Like Small pondweed (p. 123) but occurs in Shetland and Hebrides only. S1.

185. Flat-stalked pondweed *Potamogeton friesii*
Like Lesser pondweed (p. 123) but has 5-veined leaves. E3, S1, I1.

186. Sharp-leaved pondweed *Potamogeton acutifolius*
Like Blunt-leaved pondweed (p. 123) but has sharply-pointed leaves. E2.

187. Grasswrack pondweed *Potamogeton compressus*
Like Blunt-leaved pondweed (p. 123) but has 5-veined leaves, the veins joined on the leaf-tip. E2, W1, S1.

188. Slender-leaved pondweed *Potamogeton filiformis*
Like Fennel pondweed (p. 123) but has fewer whorls of flowers in the spike. W1, S2, I1.

189. Slender naiad *Najas flexilis* (Najadaceae)
Like Fennel pondweed (p. 123) but has leaves in whorls, and flowers at base of leaves. nE1, S1, I1.

190. Spiral tasselweed *Ruppia cirrhosa* (Ruppiaceae)
Like Fennel pondweed (p. 123) but has longer leaves and long, coiled flower-stalks; salt water. E2, I1.

191. Beaked tasselweed *Ruppia maritima* (Ruppiaceae)
Like Spiral tasselweed (above) but the flower-stalk not coiled; coasts. E3, W2, S2, I1.

192. Kerry lily *Simethis planifolia*
Like Snowdon lily (p. 124) but taller, with a cluster of flowers; heaths. I1.

193. Pipewort *Eriocaulon aquaticum* (Eriocaulaceae)
Like Scottish asphodel (p. 124) but has grey bracts round flowers; in water. wS1, wI1.

194. Welsh gagea *Gagea bohemica*
Like Meadow gagea (p. 125) but has solitary flowers in February–March; rocks. W1.

195. Wild leek *Allium ampeloprasum*
Like Sand leek (p. 125) but is larger, with a spherical flowerhead to 70mm. sE1, W1.

196. Blue-eyed grass *Sisyrinchium bermudianum* (Iridaceae)
Like Spring squill (p. 126) but has flattened, iris-like leaves and abruptly pointed petals. I2 and naturalised.

197. Chestnut rush *Juncus castaneus*
Like Heath rush (p. 127) but has flowers in smaller clusters, and lower bract longer than flowerhead; mountains. S2.

198. Three-flowered rush *Juncus triglumis*
Like Heath rush (p. 127) but has 3 pale flowers larger than bract; mountains. nE1, W1, S2.

199. Two-flowered rush *Juncus biglumis*
Like Heath rush (p. 127) but has only 2 flowers in the head and a longer bract; mountains. S2.

200. Round-fruited rush *Juncus compressus*
Like Saltmarsh rush (p. 127) but has flattened stems and fruit longer than tepals; marshes, fens. E3, W1.

201. Three-leaved rush *Juncus trifidus*
Like Toad rush (p. 127) but has 2–3 long bracts extending beyond flowers; mountains. S3.

202. Baltic rush *Juncus balticus*
Like Hard rush (p. 127) but grows in straight lines from creeping rhizomes, and has few flowerheads; S2.

203. Thread rush *Juncus filiformis*
Grows like Baltic rush (above) but has very slender stems; marshes. nE1, S1.

204. Sharp rush *Juncus acutus*
Like Sea rush (p. 127) but has reddish flowers and longer fruit; dunes. E2, W2, I2.

206. Dwarf rush *Juncus capitatus*
Like Bulbous rush (p. 128) but has flowers in terminal heads and small (3–4mm) tepals. sE1.

207. Pigmy rush *Juncus pygmaeus*
Like Dwarf rush (above) but has 5–6mm tepals. sE1.

208. Southern wood-rush *Luzula forsteri*
Like Hairy wood-rush (p. 128) but has upright flower-stalks. sE3.

209. Fen wood-rush *Luzula pallescens*
Like Heath wood-rush (p. 128) but has yellow-green leaves and yellowish-brown flowers. eE1.

210. Curved wood-rush *Luzula arcuata*
Like Heath wood-rush (p. 128) but has nodding, long-stalked flower-clusters; mountains. S2.

211. Sand crocus *Romulea columnae*
Like Spring crocus (p. 130) but has very narrow leaves and much smaller flowers, open only in sun. sE1.

212. Flecked marsh orchid *Dactylorhiza cruenta*
Like Early marsh orchid (p. 132) but has green parts flecked with purple, and deep purple flowers. I2.

213. Broad-leaved marsh orchid *Dactylorhiza majalis*
Like Northern marsh orchid (p. 132) but taller, with broader, bluish leaves and short-spurred flowers. W1, S2, I2.

214. Lizard orchid *Himantoglossum hircinum*
Like Man orchid (p. 132) but taller; flowers grey-purple with a very long lip. E1.

215. Dense-flowered orchid *Neotinea intacta*
Like Frog orchid (p. 132) but has dull white flowers in a dense spike. E1, I1.

216. Irish lady's-tresses *Spiranthes romanzoffiana*
Like Autumn lady's-tresses (p. 133) but has larger flowers in 3 rows spiralling round spike. S1, I1.

217. Dune helleborine *Epipactis dunensis*
Like Narrow-lipped helleborine (p. 134) but has yellowish flowers with almost closed lips. E1, W1.

218. Greater duckweed *Lemna polyrrhiza*
Like Fat duckweed (p. 135) but has larger discs, not swollen, and with several roots. E3, W1, I1.

219. Rootless duckweed *Wolffia arrhiza*
Like Common duckweed (p. 135) but tiny, with no roots. sE2.

220. Floating bur-reed *Sparganium angustifolium*
Like Unbranched bur-reed (p. 135) but has smaller, floating leaves and only 2 male flowerheads. E1, W1, S2, I2.

221. Least bur-reed *Sparganium minimum*
Like Floating bur-reed (above) but with a single male flowerhead and a short lower bract. E2, W1, S3, I2.

222. Galingale *Cyperus longus*
Like Wood club-rush (p. 136) but has fewer, narrower, flattened spikelets. sE1, W1.

223. Round-headed club-rush *Scirpus holoschoenus*
Like Sea club-rush (p. 136) but has spikelets in tight, round heads. sE1.

224. Triangular club-rush *Scirpus triqueter*
Like Common club-rush (p. 136) but has flowerhead apparently on side of stem (top of stem is a bract). sE2, I1.

225. Slender club-rush *Scirpus cernuus*
Like Bristle club-rush (p. 136) but is more delicate, with bract shorter than the greenish spike. E2, W2, S2, I2.

226. Saltmarsh flat sedge *Blysmus rufus*
Like Flat sedge (p. 136) but has rolled leaves and heads with few spikelets; saltmarshes. nE2, S3, I2.

227. Fen cotton-grass *Eriophorum latifolium*
Like Common cotton-grass (p. 136) but has no ligule at leaf-base, and rough, triangular flower-stalks; fens. E2, W2, S2, I2.

228. Slender cotton-grass *Eriophorum gracile*
Like Common cotton-grass (p. 136) but has very narrow leaves (1–2mm). sE2, I1.

229. Northern spike-rush *Eleocharis austriaca*
Like Common spike-rush (p. 137) but has more ridged stems and 5 (not 4) bristles on fruit. nE1.

230. Slender spike-rush *Eleocharis uniglumis*
Like Common spike-rush (p. 137) but has glume encircling spikelet, and flowers less crowded. E2, W2, S2, I2.

231. Many-stalked spike-rush *Eleocharis multicaulis*
Like Common spike-rush (p. 137) but is more tufted and has 3 (not 2) styles per flower. E3, W2, S4, I2.

232. Dwarf spike-rush *Eleocharis parvula*
Like Needle spike-rush (p. 137) but has greenish-white flowerheads in late summer; saline soils. sE1, W1, I1.

233. Few-flowered spike-rush *Eleocharis quinqueflora*
Like Needle spike-rush (p. 137) but has round stems and long glumes; on peat. E3, W3, S4, I3.

234. Brown beak-sedge *Rhynchospora fusca*
Like White beak-sedge (p. 137) but is creeping with darker spikelets and long bracts. sE2, W1, I2.

234. Brown beak-sedge *Rhynchospora fusca*
Like White beak-sedge (p. 137) but is creeping with darker spikelets and long bracts. sE2, W1, I2.

235. Brown bog-rush *Schoenus ferrugineus*
Like Black bog-rush (p. 137) but has shorter leaves and bracts. S1.

236. False sedge *Kobresia simpliciuscula*
Like Northern false sedge (p. 137) but has several spikes with fewer, 1-flowered spikelets. nE1, S1.

237. Dotted sedge *Carex punctata*
Like Distant sedge (p. 137) but has pale green leaves and a smooth, brown-dotted fruit. E2, W1, S1, I1.

238. Pale sedge *Carex pallescens*
Like Tawny sedge (p. 137) but has spikes all at top of stem and unbeaked fruit. E3, W3, S4, I3.

239. Smooth-stalked sedge *Carex laevigata*
Like Green-ribbed sedge (p. 137) but has broader leaves and longer spikes. E2, W3, S2, I2.

240. Large yellow sedge *Carex flava*
Like Common yellow sedge (p. 137) but has a much larger, yellow fruit. nE1.

241. Hair sedge *Carex capillaris*
Like Wood sedge (p. 138) but has stiff, narrow leaves and shorter spikes. nE1, W1, S2.

242. Thin-spiked wood sedge *Carex strigosa*
Like Wood sedge (p. 138) but has broader leaves, spike-stalks hidden by bracts, and green female glumes. E3, W1, I2.

243. Sheathed sedge *Carex vaginata*
Like Carnation sedge (p. 138) but has lowest bract with an inflated sheath; mountains. S2.

244. Starved wood sedge *Carex depauperata*
Like Carnation sedge (p. 138) but has well-spaced female spikes, each with few flowers; dry banks. sE1, sI1.

245. Slender sedge *Carex lasiocarpa*
Like Hairy sedge (p. 139) but has narrower, greyish leaves and browner female spikes; marshes, swamps. E2, W1, S3, I2.

246. Russet sedge *Carex saxatilis*
Like Hairy sedge (p. 139) but is much smaller, with dark, rounded female spikes; mountains. S2.

247. Soft-leaved sedge *Carex montana*
Like Pill sedge (p. 139) but has lowest bract like the purple-brown glumes, not leaf-like. sE2, W1.

248. Downy-fruited sedge *Carex tomentosa*
Like Pill sedge (p. 139) but has a longer lowest bract; chalk grasslands. sE1.

249. Heath sedge *Carex ericetorum*
Like Spring sedge (p. 139) but has a very short lowest bract. E2.

250. Dwarf sedge *Carex humilis*
Like Spring sedge (p. 139) but has very narrow leaves, almost hiding flowering stems. sE2.

251. Fingered sedge *Carex digitata*
Like Spring sedge (p. 139) but has slender spreading female spikes, hiding the male spike. E2, W1.

252. Bird's-foot sedge *Carex ornithopoda*
Like Fingered sedge (above) but smaller, with fruit longer than glumes. nE2.

253. Stiff sedge *Carex bigelowii*
Like Slender tufted sedge (p. 139) but has short, stiff stems; mountains. nE1, W1, S3, I2.

254. Water sedge *Carex aquatilis*
Like Slender tufted sedge (p. 139) but has several long bracts and 3–4 male spikes. nE1, W1, S3, I2.

255. Estuarine sedge *Carex recta*
Like Slender tufted sedge (p. 139) but has more reddish spikes and long-pointed glumes; estuaries. S1.

256. Close-headed alpine sedge *Carex norvegica*
Like Common sedge (p. 139) but has top spike with styles at top and anthers beneath; mountains. S1.

257. Club sedge *Carex buxbaumii*
Like Close-headed alpine sedge (above) but with spikes less crowded; mountains. S1.

258. Black alpine sedge *Carex atrata*
Like Close-headed alpine sedge (above) but with longer-stalked spikes; mountains. nE1, W1, S2.

259. Scorched alpine sedge *Carex atrofusca*
Like Common sedge (p. 139) but blackish fruit; mountains. S1.

260. Bog sedge *Carex limosa*
Like Common sedge (p. 139) but has drooping, long-stalked spikes; bogs. E2, W1, S3, I3.

261. Tall bog sedge *Carex magellanica*
Like Bog sedge (above) but with flat leaves and blunt stems. nE1, S2.

262. Mountain bog sedge *Carex rariflora*
Like Tall bog sedge (above) but with darker glumes hiding fruit. S1.

263. Fibrous tussock sedge *Carex appropinquata*
Like Greater tussock sedge (p. 139) but has much narrower, yellowish leaves. E2, I1.

264. Lesser tussock sedge *Carex diandra*
Like Greater tussock sedge (p. 139) but has narrow, greyish leaves and all spikes unstalked. E2, W1, S2, I2.

265. True fox-sedge *Carex vulpina*
Like False fox-sedge (p. 139) but has more
winged stems and reddish flowerheads. E2.

266. Gingerbread sedge *Carex elongata*
Like False fox-sedge (p. 139) but has
narrower, yellowish, grass-like leaves;
woods. E2, S1, I1.

267. String sedge *Carex chordorrhiza*
Like Brown sedge (p. 139) but grows in lines
and has very short flowerheads; bogs. S1.

268. Prickly sedge *Carex muricata*
Like Spiked sedge (p. 140) but has an all-
green stem and rounded fruit. E3, W3,
S2, I2.

269. Divided sedge *Carex divisa*
Like Oval sedge (p. 140) but not tufted;
spikes male at top not base; near sea. E2,
W1.

270. Curved sedge *Carex maritima*
Like Oval sedge (p. 140) but short and
creeping with curved stems and rounded
spikes; dunes. nE1, S2.

271. Hare's-foot sedge *Carex lachenalii*
Like White sedge (p. 140) but has blunt stem
and a shorter, denser flowerhead. S2.

272. Few-flowered sedge *Carex pauciflora*
Like Flea sedge (p. 140) but has 3 stigmas on
each flower and few (1–4) yellowish fruits;
acid peat. nE1, S4.

273. Bristle sedge *Carex microglochin*
Like Few-flowered sedge (above) but with
more (4–12) fruits on each stem. S1.

274. Wood fescue *Festuca altissima*
Like Tall fescue (p. 141) but slenderer, with
unawned spikelets; rocky woods. E2, W2,
S2, I2.

275. Various-leaved fescue *Festuca heterophylla*
Like Red fescue (p. 141) but has leaf-sheaths
open at back of stem; woods. sE2.

276. Rush-leaved fescue *Festuca juncifolia*
Like Red fescue (p. 141) but has long
runners; dunes. E2, S1.

277. Chewings fescue *Festuca nigrescens*
Like Red fescue (p. 141) but has long-awned,
hairless spikelets. Widely sown.

278. Fine-leaved sheep's fescue *Festuca tenuifolia*
Like Sheep's fescue (p. 141) but has very
narrow leaves and unawned spikelets. E3,
W1, S3, I1.

279. Blue fescue *Festuca caesia*
Like Sheep's fescue (p. 141) but has blue-grey
leaves. E2.

280. Bearded fescue *Vulpia ciliata*
Like Dune fescue (p. 141) but has clearly-
stalked flower-spikes. sE3.

281. Mat-grass fescue *Vulpia unilateralis*
Like Rat's-tail fescue (p. 141) but smaller
with shorter awns, and spike clearly
stalked. sE2.

282. Sea fern grass *Desmazeria marina*
Like Fern grass (p. 142) but unstalked
spikelets in a spike-like head; by sea. E3,
W4, S2, I3.

283. Early meadow-grass *Poa infirma*
Like Annual meadow-grass (p. 142) but has
narrow, yellowish leaves, and spikelets all
along branches; flowers early spring;
coastal sand. swE1.

284. Flattened meadow-grass *Poa compressa*
Like Bulbous meadow-grass (p. 142) but has
flattened stems; never viviparous. E4, W2,
S2, I2.

285. Swamp meadow-grass *Poa palustris*
Like Rough meadow-grass (p. 142) but has
narrower leaves and smooth sheaths; ligule
blunt. E2, W1, S1, I1.

286. Narrow-leaved meadow-grass *Poa angustifolia*
Like Smooth meadow-grass (p. 142) but has
very narrow leaves. E3, W1, S1.

287. Spreading meadow-grass *Poa subcaerulea*
Like Smooth meadow-grass (p. 142) but has
hairs at the mouth of the leafsheath, and
few flower heads. sE2, nE5, W3, S4, I2.

288. Wavy meadow-grass *Poa flexuosa*
Like Alpine meadow-grass (p. 142) but has
narrower leaves and is not viviparous. S2.

289. Glaucous meadow-grass *Poa glauca*
Like Alpine meadow-grass (p. 142) but has
bluish leaves and is not viviparous. nE1,
W1, S2.

290. Borrer's saltmarsh grass *Puccinellia fasciculata*
Like Common saltmarsh grass (p. 142) but
not sward-forming; flowerhead 1-sided.
sE2, W1.

291. Stiff saltmarsh grass *Puccinellia rupestris*
Like Common saltmarsh grass (p. 142) but
annual, prostrate, with a stiff 1-sided
flowerhead. E2, W1.

292. Lesser quaking grass *Briza minor*
Like Quaking grass (p. 143) but annual with
green spikelets; disturbed ground. sE2.

293. Small sweet-grass *Glyceria declinata*
Like Floating sweet-grass (p. 143) but has
shorter ligules, and the inner scale of each
flower toothed. E4, W4, S3, I3.

294. Lesser hairy brome *Bromus benekenii*
Like Hairy brome (p. 144) but has branches
of flowerhead arising in groups of more
than 2; woods. E2, W1, S1.

295. Field brome *Bromus arvensis*
Like Soft brome (p. 144) but has a loose flowerhead with the flowers spreading widely in each spikelet; disturbed ground. E2, W1.

296. Meadow brome *Bromus commutatus*
Like Soft brome (p. 144) but has a nodding flowerhead, and spikelets 15–25mm. E3, W2, S2, I2.

297. Smooth brome *Bromus racemosus*
Like Meadow brome (above) but with an upright flowerhead, and spikelets 10–15mm.

298. Sea couch *Elymus pycnanthus*
Like Sand couch (p. 144) but has strongly veined, hairless leaves, and pointed glumes. E4, W3, I2.

299. Glaucous hair-grass *Koeleria glauca*
Like Crested hair-grass (p. 145) but more bluish, leaves inrolled; sandy soil. Distribution EWSI not established.

300. Somerset hair-grass *Koeleria vallesiana*
Like Crested hair-grass (p. 145) but has swollen stem-bases; rocks. sE1.

301. Bog hair-grass *Deschampsia setacea*
Like Tufted hair-grass (p. 146) but has very narrow leaves and bent awn; bogs. E2, W1, S2.

302. Bristle bent *Agrostis curtisii*
Like Velvet bent (p. 147) but tufted, with very narrow leaves; heaths. swE2, sW1.

303. Black bent *Agrostis gigantea*
Like Common bent (p. 147) but taller with broad leaves; disturbed ground. E4, W2, S2, I2.

304. Narrow small-reed *Calamagrostis stricta*
Like Purple small-reed (p. 147) but has narrower, hairless leaves and a tighter flower-spike. E2, S2, nI1.

305. Scottish small-reed *Calamagrostis scotica*
Like Narrow small-reed (above) but has larger spikelets (over 4mm). S1.

306. Purple-stem cat's-tail *Phleum phleoides*
Like Timothy (p. 147) but has flower-spike tapering at the top. eE1.

307. Alpine cat's-tail *Phleum alpinum*
Like Sand cat's-tail (p. 147) but has a rounded spike; mountains. S1.

308. Alpine foxtail *Alopecurus alpinus*
Like Meadow foxtail (p. 147) but has an egg-shaped flower-spike and no awns; mountains. S1.

309. Orange foxtail *Alopecurus aequalis*
Like Marsh foxtail (p. 147) but has very short arms. E2.

310. Bulbous foxtail *Alopecurus bulbosus*
Like Marsh foxtail (p. 147) but has a swollen stem-base; saltmarshes. sE3, sW1.

311. Small cord-grass *Spartina maritima*
Like Common cord-grass (p. 148) but smaller, with shorter spikelets (less than 15mm). sE2, sI1.

SEEDS

THE NATURE OF SEEDS

The seed is a critical stage in the life-cycle of seed plants. In contrast to all other stages, the seed undergoes no growth, though there may be some development of the embryo, the young plant protected inside. The inert nature of seeds enables the plant to escape from unfavourable conditions either, in some cases, by physically moving away from a site that has become less suitable, or by allowing time to pass until more suitable conditions return. Various parts of a seed's structure have become adapted to this.

The basic structure of a seed comprises an embryo, which is derived from the fusion of part of the pollen grain with the ovule, and a surrounding coat called the testa. The embryo may be tiny and undifferentiated, as in orchids, or clearly developed into a rootlet (the radicle) and a shoot (the plumule), in which case the plumule consists of a short stalk bearing one, two or many seed-leaves, the cotyledons. It is these cotyledons which first appear above ground on germination. In addition to these two basic components, embryo and testa, there may be a store of food, the endosperm, which nourishes the young seedling in its early growth, and the human race in the form of flour and other cereal products. Some seeds, however, store food in the cotyledons, as in legumes (peas, beans and vetches); large seeds do not necessarily have an endosperm.

Seeds are individual young plants, awaiting the chance to grow and develop. Often they are produced in huge quantities, sometimes singly, but in all flowering plants they are enclosed in a fruit, which may therefore contain one or many seeds. The fruit is the outer layer of tissue (the carpel) which surrounded the ovule in the flower: the ovule gives rise to the seed and the protecting wall to the fruit. Fruits are discussed fully on p. 162.

From an evolutionary standpoint the seed-leaves (cotyledons) are the most interesting part of a seed. The most primitive seed plants, the gymnosperms (conifers and their allies) have many seed-leaves: a young pine seedling looks like a miniature green sweep's brush. The flowering plants (angiosperms), which appeared later in the evolutionary record, have either two or one. Two cotyledons characterize the dicotyledons – buttercups, campions, roses, foxgloves, daisies – and one cotyledon the monocotyledons – grasses, sedges, rushes, lilies, orchids – and the latter are generally regarded as being more recently evolved. So there seems to have been a trend to simplification, reduction in numbers of seed-leaves; such reductions are common in evolutionary history.

Seeds differ enormously in size, in the numbers produced, and in the surface of the seed-coat. All these differences relate to the ecology of the species and are described in the next pages.

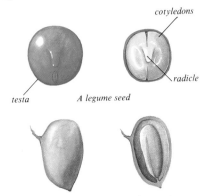

cotyledons

testa *radicle*

A legume seed

Water plantain: a monocotyledon without endosperm

THE NUMBERS AND SIZES OF SEEDS

Plants obey strict laws of economics: they make their own food by photo-synthesis and this limits the amount they pass on to the next generation as seeds. If they produce large seeds, with extensive food stores which will nurture the young seedling, they can only produce a few; the smaller the seeds, the more can be produced, but the less the chance each has of sur-vival, since its stores of food are limited. This trade-off between num-bers and size can be seen throughout the plant kingdom.

The largest seed known is that of the double coconut of the Seychelles, which weighs 10 to 20 kg; nearer home there are no seeds which approach this. Several species have very large *fruits*, such as crab apple, but the actual seeds within are comparatively small. Large seeds are commonest in plants of woodland and scrub, where the young seedling may either have to grow rapidly in height to reach the light or survive for long periods with-out proper illumination until a gap in the canopy occurs. Oaks have very large seeds, typically weighing several grams; so young oak seedlings can grow up through dense vegetation, thanks to being able to draw on the stores of food in the seed. To produce these seeds consumes a lot of the tree's resources, and foresters know

well that good seed years are poor years for timber growth. Most forest trees do not start to produce seed at all until they are 10–20 years old, and large enough to afford this great expenditure.

At the other extreme are seeds which are so small as to resemble powder, and which weigh only a few millionths of a gram (micrograms). The lightest of all is believed to be the seed of creeping lady's-tresses orchid, at around 2 micrograms; but several others', particularly of other orchids such as fragrant orchid (8 micro-grams), and of parasitic plants such as broomrapes (8–10 micrograms), are almost as minute.

Orchid seeds consist of an almost totally undeveloped embryo, with no differentiation into root and shoot, and a thin coat. They contain no food stores and indeed cannot grow unless they encounter a special symbiotic fungus which supplies them with food. This reliance on a fungal partner has enabled orchids to dispense with food stores and to concentrate on numbers rather than size. For the same reason, parasitic plants, which obtain their nourishment from another plant, also produce many small seeds. The production of very large numbers of small seeds makes the encounter of plant and partner more likely.

Other plants with very small seeds tend to be those of very disturbed habitats, which persist for only a short time, and to which dispersal is important. Annual pearlwort, so common on bare ground and paths in gardens, has seeds weighing less than 8 micrograms. But the relationship is not always so obvious: soft rush, which is a perennial and common in wet places and overgrazed fields, and *not* on disturbed and bare ground, has seeds weighing only 10 micrograms. So other considerations, which we do not fully understand, must be impor-tant too.

Most plants have seeds lying some-where between the two extremes of oak and orchid; generally, the more competitive the environment the seedling typically finds itself in, the larger the seeds.

Seeds with endosperm

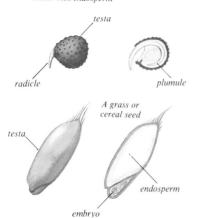

testa

radicle

plumule

A grass or cereal seed

testa

endosperm

embryo

161

FRUITS: STRUCTURE AND TYPES

The fruit is a structure unique to flowering plants (angiosperms). Conifers and their allies (gymnosperms), though also producing seeds, do not wrap them up in an outer coat to make a fruit. A fruit originates by the development of the carpel which surrounds the ovule; gymnosperms have the carpel open and it never develops into a true fruit. The seeds of some gymnosperms *appear* to be fleshy fruits – yew has a seed enclosed in a red fleshy 'fruit', and juniper has seeds in berries – but in each case the apparent fruit is formed by an outgrowth of the seed-coat, and is called an aril.

The fruits of flowering plants are very diverse: some act as protective structures, but most as dispersal agents. Just as the means of dispersal used are various, so are the adaptations of the fruits to those means.

The simplest fruits are called achenes, and in these the fruit wall is dry and simply encloses a single seed, as in meadow buttercup. Here it acts in a purely protective role, but some achenes have modifications to the fruit wall which aid dispersal, such as the persistent hooked style of herb bennet or the long feathery style of traveller's joy: the one is dispersed by animals, the other by wind, and the different structures have evolved to such distinct morphologies from a similar starting point.

Many more specialised fruits are basically achenes, but they are achenes in which the fruit wall has become developed to some particular function. The nuts of many forest trees, such as oak and beech, are simply achenes in which the fruit wall has become thickened and hard, so that it protects the nutritious seed, with its massive food store. The reason why such plants have such energy-rich seeds are discussed on p. 298; the thick fruit wall is just another consequence of their life-style.

Extensions or appendages of the fruit wall are also common. Many trees have winged fruits (ash, syca-

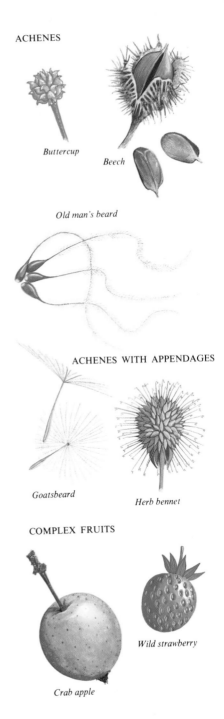

ACHENES

Buttercup

Beech

Old man's beard

ACHENES WITH APPENDAGES

Goatsbeard

Herb bennet

COMPLEX FRUITS

Wild strawberry

Crab apple

Lords-and-ladies

Gooseberry

Holly

Bittersweet

Elder

FALSE FRUITS

Yew

Juniper

CAPSULES

Foxglove

Common poppy

more, elm), and in the daisy family parachute seeds, such as in dandelions, are often found. In all these cases the basic fruit is an achene, strictly speaking a one-seeded indehiscent dry fruit.

Other dry fruits tend to contain several (often very many) seeds and to have some mechanism for distributing these, either by breaking up (dehiscing) or by opening to provide a doorway for escape. The simplest of these are those which split along one (follicles) or two sides (legumes), as in marsh marigold or broom respectively (see p. 168). Here the seeds are liberated either passively or sometimes more energetically if the fruit opens suddenly.

The commonest type of dry fruit, however, is the capsule, which opens by slits or holes of some sort, often producing a sophisticated censer mechanism. Poppies, campions, foxgloves and bluebells all have capsules. Sometimes the segments of the capsule open explosively, hurling the seeds great distances, as in touch-me-not balsam.

The most conspicuous fruits are fleshy, where the fruit wall has become succulent and attractive to animals. There are subtle differences between the fruits of cherry, bramble, holly and elder on the one hand (they are called drupes) and gooseberry, bittersweet and lords-and-ladies on the other (they are strictly berries), but they all function similarly, containing one or more tough-coated seeds which can, if necessary, often withstand passing through animal guts.

There are even more complicated fruits, where other parts of the flower become fleshy: a strawberry consists of a number of simple achenes on the surface of a fleshy structure called a receptacle (which is part of the original flower), while in apples and pears this structure surrounds a drupe (containing seeds). The pips of an apple are the seeds, and the horny bits the true fruit wall.

SEED DISPERSAL: WIND

A seed needs either to be able to travel away from its parent or to lie dormant, since the seedling cannot outcompete the adult plant, unless that dies from other causes. The actual sizes of seeds are determined by other aspects of the plant's ecology (see p. 161), but the size of a seed greatly affects its ability to disperse. Very small seeds have only to be liberated in the air, and they will be carried away by the wind. This is taken to extremes by orchids, but many other plants such as foxglove, poppies and mulleins, though larger-seeded, rely on the same mechanism. Often the fruit has a censer mechanism, which only releases the seeds when shaken, usually by wind, as in ragged robin.

Such mechanisms achieve very limited dispersal, and most of the seeds will land within a few metres of the plant. For anything more, a method of increasing the buoyancy of the seed is necessary. The simplest such method is the development of wings on the fruit or seed, as is best known in sycamore and other maples. Here the single long membranous wing gives buoyancy to what is a sizeable seed, but it provides very little lift, and the whole process depends upon liberation from a height. The ability of sycamore seedlings to spring up considerable distances from a parent tree testifies to the efficacy of such wings. When wings are associated with large fruits they act simply to delay their fall, though some very small seeds (such as those of speedwells) may have flattened edges, and

The seeds of some typical fenland plants

Marsh willowherb

Creeping willow

Marsh valerian

Marsh ragwort

Ragged robin

Broad-leaved cotton-grass

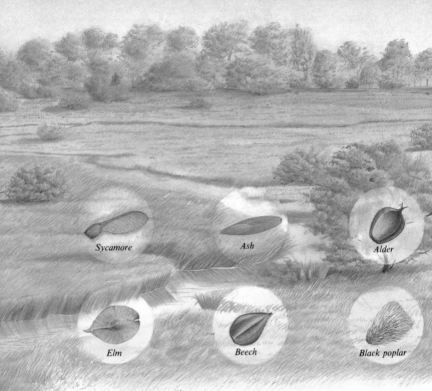

The seeds of some common trees

the slightly larger winged fruits of alder and birch can travel large distances.

Something more closely approaching flight, and hence much greater dispersal, is provided by hairs attached to the seed. These may arise in various ways and may be attached to the top (willowherbs) or the bottom (willows) of the seed. In cultivated cotton, the whole seed surface is hairy, while in common cotton-grass the hairs are modified petals and sepals. All these species have small seeds which, aided by the hairs, can travel remarkable distances.

The most sophisticated systems, however, are those involving parachutes and found mainly in the valerian and daisy families. These are simply structures of hairs arranged in such a way as to produce a very great lift for the amount of hair: the most complex and beautiful are seen in goatsbeard and in dandelions.

A few seeds may travel very great distances by these means: sycamore seeds have been known to fly 4 km, coltsfoot 14 km, poplar 30 km, and exceptionally some ragworts several hundred kilometres. These odd long-distance achievements may be immensely important in allowing a species to extend its range, but the vast majority of the seeds even of these species fall much closer to home. Only 1% of the seeds of dandelions reach 10 km, and for ash the figure is a bare 20 metres.

165

SEED DISPERSAL: WATER

Water is involved in seed dispersal in two distinct ways, as an indicator of favourable conditions and as an an actual dispersal agent. While most capsules only open when dry, there are some, particularly those of plants of wet places, such as brooklime and water forget-me-not, which open when wetted. This must lead to a limited range of dispersal, but increases the chance that the seeds will land on suitably wet ground. The same mechanism fits a very different habitat for ivy-leaved toadflax, a common plant of walls; here the restriction of seed dispersal to wet periods presumably ensures that the seeds get washed into cracks and not dispersed away from the wall.

True dispersal by water is only of value to actual water plants, for which the random movements achieved by wind would be grossly wasteful, since few seeds would actually land near water. Many water plants have buoyant seeds, achieved by layers of air-filled tissue, as in flowering rush and common water-plantain, or an actual layer of trapped air, as in white water-lily. Others simply have non-wettable coats (water forget-me-not, marsh

thistle). These floating seeds can then be dispersed along the surface by wind or by flowing water; and floating may also lead to accidental transport by waterfowl, to such seeds may adhere, which allows them to be dispersed to unconnected water bodies.

Sooner or later the seed must settle and germinate, and the mechanisms by which this is achieved have been rather little studied. Clearly such seeds cannot be stimulated into germination by water, as are those of many terrestrial species. Water violet seeds, in fact, germinate immediately they are shed into the water, but retain their buoyancy for long periods. As a result, the tiny seedlings either settle on the edge of the ditch or pond in which they are shed, or more usually are deposited on the bottom as the water level falls in summer. They then root and start to grow vigorously in the brief period before resubmergence.

Similar seedling (rather than seed) transport is found in many other water plants, including purple loosestrife, marsh woundwort and water figwort. The bottom of dried ditches often supports huge numbers of seedlings of water plants such as water

A typical water and waterside plant community

Water violet

White water-lily

Common water-plantain →

Ivy-leaved toadflax growing on a wall

crowfoot, water dropwort and water violet, along with other, more terrestrial species whose seeds have blown in. This dry period is important for their establishment, and the subsequent flooding kills off the terrestrial competitors. In places where the water level is more constant, most new colonisation is probably by re-rooting of broken fragments or the growth of rhizomes, as by reeds and yellow iris, for a seedling has little chance of growing up through any depth of water.

Sea water is also important in seed dispersal. Any Atlantic beach will sooner or later reveal exotic seeds and fruits washed up, as Linnaeus noted 200 years ago in Norway. Most, but by no means all, of these are dead, but some can certainly survive long immersion in sea-water. Saltmarsh plants, for instance, can scarcely avoid dropping their seeds into sea-water at high tide, and this must aid their dispersal. Seeds of common sea-lavender will not germinate in sea water; they must wait to be wetted by autumn rains for that, but immersion in sea water actually increases the proportion that will germinate, so the sea acts here as both dispersal agent and stimulant.

Flowering rush

← *Purple loosestrife*
Marsh woundwort
Water figwort   *Marsh thistle*

Common water crowfoot

SEED DISPERSAL: EXPLOSIVE

Many plants have their own devices for ensuring at least a limited seed dispersal: they quite literally throw their seeds away. Sometimes the seeds may subsequently be picked up by animals or, more usually, they are thrown up into more turbulent air so aiding wind dispersal; but often the whole dispersal process is achieved by the forcible ejection of the seeds.

The crackling of exploding broom fruits (the pods of legumes) is a familiar garden sound on warm days in late summer, and many others of the same family have similar mechanisms. All rely on the existence of tension between different types of cells in the fruit wall, often so arranged that when the tension is released by the rupture of the wall, the remaining flaps of tissue roll up or burst so as to fling the seeds out.

Explosive mechanisms are surprisingly common. Many plants with seeds in capsules have some limited powers to hurl the seeds out – the pods of many crucifers can do this, though some such as narrow-leaved bittercress are more effective than others. The best-known examples are the balsams, particularly touch-me-not and the introduced Himalayan balsam, cranesbills and storksbills, and violets. None of them can throw their seeds great distances: narrow-leaved bittercress and dog violet reach about 1 metre, the cranesbills 1.5 to 2 metres, and the balsams perhaps a little more.

Many of these plants with explosive fruits are woodland species: most of those mentioned so far are, as well as dog's mercury, wood sorrel and others. All grow on the ground in woods where there is usually very little wind and little chance, therefore, of wind dispersal. These explosive mechanisms may therefore be a response to the otherwise limited possibilities for dispersal open to woodland plants.

Not all plants which throw out seeds rely on these explosive mechanisms. Some achieve the same result

Broom

Meadow clary

Narrow-leaved bittercress

Touch-me-not balsam

Wood cranesbill

Candytuft

Skullcap

Common dog violet

by a type of catapult mechanism: they use the pressure applied to the plant by some outside agent. Raindrops, for example, falling on pennycress and wild candytuft pods make them act like a lever, since they have their flattened sides held horizontally. Similarly rain, wind or passing animals may operate the catapults of many labiates, including meadow clary and skullcap. Here it is the fruit-stalk which is springy and if the fruits are pressed down and released, they whip upwards, flinging out the nutlets. Interestingly, burdocks, which appear to have the sort of fruit that is dispersed by clinging to animal fur (as it will cling to clothes, to the delight of children), have in fact catapults. The hooks grip passing animals but the stalk is often strong enough not to break, and when the contact is broken the fruithead flies back, flicking out the seeds.

Mechanisms such as these, or that of the balsams, which is explosive but can be triggered by touch, may combine with animal dispersal, since the seeds are likely to stick to anything that has fired the catapult.

Dog's-mercury, lesser burdock and wood sorrel are all woodland plants which have special mechanisms for the dispersal of seeds.

169

DISPERSAL BY ANIMALS: SEEDS AND FRUITS AS FOOD

Plants and animals have influenced each other's evolution from the very beginning. Sometimes this mutual influence is so great that one can talk of co-evolution, of a situation where one can only understand the way in which one group has evolved by looking at the development of another at the same time. This is true of insects and plant pollination (see pp. 276 & ff) and also of the evolution of fruits and seed- and fruit-eaters.

Seeds, particularly those with a large store of food, are an important food source for many animals, and must have become so at an early stage in evolution. Many seeds must be consumed by grazing animals indiscriminately along with leaves and stems, but few of these are in a viable state after passing through the gut; those that do best have hard seed coats, as in red clover and fat hen. Indeed, quantities of fat hen seeds have been found in archaeological deposits in layers derived from cow dung. Some animals are specialist seed-eaters, and an even smaller proportion of the seeds they consume pass through the gut intact: pigeons, pheasants and other grain-eating birds have a crop in which the seeds are ground by stones and grit.

These animals must be of little value in dispersal, except when they hoard food. Jays may carry acorns several miles before burying them, and squirrels also have stores, though they never travel so far.

Plants which benefit greatly from animal dispersal are those where it is the fruit which is attractive and the seed is protected by a hard coat inside. Blackbirds and thrushes are particularly important in distributing these berries and other fleshy fruits, and though they travel through the bird in a few hours, limiting the possible range of dispersal, the germination of the seeds is scarcely affected.

Once these berries are seen as adapted to animal dispersal, their colours become easily explained. It is

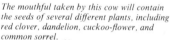

The mouthful taken by this cow will contain the seeds of several different plants, including red clover, dandelion, cuckoo-flower, and common sorrel.

A blackbird eats wild cherries.

A starling eats elderberries.

The brilliant orange seeds of stinking iris are conspicuous even in shaded hedge bottoms.

noticeable that red fruits tend to occur in summer (wild cherry, wild strawberry, raspberry, red currant) or on evergreen plants (holly, yew); in other words, they are seen against a background of green foliage, with which they contrast strongly. On the other hand, black berries tend to occur in autumn (bramble, elder, bird cherry), when the yellowing of the leaves makes red a less conspicuous colour. Most of these are mainly eaten by birds, which have well-developed colour vision but a poor sense of smell, and indeed few such fruits have a strong smell. In contrast, mammals have a good sense of smell but poor vision, and the plants with large, aromatic fruits, such as apples and pears and their relatives, are probably dispersed more by small mammals.

The production of these baits is expensive to the plant, and some have managed to avoid this expense by mimicking the appearance of an edible fruit. The brilliantly coloured seeds of stinking iris look edible, but offer little nutrition to the consumer. The plant gets the benefits of transport without the attendant costs.

Another way of reducing costs is to gain the assistance of a less demanding disperser. Ants are extremely important as seed-gatherers, and they may remove almost the whole seed production to their nests. Some plants, such as primrose, hellebores, violets, wood anemone and several other mainly woodland species, are adapted to ant dispersal by the possession of special food-bodies (called elaiosomes) attached to the seed or fruit, which is itself usually too tough for ant mandibles. The ants gather and store the seeds or fruits, consume the elaiosomes, and effectively provide both dispersal and planting of the seed by burial.

A wood ant carries a wood anemone seed to which elaiosomes are attached.

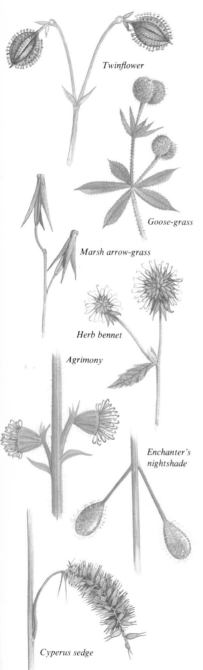

Twinflower

Goose-grass

Marsh arrow-grass

Herb bennet

Agrimony

Enchanter's nightshade

Cyperus sedge

Hooked fruits (not to scale)

SEED DISPERSAL BY ANIMALS: EXTERNAL TRANSPORT

Providing a meal is one way of getting animals to carry out the dispersal of seeds. An alternative way is to attach the seeds to the outsides of mobile animals. In practice the boundary between this and dispersal by consumption is rather hazy: when ants carry seeds to their nests they may never eat the seeds (indeed the dispersal will have been ineffective if they do), but they still gather the seeds as food. This seed must offer the ants some reward as food.

It is much cheaper to the plant to attach the seed or fruit unwittingly to a passing animal. This requires no action by the animal and so the plant needs to offer no reward. The commonest such mechanism is the possession of barbs or hooks. These may arise in many different ways, but rarely on the seed itself. Fruits covered with hooked hairs are found in goosegrass (or common cleavers) and enchanter's nightshade, while in herb bennet it is the style which persists from the flower and turns into a projecting hook. In some cases other flower parts persist, harden and become hooks, as in agrimony. It has been estimated that around 10% of all flowering plants have some such dispersal mechanism, attesting to its efficacy, and also to the fact that these hooks may serve a double purpose, protecting the seed from predators at the same time.

Sometimes the spikes on such fruits may be quite fearsome and capable of penetrating skin. Fortunately such species are rare in Britain, but the puncture vine grows in southern Europe and its fruit-spines can pierce the hooves of sheep. The pointed fruits of several grasses and sedges, including cyperus sedge, white beak-sedge and the sedge-like (but unrelated) marsh arrow-grass work on the same principle, burying themselves in passing fur.

Such viciousness is not the only way to hitch a lift, and gentler methods do occur widely. Some fruits are sticky because of the presence of glandular hairs on the surface, as in mouse-ears, while the elegant twin-flower has a pair of sticky bracts enfolding the fruit. Alternatively the seeds themselves may be embedded in a sticky gel, so that any animal feeding on them gets covered in surplus seeds; this seems to be one of the methods of dispersal used by water-lilies. Finally hairs on seeds may also permit animal dispersal, as in willows and willowherbs.

These examples give an interesting insight into the workings of natural selection. It is often assumed that every character must have been selected for its apparent function, but it is clear that most of these dispersal mechanisms have multiple functions: hooks and spikes protect as well as providing dispersal, the sticky coat of water-lily seeds makes them buoyant as well as able to stick to ducks' bills, and the hairs of willowherb seeds offer possibilities of both wind and animal dispersal. It is impossible to say that one or the other function was originally selected for; the important thing is that they provided benefits to their possessors.

Animal transport may, too, be wholly accidental. Waterfowl often have muddy feet and that mud may contain large numbers of seeds. This requires no special adaptation by the plants but may result in long-distance dispersal. The occurrence in western Britain, apparently quite naturally, of several north American species has been taken as an example of this. It is possible that pipewort, blue-eyed grass, Irish lady's-tresses orchid and a few others originally made the trip on birds' feet – interestingly they all grow in wet places.

Map of North America and Western Europe showing the distribution of blue-eyed grass (right) and Irish lady's-tresses, both of which only occur on the Atlantic fringe of Europe.

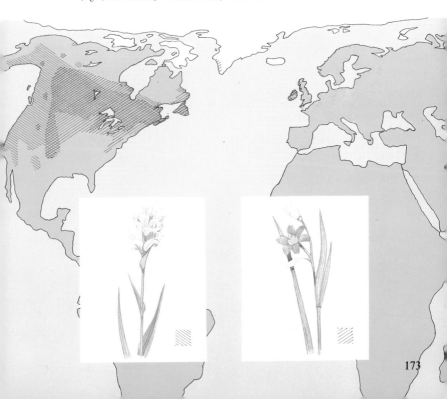

DORMANCY OF SEEDS

The importance of seeds in a plant's life-cycle varies. Some annuals may go through a phase when the whole population exists as seeds and there are no actual plants in existence – this is true of winter annuals such as rue-leaved saxifrage and common whitlow-grass, which grow in places that dry out in summer. Other short-lived plants may nevertheless maintain a permanent population, but with a very much larger hidden population in the form of a 'seed bank' in soil; this is the pattern of many common garden weeds including common field speedwell, common chickweed and groundsel.

As the life-cycle gets longer, so seeds become less significant in it, but in all species the basic role of the seed is the same: to allow the plant to find new habitats, either by moving physically away from the parent or by waiting for the return of favourable conditions. A prerequisite of such a role is the possession of dormancy, the ability *not* to germinate.

Not all seeds possess strict dormancy; some germinate on being shed. Indeed in a wet autumn seeds of white campion, for example, may actually germinate in the capsule, the censer mechanism which relies on dry weather having failed to disperse the seeds. Many seeds, however, will not germinate at first, for a variety of reasons. In some, such as wood anemone and lesser celandine, the embryo is so undeveloped that it is incapable of germination and several months must elapse before the seed is fully mature. Others have seeds potentially able to germinate but requiring some outside stimulus. The blockage may simply be a tough seed-coat, as in red clover and other legumes and in many water plants, including common water-plantain and arrowhead; these can be induced to germinate artificially by scratching the coat to allow air to penetrate, and in nature probably have to await some chance event to achieve this.

The most interesting responses are those of seeds which require a precise environmental message, usually light or temperature. Many seeds require light to germinate, a message which in nature indicates that the seed is not deeply buried. Every gardener has experienced the chastening reward of digging the vegetable patch – a massive growth of weed seedlings, such as common chickweed, activated by their sudden exposure to light. Some seeds are more subtle than this: they can detect the sort of light they receive. Light passing through leaves looks green to us, but if we could see in the infra-red, it would take on whatever hue that would be, for leaves are transparent to infra-red

Common field speedwell, common chickweed and groundsel grow together after the terrain has recently been disturbed. Many of the plants characteristic of disturbed ground have seeds whose germination is stimulated by light.

The rue-leaved saxifrage is a winter annual, and has a different annual timetable from other plants mentioned in this section. (See p. 242–245). Its seed germinates in the autumn (centre right), *and it overwinters as a young plant* (right) *to flower in the following spring* (left), *before shrivelling up and dying in the summer* (centre left).

light. Seeds of many plants will not germinate if they are in infra-red light, which is a message that they are overshadowed by other growing plants and hence that conditions are not suitable for growth. Remove the leaves covering a patch of soil in a grass field, and a crop of seedlings often appears, as they do when a forest tree falls.

Temperature gives an indication of a different aspect of the environment: the onset and passage of winter. Many seeds will not germinate unless first chilled for several weeks or months, such as trees like rowan, and herbaceous plants, including both perennials (e.g. wood sage, moschatel) and annuals (e.g. yellow rattle). This mechanism ensures that such seeds

do not germinate before the onset of winter; if they did, the seedlings would be exposed to harsh conditions at a vulnerable stage.

Some seeds have even more complex mechanisms to ensure that germination occurs at the best time. Silver birch and downy birch both have seeds which, when first shed in September and October, will only germinate if the days are long. As a result they lie dormant through the winter; once chilled for several weeks or months, however, they become insensitive to the length of the day and germinate readily. The initial need for long days ensures that, even if the winter is mild and they are not chilled, they will still germinate in the following spring.

LONGEVITY AND SEED BANKS

Most seeds live for rather a short time. Even if stored in ideal, cool, dry conditions, they die after 5–10 years. Of cultivated crops, peas and beans have some of the longest-lived seeds, only about half dying in 15 years. The longest-lived seeds generally are those of legumes, and some have been reported to remain viable for at least 50 years. These figures can be greatly extended (by how much is not yet clear) by modern storage techniques at sub-zero temperatures in very dry conditions, which put a stop to all activity in the seed, which is anyway very slight but slowly exhausts its reserves. These techniques are exploited in modern seed banks, where seed of cultivars of crop plants that are no longer sown is kept alive, so that plant breeders can still make use of them if in the future their particular characteristics (say of disease resistance) prove valuable. It may also explain the reports of extreme natural seed longevity: living lupin seeds claimed to be 10,000 years old have been found in frozen lemming burrows in cold, dry tundra.

Generally seed life-spans are much shorter, but the ability to survive for even a few years, dormant but viable in the soil, has tremendous ecological importance. Many plants are able to build up natural seed banks: the soil they grow on actually contains hundreds, often thousands, of seeds in every square metre, capable of replenishing the population of adult plants.

The simplest such seed bank is that necessary for strict annual plants, those that spend at least part of the year in seed form. Wall barley is a common roadside weed which sheds its seeds in summer; at first none will germinate, but they gradually lose their dormancy and in the autumn and winter virtually all either germinate or die. Very few survive into the following summer as seed, so here the seed bank is very short-lived, but it serves to ensure the survival of the plant over the dry summer.

In other plants the seed bank is longer-lived because the seeds require chilling over winter before they lose their dormancy (see p. 174). Himalayan balsam, yellow rattle, cow parsley and sycamore are four plants of very different ecology which have

Heather seedlings appear after a moorland fire, which actually promotes germination.

this in common, and in all cases their seeds germinate in a rush in spring, all together, when winter has created gaps, free of other plants, in which the young seedlings will do well.

Persistent seed banks occur when some at least of the seeds survive more than one year, so that there are always seeds present capable of germinating if given the right signal. Such seed banks are topped up each year by new production, and the size of the bank depends on this, on the number germinating, and on how many die or are eaten.

Heather is a good example of a plant with such a seed bank. Seeds are shed in enormous numbers from healthy stands of heather and, to start with, few germinate – they enter the seed bank. They can remain there for several years (possibly as many as ten, but certainly two or three), and will germinate if conditions are right. Many become buried by accumulating dead leaves, however, and are then dormant, often until stimulated by the heat of a managed moor fire. In the damp peat, such a fire warms the seeds to perhaps 50 or 60°C, which actually promotes germination. After such a fire thousands of seedlings can be seen. But uncontrolled fires in dry weather do huge damage, for the peat surface itself actually burns, destroying both that and the seeds in the seed bank.

Seed banks are found in plants from a wide range of habitats. They are very common in weeds and other plants of disturbed ground, where the whole adult population may easily be destroyed: good examples are nettle, curled dock, greater plantain and common chickweed, the bane of gardeners. They are also found in plants of wet ground (soft rush, great willowherb, tufted hair-grass, creeping buttercup), in many grassland plants, such as ribwort plantain, and often in plants which colonise very dry places (where again there is a risk that the adult population may not survive), including Nottingham catchfly, wild thyme and harebell.

Plants of wet meadows (such as great willowherb, soft rush, tufted hair-grass and creeping buttercup) form one of the ecological groups known to lay down seed banks.

177

GERMINATION OF SEEDS

The actual process of germination involves the liberation of the embryo from the seed-coat and the extension of the young root (the radicle) into the soil. The other part of the embryo, the cotyledons or seed-leaves (of which there are two in dicotyledons and one in monocotyledons – see p. 160), may be pushed out into the air and start to function as leaves, or may remain in the seed and simply act as a food store on which the growing seedling can draw. Where the cotyledons remain in the seed germination is said to be hypogeal (literally 'underground'), and where they emerge it is epigeal ('above ground').

In these two cases the cotyledons are performing quite different functions, the one releasing stored food, the other producing it by photosynthesis. In either case, if the seed germinates in the soil, the seedling faces the problem of pushing the young shoot into the air without damage. Roots are of course protected as they move through soil by a loose cap of tissue around the tip, which is reformed as fast as it is worn away; they are anyway well shaped for penetrating soil. Stems and leaves are not.

Where germination is hypogeal, the cotyledons remain in the seed and the young shoot itself is pushed out by the growth of the epicotyl, the part of the stem between the cotyledons and the bud that will form the shoot. This is what happens in the germination of grasses and cereals: the first green shoot to appear is in fact the first leaf; the cotyledon remains in the seed. It is protected in its passage through the soil by a translucent sheath, which is soon lost. The same is true of oak and many other plants with nut-like fruits, including horse chestnut, wild cherry and hazel: in all cases the cotyledon never emerges from the seed and serves only to pass food from the store in the seed to the young seedling. In these plants the young shoot forms a hook at the top which protects the terminal bud as it

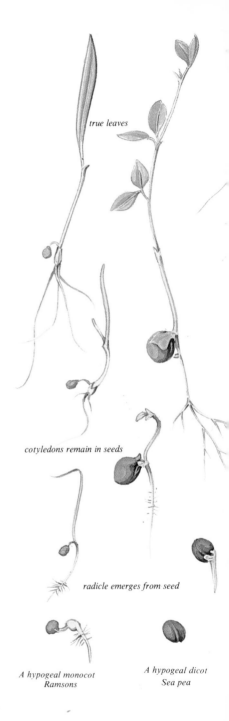

true leaves

cotyledons remain in seeds

radicle emerges from seed

A hypogeal monocot
Ramsons

A hypogeal dicot
Sea pea

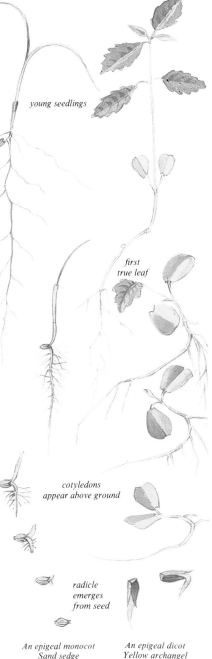

young seedlings

first true leaf

cotyledons appear above ground

radicle emerges from seed

An epigeal monocot
Sand sedge

An epigeal dicot
Yellow archangel

moves through the soil.

A slightly different situation occurs in ramsons and reedmace, in which the section of the stem between cotyledon and radicle, the hypocotyl, elongates and forms a sharp bend: this bend pushes out through the soil, carrying the seed and its embedded cotyledon with it. In these cases, the shoot then is protected either by a sheath or by forming a hook.

In epigeal germination, however, the cotyledons themselves are pushed out of the seed and the soil by the elongation of either the hypocotyl or their own stalks, and come to act as the first leaves of the young seedling. They also serve to protect the shoot-bud in its passage, again moving through the soil either bent themselves or below a bent hypocotyl.

The actual details of the germination process vary greatly, and different patterns can be found in closely-related plants. Most members of the buttercup family are epigeal, for instance, but wood anemone is hypogeal. This demonstrates that germination mechanisms were not fixed in remote evolutionary time (as, for example, the number of cotyledons was), but are a characteristic that responds to the particular ecological circumstances of the plant. Surprisingly almost nothing is known of the ecological rationale, of what are the particular advantages or drawbacks of one or other mechanism.

Stages in the germination of different types of seedling

179

GERMINATION SUCCESS

The vast majority of seeds never develop into mature plants. This is just as well, bearing in mind the numbers of seeds produced by some plants (see p. 161); and of course this fact underlies the whole concept of evolution by natural selection.

Take greater plantain, which can produce over 10,000 seeds a year and survive for at least 10 years. Yet the numbers of plantains in an area do not normally increase greatly. Of the 100,000 plantain seeds produced by each parent, only one (on average) survives to replace it; 99,999 die.

Many of these deaths will occur before germination: the seeds may simply fall into unsuitable places (in water perhaps, or on stony ground). Many will be eaten: acorns were once staple fodder for pigs, though nowadays jays and squirrels are more likely to be responsible. Other seeds and fruits suffer similar fates from beetles or the caterpillars of butterflies and moths: the seed capsules of common toadflax almost invariably produce, from eggs laid on the flowers, a tiny moth called the toadflax pug, and red and white campion capsules often contain a single larva of the campion

Toadflax pug moth and common toadflax

Of all the thousands of seeds produced by this plantain during its life, the few that survive and mature into new plants will probably be those that, by chance, find themselves in suitable 'safe sites', such as cracks in the soil. Note the sticky mucilage exuded by the seed.

moth, grown fat on a diet of seeds.

Other seeds get buried, become dormant, and never receive the right signals to germinate before they die naturally, and yet others are rotted by fungi in soil. Quite what proportion of the seeds fall victim to these hazards varies from species to species, but in all cases some survive to germinate, and it is there the next set of problems arises.

Successful germination involves a huge slice of luck, but seeds still have a few ways of improving their chances. For the seedling to survive, germination must take place in a suitable environment, but also within that in a spot where the root can penetrate a suitable soil surface. Gardeners are familiar with the problem of patchy germination: this is usually due not to patchy sowing of seed but to the fact that only certain points are suitable for germination, often cracks in the surface. Ecologists call such spots 'safe sites' and their abundance largely determines germination success.

Seeds may have a greater chance if they possess a rough seed-coat. It is at first sight an extraordinary fact that most seeds can be identified to species

(by a few experts!), by the complex patterns and sculpturing of their coats. These patterns have arisen in response to the need both to locate it in a safe site, and to hold it still while the radicle and cotyledons push out.

An essential for germination is that the seed (which is almost completely desiccated) must absorb water and this requires a good contact with the soil. Many seeds exude a sticky mucilage which helps to anchor the seed, to absorb water from the soil and pass it on to the seed, and possibly to deter predators. Such mucilages are found in plantains, purging flax, and many crucifers (including the familiar window-ledge cress).

Perhaps the most impressive mechanism for ensuring that the seed is properly embedded in soil is the twisted awn found on many grass seeds (it is well seen on sweet vernal grass) and on storksbills. This long spike becomes spirally twisted when dry and if rewetted uncoils. The fruit naturally lands with the awn pointing up, since the fruit is heavier than the awn. Once wetted, the awn begins to uncoil and quite literally screws the fruit deeper into the soil.

The seed of common storksbill falls onto the soil and screws itself in.

181

SEEDLINGS: TYPES AND FORMS

The seedling is almost as vulnerable as was the seed itself. Vast numbers of seedlings die of drought, shading, grazing or fungal infection, for at this stage the infant plant has developed few of the defences it will possess later in life.

Depending on whether germination is epigeal or hypogeal, the visible part of a seedling consists either of the cotyledons (one, two or, in the case of some gymnosperms, several) or of the first true leaves. The young leaves are usually recognisably similar to the older leaves and so the seedlings of hypogeal germinators can often be identified from that resemblance. Cotyledons, however, are almost invariably very different from true leaves.

First, they are almost always un-divided. Common storksbill, large-leaved lime and field pepperwort are three exceptions to this general rule – all have divided cotyledons. It is usually true, even for mature leaves, that plants with divided leaves tend to have the most divided ones at the top of the stem, for this shape helps them lose heat when in full sun (see p. 208). The generally undivided nature of cotyledons may therefore be a reflection of the fact that they are invariably at ground level and that overheating is not usually a problem;

Left: *A mature small nettle: even at this stage the cotyledons may still be alive and green.*

Right: *A marsh valerian plant, showing the divided upper leaves and the entire lower leaves.*

Below: *A marsh valerian seedling.*

in other words there has been no pressure through natural selection for divided cotyledons to evolve.

Despite this, several seedlings with epigeal cotyledons can be identified to the species level. The seedlings of beech with their almost semi-circular cotyledons are very distinctive as are those of Scots pine, with up to a dozen thin, needle-like cotyledons.

Most cotyledons are short-lived, withering away shortly after the true leaves are formed. Exceptions occur, paradoxically, among both the slowest and fastest growing plants. Very fast-growing weeds such as common fumitory and annual nettle may retain green cotyledons right up to the time of fruiting, if conditions are good enough for very rapid growth. At the other extreme are perennials which form underground storage organs, in which often the only above-ground structures in the first year are the cotyledons: they make food by photo-synthesis but instead of using this to make more leaves the plant sends it all to create the tuber below ground. The plant's survival will depend more on the size and vitality of this tuber than on the size of the shoot, which in any case will die back in the winter. This strategy is best seen in pignut and several other umbellifers (carrot family), as well as in a number of members of the buttercup family, particularly winter aconite.

After the seed of pignut has germinated, a weak little plant grows up, but most resources are used to form a tuber; when winter comes the young plant collapses and the tuber is dormant; in the second summer the plant reaches maturity, and flowers.

seedling   *first summer*   *first winter*   *second summer*

183

STEMS

ANATOMY OF STEMS

Green plants have the unique problem that they obtain their nutrition in two quite different places, yet are unable to move from one to the other. They must therefore somehow link the roots in the soil with the leaves above ground. This involves a sophisticated plumbing system, and all stems contain both a set of pipes which transport water and minerals from roots to leaves (the xylem) and another (the phloem) which moves the sugars made by the leaves to the growing points.

Stems, however, are more than just pipelines. In a real sense they determine the entire form of the plant. The position of the leaves on the stem is crucial to their ability to fix the energy in sunlight into sugar, and a major function of the stem can be seen as placing the leaves in suitable positions. This may be achieved in various ways – by creeping along the ground, by climbing up other plants, or simply by being tall – but always involves mechanical strength appropriate to the task. That in turn determines the anatomy of the stems.

Both the morphology and anatomy of a plant stem reflect these two dominant functions: transport and placement of leaves. Stems may be round, flat, square or ridged in cross-section and all of these shapes have particular advantages. Internally, however, rather more uniformity is found.

A young dicot stem typically has a central pith of large but simple cells surrounded by a ring of bundles of thick-walled cells: these contain the transport cells, the xylem and phloem. The xylem is composed of dead cells, now just empty tubes, up to several centimetres long and linked together by special valves; they contain water which is pulled up from the roots by the evaporation of water from the leaves. They are surrounded by other.

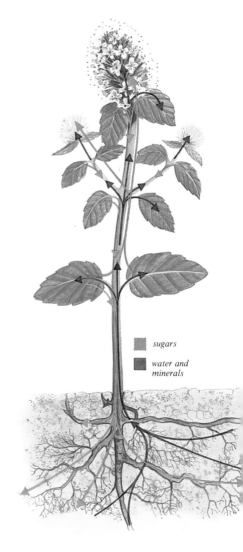

sugars

water and minerals

A whole plant of water-mint, showing the directions of the transport of substances between roots, leaves, and growing point

living cells which also have thickened walls. Outside the xylem in each bundle is found the phloem tissue, also comprising long thin transport cells, but this time living; they move sugars and other materials manufactured in the leaves to the roots, the young developing leaves and the flowers and fruits. How they do it is as yet unknown, but they can achieve remarkable feats, including moving sugars both up and down the stem.

Moving outwards, beyond this vascular tissue, we cross the cortex, which resembles the pith in being composed of simple, thin-walled cells, and finally reach the outer layer (the epidermis) which may take on many forms.

This description would apply to most dicot stems: monocots differ in having the bundles scattered through the pith, and the cortex usually much reduced.

There are many variations possible upon this basic design, however. Between xylem and phloem is found the area of dividing cells, known as the cambium. In annual stems, this serves simply to provide new transport tissue within the bundle, but in perennial stems of dicots, where xylem and phloem come to ring the pith, this cambium may go on dividing and producing new transport cells for many years, but of course only during the growth season, thereby producing annual rings. To survive, such a stem must be tough, and all long-lived stems become woody, by the thickening of the walls of cells, which soon die, so that the bulk of a tree-trunk, for example, is dead tissue.

Monocots, on the other hand, have isolated bundles, not a ring, and so cannot so easily produce the continual outward growth of the woody dicots. As a result, growth in girth is difficult for them; since growth in height requires an associated growth in girth, for simple engineering reasons, this means there are few monocots which can produce tall stems. Since the main point in having a stem which persists from year to year is to provide a springboard for new growth in height the following year, which keeps the leaves well exposed to the sun, it is not surprising that few monocots have perennial stems; only butcher's broom is woody among our monocots, though planted palms and yuccas are woody too.

These plants, however, produce their 'wood' by a quite different method. In all shoots, growth in length occurs only in a short region behind the tip; the older stems may increase in girth, but they do not expand otherwise. In woody dicots, elongation occurs at the tip and thickening further back, producing more tapering forms; in monocots, such as palms, the growth in length and width takes place simultaneously at the tip and so the old part does not alter, resulting in a cylindrical trunk.

Cross-section and vertical section of typical young, herbaceous stems, showing structure and anatomy

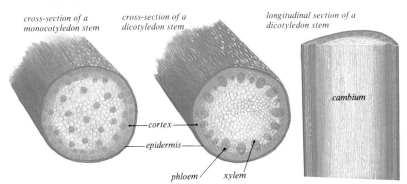

cross-section of a monocotyledon stem

cross-section of a dicotyledon stem

longitudinal section of a dicotyledon stem

cambium

cortex

epidermis

phloem

xylem

185

STEMS: STRENGTH

Inside a plant stem, some of the cells are concerned with transport (the xylem and phloem, see p. 184); those on the outside (epidermis) may have a defensive role against grazing animals and parasites, but most of them are structural. If a young seedling of hogweed is deprived of water it soon wilts and falls over; if a large flowering hogweed is similarly droughted it too will die, but it will remain standing. Indeed dead hogweed stems stand right through the winter. Clearly the mature plant has a different method of support from the seedling, which in fact relies entirely on water pressure or turgor.

Most small herbaceous plants, and all seedlings, have almost no strength other than this. They stay upright because the cell sap is much more concentrated than pure water, so that they take up water by osmosis, and this water pushes against the rigid cell walls, giving turgor strength. The thin-walled cells of pith and cortex all push against each other in this way and the whole structure is retained by the stiff epidermis. Cut a dandelion flower-stalk into a strip and it will curl up because of this considerable tension.

The next stage in strengthening is the presence of cells with thick walls, both the transport vessels (p. 185) as they mature, and special tissues called collenchyma and sclerenchyma. Collenchyma are thick-walled living cells able to resist greater turgor pressure and to provide additional support, particularly in young growing tissue; sclerenchyma, on the

Hogweed in summer and winter: the strength of the stems derives from dead tissue, and so they stand long after the above-ground parts have died.

186

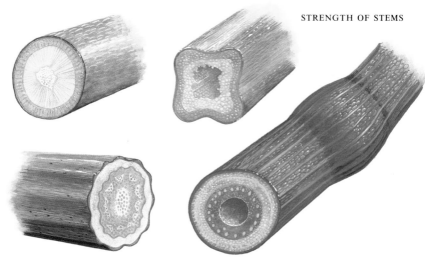

Elevations and cross-sections of stems of various types: a structural engineer would recognise many of these.

other hand, is composed of dead, woody fibres, and is associated with the bundles and often found in strands elsewhere in the stem. Taller annual stems, such as those of many composites (daisy family) and umbellifers (carrot family), contain many such cells and so remain upright even when dead. Finally the tissue may become woody (see p. 185) and develop sufficient strength to persist for hundreds of years.

A great part of the strength of many plant stems comes, however, not from the internal building materials, but from the way in which they are arranged. Engineers know well that the strongest structures are not solid rods: they suffer too readily from fractures. Rather they build with beams that are T-shaped or H-shaped in cross-section, and hollow structures are often the most resistant to stress. The typical stem structure is of a ring of strengthened tissue surrounding a soft central pith; in contrast, roots have the bundles grouped in a central strand, giving greater flexibility to an organ that need not support a load but must be flexible and able to thread its way through soil, like electric flex.

Although the commonest type of stem is round and smooth, there are many which are square or ridged. These tend to be found in particular families – labiates (dead-nettles, hemp-nettles, bugle, mints) and bedstraws always have square stems, while those of many umbellifers (hogweed, cow parsley, angelica) are ridged and hollow. The square stems have massive strengthening by sclerenchyma at the corners of the stem, while the ridges of umbellifers are largely collenchyma, a more elastic tissue, at least in the early stages.

Many cylindrical stems are hollow, for example those of many umbellifers and rushes, and have as much strength as a solid tube for a smaller investment of material, while at the same time gaining in being less brittle and so less liable to fracture when bent. Even greater strength is obtained by having joints at intervals along the stem, as is found in most grasses. It is interesting that plant breeders have recently developed special short-stemmed cereals (cereals are of course all grasses) to avoid the problem of long stems collapsing. The cultivated cereals had been bred for their grain yield and the load was too great for the strength of the stem in the older varieties.

187

HEIGHTS AND SIZES OF STEMS

The tallest plants obviously are trees: in their native forests some Douglas firs, sequoias and eucalyptus can exceed 100 m and even in Britain Douglas fir and Sitka spruce approach 60 m. This book covers only herbaceous plants and dwarf shrubs, in which either the stem dies back each year or else puts on only a small increment. Shrubs never have the dominant, upward-thrusting main stem of trees, their energies being dissipated in complex branching systems.

Many herbaceous plants do have a dominant main shoot and some can exceed 3 m in a single season's growth. Probably the tallest of these is the introduced giant hogweed, which can sometimes touch 5 m. Common reed too can be very tall in favourable conditions. Unlike tree-trunks, which grow by continually adding new tissue at the tip and by secondary growth in girth, leading to a tapering shape, these herbaceous stems are much more nearly cylindrical. The tapering column of a tree-trunk provides a degree of strength necessary for a perennial stem but not required for a herbaceous one. Nevertheless, the thickest stems are usually the tallest ones (though one of the thickest is probably that of Himalayan balsam, which rarely exceeds 2 m in height).

At the other extreme, the smallest plants may be a mere centimetre or so high. Chaffweed and allseed rarely reach as much as 5 cm and are normally about 2 cm high. Both grow in bare, damp places on very infertile soils and their minuteness is no disadvantage there. In fact in such habitats many plants never reach their

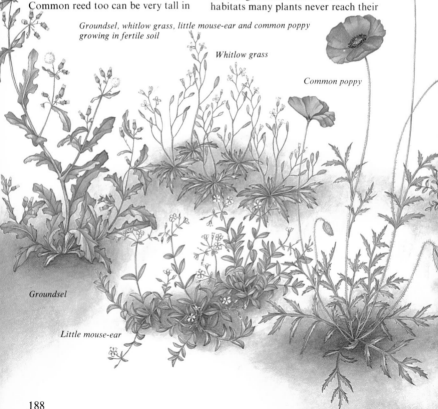

Groundsel, whitlow grass, little mouse-ear and common poppy growing in fertile soil

Whitlow grass

Common poppy

Groundsel

Little mouse-ear

188

full size. On all types of infertile soils, tiny flowering plants can be seen – groundsel in cracks in pavements, common whitlow-grass and little mouse-ear on dry sand dunes, shepherd's purse on walls. In other places, on richer, moister soils the same plants may be ten times the size and bear hundreds of times as many flowers. This ability of plants to grow to different sizes, their plasticity, is one of the most fundamental differences between plants and animals. Animals have determinate growth: they generally stop growing once their full adult size (and shape) is reached. For plants growth is much more open-ended and they can respond to stressful environments by dwarfness and to more favourable ones by greater growth.

There is an obvious advantage to a plant in most situations in being larger than its neighbours: it can intercept sunlight and shade out potential competitors. There is therefore great selection pressure to be as tall as possible. Equally there are balancing disadvantages. Tall plants must produce more stem and this may take time; if the growing season is short, or nutrients and water scarce, this may not be possible. Tall plants are more conspicuous and may be eaten more readily by grazing animals; and they are more likely to be damaged by wind.

The actual size reached by a plant is therefore a trade-off between these advantages and disadvantages. It has been reached because the evolutionary history of each species limits the environments it can grow in: shepherd's purse could never achieve a height of 2 m, and so cannot compete with really tall plants.

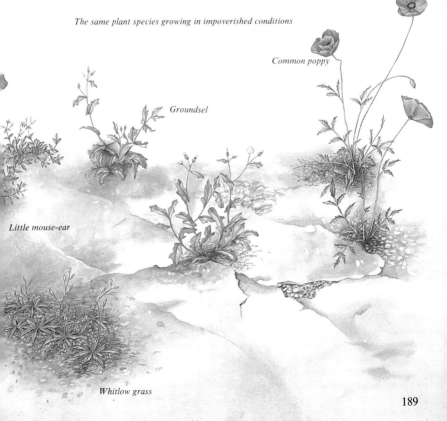

The same plant species growing in impoverished conditions

Common poppy

Groundsel

Little mouse-ear

Whitlow grass

STEMS: LIFE-FORMS

Naturalists often impress others by their ability to recognise plants and animals from afar, by their general form and behaviour, their 'jizz'. The jizz of a plant depends to a great extent on its branching pattern or architecture. The form of a daisy, with its flat rosette of leaves surrounding leafless, upright stems supporting flowerheads, is very different from that of groundsel, all of whose leaves are distributed along the same branching stems as its flowers; yet both belong to the same family, the Compositae. The differences in form conceal their evolutionary closeness but reflect the ecological pressures of the different life-styles they have adopted.

Whatever the habitat and life-style of a plant, in most environments they must withstand an unfavourable season. For most plants in our climate that is winter; elsewhere it may be a dry season. In winter, most plants cease activity and produce resting buds or seeds: the position of these buds gives great insight into the ecology of a plant. This was first recognised by the great Danish botanist Raunkiaer, nearly 100 years ago, and formed the basis of his classification of 'life-forms'.

Raunkiaer recognised seven main categories – annuals which overwinter as seeds, marsh plants, water plants, and four types of truly terrestrial perennial: phanerophytes, with buds

more than 25 cm off the ground; chamaephytes with buds less than 25 cm off the ground; hemicryptophytes with buds at ground level; and geophytes with buds underground.

Phanerophytes are trees and shrubs. They may be evergreen or deciduous, but since the stems are perennial, new growth is added each year. If this new growth comes from the continual development of a main bud, the result is a tree; but if the main shoot either grows very slowly or even dies, so that branches develop more extensively, then a shrub is formed. The more branching, the more shrubby the plant will come to seem. Leaves and flowers grow from the same stems year after year; so such plants constantly produce new branches which can bear the buds for these and for still further branches. Woody plants like this can be thought of as a colony of branches, each with its leaves and flowers, and each producing new branches.

There is no clear distinction between the smallest phanerophytes and the largest chamaephytes: dwarf shrubs such as heather and bilberry could count as either, depending on the size of the individual plant.

Left to right: River water crowfoot (a water plant); Celery-leaved buttercup (an annual which overwinters as seed); Marsh marigold (a marsh plant); Meadow buttercup (a hemicryptophyte); Wood anemone (a geophyte); Stinking hellebore (a chamaephyte); Old man's beard (a phanerophyte). The whole range of life-forms is shown here within a single taxonomic family (buttercups).

Some chamaephytes have stolons (creeping stems which run along the ground, as in yellow archangel), or simple overwintering, but low stems as in field mouse-ear, or even woody stem-bases, as in rock sea spurrey. In spring, these give rise to leafy shoots which have flowers either at their tips (as in the sea spurreys) or in between leaves and stem. These shoots live just one year, but may be extensively branched.

Hemicryptophytes typically over-winter as a rosette of leaves with the bud in the centre, which elongates rapidly in spring to form a flower-spike, sometimes leafy (bugle) and sometimes quite leafless (ribwort plantain). In some cases the over-wintering leaves are not arranged in a neat rosette, but always the general plan is similar: the leaves tend to be at the bottom and the flowers at the top, and the stem serves mainly to bear flowers, and always dies off in winter. Biennials tend to be hemi-cryptophytes, in which case they form a rosette in their first year, over-winter like that, and flower and die in the second. Obviously hemicrypto-phytes do best in short vegetation, particularly where it is grazed, when their flat rosettes are less likely to be eaten by large grazing animals than more upright shoots.

Geophytes survive the winter underground, in the form of a bulb, corm, tuber, rhizome or other storage organ. Their above-ground parts tend to be simple, often just a rosette of leaves and a central flower-stalk, as in hemicryptophytes. Spotted orchids look like rosette plants in summer, but the difference is that they dis-appear entirely in winter. Sometimes leaf and flower production are separa-ted: the leaves may be produced in spring and the flowers in autumn (autumn crocus), or the flowers followed by the leaves in spring (coltsfoot and butterbur). This enables them to exploit the best times for growing and flowering separately if these times are different.

The life-forms of plants reflect their habitats. Phanerophytes and chamaephytes are the dominant plants of favourable sites, where survival in winter is possible (either because of the climate or the lack of grazing); hemicryptophytes are particularly well suited to more open sites, often because of grazing. Geophytes, growing from stores underground, have the flexibility to grow rapidly at often difficult times of the year: almost all the early spring plants of the woodland and ground flora, which must develop very early in the year, are geophytes.

CLIMBING STEMS: SCRAMBLERS AND TWINERS

The form of a plant reflects its habitat in its resistance to winter conditions and its ability to compete with its neighbours for light. Where the second of these two considerations is dominant, plants with strongly upward-growing, dominant main shoots are found – trees and tall herbaceous plants. In these plants branching is reduced to a minimum, and growth in height, which enables them to overtop neighbours, is maximised.

Such a growth form is expensive, in that it involves the construction of a massive main stem. A very large number of plants cheat the system by using their neighbours as supports and climbing up them with stems that would be too weak to stand up by themselves. These climbers are not parasites in the sense that dodders (p. 220) are, for usually the supporting plant suffers little.

The least specialised method of climbing is by weaving leaves and stems in and out of other plants. At its simplest this can be achieved by rigidly horizontal leaves. In marsh speedwell and water chickweed the leaves are initially vertical and so can be pushed through gaps in the foliage of other plants; later they are held horizontally and so anchor the rather weak stem in position. Such an approach is greatly improved if the leaves and stems are lined with tiny, downward pointing prickles. Goose-grass, or common cleavers, is perhaps the best example of this; though a weak, sprawling annual it can totally smother the surrounding vegetation by late summer, clinging on with myriad tiny barbs.

Many longer-lived sprawling and scrambling species also have prickles: those on bramble and dog rose certainly have a protective role against animals (p. 298), but also serve to anchor the long arching stems in the tangled scrub they grow in. Again we see that natural selection produces characteristics that improve

Goose-grass

The normal technique for a dog rose is to scramble up the tangled scrub in which it grows, using its thorns as hooks; deprived of any support, it will arch over and sprawl.

the plant's overall fitness, not those that do one particular job best.

Other plants climb by twining round existing stems. Some, such as honeysuckle and bittersweet, are woody and persist from year to year; but most are either annual (black bindweed) or have annual stems from a perennial rootstock (hop, hedge bindweed). Honeysuckle grips stems with great strength; sometimes leaving scars where it has restricted the outward expansion of its support; it must of course itself be strong and elastic enough to resist this pressure which would otherwise tear its own stems. Honeysuckle is an anti-clockwise climber, as are most climbers, including hop and black bindweed. The unrelated, and much more attractive hedge bindweed for some reason climbs clockwise. There seems to be no conceivable way in which the direction of twining could affect the plant's fitness; so this difference must be due to a chance of ancestry.

Some of these twiners, like the scramblers, assist their upward march by hooks: those on the stems of hop are the most unusual for they are shaped like tiny ice-axes. Others simply rely on the rapidity and tightness with which they coil round stems As their tips grow upwards they continually wave in a circular motion in fact the growing tips of many non-climbing plants do this too, and there it can be seen as a method of sensing the direction of the best illuminated patches of the habitat. For the climbers, this waving acts to locate supporting stems. Once contact is made, the complete coil may take as little as two hours to form. If no contact is made, the climbing shoot may fall to the ground, but the tip then turns up again, now some distance from the original site, and resumes the search.

Other methods of climbing exist: ivy climbs by forming roots on the stems, Virginia creeper by small suckers, and many plants by means of twining tendrils (see p. 194).

Black bindweed

Hedge bindweed

Ivy

CLIMBING STEMS: TENDRILS

The most sophisticated climbing machinery used by plants is the tendril, a long, slender feeler that grows out from the stem or leaf and curls round supports. Climbing by tendrils is the commonest method found.

Tendrils are not always special structures with no other function. One of the most conspicuous climbers, at least on chalk and limestone soils in the south, is old man's beard or traveller's joy, our only native *Clematis*. It has woody stems and can climb as high as the tree to which it has attached itself will reach, each year keeping pace with the new growth. It achieves this entirely by using its leaf-stalks as tendrils, wrapping them around twigs and branches. But, being a deciduous, perennial climber, it encounters a problem in the winter: the leaves fall off (though the twisted stalks may persist for a while) and, therefore, so does its support. Traveller's joy relies then on the entanglement of its stems to keep it in position. In other words it uses the leaf-stalks as tendrils to do the actual climbing, but its stems for long-term support.

Old man's beard in summer and winter

Other climbers use parts of the leaf itself as tendrils. Climbing corydalis is a delicate annual, unusual in being one of the few annuals to grow in woods, where the low levels of light available normally prevent the fast rates of growth essential for the rapid completion of the annual life-cycle. Climbing corydalis gets round this problem by climbing over the existing woodland-floor plants and in this way maximises the amount of light it receives, without the expense of having to build a strong supporting stem. Its tendrils are formed from some of the leaflets at the tips of its feathery, pinnate leaves.

Climbing corydalis

Similar tendrils are found on the tips of the pinnate leaves of vetches and vetchlings, which form the largest group of herbaceous climbers in our flora. Vetches have simple round stems and usually large numbers of leaflets on each leaf, whereas vetchlings have winged stems and usually fewer leaflets; but ecologically they behave similarly. In most, what would have been the last pairs of leaflets develop into tendrils, which are therefore branched; but in some, such as slender tare, it is only the single end leaflet or its projecting midrib which forms an unbranched tendril.

Most vetches and vetchlings grow in tall grassland, fens and wood margins, using their tendrils to gain a well-illuminated position, but in a few, such as bitter vetchling, the tendrils are rather rudimentary, and it favours rather shorter vegetation; paradoxically in sea pea, which grows on almost bare shingle and has no opportunity for climbing, they are very prominent.

The tendrils of traveller's joy, climbing corydalis and the vetches and vetchlings form coils at any point along their length. In contrast, those of some other climbers are sensitive only at the tip, which continuously revolves, much like the tips of the

White bryony

stems of twining plants (see p. 192). The tendril revolutions are usually faster, however, sometimes as much as two revolutions per hour, and the speed of reaction of the tip once it contacts a support can be dramatic, often completing a coil in a matter of minutes.

The best example of such a climber is white bryony, a relative of cucumbers and gourds, which has long, unbranched tendrils arising directly from the stem, in contrast to the completely unrelated black bryony (our only member of the yam family), which has twining stems. Because of the continuous rotation of their tips, the tendrils of white bryony come to look like coiled springs, and when in contact with their supports, act in this way, giving the plant an immensely resilient strength in response to wind and other disturbances.

Slender tare

Sea pea

195

LEAVES

THE NATURE AND FUNCTION OF LEAVES

'Leaf' is one of those wonderfully useful terms that is at once instantly understood by all and yet almost impossible of definition. Leaves vary hugely in form and size and even in function. The scale-leaves on saprophytic plants (p. 230) are recognisably leaves, but contain no chlorophyll; so they cannot photosynthesise. In contrast, the green stems of broom are quite definitely not leaves, but they do contain chlorophyll, and carry out most of the plant's photosynthesis.

All plants seem to have leaves of some sort: even parasitic plants such as dodders (p. 220), which obtain their food ready-synthesised, have rudimentary scales that can be regarded as leaves, at least in terms of their evolutionary history. Most plants, however, have recognisable organs which are borne on stems and carry out most of the synthesis of sugars from air, water and light – in other words, photosynthesis.

Photosynthesis is the fundamental plant activity. Those plants that do not photosynthesise – parasites and saprophytes – can clearly be seen to have evolved from ancestors that did. In photosynthesis plants combine carbon dioxide (which is present in minute amounts in the air, around 300 parts of carbon dioxide per million of air) with water to make sugars, using the energy of sunlight. The later release of this energy, in the metabolism of plants and animals, makes all life possible.

The problem that the photosynthesising leaf has to solve is that it must allow the access of air to the inside of the leaf where photosynthesis takes place, without letting the leaf dry out. Unfortunately water vapour moves much faster out of the leaf than carbon dioxide moves in. This has necessitated two things: first a continuous supply of water from the

A leaf showing the general directions of the movement of carbon dioxide and water

water

carbon dioxide

roots in soil (normally a moderately wet environment), and secondly a control system to stop the escape of water when it is in short supply.

The control system which all higher plants possess consists of a series of pairs of cells, set in the outer layer of the leaf, which can change their shape so as to open or close a pore between them. This pore leads into a hollow chamber within the leaf, surrounded by the cells which actually do the work of photosynthesis. These pores or stomata therefore act as valves; the outer layer of cells of the leaf (the epidermis) is otherwise covered with a waxy cuticle which is quite impermeable to water vapour and to gases. When the stomata shut, no movement into or out of the leaf occurs; if they are open, the gases of the air can move in (including the vital carbon dioxide), and water vapour can move out.

The stomata are numerous and, though invisible to the naked eye, can easily be seen through a hand-lens. A square centimetre of the underside of an oak leaf may have 35,000 of them; clearly they are very small – typically each pore is around a hundredth of a millimetre long and about a third of that across. Taken all together, the open pores may make up around 2 to 3% of the total area of the leaf, but usually less than 1%.

Plants differ greatly in both the shape of their stomata (rounded, oblong or almost linear) and also in their distribution on the leaf's surface. Generally they are most numerous on the underside, protected from direct insolation which would speed the loss of water without increasing the rate of absorption of carbon dioxide.

Stomata: above *almost closed;* below *fully open*

Often the upper surface of the leaf has an obviously thick cuticle, as in the shiny leaves of ivy, which have no stomata at all there; in others there are topside stomata, but not as many as on the underside. Some plants have stomata on the topside only, but these are the exceptions. White water-lily is one such, and the explanation is simple: its leaves float on the water surface and no gas exchange could take place through the lower surface. Other water plants, such as water-plantains, which grow in water but have aerial leaves, have as many or more stomata under their leaves as on top. Since they often hold their leaves erect, there is no functional distinction between the two sides.

White water-lily

Water-plantain

THE SIZE AND SHAPE OF LEAVES

The loss of water from leaves is not just an unavoidable consequence of the need to obtain carbon dioxide from the air, as is often thought. The evaporation of water from any surface acts as a coolant, which is the principle behind the sweating of mammals. One of the problems faced by a leaf is that in exposing itself to sunlight for photosynthesis, it runs a risk of overheating. Unlike mobile animals, leaves cannot move efficiently into and out of sunlight to control their temperature (in the way, for example, that many desert animals are nocturnal), though they do have some ability to alter their position, which can help (see p. 200).

Transpiration of water is of enormous importance in cooling well-illuminated leaves. One of the earliest of all experimental scientists, Stephen Hales, published in 1727 his 'Vegetable Staticks' in which he showed that a cabbage leaf lost water at a rate of over 3 cubic centimetres for every square centimetre of leaf surface each hour; such rates can lead a large tree to lose as much as 500 litres in a day. When water supply is unlimited such rates are very effective in keeping leaves cool.

Sometimes, however, a leaf may not be able to obtain water so easily – if the soil is drying, for example – and then it will start to heat up. Leaves can only withstand a limited range of temperature, and in such circumstances another cooling mechanism becomes important. If a leaf is hotter than the surrounding air, it will lose heat by convection, just as a convection heater or a radiator warms the air in a room.

But the air around a leaf tends not to move away readily; it forms what is known as a boundary layer. This layer becomes warmed by convection and the difference in temperature between leaf and air is then less: and again cooling is slowed down. A wind will help to disperse this boundary layer.

The size and shape of a leaf determine how big the boundary layer is in the first instance. The layer is thinnest near the edge of a leaf and thickest in the centre. Large, undissected leaves therefore have very thick boundary layers and lose heat poorly by convection. Small leaves lose heat quickly in comparison and so do dissected leaves, in which no part is far from the edge. Knowing this we can understand much of variation in leaf size and shape.

Large, undissected leaves are normally found in plants that grow in wet places, like water-lilies, butterbur

Woodland plants

Water and waterside plants

Wood anemone

Butterbur

Primrose

Arrowhead

White water-lily

and arrowhead, and so have a continuous supply of water. (The very dissected leaves of plants that grow *in* water are responding to a quite different problem – see p. 202). Woodland plants, too, tend to have undissected leaves (primrose, common wintergreen, touch-me-not balsam, sweet violet), for they grow in shade where overheating is not a problem.

Plants of dry, sunny places are quite different: they have finely dissected leaves, sometimes reduced to spines. A good example is buck's-horn plantain, the only plantain to have dissected leaves, which grows in dry, sandy places. And those cranesbill species that grow in dry places, such as bloody and cut-leaved cranesbills, have more dissected leaves than those in shady places like shining and hedgerow cranesbills.

The same phenomenon can be seen on a small scale along the stem of many plants. Upper leaves are more likely to overheat than lower leaves, which are shaded by the upper. Musk mallow has very dissected leaves at the top of the stem, and they become progressively less dissected downwards. It is no coincidence that nearly all cotyledons (seed-leaves, see p. 182) are undivided: they rarely experience overheating and there has been no pressure for divided cotyledons to evolve.

Musk mallow: the leaves become progressively more deeply cut up the stem

Plants of dry places

Bloody cranesbill

Sweet violet

Buck's-horn plantain

Shining cranesbill

Cut-leaved cranesbill

LEAVES: ORIENTATION

Although plants themselves cannot move so as to position themselves in better parts of their habitat – seeds and floating plants move at random and most plants are rooted – their leaves do have a power of movement. During the course of growth, they can alter direction in relation to sources of light and the earth's gravity, so achieving the complex leaf mosaics of many plants (p. 210). But even after growth has ceased they can still show reversible movements.

The most dramatic such movements are shown by carnivorous plants such as Venus fly-trap, a north American species, whose leaves close on trapped insects in a few seconds; but the more familiar sundews and butterworts also show rolling movements to engulf their prey (p. 232). Another exotic species to have sensitive leaves is the sensitive plant, whose leaves can 'collapse' in seconds if touched, possibly giving some defence against grazing animals. There are no species

in our flora with such an ability.

Nevertheless leaf movements are common and are of two main sorts – daytime and night-time responses. Several plants with compound leaves show 'sleep movements', and they are best seen in the trifoliate leaves of wood sorrel and white clover. Here the leaves fold downwards at night, because of an unequal change in the internal pressure on either side of the base of the leaf stalk; both species have the bulk of their stomata on the lower side of the leaf, and in this way they are protected at night against dew deposition, which would delay the onset of transpiration in the morning.

These and other plants also show leaf movements in the daytime in response to the sun. These may be either movements which better expose the leaf to solar radiation, so increasing photosynthesis, or those which minimise the area of the leaf struck by the sun's rays, so reducing overheating. The first case can often be observed in fast-growing plants such as birches, where the leaves hang

Time-lapse of the sleep movements of the leaves of white clover (*left*) *and wood sorrel*

day

night

day

night

down from the stem and face the sun.

Leaf movements which reduce over-heating are more striking, though. At their simplest they may be the equivalent of the sleep movements already mentioned: this folding collapse, just as surely as the wilting collapse that occurs when a leaf loses too much water, greatly reduces the illuminated surface. Prickly lettuce, however, has a more sophisticated system. It is a plant of dry, rather bare places where water supply is rarely plentiful. Its leaves are all held vertically in a north-south plane, so that they receive maximum illumination from the early morning and late evening sun, which has least power to heat (and when the air is cool so that convection is efficient at cooling the leaf). In the middle of the day, however, when the sun is high overhead, it scarcely strikes the leaves at all. This astonishing behaviour has earned it the alternative name of compass plant.

Other leaf movements may be as much concerned with saving water as avoiding overheating. Many grass leaves roll up under hot, dry conditions, particularly in species of rather dry habitats, such as blue moor-grass, which grows in dry calcareous grassland, and marram grass, which grows in sand dunes. Plants, then, may not have the power of movement from place to place, but careful observation will reveal that they are far from motionless. Leaves are not the only responsive parts of plants: tendrils constantly revolve, almost as if they were hunting for a support (p. 194), and flowers too often follow the sun. Sunflower gets its name from that propensity, as does daisy, which is a corruption of 'day's eye', and many of their relatives, including dandelions, are sun-trackers; Jerusalem artichoke, in the same genus as sunflower, has no connection with the city, but derives from 'girasolem' – turns with the sun. The role of sun-tracking by flowers in pollination is described on p. 259.

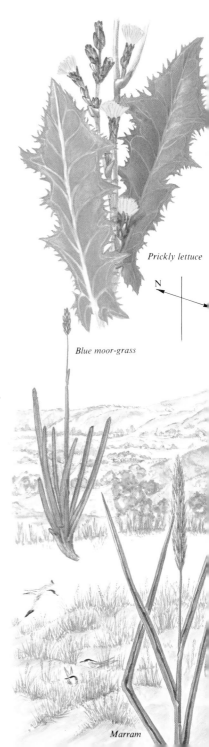

Prickly lettuce

N

Blue moor-grass

Marram

LEAVES OF AQUATIC PLANTS

One of the major evolutionary causes for the huge diversity in leaf shape and size is the relationship between habitat and the need for leaves to keep cool. The smallest and most dissected leaves tend to be found in hot, dry places where cooling by evaporation may not be possible, so that convection becomes more important. Paradoxically, similarly dissected leaves are found in plants living under water, where overheating cannot occur.

These leaves face quite a different problem. An aerial leaf obtains the carbon dioxide it needs for photosynthesis by opening its stomata so that the gas diffuses in. Because the carbon dioxide inside the leaf is continually being used up, it continues to move in. Water plants also obtain their carbon dioxide by diffusion, in their case the source being the rather small amount dissolved in the water. Unfortunately it diffuses 100,000 times more slowly in water than in air. The only solution to this is a great increase in the surface area of the leaf relative to its overall size.

Water-plant leaves are of two main types: long and thin, or feathery. Mare's-tail, Canadian pondweed, and many of the true pondweeds are examples of the first type, but perhaps the most striking is eel-grass, the only true marine flowering plant, whose ribbon-like leaves can be over 20 cm long. Other similar plants have even finer, almost needle-like leaves, as in small pondweed, fennel pondweed and slender naiad.

Such leaf-types show every gradation through the branching leaves of hornwort, into the pinnately branched leaves of spiked water milfoil and water violet. Perhaps the most dramatic development of featheriness in response to submergence is seen in the water crowfoots. In water, leaves of common water crowfoot can be seen to have complex branching patterns, not just in two planes as for most leaves, but in three, giving a structure in which a particular volume of water is efficiently exploited by the leaflets for a minimum volume of leaf. Out of the water the leaf collapses – for it is supported by the water itself – and then the structure cannot be seen. Most water crowfoots occur in still water and have short leaves, but river water crowfoot grows in fast-flowing rivers and its trailing leaves can be up to 30 cm long, on stems as much as 6 m long.

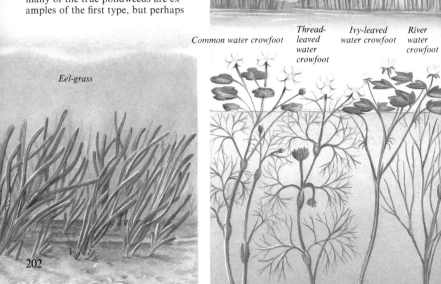

Eel-grass

Common water crowfoot

Thread-leaved water crowfoot

Ivy-leaved water crowfoot

River water crowfoot

The water crowfoots, and a few other water plants such as arrowhead, exhibit the phenomenon of heterophylly, which means having two or more different sorts of leaves on one plant. Common water crowfoot has feathery leaves which branch in two planes under water, but 'normal' oval, toothed floating leaves; arrowhead has ribbon-shaped leaves underwater, oval leaves floating on the surface, and arrow-shaped leaves above the water. All these leaf-types can be seen as adaptations to the particular problems encountered by leaves under water (slow diffusion), floating on the surface (wave movements and stresses) and in the air (maintaining safe temperatures). Not all water crowfoots show heterophylly, though: thread-leaved and river water crowfoots have no floating leaves, while ivy-leaved water crowfoot has no submerged leaves.

Many water plants have their submerged leaves finely divided and feathery: in water-crowfoots the floating leaves are of a different shape.

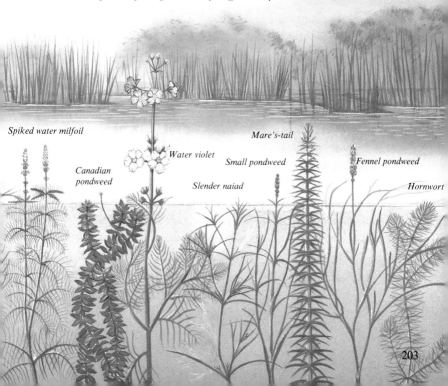

Spiked water milfoil

Mare's-tail

Water violet

Canadian pondweed

Small pondweed

Fennel pondweed

Slender naiad

Hornwort

203

SUCCULENT LEAVES

Some plants have leaves that are thick and fleshy. Unlike most plants, they do not transpire large amounts of water; rather they store it in the leaves and stems. Such plants are mainly found in two quite distinct environments: in dry places, such as the tops of walls or sandy beaches, and in wet, but salty, habitats, particularly saltmarshes. The key to this apparent paradox is the salt, for salty soils present some of the same problems to plants as do dry soils.

In dry soils, plants have difficulty in obtaining enough water simply because it isn't there. In salty soils the difficulty arises because of the effect of osmosis – the water in the plant tends to move out into the concentrated salty solution in the soil. The effect in each case is the same, that the plant has less water to expend on essential functions like cooling the leaves.

Rather, then, than cooling by evaporation they achieve lower temperatures by containing more water, not losing it. Water heats up much more slowly than solids, so the more water in the plants the more slowly they heat up (and equally the more slowly they cool down).

Inside a succulent leaf are large cells, bloated with water. It seems that they act as a temperature regulator for plants that otherwise have few methods of keeping cool.

Biting stonecrop and navelwort growing together on a wall

Cut-away of a succulent leaf showing all cells bloated

The classic succulents on dry soils are cacti. We have no native cacti, though prickly pears are common in southern Europe; but there is a group of closely related plants, mostly in the stonecrop family, which grow in very dry places and have fleshy leaves. The stonecrops themselves – whose name derives from the fact that they can grow literally on bare rock or stone – and their relatives such as hen-and-chickens houseleek and navelwort, all have succulent leaves and nearly all grow in dry places. Such taxonomic affinity is not shown by the succulents of salty soils, which occur in a wide range of families (see illustration).

Nobody is quite sure what is the underlying reason for plants of salty habitats having succulent leaves, but it seems simplest to assume that it is the same reason as on dry soils, namely that water is too hard to obtain to be used profligately, so it is stored.

Some of these plants suffer both dryness and saltiness of the soil, particularly prickly saltwort, sea sandwort, sea spurge and sea bindweed, all of which grow on sand by the sea; and oyster plant grows on shingle, an even drier habitat.

Succulence as a response to salt has evolved frequently and in widely separated families, whereas succulence as a response to dry conditions has evolved only a few times, and has spread within a few families. Why this difference should be is not clear, but certainly all these plants will suffer from one problem acutely: they grow in full sunshine – on rocks or by the sea – and so must avoid overheating.

These plants come from many families and grow on various types of seaside habitat; but they all grow on soils enriched with salt.

On shingle in the foreground is oyster plant (borage family). On sand are sea spurge (spurge family), buck's-horn plantain (plantain family), sea sandwort (pink family), sea bindweed (bindweed family) and prickly saltwort (goosefoot family). In the wet saltmarsh grow scurvy-grass (cabbage family), glasswort (goosefoot family) and sea milkwort (primrose family).

205

In a dense stand of rosebay willowherb the lower leaves are already dying as the plants come into flower.

A community of bluebells has green leaves in March, flowers in May, and the leaves are already dead by July.

EVERGREEN AND DECIDUOUS LEAVES

It is a common misconception that plants can be pigeon-holed neatly into evergreen and deciduous categories. Among trees that distinction is reasonably clear – most trees keep their leaves either for one growing season or for more than one. Herbaceous and shrubby plants, however, show much greater variation: the important thing to consider is how long individual leaves last.

Herbaceous plants die down in the winter, so that they are in a sense deciduous; but even so many retain green leaves throughout the winter. Some simply keep their previous summer's leaves; others produce a fresh crop of leaves in the autumn. In both cases, such leaves usually die off in spring when new leaves are produced.

The shortest-lived leaves are found on the fastest-growing plants, some of which are themselves short-lived. Many perennials produce tall flowering shoots each year, as in rosebay willowherb, and their lower leaves, soon over-shadowed by those above, die back quite early. For most plants, though, the leaves produced in the spring flush survive until the autumn. Some then die back totally, so that nothing remains above ground: bluebell leaves, for example, first spring from the underground bulb in February or March, form a dense clump in April and May when the trees above are still more or less leafless, and are all dead by July.

Other plants have a continuous production of leaves. Foxglove is a biennial that germinates in one year, grows steadily to produce a rosette of leaves that survive the winter, and then flowers the following summer. Its earliest leaves are already dead by the first autumn, but the later ones survive much longer. In contrast, broad-leaved willowherb, which is a perennial, develops a new rosette of leaves at the end of the summer, which overwinters, and then flowers the following summer. The leaves on the flower-stalk are summer leaves, those in the rosette winter leaves.

The longest-lived leaves are, of course, found on woody stems. Some shrubs such as dog rose are deciduous and have synchronised leaf growth in spring, and leaf-fall in autumn; others, particularly heathers, have much longer-lived leaves, which may survive several years on the stem. The link between leaf life-span and speed of plant growth is manifest here, for heathers are slow-growing plants of poor soils. Indeed, there is a general trend for plants growing in poor conditions to have evergreen leaves.

At first sight, it may seem wasteful for a plant to shed its leaves, but in fact it may be advantageous, even essential. As leaves age they become less efficient, they suffer attacks from insects and parasites, and they may become shaded by new growth above. Where this is so, the plant profits most if it withdraws scarce nutrients from the leaf and uses them to build a new leaf, better placed and more efficient. This only makes sense if the leaf has already repaid the investment the plant has made in it by providing more food than was used to build it in the first place. If conditions are poor (infertile soil, low temperatures) this will take longer, and so the leaf must survive longer. Unfortunately, the longer a leaf is around, the more likely it is to have to cope with extreme conditions (frosts, for example) and the attentions of herbivores; so such long-lived leaves may be leathery and needle-like, as in heather. This, alas, is a vicious circle, for the more like this a leaf is, the less efficient at photosynthesis it will be, and so the longer it must survive to make a net profit.

Leaves, therefore, obey simple laws of economics, and their life-spans and structures are at least partly determined by those laws.

A foxglove produces new leaves continuously throughout its biennial life-cycle.

LEAVES: SHADE DETECTION, AVOIDANCE AND SURVIVAL

Most plants grow among other plants and compete with them for light. There is always an advantage to any plant in being taller than its neighbours, so that it receives more light than them. But it follows from this that some leaves must find themselves in shade, either because the leaves of another plant are above them, or equally possibly because other leaves higher up the same stem are shading them.

To see how true this is, one can measure the area of leaves in a plant community, for example by averaging the number of leaves above any point on the ground. In grasslands this is commonly 4 or 5, but can be as high

as 10 or 12. In an oak woodland, the oak trees themselves may have 2–4 layers, the hazel shrubs underneath 1–2, and the dog's mercury carpeting the woodland floor, 3–4. Yet underneath that there are still mosses and liverworts receiving enough light to survive. Most leaves, even of plants that typically grow exposed and form the top of a leaf canopy, so-called 'sun plants', grow at least partly in the shade of other leaves.

There are a number of possible responses for a shaded leaf. The lower, shaded leaves of sun plants usually die (see p. 198); the food and mineral reserves are then withdrawn from them and shipped up to the growing point where they can build new leaves, better placed to capture sunlight. If a plant is to adopt this strategy, it is essential that its growing

Cross-section of an oak wood, showing that the mosses and liverworts on the woodland floor are shaded by perhaps three layers of dog's-mercury leaves, two layers of hazel leaves, and three layers of oak leaves.

point is always well placed; it must be able to tell the difference between being in shade and just being in dim light (which could after all result from a succession of overcast days).

Most leaves are green, because the chlorophyll which captures sunlight in leaves absorbs blue and red light much more than green. But if we could see infra-red light, leaves would not look green. They would look infra-red (whatever that might look like) because chlorophyll does not absorb infra-red at all: it is all reflected, or passes straight through. This is why infra-red satellite photography is used to detect crop diseases: the healthy leaves reflect infra-red light (and appear bright in false-colour film), but dying leaves do not.

Leaves have a remarkable pigment called phytochrome which can exist in two distinct forms and absorb either red or infra-red light, though only in minute quantities. When phytochrome absorbs the red light in unfiltered sunlight, it turns into the form that absorbs infra-red; when the infra-red light filtered through leaves falls on it, it turns back again. Since only one form of the pigment at a time is physiologically active, leaves can effectively measure the relative amounts of red and infra-red light, and so determine whether or not they are shaded by other leaves.

When they do detect such shade, sun plants, particularly those that grow among herbaceous plants, respond by growing longer stems and leaf-stalks, pushing the leaves higher and higher, and nearer the light. Shade plants, such as wood speedwell and ground ivy, however, do not; they normally live under tall trees, and no amount of upward growth would get them into the light. Selection has ensured that they make do with what they have got.

Shade plants generally survive in deep shade by growing rather slowly, since they can get little solar energy, and by having large thin leaves, which will intercept as much of the meagre sunlight as is available, for the smallest possible cost of construction. Most woodland-floor plants have

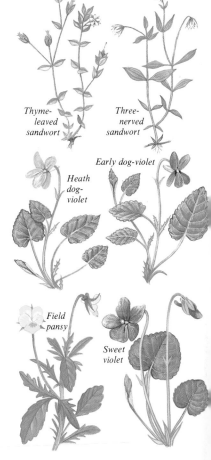

Comparison of three pairs of closely related plants: the right-hand of each pair is a woodland species; the other prefers more open habitats and has smaller leaves.

Thyme-leaved sandwort

Three-nerved sandwort

Early dog-violet

Heath dog-violet

Field pansy

Sweet violet

larger leaves than their relatives from more open habitats: compare three-nerved and thyme-leaved sandworts, or the woodland violets such as sweet violet and early dog violet with heath dog violet or field pansy.

In extreme habitats, so shaded that sufficient photosynthesis for survival is impossible, grow the so-called saprophytes (p. 230) which have no chlorophyll and rely for food on a fungal partner, which obtains it from the trees or from decomposing leaves.

PHYLLOTAXIS AND LEAF MOSAICS

Because of the problem of shading, there is much advantage to a plant in so arranging its leaves that they at least do not shade each other. This is achieved in two ways, either by spacing them out vertically along a stem, or by spreading them horizontally to make a mosaic.

Any object only obstructs the light for a certain distance from it, about 50–70 times its diameter. So if leaves are arranged along a stem at intervals of a metre or so (for typical leaf sizes) they will not shade each other. In practice, since the sun moves around the sky and so shadows move too, they can be much closer together. Even so, it is obvious that leaves on most plant stems are only a few centimetres apart; but they are arranged around the stem in a regular order, so that adjacent leaves are not on top of each other. These arrangements are known as phyllotaxis.

Geometrically the simplest arrangement is to have leaves in opposite pairs. Typically opposite pairs of leaves are displaced at right-angles to each other up the stem. This arrangement is known as opposite and decussate and is almost universally found in the pink, St John's-wort, gentian and mint families. Occasionally pairs of leaves are aligned one on top of the other up the stem, but this is usually brought about by twisting of the stem or leaf-stalks, especially on horizontal stems.

Occasionally a third leaf appears at the node, making a whorl, each leaf being spaced at 120° around the stem. Himalayan balsam and yellow loosestrife both show this variable arrangement, having either 2, 3 or rarely 4 leaves at a node. Other plants have leaves in whorls, often with many leaves at a node, as in bedstraws and corn spurrey.

But opposite and whorled arrangements of leaves can only go so far in separating one leaf from the shadow of another above, and they tend to be associated with narrow, undivided leaves, which anyway cast little shade.

Yellow loosestrife

St John's-wort

Lady's bedstraw

Isometric views of: St John's-wort with leaves in opposite pairs; yellow loosestrife whose leaves are spaced at 120° angles; lady's-bedstraw, whose leaves are in whorls

The leaves of bedstraws are almost needle-like, and none of the four main opposite-leaved families mentioned above has compound leaves.

If large and complex leaves are to be accommodated, more subtle arrangements are necessary, all variations of spiral phyllotaxis. It is striking how close this link is: all of the big families with compound (palmate and pinnate) leaves have spiral leaf arrangements, including the buttercup, rose, peaflower, cranesbill and carrot families. Here the successive leaves arise part of the way further round the stem, so that their points of insertion trace a spiral. There is a remarkable mathematical precision to the arrangements that occur, whose underlying explanation still excites debate. Many, particularly composites such as common fleabane, as well as many trees, including oak, have the leaves separated by 144°,

The leaves of a daisy are arranged in a $\frac{3}{8}$ phyllotaxy.

The leaves of common fleabane are arranged in $\frac{2}{5}$ phyllotaxy.

The leaves of a primrose grow in rosettes and are held at successively steeper angles.

two-fifths of a 360° circle. In other words, the sixth leaf is above the first, and the leaves trace two distinct spirals. Such patterns are often easiest to see in rosette plants. A daisy rosette, for example, has successive leaves separated by three-eighths of a circle, 135°; but here there are three separate spirals. The same plan occurs in raspberry, and is called $\frac{3}{8}$ phyllotaxis. If these numbers are written as fractions, then the opposite type is given as $\frac{1}{2}$ (one spiral of two leaves, so $\frac{1}{2}$ a circle each time: 180°); there are a few examples, such as hazel, alder and beech, which have $\frac{1}{3}$ phyllotaxy (one spiral of three leaves: 120°); then come $\frac{2}{5}$ (two spirals of five leaves: 144°), $\frac{3}{8}$, $\frac{5}{13}$ and so on. In this series ($\frac{1}{2}$, $\frac{1}{3}$, $\frac{2}{5}$, $\frac{3}{8}$, $\frac{5}{13}$) each successive fraction can be predicted by adding the numerators and denominators of the previous two fractions. So after $\frac{1}{2}$ and $\frac{1}{3}$, we get $\frac{1+1}{2+3}$, which is $\frac{2}{5}$; similarly after $\frac{1}{3}$ and $\frac{2}{5}$, we get $\frac{1+2}{3+5}$, or $\frac{3}{8}$. This is a well-known mathematical series, called the Fibonacci series, after its discoverer. It is intriguing that it should describe so exactly the arrangement of leaves on stems.

Although these precise geometrical arrangements serve to reduce the overlap between leaves, there are special problems posed by rosettes, where there is no vertical distance. Normally the stalks of rosette-leaves continue to elongate as long as new leaves are being formed, so that the lowest leaves project from under the upper ones, as in cranesbills and many composites. An alternative is for the angle of the leaf-stalks to become progressively steeper, so that the inner and upper leaves point more or less vertically upwards; primroses show this well.

The net effect of all these devices, particularly the ability of the leaf-stalk to provide a 'fine-tuning' of the leaf position, is usually to minimise overlap of leaves and mutual shading. The final arrangements are known as leaf mosaics, and though most clearly seen in the branches of trees can be spotted in many plants if observed carefully.

211

ROOTS

STORAGE AND SAFETY

Roots are neglected organs, partly because they are mostly hidden underground and partly because they are not recognisable as belonging to a particular species to the extent that leaves and flowers are. That in itself is an interesting fact that demands some explanation. Differences in leaf size and shape, useful for identification, can be explained in terms of avoidance of overheating (p. 198) and efficient interception of sunlight (p. 210). The soil, however, is a much more equable environment, and overheating at least is no problem, which removes at least one possible cause of variation.

There is a difference, too, in the way that sunlight, on the one hand, and water and nutrients on the other, reach plants. Light comes from a particular direction, and so the position of leaves relative to each other and to their sizes are important. Water and minerals, which roots gain for the plant, are normally well-distributed in soil and may reach the root from any direction. It matters much less, therefore, what the characteristics of an individual root are; much more significant is how much root a plant has, at what depth in the soil it is, and how much it spreads out horizontally.

Roots are not all identical, however, and differences in their form are related to their function. Roots perform three main functions – one is the absorption of water and minerals, a second the anchorage of the plant, and the third is the storage of food. Many plants have roots (and often underground shoots, too: see p. 250) modified for food storage. The advantage of underground storage is the relative protection from large

The roots of some familiar plants

Cow parsley   Dandelion   Tufted hair-grass   Lousewort

herbivores. Moles may occasionally discover such a store and eat it; but the energy required for a large animal to move about underground has precluded the evolution of a subterranean cow.

Underground storage is therefore a safe option. Some plants have swollen, but otherwise normal, roots which contain the reserves during the dormant period, including lousewort and tufted hair-grass. There is a continuous gradation between these types and the swollen taproots of cow parsley, dandelion and many other perennials. Since these food stores must represent tempting targets for mice, beetle larvae and other underground chewers, it is not surprising that they tend to be well protected with noxious chemicals. The diuretic properties of dandelion roots are well known, but many other plants, including soapwort, tormentil, wild carrot and white bryony have more or less poisonous rootstocks (at least to small animals).

One of the best-known of these chemical defences is that in the root of the great yellow gentian, so common in the mountains of central and southern Europe. In the French Massif Central, in particular, the roots are harvested on a massive scale and from them a bitter drink is brewed, reputed to have wondrous health-giving properties.

The development of a massive rootstock, a swollen main root from which the absorbing roots radiate, is one of the commonest methods by which herbaceous perennials overwinter. In many umbellifers, almost the whole of the first year's growth goes into building up this stock, on whose size the future survival of the plant depends. An obvious problem for such plants, and for plants that grow, for example, in cracks in rocks, is to ensure that the new growth at the top of the rootstock does not gradually emerge above ground where it would lose protection from climatic extremes and grazing. The solution is in the contractile properties of the roots, which in a wide range of plants including cyclamen, dog's mercury, bulbous buttercup and red clover, are able to drag the rootstock back into the soil.

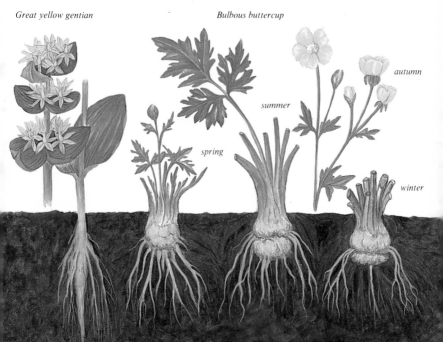

Great yellow gentian

Bulbous buttercup

autumn

summer

spring

winter

ROOTS: ABSORPTION OF WATER AND MINERALS

All plants require water and minerals, and most get them through their roots. Parasitic plants absorb them directly from their hosts (though hemiparasites use roots to do this; see p. 224), and so-called saprophytes from their fungal partner. In plants that float on water, such as duck-weeds, and in many that grow sub-merged in water, such as water violet, all or most of the absorption is directly into the leaves. Other plants use roots embedded in soil.

The structure of a root can largely be interpreted with this in mind. Water and, particularly, minerals move slowly in soil, and so it is necessary for the root to go in search of its requirements – the botanical version of Mahomet and the mountain. The root must be equipped to penetrate between particles of soil. A loose cap of tissue, continuously worn away and continuously replaced, provides this ability. The root is kept in contact with the water films surrounding the particles by delicate hairs, which may be several milli-metres long as in mouse-ear chick-weeds, though totally absent in chives and wild daffodil. Water and minerals can be absorbed over almost the whole surface and move, under the pull of transpiration, to the central core of vascular tissue, the xylem (see p. 184), which then transports them to the aerial parts of the plant.

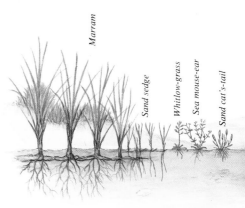

A plant community on sand-dunes in spring

Soils vary enormously in their ability to supply water to plants, and root systems are modified appro-priately. Dryness of soil may be a consequence of free-draining proper-ties of the materials (large sand parti-cles, for instance), in which case there may be water at depth. In such a soil a plant with a deeply penetrating taproot is well placed, though other, shallow-rooted plants may be able to occupy the surface layers at wetter times of year. On sand dunes, for example, there is a permanent popu-lation of deep-rooted perennials, including marram grass and sand sedge, and an ephemeral population of shallow-rooted winter annuals, including sand cat's-tail, sea mouse-ear and common whitlow-grass. The latter ones germinate in autumn, flower in spring and are dead by June.

In most habitats, there is a conspic-uous seasonal march of growth and flowering times. In lowland grass-lands, grasses such as smooth meadow-grass and sweet vernal grass, as well as several other plants includ-ing lesser celandine, are active in early spring; they are succeeded by Yorkshire fog and meadow butter-cup; and those in turn by bent-grasses, ribwort plantain, black knapweed, meadowsweet and many others. Part of the explanation for

Soil particles adhere to the roots and root-hairs of common mouse-ear

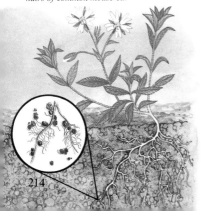

The same community in the late summer

this sequence lies in rooting depth: at the beginning of the season the surface layers warm up first and shallow-rooted plants are favoured; by mid-summer, the surface is dry and deep-rooted plants are favoured. Everyone is familiar with the sight of a droughted lawn on which the only

A lawn in the late summer: the grass has gone brown, the dandelion persists in the form of green rosettes, and the autumn hawkbit is flowering

Groundsel and curled dock, showing the extents of their root systems

green patches are of plantains and dandelions.

Plants do show large differences in rooting depth, and also, though less obviously, in root form. Generally, annuals have finely-divided, frequently-branching systems, which can rapidly explore a volume of soil. Most garden weeds, including common chickweed, fat hen, common field speedwell and groundsel, are like this. The main root dies early and their root systems resemble the branching of a shrub such as heather, upturned. Some annuals, such as weld and buck's-horn plantain, and most perennials, however, have a dominant main axis, often swollen as a taproot, the underground equivalent of the branching structure of a pine tree.

215

ANCHORAGE OF ROOTS

One of the most important functions of the root system is anchorage. At a very early stage in growth, immediately after germination, most plants concentrate on root rather than shoot growth, so ensuring both a water supply and anchorage to the ground. For most mature plants, however, the root system is far more extensive than is necessary for this purpose, so that anchorage is in effect achieved as a by-product of the need to obtain water and nutrients. In a number of particularly stressful habitats, however, special problems of maintaining stability arise.

In soils whose surface is unstable, such as the sand of young dunes, there is a problem of establishment from seed. In practice, growth is only possible by the invasion of subterranean stems, rhizomes, which can develop beneath the mobile surface layer and throw out roots and shoots, as in marram and sand couch. This of course means that most of the roots are deep in the soil; as the growth of the marram stabilises the surface, other plants invade, as seeds, and exploit the now stable surface layers, where they may intercept the rainfall and cause the marram to suffer from drought.

Even greater problems face plants growing in fast-flowing water. It is a striking fact that flowering plants have not been able to displace seaweeds from the rocky sea-shore. Seaweeds quite literally cement themselves to the rocks and so resist the

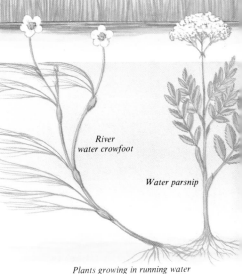

River water crowfoot

Water parsnip

Plants growing in running water

pounding of the waves. Flowering plant root systems cannot achieve this; but they do grow in fast-flowing fresh water. In these cases the root system is used almost entirely for anchorage, as almost no water is taken up (since transpiration does not occur), and minerals are absorbed direct from the water by the leaves. The real puzzle is how plants such as river water crowfoot and, in less strong currents, water parsnip, water speedwell, fennel pondweed and water forget-me-not, among others, manage to take root. Presumably they germinate and become established in periods of low flow in summer; but

Sand couch-grass establishes itself on sandy soil with a network of underground rhizomes; once it has done so, other plants may now invade on the more stable surface.

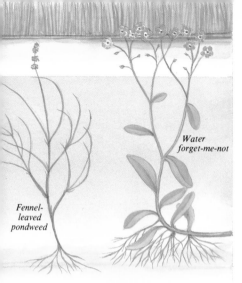

Water forget-me-not

Fennel-leaved pondweed

Creeping buttercup produces adventitious roots wherever the stolon tip settles, and a new plantlet develops

no-one seems to have studied this. In any case, the length of time available for producing a root system strong enough to withstand the resumption of strong current conditions must be very brief.

All these roots are produced in the normal way, by underground parts of plants. But some plants can actually grow roots above ground. These may act to anchor the plant onto surfaces, as in ivy, or to attach a stem to the ground. In all such cases these are adventitious roots, formed *in addition to* the main root system. Such roots may form from the stembase, as in creeping buttercup, greater plantain, and many monocots. Many plants have stems which run along horizontally, either above or below ground (rhizomes and stolons, see p. 250), and these are anchored by adventitious roots produced wherever there is a bud which may develop into a shoot, for example in white clover, wild strawberry, silverweed, New Zealand willowherb and creeping bent. In bramble, the aerial stem grows upwards initially, only bending earthwards in autumn; and it starts to produce adventitious roots before it reaches the ground, showing that contact is not essential. A few plants, notably cuckoo flower, are able to produce adventitious roots from their leaf margins, so that the leaves can act as reproductive organs. Here, contact with damp soil is a pre-requisite for root formation.

The ability to produce adventitious roots is widespread in plants, as gardeners who take cuttings well know. It has clearly evolved, not as a horticultural convenience, but as an aid to establishment of the non-reproductive parts of plants: it is notable that stems frequently root, leaves rarely, and flowers never – they are already devoted to multiplication by different means.

The cuckoo-flower can produce adventitious roots from the margins of its leaves.

SOIL TOXINS

Although soil is, in nature, an essential medium for most plants, not every soil is equally suitable for growth. In soil, a plant requires water, minerals and oxygen (for its root to breathe). The loamy soils so well-loved by gardeners provide all these, but not all soils do. Water is a particular problem: if a soil is freely-draining, usually because it is sandy and the large sand grains hold little water between them, it is likely to be too dry in summer. If not, it is probably a clay soil, in which particles are so small (a typical clay particle is a hundred to a thousand times smaller than a sand grain) that they stick together like cement. Then water accumulates and fills all the (very small) spaces between the particles, excluding the air and depriving the roots of oxygen. The same phenomenon arises on soils where the water table is high for other reasons (flooding, shallow gradients, and so on), and here peat may form, which is simply the unrotted (since rotting requires air) remains of past vegetation.

Roots growing in such waterlogged soils must obtain oxygen in some way so that they can use the sugars made by the leaves to obtain energy. Many have hollow spaces inside, down which oxygen can move from stem to root; tissue with such spaces is called aerenchyma and is found in many sedges, rushes and grasses, for example soft rush, common sedge or reed sweet-grass. An alternative is to behave like yeast, which produces the alcohol in beer or wine by growing without oxygen. This is a very inefficient process, in which sugars are converted into alcohol, not into carbon dioxide as when humans breathe; the alcohol is itself a perfectly good energy source, but is here a waste product. (Alcohol is, however, toxic to most living organisms (including drivers) and must be disposed of.) Yellow water-lily gets its alternative name 'brandy-bottle' from the alcoholic smell of its bottle-shaped fruits. It produces the alcohol in its roots, growing without oxygen in the lake-bottom mud; the alcohol is transported to the shoots and evaporates safely away.

Other soils are inimical because of acids. The acidity of a soil depends on whether it contains sufficient of the basic minerals, such as calcium, to neutralise the acids produced by other soil minerals, particularly iron and aluminium. If a soil is derived from chalk or limestone (which are largely made of the shells of long-dead animals and consist mostly of calcium carbonate), rainwater will continually dissolve the calcium. In the long term, this is the process that makes caves like those at Cheddar. Plants which prefer soils rich in calcium (calcareous soils) are called calcicoles; those favouring acid soils where the calcium has been leached away (or, if the original rock was, say, granite or greensand, was never there in the first place) are known as calcifuges. For reasons that still excite debate among ecologists, communities of calcicoles tend to be richer in species, and to contain more rare and colourful ones. Our declining chalk grasslands are good examples.

Recently man has started to accelerate the leaching process. By burning sulphur-rich fossil fuels he

Yellow water-lily

Above right: *Typical calcifuges: tormentil, slender St John's-wort and heath bedstraw.*
Below: *Typical calcicoles of chalk grassland: lady's bedstraw, salad burnet, hairy violet, common rock-rose and dwarf thistle*

creates sulphur dixoide which dissolves in rain and falls as sulphuric acid. This is acid rain. Falling on to calcareous soils it quickly removes the calcium; on acid soils it can create such acid conditions that even the resistant calcifuge plants suffer. In urban areas, sports pitches illustrate this well: often most of the pitch is dominated by slow-growing, unproductive calcifuges such as brown bent and mat grass, while the white lines, continually limed, have the normal sports-turf grasses, such as ryegrass.

Man affects soils in another way: by contaminating them with toxic metals, particularly lead, zinc and

Spring sandwort, alpine pennycress and mountain pansy growing on the spoil heap of a lead mine

copper. Where ores of these metals are mined or smelted, heaps of debris accumulate, containing so much of the toxic metals that almost nothing will grow. Man has been mining lead for thousands of years, and that is quite long enough for natural selection to get to work. On old mine workings a characteristic flora can be found. Spring sandwort, alpine pennycress and mountain pansy are all good indicators of such contaminated soils, having evolved races capable of withstanding the toxins, largely by confining them to the root cell walls, so that they never reach the more sensitive leaves and flowers. In Germany and Belgium it is wild pansies that grow on zinc mines, and they have evolved into a distinctive race sometimes regarded as a separate species.

This dramatic example of evolution in action has been observed on an even shorter time-scale, in such unlikely places as under a barbed-wire fence. Plants of brown bent under a fence in Norfolk were found to be more resistant to zinc than those a few centimetres away; the galvanising zinc had dissolved in rain over 30 years and dripped on to the grass below, and the zinc-resistant types had been selected.

INTERACTIONS

PARASITIC PLANTS

Every rule has its exception, and the rule that plants obtain their energy by fixing that in sunlight is broken by parasitic plants. Plant parasites are of two kinds: some have normal green leaves and stems, and can fix solar energy for themselves; but their roots are modified so as to tap the roots of other plants for water and minerals. Such partial (hemi-) parasites are discussed on p. 224). Full parasites have neither green leaves nor roots, and rely on their hosts for all their nutrition. Because of this they have lost during their evolution many of the characteristic features of plants, but not their flowers.

Dodders, for example, consist of nothing more than twining stems, entangled in their hosts, which bear clusters of neat, 4-petalled flowers, betraying their origins as close relatives of the bindweeds; those too are climbers, but use their supports for just that, not to gain nutrition. Perhaps some ancestral bindweed acquired the ability not just to twine around its 'host', but also to penetrate its tissues. Whenever a dodder stem touches the host stem, a sucker-like swelling develops and forces its way into the host's tissue, where it penetrates the transport cells which move sugar and other nutrients from the leaves to the host's growing points. Typical hosts are nettles for the greater dodder and gorse for the more abundant common dodder. These hosts are the source for the parasite of all the food it needs.

Both these dodders are annuals, overwintering entirely as seeds. The seeds germinate in late spring, when the hosts have already started to grow, and push out a tiny rootlet which embeds itself a few millimetres in the earth. It then elongates rapidly at the other end, waving around until it locates an appropriate living host. This growth depends entirely on the food reserves in the seed, for the plant has none of the green chlorophyll necessary for fixing solar energy. Most seedlings fail to make contact with a host soon enough, and die; but those that do quickly develop their absorbing suckers, and the contact with the soil is soon lost as the bottom of the stem withers away.

Dodder is the most simplified parasite in our flora and there are others which, though equally free of

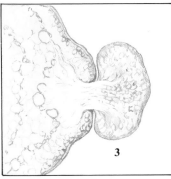

Common dodder: 1 seed root and shoot; 2 stems twined up gorse plant; 3 suckers penetrate the gorse tissue; 4 stem withers away when no longer required.

chlorophyll and dependent on their hosts for food, in other respects have a more familiar appearance. Broomrapes look rather like brownish orchids, and have bluish, reddish or yellowish flowers, the colours always somewhat muddy, perhaps because they lack some of the pigments normally associated with photosynthesis but often also found in flowers. They are most closely related to foxgloves, and this relationship shows in the form of their flowers. Broomrapes attack the roots of their hosts, not the stems, and make contact with the tissues in the host which transport food from the shoots. On germination it is a root-like probe which penetrates the soil until it finds a host root, in which it buries itself deeply. From the tuber which then develops, and which is in most cases perennial, flowering shoots emerge in summer.

Plants such as these can of course only be located when in flower, for they only emerge from the soil to be pollinated and disperse their seeds; the rest of their life is subterranean. The most abundant broomrape is the common broomrape, which is usually found parasitising clovers and a few related species, all members of the peaflower family. This restriction to a few hosts is found in all broomrapes: purple broomrape is nearly always parasitic on yarrow, ivy

broomrape on ivy, knapweed broomrape on knapweed, and so on. This specificity is very convenient to the botanist, who may find it easier to identify a broomrape from the adjacent plants than from obscure diagnostic characters of the stamens. It is in fact a common situation for both plant and animal parasites. As each host has evolved a system of defences (often chemical, see p. 240), so a particular parasite has evolved a system of overcoming them; but it is a system that will not necessarily work with any other host species.

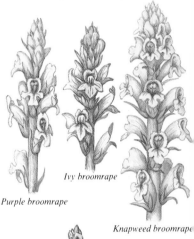

Ivy broomrape

Purple broomrape

Knapweed broomrape

Common broomrape: **1** *seed (highly magnified) sends down root which locates clover root;* **2** *tuber is formed;* **3** *new shoot;* **4** *mature plant ready to shed new seed.*

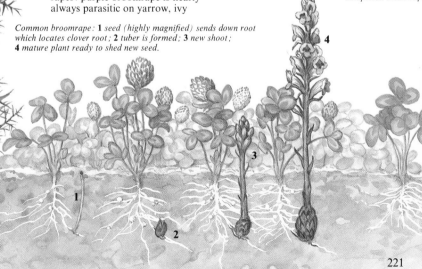

221

Other flowering plants lack chlorophyll; some are parasitic on other plants, but others, including bird's-nest orchid and the unrelated yellow bird's-nest are usually called saprophytes, which means that they feed on rotting organic matter (p. 230). They do this by harnessing the food-processing ability of fungi to their roots.

The most remarkable parasitic plant must, however, be toothwort, which is closely related to the broomrapes. It too parasitises the roots of other plants, particularly hazel and wych elm; but it does so by means of pad-like suckers which penetrate through the host's tissues into its nutrient transport system. Toothwort has extensive underground stems, liberally coated with fleshy whitish 'leaves'; at intervals these emerge to form aerial stems, which bear flowers as well as tooth-like leaves.

These leaves contain no chlorophyll and so are clearly not concerned with fixing solar energy, particularly since most are under the ground. It has been suggested that they are, in fact, complex traps for soil animals, with a central chamber lined with digestive

Toothwort parasitic on the roots of a hazel tree

The suckers with which toothwort penetrates its host's tissues

The roots of lousewort attach themselves to the roots of other plants by means of suckers.

glands, much like those of the more familiar carnivorous plants such as sundews and bladderworts (see p. 232). If so, toothwort is nutritionally about as different from other plants as is conceivable, for it is both a parasite and a predator!

It may be, however, that these glands represent the solution to a different problem. All plants transport substances within themselves dissolved in water, and when it reaches its destination, the water is lost by evaporation, typically from the leaves. Toothwort, however, is an underground plant for most of its life and so must lose water by some other means. Water naturally moves from dilute to concentrated solutions; the solution in soil is much more dilute than in plant tissues, so that the tendency is for water in soil to move into plant tissues. The leaves on toothwort's underground stems probably act to pump water out into the soil, against its natural tendency to move in the opposite direction.

HEMIPARASITES

Plants that have no chlorophyll, such as the broomrapes, dodders and toothwort on the previous page, must obviously gain nourishment in some other way: they are parasitic on other plants. Some parasitic plants, however, do have chlorophyll. Lousewort, for example, has normal green leaves, which fix energy from the sun. It has roots, too, that at first sight seem quite normal; close inspection, however, will reveal that here and there they are attached to the roots of other plants by minute white suckers – lousewort is, in fact, parasitic on these roots.

Whereas the full parasites, such as the dodders and broomrapes, have no need of normal roots or leaves, lousewort and similar plants are only partial parasites (or hemiparasites). What they do is to dispense with their own roots to a great extent, using

them simply to make contact with those of another plant, much like a broomrape. But whereas broomrapes tap the tissues in the host root that transport food from leaves to roots (the phloem, see p. 184), and so obtain a fully adequate diet, hemiparasites make contact with the xylem tissue, in which waters and minerals are moved from roots to leaves. This contains no sugars and so in effect these hemiparasites are just borrowing another plant's root system. Above ground they behave like any other plant, fixing the energy in sunlight into sugars, but they have to spend much less of their resources on making roots, leaving more, ultimately, for seeds.

One of the best known hemiparasitic plants is mistletoe, whose green leathery clumps are conspicuous on the bare winter branches of poplars and apple trees. It has long been held to have magical properties, and certainly achieves a number of interesting botanical tricks. Its root burrows into the woody stem of its host and joins with the tissue which transports water and salts from roots to leaves (the xylem). Water normally flows up the xylem only in response to transpiration by the leaves. In winter, when the host tree has no leaves,

223

Mistle thrushes eat mistletoe, then wipe their beaks on a tree-branch to remove the berries' sticky mucilage; some of the seeds will germinate in cracks in the bark, and penetrate the tree stem with a new root.

mistletoe, being evergreen, continues to transpire and draw water up the host's xylem. Hence it can grow and photosynthesise at a time when it is unshaded by the host's leaves. Its sticky white berries are distributed by birds, which wipe them off into cracks in the bark of another tree, in an attempt to clean their beaks.

The hemiparasites fall into two other families. The rare bastard toad-flax is the only British member of the Santalaceae; all the others are in the figwort family Scrophulariaceae. Only two are perennials (lousewort and alpine bartsia), and marsh lousewort is biennial. One of these hemi-parasites, alpine bartsia, has an even more complex nutritional system. It has a relatively well-developed root system and is only partly dependent on its hosts for water and minerals. It forms tiny buds on its roots in autumn, which may possibly act as traps for soil animals, rather like

those of toothwort (p. 223), for they are so structured as to present several chambers, each lined with glands. In spring these buds develop quite normally into new shoots. The glands may have the same water-excreting function as those of toothwort, but alpine bartsia's root system can still obtain its water and minerals from the soil either directly through its own roots or indirectly through those of other plants.

All the others, including eyebright, yellow rattle, red bartsia and the cow-wheats, are annual. Unusually for annuals, which normally favour disturbed ground on which they can readily re-establish from seed, without competing with existing perennials (see p. 246), these annual hemi-parasites grow in grassy places.

The link between hemiparasitism and being annual in grassland is the ability to do without extensive root systems. Eyebright seeds, for example,

germinate in spring and the young seedling produces a small, branching root which grows until it meets the root of another plant. It is not wholly dependent on this contact, for the root will function normally if necessary; but the plant only grows vigorously if it can parasitise another root system. As soon as it has penetrated the host root and the shoot has started to develop, all the growth can be concentrated there. An ordinary annual attempting to grow in a closed grassland community would have first to establish an extensive root system so as to obtain water and minerals in competition with existing plants, and all that root growth would be at the expense of shoot growth.

This explains why these (and almost only these) annuals can survive in communities otherwise composed entirely of perennials, but not why there should be so few perennial hemiparasites. The reason is probably that the roots they parasitise are rather short-lived, for much of the fine root system of most perennial plants is replaced in a burst of growth each spring, so that the longer-lived louseworts have to grow new roots themselves each season in order to find new roots to parasitise.

Alpine bartsia and its root system

a. Close-up of root-bud

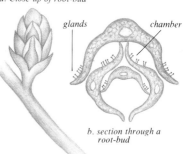

glands

chamber

b. section through a root-bud

Hemiparasites such as eyebright, yellow rattle and red bartsia often coexist in short grassland. Red clover is a typical host.

SYMBIOTIC ASSOCIATION

Root nodules

There are many instances in nature of different organisms living together in close contact and each supplying the other with something it is better fitted to obtain or make. Many of these symbiotic associations involve a plant as one of the partners, for plants are the only organisms that can use chlorophyll to turn the energy of the sun into chemical energy in the form of sugars. Thanks to this ability they usually have sugar in plentiful supply, but are limited in their growth by a shortage of minerals.

In contrast, most microbes are forced to obtain their energy by decomposing the dead (or sometimes living) bodies of other organisms. Two sorts of symbiotic associations have evolved which match together these complementary wants and abilities. The most widespread is that of fungi with plant roots (mycor-

The bacteria in lucerne's root-nodules are active in fixing nitrogen.

rhizas, p. 228), but more obvious are root nodules, which result from the association between bacteria and the roots of members of the peaflower family Leguminosae (legumes), and of a few other species.

Examination of the roots of any legume will reveal little balls at intervals. These betray the presence of a bacterium called *Rhizobium*, whose speciality is to be able to convert the nitrogen in the air (79% of the air is nitrogen gas, both in the atmosphere and in the spaces between the grains of soil) into ammonium, a form in which it can be used by plants. In return they receive from the plant the sugars they need for this and for growth. Only pink nodules actively fix nitrogen, and the pink colour is caused by a pigment almost identical to the haemoglobin which transports oxygen in the blood of animals. In the nodule it acts chemically to remove oxygen which would otherwise interfere with the complex biochemistry of nitrogen fixation. Nodules that are not pink are either very young or are inhabited by ineffective bacteria; they take the sugars but offer little or no nitrogen in return, and are effectively parasitic rather than symbiotic.

The nodule bacteria appear to be almost universally present in soils, though different strains vary in effectiveness at fixing nitrogen. When a legume root growing through soil encounters the bacteria, the two undergo a 'chemical conversation', each stimulating the other to produce a sequence of chemicals, ending in the curling of the root around the bacteria. This ensures that the root is not infected by other, possibly pathogenic bacteria, which would, of course, give the wrong chemical signals.

The advantage of nitrogen fixation to a plant is that it becomes independent of the limited supply of fixed nitrogen in soil, for which it would otherwise have to compete with other plants. The problem is that over time, the legume's leaves fall to the ground, and with their high nitrogen content, they eventually enrich the soil to a degree where it becomes suitable for

other plants which could not thrive there previously. Actively fixing plants such as red clover or lucerne can put as much nitrogen into the soil as a farmer might use as fertiliser. The advantage to the legume is then lessened, while the cost of supporting all those bacteria is the same, and so the legume loses out in competition with invading species. For this reason, legumes tend to be found on very poor soils, often those in the early stages of development, such as the sand of sand dunes. In such sites, it may take a very long time for nitrogen fixation to enrich the soil to the point at which the nitrogen-fixers are eliminated by competition.

While the symbiosis with *Rhizobium* is characteristic of legumes, there are a few other plants which can form similar associations with other microbes. Alder, bog myrtle and sea buckthorn are the only ones commonly found in Britain, and all are paired with a bacterium called *Frankia*. Unlike those of legumes, the root nodules on these woody plants are perennial and go on growing for many years, forking repeatedly, so that a large alder nodule may be larger than a tennis ball. Both alder and bog myrtle are particularly at home on waterlogged soil and are the only nitrogen-fixing plants that can grow there. Fixation normally depends upon the nitrogen in the air spaces between the soil particles, and these spaces are filled with water in a waterlogged soil; so this achievement is remarkable.

Alder is one of the few nitrogen-fixing plants that can grow in waterlogged conditions.

227

Mycorrhizas

Mycorrhizas are associations of soil fungi and plant roots and are found in most soils. They owe their ubiquity to the ability of the fungus to transport phosphorus in its tissues. Phosphorus is an essential nutrient for plants and one of the major constituents of the nucleic acids that carry the genetic information for all organisms. Unfortunately for plants, when they began to colonise land and had to obtain their minerals from soil rather than from sea water, where it diffuses relatively quickly, they encountered the problem that phosphates are almost totally insoluble and hence will scarcely move in soil. If a gardener scatters phosphate fertiliser on his lawn, it will still be there in the top few inches 50 years later, because the rain cannot dislodge it from the tight hold that the soil particles have over it. Because of this immobility, a root in soil quickly exhausts all the phosphate in the soil immediately around it and can obtain very little more.

Very early in the evolution of plants mycorrhizas evolved in response to this, as we know from the discovery of primitive plant fossils complete with mycorrhizal fungi. The fungus consists of masses of fine threads, known collectively as the mycelium, such as one sees growing over old bread or cheese, which can explore new areas of soil for phosphate at a fraction of the cost in energy to a plant of building a root system to do the same job. Hence the plant hands over some of its surplus sugar to the fungus, which builds its ramifying mycelium from it, and in turn transports phosphate ions back to the plant. The association is so effective that it has become almost universal.

The stubby, forking, mycorrhizal roots of pine have a sheath of fungus around them, which penetrates between the outer cells.

In the process two main types have emerged. Sheathing mycorrhizas can actually be seen with the naked eye, best on roots of Scots pine and most other conifers, but also on the roots of many other trees, including beech and birch. The fine roots of these trees, when infected, become thicker

Scots pine forms mycorrhizas with many different fungi. Here it is shown with an edible Boletus.

and stubby, and fork repeatedly. They are in fact coated with a web of fungal threads which is connected both to the cells of the root and to the ramifying mycelium in soil. The fungi involved here are the typical woodland toadstools, such as fly agaric which is normally mycorrhizal on birch roots. The actual toadstool is just a short-lived reproductive structure; the body of the fungus (the mycelium) is perennial in soil, and all these mycorrhizal associations are with woody perennial plants.

Herbaceous plants (and a few woody ones) form mycorrhizas with a much simpler group of fungi which form no above-ground reproductive structures and have no visible effect on the roots of infected plants. In fact these mycorrhizas (called endomycorrhizas because the structures are all inside the root) can only be seen with a microscope. Though inconspicuous they are very widespread: most wild herbaceous plants are infected, though members of the cabbage and goosefoot families tend not to be. This is perhaps because many species in these families are annual, and annuals are much less often mycorrhizal. The speed of their growth and development makes it less likely that they will have time to form and benefit from the association. Clovers, on the other hand, along with most legumes, are regularly infected, so that these plants obtain their nitrogen from a bacterium (p. 226) and their phosphate from a fungus, paying for both transactions with sugar.

Other groups of plants have special types of mycorrhizas, some of which function slightly differently. The strangest are those of orchids (see p. 230).

The fly agaric toadstool has a mycorrhizal association with birch roots, and is nearly always found in birch woods.

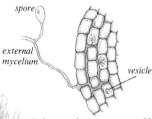

spore

external mycelium

vesicle

Endomycorrhizas cause no visible changes in infected roots; but the fungus ramifies inside the root.

229

SAPROPHYTIC PLANTS

Two sorts of plants lack chlorophyll:
one is parasitic on other plants and
includes broomrapes (p. 221), but the
other is saprophytic and lives in
association with fungi in the soil. A
few orchids – the bird's-nest orchids,
coralroot and ghost – are saprophytic, and so is the unrelated yellow
bird's-nest. All except coralroot,
which is sometimes found in the open,
live in places too shaded for green
plants dependent on sunlight to
survive in. Bird's-nest orchid and
yellow bird's-nest, for example, grow
out of the dense carpets of dead leaves
that coat the floor of beech woods, a
habitat shared with the very rare
ghost orchid. Yellow bird's-nest also
grows under pine trees.

The root systems of all these plants
are very similar: they consist of thick
branching roots, variously and fanci-
fully likened to a bird's nest or
a piece of coral (hence the names),
and they completely lack ramifying
roots. The roots are not attached to
the roots of other plants, so that it is
at first sight a mystery as to where
they obtain their nutrition. They
have no chlorophyll and so cannot
photosynthesise; without ramifying
roots they cannot obtain water and
nutrients from the soil; and they are
not parasitic on other plants. The
answer is a fungus that lives in the
soil and links to the roots with fine,
almost microscopic threads. This is a
mycorrhizal association like those
formed between fungi and more
typical root systems (p. 228), but
whereas those associations are truly
symbiotic, based on mutual benefit to
the two partners, this one appears to
be almost wholly one-way.

The benefit to the plant is very clear
– from the fungus it obtains all its
nutritional needs – but the fungus has
not yet been shown to gain anything

*Bird's-nest orchid and ghost
orchid obtain their nutrition
from a fungus within the dead
leaves of beech.*

*Coralroot is sometimes found in less shaded
conditions.*

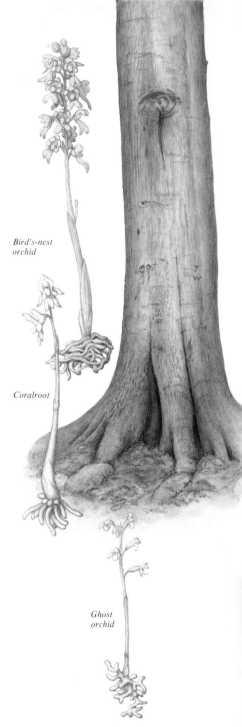

*Bird's-nest
orchid*

Coralroot

*Ghost
orchid*

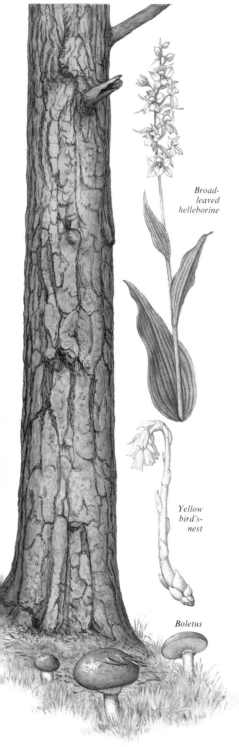

Broad-leaved helleborine

Yellow bird's-nest

Boletus

at all from the plants. Indeed it is hard to see what a leafless and rootless plant could offer! These associations seem therefore to be rather bizarre parasitisms, with the tables neatly turned: the plant is parasitic on the fungus!

Although one's attention is drawn to these odd associations by the lack of chlorophyll in the plants, they are in fact more widespread, particularly among other species of orchid. All orchids have minute seeds, so small that they contain no food reserves, and the germinating embryo is reliant on a fungal partner in its early stages. In other words, orchid seeds will not germinate unless they land next to their particular fungal partner; so at the start of their life-cycle, even the green orchids behave just like the non-green ones. One clue to this is that, very rarely, one may come across albino orchids, such as the helleborines, which have grown to maturity without chlorophyll, wholly dependent on their fungal partner. Even when apparently green and independent, though, most orchids have very limited root systems and probably rely on their fungus for some water and minerals, and possibly for some of the sugars as well.

Most of the fungi involved in these associations obtain their food, including sugars and proteins, from breaking down rotting leaves; but some take the complexity one stage further, for they are also symbiotic with other plants. It has been shown that yellow bird's-nest may be associated with a *Boletus* fungus that is itself mycorrhizal with pine trees. The mycorrhizal association of fungus and pine tree works so that phosphate moves from fungus to tree, and the sugars from tree to fungus; the yellow bird's-nest then gets both from the fungus, and so seems to be a parasite on the mycorrhizal symbiosis.

Broad-leaved helleborine, like most orchids, has a very limited root system.

A three-sided association appears to involve yellow bird's-nest, the fungus Boletus *and the roots of pine trees.*

INSECTIVOROUS PLANTS

It is a central tenet of ecology that plants are producers of energy from sunlight, and animals are consumers of that energy, either directly by feeding on plants or indirectly by eating vegetarian animals. Some plants have managed to reverse this natural order, however: while retaining their ability to photosynthesise and to gain minerals from the soil, they supplement their diet by digesting animals. Almost without exception these insectivorous plants grow on very poor soils, usually boggy areas, where the supply of minerals from the soil is poor, and it is from the nitrogen and phosphorus in the animal proteins that they particularly benefit.

Insectivory probably evolved from the defence mechanisms that some plants possess against insect grazers. Many plants have sticky hairs on their stems or leaves, for example great willowherb (p. 239), and a few, like nettles, have evolved the ability to sting. It is a fairly simple step from there to the development of hairs that first ensnare small insects and then digest them, by the release of digestive enzymes from the hairs. The simplest true insectivorous plants are the butterworts, whose long yellowish-green leaves are covered with minute glands which secrete a sticky mucilage on which small insects settle or are blown. Some of the glands then secrete digestive enzymes which in a few days wholly dissolve the proteins in the insect for absorption by the plant.

The leaves of butterworts exhibit slight movements: the edges may roll over slightly, trapping insects which settle near the edge. Sundew leaves are much more active traps. Their most striking feature is the long red hairs which cover the upper surface, each ending in a knob-like gland which secretes a sticky mucilage. Small insects attracted to this or accidentally landing on it are quite unable to escape, and the hairs around the point of contact gradually, over a period of several hours, bend inwards, both trapping the prey more effectively and bringing to bear the digestive secretions of many more glands. Individual tentacles move much faster than this: those nearest to the prey can bend towards it in about ten minutes, after which those further away start to move.

The most dramatic traps, however, are those of the bladderworts, which grow in nutrient-poor, peaty water. They are rootless and floating, and consist of green, branching stems bearing feathery leaves and the tiny bladders that give them their name. These underwater bladders are hollow and have a flap at one end, surrounded by sensitive hairs, which acts as a trap-door and can only open inwards. When the hairs are touched, usually by small swimming animals such as water-fleas, the trap-door springs open and the animal is sucked into the bladder. This astonishing event occurs because the inside of the bladder is lined with glands which actually pump water out, evacuating it and causing the inrush of water when the trap-door opens. The animal inside soon dies and its proteins, broken down by decay and digestion, are absorbed by the plant, after which the trap is re-set. The water pumping is achieved against the tendency of water to move from very dilute solutions, such as the water the bladderwort lives in, to more concentrated ones, as in the cell sap, and is a most unusual piece of physiology.

Left and below: *Bladderwort traps small swimming animals.*

Centre: *Insects are digested by the glands on butterwort leaves.*

Right: *Sundew closes up on its insect prey.*

PLANT DEFENCES

One of the most surprising things in the natural environment is the survival of plants in the face of hundreds of thousands of species of plant-eating animals. These herbivores come in all shapes and sizes, from giraffes and elephants down to tiny beetles so small that they are almost invisible to the naked eye. When you see what a few 'cabbage white' caterpillars can do to a cabbage plant, or a rabbit to a field of barley, it is surprising that any plants survive at all, for they cannot escape the attentions of these grazing animals by running or hiding.

Every plant is defended more or less successfully against grazing. The defence may be obvious – the thorns on a hawthorn or the stings on a nettle leaf – or well hidden. Many plants have defences in the form of noxious chemicals in their leaves, stems or fruits that deter animals (see p. 240). Still others rely on being simply hard to find.

Most plants are far from an ideal diet for animals, mainly because they are poor in protein. As a result, herbivores have to eat a lot of plant in order to get enough protein, and that takes time. Eating is a vulnerable activity, and the longer the herbivore takes in getting his protein, the more likely he is to be eaten, caterpillars by blue tits, rabbits by foxes. This inevitably means that there are fewer herbivores than if plants were better food. Some bits of plant scarcely count as food at all: wood has so little protein that animals that feed on it take a long time to develop. Goat moth caterpillars live on rotting willow wood and take three years to get through that larval stage; but if they are fed on a high quality artificial diet they mature in a few months.

Being poor food is a common defence, then, and many unpalatable plants have leaves full of hard, tough tissues called sclerenchyma, for example the soft rush and mat-grass,

Left: *The longer a caterpillar spends eating tough cabbage leaf, the more likely it will fall prey to a blue tit.*

Right: *A goat moth caterpillar in rotting willow*

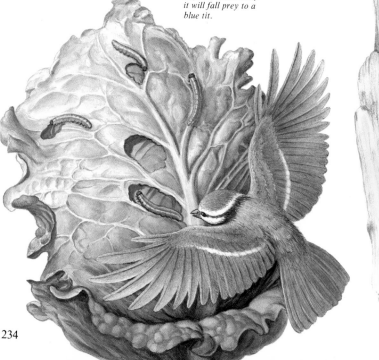

234

Clumps of soft rush are poor in food value, and are usually left uneaten by grazing cattle and rabbits.

both of which are very common in overgrazed pasture, where all the more palatable species have been killed off by grazing. Many grasses also extract silica (which in another form makes sand and glass) from the soil and form little crystals of that in their cells, which can cut the lips of grazing animals, not to mention the fingers of unwary children.

Since they cannot move, the only way plants can escape being eaten (at least by insects) is to be hard to find. Annuals live for a short time and often persist in a particular place for only a year or two, so that any specialist insects are less likely to find them; they therefore need to be less well defended. Similarly, plants that normally grow as isolated individuals

will be surrounded by other species that are unpalatable to their particular insect grazers. Such plants (and annuals too) usually have few physical defences (spines or thorns, for example) and a limited chemical arsenal.

Paradoxically, this explains why modern crop plants are so vulnerable to insect pests. They are almost all annuals – cereals, for example – and so have few natural defences. In the wild, their ancestors were hard to find, but now that they are planted in vast fields, with nothing else growing in them, the insects find them with ease, and the plants are literally defenceless.

...ne ...sses are ...rp-edged ...h silicon ...stals.

235

Gorse

Dog rose

Holly

Physical defences: thorns, spines and prickles

The most obvious defences of plants are the thorns and spines that many have on their leaves or stems, or even sometimes around their flowers and fruits.

The strongest spines are found on woody plants, particularly where the spine grows out of the wood of the stem, as in hawthorn. In gorse all the stems end in spiny points and the leaves are often reduced to scales in mature plants, the green stems doing the work of photosynthesis, so that there is nothing for a grazing animal to feed on. In other cases the spines are formed from the outer surface only of the stem and are easily detached, as in dog rose.

Leaf-spines tend to be less vicious, as they have a lesser thickness of tissue to strengthen them, but the elongated spines of spear thistle or the hard edges of a holly leaf can give a painful wound. The commonest type of leaf-spine, found in most thistles and in other unrelated plants, such as sea holly, arises from the thickening and extension of the leaf-margin. A holly leaf has a thick, toughened margin all around it and this continues round the lobes of the leaf, into the spines. It is an effective defence, rendering the leaf impervious to the attacks of most caterpillars, which typically start at the leaf edge and work their way in. Some caterpillars will eat holly leaves if the margin is cut off.

Another form of leaf-spine is where the main veins of the leaf continue beyond its margin. In spear thistle they project over 1 cm, but most of the leaf-margin is poorly protected by a few very much smaller and gentler spines. The lobes of its leaves project in all directions, however, almost vertically up (at an angle of about 75°) and obliquely down, at about 30° from horizontal. The result is that the leaves cannot easily be approached from any direction.

Similar developments of spines are found around many flowers, structures which plants must defend if they are to reproduce sexually. Many thistles have spiny bracts, which are just modified leaves around their flowers, and similar structures are found in burdocks, teasel and herb bennet. These are often interpreted as dispersal devices (see p. 172), and undoubtedly they may function in that way, but it seems likely that they also help protect the seeds from grazing.

Not all spiny plants have such fierce weapons. Spines come in all sizes, from thorns down to prickles which one would hardly notice, and indeed grade continuously into hairs (see next page) which are neither prickly nor sharp. Many leaves have fine prickles on their surface, often all over as in bristly ox-tongue, and not just around the edge, though there they can be almost saw-like, as in great fen sedge: such fine prickles probably play a role in deterring insects. Other plants have prickly stems: those of common cleavers, which give it such an ability to cling to clothing, may function as defences against grazing, or may be more important in enabling this fast-growing, scrambling annual to hook itself up over other plants and objects to get to the light.

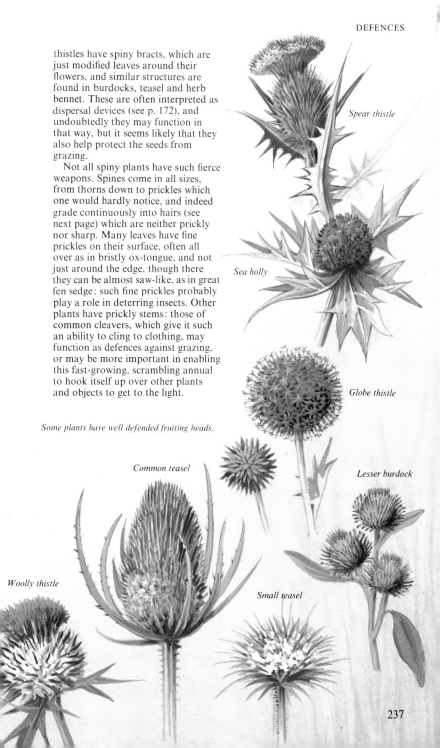

Spear thistle

Sea holly

Globe thistle

Some plants have well defended fruiting heads.

Common teasel

Lesser burdock

Woolly thistle

Small teasel

237

Hairy young sallow shoots grading back into the previous year's now hairless growth

Physical defences: hairs

Many plants have hairs on their stems and leaves, and they perform two functions. In some plants they help either to cool the surface by reflecting sunlight or, paradoxically, actually to cause it to heat up by restricting the amount of water that evaporates. The balance between these two conflicting effects depends on the type and density of hairs. Usually it is not possible to say whether the hairs on a plant perform one of these functions or whether they help to defend it. Often they probably do both; sometimes perhaps neither.

Hairs are of three main kinds: simple hairs, which are just outgrowths of one of the cells of the epidermis, the outer layer of the leaf or stem; compound hairs which are branched and consist of several cells; and glandular hairs, which are again often multicellular, and have a gland often containing chemical toxins at one end.

Simple hairs may be found almost anywhere, sometimes densely. Roots too, bear simple hairs, but these are probably responsible for maintaining contact between the root and the soil particles, allowing uptake of water. Many woody plants are hairy only on the youngest growth; as the stem matures the hairs are lost. They probably act as a defence at the most vulnerable time in the life of the shoot, before the tissues have become woody. This is why aphids cluster round the tips of rose bushes, for only there can their stylets penetrate through to the plant's transport system, the sugar-rich phloem, on which they feed. In other plants, hairs found on buds, young shoots and leaves act to prevent the aphids from getting a foothold at that critical time.

Compound hairs are commoner on leaves than stems. The dense white felt on mullein leaves, for example, is formed of masses of easily detached, branching hairs. If an animal attempts to eat a mullein leaf, the hairs stick to the lining of the mouth, causing great irritation.

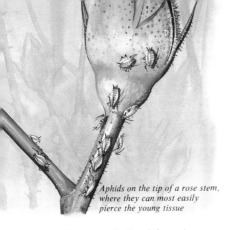

Aphids on the tip of a rose stem, where they can most easily pierce the young tissue

The most effective defence, however, is supplied by glandular hairs, such as those of great willowherb. Many of these exude sticky or irritant substances; others can inject irritants, either feebly (hedge woundwort) or powerfully (nettle). The nettle sting consists of a jointed hair which has a bent tip and contains formic acid, the same poison as in ant stings. When pressure is applied to a nettle sting, the point breaks off and the broken end acts as a small syringe, injecting the acid into the wound. As a defence it works best against large animals, though hungry ones will brave the stings. Unfortunately for nettles (but fortunately for us!), no defence is perfect, and some insects, notably the caterpillars of tortoiseshell and peacock butterflies, feed on nettle preferentially!

The surface of a mullein leaf is covered with a forest of branched hairs.

Glandular hairs and stinging hairs occupy a borderline between chemical and physical defences. They represent a stage in the development of those most complex glandular hairs found in insectivorous plants (p. 232), with their digestive enzymes and powers of movement. Not all chemical defences, however, are found in hairs; most are hidden in the plant tissue (see next page).

The caterpillar of the peacock butterfly actually prefers the nettle to other food-plants, despite the formic acid in the glandular hairs.

Chemical defences

The effects of eating deadly nightshade or hemlock are well known, but these are just two of the more dramatic examples of plant chemical defences. Most plants contain chemicals which are either unpleasant to taste or mildly or powerfully poisonous. Even some crop plants have been bred from poisonous ancestors; wild cabbage, for instance, contains cyanide-producing chemicals.

These chemicals form the last line of plant defence, and seem to be of two general kinds. Some, such as tannins, which give the flavour to tea leaves, are present in large amounts (up to 2% of the leaf weight) and make the leaf protein indigestible. They act as a general deterrent against most animals, but their production takes up a lot of the plant's energy. Others are actually poisonous or unpleasant in much smaller concentrations and so are cheaper to the plant. They act usually directly on the grazing animal, and fall into many chemical groups: alkaloids, amino-acids, cyanide-producers, and so on.

Foxglove, for example, contains a powerful cardiac glycoside, digitoxin, which acts as a muscle stimulant, and is still widely used in the treatment of heart disease; in large doses, however, it is extremely poisonous. The best-known and most virulent poisons are the alkaloids, including the atropine that makes deadly nightshade so toxic and the coniine in hemlock that killed Socrates.

Sometimes a whole plant is toxic, in others only a particular part. The seeds of many legumes contain amino-acids, the chemical building blocks of proteins, that resemble those essential in diet, but which when incorporated into a protein render it useless. The toxicity of laburnum seeds, however, is due again to an alkaloid, cytisine.

One of the most ingenious chemical defences of plants is the surprisingly widespread ability to produce cyanide. Cyanide is an extremely potent poison, active on all air-breathing organisms, and as poisonous to plants as to animals. The plant cannot therefore simply contain cyanide;

instead it manufactures two compounds, kept separate in different parts of intact cells, which give off cyanide when mixed. If a grazing animal eats such a leaf of, say, white clover or bird's-foot trefoil, it breaks the cell compartments which separate the compounds and liberates the cyanide. It has been shown that slugs prefer to eat clover leaves that do not possess this ability, even though they look identical to the cyanide-producing leaves. Unfortunately for the plant, such mixing may be brought about by the effect of frost (which causes water in cells to freeze and expand, breaking the compartments), and this leads to self-toxicity. Predictably, cyanide-producing ability becomes progressively rarer further north.

There are almost as many types of chemical defence as there are plants, and some of these chemicals are very effective. But nature is an inventive chemist, and the existence of a chemical toxin and an expanse of uneaten leaf defended by it, is a great stimulant for natural selection to produce a means of detoxifying the toxin. As a result almost every plant that is defended in this way has associated with it an insect that has learned to deal with the toxicity. Many crucifers, members of the cabbage family, for example, are poisonous to most insects, because of the potent mustard oils (related to mustard gas) that they contain: but cabbage white butterflies not only eat them with impunity, they actually locate their food plant by the smell of the mustard oil. Cinnabar moths go one better: their larvae feed on the very poisonous ragwort, which contains the alkaloids senecionin and senecin, and accumulate these so that the adult moth becomes inedible to predators by being stuffed with a plant poison.

This phenomenon explains why so many insects have specific food plants, a fact well known to butterfly enthusiasts. Over the years, insect and plant have evolved together, so that the plant is eaten only by a few herbivores (and thus is saved from devastation), while the insect has to itself a food source for which it does not have to compete with other species.

Deadly nightshade

Foxglove

Monk's-hood *Autumn crocus*

Medicinal plants

The use of wild plants as medicines has a long history: the science of botany arose as a branch of medicine and still today around half of all drugs are produced directly from plants. The medical value of a plant depends upon its possessing active chemical compounds which are almost certainly part of the plant's defensive arsenal. Foxglove, which contains digitoxin, and deadly nightshade, which contains atropine, are good examples of plants which are extremely poisonous but which contain valuable drugs. Other well-known drugs obtained from wild plants are aconitine from monk's-hood and colchicine from autumn crocus, both of which are very poisonous.

There are of course hundreds of other plants which provide milder compounds which may be used medicinally. A clue to their use is often given by the scientific name: *Anthyllis vulneraria* (kidney vetch) was used for treating wounds, *Rhamnus catharticus* (buckthorn) as a laxative, and so on, while the very common specific epithet *officinalis* (as in great burnet *Sanguisorba officinalis*, common valerian *Valeriana officinalis* or common comfrey *Symphytum officinale*) always implies a herbal use. The word 'officinal' derives from the Latin word for a store-room, and came to be used for drugs at an early date, so that when Linnaeus was coining scientific names for plants in the mid-eighteenth century, he called many drug plants *officinalis*.

Cinnabar moth caterpillars feed on the flowerheads of common ragwort; the warning red colour on the adult successfully convinces would-be predators that its body still contains the poison accumulated by the caterpillar, whose black and orange stripes are a universal warning signal in nature.

241

REPRODUCTION AND GROWTH

ANNUALS AND BIENNIALS

Plants have only limited amounts of materials to use for reproduction and growth, just as people have only limited amounts of money. People must make economic decisions as to what they will use their money for, and plants equally obey the same economic laws, without the luxury of decision-making. A poor allocation of resources, say to more leaf growth in an unfavourable environment, will lead not to poverty but to death and to the elimination of that genetic type – this is natural selection. To be successful a genetic type (or genotype) must either persist for long periods or produce successful offspring. This balance between growth and survival on the one hand and reproduction on the other, as conflicting uses of resources, is much more striking in plants than in animals, because of the ability of many plants to persist for long periods and reproduce vegetatively (see p. 248), and has resulted in the evolution of a range of life-histories, from annual to perennial.

At one extreme we have plants which complete their entire life-cycle within a year – annuals. There is an obvious disadvantage in being annual: at the end of one growing season the plant abandons the site it occupies, and new sites must be found for its seeds. Since most seeds fail to develop into new plants, very large numbers must be produced if those genes are to persist. This is achieved only by diverting a large part of the plant's resources into seed production.

This answer fails to explain why annuals should exist at all, however. The perennial, by continuing to occupy the same spot year after year (and at the same time producing some, if not so many, seeds) will always ultimately displace the annual, in a stable environment. Annuals will, therefore, only be able to survive where this perennial behaviour is impossible –

in habitats where perennials are either physically destroyed by disturbance or unable to survive because the environment is too harsh.

Disturbed habitats are the classic sites for annuals. Nowadays, the disturbance is likely to come from human activity – ploughing, digging, road-building, or simple dereliction of land – but in the past natural events such as landslides, river flooding and, on a smaller scale, mole-hills, must have been more important. The plants that grow in these places we call weeds, and they are the opportunists that colonise any bare areas and grow rapidly, producing many seeds that are, because of their numbers, more likely to find new disturbed ground.

Many of the weeds of disturbed ground are closely dependent on the

A community of 'weeds' isolated in the middle of a cereal crop, including annuals (poppy, corn marigold) and perennials

disturbances wrought by man, and since man is a recent arrival in these islands, it is not surprising that many are introduced species, some recently so (such as common field speedwell), others much more anciently; in many cases it is uncertain whether they are native or not. Common weeds such as common poppy, charlock, wild radish, field pennycress, and corn spurrey were almost certainly introduced by neolithic or later farmers along with their crops, as agriculture spread into Britain. In contrast, shepherd's purse, wild pansy, common chickweed, fat hen, common orache, knotgrass and red dead-nettle are all present in fossil deposits dating from before man colonised Britain, and so presumably survived in the limited areas disturbed by natural events.

Both groups, however, have a similar pattern of growth. They germinate either in autumn or spring, often the latter, and grow rapidly,

This part was accidentally missed by the farmer when he sprayed the field with weed-killer.

starting to flower in the early summer. The seeds often accumulate to form a seed bank (see p. 176) in the soil. Many continue to flower right through the summer, until the flowering shoot is killed by frost. Since they have formed no perennating buds, this effectively kills the plant. If, however, they have not yet reached the flowering stage in the autumn, or if they have been grown under conditions which limit flowering, many such plants will readily over-winter in a vegetative state and resume flowering the following spring. Good examples are groundsel, black medick, hairy bittercress and field pansy. These plants are not, there-fore, strict annuals, although their life-history depends on their success in producing seeds.

Often, where these 'annuals' grow naturally at high altitude (or latitude), the summer is too short for effective reproduction, and they behave there as short-lived perennials. Annual meadow-grass illustrates this well: even at low altitude populations of this common weed occur which are truly perennial – in lawns for example – but at higher altitude, on moorland paths and rocks, only short-lived perennial forms occur. It has been shown that the ability to survive into a second summer in this grass is greatest when seed production in the first summer is low.

These annuals, then, cannot be said to be avoiding winter, as is often thought, but rather to be exploiting briefly available patches of bare ground, before long-lived perennials occupy them. Equally, those plants that are strict annuals, never surviving to a second season, are avoiding not winter, but drought. Survival in a dry habitat requires a large root system, and to build such a system involves a cost in resources which cannot then be used for reproduction. Two possible ways of surviving there as a species are available: as a perennial, which produces a large root system and grows for many years, flowering only occasionally; and as an annual, growing in the wettest part of the year – the winter – and flowering in spring and surviving the dry summer as seed.

This second approach is wide-spread. Many of our common native annuals grow in this way, including common and wall whitlow-grass, shepherd's cress, sand cat's-tail, early hair-grass, spring vetch and early forget-me-not. All produce seeds which are unable to germinate on shedding in May and June, but after several months become fully ripe. They germinate in September or October and in a mild autumn achieve much of their vegetative growth before the winter. In a mild winter they will continue to grow, until they start to flower in April. By June, as the soil dries out, they have finished

flowering, and die. These plants are often called winter annuals, because their main period of growth is in and around winter, which is actually the most favourable season for them. Typical habitats are lowland rocks, walls, dry roadsides, sand dunes and other places with very thin soil which is unable to supply water in high summer.

Annuals, then, fall into two groups: those that flower once and then die, which are in a sense pre-programmed annuals; and those that die only when the environment deteriorates suffi-ciently, which might be called en-forced annuals. This distinction in fact applies to all plants, not just annuals. Some grow vegetatively for

The life-cycles of three monocarpic plants: a summer annual which passes the winter as a seed; a winter annual which passes the summer as a seed; and a biennial which flowers in its second summer.

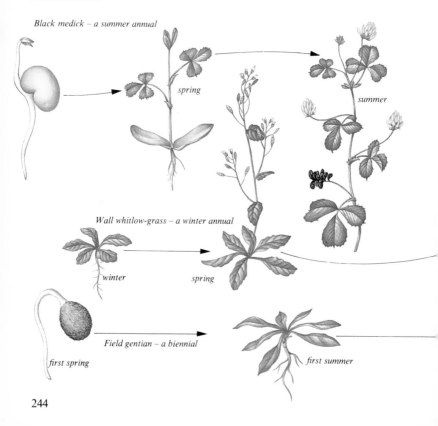

Black medick – a summer annual

spring

summer

Wall whitlow-grass – a winter annual

winter   spring

Field gentian – a biennial

first spring

first summer

a while, flower and die; others continue after flowering and may flower many times. The first sort are known as monocarpic, but perennials can be that too. The most familiar examples of monocarpic perennials are those that grow vegetatively for one year and flower in the next – biennials.

The best known biennial is the foxglove. Its seeds germinate in autumn or spring; spring-germinating seedlings grow vegetatively for a year, produce a massive rosette of leaves, which overwinters and in the following summer develops a long flower spike, which may produce several hundred thousand seeds. Exceptionally, the rosette may survive over another winter, but normally it withers and dies after flowering. Because it puts so much of its resources into seeds, it does not save enough as reserves in the rootstock and so cannot overwinter; alternatively one could say that, because it puts so few resources into an overwintering rootstock, it can therefore liberate many more seeds. This biennial pattern is not really so clear-cut, however: autumn-germinating seeds may overwinter as a small rosette and then behave like those that germinate in spring, but if they get large enough before the first winter they will flower in the following summer and die, thus becoming a winter annual. At the other extreme, foxglove rosettes on poor soil or in deep shade may

require two summers' growth before they flower; these are presumably triennials.

In practice, nature does not allow itself to be categorised too neatly. Selection has acted on plants so that those which survive and reproduce best under particular conditions are preserved. Since the conditions plants encounter vary, this may require flexibility, not only of morphology (cf. stems, pp. 184 & ff) but also of life-history. A plant such as hawkweed ox-tongue, for example, is generally said to be perennial, though it rarely lives more than a few years. It is quite capable of behaving as an annual or a biennial as well, though. Great mullein and field gentian are normally biennial, but can be annual or rarely perennial; many umbellifers (wild carrot, wild parsnip, hogweed) are biennials that can persist for a year or so; and sand spurrey is an annual that can be biennial. One very striking thing, however, is how restricted the biennial habit is. It is common in the umbellifers, mulleins and a few gentians. Weld and mignonette are either biennial or short-lived perennials, and so are a few legumes, mainly tall and ribbed melilot. Many more plants are indeterminate annuals behaving as biennials, or biennials behaving as perennials, under particular conditions.

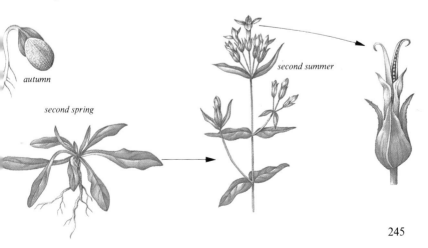

autumn

second spring

second summer

PERENNIALS – LONGEVITY AND CLONES

Annuals, biennials and other short-lived plants are the exception in the plant kingdom. They thrive only in special habitats, primarily disturbed ones. Because we, as a species, are strongly associated with disturbance, we see annuals as a more prominent feature of the plant kingdom. Where disturbance is less frequent, however, annuals fare poorly and perennials thrive, for they have the great advantage that they do not have to abandon the site they have gained and start all over again from seed.

In Britain and most of Europe, sites that are not disturbed frequently by man quickly develop a cover of trees, usually within 20 to 30 years. There are exceptions to this rule – mountain tops, saltmarshes and river shingle, for example – but these environments are usually either naturally disturbed or harsh. The communities of stable sites are dominated by long-lived plants. Woodlands comprise trees and shrubs, which as woody plants are often very long-lived, but also a ground layer of shade-tolerant plants. Few of these are annuals: mostly they are slow-growing perennials such as dog's mercury or wood sorrel, or else bulb-forming species which grow in the brief light period before the tree leaves develop – bluebells, for example. Woodland annuals are rare: only three-nerved sandwort, climbing corydalis and touch-me-not balsam are native, though the introduced balsams, particularly small balsam, also grow in shade. The main problem for an annual in shade is to grow fast enough in one season to produce enough seeds to perpetuate the species.

If the perennial habit is the norm in undisturbed habitats, the term conceals a great range in life-span. Surprisingly, although much is known of the life-spans of many animals and of some plants, notably trees, few herbaceous and shrubby species have been well studied. Some perennials such as carline thistle are indubitably

A green-winged orchid may spend several years without flowering, in some years producing a non-flowering rosette, and in others not appearing above ground at all.

short-lived, persisting perhaps only 4–5 years; others appear to survive much longer. Orchids in particular are renowned for their ability to disappear from a site, only to be rediscovered 20 or 30 years later. Green-winged orchid and lizard orchid both display this erratic behaviour, apparently because in some sites in most years the plant fails to flower and so is not observed.

The main problem in determining the longevity of most herbaceous perennials lies in defining the individual. An oak tree develops from an acorn, grows a single large trunk bearing a crown of branches, lives for perhaps 300 years, and dies. A rosebay willowherb seed grows into a plant with an erect, annual stem and a ramifying perennial system of rhizomes underground. In the second year this rhizome system puts up several stems; in the third, many, and so on. Is this one individual, or many? One might say that as long as all the above-ground shoots are linked by below-ground connections, the whole patch represents a single individual;

alternatively it could be seen as a clone of genetically identical individuals.

Definition becomes more difficult when the below-ground connections are severed, either physically or naturally, as the clone matures. Then the clone may develop into a series of patches, possibly well separated, but all genetically identical. Each patch is as closely related to all other patches as the stems within a patch are to each other. It is easy to see that such clonal plants are potentially immortal, in the sense that some part of the super-individual that makes up the clone may survive. Patches of bracken, which spread by rhizomes, have been shown by careful investigation to be one or two thousand years old; and in one study the red fescue plants in an ordinary (but ancient) pasture were shown to belong to a number of distinct clones, the oldest of which was estimated at around 800 years – probably the time at which the field was first created from the original wildwood.

This capacity to form clones only occurs in plants that possess the capacity to reproduce vegetatively.

The methods of vegetative reproduction are numerous (see p. 248), but have in common the avoidance of the sexual process, which would mix up the genetic system. Hence all vegatively produced offspring are identical genetically (although the action of distinct environments on them may produce different *looking* plants), and from this arises the problem of knowing what an individual of such a plant is.

As with all plant activities, however, vegetative reproduction involves the diverting of resources from other activities. Plants that produce rhizomes cannot use those resources for flowers, leaves or roots. Vegetative reproduction – the production of new 'individuals' – is an alternative to sexual reproduction and to normal growth, though not an exclusive alternative: all three can occur simultaneously. Some perennials have no means of vegetative reproduction: they are usually short-lived – lesser hawkbit or ploughman's spikenard, for example – and lie between annuals and biennials on the one hand, and the really long-lived perennials, which almost always have some such means, on the other.

The spread of rosebay willowherb by means of underground rhizomes may produce a patch of the plant. Is each patch one individual, or many?

VEGETATIVE REPRODUCTION

An annual at the end of the growing season needs to put as much as possible of its resources into seeds. It is common to find flowering and fruiting individuals of plants such as groundsel and shepherd's purse, growing in cracks in pavements or on gravel paths where the nutrient supply is limited, which possess only one or two leaves and a meagre root system, but several flowers. A perennial in the same situation would almost certainly fail to flower, for the perennial life-style depends upon maintaining occupation of the site – the ecological equivalent of 'possession is nine-tenths of the law'.

This requirement by perennials means that spare resources must be stored for the next growth season, to give the plant a head-start. This is why some umbellifers produce little more than a pair of cotyledons (seed-leaves) above ground in their first year, all the production being used to build a food-rich taproot which can fund the next year's growth (p. 213). For reasons of safety, such storage nearly always takes place below ground where it is hidden from the large above-ground herbivores.

The simplest form of overwintering organ is a swollen rootstock, and is found in many composites (e.g. dandelion, wall lettuce, goatsbeard), plantains (e.g. ribwort plantain) and umbellifers (e.g. angelica) and in many species of the rose and butter-cup families. Equally simple are those shrubby or woody plants which survive above ground in winter with woody stems. These may be quite short-lived as in snapdragon, or much more persistent as in heather or crowberry. Some plants manage the same effect without woody stems, but usually only in mild, often maritime conditions, for example sea milkwort.

These methods, however, usually achieve only the survival of the individual in its original site. Much more frequent is the adaptation of the perennating structure to perform a

second function – dispersal and multiplication. For example, many plants which overwinter by means of a rootstock, have in fact a branching stock, each branch of which may form a new plantlet above ground, so that the original individual rapidly becomes a colony. Branching stocks are found in several campions and allies (white and sea campions, Nottingham catchfly, ragged robin) in the pink family, in many members of the rose family (tormentil, lady's-mantle), in several perennial stonecrops (roseroot, orpine), in grass of Parnassus, common sea-lavender, thrift, some bellflowers and many composites (goldenrod, ox-eye daisy).

Although a branching stock can, in time, allow the plant to spread some distance, it largely results in a dense colony at a particular point, giving a very clumped pattern. The disadvantage of this is that all the new 'individuals' are in effect competing with each other for living space. The advantage is simply that the vigorous

Above: *In poor conditions, an annual such as shepherd's purse* (left) *will channel its resources into the flowers, which are for reproduction, at the expense of its roots and leaves; wall lettuce* (right) *survives the winter as a swollen rootstock.*

colony so produced is very resistant to competition from other species, and many of the species given as examples are able to survive in one place for long periods.

Greater dispersal requires the development of long thin structures and these are of two main kinds – rhizomes and stolons (p. 250). Rhizomes are long-lived, and stolons are annual structures, though they are produced by perennial plants. The same effect is produced in a few plants by the development of buds on wide-ranging roots, as in fen violet. In all these the advantage of dispersal is clear-cut, but the disadvantage is more subtle.

The new plants produced by rhizomes and stolons are all genetically identical to the parent. The parent landed (by seed) or was placed (by rhizome or stolon) in its site quite randomly. The site was obviously not unfavourable, for it survived, though many of its fellows may have perished in nearby, but less suitable places. In a sense, natural selection has matched plant to site. As the rhizome or stolon grows away from the parent, it is more and more likely to encounter different, less favourable, conditions. Since there is no genetic variation here, the new plantlets will be selected against in such conditions.

This can be seen happening in white clover, one of the most mobile of all plants. Take a time-lapse film of your lawn over several years and you will see the clover wandering through it quite nomadically as the stolons grow continuously at one end, and die back at the other. Yet the clover in your lawn probably comprises several clones, and in one field it was found that each clone grew best with a particular species of grass. As those clones wandered through that field, they must continually have been moving through patches of different grass species, sometimes therefore finding themselves in a favourable patch and sometimes in an unfavourable one.

Left: *The branching rootstocks of sea campion, sea pink (thrift) and sea mayweed produce clumps and cushions of individual plants.*

249

RHIZOMES AND STOLONS

Rhizomes and stolons are horizontal stems that produce new plants at intervals along their lengths. Rhizomes are long-lived and as a result often double up the functions of dispersal and storage – yellow iris rhizomes, for example, are thick and full of stored food; stolons are short-lived and normally wither away once the new plantlet has established its own roots and leaves. While they persist they serve as a channel for nutrients from the parent to its vegetative offspring.

Rhizomes are almost invariably underground, and the resistance offered by soil, coupled with their generally greater diameter associated with food storage, probably explains the shorter distance covered annually by rhizomes as opposed to stolons. Violets display a complete range of rhizome and stolon production: marsh violet has a long rhizome, spreading about 20 cm a year; heath dog violet and hairy violet have a much shorter rhizome, covering only 1 or 2 cm a year; common dog violet has no rhizome at all, but can produce plants from buds on its roots; and sweet violet has both a short rhizome and long stolons which root at the ends and reach 30 to 40 cm.

Other plants manage much greater distances: the rhizomes of butterbur and rosebay willowherb can both reach over a metre underground, though 20 to 30 cm is much more usual, as in sand sedge, water mint, ground elder and nettle. Sand sedge is unusual in that its rhizomes can

Yellow flag (yellow iris) and its rhizome

travel in almost perfect straight lines for years at a time, rarely branching, enabling it to colonise patches of bare sand created by wind on sand dunes. Its progress is marked by a tuft of shoots every 10 to 20 cm. In more closed communities, however, it branches more frequently, forming a network rather than a line. By excavating the sand from around a sand sedge rhizome one can follow its progress: it stays strictly 10 cm or so below the surface, even where that is sloping. It is a moot point how the rhizome achieves this; probably it detects daily changes in temperature, which would get more and more marked nearer to the surface.

Sand sedge spreading over a dune 'blow-out' by means of a network of underground rhizomes

Many rhizomatous plants are capable of forming dense stands that exclude all other species, by filling the space with a network of shoots. Wood small-reed and common reed are two grasses adept at this, the latter forming enormous reed beds in wet places; others with this ability are pestilential weeds, such as creeping thistle, nettle and ground elder. The network of branching rhizomes exhibits a predominance of 120° angles; by branching thus they form hexagonal shapes, and hexagons are the only regular shapes apart from triangles and rectangles which can completely fill an area of ground.

Some stolons, too, spread underground, where they are perhaps less vulnerable to grazing animals. Many are aerial, however, and in some cases may be borne well clear of the ground, only rooting where the tip returns to earth, when they are called runners. There are many plants with above-ground stolons and runners which spread easily a metre or more each year – wild strawberry, creeping cinquefoil and silverweed are all closely related examples, and ground ivy can manage a similar distance. The longest reach of all, however, is undoubtedly achieved by brambles, whose arching stems may hit the ground five metres or more from the parent. Most of these plants are members of the rose family, but stolons are widely found: creeping buttercup, white clover, water forget-me-not and smooth meadow-grass are all stoloniferous and cover the whole taxonomic range.

More important, perhaps, than the length of the stolon, is the number of plantlets produced along it. Stolons of creeping buttercup can easily produce five new plants in a season, with intervals of around 20 cm between them, shorter in thick vegetation, longer on bare soil. If a single plant sends out two runners, producing 10 plantlets, and the following season each of those does the same, in a short time a large area can be filled with creeping buttercup plants. This often happens in poorly cultivated gardens.

Rhizomes and stolons, then, achieve both multiplication and dispersal, often over considerable distances. They give the new plant a high chance of survival because in its early life it can be supported by nutrients transported from the parent plant. This explains why such plants are so effective at colonising and excluding other species from small patches of ground.

Wild strawberry and creeping buttercup both spread by means of stolons and runners.

251

BULBS, CORMS AND TUBERS

The contrast between the two roles of vegetative reproduction – dispersal, and storage for persistence – is well seen in the range of form of rhizomes. Many plants have long rhizomes which distribute new plantlets over a wide area (see p. 250); equally commonly, however, the rhizome is so short that it cannot achieve this, and the storage function is obviously predominant.

Short rhizomes, corms and tubers are all swollen, underground stems: rhizomes last for more than one year, corms last for one year and form new corms in the axils of the scale-leaves they bear, and tubers also last for one year and are simply formed by the swelling of the stem-base, in no particular relationship to last year's tuber. The distinction, though, between the three is often made, but equally often hard to apply. Strictly, gladiolus and meadow saffron (or autumn crocus) have a corm, lords-and-ladies and bulbous buttercup a tuber, and violet helleborine a vertical rhizome.

The result is in all three cases the same, however, and moreover is ecologically more or less indistinguishable from the possession of a vertical rootstock (see p. 213) or of root tubers, as in common spotted orchid, or of adventitious buds on roots, as in common dog violet. Evidently during evolution many different methods have been adopted to achieve the same end result, and some may represent evolutionary steps towards others. All those methods differ considerably in structure, though again not in function, from bulbs. Bulbils are swollen leaf-bases, full of stored food, and

wrapped around a series of buds, one of which, the terminal bud, is usually much the biggest. We can perhaps see a stage in the evolution of bulbs in the swollen leaf-bases of wood sorrel, scattered along its overwintering rhizome. In bulbous plants the stem is contracted and the leaf-bases gathered together, as in snowdrop. The above-ground parts of plants such as snowdrop consist of leaves, flower-stem and flower-stalk, but no stem, which is confined to the bulb.

Although the same result – storage of food without dispersal – is achieved by so many different morphological adaptations, there is a common ecological thread linking many of these plants. Northern Europe is rather poor in bulbous and similar plants: irises, crocuses and daffodils are much more characteristic of mediterranean regions, where early spring is the most favourable time for growth, and the summer is too dry. There these plants undergo rapid growth and flowering during the wet season and then die back above ground, withdrawing nutrients back into the bulb or corm.

One or two such plants penetrate northwards (including gladiolus and grape hyacinth), but the majority of them are found in what is apparently a quite different habitat: deciduous woodland. Many of the classic flowers of the spring woodland floor grow from such storage organs, including snowdrop, bluebell, ramsons, marta-

Common dog violet: adventitious bud on root

Snowdrop: bulb

Wood sorrel: swollen leaf base along rhizome

Autumn crocus: corm

gon lily and yellow star of Bethlehem (bulbs), lords-and-ladies and early purple orchid (tubers), and primrose, wood anemone, lily-of-the-valley and common solomon's seal (rhizome). In that habitat there is a brief window from about March to May, when the sun is high enough to allow rapid growth before the trees have leafed up. To exploit it these plants must be able to present a fully developed set of leaves as early as March: February is usually too cold to make these from scratch, and so the stored food (and often the pre-formed leaves themselves) inside the bulb or corm are used to create them rapidly.

Most perennials, then, have some form of vegetative reproduction, though it is often as much concerned with survival as multiplication. Almost every part of a plant has in one species or another been turned to this purpose, even the flowers in some viviparous species (see p. 292). Sometimes the adaptations involve great specialisation; in other cases they involve simply the ability of a bit of a plant to generate roots and continue growth. All gardeners know that many woody plants will 'take' from cuttings. This can happen in the field, where crack willow branches, which

break off readily in a gale, may embed themselves in the ground and root. More surprisingly, some leaves can do this too: cuckoo flower leaflets pressed onto damp earth will readily develop tiny roots and a new stem, by effectively generating new buds along the margin. This seems to be quite a common phenomenon in the wild in cuckoo flower, and, though probably rarer, it is known in watercress, marsh yellowcress, greater celandine, and bog orchid. There is a continuous series of types ranging from these adventitious buds, formed opportunistically, to the bulbils habitually produced on leaves or in leaf-axils of a range of plants, including lesser celandine, whose shade-loving subspecies produces bulbils, but in which the type found in full sun never does.

These examples simply serve to emphasise the importance of vegetative reproduction in the normal growth of most perennials.

Many mechanisms of vegetative propagation in plants have more to do with survival than with dispersal.

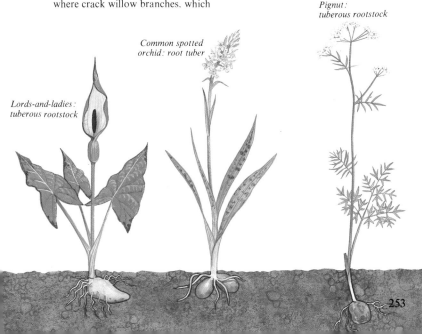

Pignut:
tuberous rootstock

Common spotted orchid: root tuber

Lords-and-ladies:
tuberous rootstock

SEXUAL REPRODUCTION: PROBLEMS

The distinguishing feature of the flowering plants is their method of sexual reproduction. The flower is a structure that has evolved under the pressure of the need to transfer male sex cells to female ones. All flowering plants possess flowers, though in some they have been modified to perform a non-sexual reproductive act (vivipary p. 292, apomixis p. 290). Yet nearly all perennial flowering plants also possess means of vegetative reproduction, suggesting that the sexual method is not always the best. In fact, sexual reproduction poses some very great problems.

An individual flowering plant, if it survives to maturity, must be adequately fitted to its environment. Consider that many plants can produce hundreds of thousands of seeds in their lifetime (see p. 161), of which on average only one survives (or there would be a tendency for the population to increase or decrease). Many of those that fail to survive will be perfectly capable of growing in suitable places but will simply never find them, or else will be killed by some wholly fortuitous event, unconnected with their fitness, such as being swept away by a landslide or run over by a lorry. Despite this large element of chance, the concept of natural selection and common sense both dictate that the lone survivor will be well adapted.

Sexual reproduction, however, involves destroying that well-adapted mixture of genes and producing hundreds of new ones. The old combination may turn up in them, in all important respects, and some of the new ones may be actually better adapted (though chance events may eliminate them). Many, however, will be less well adapted. Sexual reproduction, therefore, may equally result in a reduction in adaptedness as in an increase in it, whereas vegetative reproduction simply copies the genes of the parent exactly, and so preserves the already successful combination. Sexual reproduction is, therefore, a

A clump of yellow archangel progresses vegetatively very well, but for sexual reproduction its seeds will be faced with myriad problems: they may fall on a road or in water; where it is too dry or too wet; too shaded or too cluttered with other plants; or it may be eaten by mammal or bird.

high risk activity, though of course if environmental conditions are changing the range of new genetic types it offers allows evolutionary change to occur, possibly resulting in better adapted types.

It is hard for us to observe these sorts of changes in nature, but where man alters the environment he creates new conditions. Soils contaminated with metals by mining (mainly lead, zinc and copper: see p. 218) show it happening. They have been colonised by newly-evolved populations of grasses such as common bent and red fescue, resistant to the toxic metals. Significantly, these grasses reproduce both sexually and vegetatively, the former allowing the new types to appear, the latter their propagation without alteration.

Another problem of sexual reproduction lies in its association with seeds. The seed has evolved as a dispersal structure, allowing plants to migrate to new habitats literally in

space and figuratively (by dormancy) in time. This sets limits on its size. Although some seeds are large, with weights of 10 grams or more, most are much smaller, weighing a few milligrams, and many are lighter still (p. 161). A small seed has little in the way of food reserves for the developing seedling, which is consequently vulnerable; it is no accident that in most plants the bulk of the massive mortality occurs in the seed and seedling phases. In contrast, vegetative reproduction normally involves a phase in which the offshoot is connected to the parent and can be directly nurtured by it.

Perhaps the subtlest problem of sex, however, lies in its effect on the propagation of genes. The theory of evolution by natural selection depends upon the idea that evolutionary change comes from the transmission of gene combinations from one generation to the next: those that get through are selected for, those that do not are selected against. Gene combinations will be more favoured by selection, therefore, if all their genes are transmitted than if only some are. We have already seen that on average each individual leaves just one offspring; in a sexually reproducing individual that offspring will have only half of each of its two parents' genes. In vegetative reproduction it will have all of its one parent's genes. In that case, gene combinations which involve vegetative reproduction will be favoured, as they come through to the offspring twice as often, all other things being equal.

In practice, they are *not* equal. The lack of flexibility in response to environmental change offered by vegetative reproduction condemns a species limited to that alone to earlier extinction, however successful it may be in the short term. But the advantages of vegetative reproduction ensure that most perennials use both methods.

255

POLLINATION AND FERTILISATION

The essential act of sexual reproduction in plants is the fusion of a cell nucleus within the pollen grain with another in the egg cell. Achieving this involves the transport of the pollen grains from the anther, where they are formed, to the stigma, the receptive surface connected to the ovary by the style. On arrival the grains germinate, just as moss spores do on damp soil, and the tube produced by each grain grows down the style connecting stigma to ovary, until one tube reaches the egg cell.

This journey is wonderfully improbable. The likelihood of a pollen grain reaching the style is so small that millions must be produced. The vast majority will not even reach a stigma, and many that do will land on one of the wrong species. Those grains usually fail to germinate at all and, even if they do, they fail to grow down the style. That growth is a quite extraordinary event, akin to the growth of a parasitic fungus. Just as human tissues produce antibodies to resist infection by pathogenic organisms, so plant tissues can repel invaders. Yet they not only allow the growth of the pollen tube of their own species; they actually stimulate its germination and growth by specific chemical secretions. To understand how this occurs we need to look at the pollen more carefully.

Pollen is formed inside the anthers and each grain is in fact a spore (see p. 12). The individual pollen grains vary greatly in size, from less than 10 micrometres (thousandths of a millimetre) in the borage family – forget-me-nots, buglosses and comfreys – to nearly a hundred micrometres in herb robert and hedge bindweed. Some cultivated plants, such as melons and marrows, have larger grains still, often over one-fifth of a millimetre (200 micrometres).

The grains differ between species, however, in much more than size. Even under a simple lens, differences in shape can be seen, from the spherical grains of grasses and pondweeds

The flowers of rosebay willowherb, showing the sexual parts and the mechanisms for cross-pollination

anthers mature

pollen

stigmas mature

to more or less triangular or elongated forms. Much the greatest and most surprising differences appear, however, if the grains are looked at under a microscope, when the walls turn out to be minutely textured and sculptured. Remarkably, these patterns are so distinctive that virtually all pollen grains can be identified to the family of plants they come from, most to the genus, and many to the species.

The patterns consist of a number of pores or furrows, which run across the surface, and a finer-scale sculpturing of the areas between the furrows. One pore or furrow is the point where the pollen tube emerges from the grain; if there are others they are the sites at which chemicals involved in the recognition of grains by stigma are exuded (p. 273). In addition, the pores or furrows may be scattered over the surface of the grain, or grouped either around its equator or at one or more poles. Add to this the fact that some grains habitually occur in pairs, or in groups of four (heather, bulrush) or more (orchids), and the complexity of the system is obvious.

Sometimes large genera or whole families have similar grains. Pondweeds all have simple spherical grains with no pores nor furrows, and sedges and grasses (whole families) have a single pore. Meadow saffron has two pores, willowherbs three, and grass of Parnassus has three furrows. With so few features there is little scope for variation here, but grains with more pores and furrows can be very different in appearance. With four, there can be four pores around the equator (harebell and some other bellflowers),

four at the poles (water milfoil), or four scattered on the surface (nettle); or there may be four furrows symmetrically places (mare's-tail), four furrows scattered (buttercups), or even two furrows and two pores (docks). With five or six apertures there is equally great variation; deadnettles, bedstraws, violets, plantains and spurreys are examples. Finally there are grains with large numbers of pores (goosefoots), furrows (primrose) or both (bladderworts); some of these can be exquisitely beautiful objects.

Added to this (though best seen under a scanning electron microscope) there is the detailed sculpturing of the wall between the apertures. A few grains are quite smooth (monk's-hood), some are finely pitted (bindweeds, chickweeds), but most have minute projections, which may be very regular (dogwood), pointed (mallows, bellflowers), in a parallel arrangement (cinquefoils) or a network (crucifers, yellow iris), and so on.

All this astonishing variation is not just decoration. It plays an important role in the complex process by which the stigma recognises pollen as being of the same or a different species. It also, quite incidentally, enables scientists to reconstruct ancient vegetation from the pollen preserved in lake sediments and peat bogs, for the pollen grain wall is not only very recognisable, but also very resistant to decay.

There is infinite variety in the form of pollen grains; these are magnified 1,000 times.

PROTECTION OF POLLEN

The requirement for pollination – that
the pollen be transferred to a stigma –
means that the pollen must be dis-
played to an appropriate vector. This
may be the wind (p. 274), insects
(p. 218), water (p. 276), or other
agents; but this act of display renders
the pollen susceptible to damage from
sudden showers, low temperatures or
other physical hazards. Clearly anything which reduced these hazards
would be advantageous, and though
it is hard to prove the point, there
are a number of features of flowers
which are easiest to explain in this
way.

The simplest solution is an arrangement of the flowers so that they
cannot be wetted, for example. A
large group of plants has bell-shaped,
hanging flowers, notably in the
heather family: heather, bilberry,
cowberry and cranberry are all like
this and all tend to grow in wet
climates. Snowdrops, too, hang down
in flower. Equally, the structure of the
flower may be such as to protect the
anthers and stigmas; many plants,
notably in the labiate and figwort
families have lips, the anthers often
sitting tightly in the upper lip, or in
the keel of peaflowers. It is just as
likely that such an arrangement has
been selected in response to insect
pollination, but an additional advantage may have accrued from pollen
protection. It is important to remem-
ber that characteristics are selected
because they improve the plant's
survival overall, not only because they
do one particular job well.

Many plants, however, have flowers
permanently 'face-up'. Some of these
are constructed in such a way that
pollen movement is possible, but
water cannot enter. Globeflower
flowers never open; their many petals
(which are actually petal-like sepals)
form an overlapping roof to the
flower, which raindrops cannot penetrate, though sufficiently determined
insects can.

A more widespread structure is for
the stamens and styles to be inside a
narrow tube in the centre of the

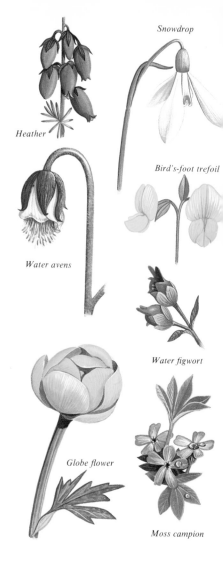

Pollen may be protected by nodding, tubular or
closed flowers.

flower (as in alpine gentian, moss
campion, or bird's-eye primrose),
whose opening is too narrow to admit
a raindrop. It is common to see a pool
of water sitting atop this tube after
rain, while the tube itself remains dry
inside.

The most striking protective responses, though, are those that in-

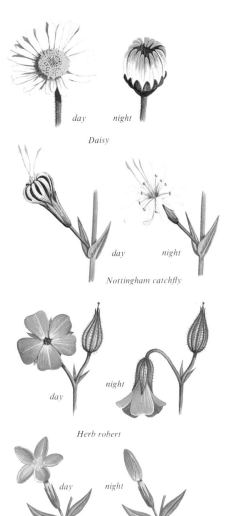

day   *night*

Daisy

day   *night*

Nottingham catchfly

night

day

Herb robert

day   *night*

Common centaury

The 'sleep movements' in various flowers.

volve movement. The 'sleep' movements of leaves are most likely an anti-frost and -dew device (see p. 200); the similar movements of flowers probably have the same effect. Common centaury, clustered bellflower and hepatica are three unrelated plants all of which have petals that close over the centre of the flower at

night, though the best-known examples are all composites. Daisy gets its name (a contraction of 'day's eye') from the fact that its flowers only open in bright weather; they close always at night and open fully in sunshine; on wet mornings they never open at all, unless very old. The same happens in dandelions, nipplewort, wall lettuce, goatsbeard and chicory. All these, of course, have compound flowerheads and it is the outer, straplike flowers, which take on the protective function and bend over to enclose the inner tubular ones. In other cases it is the flower-stalk that moves, being erect in the day and drooping at night, as in herb robert.

These movements are all reversible; but in some plants they are part of the normal course of growth. A foxglove stem in full flower has unopened buds at the top, flowers in the middle and fruits at the base. The stalks of the buds point upwards, those of the flowers downwards and those of the fruit straight out or up again, and the same can be seen in yellow loosestrife, wintergreen, columbine and water avens, linked only by their type of flowerhead – a long, stalked spike. It is perhaps too simplistic to assume that this achieves all the necessary advantages: exposure to the sun for the developing bud and the ripening fruit, and protection from rain for the flower. Certainly an upward-pointing foxglove flower would fill with water in the first shower. Interestingly, bumble-bees often spend the night in foxglove flowers: since they point downwards rather than towards the sky, their interior will not lose heat by radiation to a clear sky so quickly.

Needless to say, plants which are pollinated by night-flying moths should show no such responses. The best examples are either horizontal tube-flowers such as honeysuckle, or erect flowers with the stamens and styles in a central, narrow tube, as in white campion. Some campions go to the extreme of only unrolling their petals at night – in hot sun Nottingham and night-flowering catchflies are both unattractive, but at night have elegant and conspicuous flowers.

SELF-POLLINATION

All that is essential for seed formation in many plants is that pollen from a plant of that species should fall onto the stigma. In others, however, it is essential for the pollen to come from a different plant of the same species – in other words, only cross-pollination is achieved, not self-pollination. The reasons for this lie in genetics.

There is a widespread belief that inbreeding is bad. In human societies that is best exemplified by the almost universal taboo on incest, but also at a more trivial level by such myths as that the Hapsburg Emperors became steadily more and more dotty as they continually inbred. Inbreeding in plants in the strict sense implies self-pollination (selfing), but the same genetic effect is achieved over many generations by cross-pollination (crossing) between a small, self-contained population of plants, within which the total set of genes available is very restricted.

It is certainly not an unreservedly bad thing: breeders of crop plants rely on inbred lines for achieving good results. What the plant breeders, at least, are trying to achieve is a lack of variability. They want to ensure that each wheat plant in a seed-lot carries the same set of genes – for disease resistance, high yield, protein content and so on – and they do this by continual selfing, which eliminates variation.

In wild plants exactly the same thing happens. Every time a plant selfs, exactly half the variability is lost, since each parent has two sets of genes (which may be different) but each sex cell (gamete) has only one. When they fuse, some of what were pairs of different genes will become pairs of identical ones, but no new pairs of different genes will be created. In the long run, then, inbreeding reduces variability and, since the environment will ultimately most certainly change, complete inbreeding means certain extinction. This exactly parallels the balance that determines whether plants reproduce sexually or vegetatively (p. 254). Inbreeding, like

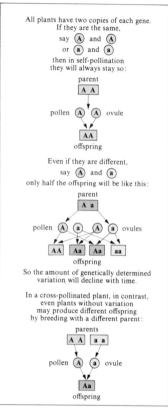

All plants have two copies of each gene. If they are the same,
say (A) and (A)
or (a) and (a)
then in self-pollination they will always stay so:

parent
A A
pollen (A) (A) ovule
AA
offspring

Even if they are different,
say (A) and (a)
only half the offspring will be like this:

parent
A a
pollen (A) (a) (A) (a) ovules
AA Aa Aa aa
offspring

So the amount of genetically determined variation will decline with time.

In a cross-pollinated plant, in contrast, even plants without variation may produce different offspring by breeding with a different parent:

parents
A A a a
pollen (A) (a) ovule
Aa
offspring

vegetative reproduction, does offer the advantage (exploited by the plant breeder) of perpetuating a successful genetic type; so successful inbreeders will be at an advantage in the short term, and doomed to extinction in the long term.

One solution to this paradox is, as with the sexual/vegetative conundrum, to do both. The majority of flowering plants reproduce sexually both by outbreeding and inbreeding. They are remarkably well suited to doing this: the great majority have hermaphrodite flowers with both stamens and styles. It is physically no problem, then, for the pollen to get to the stigma in the same flower. Nevertheless, many flowers appear to go to great lengths to ensure that that does not happen, that selfing is prohibited. The various mechanisms include differences in the time at which stamens and styles mature (p. 262), structural separation of stamens and styles (p. 266), chemical barriers which stop selfing pollen tubes from growing (p. 268) and, in the extreme, separation of stamens and styles into separate flowers on separate plants (p. 270).

Many of these devices are, however, only partial. They favour outcrossing: but if pollen from another plant fails to materialise, they do not prohibit selfing – better some selfed seeds than none at all. At the other extreme lie flower types in which *only* selfing is possible: these are called cleistogamous flowers and their sepals and petals never open, so that there is neither access nor escape for the pollen.

Cleistogamous flowers are found on many plants, but all have normal, open flowers as well which allow cross-pollination if possible. They range throughout the taxonomic spectrum: sweet violet, wood sorrel, knotgrass, sundews, field gentian, trailing St John's-wort, corn spurrey, germander speedwell, touch-me-not balsam, water violet, bogbean and toad rush are a few examples. Often the 'normal' flowers are very showy and the much smaller cleistogamous flowers may be hard to spot.

There seems to be no clear-cut ecological pattern here: plants of almost all types of habitat are represented, though deep shade (sweet violet, touch-me-not balsam) and water (water violet, mudwort, blinks) are particularly well represented. Many of the species involved are annuals, too, and there is an advantage to an annual in selfing. Since their habitats are short-lived, dispersal is their normal way of life, and by chance individuals may often find themselves growing isolated from others, when cross-pollination will be impossible.

Many colonising annuals self-pollinate, sometimes through truly cleistogamous flowers (knotgrass, corn spurrey), and sometimes simply because their flowers are so small and inconspicuous that insect visits are unlikely (thale cress, common whit-

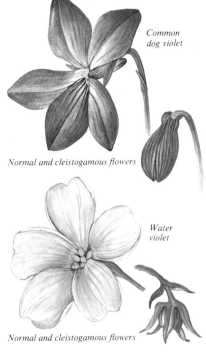

Common dog violet

Normal and cleistogamous flowers

Water violet

Normal and cleistogamous flowers

Small-flowered cranesbill: the anthers are so close to the stigmas that self-pollination is almost inevitable.

low-grass, early forget-me-not, corn-salad, dove's-foot cranesbill). They must often find themselves reduced to small populations, when selfing may be the only route to survival. The flowers of many of these plants, such as small-flowered cranesbill and chaffweed, have anthers so close to stigmas that selfing is almost inevitable.

261

CROSS-POLLINATION: DICHOGAMY

The simplest way of ensuring cross-pollination in a typical hermaphrodite flower is for the stamens and styles to mature at different times – this is known as dichogamy. Where the stamens mature first the term is protandry (literally, male first), and where the styles mature first it is protogyny. Of course such an arrangement does not prevent pollen from an adjoining flower on the same plant from being transferred to the stigma, but it at least prohibits the accidental transfer of pollen from anther to stigma *within* a flower, which is the most likely source of self-pollination.

Protandry and protogyny are most easily seen on plants which have their flowers in long spikes typically opening from the base upwards. Sometimes whole families have the same arrangement: the crucifers are all protogynous, and wild cabbage, cuckoo flower and garlic mustard show this well, as do common toad-flax, nightshades, most of the rose family, including agrimony and herb bennet, valerians, heathers and Jacob's ladder. Protandry is equally widely distributed and is clearly seen in rosebay willowherb and foxglove, but is also found in meadow cranesbill, and most of the umbellifers, saxifrages, composites, pink, pea-flower, mallow, bellflower and dead-nettle families. There seems to be no clearly-defined significance in whether a plant is protandrous or protogynous. Within a family or even a genus, both types may occur (meadow cranesbill *Geranium pratense* is protandrous but herb robert *G. robertianum* is protogynous).

Hermaphrodite flowers in which anthers and styles mature simultaneously, which would almost certainly result in automatic selfing, are rare. Clearly there is strong selection pressure for the anthers and stigmas to mature at different times. Protogyny is the more reliable mechanism, since in the initial phase (when only the stigmas are mature) only cross-pollination may occur. Unless protandry is complete, so that the anthers are withered before the stigmas mature, there will be a phase when the stigmas are receptive and the anthers still shedding pollen, so that selfing is likely. Many plants have evolved complex pollination mechanisms which avoid this problem.

Complete dichogamy, where one set of sexual organs has ceased to function before the other becomes active, is rather rare. Wood and meadow cranesbill flowers have mature anthers while the stigmas are still hidden; after the anthers have released their pollen, they fall off their filaments and then the tip of the style unfurls and reveals the five stigmas. The same thing happens in grass of Parnassus, spring sandwort and common valerian. The opposite case – complete protogyny – is apparently rarer, but certainly occurs in pellitory-of-the-wall and marsh arrow-grass.

Most hermaphrodite flowers show a much smaller separation than this, with a period when anthers are shedding pollen and stigmas are receptive to it. In protogynous flowers this enables the plant to fall back on selfing if cross-pollination of the stigma in the initial phase has failed. In protandrous plants, achieving this fail-safe policy involves much more complex arrangements, for if the possibility of cross-pollination is to be allowed, there must be three phases: first the anthers mature and liberate pollen, then the stigmas become receptive, and only then, if crossing has failed, is selfing admitted.

In protogynous forms such as crucifers (thale cress, hoary cress, scurvy-grasses) the stamen filaments elongate after the stigmas have first matured, so depositing pollen on the stigma, but having first allowed crossing. The small cranesbills – herb robert, shining cranesbill, long-stalked cranesbill – are also protogynous: five of the anthers are adjacent to the stigma anyway and pollinate it a few hours after the flower opens. The other five then elongate, protrude from the flower, and make pollen available for crossing.

Time-lapse of protandry in wood cranesbill: the anthers are withered by the time the stigmas open.

Time-lapse of protogyny in long-stalked cranesbill: half the anthers effect self-pollination, and the others make pollen available for cross-pollination.

Members of the pink family also have two sets of stamens, but they are all protandrous. In sand catchfly, water chickweed, common chickweed and corn spurrey, for example, the first ring of five stamens shed pollen as soon as the flowers open; at this stage the stigmas are stuck together and unavailable. Soon the stigmas unfurl and become receptive, and the filaments of the remaining anthers then elongate and move inwards so that their anthers sit next to the stigmas. If cross-pollination has failed, as in many of these plants it often has, selfing is guaranteed.

Such stamen movements, achieved by the elongation and bending of the filaments, are very common. Stamens that bend in to the centre of the flower are found in many umbellifers (e.g. fool's parsley), in enchanter's nightshade, agrimony, hedge bed-straw, greater celandine, brooklime and common star of Bethlehem for example. The mechanisms which control the precision of such movements

is, however, still obscure. The same result could be achieved by style movements.

In a number of protandrous species the anthers shed pollen onto the non-receptive stalk of the style; later the stigma lobes unfurl and become receptive. In bellflowers and many composites, including knapweeds and ragworts, the stigma lobes, if not cross-pollinated during this phase, roll back on themselves and so come into contact with pollen already deposited on the stalk of the style. The same result is often achieved in protandrous flowers where the anthers remain active for long periods (e.g. rosebay willowherb), and in protogynous flowers (yellow rattle, eyebright, lady's-mantle and many others) the stigma lobes may finally bend back to touch the anthers, still containing pollen.

The mechanisms described here are complicated and diverse, but in all cases the result is the same: cross-pollination is given priority, but if it fails, selfing is assured.

Time-lapse of protandry in clustered bellflower: in the final stage the stigma lobes curl down and pick up pollen on the style.

263

THE ARRANGEMENT OF FLOWERS

Most plants have floral devices that favour cross-pollination in the sense that there is a period when it is more likely for pollen from another flower to reach the stigma than pollen from within that flower (p. 262). In extreme cases, there may be mechanisms which stop the 'home' pollen from growing (incompatibility, p. 268), or the stamens and styles may be in separate flowers on separate plants (dioecy, p. 270). Incompatibility and dioecy do prevent selfing altogether, but interestingly the other mechanisms do not, because whatever happens within the individual flower, most plants have several, often many, flowers open at one time, and so pollen can still be transferred between those flowers. In genetic and evolutionary terms, there is no difference between that and within-flower selfing.

Meadow cranesbill is a good example of a completely protandrous plant (p. 262). The anthers have actually disappeared by the time the stigmas are receptive, but at any one time a plant may have 10 or 20 open flowers, some with mature anthers, some with receptive stigmas. It is pollinated by bees and, since bees usually visit several flowers on one plant, it is obviously more likely that pollen will move from flower to flower on a plant, than that it will move from plant to plant. Some plants are monoecious, that is to say have separate male flowers (with stamens) and female flowers (with styles) on the same plant, such as annual nettle, bur-reeds, reedmaces and sedges. This at first seems to be a mechanism which prevents selfing; but of course it is not, because it does not stop inter-flower pollination on the same plant. Interestingly, many monoecious plants are wind-pollinated.

One way around this is for the male flowers and the female flowers to behave as a block, all the males maturing before the females. This happens in sedges. Cotton-grasses get their name from the long, woolly bristles attached to the fruit, and they are easily recognised by this. The peat moors of upland Britain are often white with the fruiting-heads of hare's-tail cotton-grass in June. In April they look quite different, for then the yellow anthers of the male flowers predominate, and the female are as yet inactive. This is a special form of protandry, in which all the flowers are synchronised.

A quite different situation occurs in those rather few plants that bear solitary flowers, so that the chances of self-pollination are remote. Alter-

Hare's-tail cotton-grass on a peat moor in April (left) and June

male flowers · fruits

Male water parsnip flowers elongating

natively the plant may produce many short-lived flowers, of which only one will be open at one time. Common poppy flowers last a single day, and anthers and stigmas mature together; self-pollination is prevented by an incompatibility system, and the fact that individual flowers are so ephemeral means that the transfer of pollen between flowers on a plant is most unlikely.

The arrangement and distribution of flowers is very important. It is striking how many different arrangements exist, from solitary flowers to clusters, spikes, dense heads, umbels and so on. Two of the most complex types are the umbels of umbellifers and the extraordinary flowerheads of composites. Umbels comprise whorls of branches of similar length, each of which ends in a new whorl and so on. In hogweed the flowers behave synchronously, the anthers of all maturing before the styles, though all the individual flowers are hermaphrodite. Sweet cicely adds a sophistication to this by having a few male flowers which open later, so ensuring selfing if crossing fails, and in cow parsley and water parsnips these last male flowers elongate to a position above the style of the hermaphrodite ones, so that the pollen falls directly on to them.

Composites have the most remarkable flowerheads. A daisy 'flower' may look like one flower, but is in fact many, tightly packed together, with the outer flowers modified so as to look and function like petals. They are so close that visiting insects will inevitably carry pollen

from flower to flower if it is available. The packing is so tight that in most cases even this is unnecessary – the styles are long enough to pick up pollen from adjacent florets. The arrangement of florets is like a spiral honeycomb, so that distances between florets are very small. Individual florets in plants such as autumn hawkbit and beaked hawksbeard are protandrous, reducing the possibility of within-flower selfing; but maturation progresses into the centre from the edge so that the outer flowers can always collect pollen from the inner.

In practice, arrangements of flowers in flowerheads may often have evolved so as to guarantee between-flower selfing, where within-flower selfing (which, if it is at all possible, will be automatic) is discouraged. Some plants have spikes of flowers, but with all the flowers arranged along one side of the spike – toothwort and toothed wintergreen for example. Toothwort is protogynous and matures from the bottom of the spike upwards. Insect pollination may occur, but if it fails the pollen can be dispersed a short distance by wind – the close juxtaposition of the flowers means that pollination from a flower immediately below is likely.

Spike of toothed wintergreen

Coltsfoot flower

265

AVOIDING
SELF-POLLINATION

Positions of stigmas and anthers
In many flowers differences in the time of maturity of anthers and stigmas ensure that cross-pollination is favoured (p. 262). In others it is the position of the stigma that is important. It is common to see long styles protruding far from the mouth of a flower, as in clustered bellflower, figwort, common comfrey, common wintergreen or St Bernard's lily. This obviously reduces the chances of self-pollination, since the pollen cannot simply fall on to the stigma. Even in flowers where the distance between the anthers and stigma is much smaller, their relative position may make self-pollination unlikely. Many flowers are held horizontally, such as those of most labiates (e.g. self-heal, bugle, white dead-nettle or hedge wound-wort), and in the figwort family (e.g. figworts, foxgloves, monkey flower or speedwells) and in violets. Mostly these are tubular flowers, and a small horizontal displacement of anthers

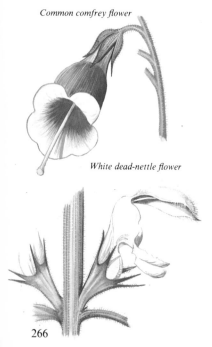

Common comfrey flower

White dead-nettle flower

and stigma suffices. Flowers held vertically again may require that the anthers are not directly above the stigmas. That this would be more difficult to achieve with a tubular flower may partly explain why these are normally arranged horizontally.

A few plants have, however, adopted a much more sophisticated system in which different flowers have distinct arrangements of stamens and styles, a phenomenon known as heterostyly. It is easiest to see in primroses: any group of primrose plants will show some in which there is a conspicuous pinhead-like stigma in the mouth of the petal tube and others in which the mouth is fringed by a ring of anthers. Very rarely (and for some unknown reason particularly in one area in Somerset and one in the Chilterns), flowers with both anthers and stigma at the same level occur. In section, the heterostyled flowers show that they contain both anthers and stigmas, but at different levels. Where the stigma is easily visible, the anthers are on short filaments at the bottom of the tube – these are called 'pin' flowers. 'Thrum' flowers have the opposite combination.

Heterostyly appears to be a device which ensures cross-pollination, not only between flowers but between plants, since all flowers on one plant are either pin or thrum. The mechanism seems to be that a visiting insect at a thrum flower gets dusted with pollen in such a way that it is more likely to transfer it to a pin flower's stigma, which is at the same level as the thrum flower's anthers.

This pin-thrum system is found in several relatives of the primrose, including cowslip, oxlip and bird's-eye primrose, but has been lost in Scottish primrose. Probably this is because Scottish primrose lives in a less insect-rich environment and has come to rely on selfing, which heterostyly acts to prevent. The water violet, which is a relative of the primrose despite its name, is also heterostylous, as are some members of the gentian family (Chiltern gentian), bogbean, bastard toadflax, several species in the borage

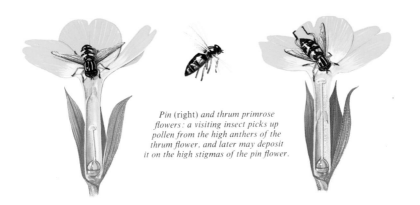

Pin (right) *and thrum primrose flowers: a visiting insect picks up pollen from the high anthers of the thrum flower, and later may deposit it on the high stigmas of the pin flower.*

family (including lungwort and oyster plant) and perennial flax. It is not, however, fail-safe: obviously, in a thrum plant, pollen can fall from the anthers on to the stigma below. If this happens, pollination does not actually take place, because the morphological difference is backed up by an incompatibility system (see p. 268), which means that only cross-pollination can succeed in any case. The morphological difference may have evolved to increase the efficiency of an existing incompatibility system, reducing the chance of pollen being transferred to a stigma where it cannot grow and will be wasted.

Some plants have even more complex hererostyly. Purple loosestrife has three sorts of flowers: the style may be short, mid-length or long, and the stamens take up the remaining two positions. The complexity goes further because the anthers on long stamens produce much larger pollen grains and those of the shortest stamens much smaller pollen grains than the others. Good pollination and

seed-set are only achieved if pollen is transferred from long stamens to long styles, mid to mid and short to short. Whereas in a simple case of heterostyly with two different flower types, such as primrose, only half of the possible combinations are 'legitimate', in the tristylic flowers of purple loosestrife two out of every three will work, because the long styled flower can accept pollen from the long stamens in either short or mid-styled flowers.

These heterostylous systems are very similar in action to the many flowers in which movements of the stamens and styles produce at different times conspicuous anthers or stigmas (p. 264). In those, however, the function seems usually to be to promote cross-pollination if possible, but to ensure selfing if not. Heterostyly is always associated with incompatibility, however, which prohibits selfing, and it seems to have evolved as a means of ensuring the correct transfer of pollen.

Sections through the three sorts of purple loosestrife flowers

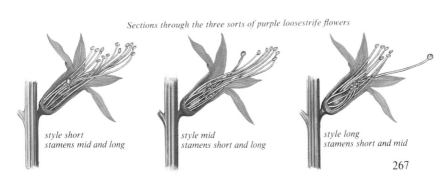

style short
stamens mid and long

style mid
stamens short and long

style long
stamens short and mid

267

Incompatibility

Gardeners are familiar with the problem of getting single apple trees to fruit. Nearly all of the various cultivated apple varieties carry genes that make it impossible for the pollen they produce to grow in their own styles and as a result they have to be grown with another variety. Only certain varieties will do, however, for some carry the same genes and are therefore incompatible. This whole phenomenon of incompatibility is widespread and an important method of ensuring that selfing does not occur.

Strictly one should distinguish self-pollination from self-fertilisation. In self-pollination, pollen is deposited on the stigma from anthers on the same plant (or even the same flower); in self-fertilisation, that pollen produces an effective pollen tube which grows down the style and fertilises the egg. Where selfing is to be avoided, it is self-fertilisation that is the important part; self-pollination is simply a waste of pollen in these circumstances. One would expect, therefore, the two mechanisms to be closely associated in some cases.

The heterostyly of primroses is described on p. 267. The two different flower structures can be seen as a way of ensuring that pollen from one type of flower is transferred to the other type on a different plant. In other words, the morphological difference is an aid to cross-pollination. The lack of self-fertilisation is ensured by a chemical incompatibility mechanism, which prevents pin pollen growing in pin styles and thrum pollen in thrum styles. Here the self-incompatibility is probably the original phenomenon, and the morphological difference has evolved as a means of stopping the wasteful transfer of pollen to the wrong style type.

The opposite may be true, however, in some plants, where the incompatibility seems to have evolved because the floral structure almost guarantees self-pollination (i.e. deposition of pollen onto the stigma in the same flower). All peaflowers

In one type of incompatibility system, each pollen grain carries one of two genes in its parent. If either is the same as one of the two genes in the style, pollination will fail

AB parent produces
(**A**) and (**B**) pollen

both fail on
an **AB** style

only **A** successfully
pollinates a **BC** style

both successfully
pollinate a **CD** style

have the same highly characteristic flower structure, with the stamens and styles enclosed in a folded petal, the keel. This operates as a mechanism to achieve insect pollination (see p. 276), but the associated self-pollination is prevented from becoming self-fertilisation by a self-incompatibility system in bird's-foot trefoil, sainfoin and the larger clovers, particularly red and white clover. In contrast, some of the smaller clovers, such as

In the other type, the pollen has the same characteristics as the parent, and again only pollen from a distinct parent can successfully pollinate a style

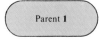

Parent 1

all pollen bears the same chemical message

pollen fails to grow
in a similar style

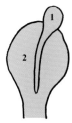

pollen successfully grows
in style of a
different type of plant

pollen grains carry only one of the two possible sets of genetic information (i.e. they are haploid; see p. 12), while styles being parental tissue carry both (i.e. they are diploid – only the actual egg cell is haploid), incompatibility occurs if the gene in the pollen grain is the same as either of those in the style tissue.

If there were only two genes then half of all possible pollinations would fail: this is what happens in primrose. The more genes there are, the less likely it is that the one in the pollen grain is the same as one of the two in the style. So the more genes involved, the greater the chances there are of successful pollination and fertilisation. The incompatibility system in clover involves hundreds of genes, and similar systems occur in many other plants. Families in which incompatibility is widespread include the buttercup, saxifrage, rose, pea-flower, willowherb, figwort, bell-flower, orchid and grass families.

It is also possible for the chemicals responsible for the incompatibility in the pollen to come not from the haploid pollen itself, but from the diploid parent plant of the pollen. As the pollen matures, the anther walls (which are diploid, just as the style is) may stick the chemicals onto the pollen, which is where the complex sculpturing of the pollen wall (p. 257) becomes important, to retain these deposits. In these cases the two genes from each parent must match exactly if there is to be an incompatibility reaction. This type of incompatibility is particularly common in composites, but is also found in the crucifers (e.g. wild cabbage), and in the cranesbill family.

Self-incompatibility then ensures that successful pollen must come from a genetically different plant. It is worth remembering that, thanks to the powers of vegetative reproduction in most perennials, many form clones, where all the plants in a clump are genetically identical. In these, incompatibility will necessitate long-distance pollination, if sexual reproduction is to take place.

slender trefoil and knotted clover, have no incompatibility system and are almost always selfed.

Incompatibility works in much the same way as our own immune system. Chemicals in the pollen grain interact with others in the style and only if the combination is correct will the pollen grain germinate and grow successfully. The pollen grain chemical can be thought of as an antigen and that in the style as an antibody. Because

Separation of the sexes

The most effective safeguard against self-fertilisation is the one adopted by most higher animals – the existence of separate male and female individuals. This is surprisingly rare in higher plants in which the underlying structure is clearly the hermaphrodite flower with stamens and styles together. Plants which have quite distinct male individuals (with stamens) and females (with styles) are termed dioecious.

Examples of strictly dioecious plants include hop, nettle, common and sheep's sorrels, and dioecious sedge, and in these only cross-pollination can occur. It is noticeable that all of them have effective methods of vegetative reproduction – sheep's sorrel produces buds on long roots, dioecious sedge has a creeping rhizome, nettle has creeping stems that root at the nodes – and none is annual: annual mercury is one of the very few dioecious annuals. The price that is paid for the guarantee of cross-pollination is the reduced chance of pollination occurring at all. The animals that have separate male and female individuals are generally mobile, so that they can seek each other out; sessile animals are often, like plants, hermaphrodite.

Strict dioecy, the existence of purely male and purely female individuals, is rare in flowering plants. It represents one end of a continuous series of possible combinations of sexual types. At the other end of the series are the strictly hermaphrodite flowers, which contain both stamens and styles. This is the commonest situation. Between the two, however, is a remarkable array of other combinations. It is quite common to find either male or female flowers on otherwise hermaphrodite individuals. These single-sex flowers may have no trace of the organs of the other sex, but commonly they have come about through the atrophying of either stamens or styles. Sometimes, indeed, there may be quite normal-looking stamens present, which simply produce no pollen. Some flowers of broad-leaved dock may actually produce pollen in some of its flowers which is unable to grow, whereas a flower of annual knawel may have any number of its ten anthers shrivelled up and empty of pollen, so that the flowers may be truly hermaphrodite, effectively female, or anywhere in between. Alternatively the apparently male or female flowers may still have traces of the other set of organs visible: shrubby cinquefoil and marsh valerian are apparently dioecious, but the male flowers on one plant have rudimentary (and wholly non-functional) styles, while the female flowers on another bear similar ineffective stumps of stamens.

Flowers, then, may be purely single-sex (male or female), effectively so, or truly bisexual (hermaphrodite).

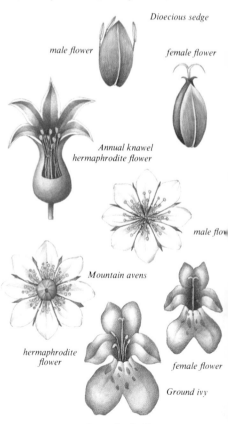

Dioecious sedge

male flower

female flower

Annual knawel hermaphrodite flower

male flow

Mountain avens

hermaphrodite flower

female flower

Ground ivy

hermaphrodite flower

All possible combinations seem to occur. Dioecious plants have already been described, but androdioecious plants which have both hermaphrodite and male individuals occur (e.g. mountain avens), as do gynodioecious plants, such as field scabious, sticky catchfly and many labiates, including ground ivy, self-heal, thymes, marjoram and water mint. Gynodioecy is in fact much commoner than androdioecy, presumably because wholly male individuals are less effective at producing offspring than wholly female ones.

Some plants go the whole way and have all possible sexual types – hermaphrodite, male and female individuals. Such polygamous species include several campions and catchflies (moss campion, Nottingham catchfly, Spanish catchfly) and salad burnet, which has almost all conceivable combinations of flower types on different individuals.

Other plants have different combinations of flower types all on the same individual. Many simply have separate male and female flowers on the same plant, which reduces the chance of selfing, but does not prohibit it (p. 264). These monoecious species include annual nettle, water milfoil and many monocots – arrowhead, bur-reeds, reedmaces and almost all sedges, including the large and conspicuous greater pond-sedge and greater tussock sedge. In most sedges the male flowers appear first (i.e. they are protandrous, see p. 262), and this is when low-growing sedges like spring sedge are most conspicuous, the yellow anthers making a good display.

More complex arrangements are found on andromoneocious plants, which have hermaphrodite and male flowers on one individual, as in bistort, crosswort, several umbellifers, including cow parsley, sanicle and rough chervil, and some grasses, such as false oat-grass and creeping soft-grass. The parallel condition is gynomonoecy – female and hermaphrodite flowers together – and this group includes mountain sorrel and many composites, in which the outer ray-florets are female and the inner disc-florets hermaphrodite (sea aster, goldenrod, blue fleabane, leopard's-bane). Since the outer florets open before the inner, gynomonoecy here results in protogyny (female flowers first, see p. 262). Whereas androdioecy is rare because of the reproductive problems of wholly male plants, andromonoecy is probably commoner than gynomonoecy, for the problem of failing to reproduce does not apply when both flower types are on one individual.

All these arrangements are probably best seen as various solutions to the problem of obtaining an appropriate balance between self- and cross-fertilisation.

Marsh valerian
male flower
female flower
hermaphrodite flower
male flower

Salad burnet
female flower

female ray floret
gynomonoecious flowerhead
Sea aster
hermaphrodite disc floret

WIND POLLINATION

Many of the features of flowers, such as the separation of anthers and stigmas either in time of development or even onto separate plants, are best understood as mechanisms which promote cross-pollination. More accurately, they make self-pollination less likely or sometimes impossible; cross-pollination requires a positive contribution: something must transport the pollen from one plant to another. That something may either be an animal, and in temperate regions that almost invariably means insects (see p. 276), or a physical agent, normally wind but occasionally water (p. 274).

Wind pollination is an extremely haphazard mechanism. Once liberated, the pollen grain will simply follow wind currents, and the chances of its reaching a stigma are minute. This necessitates a massive production of pollen grains: a single flowerhead of a grass such as creeping bent may produce 10 million grains. But these grains are then dispersed into a volume of air that rapidly dilutes them, and if each grain from such a spike travels a metre away, the paths they all traverse will represent less than 0.1% of the volume of space surrounding that spike. The chances of one hitting a stigma are not high.

Pollen is distributed by wind in a very characteristic fashion. Most falls within a few metres of the flower, but a small amount gets carried a remarkably long way. Because most wind-pollinated plants produce many flowers and often grow in dense patches, enough contacts are made between pollen and stigma. Nevertheless, it is a risky business and a number of other adaptations are important.

First it is often the case that the whole flower or flowerhead is well exposed to the wind. Many trees are wind-pollinated and have catkins that hang loosely and may be jarred by air currents, so releasing pollen. In herbaceous plants wind-pollinated species tend to have more conspicuous flowerheads, even though the individual flowers may be less showy;

compare docks and knotgrasses, where the wind-pollinated docks have tall spikes and the knotgrasses small flowers in the leaf-junctions. There are few, if any, truly creeping and ground-hugging plants that are wind-pollinated.

If the whole flowerhead is not presented like a catkin to respond to air movement, the stamens of the individual flowers often are. The anthers typically project a long way from the flower on long filaments, either rigidly as in ribwort plantain or hanging down as in many grasses, particularly false oat-grass. In either case it is important that pollen is only released when conditions favour dispersal – i.e. dry with a light breeze.

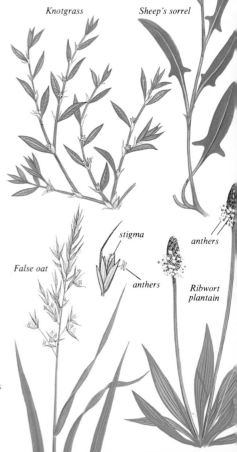

Knotgrass

Sheep's sorrel

False oat

stigma

anthers

anthers

Ribwort plantain

stigmas

anther

Marsh arrow-grass

Meadow fescue

Broad-leaved dock

leaved dock, or be actually feathery in appearance as in false oat-grass and meadow fescue.

A final corollary of wind pollination is the absence of the need to attract insects, and hence often of the devices that serve to do so – colourful petals, strong scents, copious nectar (see p. 282). The selection pressure against these wasteful characteristics must be strong, since wind pollination has almost certainly evolved several times, and the same developments appear to have occurred each time. The most important groups are the grasses, sedges and rushes which are all related, and the plantains, docks and goosefoots which are not. In addition, wind-pollinated species turn up occasionally in other families – mugwort is a composite, and meadow-rues are in the buttercup family.

Most interesting of all are those cases where species are apparently in the process of evolving to or from wind pollination. Salad burnet in the rose family and heather are two good examples. Heather flowers produce masses of nectar but, if insect pollination fails, the stamens elongate and the pollen can be transferred by wind. In fact a small amount of wind pollination is probably not uncommon in many normally insect-pollinated flowers, so the potential is always there for selection to act on.

Many wind-pollinated species have explosive anthers that only dehisce when the weather is dry. Nettles release pollen like this, and in good light little puffs of dust-like pollen can be seen rising from a nettle patch. Timing release to coincide with breezes is more difficult, but breezes tend to occur in the early morning which may explain why so many grasses (e.g. foxtails, timothy, cock's-foot, sweet vernal grass, meadow-grasses, quaking grass and tufted hair-grass) release pollen between about 5 and 9 a.m.

A further modification which clearly enhances the chances of successful pollination is the development of a feathery stigma, with a greatly increased surface area that is more likely to entrap pollen grains. The stigma may consist of many fine hair-like points, as in marsh arrow-grass, simple branching lobes, as in broad-

If insect pollination fails, the stamens of heather flowers elongate, which makes wind pollination possible.

273

WATER POLLINATION

Plants that actually grow in water possess many different pollination mechanisms. Some, such as water-lilies, water crowfoots and bladder-worts rely on insects and face no unusual problems, other than that of ensuring that the anthers are held well clear of the water surface and so available to insects. Others, however, are wind-pollinated, including pond-weeds, eel-grasses, Canadian pond-weed and water starwort, and these have taken advantage of a special feature of their environment.

The distance to which dispersal of pollen by wind is possible depends upon the balance between gravity and the lifting power of air currents; eventually the pollen grain must land. In dry habitats pollen that has landed is no longer capable of reaching a stigma; in water, however, it may float and continue to be dispersed. This actually opens the way to a much greater chance of pollination, for if the pollen in fact moves in two dimensions along the water surface it is much more likely to reach its target than a grain moving randomly through a three-dimensional space in the air. This requires, however, that the stigmas be at the water surface too, so that the whole process of pollination takes place effectively in two dimensions at the water surface.

It is noticeable that insect-pollina-ted plants often have tall flower-spikes, projecting well away from the water (water violet, bladderwort) or cup-shaped flowers which act like boats (water-lilies). Wind-pollinated water plants, however, have short spikes scarcely appearing above the

Bladderwort

Lesser pondweed

Fennel pondweed

water, as in pondweeds. Some pond-weeds do have stiffly erect flower-spikes and seem to rely on normal wind dispersal, as in broad-leaved pondweed, but others have obviously adopted the trick of using the water surface; the flower-spike of fennel pondweed actually floats on the surface and those of small pondweed and lesser pondweed scarcely break it

A similar effect occurs in Canadian pondweed, though it is scarcely ever observed because this species is dioe-cious and mainly spread by vegetative growth, so that populations tend to

Canadian waterweed

be huge, genetically identical clones (see p. 246). Male plants are extremely rare in Britain, possibly because those originally introduced from North America were female. Where pollination does occur, however, it too relies on the surface film. The female flowers are on the ends of long stalks and 'walk' on the water by means of the curled, water-repellent stigmas. The pollen, too, is non-wettable thanks to its minutely spiny surface, and is blown across the water surface until it reaches the stigmas.

This sort of pollination is really a specialised form of wind pollination, relying on floating pollen and surface-borne stigmas to reduce the number of dimensions in which the search must take place from three to two. It works well on still water, but obviously would be less effective in flowing water, where the plants at the top of the stream would never get pollinated and those at the bottom would never pollinate anything. Not surprisingly most of the species involved live in ponds and lakes.

The same argument might apply to the only truly marine flowering plant – eel-grass. This lives below the low-water mark on muddy shores and has monoecious flower-spikes which are protogynous. The anthers liberate curious long, slender grains which are washed up and down the shore by the tides and wrap themselves around the stigmas if they meet. This tendency for pollen grains to be long and thin is widespread in plants relying on water-surface pollination, and again increases the chances of grain meeting stigma.

If this mechanism is not true water pollination, since the pollen (except in eel-grass) is actually moved by wind, then water starwort apparently *can* achieve pollination under water, although there is some controversy over this. There are in fact several species of water starwort, all extremely difficult to distinguish from one another. Some species are certainly wind-pollinated, but others apparently can set viable seed in flowers that remain continuously submerged. Some believe that this is

Eel-grass

achieved by cleistogamous flowers (p. 261), that never open but self-fertilise.

True underwater pollination does, however, definitely occur in hornwort, where the anthers float to the surface and release the pollen grains, which then sink slowly past the receptive but submerged stigmas. Again, however, this will only achieve self-pollination unless the floating anther is moved by wind across the water surface before releasing the pollen.

Wind and water pollination are therefore closely linked, and water pollination is really a clever trick adopted by wind-pollinated water plants to improve their chance of successful cross-pollination.

Hornwort

ANIMAL POLLINATION

Although some flowers rely on purely physical mechanisms to transfer pollen from flower to flower (wind, p. 272 or water, p. 274), these are quite out of the control of the plant. Most plants rely on animals as pollinators, and simply because they are the right size for most flowers, insects are the most widely used vectors. The plant cannot control the behaviour of the insect directly, but by offering appropriate stimuli and rewards, and by taking advantage of the pollinator's behaviour patterns, it can exercise considerable indirect control.

Four orders of insects are important pollinators: the beetles (Coleoptera), flies (Diptera), bees and wasps (Hymenoptera) and butterflies and moths (Lepidoptera). Their behaviour and method of feeding vary greatly and so the morphology of particular flowers will be more or less suitable for each group. Nevertheless there are some common requirements: the flower must advertise itself in some way, so that the insect can discover it; it must offer some reward so that the insect will visit it; it must make it possible for the insect to land; and it must transfer pollen from anther to insect.

Beetles are very unspecialised pollinators. They have biting not sucking mouthparts and so tend to feed on pollen rather than nectar, and in addition they fly less often and usually less far than most other pollinating insects, and so are less likely to transfer pollen between flowers. Nevertheless, beetles are often found in or on flowers, and some are closely associated with particular species, particularly in the carrot family. Chrysomelid and cantharid beetles, such as the common soldier beetle, are common, though the latter are carnivorous and their pollinating activity must be incidental.

Flies are much more significant pollinators than beetles and range from large species, such as craneflies and hoverflies, down to the tiny gall-midges, blackflies and other midges.

Many flies have piercing mouthparts and feed on animals, and of those that have only sucking mouthparts, many go for carrion and other rotting material. Nevertheless there are many predominantly nectar-feeding small flies. They are particularly important in primitive, flat and open flowers where the nectar is easily reached and no long proboscis nor other adaptation is necessary. Grass of Parnassus, mossy saxifrage in the saxifrage family, hemlock water dropwort in the carrot family, wood spurge in the spurge family, tormentil in the rose family, and lesser celandine in the buttercup family are all good examples of flowers in which the nectar is readily accessible and of which flies are important pollinators.

The large flies such as hoverflies are, however, much more like bees in their pollination action. They have a

Small fly on tormentil flower

Hoverfly on devil's-bit scabious flower

proboscis which can extract nectar from tubular flowers such as ragged robin, cuckoo flower, devil's-bit scabious or marsh thistle. Autumn hawkbit, germander speedwell and enchanter's nightshade are well known as favourites of hoverflies, and the last two have protruding stamens to which the insect clings, so bending them that they deposit pollen on its back.

The Hymenoptera (bees, wasps, ants and sawflies) are, however, the most important group of pollinators, and of them the bees are the champions. There are over 200 species of bee in Britain, just one of which is utilised by man; bumble-bees are important pollinators too. Bees feed on both pollen and nectar, and honey-bees gather pollen in special sacs on their legs. Flowers favoured by bees tend to be those which offer large amounts of both nectar and pollen, particularly those in the daisy and peaflower families. In both these families the anthers are at the base of

Honey-bee on toadflax flower

Bumble-bee in self-heal flower

Meadow brown butterfly on bugle flower

Elephant hawk-moth at honeysuckle flower

the passage along which the bee crawls to get nectar and so well-suited to offering pollen to the pollen brush on the underside of the bee's abdomen.

Bees are large and heavy insects and, unlike the other group of large insect pollinators, butterflies and moths, always land on the flower. Bee flowers therefore need to be relatively strong and short-stalked; flat heads of flowers such as those of the daisy and teasel families, and large tubular flowers such as foxglove, self-heal and other members of the figwort and labiate families, are typical bee flowers. Even many saucer-shaped flowers are bee-pollinated too, the flat petals acting as ideal landing platforms. The strength of bees, too, enables them to penetrate flowers where the lips close, such as toad-flaxes, or where the petals enclose the stamens, as in peaflowers. Such flowers are of little use to feebler insects.

The last group of insects are the butterflies and moths whose special feature is a long proboscis. Almost all are nectar feeders and they can typically obtain nectar from depths of 10–20 mm in tubular flowers, twice as deep as most flies and bees. Flowers for which butterflies and moths are important pollinators are common in the daisy family (golden-rod, hemp agrimony, ragworts, knapweeds, thistles), and others in-clude valerians, campions, bramble and raspberry, wild thyme, bugle and several orchids, including fragrant orchid. Several of these are white-flowered and are favoured by night-flying moths. All tend to be strong-scented. Perhaps the best-known example of a Lepidoptera flower is honeysuckle, with its very long petal-tube, which is said to be especially adapted for pollination by hawk moths, which have very long probos-ces. Certainly hawk moths do polli-nate honeysuckle; but since the plant occurs and fruits freely in areas where hawk moths are far from abundant, it is clearly not dependent on them.

277

ATTRACTING INSECTS: COLOUR AND SCENT

An insect-pollinated flower must first attract insects, either by scent or colour. Flowers vary greatly in the amount and type of scent they produce, and in colour, and much of this can be explained by looking at the responses of the pollinators to these.

Scent plays a role for all groups of pollinators, but in a rather haphazard way. In most flies, butterflies and bees it appears to enable the insect to distinguish different species of flower at close range, whereas the initial location is based upon colour and other visual stimuli. On the other hand some flowers have no detectable scent at all, but they are usually visually conspicuous (for example most gentians), while some that are strongly scented are rather dull in appearance. It is rash to assume, though, that flowers that are scentless to us are so to insects. Many flowers which can affect bees by their smell appear to the human nose to be almost unscented, for example white bryony. There are also definite differences in the scents of flowers frequented by flies, bees and Lepidoptera. Fly-pollinated flowers are often rather unpleasant-smelling (for example alexanders), perhaps attracting by the similarity to carrion. Bee-pollinated flowers tend to be sweet and honey-like, as in sweet violet, white clover and gorse, while butterfly- and particularly moth-pollinated flowers have stronger, heavier odours, as is so well illustrated by honeysuckle.

Not only do plants produce a wide range of different aromas which attract insects, they also time their release to coincide with the time their pollinators are flying. Many plants are scented only in the daytime, often only in sunshine, as in broom and grass of Parnassus, but some, which are pollinated by night-flying moths, do the opposite. Honeysuckle is evening-scented and white campion and Nottingham and night-flowering catchflies are night-scented, coinciding with the flight period of their main pollinators.

Although scent is important, particularly in flower recognition, in most cases the visual signal seems the more important. For flies, and particularly for butterflies, yellow and blue are the most favoured colours; many species are certainly able to distinguish colours. It is the colour vision of bees, though, that has been most closely investigated.

Bees see further into the ultra-violet part of the spectrum than we can, but less far into the red end, their range spanning ultra-violet, violet, blue, green, yellow and orange. This means that colours perceived by bees are very different from those we see. An object has a particular colour if it reflects light of the wavelength associated with that colour: many flowers do reflect ultra-violet light and so can be seen by bees, normally in combination with other types of light. Just as we see a mixture of red and blue as purple, bees see a mixture of yellow and ultra-violet (each just down the rainbow from red and blue) as 'bee-purple', and a mixture of blue-green and ultra-violet as 'bee-white'.

White flowers (which reflect all types of light) may be distinguishable to bees depending on the amount of ultra-violet they reflect, while yellow flowers may appear simply yellow (e.g. cowslip) or 'bee-purple' (creep-

A bee sees the flowers of cowslip and tormentil as different colours.

ing cinquefoil), because the latter also reflects ultra-violet. Equally, though we can distinguish blue and purple flowers, to a bee both will seem blue (unless they also reflect ultra-violet), since it cannot see the red in the purple.

Almost certainly these responses of pollinators to flower colours explain the obvious changes in preponderance of different colours at different times of year. In early spring white is commonest (e.g. wood anemone, snowdrop), at a time when few pollinators, and those mainly flies, are to be found. In late spring yellow becomes commoner, then blue, and finally red. That red flowers occur almost exclusively in high summer (e.g. poppies) is probably explained by the facts that few insects can see red; poppies reflect ultra-violet and so are 'visible' to bees, and bees fly in summer.

Many flowers, however, are not just one simple colour, but are patterned or multi-coloured. It is common to find a highlighted ring around the mouth of the petal tube, as in forget-me-nots and speedwells, which appears to act to direct pollinators to their proper goal, and the stripes and lines of spots on eyebright, wild pansy and many others serve the same purpose. Other honeyguides may be present, invisible to us

A bee sees the flowers of purple loosestrife and germander speedwell as the same colour.

'Honey-guides' in the flowers of forget-me-not (top left), speedwell (top right), wild pansy (centre left), eyebright (centre right). The honeyguides in the flower of evening primrose (bottom) can only be seen by humans under ultra-violet light (bottom left).

but visible to ultra-violet vision. A flower that appears to us to be purely white may, to a bee, have a complex pattern.

The role of flower colour in pollination is immense. The contrast between flower colour and the background (whether green leaves, dark stems or brown leaf-mould) is certainly important but little investigated; and the relationship between colour and the gathering of flowers into heads or spikes, which increases their conspicuousness, would repay investigation. There is some evidence that similar flowers blossoming simultaneously may compete with one another for pollinators and the whole gamut of flower colour, scent, arrangement and timing may have been brought about by natural selection acting to reduce that competition.

279

REWARDS FOR POLLINATORS

Pollen

Pollen is a most valuable food for insects, for it is rich in protein. Plants therefore face a dilemma: many use insects to transport their pollen, but that will not be achieved if the insect devours it all first. The pollen cannot be hidden away: it must be available to the right insects and somehow unavailable to the rest. The more complex mechanisms by which this is achieved are discussed on p. 284, but even in simpler flowers the same effect can be achieved.

The ideal pollinators are sucking insects such as butterflies and hover-flies which feed only on nectar. Here the problem is to ensure that they do actually pick up some pollen. Bees are effective pollinators because they feed on both pollen and nectar, but become so dusted with pollen that they can transfer it to another flower. There are, though, many other insects that feed on pollen and they vary in effectiveness as pollinators from beetles (which are only moderately effective), down to springtails, tiny wingless insects mainly found in soil and litter, which are almost totally ineffective. The value of a pollinator depends on the chance of its moving to another flower while still carrying the pollen. Beetles do fly, but tend to remain on one flowerhead for long

A bee on a common poppy flower

periods; wingless insects will rarely move from flower to flower. Many plants have mechanisms which pre-vent small crawling insects from reaching the pollen, or even the flowers. Catchflies get their name from the sticky hairs on their flower-stems, which occasionally entrap flies. Sticky catchfly has bands of sticky hairs just below the leaves on each flowering stem, which by analogy with the bands that fruit-farmers place on apple-tree trunks, seem to serve to stop crawling insects climbing to the flowers. Many other plants, such as field mouse-ear and hoary willowherb, are hairy all over, but only have the sticky glandular hairs at the top of the stem or on the

Small crawling insects may be unable to cross the sticky bands below the leaves of sticky catchfly.

A rose-chafer beetle bites through the back of a bramble flower.

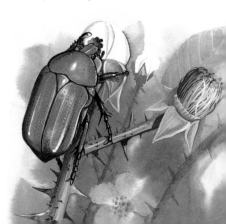

flower-stalks. It is common, too, to find sticky hairs on the outside of the sepals. All these hairs may serve several functions – against heat loss (p. 242), against seed-eating animals (p. 173), or against pollen-feeding insects. They may even act in all these ways; to the plant the important result is that they increase its fitness.

Against some attacks, however, such defences will be inadequate. Many beetles and several bees and other insects avoid them by biting through the back of the flower and consuming its contents, sometimes before the bud has opened.

Not all pollen-eating is deleterious to the plant. There is a large group of flowers which produce no nectar at all, and rely solely on pollen production to reward pollinators. One of the best-known examples is common poppy, which also produces one of the largest quantities of pollen among insect-pollinated flowers, more even than many wind-pollinated species, normally the most profligate. Common poppy has large, saucer-shaped flowers, each of which lasts just a day. The pollen is in a ring of anthers around the central disc along which the stigmas radiate; it is easily accessible and the flowers are visited by large insects such as bumble-bees, as well as many smaller beetles and flies. The bees simply walk around the central disc collecting as much pollen as they can and becoming thoroughly dusted in the process. The whole process is extremely messy and unsophisticated, and much pollen must end up on the stigmas, so it is not surprising to find that common poppy is self-incompatible.

The poppy family has some of the simplest flowers; buttercups and their allies are similar. Such simple flowers have few devices for concealing pollen from predators and delivering only to specialised pollinators. Wood anemone has a very similar flower structure to the poppy and also relies on pollen to attract its insect pollinators, while common meadow-rue, another member of the buttercup family, has flowers reduced to little more than styles and stamens, but

The flowers of wood anemone and meadow rue, two plants that use pollen as the reward for pollinators

clustered together so that the yellow anthers give the visual signal. It too relies on pollen alone.

As flowers become more complex (see p. 284), one of the main developments is the production of nectar as a reward, and its concealment so that only specialised pollinators find it. The simplest version of this is perhaps seen in buttercups and spearworts, which also have simple, open flowers, but with tiny pockets at the base of the petals in which the nectar is produced.

Greater spearwort flower

Nectar

Most insect-pollinated flowers reward their visitors by supplying nectar, a name which is redolent of complex culinary delights, but in fact refers to a simple sugar solution. Sugar is something that plants can usually make in abundance directly by photosynthesis. It contains almost none of the minerals of which plants are usually so short, unlike pollen which is rich in protein and so contains much nitrogen. It is in effect a plant waste-product, just as is the honeydew which drops from the aphids on a lime tree. It is produced by the plant by simple secretion, often at the bases of the petals, sometimes at the end of the petal tube, and sometimes by special tissues called nectaries.

Because of the function of nectar, its production can only be understood by looking at where it is produced in the flower in relation to the structure of the flower and the types of pollinators it attracts. Open, cup-shaped flowers tend to benefit from short-tongued insects and their nectar is typically readily accessible. The commonest arrangements are for the nectar to be produced at the bottom of the filaments of the stamens (in storksbills and cranesbills, and in many of the pink family, including corn spurrey and spring sandwort, for example); or for it to be secreted at the base of the petals (as in pasque flower, meadow buttercup, stinking hellebore and many others in the buttercup family); or at the base of

the ovary (as in most of the cabbage family, e.g. field pennycress, and some of the rose family, e.g. bramble and raspberry); or on top of the ovary in the centre of the flower (as in golden saxifrages, ivy and most umbellifers).

In all these cases the unsophisticated nature of flower and pollination mechanism go together with the rather readily accessible nectar. There are many flowers, however, in which the nectar is very well concealed, and most of them are tubular, which is generally regarded as being more advanced in an evolutionary sense. Commonly the nectar is produced at the end of the petal tube and sometimes this is elongated into a spur. A foxglove flower, for example, is a simple tube and the nectar is produced at its very top, beneath the

The flowers of a variety of species which offer nectar in different ways

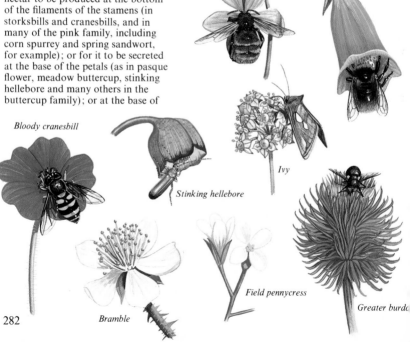

Marsh violet

Foxglove

Bloody cranesbill

Stinking hellebore

Ivy

Field pennycress

Greater burdo

Bramble

ovary, much as in a simpler, cup-shaped flower; but here the insect must crawl past anthers and stigma to reach the nectar.

Spurred flowers are particularly suitable for pollination by butterflies and other long-tongued insects. Short spurs are found in valerians, where they seem almost as protrusions on the side of the petal tube, and in violets. In the latter the spur is wide enough for bees to crawl into it. Long spurs such as those of common toad-flax and fragrant orchid give a very high degree of protection to the nectar, and as in many of these cases access to the concealed nectar is restricted by some form of doorway. In toadflaxes and fluellens this is achieved by having the two lips of the petal tube closed together, so that only strong insects such as bees can

force their way in. This is found in fumitories and climbing corydalis as well. In other cases the closure of the spur or tube is due to scales at its mouth, as in hound's-tongue.

In all cases the nectar is produced below or beyond the anthers so that any insect that tries to reach it should first pass them and co-operate in the pollination process, though many, particularly those with biting or piercing mouthparts, may cheat the plant by cutting through the flower from outside: such flower-burglars serve no purpose for the plant and are often discouraged by structures on the sepals or bracts surrounding the flower. The spiny bracts around burdock and spear thistle flowerheads and the hairy sepals of bird's-foot trefoil and hedge woundwort may well serve this purpose.

It is possible too that the gathering of flowers into tight heads may be as much a response to the activities of flower-burglars as to the increased conspicuousness that it affords. Tubular flowers which store or produce nectar at the ends of tubes or spurs are obviously vulnerable to insects which bite through these. The composites are an entire family in which tubular flowers are aggregated like this, but the same is found in scabiouses, teasels, and many clovers. Alternatively, such flowers may be in dense heads with the bases of the tubes hidden by long bracts or sepals, as in mulleins, mints and many of their relatives.

Common fumitory

Corn mint

Bird's-foot trefoil

Fragrant orchid

Small scabious

Houndstongue

283

POLLINATION IN
COMPLEX FLOWERS

Most open and bell-shaped flowers
have a rather crude pollination
mechanism. Often it involves little
more than ensuring that visiting
insects become dusted with pollen so
that there is a good chance of them
transferring some to the stigma of
another flower. The plants that
appear at the beginning of the
Directory section of this book
(buttercups, poppies, stitchworts,
cinquefoil) tend to be like this; towards the end of that section more
complex flowers that are not radially
symmetrical appear. These have much
more sophisticated pollination mechanisms.

Horseshoe vetch flower

Common melilot flower

Bilateral rather than radial symmetry (which most commonly involves having two lips) means that
visiting insects cannot approach from
any angle but must follow a route
directed by the flower. Two quite
clearly defined types exist, depending
on whether the anthers are beneath
the passage into the flower and so
dust the underside of the insect, or
above it and so put pollen on its back.
The best examples of the first type are
peaflowers. The British species of the
peaflower family (legumes) all have a
similar floral structure. The five
petals are arranged with one on top,
more or less upright like a sail or a flag,
and called the standard; two spreading on either side called wings; and
two interlocking in the centre and
pointing straight forward, called the
keel. The keel encloses the style and

stamens; nine of the ten stamens are
joined into a rather rigid tube. When
an insect visits a flower of ribbed
melilot for example, it clings to the
wings or keel and tries to reach the
nectar at the base of the stamen tube;
in doing so, it forces the keel petals
down, exposing the anthers and picking up pollen. Since anthers and
stigma are close together, though
receptive at different times, the pollen
is ideally placed on the insect's body
to be transferred precisely to the
stigma of another flower.

Other legumes have a more complex system like a piston-pump. In
bird's-foot trefoil, horseshoe vetch
and rest-harrow, the wings arch over
the keel which forms a tube narrowing down to a spout at its tip. When a
bee lands on the wings, which are
jointed onto the keel, the pressure
forces the stamens inside the keel
towards the hole at its apex and ejects
a small mass of pollen from there,
which adheres to the bee. Some
legumes have the stamens held back
under tension in such a way that
pressure on the keel causes them to
spring up, throwing the pollen out
violently: such an explosive mechanism occurs in broom, gorse, petty
whin, dyer's greenweed and purple
milk-vetch.

These clever mechanisms are required where the pollen is held beneath the insect's path. If the anthers
are above the insect, however, gravity
can do much of the job. Nevertheless,
many such flowers do have more
subtle devices. Most labiates have
two-lipped flowers, with the lower lip
acting as a landing platform for bees

and other large insects, and the upper
shielding the stamens and style. In
many the gap between the two lips is
such that large bees must brush
against the anthers to reach the pollen
and become dusted with pollen. The
flowers are protandrous, and in
another flower pollen may be transferred to a receptive style in the same
position. Bugle, wood sage, dead-
nettles and yellow archangel have this
simple system, but meadow clary and
the related Jupiter's distaff (both
Salvias) are more sophisticated. Here
the stamens are hinged to the lower
lip of the petal-tube, and a heavy bee
actually causes the anthers to bend
down and deposit pollen on its back.
Later the style, which at this stage
points out of the upper lip, bends
down and forms a gate to
intercept pollen-laden bees.

It is of course essential for successful pollination that pollen not only
gets onto the insect, but is later
transferred to a stigma. This may be
achieved by the sort of mechanisms
already described, and is often aided
by the stickiness of the stigma, as in
most umbellifers and members of the
heather family. In others the stigma
itself may be capable of movement:
in monkey flowers the 2-lobed stigma
stands at the flower entrance, receives pollen from a visiting insect,
and then promptly closes up, so that
the pollen that the insect picks up
from the anthers further into the
flower is not transferred to the style
as the insect leaves, but instead goes
to the next unpollinated monkey
flower it visits.

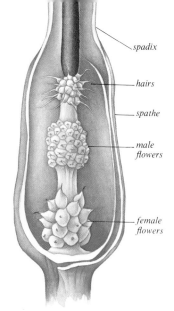

Lords-and-ladies flowerhead

Remarkable though these devices
are, they seem straightforward in
comparison with those of orchids
(p. 286) or of lords-and-ladies. This
extraordinary plant actually traps
flies in its 'flowers', which comprise a
leaf-like 'spathe', encircling the
purple, finger-like spadix which
arises from the concealed 'flower'
proper. Inside the hollow spathe are
successive rings of sterile flowers
modified into hairs, male flowers
containing just a single stamen; and
finally female flowers comprising
simply ovary and style.

The spathe opens in the daytime
and actually generates heat, which
helps to disperse a faint but, to
humans, unpleasant smell, which
nevertheless attracts a few species of
small flies. These enter the chamber
beneath the spadix and slide past the
hairs, the surfaces being smooth and
acting as insect ski-slopes. Once they
are inside, the hairs prevent their
escape, and if they have already
visited another plant, they can now
pollinate the receptive female flowers.
The next day the stamens mature and
shed pollen on the flies, the bristles
wither and allow their escape, and (if
all goes well for the plant) they head
for another plant.

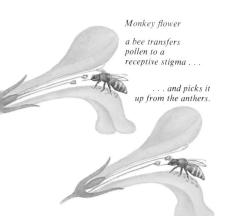

Monkey flower

*a bee transfers
pollen to a
receptive stigma . . .*

*. . . and picks it
up from the anthers.*

285

POLLINATION IN ORCHIDS

Orchids have an enormous fascination: the complexity of their flowers, which may resemble manikins (as in monkey, military and lady orchids), or insects or even spiders (as in bee, fly and spider orchids), or may have long tails or other strange appendages as in lizard orchid, makes them attractive to naturalists and gardeners alike. But these floral modifications are intimately related to the function of the flower and its mode of pollination.

All orchid flowers have six 'tepals' (i.e. structures that cannot be easily determined as either petals or sepals), an outer and an inner ring of three. One of the three inner tepals is usually greatly modified and forms a lip (the labellum), which often acts as a landing platform for insects. The stamens and styles are arranged quite differently from those of other flowers: they occur together on a central column, which has the stigma (a flat plate) on one surface, separated from the single functional anther by a projecting peg called the rostellum. The single anther (there are two in lady's slipper orchid) bears two pollen masses called pollinia which adhere intact to a visiting insect and are transferred as such. Normally the pollinia are shed from the anther and retained on the sticky rostellum, from which they are easily removed.

The simplest orchid flowers are those of the helleborines, many of which are mainly self-pollinated. They have rather unshowy flowers in which the lip is poorly developed. Broad-leaved helleborine, which has dull green and purple flowers, is

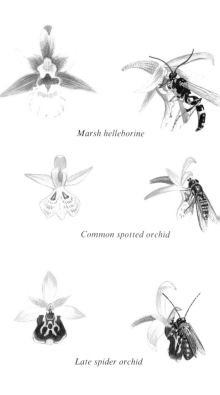

Marsh helleborine

Common spotted orchid

Late spider orchid

Wasp's-eye view of the flower of broad-leaved helleborine

apparently mainly visited by wasps. The wasp's-eye view of the flower shows the two pollinia just above the stigma on the central column, and the rostellum in between. The rostellum produces a sticky secretion, which serves to stick the pollinia to the wasp's head as it probes for the nectar in the lip. This 'glue' is not, however, strong enough to prevent the pollinia flopping down over the wasp's face and when it visits the next flower, the pollinia are placed exactly so as to be transferred to the stigma. The same change of position is achieved in marsh helleborine by the lip being hinged and depressed under the weight of a bee: as the bee leaves the flower the lip springs back, forcing the bee to brush against the rostellum, picking up the pollinia. When it lands on another flower the depression of the lip ensures that the

Common twayblade

Greater butterfly orchid

Fly orchid

pollinia, fixed to the bee's head, are now lined up against the stigma.

Various other devices occur in other orchids: in common twayblade the rostellum is bent over in front of the stigma and visiting insects (mainly small ichneumon wasps and beetles) crawl up the lip, removing nectar until they touch the rostellum. It then produces a drop of an extraordinary natural 'superglue' which actually rapidly cements the two pollinia (which lie atop the rostellum) to the insect. Once the pollinia are removed, the rostellum springs back.

Extraordinary though these devices are, the most remarkable mechanisms occur in the genera *Orchis*, *Dactylorhiza* and *Ophrys*. In the first two (in, for example, common spotted orchid or early purple orchid) insects, seeking nectar in the short spur into which the lip projects, pick up the

two pollinia from the rostellum. Once again the 'glue' dries rapidly but in doing so twists the pollinia round by 90°, so aligning them to touch the sticky stigmatic disc of the next flower to be visited. Some related species have very long spurs, as in pyramidal, fragrant and greater and lesser butterfly orchids. These are mainly pollinated by butterflies and, in the case of the white-flowered butterfly orchids, rather paradoxically by night-flying moths. The narrowness of the flower admits their proboscis readily, but excludes larger insects.

The most remarkable flowers, however, are those of the 'insect' orchids – fly, bee, and early and late spider orchids. Their flowers are remarkably like insects, and in the case of the inaptly named fly orchid, attract by scent a few species of solitary wasp which are sufficiently duped by the flower to attempt to mate with it. In doing so, the wasp picks up the pollinia, and when it finally gives up the attempt, it moves on and transfers them to another plant. In experiments male wasps have been shown to prefer mating with fly orchid flowers than with actual female wasps!

The two spider orchids appear to play the same trick on particular species of bee (which they resemble much more than spiders), but the bee orchid, though a good insect mimic, is in fact self-pollinated. It seems to have evolved selfing as a secondary device but one that is much more reliable, for it almost invariably sets ample seed and it is probably the commonest species in the group. The insect mimics are much commoner in warmer climates, and in northern Europe are at the edge of their range, perhaps limited by the distribution of their insect partners. It is in that light that the selfing of the bee orchid should be seen.

HYBRIDS

In evolutionary terms, we can measure an individual's success by its fitness, which means the number of offspring it leaves to the next generation, and so to successive generations after that. All aspects of reproduction are important here. Pollination is successful if pollen is transferred to a receptive stigma, but this must be followed by fertilisation, seed maturation, dispersal and germination. Only then can a new plant be seen to have been left by the parent. But if this new plant fails to reproduce, all the previous stages will have been in vain. That failure could be due to many causes, but one possibility is the genetic incompatibility of the pollen and egg of its two parents.

Considering how imprecise most pollen distribution is, it is very likely that pollen from plants of many species will land on other species' stigmas. Most of that pollen fails to grow, and, even if it does, fails to fertilise the egg. But sometimes a pollen grain of a different species achieves this, and forms an interspecific hybrid. Even then its troubles are not over: the very different genetic information in pollen cell and egg cell may prevent the seed from forming, or the plant from growing, or finally a plant that does grow from reproducing itself.

Because of all these barriers, hybrids are rather rare, and because most pollen transferred to other species is therefore wasted, there has been strong selection to prevent such transfer. If a plant pollinates another species and nothing happens, the only loss is that of the pollen. But if it produces a sterile hybrid, that plant may compete with it (or its offspring) without perpetuating its genes.

Nevertheless, hybrids are found in many different genera. Mostly they are between closely-related species in a single genus, as the genetic differences between genera are likely to be too large to permit the hybrid to develop normally. Inter-generic hybrids are found in orchids (between fragrant and frog, common spotted and southern marsh orchids,

Red campion is a native and white campion an ancient introduction; the hybrid between them is now commoner than the parents in some parts of the country.

Oxford ragwort (left), an introduced species, and the native groundsel (right); the rayed form of groundsel (centre) has probably arisen within the last two hundred years by hybridisation of these two species.

for example), but are rare elsewhere. Indeed, the strict definition of a species is that it cannot interbreed with other species, let alone genera. Probably it is the complex mechanisms that orchids erect (see p. 286) to avoid incorrect pollinations that has led to their failure to evolve barriers to hybrid production when the pollination barrier *does* fail.

The occurrence of hybrids varies greatly between families. They are very rare in the buttercup family, for example, but common among docks and thistles. There is no simple explanation for this, but wherever hybrids occur abundantly it is likely that there is some outside factor involved, often man. Red and white campion, for example, freely interbreed, producing fully fertile hybrids that can themselves interbreed with either parent. In some parts of the country this had led to the campions becoming a complex mixture of species and hybrids, with few individuals easily recognisable. Only the red campion is native; it is a plant of shaded habitats and wood margins. White campion was introduced by early farmers as an arable weed. The two species never met naturally, therefore, and so had never evolved a barrier to crossing. When they came into contact through the spread of agriculture into wooded areas, the hybrids appeared.

A similar case involves Oxford ragwort, introduced from the Mediterranean and now a common urban weed. Like most ragworts, but unlike groundsel (another *Senecio* species), it has both disc- and ray-florets. The recent increase of populations of groundsel which *do* have ray-florets is thought to be the result of hybridisation with Oxford ragwort.

Hybridisation can therefore introduce genetic novelty and be a stage in the evolution of new species. This has been definitely shown in the recent appearance of common cord-grass, a wholly new species, which resulted from the hybridisation of the native small cord-grass and the introduced American species smooth cord-grass in Southampton Water. The first hybrids produced were sterile, and only survived by vegetative growth – that hybrid, known as Townsend's cord-grass still exists – but some time around 70 to 80 years ago it underwent an internal doubling of its chromosomes and produced the new species, common cord-grass, which is fully fertile, and now much the commonest saltmarsh grass.

Cord-grass in Southampton harbour: (left) *small cord-grass,* (right) *smooth cord-grass,* (top) *Townsend's cord-grass,* (bottom) *common cord-grass.*

289

APOMIXIS

The difference between sexual reproduction and vegetative growth and
reproduction has been emphasised on
p. 254), and the close link between
sexual reproduction and seed production stressed. Normally seeds are
produced sexually by the fusion of the
male gamete (from the pollen) with
the female (the egg). This means that
for most plants the advantages and
disadvantages of reproduction by
seed are inextricably linked with those
of sex. A few plants, however, have
found a way of breaking that link.

To the casual observer one dandelion looks much like another, and
even experienced botanists will only
recognise four of five different types
in our flora. The commonest type is
the coarse, large-flowered one so
common in grassy places and gardens; but there are small-flowered,
more elegant dandelions that grow on
dry hillsides, and red-veined types in
fens and marshes. The real specialist,
though, will recognise hundreds of
different species of dandelion – over
150 in Britain alone. They differ from
each other in much finer detail than
most closely related species do; but
the differences are fixed, and persist
from generation to generation.

The reason why dandelions are so
different from normal species is that
although their flowers look similar to
those of many other composites, and
produce typical composite seeds with
their characteristic parachutes, those
seeds are produced without pollination taking place, by a process known
as apomixis. In normal sexual reproduction the egg cells and pollen cells
are produced by a halving of their
genetic complement, so that when
they fuse the normal complement is
restored. In apomixis, the egg cell is
just like any other cell in genetic
terms, in having a full complement of
genes: it does not require fertilisation
by pollen, and it develops directly
into a seed. That seed is therefore
genetically identical to the single
parent, just as are vegetatively produced offspring (from rhizomes or
stolons, for example). Apomixis

*On dry hillsides dandelions are
small-flowered and elegant.*

*The commonest type of
dandelion, found in gardens and
roadsides, is coarse
and vigorous.*

*In fens and mar
dandelions often
have red leaf-ve*

combines the advantages of vegetative reproduction with those of seeds: in other words, the ability of the former to preserve well-adapted genetic types with the latter's dispersal and dormancy characteristics.

The reason why this system produces such myriads of 'microspecies' is that, whereas normal sexual species contain a great range of slightly different genetic types, all of which can interbreed, interbreeding (and so mixing of genes) cannot occur in apomictic species. Every time a new type arises (by mutation or in some cases by a temporary reversion to sexual behaviour), it can be preserved precisely by apomixis.

Dandelions are not the only apomictic group, though they are certainly one of the most successful. Other genera which adopt the same method include hawkweeds, lady's-mantles and whitebeams. Interestingly, they fall mainly in two families, the daisies and the roses, suggesting that some sorts of plants are better able to achieve this trick than others.

Where apomixis is strict, and no sexual reproduction seems ever to occur, as in most lady's-mantles, the differences between the microspecies can be reasonably distinct, though even in this genus there are known sexual species. Some apomict genera, though, quite frequently revert to brief bouts of sexual reproduction, which of course mixes up the genes of the previously distinct types and may cause great confusion. This

appears to happen in spring and alpine cinquefoils, two very similar species which occur respectively on dry limestone areas in the lowlands and on base-rich rocks in the hills. The main difference between them is that spring cinquefoil has creeping, rooting stems and forms mats. Sometimes, where the distributions of the plants overlap, intermediates are found. Normally these would be interpreted as hybrids, but they turn out to arise from the fusion of a pollen cell with half the normal genetic complement (as in ordinary sexual reproduction) and an egg cell with the full complement (as in apomixis). Quite what the evolutionary future is of such offspring is unclear, but they emphasise that apomixis may be combined with normal sexual reproduction to provide a very flexible system. The abundance of dandelions certainly shows that it can be successful.

Alpine cinquefoil (right) *occurs in the hills,*
spring cinquefoil (below) *in the lowlands.*

291

VIVIPARY

To the casual glance, the operation of the flower seems obvious. It contains male and female organs, and fusion of the gametes they produce results in the seed, which contains the embryo of the new plant. There may be subtle devices to ensure cross- or self-pollination; but in all cases the basic process seems similar. Apomictic flowers (p. 290), in which seeds can develop directly from the egg cell without the need for pollination, show that there may be other routes to seed production; and there is one step further down the road of modification of flower behaviour, which reduces the flower to a wholly vegetative structure, and that is vivipary.

Vivipary is in truth a misnomer. In animals it implies giving birth to live young, and the appropriate analogy in plants should presumably be where seeds germinate before being shed. That does happen quite frequently (in white campion and many annual grasses, for example) when the seedhead becomes wet, either through heavy rain or through being pressed against wet soil. But in plants the term 'vivipary' is used to indicate the replacement of the flowers in the flowerhead by tiny plantlets, which can become detached and grow immediately into new plants.

This phenomenon is best seen in viviparous fescue, a common mountain grass; indeed it is one of the best indicators of the arrival of alpine conditions as one climbs a mountain – when viviparous fescue starts turning up, other alpine plants are likely to be around too. In the fescue, and in other grasses and rushes which do the same thing, the flowers develop a few glumes (the grass equivalent of petals and sepals), but the other parts of the flower turn instead into tiny leaves. This part then falls off, grows roots and is immediately capable of an independent existence.

Viviparous fescue is the only common grass that is always exclusively viviparous, but several other mountain grasses are either usually so or mainly so. Alpine meadow-grass

Alpine plants, such as viviparous fescue (right) and alpine hair-grass, avoid problems of short growing seasons and low temperatures by refraining altogether from seed production: the flowers are replaced by tiny plantlets.

occasionally has normal flowers, and alpine hair-grass, which is a subspecies of tufted hair-grass usually has flowerheads containing both normal and viviparous flowers. Several common lowland grass species produce occasional individuals which are viviparous, including cock's-foot and crested dog's-tail, but mostly it is found in mountain plants, where, presumably, the chances of successful pollination, and conditions suitable for seeds to mature, may not occur very often. In such cases the production of offshoots in place of flowers may be a great advantage.

Although viviparous fescue is always listed as a good species in floras, it is almost certainly a collection of viviparous forms of a number of different species of fescue. Both sheep's fescue and fine-leaved sheep's fescue certainly have viviparous forms and, the fescues being an obscure and difficult group of species, probably several others do too. The problem is that if they fail to produce flowers then the characters which are used to distinguish the normal species simply vanish, and the botanist is then left with a real problem in deciding what to do with the non-flowering plants he finds.

Most viviparous plants grow either in upland areas where the growing season is short or in very shady places where, possibly, there are too few insect pollinators. Only grasses and a few rushes, such as bulbous rush, which is a widespread lowland species, replace the flowers with little plantlets, but several bistorts, saxifrages and garlics have some or all of the flowers replaced by tiny bulb-like propagules called bulbils. These grow roots and leaves once detached from the plant, and in some cases (as in crow garlic) may actually sprout leaves while still in the flowerhead. Alpine bistort and drooping saxifrage both habitually have most or all of the flowers in the spike replaced by bulbils; both grow at high altitude and in the far north.

The dividing line between these forms of vivipary and other forms of vegetative reproduction is far from clear. Coralroot bittercress is a relative of cuckoo flower that grows in deep shade, often in beechwoods. Although it normally produces several normal flowers, most of the upper stem leaves bear bulbils rather than flower-branches. Whether these replace flowers or not is unclear, although in a plant like the shade form of lesser celandine, which bears a few flowers and bulbils deep down, almost at soil level beneath the leaves, they only replace the flowers in the sense that the plant produces fewer flowers as a result.

Vivipary may also act as a compensation for lack of light: coralroot bittercress is a deep-shade plant; the shade form of the lesser celandine has fewer flowers than its non-shade counterpart.

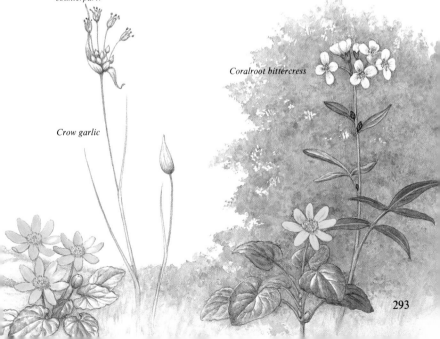

Coralroot bittercress

Crow garlic

293

THE GREEN PARTS OF FLOWERS

Most of the parts of a typical flower have fairly obvious roles to play. The stamens and styles are the reproductive organs, the nectaries provide rewards for visiting insects attracted by the petals, and so on. Many flowers are, however, surrounded by green parts that sometimes have less obvious functions.

Two sorts of green parts are commonly found: bracts and sepals. Sepals are a true part of most flowers and are often not green. They lie immediately outside the petals and are sometimes indistinguishable from them, as in globeflower, ramsons or wild daffodil. In other cases the petals may not be there at all and, if the sepals are their normal green colour, this gives a very inconspicuous flower, for example annual pearlwort. Sometimes it is impossible to say whether the parts of a flower are petals or sepals, and they are called tepals (or strictly perianth segments, the perianth being the botanical name for the sepals and petals together); marsh marigold is a good example, which has five or more bright yellow perianth segments.

Bracts, on the other hand, are not strictly part of a flower at all, but leaves from the base of which the flower springs. The junction of leaf and stem is the axil, and flowers most often arise in the axil of a leaf. Often that leaf is like the other leaves of a plant, but frequently it is different in form or colour: then it is known as a

The 'petals' of dwarf cornel are actually bracts, as is seen when the 'flower' matures to give several fruits.

When the flower-head of wheat is at an early stage, the whole plant is green; before the flowerhead has had time to ripen, the rest of the plant is dying, leaving the 'ear of corn' to photo-synthesise for itself before it too turns golden brown.

The cream-yellow bracts of carline thistle surround a cluster of individual flowers.

bract. Bracts are usually green and to that extent leaf-like, but in some plants they take over the role of the petals. Dwarf cornel and carline thistle both seem to have conspicuous flowers or flowerheads, the former apparently with four large white petals: they are in fact bracts which have changed to look like petals, and in their centre are not the stamens and styles of a single flower, but a group of very small flowers. In fruit the bracts fall away and each flower matures to a bright red berry, giving a clue to the compound nature of the original 'flower'.

Typically, however, bracts and sepals are green, and as such seem to have two main roles – protection and nourishment. When they are green, it is not surprising to find that they can photosynthesise just like a green leaf (see p. 196), and in some plants this of the fruit. In many annuals the lower leaves begin to die before the seeds have ripened and, by the time all the seeds are ripe, the whole plant may be brown. This is dramatically obvious with a field of wheat, and it is known that the young green ears of wheat can actually make almost half of their needs by their own photosynthesis. Wheat has been heavily modified by centuries of selective breeding, and may not be typical of wild plants; but this example shows that the greenness of bracts and sepals implies a real ability for a flower to be nutritionally self-sufficient.

Their other role is protection. To achieve its function a flower must survive to maturity. Whereas a leaf that is eaten while still green may have contributed substantially to the plant, a flower that is eaten before the seeds are ripe has achieved nothing. Few flowers are heavily protected against large grazing animals, although the spiny bracts of sea holly, burdock or spear thistle must be fairly discouraging. But the less well developed sepals and bracts of many flowers serve to protect unopened flowers in bud, and to make robbing of pollen or nectar from the base of the flower by large insects, such as bumble-bees, more difficult.

In some plants where the sepals form a tube, they are inflated so that the stamens, styles and nectaries are well separated from it, as in the centre of a balloon. This is particularly obvious in bladder campion and sea campion, and may prevent insects from robbing the flowers of nectar by biting the back of the flower and so failing to pick up and transfer pollen. The distance through the sepal tube to the nectar is almost twice as great as the length of the proboscis of the bumble-bees that can rob other flowers in this way.

Sometimes the sepal tube becomes inflated in fruit, as in yellow rattle, lousewort and marsh lousewort. This may help to protect the seeds in the same way, or maybe assist in seed dispersal.

The flower of bladder campion

sepal tube

The flower of yellow rattle

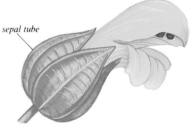

sepal tube

THE RIPENING OF FRUITS

The culmination of the process of sexual reproduction is the mature seed, from which the life-cycle re-starts. At its simplest the seed consists of an embryo – the new plant – surrounded by a coat. This is the case in orchids (such as creeping lady's-tresses) and in some parasitic plants such as dodders and broomrapes. The orchids, too, are dependent on a fungal partner, at least in the early stages of their growth, and so in a sense are parasitic too. In non-parasitic plants, the seed usually contains some food stores as well and the embryo may be much better developed than it is, for example, in orchids. To lay down these stores and to permit the early growth of the embryo in the seed, the connection to the parent plant is necessary.

In a seasonal environment, conditions will only be favourable for the ripening of seeds and fruits for part of the year. The flowering time of a plant will therefore be dependent both on the best time to grow and produce flowers and on whether there is time left in the good season to ripen fruits. Early-flowering plants, such as snowdrops or celandines, have the problem of producing flowers early in the season, when conditions may be unfavourable for growth – their seeds will be shed by April or May, though. Late-flowering plants have the opposite problem, and there are very few

On one plant of Himalayan balsam, dehisced seed-pods, green seed-pods, flowers and buds can all be found at the same time.

plants which come into flower for the first time later than August. There are many which flower all year round, mainly weeds such as red dead-nettle, common chickweed and com--mon field speedwell, as well as a few grassland plants, notably daisy; others flower all summer, only stopping when the first frosts kill the flowers – ragwort, autumn hawkbit and yarrow are good examples. Himalayan balsam is an annual that starts flowering in July and also continues until it is killed by frost, but the flowers that set fruit after the end of August will only shed ripe seed in a year when the first frosts are exceptionally late. As the days cool and shorten in the autumn, so the length of time needed for the seeds to mature increases and the chance of it happening declines very quickly. These late produced flowers are opportunistic, therefore, and able to take advantage of an exceptional year. In an annual

Red dead-nettle flowering in mid-winter

it makes sense for the plant to go on flowering right up to the end, since any growth it achieves in the autumn is wasted anyway. In a perennial it seems less clear why it should be any advantage, since the plant could be using the energy it spends on these late flowers on building up its over-wintering energy reserves.

The length of the growing season is therefore a major factor limiting the distribution of plants. Many plants have the northern edge of their range determined not by the severity of the frosts, but by the length of the growing season and the chances of their producing ripe fruits. This can easily be seen in August as one climbs a mountain. A plant like heath rush, which grows from sea level to nearly 1,000 m sets a profusion of seed at

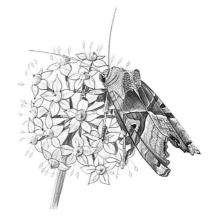

Angle shades moth on ivy flower

Lowland and upland individuals of heath rush

low altitude; but as one goes up seeds become fewer and fewer. Many plants overcome this by adopting vegetative reproduction where growth conditions are poor (see p. 254).

The few plants which do actually have their flowering season in the autumn, therefore deserve attention. Ivy flowers from September to November, and is of great importance as a source of nectar to the few moths which are active at that time, and to flies: common cord-grass, too, is a September flowerer, and in its maritime environment can perhaps expect a longer growing season. Both species are well capable of vegetative growth, and it seems likely that reproduction from seed is of minor importance, certainly in the cord-grass. Ivy near its northern limit of distribution scarcely flowers at all, but even where flowers are produced it has a way round the problem of seed maturation in winter. Ivy seeds, when shed, contain a very immature embryo and cannot germinate. Growth of the embryo takes place after dispersal and when temperatures recover, and germination typically takes place in early summer. Interestingly the same delayed maturation of the embryo is found in several woodland plants which flower in spring and die down when the tree leaves emerge, including lesser celandine and wood anemone. Here it is the deep shade of summer rather than the cold of winter that limits the growing season.

THE PROTECTION OF FRUITS

Most seeds and fruits face a dilemma: those that are distributed by wind (see p. 164) must be exposed to the elements, but somehow protected from, for example, rain. Those that are dispersed by animals that eat them for the fruit, must avoid being eaten either before they are mature or by animals that will consume and destroy both seeds and fruit. All seeds, too, must face the general problem that they are a high quality food source. Once dispersed, they must rely on their inbuilt defences (vetches and other legumes may have toxic chemicals in their seeds, for example and many seeds have tough coats – see p. 170); but, before dispersal, the parent plant can provide defence against grazing and chewing animals.

Of course many such defences will be part of the normal defensive machinery of the plant, and not serving exclusively to protect seeds. The hairs on the sepals of many plants may prevent robbery of nectar and pollen (p. 280) and later protect the seeds too. The prickles on dog rose stems and the spiny leaves of gorse must help ward off attacks on their fruits in addition to their general defensive function. Dog rose, particularly, has seeds that are dispersed by birds, which are attracted to the conspicuous red hips. Because birds simply swallow the seeds they pass through the gut undamaged; but mice and voles also readily consume rose hips and with their teeth can actually break the seed-coat and digest the seeds as well. They would find it hard, however, to climb a dog rose stem, with its array of downward pointing prickles.

Surprisingly few seeds are well-protected against animals while still on the parent plant. A number of species have flowerheads armed with spiny bracts – for example sea holly, teasel and many thistles – and a very few actually have spiny fruits: corn buttercup is one case, which may be as much concerned with dispersal as defence. For some reason spiny

The seeds of rose-hips pass undamaged through the gut of a fieldfare; the more destructive mouse finds it difficult to reach the hips because of the down-pointing thorns.

fruits are commoner in trees: sweet chestnut and horse chestnut are good examples.

It is much commoner to find that the seeds are protected against the elements than against animals. Many wind-dispersed seeds rely on a type of censer mechanism for dispersal (see p. 164), and for this to work it is obviously necessary for the seeds to be quite dry. In many members of the pink family, including campions, catchflies and chickweeds, the capsule opens by a series of teeth that are hygroscopic, and close up entirely in wet weather. In other cases the capsule hangs downwards and the openings are at its base, which is therefore at the top of the inverted capsule, as in bellflowers and wintergreens. Again the slits open only in dry weather and close again in the wet.

Despite all these precautions, many seeds do fall victim to various hazards. If you collect a few fruiting heads of common toadflax in August, they will almost certainly produce within a few weeks several tiny moths, known as toadflax pugs, whose caterpillars were feeding in the pods and pupated there. Similarly it is common to find capsules of red and white campion containing not seeds, but a caterpillar of the campion moth. This example, however, if studied in detail, should give us cause to realise that the life-histories of plants and their interactions with animals are complex phenomena.

The campion moth is one of several closely related species that are wholly dependent on the seeds of campions and a few related species for their food. The campion moth itself feeds mainly on red and white campion and ragged robin, as does the very similar lychnis moth; the grey and the marbled coronet on the other hand feed primarily on bladder and sea campions, and so are commonest near the coast, while the white spot only devours seeds of the scarce Nottingham catchfly and the viper's bugloss (despite its name) is confined to seed capsules of the extremely rare Spanish catchfly (p. 1). The distribution of the last two moth species therefore closely mirrors the very limited distribution of their food plants.

At first sight these moths may seem simply to be predators of seeds of their host plants, and so wholly detrimental. In fact the relationship is more nearly one of mutual benefit, a kind of symbiosis (cf pp. 226–9). Most of these campions and catchflies rely on the moths to pollinate their flowers, for when the moth visits a flower to lay its eggs in the young seed capsule it simultaneously picks up pollen from the protruding stamens, and transfers it to the next flower it visits. It visits many more flowers for nectar than to lay eggs and so, although the plant in this arrangement loses a part of its potential seed production, it at least guarantees the pollination necessary for that production. It would be simplistic to presume that this remarkable arrangement is in some way deliberate; the plant still suffers the loss of some of its seeds, though obviously not enough to render any of the species extinct. Rather it is presumably a chance interaction, beneficial to the moth in an obvious way, and sufficiently so to the flower for it to have persisted and spread. There must be many other interactions between plants and animals of which we as yet know nothing.

A marbled coronet moth picks up pollen from, and lays its eggs in, the flower of bladder campion; when the egg hatches, the caterpillar eats most of the seeds.

EPILOGUE

The theme that runs through this book is of the adaptation of flowering plants to their way of life. Before Darwin, it was customery to see the often astonishing adaptations of living organisms as evidence of the hand of the creator. Indeed there is some irony in the fact that it was the proponents of this concept of 'natural theology' who accumulated much of the knowledge of the natural history of plants and animals which evolutionists were later to use as the convincing evidence for evolution by natural selection. The view of adaptation that we see from an evolutionary perspective is surely much richer. It is true that many plants are astonishingly well adapted to their way of life. The traps by which bladderwort catches its prey, or the pollination mechanisms of orchids, are spectacular examples of such superb adaptation, and these examples of 'perfection' often lead people still to question the idea that a chance mechanism could have given rise to them.

Natural selection, of course, is no chance mechanism. The origin of variation, in the mutations of DNA, may be random; but the selective pressures of the environment on the varying structures of plants are far from random. Perhaps equally striking is the curious *lack* of perfection in so many structures and activities. Why do some plants produce so many millions of seeds (of which only one or two can survive on average), while others produce only a few? Is it not curious that no plant is able to fix atmospheric nitrogen? Those that can all live symbiotically with a bacterium that is the real fixer. Why do dandelions still produce showy flowers, just like their insect-pollinated relatives, even though their seeds are formed by a completely asexual mechanism?

Natural selection has only ever acted on what it has been offered, and often that produced a rather second-best solution to an ecological problem. It does not act by producing the best solution to any one problem, but by increasing the frequency of genotypes that can solve all the problems of survival. So it is dangerously facile to look for a single facet of the environment which can be said to be responsible for a particular feature of a plant. In several places in this book, I have pointed out 'adaptations' which could be seen as dealing with several problems: a good example is the hairs on a leaf, which might both help the plant to save water by reducing transpiration, and at the same time deter leaf-eating insects. Neither factor can be regarded as the only stimulus which led to the evolution of hairs, but both have probably contributed. In the end, the characteristics that win through are those that overall are better at ensuring successful propagation than any others available.

The result may be far from perfect: the case of the moths that lay their eggs in the seed-pods of campions, but in doing so pollinate the flowers, is perhaps the epitome of this view of the pragmatism of nature. Such interdependence is commoner than is often believed, but still may not lead to long-term success. The viper's-bugloss moth lays its eggs only in the seed-pods of Spanish catchfly (see p. 1), a campion now almost extinct in Britain, and confined to the Breckland of East Anglia. The decline of the plant and that of its pollinator and predator are inextricably linked.

GLOSSARY

Page numbers refer to principal entries

Achene: a dry, one-seeded indehiscent fruit (p. 162).

Acid rain: rain with a high level of acidity caused largely by the emission of sulphur dioxide during the burning of coal- and oil-based fuels and its subsequent conversion to sulphuric acid (p. 219).

Acid soils have few basic minerals and are formed on rocks such as sandstone; peaty soils are usually acid (p. 218).

Adventitious: arising in an uncharacteristic position, e.g. of roots that grow from a stem or runner (p. 215).

Aerenchyma: plant tissue with air spaces between individual cells, as in many aquatic plants (p. 218).

Algae: a diverse group of mainly aquatic plants that differ from others by their simple structure and single-celled sex organs (p. 10).

Alpine conditions are those characteristic of high mountainous areas throughout the world (p. 292).

Alternate leaves arise singly in series along a stem, with each leaf on the opposite side of the stem from that below or above it (p. 22).

Androdioecious plants have hermaphrodite and male flowers on separate individuals (p. 271).

Androdioecy: *see* Androdioecious.

Andromonoecious plants have hermaphrodite and male flowers on the same individual (p. 271).

Andromonoecy *see* Andromonoecious.

Angiosperm: a flowering plant, a member of the Angiospermae, whose seeds are enclosed in a carpel (p. 11).

Annual plants live for a year or less; they are usually shallow-rooted and are never woody (p. 242).

Anther: the part of the stamen in which pollen grains are produced (p. 14).

Apomict: a plant that reproduces by apomixis (p. 291).

Apomixis: asexual reproduction, usually the formation of a seed without fertilisation by a male sex cell (p. 290).

Aril: an extra covering, often fleshy and brightly coloured, of a seed (p. 162).

Awn: one of the bristle-like, spiny projections found on the flowering parts of some grasses (p. 181).

Axil: the junction of leaf and stem (p. 294).

Base-poor: of soils and rocks that have few basic minerals.

Base-rich: of soils and rocks that are rich in basic minerals.

Berry: a fleshy fruit with many seeds (p. 162).

Biennial plants live for two years, usually growing in the first year and setting seed in the second (p. 242).

Bilateral symmetry: symmetry in one plane only, as in the flowers of orchids (p. 19).

Bisexual flowers have both male and female parts (p. 270) – *cf* hermaphrodite.

Bogs are formed on wet, acid peat and are often dominated by sedges and *Sphagnum* mosses (p. 52).

Bract: one of the small, leaf-like organs at the base of a flower and from whose axil the flower arises (p. 15).

Bryophyte: a plant that has stems and leaves but no vascular tissue. Bryophytes require water for reproduction and so, like mosses and liverworts, are mainly confined to moist habitats (p. 10).

Bud: an undeveloped shoot containing parts of young leaves or flowers (p. 190).

Bulb: an underground storage organ consisting of densely packed fleshy leaves (p. 252).

Bulbil: a small, bulb-like organ, at the base of leaves or in place of flowers, that breaks off to form a new plant (p. 252).

Calcareous soils are rich in calcium carbonate (lime) (p. 218).

Calcicole: a plant that flourishes on lime-rich soils (p. 218).

Calcifuge: a plant that prefers acid soils, with little lime (p. 218).

Calyx: the sepals as a whole, usually when they are joined, which constitute the inner layer of the perianth (p. 14).

Cambium: the layer of dividing cells between the xylem and phloem of a stem or tree trunk (p. 185).

Canopy: the top layer of leaves in a plant community, in woodland consisting of the crowns of trees (p. 161).

Capsule: a dry fruit, containing several carpels, that opens by pores or slits (p. 163).

Carpel: the female reproductive part of a flower, usually consisting of an ovary, style and stigma (p. 14).

Casual plants appear irregularly, without fixed localities (p. 31).

Catkin: a hanging flower-spike (p. 19).

Cell: the basic unit or organic matter, con-sisting of protoplasm surrounded by a membrane. Unlike animal cells, plant cells have cell walls (p. 12).

Cereal: a plant of the grass family Gramineae that produces edible grain (p. 178).

Chamaephyte: a low-growing, herbaceous or woody plant whose buds are borne less than 25cm from the ground (p. 190).

Chlorophyll: the green pigment of plants that absorbs energy from light for photosynthesis (p. 196).

Chromosome: one of several microscopic, thread-like structures in the nucleus of a cell that carry the genetic information (p. 289).

Claw: the narrow upright part of the elongated petals found on some flowers (p. 18).

Cleistogamous flowers are capable only of self-pollination; their petals and sepals never fully open (p. 261).

Clone: a set of genetically identical individuals descended from a common ancestor, as in plants that reproduce vegetatively (p. 246).

Cluster: a loose group of flowers (p. 24).

Collenchyma: the tissue of thick-walled living cells that helps to support the stems of plants (p. 186).

Community: a group of plants growing together (p. 208).

Composite: a member of the daisy family Compositae (p. 110).

Compound leaves are divided into several individual leaflets (p. 200).

Conifer: a cone-bearing plant, a member of the Gymnospermae (p. 30).

Corm: a bulb-like underground storage organ, consisting of a swollen stem, that persists for up to one year (p. 252).

Corolla: the petals as a whole, particularly when they are joined, the inner ring of the perianth (p. 14).

Corolla tube: the lower part of a corolla where the petals are joined in a tube (p. 15).

Cortex: the layer of tissue, consisting of simple, thin-walled cells, between the vascular tissue and the epidermis of a stem or root (p. 185).

Cotyledon: a seed-leaf, arising from the embryo of a seed (p. 160).

Cross-pollination: the pollination of one plant by another, normally of the same species (p. 262).

Crossing: *see* Cross-pollination.

Crucifer: a member of the cabbage family Cruciferae (p. 46).

Cultivar: a variety of a plant produced by human cultivation and which does not occur in natural populations (p. 176).

Cuticle: the waxy outer layer of leaves and green stems that is secreted by the epidermis (p. 196).

Cyme: an inflorescence of lateral branches whose growing points are terminated by flowers (p. 22).

Deciduous plants shed their leaves at the end of each growing season (p. 206).

Decussate leaves arise in pairs at each node, one on either side of the stem (p. 163).

Dehisce: of a fruit, to split open along a line and so release the seeds (p. 163).

Desiccated: dried out (p. 181).

Dichogamy: the maturation of stamens and styles at different times in the same flower (p. 262).

Dicot: an abbreviation for Dicotyledon.

Dicotyledon: one of the main groups of flowering plants (Angiosperms), distinguished by its seeds having two cotyledons, or seed-

leaves (p. 160).

Diffusion: the movement of molecules in a fluid from areas of high concentration to those of low (p. 202).

Dioecious plants have male and female flowers on separate individuals (p. 270).

Dioecy: *see* Dioecious.

Diploid cells are the normal vegetative state; they have two sets of chromosomes – twice the base or haploid number found in sex cells (p. 12).

Disc-floret: in the daisy family Compositae, a flower in the central part of the flower-head whose petals are joined together in a tube ending in five short teeth (p. 271) – *cf* ray-floret.

Dissected leaves have an indented margin, either regularly or irregularly lobed, so that no part is far from the edge (p. 198).

Dormancy: an inactive period before growth begins (p. 174).

Downy: covered with soft hairs (p. 37).

Drupe: a fleshy fruit whose seed or seeds are surrounded by a tough, stone-like wall (p. 163).

Ecology: the study of organisms in relation to each other and to their environment (p. 164).

Ectomycorrhiza: a mycorrhizal association in which the fungus forms a sheath around plant roots (p. 230).

Egg cell: an ovule or female gamete (p. 256).

Elaiosome: a special food-body attached to a seed or fruit.

Embryo: the young plant inside the seed (p. 160).

Endomycorrhiza: a mycorrhizal association in which the fungus penetrates the cells of the host plant's roots (p. 229).

Endosperm: storage tissue in the seed which nourishes the young seedling in its growth (p. 160).

Entire leaves have no lobes (p. 33).

Enzyme: a protein molecule that catalyses biochemical reactions (p. 233).

Ephemeral: short-lived (p. 49).

Epicalyx: a ring of sepal-like organs just below the true sepals (calyx); common in the rose family Rosaceae (p. 73).

Epicotyl: the part of the stem in an embryo or seedling between the cotyledons and the bud that will form the shoot.

Epidermis: the outer layer of cells of a leaf, stem or root (p. 197).

Epigeal: of germination in which the cotyledons are borne above the ground (p. 178).

Evergreen plants retain their foliage throughout the year (p. 206).

Evolution: the process of genetic change in successive generations of organisms resulting from the selection of different genotypes, and by which all the great diversity of living organisms has arisen (p. 16).

Family: a unit in the classification of organisms, consisting of related genera (p. 16).

Fertilisation: the fusion of male and female sex cells (p. 256).

Filament: the stalk of a stamen, bearing the anther (p. 14).

Flora: the total set of plant species of a particular area (p. 190).

Floret: a small flower, part of a compound flowerhead, as in the daisy family Compositae (p. 271).

Flower: the reproductive structure of a flowering plant (p. 14).

Flowerhead: an inflorescence at the tip of a stem consisting of many densely packed florets (p. 15).

Flower-spike: a spike-shaped inflorescence with sessile flowers (p. 191).

Flower-stalk: the stalk joining flower to stem (p. 206).

Flower-stem: a stem from which flowers arise (p. 252).

Flower-branch: a branch of a woody plant from which flowers arise (p. 293).

Follicle: a dry, dehiscent fruit with one carpel, which on opening splits along only one side (p. 163).

Fruit: the seed-containing organ of flowering plants (p. 162).

Fruit-spike: a collection of fruits arising from a single spike (p. 122).

Fruit-stalk: the stalk joining fruit to stem (p. 169).

Fruiting-head: a collection of fruits arising from the tip of a stem (p. 264).

Fungus: one of the kingdom of organisms that differ from plants in that they lack chlorophyll, do not photosynthesise, are dependent on other organisms for food and usually contain chitin in their cell walls (p. 228).

Gamete: a sex cell; in some plants gametes can develop into new individuals without the need for sexual reproduction (p. 12).

Gene: the basic unit of material inheritance, in the form of a length of DNA in the chromosome (p. 12).

Gene-pool: the sum total of a particular population's genes (p. 260).

Genera: *see* Genus.

Genotype: the genetic composition of an organism as opposed to its physical characteristics (p. 242).

Genus (pl. genera): a unit of classification comprising a group of related species (p. 289).

Geophyte: a plant whose resting buds are underground (p. 190).

Germination: the onset of growth in a seed or spore (p. 178).

Gland: a group of cells at or near the surface of a plant that secrete various substances (p. 222).

Glandular hairs are often many-celled and have a gland at the tip (p. 238).

Glume: one of the small bracts that occur at the base of a grass or sedge spikelet (p. 222).

Gymnosperm: a seed-bearing plant, a member of the Gymnospermae, whose unprotected seeds have no carpellary structure, e.g. in conifers (p. 11).

Gynodioecious plants have hermaphrodite and female flowers on separate individuals (p. 271).

Gynodioecy: *see* Gynodioecious.

Gynomonoecious plants have hermaphrodite and female flowers on the same individual (p. 271).

Gynomonoecy: *see* Gynomonoecious.

Habitat: the environment in which an organism lives (p. 161).

Hairs: simple or branched, straight or curved, one- or many-celled outgrowths from the surface of a plant (p. 238).

Haploid cells have only one set of chromosomes (p. 12).

Heaths are usually formed on dry, acid soils and dominated by heather, gorse or similar shrubs (p. 51). Wet heaths are on damp, shallow peat.

Hemicryptophyte: a plant whose buds are at ground level (p. 190).

Hemiparasite: a partial parasite, usually a plant whose roots parasitise those of another but whose parts above ground behave normally (p. 224).

Herbaceous plants are soft-stemmed and fleshy rather than woody (endpaper).

Herbivore: a plant-eating animal (p. 234).

Hermaphrodite flowers have both male and female reproductive parts (p. 14).

Heterophylly: of plants that have two or more different kinds of leaves.

Heterostylous: having two or more different arrangements of stamens and styles on flowers of the same species (p. 266).

Heterostyly: *see* Heterostylous.

Hip: the fruit of some members of the rose family Rosaceae (p. 300).

Homogamous: having anthers and stigmas that mature simultaneously in the same flower (endpaper).

Honey-dew: a sugary secretion produced by aphids (p. 282).

Hybrid plants are strictly the result of cross-fertilisation between two genetically unlike parents, but the term is usually reserved for crosses between distinct species (p. 288).

Hygroscopic: tending to take up moisture (p. 300).

Hypocotyl: the part of a stem of an embryo or seedling between the cotyledons and the radicle (p. 179).

Hypogeal: of germination in which a seed's cotyledons remain underground (p. 178).

Inbreeding: reproduction between closely related individuals; in some plants involving self-fertilisation by the same individual (p. 260); or cross-pollination between genetically identical members of a clone.

Incompatibility systems are chemical interactions between pollen and the female sex organs by which plants avoid inbreeding (p. 268).

Incompatible plants are unable to breed with

one another (p. 268).

Indehiscent: not dehiscent (p. 163).

Inflorescence: the part of a plant that bears the flower or flowers (p. 22).

Insectivorous plants are able to entrap and digest insects for food (p. 233).

Insectivory: *see* Insectivorous.

Insolation: exposure to the rays of the sun (p. 197).

Inter-generic hybrids are those between two species of different genera (p. 289).

Inter-specific hybrids are those between two species of the same genus (p. 288).

Introduction: a plant that is not native to an area but which has been introduced by man.

Keel: the two lower petals of a peaflower, a member of the pea family Leguminosae, which are joined together and conceal the stamens and styles (p. 284).

Labellum: the 'lip' formed by the lower petal or fused petals of some flowers, particularly orchids (p. 286).

Labiate: a member of the labiate family Labiatae (p. 93).

Leaf: the organ of photosynthesis and trans-piration in most green plants (p. 196).

Leaf-axil: the junction of stem and leaf (p. 253).

Leaf-lobe: the lobe-shaped parts of some leaves (p. 78).

Leaf-margin: the edge of a leaf (p. 236).

Leaf mosaic: the geometric arrangement of leaves on a plant (p. 210).

Leaf-rosette: a rosette-shaped arrangement of leaves, usually at the base of the stem (p. 75).

Leaf-spine: a thin, sharp organ on the surface of some leaves (p. 236).

Leaf-stalk: the stalk that connects a leaf to a stem (p. 194).

Leaflet: a leaf-like part of a compound leaf (p. 194).

Legume: a member of the pea flower family Leguminosae, or the seed pod of one (p. 63).

Life-cycle: the changes that occur in an organism from one stage of development to the same stage in the next generation (p. 12).

Life-form refers to a classification of plants in relation to their behaviour in unfavourable seasons (p. 190).

Limb: the flattened part, at right-angles to the claw, of the elongated petals of some flowers (p. 19).

Limestone contains calcium carbonate and soils formed on it are therefore calcareous (p. 218).

Lime: strictly, calcium oxide (which is not found as such in soils), but commonly used to include calcium carbonate – *see* Limestone.

Linear leaves are narrow and parallel-sided (p. 129).

Lip: *see* Labellum.

Loamy soils contain an even mixture of different-sized soil particles.

Lobed leaves are deeply indented but are not formed of separate leaflets (p. 24).

Long-plumed: having a long, plume-like appendage (p. 42).

Margin: the edge of a leaf; *see* Leaf-margin.

Mats are dense carpets of growth (p. 291).

Metabolism: the sum of an organism's bio-chemical processes (p. 196).

Microspecies: a term used where the morpho-logical distinctions between species are obscure, usually because of an apomictic breeding system (p. 291).

Midrib: the major vein along the centre of a leaf (p. 195).

Monocarpic plants flower and set seed only once in their lifetime (p. 245).

Monocot: an abbreviation of Monocotyledon.

Monocotyledon: a flowering plant, a member of the Angiospermae, whose seeds have only one cotyledon, or seed-leaf (p. 160).

Monoecious plants have separate male and female flowers on the same individual (p. 264).

Monoecy: *see* Monoecious.

Moors are the upland equivalent of heaths, and usually wetter and heather-covered (p. 82).

Morphology: the study of an organism's structure and form (p. 245).

Mucilage: a slimy substance secreted particularly by the roots of plants (p. 181).

Mutation: a change in the genetic structure of an organism (p. 291).

Mycelium: the mass of threads that constitute a fungus (p. 228).

Mycorrhiza: a non-pathogenic association between a fungus and the roots of a plant (p. 228).

Natural selection: Darwin's theory of evolu-tionary change, by which those individuals most suited to an environment will survive and reproduce more successfully than others (p. 173).

Nectar: a sugary solution secreted by many plants (p. 282).

Nectary: a nectar-secreting gland, usually in the flowers of a plant (p. 282).

Nitrogen fixation: the conversion of atmospheric nitrogen to organic nitrogen compounds, e.g. by the activities of soil-inhabiting bacteria in nodules on the roots of some plants (p. 226).

Nodule: a swelling on the roots of a plant caused by the action of nitrogen-fixing bacteria (p. 226).

Nucleic acid: a complex organic compound that carries the genetic information in all living things (p. 228).

Nucleus: the part of the cell that carries the genetic information (p. 256).

Nut: a dry, indehiscent fruit with only one seed (p. 162).

Node: the point on a stem from which a leaf arises; often swollen and hard. Creeping plants may also root from nodes (p. 210).

Ochrea (pl. ochreae): a tubular sheath around the stem of a dock or knotweed (Polygon-aceae) (p. 30).

Offshoot: a plant derived vegetatively from another.

Opposite leaves arise in pairs at each node, one on either side of the stem (p. 210).

Osmosis: the passage of water from a solution of high concentration to one of low concentration across a semi-permeable membrane (p. 186).

Outbreeding: breeding between individuals that are not closely related to one another (p. 260).

Outcrossing: cross-pollination between individuals that are not closely related to one another (p. 261).

Ovary: the part of the carpel of a flower that contains the ovules (p. 256).

Ovule: the part of the ovary containing the female sex cell that after fertilisation develops into the seed (p. 14).

Palmate: branched or lobed like the fingers of a hand (p. 210).

Pappus: an arrangement of fine hairs on the surface of some fruits that aids in wind dispersal (p. 109).

Parasite: a plant, usually without chlorophyll, that obtains nutrients from other plants (p. 220).

Pathogenic organisms cause disease in others (p. 226).

Peaflower: a member of the peaflower family Leguminosae (p. 58).

Peat: the undecayed remains of plant matter, deposited where microbial activity is inhibited, usually in waterlogged sites (p. 218).

Perennating plants, or parts of them, live from one growing season to another (p. 243).

Perennial plants survive for more than two years; if the above-ground parts survive throughout the year (phanerophytes), they are woody (p. 246).

Perianth: the collective term for the petals and sepals of a flower (p. 14).

Petal tube: an arrangement in which the petals of a flower combine to form a tube (p. 19).

Petals: often brightly coloured, variously-shaped organs that form the corolla of a flower and surround its reproductive parts (p. 14).

Phanerophyte: a plant whose buds are more than 25cm from the ground (p. 190).

Phloem: the tissue of a plant that conducts sugars and other nutrients made by the leaves to its growing points (p. 190).

Photosynthesis: the process by which green plants, using energy absorbed by chlorophyll from sunlight, synthesise carbon dioxide and water to make organic compounds (p. 196).

Phyllotaxis describes the arrangement of leaves on a stem (p. 210).

Physiology: the study of the processes and functions of organisms (p. 233).

Phytochrome: a light-sensitive pigment in the leaves of green plants (p. 209).

Phytoplankton: the plant members of plankton, mainly algae (p. 10).

Pigments: coloured substances that in plants absorb energy from sunlight (p. 209).

Pin: of a heterostylous flower whose anthers are below the stamens (p. 266).

Pink: a member of the pink family Caryophyllaceae (p. 40).

Pinnate leaves have two rows of leaflets, one on either side of the midrib (p. 210).

Pith: the central tissue of the stems of non-woody plants (p. 184).

Plankton: the micro-organisms, including plants, that float freely in salt and fresh waters (p. 10).

Plasticity: the ability to change form in response to different environmental conditions (p. 189).

Plumule: the shoot of an embryo (p. 160).

Pod: a thin, dry fruit from one carpel that opens by a seam around both sides (p. 168).

Pore: a small hole, for example on the surface of a leaf or on a seed-capsule (p. 196).

Pollen consists of minute grains, produced by the anthers of a flower, each one giving rise to a male sex cell (p. 256).

Pollen tube: the thread-like outgrowth of the pollen grain that grows down the style towards the female sex cell (p. 256).

Pollination: the transfer of pollen from male to female reproductive organs (p. 256).

Pollinium (pl. pollinia): a mass of pollen grains that are transferred together during pollination (p. 286).

Prickle: a sharp-pointed outgrowth (p. 236).

Procumbent plants are weak-stemmed and trail loosely on the ground (p. 33).

Propagation: natural or artificial reproduction, usually vegetative (p. 242).

Propagule: a seed, spore or other part of a plant that gives rise to a new individual (p. 293).

Prostrate: growing along the ground (p. 34).

Protandrous flowers have stamens that mature before the styles (p. 262).

Protandry: *see* Protandrous.

Protogynous flowers have styles that mature before the stamens (p. 262).

Protogyny: *see* Protogynous.

Pustulate: with small swellings (p. 107).

Raceme: a long inflorescence with flowers on either side, which continually grows at the tip so that the old flowers are at the base (p. 23).

Radial symmetry describes a flower whose parts are arranged equally around a central point, like the spokes of a wheel (p. 19).

Radicle: the root of the embryo (p. 160).

Ray-floret: in the daisy family Compositae, a flower whose petals are elongated into a strap-like tube (p. 271).

Receptacle: the expanded tip of the flower-stalk from which the flower (and later the fruit) arises (p. 163).

Reflexed: bent sharply backwards (p. 70).

Rhizome: a horizontal underground stem,

bearing buds and producing roots and shoots, that persists for more than one year (p. 250).

Root: the part of a plant that grows down into the soil, absorbing water and nutrients and sometimes acting as a storage organ (p. 212).

Root-bud: a bud arising from a root (p. 74).

Root-cap: the protective sheath that covers the growing tip of a root (p. 214).

Root nodule: see Nodule.

Rootstock: the swollen and often long-lived base of the root-system (p. 213).

Root tuber: see Tuber.

Rosette: a flattened, rose-like group of leaves at the base of a stem arising from the roots (p. 211).

Rosette leaf: one of the leaves that forms a rosette (p. 211).

Rosette plant: a plant whose leaves are in a rosette.

Rostellum: an outgrowth, for example in the flowers of orchids one that separates stigma from anther (p. 286).

Runner: a creeping above-ground stem that can root at its nodes to form new plants (cf stem) (p. 251).

Safe site: a place suitable for the germination of seeds (p. 181).

Saltmarsh: a coastal, estuarine habitat subject to flooding at high tides (p. 167).

Sand dunes are usually wind-blown and formed of calcareous shell-sand (p. 32).

Sap consists of the water and nutrients that circulate in a plant (p. 186).

Saprophyte: a plant that feeds on dead organic matter (p. 230).

Scale: a small flap of tissue, often papery and brown; not leaf-like (p. 14).

Scale-leaf: a small, scale-like leaf at the base of the stem or on underground parts of a plant (p. 196).

Sclerenchyma: a strengthening tissue composed of thick-walled cells in the stems of plants (p. 186).

Seed: the fertilised ovule, comprising an embryo, testa and, often, an endosperm (p. 160).

Seed bank: a collection of dormant seeds in soil (p. 176).

Seed capsule: see Capsule.

Seed-coat: see Testa.

Seed-leaf: see Cotyledon.

Seed plant: a spermatophyte (p. 11).

Seedling: a young plant (p. 182).

Self-fertilisation: fertilisation of a flower by itself or by other flowers on the same plant (p. 260).

Self-incompatible: see Self-incompatibility.

Self-incompatibility: of plants in which fertilisation can only occur between genetically distinct individuals (p. 268).

Self-pollination: pollination within the same flower, or between flowers on the same plant (p. 260).

Selfing: see Self-pollination.

Sepals are known collectively as the calyx and form a ring immediately below the petals; usually brown or green and less conspicuous than petals (p. 14).

Sepal tube: an arrangement in which the sepals of a flower are formed together in a tube-like shape (p. 295).

Sexual reproduction: the production of offspring by the fusion of male and female sex cells (p. 12).

Sheath: a protective structure, such as the lower part of a leaf which is wrapped around the stem, often forming a tube (p. 28).

Sheathing mycorrhiza: a mycorrhizal association in which the roots of plants are coated with fungal threads (p. 228).

Shrub: a much-branched woody plant, shorter than a tree.

Silicula: a dry fruit derived from two carpels that is less than three times as long as broad, as in members of the cabbage family Cruciferae (p. 23).

Siliqua: like a silicula, but longer and narrow (p. 23).

Simple leaves are entire, not divided into leaflets (p. 22).

Solitary flowers are borne singly, not in clusters (p. 265).

Spadix: a fleshy spike bearing many sessile flowers (p. 285).

Spathe: the large hooded bract that encloses a spadix (p. 285).

Species: the basic unit of classification, comprising a group of similar individuals capable of interbreeding (p. 289).

Spermatophyte: a member of the class Spermatophyta, the seed plants, which includes the angiosperms and gymnosperms (p. 11).

Spike: a long inflorescence with sessile flowers arising from the central axis (p. 259); a stalked spike has stalked flowers.

Spikelet: the basic unit of a grass or sedge inflorescence, bearing one or more flowers (p. 140).

Spine: a sharp-tipped appendage (p. 236).

Spore: the propagule by which the haploid generation of a plant reproduces; spores are the main reproductive agents in mosses and liverworts; in flowering plants the pollen-grains are strictly spores (p. 12).

Spur: a tubular projection from a petal or sepal (p. 14).

Stamen tube: an arrangement in which the stamens are formed together in a tube-like shape (p. 284).

Stamens are the male organs of a flower, consisting of a filament and anther bearing the pollen; distinguished from the styles by lying outside the centre of the flower, usually in a ring, and by the often coloured anthers (p. 14).

Standard: the upper petal of a peaflower (p. 284).

Stem: the part of a plant bearing leaves, buds or reproductive parts; some stems grow below the ground (p. 184).

Stem-tuber: *see* Tuber.

Stigma: the tip of the style which receives pollen (p. 14).

Stigma lobe: an appendage of the stigma which can trap pollen (p. 263).

Stipule: scale- or leaf-like organ at the base of a leaf-stalk (p. 22).

Stolon: a short-lived creeping stem that can produce new plants at its nodes; most stolons are above the ground (p. 250).

Stoloniferous: of a plant with stolons.

Stomata (sing. stoma): the pores on the surface of a leaf through which water and carbon dioxide move (p. 197).

Style: the filament that connects the stigma to the ovary, the female organ; styles lie in the centre of the flower, within the ring of stamens (p. 14).

Subspecies: the unit of classification immediately below the species; subspecies differ from one another in form and appearance and are usually geographically separated, but interbreed freely if brought together (p. 253).

Succulent leaves are thick and fleshy, storing water in their cells (p. 204).

Suckers are new shoots that develop from the roots of a plant and are therefore a means of vegetative reproduction (p. 56).

Summergreen plants remain green throughout the summer (p. 40).

Sun plants occur in unshaded habitats (p. 208).

Symbiosis: a close physical relationship between two organisms, as in mycorrhiza (p. 226).

Symbiotic: *see* Symbiosis.

Systematic order: a classification of organisms representing a pattern of evolutionary relationship (p. 16).

Tap-root: a strongly-developed. downward-growing main axis of a root system (p. 213).

Taxonomist: a scientist who classifies organisms on the basis of the similarities and differences between them (p. 16).

Tendril: a long, slender feeler, often spirally twisted, developed from a leaf or stem (p. 194).

Tepals are petals and sepals that cannot be distinguished (p. 15).

Terminal bud: the bud at the end of a shoot (p. 178).

Testa: the tough, protective outer covering of a seed (p. 160).

Thorn: a sharp, pointed, woody outgrowth (p. 236).

Thrum: of a heterostylous flower whose stamens are above the styles (p. 266).

Toothed leaves have shallow but sharp lobes (p. 203).

Transpiration: the evaporation of water from the leaves and other surfaces of a plant (p. 198).

Tree: a tall woody plant with a well-developed main stem (p. 10).

Trefoil leaves consist of three leaflets (p. 23).

Tristylic flowers have three styles (p. 267).

Tuber: a swollen, fleshy underground stem or root that acts as a storage organ and lasts for more than one year (p. 252).

Tubercle: a small nodule or swelling (p. 31).

Umbel: a flowerhead shaped like a flattened umbrella with the flower-stalks all arising from the same point (p. 77).

Umbellifer: a member of the carrot family Umbelliferae characterised by having the flowers in umbels (p. 77).

Undifferentiated: not developed into distinct parts (p. 160).

Undissected leaves are entire, without lobes (p. 198).

Unisexual: of one sex only (p. 17).

Valve: one of the parts that make up a seed capsule, as in the dock family Polygonaceae (p. 30).

Variety: a distinct form of a plant, of lower rank than a subspecies and not geographically defined (p. 268); often the product of a single mutation.

Vascular tissue consists of the xylem and phloem, which move water and nutrients from one part of the plant to another (p. 185).

Vector: an agent that transfers pollen from one plant to another (p. 258).

Vegetative reproduction is asexual; a plant can generate new individuals without the need for sexual reproduction (p. 248); the individuals formed in this way comprise a clone.

Veins: the lines to be seen on a leaf; they transport water and nutrients (p. 236).

Viviparous plants can reproduce vegetatively by means of tiny plantlets on the flowerhead in place of some or all of the flowers (p. 292).

Vivipary: *see* Viviparous.

Weeds are plants that grow where they are not wanted, usually to the detriment of cultivated plants (p. 174).

Whorl: where three or more organs arise at the same point on a stem (p. 210).

Wing: one of the two spreading side petals of a peaflower (p. 284).

Winged seeds have appendages to aid in their dispersal by wind (p. 162), and winged stems have flaps of tissue running down from the leaf-junctions.

Winter annuals have their main period of growth in winter and complete their life-cycle by early summer (p. 244).

Wintergreen plants remain green through the winter (p. 34).

Woolly: with soft, thick hairs (p. 28).

Xylem: vascular tissue that conducts water and nutrients from roots to leaves (p. 184).

INDEX

This index is largely restricted to the names of species. Figures in bold refer to the main entry in the DIRECTORY. Scientific names are indexed only to the DIRECTORY, since they are not used elsewhere in the book. Topics are not indexed here: they can be located through the contents pages 5–7 or through the glossary pages 301–7.